Risk and Resilience in Childhood

An Ecological Perspective

2nd Edition

Risk and Resilience in Childhood

An Ecological Perspective

2nd Edition

 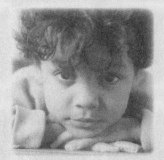 

Mark W. Fraser, Editor

NASW PRESS

National Association of Social Workers
Washington, DC

Gary Bailey, MSW, *President*
Elizabeth J. Clark, PhD, ACSW, MPH, *Executive Director*

Cheryl Y. Bradley, *Publisher*
Paula L. Delo, *Executive Editor*
Andre Barnett, *Editor*
Christina Bromley, *Editorial Assistant*
Alison Peña, *Copy Editor*
Robin Bourjaily, *Proofreader*
Bernice Eisen, *Indexer*

Library of Congress Cataloging-in-Publication Data

Risk and resilience in childhood: an ecological perspective / Mark W. Fraser,
    editor.—2nd ed.

      p. cm.
Includes bibliographical references and index.
ISBN 0-87101-356-8 (pbk.)
    1. Problem children—United States.   2. Social work with children—United
States.   I. Fraser, Mark W., 1946–

HV741.R565   2003
362.74—dc21

                                        2003052073

Printed in the United States of America

Contents

List of Tables and Figures

TABLES

FIGURES

Acknowledgments

Iam in debt to my many colleagues and friends who so greatly contributed to this book and who withstood with humor and grace my comments on preliminary manuscripts. Their dedication and scholarship have given our coverage of risk and resilience an unexpected breadth and depth. Maeda Galinsky, Kenan Professor at the School of Social Work, University of North Carolina, Chapel Hill, has been a constant source of inspiration and support. She cowrote the final chapter. Special thanks to her and to Maritza Penagos who assisted in editing manuscripts. Finally, very special thanks to Mary, who supports my propensity to hide out when I shouldn't, and to Alex and Katy, who keep me involved in the real world of street chalk, guinea pigs, and video games.

1

The Ecology of Childhood:
A Multisystems Perspective

Mark W. Fraser

Despite impressive improvements in public health, social services, and education during the 20th century, the social record of America is clouded by declines in the quality of life for children in the 1980s and 1990s. Coming as they did at the end of a century of remarkable advancements, these declines stunned both experts and advocates. The declines in quality of life placed millions of children at risk of serious health problems, violence, substance abuse, and school failure. Beginning in the last quarter of the century, both the relative and official rates of childhood poverty climbed. The poverty rate reached a high of 22.7 percent in 1993, up from 17.1 percent in 1975 (U.S. Census Bureau, 2002a). In big cities, in little towns, and in the open expanses of cattle, farm, and tribal lands, children were at increased risk in America.

Recent data, however, suggest that conditions may be improving for the nation's 72 million children, who account for about 26 percent of the population (U.S. Census Bureau, 2002a). After the overall childhood poverty rate peaked in 1993, it declined to 16.1 percent in 2000, the lowest level since 1978 (U.S. Census Bureau, 2002b). In the 1990s, the percentage of children in poverty was down some 24 percent (to 9.3 percent) for white, non-Latino youths; down some 32 percent (to 30.6 percent) for African American youths; and down some 27 percent (to 28.0 percent) for youths of Hispanic origin (U.S. Census Bureau, 2002b). The decrease was particularly apparent for female-headed households with children, of which 44.5 percent fell below the poverty level in 1990 (U.S. Census Bureau, 2002c). In 2000 the poverty rate had decreased to 32.5 percent, which is still far too high but an improvement nonetheless. Although the direction of these changes is promising, 41 percent of African American, 41.4 percent of Latino, and 23.9 percent of white, non-Latino children in female-headed families lived in poverty in 2000 (U.S. Census Bureau, 2002c).

For children, the effects of poverty are both direct and indirect. Poverty directly reduces the quality of food, shelter, health care, education, and transportation that a family can afford and to which children have access. Poor children live in less safe and more hostile physical environments (Evans & English, 2002; Sherman, 1994). Poverty affects children indirectly by placing parents in "often impossible circumstances" (Lamer & Collins, 1996, p. 72). When they are exhausted from low-paying jobs and enervated by the sheer demands of coping with inadequate resources, parents simply find it harder to provide consistent supervision and monitoring, to be responsive to children's needs, and to make available a range of socially and educationally stimulating experiences (Duncan & Brooks-Gunn, 1997, 2000; Duncan, Brooks-Gunn, & Klebanov, 1994; Hart & Risley, 1995; Klebanov, Brooks-Gunn, & Duncan, 1994). In a longitudinal study of African American and European American infants weighing between 1,000 and 2,500 grams at birth (that is, low birthweight), maternal parenting fully mediated the effects of poverty and maternal emotional health on the cognitive ability of children at both three and five years of age (Linver, Brooks-Gunn, & Kohen, 1999). The depth and duration of poverty clearly affect children directly, but research strongly suggests that a significant increment of risk accrues through the indirect effect of poverty on parenting and on other family factors.

Despite reductions in the rate of childhood poverty at the turn of the century, many children today continue to live in poverty and to be exposed to conditions that disrupt child development. Low-birthweight infants have a significantly higher risk of death and illness when compared with normal-birthweight infants. The percent of low-birthweight infants increased throughout the 1990s, leveling off from 1998 to 2000 at its highest rate (7.6 percent) since 1981 (Martin, Hamilton, Ventura, Menacker, & Park, 2002, p. 79). Despite widespread prevention activities, the rate of daily cigarette smoking by adolescents is similar today to what it was from 1984 to 1985 (Monitoring the Future, 2002b). Illicit drug use (of marijuana, cocaine, heroin, and other nonprescribed drugs in the past 30 days) among twelfth-graders has declined since 1980, but it is up significantly since 1990 (Monitoring the Future, 2000a). In education, modest improvements in math and reading test scores have been achieved at the same time that fewer children are completing diploma programs. Overall, increases in the percentage of young adults who have completed high school are related to the growth of alternative programs offering equivalency exams, such as the GED test (Federal Interagency Forum on Child and Family Statistics, 2001, p. 108). On the plus side, the percentage of high school graduates who go on to obtain a bachelor's degree has increased 25 percent since 1980 for white, non-Hispanic young adults; 38 percent for Hispanic young adults; and 33 percent for African American young adults (Federal Interagency Forum on Child and Family Statistics, 2002, p. 113). Finally, after peaking in 1994 at 527 violent crime arrests per 100,000 youths (ages 10 to 17), arrests for violent crime decreased to 309 per 100,000 youths in 2000, slightly less than the violent crime arrest rate for juveniles in 1980 (Office of Juvenile Justice and Delinquency Prevention, 2002). So, the picture is mixed. Amid important improvements in childhood poverty, education, and crime prevention, major indicators of child well-being suggest that large numbers of American children continue to be at risk.

What happened in the latter part of the 20th century to produce declines in the quality of life for children in the United States? Some scholars argue that the U.S. labor market had changed. Due in part to macroeconomic forces in the food industry worldwide, not only have many family farms failed or disappeared, but, in what amounted to a second labor-related revolution in the 20th century (the first being the decline of family farms), the smokestack industries—such as steel mills, where many former farmers and their children worked in the first half of the century—have gone out of business. Low-paying service and high-paying technology-related employment now characterize the U.S. labor market. But high-technology jobs require higher education, so, for many displaced workers, immigrants, and young adults trying to enter the labor force, service-, sales-, and agriculture-related work have been the principal options. Work alienation and joblessness rose in the 1980s and 1990s, and real wages stagnated. In fact, after rising sharply in the 1950s and 1960s, real wages for young adults and poorly educated workers actually fell during the 1970s and 1980s (Haveman &

Wolfe, 1994). In 1970, for example, a young worker with a full-time job earned about $17.50 per hour. In 1986, however, that same worker earned only $14.20 per hour, after adjustments for inflation (Duncan, 1991). More recently, in the 10-year period from 1989 to 1999, real wages rose modestly (11.6 percent) for the lowest earnings groups, but most of this increase was due to wage increases in 1998 and 1999. For middle-earning groups, wages and salaries increased only 2.4 percent between 1989 and 1999, with positive changes emerging only at the end of the period (Ilg & Haugen, 2000). Thus, real earnings accelerated only at the end of the 1990s, about the same time declines in the childhood poverty rate emerged. Before the period of 1998 to 2000, earnings languished and even declined precisely for the population of workers most likely to be having children. It was possible to work and still be poor. Inadequate earnings, together with increased joblessness, produced a lower quality of life for millions of American children.

But the labor-market argument is complicated by significant changes in the social landscape of America. Wage stagnation covaried with large increases in the divorce rate and the percentage of single-parent households; with more permissive norms regarding sexual activity for men and women; with declining public support of social, education, and health programs; with the growth of illicit drug markets in urban areas; and with decreases in the traditional authority of schools, religious organizations, and community agencies. Whether the decline in the 1980s and 1990s in the well-being of children and recent (selective) reversals in indicators of the health and well-being of children are attributable to fluctuations in the labor market or to broader social and technological changes in society is hotly debated. Although the ecology of childhood improved dramatically in the 20th century, many children today are exposed to adverse, hostile conditions that compromise healthy child development.

A RISK AND RESILIENCE PERSPECTIVE

Social workers and other professionals are confronted daily with the effects of poverty, poor housing, inadequate health care, crowded schools, and dangerous neighborhoods. If anything, the work of social workers in child welfare agencies, hospitals, mental health centers, neighborhood storefronts, residential treatment and correctional facilities, schools, and youth service organizations has intensified. Large numbers of children are failing in school, getting in trouble with the courts, using illicit drugs, engaging in unprotected sex, joining gangs, getting shot, and attempting and committing suicide. Parents are at their wits' end. Voters are concerned about crime, drugs, and public safety. Frustrated employers challenge schools to produce graduates who have more market-ready skills. And legislators, leery of the costs of social and health services, demand evidence of effectiveness. Health and human services workers face a pressure cooker of problems.

How are we to respond? Without major social structural reforms that significantly affect rates of poverty, there are few good answers. However, recent research on risk and resilience in childhood offers important new guidance on the design and delivery of social and health programs. Clearly, services can and must better address the individual (both biological and psychological), family, neighborhood, and broader contextual conditions that produce childhood problems. Two familiar perspectives—ecological and systems theories—offer useful frameworks for understanding the risks faced by children and their families. Coupled with these theories, the epidemiological methods used in the field of public health provide a foundation both for developing more comprehensive case assessments and for designing more effective services. The purpose of this book is to describe this risk and resilience perspective.

DEFINITION OF RISK

Each chapter in the book employs the term "risk factor," which means any influence that increases the probability of harm (the onset), contributes to a more serious state, or maintains a problem condition (Coie et al., 1993). In the social and health sciences, risk factors are used to predict future outcomes, and they are usually expressed as probabilities. Of course, one can never predict with certainty, but the combination of several risk factors may lead to the conclusion that a child is at "high" risk for a certain outcome, such as alcohol abuse or mental illness. Conversely, the absence of risk factors may lead to the conclusion that a child is at "low" risk for a certain outcome. For exactly the same risk factor, the probability of the occurrence of a future problem may vary by the race or ethnicity, gender, and age of a child. The fact that we are beginning to understand these race or ethnicity, gender, and age differences is a most promising development. But, as with any discussion of human behavior, the concept of risk and its cousin, protection, is continually being refined. Understanding risk factors and their relative effects is the subject of a rapidly growing body of research, which we will try to summarize throughout this book.

Although there is some evidence that childhood problems are highly interrelated and stem from one aggregate risk pattern (Jessor, 1987, 1993), there is stronger evidence that childhood problems have both common and unique risk structures (Loeber, Farrington, Stouthamer-Loeber, & Van Kammen, 1998; Mrazek & Haggerty, 1994). In other words, over and above a set of what might be called crosscutting or generic risk factors for all childhood problems, different individual, family, school, neighborhood, and contextual conditions contribute to different kinds of problems. Chapter 2 reviews the generic or common risk factors thought to underlie many childhood problems, and it discusses the important notion of cumulative risk—the idea that whether a risk factor is unique to a problem or whether it affects many problems, developmental outcomes in childhood are affected more by the number of risk factors than by any specific single risk factor. Building on this risk factor perspective, each subsequent chapter uses the same risk-centered terminology and introduces risk factors for different childhood problems.

SUCCESS AGAINST THE ODDS: RESILIENCE AND PROTECTIVE FACTORS

Many texts examine risk factors, but few examine the puzzling issue of why some children prevail over great adversity. Although poverty is a risk factor for poor academic achievement, not all poor children fail in school (see, for example, Duncan et al., 1994; Furstenberg, Cook, Eccles, Elder, & Sameroff, 2000). What protects some poor children from school failure? And although exposure to violence is a risk factor for violence, not all children exposed to violence develop aggressive and coercive interpersonal styles. What protects these children from delinquency? Something operates to mitigate the risks for these children (see, for example, Bowen, Bowen, & Cook, 2000; Stouthamer-Loeber, Loeber, Wei, Farrington, & Wikstrom, 2002). These children appear to be "resilient" in the face of risk.

This book begins to define and deal with the idea of *resilience,* which arises from the strengths that are usually incumbent in the environments of high-risk children. Conceptually, we call these strengths "protective factors." *Protective factors* are those internal and external resources that promote positive developmental outcomes and help children prevail over adversity. Like risk factors, protective factors include dispositional, familial, and extrafamilial characteristics. In aggregate, they are the positive forces that contribute to adaptive outcomes in the presence of risk (Garmezy, 1993). Chapter 2 further describes and discusses protective factors and resilience.

HIGH-RISK BEHAVIOR VERSUS HIGH-RISK ENVIRONMENTS: NEED FOR AN INCLUSIVE FRAMEWORK

In common parlance, risk is often defined after the fact; that is, a child is viewed as at risk because he or she already has gotten into trouble, been victimized, or failed in some way. There are two problems with this reasoning. First, it begs the question of predictability because the behavior has already occurred. True, prior behavior is one of the best predictors of subsequent behavior, but to plan early intervention services, we need to rely on risk factors that exist before a child gets into trouble—before a negative outcome cues us that something is amiss. If we can identify the predictors of problems, we may be able to intervene early. Second, a definition of risk that relies only on engagement in "risky" behavior ignores the other conditions—the family, school, peer, and neighborhood environments—that predispose children to certain kinds of problems (Resnick & Burt, 1996). All of these factors are useful in thinking about the problems of children. Thus, to give some order to the growing body of research on risk and resilience, we need a conceptual frame of reference that incorporates both individual and contextual conditions affecting children.

ECOLOGICAL THEORY: A MULTISYSTEMS, TRANSACTIONAL PERSPECTIVE

Ecological theory has this inclusive characteristic and is fully compatible with a risk and resilience perspective. Ecological theory focuses both on the individual and on the context. As an early proponent of ecological theory, Bronfenbrenner (1979, 1986) argued that children's development is strongly influenced by the family, school, peer, neighborhood, and community contexts in which they live. Based on the interplay among genetic predisposition, physiological influences (neurochemical imbalances or exposure to a disease, for example), and often conflicting forces in the social environment, human behavior is thought to be transactional and subject to the dynamics of social exchange. In the context of biological influences, the theory posits that children develop and adapt through transactions with parents, siblings, peers, teachers, coaches, religious leaders, and a variety of others who, sometimes for better and sometimes for worse, people their lives. This person-in-environment perspective, in which transactions between organism and environment are thought to produce behavior, lies at the heart of social work and other helping professions (see, for example, Council on Social Work Education, 2001; Germain, 1991; Hepworth, Rooney, & Larson, 2002).

From this perspective, the social ecology of childhood can be conceptualized as consisting of interdependent and often nested parts or "systems." A child usually lives in a family. A family lives in a neighborhood. As they grow up, children in a family attend schools, and later, teenage children may work in the community. Each is a system, an "organized collection of activities and resources that exists within definable social and physical boundaries" (Berger, McBreen, & Rifkin, 1996, p. 42). And each exerts an influence on children. Systems such as the family and school have purposes and usually regulate social exchange. Whether open or closed, they have rules, roles, and power that determine activities and the use of resources.

This book employs the concept of multiple systems of influence; moreover, the authors argue that the central systems in children's lives make up an "ecology of childhood." However, we do not fully invoke the typology of general systems theory. Whereas Bronfenbrenner and others have proposed a layering nomenclature for various types of systems (microsystems, mesosystems, macrosystems, and exosystems), we adopt a simpler "multisystems" perspective. At some level above the family, it becomes quite difficult to identify higher- and lower-order systems. What constitutes the school system? Is it the local elementary or middle school that a particular child attends? Or is it the entire school district? How does the school system relate to the neighborhood? To the community? Which is superordinate? Instead of positing a nested structure of contextual influences, we simply identify risk and protective conditions that affect children across three systems-related domains. Introduced in chapter 2 and used throughout the text, these domains include (1) individual psychosocial and biological characteristics; (2) family factors; and (3) environmental conditions, including school and neighborhood factors.

RISK AND CAUSATION: A MULTISYSTEMS VIEW

The multisystems perspective has one further characteristic that makes it attractive. Patterns in systems are thought to arise from reciprocated causation. That is, behaviors are viewed as "a function of dynamic interactions of elements of the whole system and the system's transactions with the surrounding ecology" (Henggeler, Schoenwald, Borduin, Rowland, & Cunningham, 1998, p. 12). From this perspective, persons A, B, and C can be influenced by each other mutually and simultaneously, and they can also be influenced by concentric circles of environmental factors ranging from family and peers to school, neighborhood, and community.

In sorting out the relative influences of biological factors, learned patterns (for example, cognitive schemata and heuristics), social interactions, and various contextual conditions, it may never be possible to identify causes and their effects fully. In the face of such complexity, causal order, at least in its traditional sense, may not exist. In any event, because the uncertainty is so great and our capacity to measure is so limited, a perspective that does not require notions of simple, linear causation is desirable.

The multisystems ecological perspective admits to reciprocated causation; in so doing, it permits risk and protective factors to operate without the attendant baggage of being thought of as causes. Some risk and protective factors may truly be causes, of course, and the identification of causes is important in the context of developing social programs and scientific theories. But other risk factors may simply be markers that covary with true, though latent, causes. They are useful because they often mark the changing status of problems and signify the need for intervention. On balance, when we invoke an ecological and multisystems paradigm, we do not assume that all risk and protective factors operate as direct causes of child behavior or health.

STRUCTURE OF THE BOOK

Each chapter in the book builds on an ecological and multisystems perspective by introducing and reviewing risk and protective factors for various problems and disorders in childhood. Each chapter follows a similar outline:

- *Description of the problem*: delineating national trends for the topic of the chapter; presenting incidence and prevalence data on differences by age, by race or ethnicity, by gender, and by socioeconomic status, if available.
- *Description of risk and protective factors*: building on the common risk and protective factors discussed in chapter 2, a review of risk and protective factors specific to the topic of the chapter.
- *Description of differences in risk and protective factors*: to the extent they are known, exploring differences in risk and protective factors by child age, by gender, by race or ethnicity, and by sexual orientation.
- *Methods for assessing risk and protective factors*: reviewing briefly those measurement instruments that may be useful in assessing risk and protective factors; some chapters give a detailed exploration of methodological issues in measurement and case assessment.
- *Implications for prevention, early intervention, or treatment:* based on a risk and resilience perspective, discussing implications for practice, including the design of prevention, early intervention, or treatment services.

This book contains 13 chapters. Chapter topics were chosen because they represent common conditions, disorders, and social or health problems encountered by practitioners who work with children and their families. In selecting topics, we could not be exhaustive. For example, we included a chapter on depression, but we did not include a separate chapter on the closely linked topic of eating disorders. And even though they may be heritable or have developmental markers in early childhood, important problems that arise frequently in young adulthood or in marital relationships, including schizophrenia and family violence, are not addressed in the text. Similarly, problems that are quite serious but affect a comparatively small number of children, for example, Asperger's and Rett's disorders, are not included. The chapters are designed to be exemplars of the application of a risk and resilience perspective, and readers are encouraged to apply the methods described in the book to other problems occurring in childhood.

In chapter 2, Mark Fraser, Laura Kirby, and Paul Smokowski explore the concepts of risk, protection, and resilience. They define terms, describe types of risks, review the concept of resilience, and develop a model for common risk and protective factors thought to underpin many childhood problems. This chapter lays the foundation for other chapters in the book.

In chapter 3, James Nash and Karen Randolph outline methodological issues in measuring and comparing risk and protective factors. This chapter contains many examples of the estimation of odds, odds ratios, and relative risks, the central ways that risk and protective factors are compared in the social and health sciences. The chapter also introduces life tables and survival analysis, advanced methods of analysis that are used increasingly by social workers and others who study risk and resilience.

In chapter 4, Barbara Thomlison discusses risk factors both for child maltreatment and for recovery from child maltreatment. Reports of child abuse and neglect have soared in recent years (Curtis, Boyd, Liepold, & Petit, 1995; U.S. Department of Health and Human Services, 1996, 2001). Each year about 1 million reports of child maltreatment are substantiated (U.S. Department of Health and Human Services, 2001), and longitudinal studies indicate that child maltreatment is a risk factor for a variety of adjustment disorders, including both internalizing (for example, major depressive disorders) and externalizing (for example, delinquency) problems (Kaufman & Charney, 2001; Weiss, Longhurst, & Mazure, 1999; Widom, 1989a, 1989b, 1989c, 1999). Thomlison discusses methods to assess risk of maltreatment, and she explores the elements of service that are essential to promote recovery from victimization.

In chapter 5, Jack Richman, Gary Bowen, and Michael Woolley investigate research on educational resilience. This chapter uses census data to discuss trends in education. The chapter might well be entitled "School Success" because the authors focus on academic achievement, a factor that protects many children who are exposed to high risk, as well as truancy and dropout. Richman, Bowen, and Woolley conclude by reviewing the "School Success Profile," a comprehensive assessment and intervention-planning instrument for identifying the needs of youths in middle and high school.

Each year thousands of children are born with serious developmental disabilities, including autism. Whether these disabilities are caused by genetic risk, maternal substance abuse, environmental contaminants (lead, for example), or other factors, the birth of a child with a developmental disorder poses special challenges in parenting, child care, and education. In chapter 6, Irene Nathan Zipper and Rune Simeonsson discuss the challenge of creating means for children of all abilities to participate fully in community activities. Using a risk factor perspective, they review recent legislation, emerging concepts of inclusion, and barriers to more effective services.

In chapter 7, Jeffrey Jenson explores alcohol and drug abuse, a problem that has mushroomed in importance. The growth of international cartels exclusively devoted to the sale of illicit drugs has resulted in extensive law-enforcement efforts and programs for federal interdiction and foreign eradication of drugs. Jenson argues that demand-side strategies designed to prevent alcohol and drug abuse show great promise. He discusses risk and protective factors for the use of psychoactive substances. He then outlines risk-focused principles for the design of more effective programs for prevention and early intervention.

In chapter 8, James Herbert Williams, Charles Ayers, Richard Van Dorn, and Michael Arthur discuss recent studies of risk factors for delinquency and conduct disorder. Their chapter, which is rich in theory and in practice implications, builds on the work of David Hawkins and Rico Catalano of the Social Development Research Group, School of Social Work, University of Washington (see, for example, Catalano & Hawkins, 1996; Huang, Kosterman, Catalano, Hawkins, & Abbott, 2001). They outline the individual, family, school, and community conditions that promote antisocial, aggressive behavior. From the perspective of social development, they then explore issues related to the prevention of conduct problems in childhood and adolescence.

No public health problem has more serious consequences for children than AIDS. Children who are born with AIDS or who develop it through sexual contact are at enormous risk. In chapter 9, Kathleen Rounds discusses AIDS and sexually transmitted infections (STIs) from a public health perspective. She reviews recent data on the incidence and prevalence of major STIs, including AIDS. Then she explores our growing knowledge about the behaviors, beliefs, and conditions that increase the odds of contracting an STI. Finally, she discusses research findings from promising prevention and early intervention programs.

In chapter 10, Cynthia Franklin, Jacqueline Corcoran, and Mary Beth Harris address the problem of adolescent pregnancy. Although births to young women ages 15 to 17 have dropped to record low levels (Federal Interagency Forum on Child and Family Statistics, 2001), pregnancy and giving birth are life-shaping events for many young women (Maynard, 1996). Franklin and her colleagues review the risk and protective factors for adolescent pregnancy. They discuss the effect of adolescent pregnancy on educational achievement, economic security, maternal and child health, and social relations. After reviewing case-assessment instruments, they explore a range of services that both prevent pregnancy and help young mothers and fathers respond to the tasks of child rearing.

In chapter 11, Carlean Gilbert reviews the literature on the problem of childhood depression. Arguing that mental illness is best conceptualized as arising from the interaction between biological predisposition and environmental risk, Gilbert discusses the historical controversy over childhood depression. She outlines the findings from recent research, describes case-assessment instruments for measuring levels of depression, and proposes guidelines for practice with children at risk of depression.

Although infant, child, and adolescent mortality rates have declined over the past two decades (due in part to the use of restraint systems that reduce injuries in automobile accidents), suicide is a major cause of death among adolescents, particularly white, non-Hispanic and American Indian–Alaska Native adolescents (Federal Interagency Forum on Child and Family Statistics, 2001). In chapter 12, Mark Macgowan reviews recent research on suicide and suicide attempts. In this chapter, he describes suicide-related risk factors that every social worker who works with children should know. Then he reviews strategies for intervention to prevent suicide and to work with children who may have attempted suicide.

Finally, in chapter 13, Mark Fraser and Maeda Galinsky revisit the central concepts of risk and resilience, framing issues and challenges in the context of evidence-based practice. Because much of social work practice involves working with and designing programs for children and families at risk, the concept of resilience is particularly relevant. In clinic, community, correctional, hospital, residential, and school settings, the purpose of social work practice with children is to develop strategies—interventions—to help children who are exposed to risk. Resilient children are exposed to high risk, but, through internal and external resources, they manage to beat the odds. Understanding their success and understanding the protective factors that interrupt risk mechanisms hold the potential to significantly inform social work practice. Knowledge about resilience cannot replace knowledge related to developmental deficits, psychopathology, and hostile environmental conditions. But it contributes to our understanding of problems by focusing on the assets and strengths—the protective forces—that disrupt risk processes. In chapter 13, Fraser and Galinsky explore the implications of our growing knowledge of risk and protection for evidence-based practice with children and their families.

REFERENCES

Berger, R. L., McBreen, J. T., & Rifkin, M. J. (1996). *Human behavior: A perspective for the helping professions.* White Plains, NY: Longman.

Bowen, G. L., Bowen, N. K., & Cook, P. G. (2000). Neighborhood characteristics and supportive parenting among single mothers. *Families, Crime, and Criminal Justice, 2,* 183–206.

Bronfenbrenner, U. (1979). *The ecology of human development: Experiments by nature and design.* Cambridge, MA: Harvard University Press.

Bronfenbrenner, U. (1986). Ecology of the family as a context to human development: Research perspectives. *Development Psychology, 22,* 723–742.

Catalano, R. F., & Hawkins, J. D. (1996). The social development model: A theory of antisocial behavior. In J. D. Hawkins (Ed.), *Delinquency and crime: Current theories* (149–197). New York: Cambridge University Press.

Coie, J. D., Watt, N. F., West, S. G., Hawkins, J. D., Asarnow, J. R., Markman, H. J., Ramey, S. L., Shure, M. B., & Long, B. (1993). The science of prevention: A conceptual framework and some directions for a national research program. *American Psychologist, 48,* 1013–1022.

Council on Social Work Education. (2001). *Educational policy and accreditation standards.* Washington, DC: Author.

Curtis, P. A., Boyd, J. D., Liepold, M., & Petit, M. (1995). *Child abuse and neglect: A look at the states.* Washington, DC: Child Welfare League of America.

Duncan, G. J. (1991). The economic environment of childhood. In A. C. Huston (Ed.), *Children in poverty: Child development and public policy* (pp. 23–50). New York: Cambridge University Press.

Duncan, G. J., & Brooks-Gunn, J. (Eds.). (1997). *Consequences of growing up poor.* New York: Russell Sage Foundation.

Duncan, G. J., & Brooks-Gunn, J. (2000). Family poverty, welfare reform, and child development. *Child Development, 71*(1), 188–196.

Duncan, G. J., Brooks-Gunn, J., & Klebanov, P. K. (1994). Economic deprivation and early childhood development. *Child Development, 65,* 296–318.

Evans, G. W., & English, K. (2002). The environment of poverty: Multiple stressor exposure, psychophysiological stress, and socioemotional adjustment. *Child Development, 73*(4), 1238–1248.

Federal Interagency Forum on Child and Family Statistics. (2001). *America's children: Key national indicators of well-being, 2001.* Washington, DC: U.S. Government Printing Office.

Federal Interagency Forum on Child and Family Statistics. (2002). *America's children: Key national indicators of well-being, 2002.* Washington, DC: U.S. Government Printing Office.

Furstenberg, F. F., Jr., Cook, T., Eccles, J., Elder, G. H., & Sameroff, A. J. (2000). Managing to make it: Urban families and adolescent success. Chicago: University of Chicago Press.

Garmezy, N. (1993). Vulnerability and resilience. In D. C. Funder, R. D. Parke, C. Tomlinson-Keasey, & K. Widaman (Eds.), *Studying lives through time* (pp. 377–398). Washington, DC: American Psychological Association.

Germain, C. B. (1991). *Human behavior in the social environment: An ecological view.* New York: Columbia University Press.

Hart, B., & Risley, T. R. (1995). *Meaning differences in the everyday experience of young American children.* Baltimore: Paul H. Brookes.

Haveman, R., & Wolfe, B. (1994). *Succeeding generations: On the effects of investments in children.* New York: Russell Sage Foundation.

Henggeler, S. W., Schoenwald, S. K., Borduin, C. M., Rowland, M. D., & Cunningham, P. B. (1998). *Multisystemic treatment of antisocial behavior in children and adolescents.* New York: Guilford Press.

Hepworth, D. H., Rooney, R. H., & Larson, J. A. (2002). *Direct social work practice: Theory and skills* (6th ed.). Pacific Grove, CA: Brooks/Cole.

Huang, B., Kosterman, R., Catalano, R. F., Hawkins, J. D., & Abbott, R. D. (2001). Modeling mediation in the etiology of violent behavior in adolescence: A test of the Social Development Model. *Criminology, 39*(1), 75–108.

Jessor, R. (1987). Risky driving and adolescent problem behavior: An extension of problem behavior theory. *Alcohol, Drugs, and Driving, 3*, 1–11.

Jessor, R. (1993). Successful adolescent development among youth in high-risk settings. *American Psychologist, 48*, 117–126.

Kaufman, J., & Charney, D. (2001). Effects of early stress on brain structure and function: Implications for understanding the relationship between child maltreatment and depression. *Development and Psychopathology, 13*(3), 451–471.

Klebanov, P. K., Brooks-Gunn, J., & Duncan, G. L. (1994). Does neighborhood and family poverty affect mothers' parenting, mental health, and social support? *Journal of Marriage and the Family, 56*, 441–455.

Lamer, M., & Collins, A. (1996). Poverty in the lives of young children. In E. J. Erwin (Ed.), *Putting children first* (pp. 55–75). Baltimore: Paul H. Brookes.

Linver, L. R., Brooks-Gunn, J., & Kohen, D. (1999). Parenting behavior and emotional health as mediators of family poverty effects upon young low-birthweight children's cognitive ability. *Annals of the New York Academy of Sciences, 896*, 376–378.

Loeber, R., Farrington, D. P., Stouthamer-Loeber, M., & Van Kammen, W. B. (1998). *Antisocial behavior and mental health problems: Explanatory factors in childhood and adolescence.* Mahwah, NJ: Lawrence Erlbaum.

Martin, J. A., Hamilton, B. E., Ventura, S. J., Menacker, F., & Park, M. M. (2002, February 12). *Births: Final data for 2000 National Vital Statistics Reports* (Vol. 50, No. 5). Hyattsville, MD: National Center for Health Statistics. Retrieved from http://www.cdc.gov/nchs/fastats/birthwt.htm on June 17, 2002.

Maynard, R. A. (Ed.). (1996). *Kids having kids: A Robin Hood Foundation special report on the costs of adolescent childbearing.* New York: Robin Hood Foundation.

Monitoring the Future. (2002a). *Long-term thirty-day trends in prevalence of various drugs for twelfth graders.* Retrieved from http://monitoringthefuture.org/data/ 01data.html#2001data-drugs on June 17, 2002.

Monitoring the Future. (2002b). *Long-term trends in prevalence in use of cigarettes.* Retrieved from http://monitoringthefuture.org/data/01data.html#2001data -cigs on June 17, 2002.

Mrazek, P. J., & Haggerty, R. J. (Eds.). (1994). *Reducing risks for mental disorders: Frontiers for preventive intervention research.* Washington, DC: National Academy Press.

Office of Juvenile Justice and Delinquency Prevention. (2002). *Juvenile arrest trends.* Washington, DC: U.S. Department of Justice. Retrieved from http://ojjdp.ncjrs. org/ojstatbb/asp/JAR_Display.asp?ID=qa2201012002 on July 14, 2002.

Resnick, G., & Burt, M. R. (1996). Youth at risk: Definitions and implications for service delivery. *American Journal of Orthopsychiatry, 66,* 172–188.

Sherman, A. (1994). *Wasting America's future: The Children's Defense Fund report on the costs of child poverty.* Washington, DC: Children's Defense Fund.

Stouthamer-Loeber, M., Loeber, R., Wei, E., Farrington, D. P., & Wikstrom, P. (2002). Risk and promotive effects in the explanation of persistent serious delinquency in boys. *Journal of Consulting and Clinical Psychology, 70*(1), 111–123.

U.S. Census Bureau (2002a). *DP-1: Profile of general demographic characteristics, 2000* [Table]. Retrieved from http://factfinder.census.gov/servlet/QTTable?ds_ name=DEC_2000_SF1_U&geo_id=01000US&qr_name=DEC_2000_SF1_ U_DP1 on July 16, 2002.

U.S. Census Bureau (2002b). *Historical poverty tables.* Retrieved from http://www .census.gov/hhes/poverty/histpov/hstpov3.html on June 16, 2002.

U.S. Census Bureau (2002c). *Historical poverty tables.* Retrieved from http://www .census.gov/hhes/poverty/histpov/hstpov4.html on June 16, 2002.

U.S. Department of Health and Human Services, Administration on Children, Youth, and Families. (1996). *Child maltreatment* 1994: *Reports from the states to the National Center on Child Abuse and Neglect.* Washington, DC: U.S. Government Printing Office.

U.S. Department of Health and Human Services, Administration on Children, Youth, and Families. (2001). *Child maltreatment* 1999: *Reports from the states to the National Center on Child Abuse and Neglect Data System.* Washington, DC: U.S. Government Printing Office.

Weiss, E. L., Longhurst, J. G., & Mazure, C. M. (1999). Childhood sexual abuse as a risk factor for depression in women: Psychosocial and neurobiological correlates. *American Journal of Psychiatry, 156,* 816–828.

Widom, C. S. (1989a). Child abuse, neglect, and violent criminal behavior. *Criminology, 27,* 251–271.

Widom, C. S. (1989b). The cycle of violence. *Science, 244,* 160–166.

Widom, C. S. (1989c). Does violence beget violence? A critical examination of the literature. *Psychological Bulletin, 106,* 3–28.

Widom, C. S. (1999). Childhood victimization, running away, and delinquency. *Journal of Research on Crime and Delinquency, 36*(4), 347–370.

2

Risk and Resilience in Childhood

Mark W. Fraser, Laura D. Kirby, and Paul R. Smokowski

Early developmental theorists recognized the importance of studying both atypical and normative development to gain a more complete understanding of
human functioning and adaptation (Cicchetti, 1990). In other words, they
believed that knowledge about the etiology of problem behavior could inform efforts to
promote or to enhance adaptive functioning. Similarly, in an effort to influence health
and rates of illness in general, the emerging field of epidemiology explored factors
related to the presence or absence of disease across populations. The story of John
Snow and the town pump illustrates this point. When Snow removed the handle from
the Broad Street water pump in 19th-century London, the spread of cholera was
stopped (Lilienfield & Lilienfield, 1980). With little understanding of how the disease
was spread, Snow based his action on observed behavioral differences of individuals
with and without the disease. He succeeded in slowing the spread of cholera by identifying and then interrupting the route of transmission of the disease.

As a discipline, epidemiology is an outgrowth of the study of the developmental pathways of health problems, and the search for factors that increase risks for social
problems grew out of that tradition (Garmezy, 1985). In the middle part of the last century, experts interested in the genesis of social and health problems began to focus on
the relationship between adversity and adaptation. Some scholars, for example, placed
great emphasis on parent-child attachment, and disrupted attachments were thought to
contribute to many kinds of childhood disorders (Svanberg, 1998). More recently, attention has shifted, or perhaps a better word would be "broadened," to consider the characteristics of family life, schools, and neighborhoods as factors that contribute to the
development of social and health problems (Sroufe, Carlson, Levy, & Egeland, 1999).

One of the important findings from recent studies is that there is remarkable
variability in the reactions of children to adversity. Although children exposed to major
stressors often develop problems, some children do not. Initially, researchers were
puzzled to find children who manifested positive, rather than pathological, adaptation
in the face of hostile environments and significant personal disadvantage. These
"invulnerable," "stress-resistant," or "resilient" groups of children fascinated scholars. Studies of these children are leading to a conceptual shift from the traditional
investigation of pathology to more recent investigations of successful adaptation. The
term "risk" reflects the fact that children in a particular group, for example, children
exposed to neighborhood violence, may have an increased probability of a poor developmental outcome. But, as a *probability*, risk also expresses the idea that children who
have similar biological or behavioral characteristics or who are exposed to similar sociocultural conditions may vary in their actual vulnerability to social and health problems
(Ingram & Price, 2001).

13

This chapter examines risk and resilience phenomena using an ecological, transactional model (Bronfenbrenner, 1979, 1986; Sameroff, 1995). Important conceptual issues in risk and resilience are reviewed. Then, a model for common risk and protective factors is proposed. This model is inclusive, providing an overarching framework for assessing social and health problems. Building on this model, subsequent chapters in this book will provide more specific information that focuses on particular problems faced by children and youth.

RISK FACTORS

The chapters in this book use the concept of developmental risk and, in so doing, rely on a broad definition of risk factors. On the basis of work by Coie and others (see, for example, Coie et al., 1993), we define *risk factors* as any influences that increase the chances for harm or, more specifically, influences that increase the probability of onset, digression to a more serious state, or maintenance of a problem condition. Risk factors range from prenatal biological complications to toxic environmental conditions that affect children. For example, perinatal trauma has been shown to be a biological risk factor for later academic difficulties (Lotspeich, 1998; O'Dougherty & Wright, 1990; Rutter, 2000b). Poor academic achievement is a risk factor for delinquency, and association with peers who are delinquent may lead to the maintenance of antisocial, aggressive behavior. Quite separately, the broad environmental conditions associated with public housing elevate risk for violent behavior (Office of Juvenile Justice and Delinquency Prevention, 1995; U.S. Department of Health and Human Services, 2001; Wikstrom, 1998; Wikstrom & Loeber, 2000). Each of these affects the probability of a poor developmental outcome for children. Each is a risk factor.

Some risk factors are directly related to negative outcomes, whereas others, called "markers," simply represent other processes responsible for potential negative outcomes. Being male, for example, is often identified as a risk factor for various types of psychiatric and behavioral disorders, including conduct disorder (Mrazek & Haggerty, 1994). However, there is little evidence that a singular gender difference explains the heightened vulnerability of boys for conduct disorder. More likely, gender is a marker for one or more other risk factors—some of which may be physiological but some of which may relate to the ways boys are socialized—that increase the probability of developing a behavior problem.

BEYOND RISK TRAITS: GENE–ENVIRONMENT INTERACTIONS

A *risk trait* refers to an individual predisposition toward developing a specific problem condition (Pellegrini, 1990). Genetic markers are often thought of as risk traits. For example, children born to parents with schizophrenia are more likely than other children to develop symptoms of schizophrenia (Rende & Plomin, 1993). Although genetic research has provided strong evidence for the existence of specific genes that increase the probability of developing some mental and medical disorders (including schizophrenia and major depressive disorders), it also supports a multifactorial model of risk (Rende & Plomin, 1993; Rutter, 2000a). Environmental and interpersonal factors are believed to play a key, sometimes triggering, role in determining outcomes for children with genetic risk. Genetic risks for many social and health problems may be mediated by—or expressed through—temperamental characteristics, such as a high basal arousal rate and low behavioral inhibition, that are sensitive to environmental conditions (Plomin, De Fries, McClearn, & Rutter, 1997). Moreover, both actively and passively, genetic influences may affect environmental conditions related to social and health problems (Rutter et al., 1997).

The influence of genetic risk—once thought to be an invariant trait—on environmental factors has led to the concept of *gene–environment interaction*, in which a genetic influence is conceptualized as having both direct and environmental components. That is, genetic influences may be expressed directly as a disorder or reflected in temperamental characteristics, for example, and they may be expressed indirectly through their influence on environmental conditions that potentiate the expression of disorders or problems. A temperamental child whose stubborn, disruptive behavior has genetic links may create such stress for parents that child monitoring is weakened and parent–child attachments are worn thin. Genetic risk, in such a case, potentiates the expression of a disorder both directly through temperament and indirectly through transactions with environmental conditions. Recent studies support both kinds of effects (Rutter, 2000a), although the comparative influence of direct versus gene–environment interactions is not well researched (see, for example, Meyer et al., 2000; Roy, Rutter, & Pickles, 2000; Rutter, Pickles, Murray, & Eaves, 2001). What this means is that children who have high genetic risk may vary significantly in their vulnerability at different points in development. Their risk exposure may operate, at least partly, through environmental conditions that vary over time and are subject to social intervention. This complex process leads to a dynamic transactional model of child development. Sameroff (1995) writes, "The child's behavior at any point in time is a product of the transactions between the phenotype (the child), the environtype (the source of external experience), and the genotype (the source of biological organization). This regulatory system is reciprocally determined at each point in development" (p. 667).

Research on the cycle of violence in child maltreatment offers a case in point. It is widely known that children who have been abused are more likely than children who have not been abused to experience conduct problems in adolescence (Rutter, Giller, & Hagell, 1998; Widom, 1989, 1999). Still, although their rates are significantly higher, most children who are maltreated do not get into trouble (Shields & Cicchetti, 2001; Widom, 1999). What accounts for the wide variation in responses to maltreatment? Social researchers have discovered that children who are abused are more likely, when compared with nonabused children, to demonstrate significant problems in regulating their emotions, displaying empathy, assessing their own arousal, and interpreting social information (Dodge, Bates, & Pettit, 1990; Shields & Cicchetti, 2001). Children recovering from abuse are less skillful in regulating anger and accurately interpreting the intentions of others. This could derive from differential experiences of trauma and the hypervigilance that trauma sometimes creates. Errors in interpreting others' actions and in controlling emotions may lead to greater risk of getting into fights, using force to resolve disputes, and obtaining social position through aggressive behavior (Dodge et al., 1990; Shields & Cicchetti, 2001). Other mediating factors may also be at work because neighborhood, school, and peer influences affect behavioral trajectories (see, for example, Moffitt, Caspi, Rutter, & Silva, 2001).

But could there be a latent genetic component in this sequence of behavioral risk factors? Research suggests that this may be the case. The monoamine oxidase (MAOA) gene is on the X chromosome (Xp11.23-11.4), and it controls the MAOA enzyme, which renders inactive neurotransmitters such as norepinephrine, serotonin, and dopamine. Although the causal processes are complicated and may involve other genes or alleles (slight variants of the same gene), the absence of MAOA has been associated with impulsive, aggressive behavior in both humans and animals (Rowe, 2001). MAOA seems to reduce reactivity and sensitivity to stress. Therefore, its absence means that a child is more quickly aroused in the presence of stress, and its presence suggests that a child is more capable of conscious self-control (Clark & Grunstein, 2000). In a sample of 442 New Zealand boys who were tracked from birth to age 26, Caspi and colleagues (2002) examined the relative influence of MAOA activity level and maltreatment severity on subsequent antisocial behavior. After dividing the sample into groups of no maltreatment, probable maltreatment, and severe maltreatment, they estimated MAOA activity and found no significant differences across the three levels of maltreatment. Because maltreatment groupings did not differ on MAOA activity, the researchers believed that genotype alone did not influence exposure to maltreatment. Next, they divided each of the three maltreatment groups into low and high MAOA activity subgroups and estimated antisocial behavior within maltreatment groupings. Across four measures of conduct problems—(1) diagnosis of conduct disorder in adolescence, (2) conviction for a violent offense as an adult, (3) diagnosis of antisocial personality as an adult, and (4) disposition toward violence as an adult—high MAOA activity distinguished prosocial from antisocial adults in the severe maltreatment group, but not in the other two maltreatment groups. The effect of child maltreatment on antisocial behavior was significant overall (that is, a greater percentage of boys who were maltreated had conduct problems), but the effect was much weaker for the high MAOA group exposed to severe maltreatment than for the low MAOA group exposed to severe maltreatment. In other maltreatment groups, MAOA level failed to distinguish behavioral outcomes. In other words, the interaction between MAOA activity and maltreatment severity was startlingly strong. Compared with individuals who had not been maltreated, the risk for being convicted of a violent crime was 10 times higher when the individual had the combination of low MAOA activity and a history of severe maltreatment.

The findings provide intriguing evidence that a gene may moderate the impact of child maltreatment on the future behavior of some children and that genetic effects interact with environmental conditions to affect vulnerability. In this case, a poor developmental outcome depends on an interaction between environment (exposure to severe maltreatment) and a child's genotype (low MAOA activity). What is especially interesting from the perspective of resilience is that high MAOA appears to confer a measure of protection against a poor developmental outcome in boys who are severely abused. Clearly, additional research is needed to replicate this study with other populations and to extend it to girls. We use it to represent a thread of biobehavioral research that is beginning to explicate the intertwined influences of biological and environmental factors on child development. Parenthetically, these studies imply that combinations of pharmacological interventions (for example, to increase levels of MAOA) and social interventions (for example, to train maltreated children to regulate arousal and more accurately interpret social information) may hold potential to improve the effectiveness of child welfare practice in the not-to-distant future.[1]

Historically, the term "risk trait" was used to describe a wide range of risk conditions that were thought to exert relatively predictable effects (see, for example, Zubin & Spring, 1977). In addition to genetic effects, the term was sometimes used to describe attributes of individuals, such as having a low IQ, or the presence of a specific disorder, such as attention-deficit hyperactivity disorder, which may function as a marker of risk for a subsequent problem or disorder. Research is beginning to suggest that the term "trait" is a misnomer, even for genetic influences such as the influence of MAOA activity. Sensitivity to risk appears to vary and is often related to environmental or "contextual" conditions. Thus, the term "risk trait," even when used to describe genetic influences, must be conditioned on the idea that there is great variation in susceptibility to risk.

CONTEXTUAL EFFECTS

Contextual effects are environmental conditions that affect vulnerability. The social and environmental context can create and maintain poor functioning by exposing children to damaging experiences; alternatively, it can promote high functioning by exposing children to supportive others and opportunities for advancement. These contextual effects include the influences of being a member of particular groupings or clusters. For example, they can include the effect of being in a particular classroom with a teacher who may have a special affect (for example, a caring and understanding versus hostile demeanor) or living in a particular neighborhood with a special characteristic, perhaps a neighborhood that prides itself in having a Greek, Korean, Mexican, Puerto Rican, or Samoan tradition wherein children learn about their ethnic heritage and wherein religious or spiritual ceremonies mark major community events. Contextual effects are nested and multidimensional. Family factors, such as family size and cohesion, affect parenting. In turn, family factors are nested in the influence of neighborhood factors, such as neighborhood safety and cohesion, which often influence the capacity of parents to supervise children and support their efforts in school, in sports, or in other activities (Bowen, Bowen, & Ware, 2002). The relative influences of contexts broaden, differentiate, and deepen as children grow (Richman & Fraser, 2001). Contextual effects deflect stress or contribute to it by regulating social and tangible resources requisite for meeting fundamental needs (Boyce et al., 1998).

Contextual effects are sometimes thought of as providing the "three Rs": *rules* (local expressions of expectations), *resources* (human and concrete assets for problem solving), and *routines* (behavioral patterns for sustained social interaction; Wikstrom, 1998). They include, for example, the special effects of attending a magnet school that has rules, resources, and routines related to developing competencies in, say, the fine arts. In the workplace, contextual effects include the "organizational climate" and its influence on workers and, by extension, the community. Sometimes, too,

---

[1]For a discussion of the practice implications of biologic risks in adopted children, including both genetic liability and physiological insult during prenatal and postnatal periods, see Barth (2002).

contextual effects include the impact of being in neighborhoods that have differing degrees of collective efficacy—shared beliefs and the capacity to take action on behalf of neighborhood members (Sampson, 2001).

Neighborhood poverty is one of the more commonly researched contextual influences. It directly affects children by lowering the quality of their food and shelter. It has indirect effects on children by placing parents under such constant strain that they find it difficult to respond consistently to a child's needs. Contextual effects often appear to be mediated by or, at least, entangled with variables at the family and individual levels (for detailed discussions, see Duncan & Raudenbush, 2001; McLoyd, 1990; 1998). For example, results from the Pittsburgh Youth Study, a study of 506 boys in public school, indicate that neighborhood effects on delinquency are largely mediated by such variables as hyperactivity and quality of parental supervision (Peoples & Loeber, 1994). Contextual effects appear to be like other risk factors in that they may exert strong effects in some settings and at some times and weak effects in other settings and times (Booth & Crouter, 2001).

STRESSFUL LIFE EVENTS: FROM TURNING POINTS TO DAILY HASSLES

One approach to studying risk has been to assess the impact of stressful life events, such as becoming pregnant, getting arrested, or witnessing a disaster. Some life events are so pivotal that they alter developmental trajectories. These "turning point effects" are so potent that they immediately alter individual capabilities and environmental conditions—a dramatic and abrupt transition. The effects of a disabling automobile accident or an arrest that is followed by disposition to secure care can drastically alter a child's life course.

Turning point effects dramatically alter risk by significantly altering the context or by altering the individual's personal perceptions (for example, feelings of self-efficacy, self-esteem, or optimism). Turning points affect development both negatively and positively. For example, military service may remove an adolescent from a violent neighborhood or a delinquent peer group (Sampson & Laub, 1996). In a longitudinal study of some 698 children from the island of Kauai, Werner and Smith (1982, 1992) found army service to have its greatest positive effect on boys from the most disadvantaged backgrounds. For these boys—more than for boys from more advantaged environments—the training and travel afforded by the army was a turning point. It provided opportunities and rewards that were unavailable to these boys through their families or in their communities.

As turning point effects, marriage (when stable and harmonious) and employment have been shown to reduce criminal activity (Laub, Nagin, & Sampson, 1998). They are positive turning points. In the same way, spiritual conversion may dramatically alter the attachments and activities that shape a person's behaviors and beliefs. After he conducted in-depth interviews with dozens of boys sent to maximum security prisons for murder, Garbarino (2001, p. 93) concluded, "What is left for them? What can they do? They can only go upward and inward, through a process of reflection, introspection, meditation, religious involvement, spiritual concern, and reading." In Garbarino's view, a turning point related to religious conversion may be all these boys have left. Such turning point effects radically alter risk factors. They hold the potential to reduce risk and present new opportunities. In one sense, the purpose of social intervention is to create turning-point effects—to remove a child from a harmful home situation or to place an adolescent mother in a school program where she can continue her education, learn to be a parent, and receive support for positive parenting. Turning point effects significantly alter developmental outcomes.

In contrast to turning point effects, a second approach to the study of stress has been to consider the effects of repeated annoying events, daily hassles, and accumulated stress on developmental outcomes. These can range from experiences in the home (for example, living in an apartment where local trains and trucks make loud noises at all hours of the day), in the school (for example, being scared of bullies and taking circuitous routes to classes), with peers (for example, having friends who are constantly in need of help), and in the neighborhood (for example, having to walk past drug dealers on the way to school; Seidman et al., 1998). A family-focused measure of 44 social and economic life stresses was found to predict early onset conduct problems in a 20-year longitudinal study of 180 children who, starting at birth, attended a public health clinic in Minneapolis (Aguilar, Sroufe, Egeland, & Carlson, 2000). In the same study, a measure of daily stress experienced by the children when they reached 16 years old predicted the development of late onset conduct problems in high school.

The effects of stressful life events on adolescent development are only now being thoroughly investigated. Research on bullying is, perhaps, a case in point. In a study of 15,686 U.S. students between the ages of 12 and 16, Nansel and colleagues (2001) reported that 8.5 percent were bullied "sometimes" and 8.4 percent were bullied "one or more times a week." Bullying was defined as repeated teasing in a way not liked or being the object of nasty and unpleasant things said by another student or students. In aggregate, nearly 30 percent reported moderate or frequent involvement in some type of bullying (13.0 percent as a bully, 10.6 percent as a victim of a bully, and 6.3 percent as both). Until recently, these types of life events have been largely ignored in the United States, but studies in Europe suggest that children who are bullied are at greater risk of poor social and academic developmental outcomes (Astor, Benbenishty, Pitner, & Meyer, 2004). Many bullies experience mental health difficulties including attention-deficit disorder, depression, and oppositional–conduct disorder (Kumpulainen, Rasanen, & Puura, 2001). Also, research has found that bullies tend to engage in frequent, excessive drinking and substance use more often than victims or bully–victims (Kaltiala-Heino, Rimpela, & Rimpela, 2000). As adults, research has found that bullies often display externalizing behaviors, hyperactivity, and antisocial characteristics (Kumpulainen & Rasanen, 2000; Olweus, 1994; Roberts & Morotti, 2000). Victims also experience difficulties as a result of being bullied. As adults, former victims have lower levels of achievement than their peers. In addition, at age 23, former victims tend to be more depressed and have poorer self-esteem than nonvictimized young adults (Olweus, 1995). Research has also indicated that former victims experience various psychosocial difficulties during adulthood as well as problems in their sexual relationships (Carney & Merrell, 2001; Gilmartin, 1987; Hazler, 1996). Furthermore, in adulthood, former victims sometimes carry out acts of retribution against former bullies (Carney & Merrell, 2001).

Identifying causal relationships between annoying, embarrassing, demeaning, or aggravating daily events and long-term outcomes is difficult. But research on bullying suggests that repeated harassment exacts a developmental toll that, while not as precipitous as turning point events, is certainly harmful. Both kinds of stressful events—turning point events and daily hassles—appear to be related to the development of social and health problems in childhood.

CUMULATIVE EFFECTS: THE BUNDLING OF RISK

There is growing evidence that the cumulation of stress has a major effect on child development (Coie et al., 1993; Garmezy, 1993a; Rutter, 2001; Seifer, Sameroff, Baldwin, & Baldwin, 1992). One oft-heard hypothesis regarding stress is that prolonged exposure to a risk factor increases the likelihood of negative outcomes (Stouthamer-Loeber et al., 1993). School failure, for example, may not be associated with aggressive, antisocial behavior in early grades, but it may become associated with behavior problems as failures are repeated over time (see Farrington et al., 1993; Loeber & Farrington, 2000; Loeber, Farrington, Stouthamer-Loeber, & Van Kammen, 1998a; Loeber & Stouthamer-Loeber, 1996).

Risk factors frequently occur together or cluster to produce heightened vulnerability (Dishion, Capaldi, & Yoerger, 1999; Pellegrini, 1990; Rutter, 2001). Children who lose a parent to death or divorce, for example, often suffer economic strains and a decline in social status as a consequence (Crook & Eliot, 1980). In the same vein, there is evidence that adolescent drug abuse clusters with other adolescent problems, such as delinquency, attention deficit, pregnancy, school misbehavior, depressed mood, and dropping out (Hawkins, Catalano, & Miller, 1992; Loeber, Farrington, Stouthamer-Loeber, Van Kammen, 1998b). Furthermore, some broad contextual variables such as poverty represent a latent clustering of risk factors, including, for example, low maternal education, low-status parental occupation, large family size, and the absence of one parent (Luthar, 1991). In short, risk tends to cluster, and children who are high on two or three risk factors are likely to be high on other, perhaps unobserved, risk factors. This phenomenon is sometimes called "bundling" (Rutter, 2000b).

As the number of risk factors increases, the cumulation exerts an increasingly strong influence on children (Dishion, Capaldi, & Yoerger, 1999; Greenberg, Speltz, DeKlyen, & Jones, 2001). Rutter (1979) found that the presence of a single family stressor had a negligible effect on the rate of psychiatric disorder among children. The presence of two or more risk factors, however, multiplicatively increased the rate of disorder among children. In a longitudinal study, Fergusson and Lynskey (1996) developed an index of family stress; then, using this index, they compared youths at age 15 on measures of delinquency, substance abuse, and other social problems. The relationship between the number of family stressors and the presence of social problems was positive but nonlinear. One or two family stressors seemed to make little difference, but several created high odds for serious behavioral problems. Similarly, in a study of 78,710 sixth- through 12th-grade children from Kansas, Maine, Oregon, South Carolina, and Washington, Pollard, Hawkins, and Arthur (1999, p. 151) found substance abuse, school problems, and delinquency to be strongly related to risk exposure, with "steep [curvilinear] increases in prevalence associated with the highest levels of risk. . . ."

Thus, the effect of exposure to several risk factors is not simply additive. Although the effect of a single stressor may be negligible, the effect of three or four stressors may be far greater than a threefold or fourfold increase in vulnerability.

RISK MECHANISMS

Risk factors that occur or exist at one moment in time, such as a stressful life event, may be useful to determine the risk status of children, but they provide little information about how a child came to be at risk. The term "risk mechanism" refers to the process whereby a risk factor contributes over time to heightened vulnerability. At the practice level, a child's vulnerability is perhaps most precisely understood only in the context of knowledge of the mechanisms that cause social and health problems. Understanding endogenous risk processes that are directly related to the development of disorders is a central ingredient in estimating individual vulnerability (Ingram & Price, 2001). For example, poor parenting is a commonly identified risk factor. The risk mechanism that underlies poor parenting probably involves inadequate supervision of children, inconsistent responses to children's behavior, and constant nagging or nattering (Patterson, 1982). No single "poor parenting" event produces a negative outcome. Rather, interactional processes shape behaviors and problems over time. Even though cumulative risk appears to predict many developmental outcomes, the understanding of particular risk mechanisms is vital for targeting intervention and prevention programs. The separation of vulnerability-enhancing mechanisms from risk indicators is a major challenge.

RISK CHAINS AND CAUSAL MODELS

At least in principle if not practice, the health and social sciences have relied on causal chains or models to establish a logical foundation on which to base prevention and other intervention efforts (Simeonsson, 1994). Relationships among risk factors and social problems are complex, however, and clearly defined causal chains are difficult to identify and often the subject of heated debate. Nevertheless, the causal modeling concept can be modified to identify sequential, though not necessarily causal, risk chains (Mrazek & Haggerty, 1994; Simeonsson, 1994). In a social development model of antisocial behavior proposed by Huang, Kosterman, Catalano, Hawkins, and Abbott (2001), for example, risk chains represent linkages of conceptually distinct risk factors. Sequenced or chained risk factors for antisocial behavior include perceived opportunities for antisocial interactions, interaction with antisocial others, and perceived rewards for antisocial behavior. Linked together, they represent one of many logical, sequential pathways that lead children to antisocial behavior. Risk chains of this nature are testable and disrupting them can be a target of prevention, early intervention, or treatment.

The concept of risk is continually being refined. It is widely agreed that different types of risk exist, including individual and contextual risks plus stressful life events. Understanding risk is further complicated by related concepts, such as cumulative risk, risk chains, and risk mechanisms. What is clear is that risk is probabilistic, meaning that children exposed to risk factors are more likely to experience negative outcomes. It is equally certain that some children who are exposed to a high level of risk manage to overcome the odds (Rutter, 2001; Werner & Smith, 1992). They are resilient.

CONCEPT OF RESILIENCE

The study of resilience emerged as a by-product of the search for risk factors. Curiously, researchers consistently found that some children who faced stressful, high-risk situations fared well in life (Garmezy, 1971, 1985; Rutter, 1987; Werner, 1984; Werner & Smith, 1977, 1982, 1992). For example, research showed that some children who were born prematurely and at low birthweights succeeded in school as well as in other social settings. Other children who were victims of abuse or neglect were found to be quite successful in developing positive, productive, and intimate relationships with others later in life. Research indicated that children's responses to stress varied markedly. This led Garmezy (1971), Rutter (1979), Masten (1987), Luthar (1991), Sameroff (1995), Elder (1974), and others to focus on positive as well as pathological outcomes in groups of children thought to be at high risk. The concept of resilience arose from this work. Resilience is defined as observing a normal or even exceptionally positive developmental outcome in spite of exposure to major risk for the development of serious social or health problems. The main question resilience researchers have posed is, "Why are certain (resilient) children able to sustain adaptive functioning under significant duress while other children are not able to manifest this level of adaptation?" The term "resilient" has come to be used to describe children who achieve positive outcomes in the face of risk. This implies that children have been exposed to risk and have made adaptations or have benefited from environmental assets that produced good developmental outcomes.

TYPES OF RESILIENCE: INVULNERABILITY?

Are resilient children invulnerable? Do they have such strength of character or such extraordinary skill that they overcome adversities to which the vast majority of others succumb? Pines (1975), Anthony (1987), and others labeled resilient children "invulnerable" based on their apparent ability to maintain emotional competence despite severe or prolonged adversity. But the concept of invulnerability is controversial. There is little evidence to support the implication that some children are simply not vulnerable to the effects of risk factors (Fisher, Kokes, Cole, Perkins, & Wynne, 1987; Pellegrini, 1990). In fact, among children exposed to risk, those who have the least exposure—that is, children exposed to the least cumulative risk—appear to fare the best. Those with the highest levels of exposure are the least likely to produce adaptive behavior (Pollard et al., 1999; Rutter, 2000a, 2000b). Rather than being invulnerable, this suggests that children have individual thresholds for risk and resilience. Some children may be able to endure more adversity than others, but under great stress, all children have limits and few, if any, remain unaffected.

Terms like "stress resistant" or "invulnerable" promise too much (Garmezy, 1993a). Far from being invulnerable, resilient children are affected by stress like everyone else, but they are more able to adapt or recover, returning to prior levels of adjustment, than their less resilient peers. Garmezy emphasizes this by stressing that accumulated risk or "pileup" can overwhelm even the most resilient children or adolescents. This point of view argues for a threshold or "breaking point" conception of resilience.

On balance, the term *invulnerable* has been superseded by the broader concept of resilience. Whereas invulnerability suggests that some children are unaffected by a risk factor that affects most children or that some children's responses to adversity are exceptional or even superhuman, resilience is defined by the presence of risk factors in combination with positive—often quite intuitive and colloquial rather than esoteric—forces that contribute to adaptive outcomes (Garmezy, 1993b). Resilience emerges from "the everyday magic of ordinary, normative human resources in the minds, brains, and bodies of children, in their families and relationships, and in their communities" (Masten, 2001, p. 235).

Within that framework, three types of resilience have been described (Masten, Best, & Garmezy, 1990). The first, commonly referred to as "overcoming the odds," is defined by the attainment of positive outcomes despite high-risk status. For example, a preterm infant is considered high risk by virtue of the correlation between prematurity and negative health outcomes. A preterm infant who does not experience negative outcomes may thus be described as overcoming the odds. This notion of resilience grew most directly out of the risk literature described above. The second concept of resilience, grounded in the literature on stress and coping, refers to "sustained competence under stress." In families where conflict is high, for example, resilient children will display an ability to cope with chronic environmental and interpersonal stress. Coping in this sense refers to a child's efforts, including both thought and action, to restore or maintain internal or external equilibrium (Masten, Best, & Garmezy, 1990). The third conception of resilience refers to "recovery from trauma." This type of resilience is evident in children who function well after an intensely stressful event, such as sexual abuse or exposure to street violence. Many child survivors of World War II concentration camps have been recognized as resilient in this way. To capture these three subtypes in an overarching framework, resilience is best defined as "successful adaptation despite adversity" (Begun, 1993; Benard, 1993; Cowan, Wyman, Work, & Parker, 1990; Masten, 1994; Rutter, 2000b, 2001; Werner & Smith, 1992).

Is resilience an individual characteristic? Certainly, resilience is often associated with having a "resilient temperament" or with personal characteristics, such as resourcefulness, achievement motivation, efficacy, high intelligence, and humor. But, although resilience emerges in some children from a tenacity of spirit and other personal attributes, resilience appears to be less a personality trait than the product of dynamic interplay between adversity and a variety of *both* personal and environmental assets that suppress or mediate risk. Complex transactions between environmental assets and individual attributes are required for producing resilience. Studies of children in Rochester and Philadelphia by Sameroff, Bartko, Baldwin, Baldwin, and Seifer (1998, p. 183) found, ". . . the effects of . . . individual competencies do not overcome the effects of high environmental risk." A child with a tenacious spirit will have great difficulty maintaining motivation in bleak environments that offer no options for positive development. At the same time, however, resilient children are resourceful in seeking out environmental niches to nurture their abilities.

One finding is consistent in studies of children: Individual behavior, whether resilient or not, is the result of continuous transactions between children and their experiences in their families, schools, and neighborhoods. This has important implications for intervention because we cannot dismiss children who have poor developmental outcomes as children who lack resilient dispositions. Indeed, it is the environment that appears most important for planning prevention and intervention services. When resilience in children is observed, exceptional interpersonal and environmental resources are almost always found. Early childhood intervention research supports this contention. For instance, Reynolds, Temple, Robertson, and Mann (2001) reported findings from a 15-year longitudinal investigation of disadvantaged children in Chicago. Children who participated in Chicago's Child–Parent Center (CPC) program, relative to a matched comparison group, had higher rates of high school completion; higher rates of completed education; and lower rates of juvenile arrest, violent arrest, and dropping out of high school. The CPC program was an exceptional environmental resource that provided comprehensive education, family, and health services for high-risk children ages 3 to 9. The program also heightened parent involvement in children's lives and enhanced parent and child attachments to school. Through understanding the environmental factors that promote competence in the face of high risk, it may be possible to design more effective services.

RESILIENCE AND COMPETENCE

Various perspectives on resilience have emerged in the literature. As suggested in the previous section, resilient children are often described as "competent." Competence refers to the effectiveness of individual adaptation to environmental constraints at a given point in child development and within a particular cultural context (Garmezy & Masten, 1991; Masten & Coatsworth, 1995). Competence thus incorporates expectations for behavior that are age appropriate within the meaning–giving schema of a child's nationality, culture, religion, and language. The processes that contribute to adaptational success are clearly multidimensional, involving the integration of cognitive, emotional, physical, and social skill (Masten & Curtis, 2000). And they are transactional, involving interaction between individual capabilities and the environment. From this perspective, adaptational failure can have roots in individual attributes, for example, genetically related cognitive capabilities or insult to cognitive capabilities as a result of a traumatic accident, or environmental conditions that present insurmountable barriers. In thinking of competence, there is no assumption that adaptation is related solely to individual characteristics. Far from it, in fact, adaptation and competence are viewed as the outcomes of transactions between individual capability and environmental conditions.

Competence implies good, not necessarily superb, adaptation within a particular ecological context during a particular developmental stage. To be competent, a child or adolescent does not need to be resilient. Competence in some domains may come easily, with or without strenuous effort. Competent behavior may simply be a function of practice, intuition, or natural finesse or an appropriate response to environmental stimulation. Such is the case for the gifted student or the musician with natural talent. Resilience, in contrast to competence, is good adaptation despite significant individual or environmental adversity. To be considered resilient, a child or adolescent must manifest competence even though she has experienced important challenges on the road to adaptation (Masten & Coatsworth, 1995). Without risk, there is no possibility or need for resilience, but competence, regardless of risk, is always possible and usually necessary for positive adaptation.

Being resilient or competent does not imply that children survive without pain or anxiety. Significant psychological distress has been observed in children who were behaviorally competent (Farber & Egeland, 1987; Luthar, 1991). Similarly, definitions of resilience based on competence in a single functional domain, for example, academic success, may give a false impression because competence in one area represents only a small part of what may be considered successful coping (Luthar, Doernberger, & Zigler, 1993). Werner and Smith (1992) found that many "invulnerable" children had painful memories, nightmares, and other adjustment problems. Likewise, in a study of 150 ninth-grade youths from inner-city schools, Luthar, Doernberger, and Zigler (1993) found that high-performing, resilient children had depressive symptoms comparable to low-performing, highly stressed youths. It appears that an adequate coping response in one situation does not necessarily spill over to other situations. Although there is some evidence that resilience in one developmental sphere may generalize to other spheres (Masten et al., 1999), the prevalence of spillover effects is not well documented. In fact, among apparently resilient children, the unevenness of functioning across developmental domains has spawned a number of new terms: "educational resilience" (Brown, D'Emidio-Caston, & Benard, 2001; Wang, Haertel, & Walberg, 1994), "emotional resilience" (Kline & Short, 1991a, 1991b), and "behavioral resilience" (Carpentieri, Mulhern, Douglas, Hanna, & Fairdough, 1993). Moreover, the term "resilience" has recently been applied to competence in the systems supporting children—family resilience (Walsh, 1998), couples resilience (Conger, Rueter, & Elder, 1999), and community resilience (Sonn & Fisher, 1998).

Developmental processes represent another potential source of variation in childhood resilience. Although risk is ubiquitous in the lives of many children, children respond differently to risk over time. Vulnerability appears to shift as a function of developmental or maturational changes. The fluctuating nature of vulnerability may result from the interaction of individual and environmental conditions that change as children enter school, develop friendship networks, explore sexuality, and so on. Developmentally, constitutional or individual factors appear more important during infancy and childhood, and interpersonal factors appear more important during adolescence (Grizenko & Fisher, 1992). In the Kauai study (Werner & Smith, 1977, 1982, 1992), children were variably exposed to a number of risk factors, including perinatal stress, chronic poverty, family discord, and parental psychopathology. About one-third of the total group was identified as high risk. Somewhat fewer than one-third of the high-risk children grew into competent, confident, and caring young adults and were classified as resilient. Clusters of protective factors were identified for these resilient children, including both individual characteristics (such as having a positive social orientation and being affectionate, active, and good-natured) and environmental characteristics (such as the presence of a warm, supportive home environment). However, in a long-term follow-up, Werner (1992) observed that most of the high-risk youths who developed serious coping problems in adolescence could be described as resilient by the time they reached their early 30s. On the basis of these and other similar data, it appears that resilience is not a fixed attribute, but rather a dynamic characteristic that changes with social circumstances. It may emerge even after poor interim outcomes.

Understanding resilience in environmental and cultural contexts is key to understanding children at risk. This book focuses on the wide range of risk conditions that affect children and that interact with children's personal and environmental resources to produce developmental outcomes. Understanding the sources of competence and resilience in childhood holds the potential to inform the development of innovative, more effective social and health services. So, this book conceptualizes developmental outcomes in terms of successful adaptation, rather than developmental deficits, and normative social functioning, where children reach developmental milestones at age-appropriate times and in appropriate sequences without experiencing serious social problems. In other words, we focus on the factors that produce positive life course outcomes among children at risk.

RESILIENCE, RISK, AND CULTURE: DYNAMIC INTERACTION OVER TIME

In relying on normative functioning to define resilience, we must recognize that culturally determined behavior is a potential source of variation in outcomes. In other words, behavior considered adaptive and normative in one culture may not be similarly adaptive and normative in other cultures (Coie et al., 1993; Coll & Magnuson, 2000). Consider the example of "difficult" temperament. In some cultures, assertiveness is not highly valued and may be viewed as improper, if not dysfunctional, behavior. But in other cultures, an assertive and demanding temperament may be adaptive and perhaps even required for survival (Masten et al., 1990).

Similarly, some risk factors, the way they are defined, and their relationships to developmental outcomes may be unique to specific populations (for a discussion, see Barrera, Castro, & Biglan, 1999). For example, in the Hopi Indian culture, significant social stigma used to be attached to traditionally disapproved marriages, such as marriage across tribes, mesas, and clans of disparate social status. Levy and Kunitz (1987) observed that children of parents who entered into such marriages were at increased risk of suicide (Mrazek & Haggerty, 1994). For Hopi children, then, cross-mesa marriage constituted a risk factor; for children from other backgrounds, it was less important.

In the same vein, some risk factors may operate differently for children in African American families than for children in European American families. Though there is variation, African American females become single parents, sole heads of the household, and bear more children at an earlier age than European American females. Viewed without assessing the contribution of culture, this is often thought to place many African American children at risk (McAdoo, 1998). African American culture, however, has traditionally included other family members (especially other females, such as grandmothers) in caregiving roles and commonly fosters wide social support systems within the African American community. Large extended family networks and "fictive" kin networks, in which nonrelatives are treated as kin, are common within African American communities (Thornton, 1998). Consequently, African American children often experience a wider variety of caregiving relationships than European American children. The presence of a maternal grandmother, for example, has been noted as a key factor in ameliorating the negative effects of teen parenting (Cantwell & Jenkins, 1998; Garcia Coll, Sepkoski, & Lester, 1982). Religious participation, spirituality, access to a supportive network, and attitudes that boldly challenge societal values that exclude African Americans also appear to buffer stress (Bagley & Carroll, 1998; McLoyd, 1990). Because of cultural differences in the ways children are raised and the coping mechanisms used by parents, single parenthood may hold less potential for harm for African American children than for European American children. In short, the meaning and potentiating capacity of risk factors must be interpreted in the context of cultural motifs and norms, religious beliefs, social support, racial and ethnic socialization, and other factors that affect child rearing.

On the basis of resources, beliefs, expectations, and support structures within particular cultural groups, the same risk factor may differ in its impact. Acculturation, for example, can be a risk-laden process for many immigrants. There is clearly a link between acculturation stress and subsequent social maladjustment, psychopathology, and substance use (for example, see Al-Issa, & Tousignant, 1997; Delgado, 1998; Gil, Vega, & Dimas, 1994; Szapocznik, & Kurtines, 1980). However, acculturation processes and outcomes vary considerably both between and within groups of immigrants. Within-group comparisons illuminate important differences. For example, the estimated proportion of the U.S. Latino population with at least a high school degree ranges from about 73 percent for people with Cuban heritage to about 51 percent for people with Mexican heritage (U.S. Census Bureau, 2000). This difference in educational attainment may be connected to acculturation risk. Further complicating this process, there appears to be a curvilinear relationship between psychosocial problems and acculturation, with children and adolescents at high and low acculturation levels exhibiting more problems than children in the mid-range of acculturation (LaFromboise, Coleman, & Gerton, 1993; Rogler, Cortes, & Malgadi, 1991). In comparison to less acculturated peers, more acculturated Latinos display higher levels of alcohol use; less consumption of balanced, healthy meals; and more consumption of marijuana, cocaine, or both (Amaro, Whitaker, Coffman & Heeren, 1990; Marks, Garcia & Solts, 1990; Vega et al., 1998). However, researchers have linked low acculturation levels with psychological difficulties, such as depression, social withdrawal, familial isolation, despair, obsessive–compulsive behavior, hostility, anxiety, and posttraumatic stress disorder (Miranda, Estrada, & Firpo-Jimenez, 2000; Szapocznik & Kurtines, 1980; Torres-Matrello, 1976). Moderate acculturation levels that manifest in biculturalism are linked with the least detrimental and most adaptive outcomes—higher quality of life, affect balance, social interest, and psychological adjustment with concomitant lower problematic behavior (Gil, Wagner, & Vega, 2000; Lang, Munoz, Bernal, & Sorensen, 1982; Miranda et al., 2000; Rogler et al., 1991; Szapocznik & Kurtines, 1980). Thus, bicultural individuals demonstrate resilience in handling acculturation stressors and being able to access resources from two cultural systems. The implication for practice is clear: Variation across and within cultures must always be considered. Both vulnerability and adaptation are deeply embedded in cultural systems.

CONCEPT OF PROTECTION

In the face of growing dissatisfaction with pathology- and deficit-focused intervention strategies, professionals from mental health and other fields have joined public health practitioners in the search for factors that might promote successful adaptation—resilience—in children. In part, the assets and strengths perspectives in social work and allied health disciplines represent this view (Saleebey, 1996, 1997, 2000). Because assets and strengths are conceptualized as protecting children from risk, protective factors occupy an increasingly important position in developing our understanding of psychopathology and other social problems.

But in spite of its growing salience, the term "protective factor" has not been clearly or consistently defined. Some scholars distinguish between "resilience factors" as those that are internal to a child and "protective factors" as those that are external (Seifer et al., 1992). Others argue that protective factors are preventive in relation to risk, whereas resilience factors aid the individual in recovering from a stressor or crisis event (McCubbin, McCubbin, Thompson, Han, & Allen, 1997). Others have adopted a broader definition in which individual protective factors are differentiated from environmental protective factors. Still others have argued that protective factors can be defined only in concert with risk factors because of their interrelatedness (Rutter, 1979). Drawing on statistical models for expressing interactions, Luthar, Cicchetti, and Becker (2000) posit a variety of protective effects: direct (main and mediating) protective, protective-stabilizing, protective-enhancing, protective but reactive, vulnerable–stable, and vulnerable–reactive effects. From this perspective, for example, the protective value of wearing a bicycle helmet, which is realized only in the presence of an accident (a high-risk situation when use of a helmet may reduce injury), is a protective-enhancing effect. It confers enhanced protection at the point of great risk and it provides little added protection in the absence of risk. Recognizing that protection can arise from personal attributes and environmental assets, we will define protective factors as both *internal and external resources that modify risk*. The defining feature of protective mechanisms is a modification of the risk situation. This requires some form of "amelioration (protection) of the reaction to a factor that in ordinary circumstances leads to a maladaptive outcome" (Rutter, 1987, p. 317).

Like risk factors, protective factors may be domain specific. That is, they may operate principally within specific domains of development and have limited spillover to other domains. While some protective factors, such as self-efficacy, appear to have a widespread effect on functioning, other protective factors are more specific. For instance, academic achievement, one of the most prominent developmental outcomes throughout childhood and adolescence, appears to be promoted by having more individual resources and social capital (Coleman, 1988). Competence in the academic domain is influenced by IQ, motivation to succeed, beliefs in one's abilities, and positive attitudes about school (Masten & Coatsworth, 1998). Cognitive patterns attributing success to hard work and effort (and failure as the lack of hard work) also facilitate academic achievement by fostering an internal sense of control over personal achievement (Stevenson, Chen, & Lee, 1993). In contrast, socioemotional functioning, another important developmental outcome, has been associated with higher IQ and positive academic achievement (Hartup, 1983; Masten & Coatsworth, 1995). But factors that promote adaptive development in this domain appear to be more rooted in environmental interactions with parents, teachers, and peers (Masten & Coatsworth, 1998).

Three broad categories of protective variables promote resilience in childhood (Garmezy, 1985). The first refers to dispositional attributes, including neurophysiological and temperamental factors, social orientation and responsiveness to change, cognitive abilities, and coping skills. Variation in hypothalamic, pituitary, and adrenal functioning, which relates in turn to the secretion of cortisol, a stress-related hormone, is probably related to adaptive capacity (for a review of neurobiological mechanisms, see Lewis & Ramsay, 2002; Vance, 2001). This could be considered a biologically based dispositional attribute. The second general category of protective factors is the family milieu. A positive relationship with at least one parent or a parental figure serves an important protective function. Other important family variables include cohesion, warmth, harmony, supervision, and absence of neglect. The third category of protective influences in childhood encompasses attributes of the extrafamilial social environment. These include the availability of external resources and extended social supports as well as the individual's use of those resources.

In the same way that the term "risk factor" describes the point at which a social influence becomes harmful to child development, a "protective factor" describes the point at which a social influence lowers vulnerability for a poor developmental outcome. In common parlance, the terms "risk factor" and "protective factor" are often used for describing the opposing or, perhaps, counterbalancing effects of significant individual attributes and social conditions. They are conceptualized as opposite ends of a continuum. Positive parenting, for example, is thought to produce good outcomes; negative parenting is thought to produce poor outcomes. Positive parenting can thus be described as a protective factor; negative parenting, a risk factor. When used as antonyms, risk and protection express the idea that at one pole of an indicator quite desirable outcomes are observed, while at the other pole quite undesirable outcomes are observed. Using a polar opposites approach, Felix-Ortiz and Newcomb (1992) defined exposure to a factor as a score in the uppermost (risk) or lowermost (protection) 20 percent of a distribution. They then summed aggregated risk and protective scores across a variety of scales. Similarly, in a Philadelphia study of nearly 500 youths ages 11 to 14, Sameroff and colleagues (1998) created 20 "promotive factors" by scoring as protective effects the lowest (most prosocial) quartile of each risk dimension and 20 risk factors by scoring the highest quartile of each risk dimension. After examining the relationships between aggregated protection and five outcomes—(1) psychological adjustment, (2) self-competence, (3) problem behavior, (4) activity involvement, and (5) academic performance—they concluded "there does not seem to be much difference between the influence of risk and promotive variables . . . aiding child development at one end and inhibiting it at the other" (Sameroff et al., 1998, p. 172). This "dimensional" view of risk and protection is common.

Notwithstanding, some experts are uncomfortable with this perspective (Roosa, 2000). The authors of a Surgeon General's Report (U.S. Department of Health and Human Services, 2001, p. 62) observed that this approach "blurs the distinction between risk and protection, making them essentially the same thing." Rutter (2000b, p. 658), too, argued, ". . . there is not much to be gained, apart from the introduction of unhelpful confusion, calling the low risk end of a risk dimension a protective factor."

In response, experts have attempted to define separate, conceptually distinct protective and risk constructs. According to this view, the labeling of risk and protective factors should be rationalized by an understanding of the relationship between a purported risk-protective factor and its influence on developmental outcomes. It is argued that there are some factors that have principally risk–increasing or principally risk-reducing (protective) effects. When the nature of the effect is known, the most potentiating pole can be scored and indexed as either a risk or protective factor. Although there may be few true single-pole effects, this perspective represents also the idea that the effects of individual attributes and environmental circumstances may not be linear. Threshold effects may demark points wherein risk or protection elevates geometrically. For example, although parents use styles of discipline that range from verbal reprimand to spanking to harsh physical punishment, research suggests that, when compared with other types of discipline, harsh physical punishment has a multi-fold negative effect on children's development, especially the development of conduct problems (Patterson, Reid, & Dishion, 1992; Reid, Patterson, & Snyder, 2002). "Harsh physical discipline," then, might be labeled a risk factor because it indexes significantly higher odds for a poor developmental outcome. In a study designed to estimate the relative effects of risk versus protective factors in adolescence, Pollard and colleagues (1999) used this approach when they broke 28 factors predictive of adolescent substance abuse into 20 risk constructs and eight protective constructs. As factors associated with prosocial outcomes, protective constructs included: high perceived rewards for community involvement, many opportunities for school involvement, high perceived rewards for involvement in school, high degree of family attachment, high perceived opportunities for family involvement, high perceived rewards for family involvement, belief in moral order, and high degree of social problem-solving skill.[2] To create a measure of aggregate protection, individual scores across all eight constructs were summed into a mean protection score for each student.

PROMOTIVE VERSUS PROTECTIVE FACTORS

Clearly, progress is being made in operationalizing terms in the field of risk and resilience. Still, there continues to be no consensus on how to define a protective factor. Originally, the term was reserved for use in conjunction with high risk (Rutter, 1987). That is, protection was conceived as possible only in the presence of adversity or threat. Statistically speaking, then, it was reserved as a term to describe interactions. However, with the rise of person-centered and qualitative analyses, wherein low- and high-functioning children in at-risk populations are compared, protective factors are defined as positive attributes and resources that distinguish adaptive from maladaptive children (see, for example, Bowen & Flora, 2002; Brodsky, 1999; Smokowski, Reynolds, & Bezrucko, 1999; Werner & Smith, 1982, 1992). In part, this led Sameroff and Fiese (2000, p. 140) to argue, ". . . in most cases protective factors simply appear to be the positive pole of risk factors. In this sense, a better term for the positive end of the risk dimension would be *promotive* rather than protective factors."

Promotive factors influence positive developmental outcomes in general—independent of risk—and, from this perspective, the term protective factor is reserved to describe attributes and conditions that lower the chances of poor developmental outcomes in the presence of risk. In a longitudinal study of 967 boys in Pittsburgh, Stouthamer-Loeber, Loeber, Wei, Farrington, and Wikstrom (2002) trichotomized predictors of delinquency into promotive effects (25th percentile or below: the most prosocial quartile), neutral effects (middle 50 percent), and risk effects (75th percentile or higher: the most at-risk quartile). Of 28 significant child, family, school, peer, and neighborhood predictors, nine had risk-only effects, nine had promotive-only effects,

---

[2]Risk constructs were not defined as the opposites of protective constructs. They included, for example, low neighborhood attachment, low degree of commitment to school, poor supervision by family, poor family discipline, high degree of family conflict, family history of antisocial behavior, parental attitudes that promote drug use, high degree of rebelliousness, attitudes favoring drug use, peer drug use, and high degree of sensation seeking.

and 10 had both risk and promotive effects (Stouthamer-Loeber et al., 2002). Similar to the approach used by Felix-Ortiz and Newcomb (1992), this approach seems to be useful because it recognizes the dual-pole effects of some predictors of developmental outcomes. Moreover, it preserves the possibility that through interactions some promotive variables may reduce risk, that is, have an added nonlinear effect in the presence of adversity (see also Sameroff & Gutman, 2004). But we caution readers that, while it seems to make a useful distinction, the term *promotive factor* is not yet widely used. Many important conceptual and methodological issues remain unresolved.

PROTECTIVE MECHANISMS

The concept of modifying risk—protection—becomes especially useful for designing services when the focus turns to processes or mechanisms. Although many different kinds of protective processes appear to exist, four have been consistently cited in the risk and resilience literature (Rutter, 1987): (1) *Reduction of risk impact* includes processes that alter exposure to a risk condition. For example, consistent parental supervision and regulation of children's activities outside the home would probably reduce the risk of drug abuse for children raised in high-risk environments (Hawkins et al., 1992). In the context of higher risk, a protective factor moderates the relationship between risk and outcome. Sometimes, too, the protective factor is activated only in the presence of risk. For example, an automobile seat belt reduces the risk of harm only in the presence of an accident. (2) *Reduction of negative chain reactions* involves disrupting the linkage between a stressor and an outcome. For example, support from one parent following the death of another parent may protect a child from vulnerability to a chain of stressors, which often follow the loss of a parent. (3) *Development of self-perceptions, especially self-esteem and self-efficacy,* is characterized by any activity that promotes self-confidence and effectiveness. Self-esteem may be enhanced through secure relationships with parents, for example, or through task accomplishments, such as school successes. Self-esteem incorporates the concept of self-efficacy, or a capacity to regulate emotions, develop plans, and control outcomes in various settings. In school and on the streets after school, a sense of self-efficacy may protect children by promoting adaptive behavior in the face of bullies, gangs, or other threats. (4) *Opening of opportunities* through social structural reforms operates at a societal level, but it can have individual effects. For example, changes in school policies may boost graduations from high school, which expand opportunities for graduates who might not have completed high school under earlier policies.

CUMULATIVE PROTECTIVE EFFECTS

Like risk (and promotive) factors, protective factors probably have cumulative effects. In a study of 243 premature, low-birthweight children living in poverty, Bradley et al. (1994) found that the presence of three or more protective family factors, including parental warmth, acceptance, organization, and infant stimulation, differentiated resilient children from nonresilient children. Although support for the view that protective factors exert a nonlinear effect on child outcomes is mixed, these data suggest that there are at least cumulative, additive effects across protective conditions.

MODELS OF RESILIENCE: HOW DO RISK AND PROTECTIVE FACTORS INTERACT?

It is widely believed that resilience results from the interplay between risk and protective factors, but the nature of the dynamics that produce resilience is poorly understood and inconsistently described in the literature. Building on the idea of modifying risk, two basic models of resilience have emerged, although the terminology varies. They are the additive and interactive models.

ADDITIVE MODELS

Additive models, in which protective factors are said to exhibit main or compensatory effects, posit that the presence of a risk factor directly increases the likelihood of a negative outcome and the presence of a protective factor directly increases the likelihood of a positive outcome (Luthar, 1991; Masten, 1987; Pellegrini, 1990). Risk and protection are often seen as polar opposites with protective factors promoting normative developmental outcomes (for an exception, see Ladd & Burgess, 2001). Ipso facto, high protection is thought of as lowering or even eliminating risk. Along a continuum of neighborhood risk (for example, the degree of drug trafficking), the protective factor of high parental supervision is seen as exerting a similar effect in both low drug trafficking and high drug trafficking neighborhoods. It has a "main" or "additive" effect; its effect is consistent in adding protective value across all levels of risk. In this case, parental supervision could also be thought of as a "promotive factor." The idea of a *compensatory effect* is related to interventions based on additive models. If enough resources can be marshaled, the protection afforded by increasing assets or strengths will offset or compensate for the presence of risk (Masten et al., 1999). Resilience, then, is the result of the relative influence of risk conditions versus resources that promote positive outcomes.

INTERACTIVE MODELS

The term "interaction" is used often to describe risk and protective dynamics. It emphasizes the moderating role of protective factors (see, for example, Fraser, Richman, & Galinsky, 1999; Pollard et al., 1999; Rutter, 1979, 1983, 2000b, 2001). In interactive models, protective factors have effect only in combination with risk factors. In other words, protective factors are thought to exert little effect when stress is low. Their effect emerges when stress is high (Masten, 1987). Immunization against disease provides a useful analogy for this process: Immunization does not directly promote positive physical health; rather, it provides protection from disease following exposure to a pathogen.

Within an interaction framework, moderation occurs when a relationship between a risk factor and an outcome is weakened by the presence of a protective factor. Different from risk, protection has been conceptualized in three ways. First, it may *buffer risk factors*, serving as a cushion against the negative effects or risk factors. Social support is thought to moderate the effect of a high-risk environment in this way. For example, the nurturing and supportive parenting provided to girls participating in "Project Competence," a Minneapolis project for school-age children, appeared to moderate the extent to which exposure to high risk was linked to disruptive behavior in school (Masten, 1987). Second, protection may *interrupt a risk chain* through which risk factors operate. Interventions that aim to reduce family conflict, for example, may interrupt a chain of risks connecting family environment with youths' peer affiliations and drug use. In other words, reducing family conflict may prevent early experimentation with drugs, which is a risk factor for greater and more persistent use of psychoactive substances (Hawkins et al., 1992). Third, protection may operate to *prevent the initial occurrence of a risk factor*. Positive temperamental characteristics, such as being easy to soothe, affectionate, and good-natured, may protect children from abuse or neglect by enabling them to elicit positive responses from caregivers who have high risk to be abusive parents (Morriset, 1993).

  Although this interaction conceptualization of protection continues to hold promise, it is not fully satisfying. Interaction effects can be tested with multiple regression (and other) analyses, wherein an equation with only main effects is compared with an equation that includes both main and interaction effects (Cohen & Cohen, 1983). Although only a few studies have done these analyses, interaction effects have not consistently been found to be statistically significant. Because of methodological issues in testing interactions, they are hard to detect (Luthar et al., 2000). Moreover, the increase in variance explained by interactions is almost always small (see, for example, Felix-Ortiz & Newcomb, 1992; Ladd & Burgess, 2001; Luthar, 1991; Moran & Eckenrode, 1992; Myers, Taylor, Alvy, Arrington, & Richardson, 1992). For example, in a study of adolescent drug use, Felix-Ortiz and Newcomb (1992) found that the interaction between a risk factor index and a protective factor index explained only 4.2 percent of the variance in alcohol use.[3] It is not clear that statistical modeling of interactions adequately represents the modifying, suppressing, buffering, strengthening, and catalyzing effect of protective factors and mechanisms (Rutter, 2000a, 2000b). More work is needed. Nevertheless, the existing data indicate that protective factors do indeed moderate risk factors, making it clear that processes whereby risk and protective factors lead to resilience are complex and, at least in part, nonlinear. Interactive modeling of protective factors is promising because it allows investigators to identify potentially malleable factors that, if fostered by a program, could reduce social and health problems in high-risk children—precisely the children with whom social workers and other professionals often work.

SYSTEMS OF INFLUENCE: PROXIMAL VERSUS DISTAL EFFECTS

  Interactions among risk and protective factors are further complicated by the fact that they are embedded in systems at many different levels in the ecology. Risk and protective factors have been identified within the individual, in the family, in the school environment, in the neighborhood, and in the broader social context (Garmezy, 1985; Rutter, 1987; Werner & Smith, 1982, 1992). In the ecology of human behavior (Bronfenbrenner, 1979, 1986), resilience can be conceptualized as resulting from the relative balance of risk and protective factors across multiple system levels (O'Keefe, 1994).

---

[3]Critics argue that this is quite small, and it certainly seems to be. However, suppose 4.2 percent of adolescent alcohol use could be affected. This might translate into hundreds of prevented automobile accidents, alcohol-related fights, and alcohol-related date rapes. Because the problems are potentially quite large, small percentage changes can have significant practice and public policy effects.

Risk researchers debate which of the system levels has the greater effect on resilience (Seifer & Sameroff, 1987). However, it is widely believed that "distal factors," or those that are situated farther away from the child, are less influential than "proximal factors," which impinge directly on the child (Baldwin, Baldwin, & Cole, 1990; Garbarino, Kostelny, & Dubrown 1991; Myers et al., 1992). Poverty, for example, is often considered a distal variable that limits opportunities and indirectly places children at risk. Through risk chains, however, poverty may lead to other more proximal risks. For example, a single mother's irritability and exhaustion caused by full-time work at a low-paying job may directly affect the parent–child relationship. An ecological framework that simultaneously considers a broad range of variables in individual, family, school, and neighborhood systems can help organize attempts to identify all the factors that may affect a child's life (Luthar & Zigler, 1991; Seifer & Sameroff, 1987). This book uses an ecological, multisystems perspective throughout.

RESILIENCE: OVERCOMING THE ODDS?

Resilience is a touchstone of literature, and it is the lodestone of prime-time television. With exceptional skill, daring, perseverance, and humor, film and TV stars overcome seemingly impossible odds. But does this happen to real people in real life? Yes, however, caution is warranted. Across 20 risk factors and eight protective factors, Pollard and colleagues (1999) cross-classified 78,710 middle and high school students by quintiles (that is, five categories of risk and five categories of protection). Across all youths, risk and protection was negatively related ($r = -.66$), indicating that students with higher risk scores had lower protection scores. Embedded in the findings was a sobering story. At the highest level of risk (the top 20 percent), fewer than 5 percent of the youths had protection scores in the third, fourth, or fifth quintiles. For the highest risk youths, protection was rare. Similarly, in a study of 213 children from low-income families, of which 133 families had been reported for child maltreatment, Cicchetti and Rogosch (1997) found two (1.5 percent) adaptive maltreated children and eight (4.3 percent) adaptive nonmaltreated children, when "adaptive" was defined as scoring in the upper one-third on standardized measures of interpersonal behavior, conduct problems, and school success. To date, research suggests that the percent of children who function adaptively—who are resilient—following severe trauma, such as repeated maltreatment, may be substantially smaller than the percent of children who function adaptively following more prevalent and less severe adversities. Thus, level of risk and how we define successful adaptation are critical ingredients in understanding resilience. Some children experience such extreme adversity that successful adaptation is quite remarkable and rare. When risk is less severe, more children are likely to adapt successfully.

SENSITIVITY TO RISK: STEELING EFFECTS AND BENEFITS FROM ADVERSITY?

Sensitivity to risk is the degree of vulnerability to a risk factor or set of factors. Is it possible that exposure to adversity has benefits, or *steeling effects*, making some children more resistant to stress? In the same way that a child who survives exposure to many pathogens builds a strong immune response system, could exposure to poverty or other risks decrease sensitivity to risk? Or in a similar way that roofers and construction workers learn to work at dizzying heights, can exposure to adverse circumstances "steel" us to future adversities of a similar nature? If we survive, can we benefit from the adversities of serious illness, combat, and accidents of fate? Elder's well-known study, *Children of the Great Depression* (1974), showed that adolescents who stopped school to work to help their families became stronger. But his study also showed that work negatively affected younger children. The developmental timing of the stressor was a critical component for determining how it affected life outcomes.

Life event researchers have investigated the possibility of deriving benefits from adversity. In a review of this literature, McMillen (1999) reported that 45 percent to 90 percent of survivors of traumatic events say they have derived some benefit from the adversity they experienced. Prevalence rates vary by stressor or life event, typically ranging from 47 percent for adult survivors of child sexual abuse to more than 90 percent for cancer survivors. Individuals who derived a benefit from adversity commonly report enhanced self-efficacy, changed health behaviors, heightened feelings of interpersonal support and trust, or transformed perceptions with a deeper sense of meaning. Resilient individuals have also been found to have higher levels of self-understanding relative to their nonresilient peers (Beardslee, 1989). Benefits from adversity appear more likely to occur at moderate levels of stress for individuals with intermediate levels of coping skills. Individuals with low levels of coping skills who experience severe or chronic stressors are less likely to derive a benefit from their experience (McMillen, 1999).

In the same vein, success is required for an experience to have a beneficial or steeling effect. It is possible that children who prevail over developmentally appropriate challenges enhance skills in planning and working with others and develop a sense of control over the environment that builds self-confidence and bolsters chances for future successes. This, in part, is the theory behind wilderness challenge programs, in which youths are involved in ropes courses, desert hikes, wagon trains, or river trips that require cooperative problem solving, creativity, and tenacity. These programs supervise conditions to ensure that challenges are modulated. For some children, however, challenge is not modulated in real life. Although children do indeed prevail over adversity and appear to be strengthened by the experience, steeling effects probably operate for few children at the highest levels of risk.

A MODEL FOR COMMON RISK AND PROTECTIVE FACTORS

We are learning more and more about the ways that risk and protective factors interact to produce resilience. A general model of resilience is emerging from research. On balance, evidence supports the presence of both additive and interactive effects, perhaps with additive effects that promote developmental outcomes across various levels of risk playing the more important role (for example, Ladd & Burgess, 2001; Sameroff & Gutman, 2004). To account for the presence of effects at multiple system levels, risk and protective factors must be understood within an ecological framework. Moreover, a developmental framework must be used both to allow for changes in resilience in individuals at different points in time and to explain the cumulative effects of risk.

Dozens of studies now identify risk and protective factors related to childhood problems, and some risk and protective factors appear to be common to many different problems (for reviews, see Coie et al., 1993; Fraser et al., 1999; Luthar et al.,

2000; Luthar & Zigler, 1991; Mrazek & Haggerty, 1994). This set of crosscutting risk and protective factors—including some promotive factors that represent a prosocial or positive pole of a risk dimension—is shown in Table 2-1 and discussed briefly in the next section. Risk and protective factors are shown in the table at the system level where they occur, either as psychosocial and biological characteristics of individual children or as contextual factors in the family, school, neighborhood, and larger systems. Consistent with ecological theory, the classification schema reflects the idea that a child's social ecology consists of many different systems, each of which has the capacity to influence developmental trajectories.

Identifying the common factors that produce risk and resilience in children is a first step both in conducting an ecologically based assessment and in designing ecologically focused services. Setting aside, for the moment, problem-specific risk and protective factors (these are reviewed in later chapters in the book), Table 2-1 focuses on those common factors that place children at risk and appear to protect children in the context of high risk.

Table 2-1. Common Risk and Protective Factors for Serious Childhood Social Problems: An Ecological and Multisystems Perspective

SYSTEM LEVEL	RISK FACTORS	PROTECTIVE FACTORS
Broad environmental conditions, including neighborhood and school	Few opportunities for education and employment Racial discrimination and injustice Poverty	Many opportunities for education, employment, growth, and achievement Collective efficacy Presence of caring adult
Family conditions	Child maltreatment Interparental conflict Parental psychopathology Harsh parenting	Positive parent–child relationship Effective parenting
Individual psychosocial and biological characteristics	Gender Biomedical problems, including genetic liability	"Easy" temperament as an infant Self-esteem and hardiness Competence in normative roles: self-efficacy High intelligence

COMMON RISK FACTORS

BROAD ENVIRONMENTAL RISK FACTORS

Few Opportunities for Education or Employment

The environment is the context for child development. It provides children with opportunities to learn. It exposes them to adults who make meaningful contributions to their communities and who serve as role models and mentors. It provides incentives and disincentives for behaviors. And it is a source of social and economic support for families. When the environment is impoverished, children suffer.

Historically, the term "social disorganization" was used to describe communities whose core socialization structures—schools, businesses, religious organizations, and health care services—had failed under the weight of widespread poverty, residential instability, unemployment, racial–ethnic tension, and crime (Shaw & McKay, 1942). In studies in Chicago and many other cities, Shaw and McKay (1942), Cloward and Ohlin (1960), and others found that disorganized neighborhoods failed to provide an adequate range of opportunities to ensure that legitimate social goals (for example, obtaining a well-paying job) could be reached by commitment to traditional social processes (for example, graduating from school). The hypothesis that limited or "blocked" opportunities in work, school, and other settings place children at risk is derived, in part, from these studies, and it is augmented by recent studies, described below, of collective efficacy in effective communities in which social processes operate to promote child development (for reviews, see Herrenkohl, Hawkins, Chung, Hill, & Battin-Pearson, 2001; Sampson, Raudenbush, & Earls, 1997). On the basis of a large body of research, these theories posit that nearly all children develop high expectations for social, educational, and economic success (Agnew, 1993; Farrington et al., 1993). But as a result of unfavorable neighborhood and school conditions (for example, a poorly trained or hostile teacher) where there are few opportunities for advancement and where social institutions operate poorly, some children fail to learn skills necessary for advancement and others, who try to make the systems work, learn that the odds against their success are high (for specific discussion of schools, see Gottfredson, 2000; for a broader application to schools and neighborhoods, see Huang et al., 2001). The discrepancy between what a child hopes to achieve and what he or she actually expects to achieve through legitimate means is thought to be the source of frustration and anger (see, for example, Merton, 1938). And at the end of the risk chain, according to these structural, strain, and opportunity theories, defeat, frustration, and anger cause high rates of alienation. In turn, these contribute to the formation of gangs; the development of drug-trafficking subcultures; and the emergence of alternative illicit opportunities through laundering money, selling illegal weapons, fencing stolen goods, and prostitution.

Racial Discrimination and Injustice

As a result of a long history of racial discrimination, African American and other people of color bear a disproportionate share of the burden of poverty and unemployment in the United States (Nettles & Pleck, 1994; Taylor, 1994). Thus, these children experience increased vulnerability to the effects of low income and low socioeconomic status (SES). Moreover, significant noneconomic aspects of racism further place many children of color at risk (Kreiger, Rowley, Herman, Avery, & Phillips, 1993). These include differential opportunities for health care, employment, and education, plus the psychosocial effects of facing discriminatory behavior from individuals and institutions. For many children, the experience of repeated rejection and hostility inhibits self-esteem and contributes to high levels of frustration and anger (Jarrett, 1995).

Poverty (and Collective Poverty)

Poverty, including low SES, has an individual and a collective effect. It has been identified as a risk factor for a range of poor outcomes, including child abuse and neglect (Vondra, 1990), delinquency (Hawkins et al., 1992), externalizing behavior disorders (Velez, Johnson, & Cohen, 1989), and socioemotional and educational maladjustment (Felner et al., 1995). The definition of SES, which is a complex measure of economic, educational, and occupational station, differs slightly from that of poverty or low income. However, the two indicators—poverty and low SES—operate similarly to place children at risk.

The significance of poverty as a risk factor is thought to lie in the presence of multiple stressors associated with inadequate resources (Bradley et al., 1994; McLoyd, 1990; Schteingart, Molnar, Klein, Lowe, & Hartman, 1995). Children living in poverty are more frequently exposed to such risks as medical illnesses, family stress, inadequate social support, and parental depression (Parker, Greer, & Zuckerman, 1988). Because poverty is a condition that rarely changes quickly, the cumulation of stressors over time may magnify risk (Garmezy, 1993a, 1993b).

At least three mechanisms operate in making poverty a common risk factor (Bradley et al., 1994). First, poverty circumscribes a family's resources; that is, the most direct effect of poverty is that it increases the potential that a child will lack adequate food, clothing, shelter, and other basic necessities. Second, poverty limits access to adequate health services. Poor children often do not receive preventive care, and when they need health services, they tend to use the most expensive form of care—emergency room treatment. Finally, poverty is thought to act as a risk factor because it is associated with unsupportive, unstimulating, and chaotic home environments (Hart & Risley, 1995). Studies have shown that economic hardship is both correlated with parental psychological distress and poor family management practices (Duncan, 1991; Lamer & Collins, 1996; McLoyd, 1990).

Collective poverty is a central element in neighborhood disadvantage. Neighborhood disadvantage consists of a multidimensional cluster of characteristics, such as high unemployment, high crime and violence, frequent resident mobility, cultural conflict, broken families, and restricted access to resources. Each of these contributes independent explanatory power to models of neighborhood disadvantage. Yet, they often load on one factor, neighborhood poverty, when examined using factor analyses. Consequently, there commonly exists a "pileup" of contextual stress in disadvantaged neighborhoods. Elliott and colleagues (1996) write:

> Poverty, single parent families, high mobility, limited job opportunities, and cultural diversity not only result in an attenuation of social and cultural neighborhood organization but also increase the likelihood of the emergence (and lack of effective control) of illegitimate opportunity structures and dysfunctional lifestyles, including an illicit economy (gambling, prostitution, extortion, theft, drug distribution networks), substance abuse, violence and delinquent gangs. The presence of deviant groups and illegitimate opportunity structures provides alternative opportunities and rewards for involvement in the illicit economy and support networks that encourage or at least tolerate health compromising lifestyles. (p. 394)

Within this milieu, conventional societal norms and values may not be rejected on ideological grounds, but rather because they lack salience for individual survival (Wilson, 1996).

Neighborhood disadvantage may also be associated with distinct developmental outcomes. In predicting academic functioning, the percentage of affluent neighbors has more power than the percentage of low-income neighbors in a community (Brooks-Gunn, Duncan, Klebanov, & Sealand, 1993; McLoyd, 1998). Adolescents in affluent neighborhoods tend to drop out of school less frequently and complete more years of school than adolescents in less-advantaged neighborhoods. Such findings tend to support resource and collective socialization theories that emphasize how access to high-quality schools, health care, role models, and so on benefit developmental competence and prevent social problems (for example, Herrenkohl, Guo, et al., 2001). In elementary-school children, some evidence has shown neighborhood effects to be seasonal. Controlling for family resources, Entwisle, Alexander, and Olson (1997) found neighborhood resources positively affected academic growth during summers, but they had no positive effect when schools were in session. Further, the beneficial effect for resources during summer was stronger for more affluent neighborhoods.

Low-income neighborhoods may also have an effect on socioemotional functioning. In a sample of five-year-olds, Duncan, Brooks-Gunn, and Klebanov (1994) found more externalizing aggressive behavioral problems among children with a higher percentage of low-income neighbors. Even after controlling for a variety of family variables, the effect of neighborhood was strong. What is the risk mechanism related to neighbors? It is not clear, but a number of factors may be at work, such as lower adult supervision, greater modeling by aggressive peers, less prohibition against acting out, or increased need for children to defend themselves aggressively in a hostile environment. Many experts agree that the effects of poverty and other sociocultural risk factors are mediated, at least in part, through risk chains (Bradley et al., 1994; Felner et al., 1995; McLoyd, 1990). Low SES, for example, may increase family stress, which can lead to inconsistent parenting and which, in turn, places children at risk of behavioral difficulties (see, for example, Duncan et al., 1994). Thus, in conceptualizing the effect of poverty on childhood, one must think in terms of linkages between and across individual, family, school, and neighborhood risk factors.

FAMILY RISK FACTORS

Child Maltreatment

All forms of child maltreatment—neglect, physical abuse, sexual abuse, and psychological abuse—place children at risk. Annually, about 4 percent of all children are reported to U.S. child welfare services as victims of alleged abuse or neglect (U.S. Department of Health and Human Services, 1999). Recent data strongly suggest that abused and neglected children are more likely than children who have not been victimized to engage in antisocial, aggressive acts, including delinquency, and physically, sexually, and verbally abusive relationships with peers (Aguilar et al., 2000; Office of Juvenile Justice and Delinquency Prevention, 1995; Shields & Cicchetti, 2001; Wekerle & Wolfe, 1998; Widom, 1989). Overall, too, they are at greater risk for a variety of psychosocial and mental disorders, including drug use, low grade-point average, running away, and pregnancy (Kelley, Thornberry, & Smith, 1997; Mrazek & Haggerty, 1994; Widom, 1999; Youngblade & Belsky, 1990).

Two different mechanisms, both with theoretical underpinnings, appear to explain how maltreatment increases vulnerability in children. The first explanation is derived from attachment theory. It suggests that problems in infant–caregiver attachment prevent the successful adaptation of children (Youngblade & Belsky, 1990); that is, maltreatment by a parent inhibits bonding between the infant and parent, and adequate bonding is viewed as necessary for healthy child development, including the formation of friendships with peers.

The second mechanism is derived from social learning and cognitive theories in psychology. With roots in the biologic insult that maltreatment may have on brain chemistry (Barth, 2002), this hypothesis argues that children develop maladaptive cognitive schemas as a result of abuse. Abused children learn to be suspicious of and hostile toward other children and adults, particularly strangers. They develop negative self-images and low self-esteem (Rutter, 1994; Widom, 1989, 1999; Youngblade & Belsky, 1990). Moreover, there is modest evidence that the experience of maltreatment leads children to evaluate aggressive behavior as an effective interpersonal tool in achieving personal goals (Dodge, Bates, & Pettit, 1990; Shields & Cicchetti, 2001). Thus, many abused and neglected children view the world as hostile, and for reasons that are far from clear (and may involve genetically influenced factors such as level of MAOA; Caspi et al., 2002), they may develop aggressive interpersonal styles that place them at risk of school failure, delinquency, and other social problems.

Interparental Conflict

A great deal of evidence suggests that high levels of conflict between parents are linked with children's psychological difficulties; conflicts at school with teachers and peers; and antisocial, aggressive behavior (Emery & Forehand, 1994; Farrington et al., 1993; Hawkins et al., 1992; McCloskey & Stuewig, 2001; Office of Juvenile Justice and Delinquency Prevention, 1995; O'Keefe, 1994; Rae-Grant, Thomas, Offord, & Boyle, 1989). In a study of 117 low-income boys from a Women, Infant, and Children Nutritional Supplement Program in Pittsburgh, Ingoldsby, Shaw, and Garcia (2001) found that interparental conflict when the boys were approximately 3½ years of age predicted poor parent–child relationships at age 5 and both child–peer and child-teacher conflicts at age 6. Frequent interparental hostility and fighting may desensitize children to conflict, teach them to make (what may be appropriate) hostile attributions about parents (who may pose a threat); impair parent–child attachments; and provide models of poor problem solving that "spread" to relationships with siblings, peers, teachers, and others (Emery & Forehand, 1994; Ingoldsby et al., 2001; MacKinnon-Lewis, Lamb, Hattie, & Baradaran, 2001; McCloskey & Stuewig, 2001). More generally, interparental conflict may act as a barrier to effective parenting, thereby leaving children vulnerable to environmental conditions and negative peer influences (Emery & Forehand, 1994).

PARENTAL PSYCHOPATHOLOGY

Various forms of parental psychopathology, including conduct problems, depression, substance abuse, and other serious mental illnesses, also appear to place children at risk of psychosocial problems (Jaffee, Caspi, Moffitt, Belsky, & Silva, 2001; Munson, McMahon, & Spieker, 2001; Sameroff & Seifer, 1990; Velez et al., 1989; Werner & Smith, 1982). However, parental psychopathology cannot be relegated to any one risk chain. The mechanisms by which parental psychopathology and criminality may influence child development range from genetic transmission of heritable attributes to parental modeling of inappropriate, learned behaviors (Factor & Wolfe, 1990). Because of the symptoms of their illnesses, parents with severe mental disorders may have difficulty providing consistent care and appropriate discipline (Masten et al., 1990). In a study of 93 single African American mothers of preschool children, Jackson, Brooks-Gunn, Huang, and Glassman (2000) found maternal education and social support in solving problems to be negatively related to financial stress. Financial stress, in turn, was significantly correlated with depressive symptoms, which directly affected parenting—consistency in family routines, intellectual stimulation of children, and the degree of emotional support provided to children. Finally, at the end of this risk chain, quality of parenting was significantly related to children's problem behaviors, including hitting, fighting, teasing, and disobedience. These results underscore the interaction of environmental factors (financial strain and social support) as potential triggering and buffering measures for depression, which has heritable and social environmental elements (Rutter, 2000b).

Harsh Parenting

Poor parenting is a common risk factor for problem behaviors, including peer conflicts, loneliness, delinquency, teenage pregnancy, and substance abuse (Denham et al., 2000; Hawkins et al., 1992; Jaffee et al., 2001; McCloskey & Stuewig, 2001; Moffitt & Caspi, 2001; O'Donnell, Hawkins, & Abbott, 1995). Poor parenting is a multidimensional construct consisting of poor communication, problem solving, monitoring skills, and hostile affect. In his studies of white families who experienced the Great Depression, Elder (1974) found that heavy economic loss made fathers more irritable, explosive, and punitive in interactions with their children (see also Elder, Nguyen, & Caspi, 1985). Having fathers display inconsistent, arbitrary discipline and other negative parenting behaviors predicted several socioemotional problems in children. Central to the construct of poor parenting is the use of harsh and inconsistent family management practices, which forms the basis for Patterson's theory of coercive family processes (Patterson, 1982; Patterson et al., 1992). Based on social learning theory, the coercion model of poor family management posits that parents, by responding to children's behavior inconsistently and noncontingently, teach children to use aversive behavior to meet social goals in the family, at school, and in other settings (Patterson, Forgatch, Yoerger, & Stoolmiller, 1998; Reid et al., 2002). Although poor family management practices may not cause childhood problems that have biological origins, they can exacerbate them.

INDIVIDUAL PSYCHOSOCIAL AND BIOLOGICAL RISK FACTORS

Biomedical Problems

Biomedical problems affect children in at least two ways (O'Dougherty & Wright, 1990). First, some infants and children have serious disorders that significantly impair cognitive abilities or increase emotional lability (Masten et al., 1990). Because of their lack of supportive family and educational environments, these children often experience developmental delays. Second, some children experience prenatal, perinatal, neonatal, or early developmental events that insult the developing central nervous system and increase risk for future disorders (Graham, Heim, Goodman, Miller, & Nemeroff, 1999; Moffitt & Caspi, 2001). These include maternal health and substance use during pregnancy, birth complications, feeding patterns, nutrition, and infant health during the first year of life (Allen, Lewinsohn, & Seeley, 1998; Cadoret & Riggins-Caspers, 2000). Other children have high genetic liability for neurobehavioral features, for example, autonomic hypoactivity, such as low skin conductance, low heart rate responses, and low behavioral sensitivity to aversive consequences, and low amplitude electrocortical brain activity, which place them at risk of serious mental disorders and substance abuse. Compared with children not experiencing birth-related problems, for example, low birthweight or premature infants appear to be more vulnerable to life stressors (Grizenko & Pawliuk, 1994; Mrazek & Haggerty, 1994; Office of Juvenile Justice and Delinquency Prevention, 1995; Werner & Smith, 1992). Findings from the Minnesota Twin Family Study, which has tracked approximately 2,700 adolescent twins and their families, suggest that up to 23 percent of the variation in adolescents' tobacco, alcohol, and drug use may have genetic origins in neuromechanisms (Iacono, Carlson, Taylor, Elkins, & McGue, 1999). For both categories of biomedical risk, research suggests that outcomes are largely determined by the interplay of biological and environmental factors (Mrazek & Haggerty, 1994; Werner, 1992; Werner & Smith, 1982). That is, individual, family, and other contextual factors often mediate the expression of biomedical risk. However, research suggests also that biologic factors, such as fetal alcohol exposure, can have direct and enduring effects on child development (Cadoret & Riggins-Caspers, 2000).

Gender

Gender clearly affects risk chains. In response to a variety of stressors, including family discord, divorce, and out-of-home day care, boys often show more severe and prolonged disturbances than do girls (Luthar & Zigler, 1991; Morisset, 1993; Wangby, Bergman, & Magnusson, 1999). Boys are also more likely to engage in aggressive, antisocial behavior (Compas, Hinden, & Gerhardt, 1995; Patterson et al., 1992). However, adolescent girls often have relatively more difficulties in school, and girls have a higher risk for some mental health disorders, including depressive mood and eating disorders (Johnson, Roberts, & Worell, 1999; Werner & Smith, 1982).

Gender may be a marker for certain conditions, but it is not clear whether it is a cause. Unquestionably, the social expectations and opportunities for boys and girls have changed over the past century. During this time, the comparative rates of social and health problems have also changed. Different risk chains may operate for boys and girls; moreover, the risk and protective factors that comprise these chains may have changed over the years. Thus, gender differences probably reflect both fundamental biological differences between boys and girls and changing beliefs, values, norms, and opportunities (Silverthorn & Frick, 1999). Understanding the different and common forces that affect girls and boys is a major research challenge. Recent research suggests that many of the same factors that place boys at risk also place girls at risk. For example, although girls, as compared with boys, are less likely to be overtly aggressive, a study of 466 European American and 100 African American kindergarten children who were tracked through the fourth grade found no gender differences in the kinds of risk factors predictive of conduct problems (Deater-Deckard, Dodge, Bates, & Pettit, 1998). Despite mean differences in girls' and boys' problem behavior, this suggests that the individual, family, school, and community risk mechanisms that cause conduct problems may be similar for boys and girls in elementary school (for similar findings regarding adolescence-limited conduct problems in girls and boys, see Moffitt & Caspi, 2001; Moffitt et al., 2001; for alternative views, see Artz, 1998; Kempf-Leonard, Chesney-Lind, & Hawkins, 2001; Shaw, Vondra, Hommerding, Keenan, & Dunn, 1994). Gender effects such as these are discussed in subsequent chapters.

COMMON PROTECTIVE FACTORS

BROAD ENVIRONMENTAL PROTECTIVE FACTORS

Many Opportunities for Education or Employment

Children and adolescents who have many opportunities for education, employment, growth, and achievement are less likely than those without such opportunities to reject prosocial values out of frustration and anger. They are more likely to expect to achieve their hopes and aspirations. Moreover, through involvement and commitment to school, faith organizations, and community, youths develop attachments to other youths and adults who share similar values and beliefs. In a study of 976 adolescents from Upstate New York, regular religious participation, for example, was associated with a 27 percent reduction in the likelihood of marijuana initiation, controlling for parent attachment, parental drug use, peer beliefs, sibling liquor use, and personality characteristics ("unconventionality"; Brook, Kessler, & Cohen, 1999). Similarly, a two-year prospective study of 77 children of parents who abused opioids and cocaine showed a neighborhood opportunity measure—the percent of adults employed in management or higher positions—to predict academic achievement for girls, who, by most accounts, would be considered at high risk (Luthar & Cushing, 1999). This research and many other studies suggest that, when the context for child development is characterized by many opportunities for involvement, children, including those at high risk, may be motivated to do well in school to resist negative peer influences, to delay childbearing, and to engage in other prosocial behaviors (for example, Huang et al., 2001).

Collective Efficacy: Social and Tangible Support

In an early review of resilience, Garmezy (1985) identified the existence and use of social supports as one of three broad categories of protective factors for children at risk. The growing body of evidence since then suggests that social support has both direct and indirect effects on child behavior. Feeling supported and having the emotional and tangible resources that derive from caring social relationships have been found to promote child development for both normal-term and preterm infants (Crnic, Greenberg, Ragozin, Robinson, & Basham, 1983), for children of depressed parents

(Pellegrini et al., 1986), and for children experiencing other types of environmental stress (McLoyd, 1990; Seifer et al., 1992; Werner & Smith, 1992). In addition, a large body of literature indicates that intervention programs offering supporting services to high-risk children and their families promote positive outcomes, which strongly suggests that social support serves a protective function (Luthar & Zigler, 1991).

Supportive, collaborative relationships with others provide webs of resources or ties that strengthen parenting. Supportive ties may be close and strong, the sort that characterizes relationships with relatives and good friends. Ties may also be more distal— some might say, weak ties—of the sort that characterize acquaintances who are contacted in relation to particular problems, such as finding adequate child or health care or dealing with an immigration issue. Strong ties are based on involvement with and attachment to significant others. Weak ties do not require strong bonds of attachment, but both types of ties are based on shared values. Shared values and beliefs are central elements in social connectedness.

Positive interpersonal relationships and social support may mitigate the effect of stressful life events for children in much the same way that they do for adults (Morisset, 1993). That is, supportive relationships may serve as a buffer against life stressors (Jarrett, 1995; Smokowski, Reynolds, & Bezrucko, 1999). Supportive families may also protect children by providing models of and reinforcement for skills that improve problem solving, motivation, academic achievement, and later socioeconomic opportunities (Masten et al., 1990). And at the community level, ties that develop through schools, churches, synagogues, temples, wards, and other organizations may serve a protective function by providing settings for supportive relationships (Masten, 1994).

At the community level, recent research has coined the term "collective efficacy" to reflect the ways in which extrafamilial social support and connectedness affect child development. From this perspective, one begins with the assumption that the context for child development extends beyond the family. That is, the family is nested in a neighborhood system that provides support, or fails to provide support, for child rearing. The provision of support is thought to be a characteristic of effective neighborhoods. It consists of the degree to which members of a neighborhood share values, beliefs, and expectations and the degree to which neighbors are willing to take action on behalf of others (for example, to correct the behavior of a neighbor's child in a parent's absence). The first is related to social cohesion, and the second is a form of social control. In a longitudinal study of 343 neighborhoods in Chicago, Sampson (2001) found that neighborhoods characterized by high levels of shared obligations ("I'll watch your child, if you'll watch mine later."), expectations ("Working together, we can make our streets safer."), and interlocking social networks ("Do you know a Spanish-speaking dentist who would be willing to see my mother? She has a toothache and hasn't seen a dentist in years.") had significantly lower levels of crime and low-weight births. Drawing on Bandura's (1977, 1982) work related to self-efficacy and labeling the phenomenon collective efficacy, Sampson, Raudenbush, and Earls (1997) found collective efficacy to operate protectively while controlling for population density, neighborhood disadvantage, residential instability, race–ethnic composition, and other well-known structural measures. That is, holding poverty and other structural disadvantages constant, neighborhoods in which there was greater social cohesion and informal social control observed lower crime rates and fewer low-weight births.

Though preliminary, these findings suggest that the collective disadvantage of poverty is mediated, in part, by social processes that cause social cohesion to breakdown and that "depress shared expectations for efficacious action" (Sampson, 2001, p. 23). The presence of supportive, helpful others appears to promote positive developmental outcomes even in the face of poverty and other neighborhood-level risks.

Presence of a Caring Adult (including a Mentor)

The presence of at least one caring adult who offers social support and connectedness has been consistently identified as a protective factor for children across a variety of risk conditions. For example, following the death of a parent or in the face of chronic family discord, the presence of a caring, supportive adult is widely acknowledged for helping children positively respond to and recover from loss, trauma, and stress (Brooks, 1994; Grizenko & Pawliuk, 1994; Rutter, 1987, 2000a; Werner, 1993). The caregiver need not be a parent and is often a grandparent or other extended relative, a teacher, a human services worker, or a volunteer from community groups and agencies. The effects of mentoring programs in which children are paired with an adult (often a young adult) are similarly positive but more modest. The differential findings from evaluations of mentoring projects are probably related to programmatic factors, such as the quality of ongoing training for mentors, frequency of contact between the mentor and child, use of structured activities, involvement of parents, and monitoring of implementation (DuBois, Holloway, Valentine, & Cooper, 2002). Although poorly implemented mentoring programs can have negative effects, programs in which youths are able to form enduring attachments appear to have positive effects on school acceptance, academic achievement, interpersonal relationships, and prosocial behavior (Grossman & Rhodes, 2002; Grossman & Tierney, 1998). Mentoring that occurs naturally in the lives of adolescents appears to have equivalent effects (Zimmerman & Bingenheimer, 2002). Mechanisms whereby relationships with caring adults and mentors protect children appear to include modeling prosocial skills and behavior, helping the child to build self-esteem, providing information and access to knowledge, providing guidance, and offering a source of protection against environmental stressors (Masten, 1994).

FAMILY PROTECTIVE FACTORS

Positive Parent–Child Relationship

Similarly, a good relationship with at least one parent has been shown to diminish the effects of interparental conflict (Emery & Forehand, 1994; Neighbors, Forehand, & McVicar, 1993; O'Keefe, 1994; Rutter, 1979) and promote childhood resilience (Demos, 1989; Feldman, Stiffman, & Jung, 1987; Franz, McClelland, & Weinberger, 1991). It also appears to function protectively against more generalized life stressors, such as economic hardship or stressful life events (Graham & Easterbrooks, 2000; Radke-Yarrow & Sherman, 1990; Werner & Smith, 1982). In Rutter's (1979) study of troubled families, three-quarters of children who did not have a good relationship with one parent displayed conduct problems. In comparison, one-quarter of those who had a good relationship developed behavioral difficulties. While studying alcoholic families, Berlin and Davis (1989) found an affectionate bond to a nonalcoholic parent to be the most important variable in fostering adaptation. Positive parent–child relationships help children feel secure, and they promote more consistent supervision and discipline. Moreover, they contribute to cognitive and social development both through direct instructional activities, such as helping with homework, and through the indirect processes associated with mentoring, caring, and nurturing (Masten et al., 1999; Neighbors et al., 1993).

Effective Parenting

Werner (1993) concluded that the effects of several risk conditions, including poor birth outcomes, such as low birthweight, were almost totally mediated by the quality of child-rearing conditions. For very young children, effective parenting may promote self-efficacy and self-worth through the development of secure infant–caregiver attachments, providing a basis for subsequent cognitive development and social adaptation (Masten et al., 1990; McGroder, 2000; Morisset, 1993; Rutter, 2000b). Furthermore, effective parents provide children with a model for effective action, provide opportunities for children to experience mastery, and may persuade children of their own effectiveness, thereby increasing feelings of self-efficacy (Bandura, 1982). For older children, parental closeness, warmth, (clear and supportive) instruction, limit setting, and involvement also appear to influence important developmental outcomes (Denham et al., 2000). Recent studies suggest that these qualities suppress conduct problems, promote academic achievement, and contribute to positive social relationships (for example, having close friends and an active social life; Masten & Coatsworth, 1998; Masten et al., 1999).

In high-risk neighborhoods, parental supervision and monitoring appear to be crucial factors in protecting children from harm and in promoting resilient outcomes (Jarrett, 1995). Spencer (2001) recently studied 219 African American males in grades 8, 9, and 10 in a southeastern metropolitan area. She found that exposure to stressful events and daily hassles distinguished boys who subsequently graduated from high school from those who did not graduate. But boys who graduated reported significantly more parental monitoring of their activities and their friends, suggesting that parents helped buffer boys from negative experiences. In Philadelphia, Furstenberg and his colleagues (1999) found "preventive parenting strategies" promoted adolescent success in disadvantaged teens. These strategies included knowing who the child was with, keeping the child at home as much as possible, and pointing out how neighborhood dangers have destroyed others' lives. These preventive parenting "speeches," coupled with encouraging messages about the child's ability to overcome adversity, appear to be critical components of effective parenting in high-risk environments (Smokowski et al., 1999).

INDIVIDUAL PSYCHOSOCIAL AND BIOLOGICAL PROTECTIVE FACTORS

Easy Temperament

One of the most frequently cited protective factors is a positive or "easy" temperament (Cowan et al., 1990; Grizenko & Pawliuk, 1994; Moffitt & Caspi, 2001; O'Keefe, 1994; Werner, 1993). Temperament refers to stable and probably physiologically related differences in arousal, emotional regulation, and what some have called "effortful" control—the ability to moderate impulsivity and responses to social circumstances (Rothbart & Ahadi, 1994). For infants, this includes such attributes as activity level, feeding patterns, adaptability, and intensity of reactions to stimuli. In older children, an easy temperament has often been defined simply as general cheerfulness, happy mood, and positive outlook. In a study of 223 mothers and their children (ages 9 to 12 years) who had recently experienced divorce, Lengua, Sandler, West, Wolchik, and Curran (1999) found such a measure to distinguish children who had avoided depressive symptoms and conduct problems from those who had not. Increasingly, however, temperamental characteristics are defined as processes of "initiating, maintaining, modulating, or changing . . . internal feeling states . . . in service of accomplishing one's goals" (Eisenberg et al., 2000, p. 1367). In a cohort study of 146 kindergarten to third-grade children who were assessed two years after an initial assessment, behavioral control (for example, not cheating on a puzzle problem where cheating would be easy) and attentional control (for example, ability to regulate desires and complete a task in the face of an enticing diversion) predicted future conduct problems (Eisenberg et al., 2000). More skillful children were less likely to develop behavioral difficulties. Although rooted in neurochemical basal arousal and other physiological characteristics, temperament is seen more and more as a set of discrete cognitive, regulatory skills that operate directly as protective factors by influencing a child's perception of and reaction to stressors, and indirectly by enabling children to elicit positive responses from caretakers and peers (Morisset, 1993; Rutter, 1987).

Competence in Normative Roles: Self-Efficacy with Peers and in School

Bandura (1977, 1982, 1995, 1997) conceptualized a process by which competence serves a protective function for children through the development of self-efficacy (a belief in one's personal effectiveness). He argued that success in one developmental setting increases a child's view of herself or himself as effective, in turn enhancing the motivation to act positively in other developmental settings. In this sense, then, self-efficacy is thought to promote adaptation, coping, and achievement across settings and systems. Empirical evidence supports the idea that experiences of success lead to increased self-efficacy (Brooks, 1994; Morisset, 1993; Rae-Grant et al., 1989; Rutter, 1985; Wills, Baccara, & McNamara, 1992). Although it is not clear whether self-efficacy and social competence predict social adjustment overall, recent data suggest that academic efficacy (capability to manage learning and master various subjects), social efficacy (ease in managing peer and other social relationships), and self-regulatory efficacy (ability to resist pressure from peers to do things you disapprove) lead to higher social acceptance (reduced peer rejection), psychological wellness, academic aspirations, and achievement (Bandura, Barabranelli, Caprara, & Pastorelli, 2001; Eisenberg, Fabes, Guthrie, & Reiser, 2002; Epstein, Griffin, & Botvin, 2002; Hanish & Guerra, 2002; Lengua, 2002; Miller-Johnson, Coie, Maumary-Gremaud, Bierman, & Conduct Problems Prevention Research Group, 2002). Relatedly, it is clear that success in school and in social relationships with peers protects children against delinquency, substance abuse, teen parenting, and other social and health problems (Carnahan, 1994; Epstein, et al., 2002; Hanish & Guerra, 2002; O'Donnell et al., 1995; Scott-Jones, 1991).

Self-Esteem and Hardiness

Self-esteem has been cited as a major protective factor for recovery from child maltreatment (Moran & Eckenrode, 1992) and a variety of other social and health problems (Garmezy, 1985; Masten et al., 1990; Rutter, 1979; Werner & Smith, 1992). According to Brooks (1994), "Self-esteem may be understood as including the feelings and thoughts that individuals have about their competence and worth, about their abilities to make a difference, to confront rather than retreat from challenges, to learn from both success and failure, and to treat themselves and others with respect" (p. 547). As defined here, self-esteem incorporates the elements of self-efficacy. Enhancement of self-esteem may represent the protective mechanism through which many commonly cited protective factors, such as participation in hobbies (Grizenko & Pawliuk, 1994), responsibility for regular household chores (Werner & Smith, 1992), or good performance in school (Carnahan, 1994) operate.

Critics have argued that self-esteem focuses too much on a personal attribute rather than on the transaction between child and environment. The concept of *hardiness,* they argue, better describes the relationship between an individual tenaciousness of spirit and stress-producing contexts in development, particularly in adolescent development (Debold, Brown, Weseen, & Brookins, 1999). Hardiness has three elements:

1. Control: the ability to understand a social circumstance, draw appropriate inferences taking into account the context, select an adaptation strategy, and implement it.
2. Commitment: a set of values and beliefs that impart a sense of purpose.
3. Challenge: a response to stress such that a child feels motivated and capable in solving problems.

Hardiness is a useful elaboration of self-esteem because it implies that self-esteem is dependent on the capacity to perceive social cues, make appropriate interpretations, set relational as well as concrete goals, select an appropriate interpersonal strategy, and have sufficient skill to implement the strategy in context. Thus, the processes that underlie self-esteem and hardiness involve interpreting social information and implementing a problem-solving strategy. Self-esteem and hardiness develop in the context of opportunities for learning these skills from family, friends, and others. Moreover, they are probably related to the presence of rewards from family and friends for persevering in the face of challenge. These may be malleable and subject to intervention (see, for example, Fraser, Nash, Galinsky, & Darwin, 2000).

Intelligence

Finally, as measured by IQ and other tests, intelligence appears to be moderately negatively associated with some social and health problems (Masten et al., 1999; Wicks-Nelson & Israel, 1997; Woodward & Fergusson, 1999). Controlling for race or ethnicity and SES, low intelligence is often correlated with aggressive, antisocial behavior, including various forms of delinquency (Farrington et al., 1993; Loeber et al., 1998a). In turn, high intelligence is often cited as a protective factor against antisocial behavior (Masten, 1994). Studies have also demonstrated the protective effects of high intelligence against generalized life stress (Radke-Yarrow & Sherman, 1990). In pondering such findings, Rutter (1979, 1985) speculated that high intelligence operates as a protective factor through two pathways. First, he suggests that high intelligence may lead to academic success, which in turn leads to higher self-esteem and self-efficacy. Second, he argues that more capable children may develop more sophisticated problem-solving skills, which in turn give rise to more effective responses to stressful situations.

Conclusion

This chapter has defined the basic concepts of risk, resilience, and protection that characterize a new way to understand human behavior and the ecology of childhood. Employing both ecological and multisystems perspectives, it discussed risk traits, stressful life events, cumulative risk, and risk chains. The interplay of risk and protective factors was then explored from the viewpoint of resilience. Finally, the chapter addressed risk and protective factors that appear to be common to many childhood disorders and problems. This model of common risk and protective factors serves as the basic reference for the chapters that follow.

References

Agnew, R. A. (1993). Why do they do it? An examination of the intervening mechanisms between "social control" variables and delinquency. *Journal of Research in Crime and Delinquency, 30*, 245–266.

Aguilar, B., Sroufe, L. A., Egeland, B., & Carlson, E. (2000). Distinguishing the early-onset/persistent and adolescence-onset antisocial behavior types: From birth to 16 years. *Development and Psychopathology, 12*(2), 109–132.

Al-Issa, I., & Tousignant, M. (Eds.). (1997). *Ethnicity, immigration, and psychopathology.* New York: Plenum Press.

Allen, N. B., Lewinsohn, P. M., & Seeley, J. R. (1998). Prenatal and perinatal influences on risk for psychopathology in childhood and adolescence. *Development and Psychopathology, 10*(3), 513–529.

Amaro, H., Whitaker, R., Coffman, G., & Heeren, T. (1990). Acculturation and marijuana and cocaine use. *American Journal of Public Health, 80*(Suppl.), 54–60.

Anthony, E. J. (1987). Risk, vulnerability, and resilience: An overview. In E. J. Anthony & B. J. Cohler (Eds.), *The invulnerable child* (pp. 3–48). New York: Guilford Press.

Artz, S. (1998). *Sex, power, and the violent school girl.* Toronto: Trifolium Books.

Astor, R. A., Benbenishty, R., Pitner, R. O., & Meyer, H. A. (2004). Bullying and peer victimization in schools. In P. Allen-Meares & M. W. Fraser (Eds.), *Intervention with children and adolescents: An interdisciplinary perspective* (pp. 417–448). Needham Heights, MA: Allyn & Bacon.

Bagley, C. A., & Carroll, J. (1998). In H. I. McCubbin, E. A. Thompson, A. I. Thompson, & J. A. Futrell (Eds.), *Resiliency in African-American families* (pp. 117–142). Thousand Oaks, CA: Sage.

Baldwin, A. L., Baldwin, C., & Cole, R. E. (1990). Stress-resistant families and stress-resistant children. In J. Rolf, A. Masten, D. Cicchetti, K. H. Nuechterlein, &

S. Weintraub (Eds.), *Risk and protective factors in the development of psychopathology* (pp. 257–280). New York: Cambridge University Press.

Bandura, A. (1977). Self-efficacy: Toward a unifying theory of behavioral change. *Psychological Review, 84*, 191–215.

Bandura, A. (1982). Self-efficacy mechanisms in human agency. *American Psychologist, 37*, 122–147.

Bandura, A. (1995). *Self-efficacy in changing societies.* New York: Cambridge University Press.

Bandura, A. (1997). *Self-efficacy: The exercise of control.* New York: W. H. Freeman.

Bandura, A., Barbaranelli, C., Caprara, G. V., & Pastorelli, C. (2001). Self-efficacy beliefs as shapers of children's aspirations and career trajectories. *Child Development, 72*(1), 187–206.

Barrera, M., Castro, F. G., & Biglan, A. (1999). Ethnicity, substance use, and development: Exemplars for exploring group differences and similarities. *Development and Psychopathology, 11*(4), 805–822.

Barth, R. P. (2002). Outcomes of adoption and what they tell us about designing services. *Adoption Quarterly, 6,* 45–60.

Beardslee, W. R. (1989). The role of self-understanding in resilient individuals: The development of a perspective. *American Journal of Orthopsychiatry, 59*(2), 266–278.

Begun, A. L. (1993). Human behavior and the social environment: The vulnerability, risk, and resilience model. *Journal of Social Work Education, 29,* 26–35.

Benard, B. (1993). Fostering resiliency in kids. *Educational Leadership, 51*(3), 44–49.

Berlin, R., & Davis, R. (1989). Children from alcoholic families: Vulnerability and resilience. In T. Dagan & R. Coles (Eds.), *The child in our times: Studies in the development of resiliency* (pp. 81–105). New York: Brunner-Mazel.

Booth, A., & Crouter, A. C. (Eds.). (2001). *Does it take a village?* Mahwah, NJ: Lawrence Erlbaum.

Bowen, N. K., Bowen, G. L., & Ware, W. B. (2002). Neighborhood social disorganization, families, and the educational behavior of adolescents. *Journal of Adolescent Research, 17*(5), 468–490.

Bowen, N. K., & Flora, D. B. (2002). When is it appropriate to focus on protection in intervention for adolescents? *American Journal of Orthopsychiatry, 72*(4), 526–538.

Boyce, W. T., Frank, E., Jensen, P. S., Kessler, R. C., Nelson, C. A., Steinberg, L., & the MacArthur Foundation Research Network on Psychopathology and Development. (1998). Social context in developmental psychopathology: Recommendations for future research from the MacArthur Network on Psychopathology and Development. *Development and Psychopathology, 10*(2), 143–164.

Bradley, R. H., Whiteside, L., Mundfrom, D. J., Casey, P. H., Kelleher, K. J., & Pope, S. K. (1994). Early indications of resilience and their relation to experiences in the home environments of low birthweight, premature children living in poverty. *Child Development, 65,* 346–360.

Brodsky, A. E. (1999). Making it: The components and process of resilience among urban, African-American single mothers. *American Journal of Orthopsychiatry, 69*(2), 148–160.

Bronfenbrenner, U. (1979). *The ecology of human development: Experiments by nature and design.* Cambridge, MA: Harvard University Press.

Bronfenbrenner, U. (1986). Ecology of the family as a context to human development: Research perspectives. *Development Psychology, 22*, 723–742.

Brook, J. S., Kessler, R. C., & Cohen, P. (1999). The onset of marijuana use from preadolescence and early adolescence to young adulthood. *Development and Psychopathology, 1*(4), 901–914.

Brooks, R. B. (1994). Children at risk: Fostering resilience and hope. *American Journal of Orthopsychiatry, 64*, 545–553.

Brooks-Gunn, J., Duncan, G., Klebanov, P., & Sealand, N. (1993). Do neighborhoods influence child and adolescent development? *American Journal of Sociology, 99*, 353–395.

Brown, J. H., D'Emidio-Caston, M., & Benard, B. (2001). *Resilience education*. Thousand Oaks, CA: Corwin Press.

Cadoret, R. J., & Riggins-Caspers, K. (2000). Fetal alcohol exposure and adult psychopathology: Evidence from an adoption study. In R. P. Barth, M. Freundlich, & D. Brodzinsky (Eds.), *Adoption and prenatal alcohol and drug exposure* (pp. 83–113). Washington, DC: Child Welfare League of America.

Cantwell, M. L., & Jenkins, D. I. (1998). Housing and neighborhood satisfaction of single-parent mothers and grandmothers. In H. I. McCubbin, E. A. Thompson, A. I. Thompson, & J. A. Futrell (Eds.), *Resiliency in African-American families* (pp. 99–115). Thousand Oaks, CA: Sage Publications.

Carnahan, S. (1994). Preventing school failure and dropout. In R. J. Simeonsson (Ed.), *Risk, resilience, and prevention: Promoting the well-being of all children* (pp. 103–124). Baltimore: Paul H. Brookes.

Carney, A. G., & Merrell, K. W. (2001). Bullying in schools: Perspectives on understanding and preventing an international problem. *School Psychology International, 22*, 364–382.

Carpentieri, S. C., Mulhern, R. K., Douglas, S., Hanna, S., & Fairdough, J. (1993). Behavioral resiliency among children surviving brain tumors [Special issue]. *Journal of Clinical Child Psychology, 22*, 236–246.

Caspi, A., McClay, J., Moffitt, T. E., Mill, J., Martin, J., Craig, I. W., Taylor, A., & Poulton, R. (2002). Role of genotype in the cycle of violence in maltreated children. *Science, 297*, 851–854.

Cicchetti, D. (1990). A historical perspective on the discipline of developmental psychopathology. In J. Rolf, A. Masten, D. Cicchetti, K. H. Nuechterlein, & S. Weintraub (Eds.), *Risk and protective factors in the development of psychopathology* (pp. 2–28). New York: Cambridge University Press.

Cicchetti, D., & Rogosch, F. A. (1997). The role of self-organization in the promotion of resilience in maltreated children. *Development and Psychopathology, 9*, 797–815.

Clark, W. R., & Grunstein, M. (2000). *Are we hardwired? The role of genes in human behavior*. New York: Oxford University Press.

Cloward, R. A., & Ohlin, L. B. (1960). *Delinquency and opportunity: A theory of delinquent gangs*. New York: Free Press.

Cohen, J., & Cohen, P. (1983). *Applied multiple regression/correlation analysis for the behavioral sciences* (2nd ed.). Hillsdale, NJ: Lawrence Erlbaum.

Coie, J. D., Watt, N. F., West, S. G., Hawkins, J. D., Asarnow, J. R., Markman, H. J. Ramey, S. L., Shure, M. B., & Long, B. (1993). The science of prevention:

A conceptual framework and some directions for a national research program. *American Psychologist, 48*, 1013–1022.

Coleman, J. S. (1988). Social capital in the creation of human capital. *American Journal of Sociology, 94*(Suppl.), S95–S120.

Coll, C. G., & Magnuson, K. (2000). Cultural differences as sources of developmental vulnerabilities and resources. In J. P. Shonkoff & S. J. Meisels (Eds.), *Handbook of early childhood intervention* (2nd ed., pp. 94–114). New York: Cambridge University Press.

Compas, B. E., Hinden, B. R., & Gerhardt, C. A. (1995). Adolescent development: Pathways and processes of risk and resilience. *Annual Reviews in Psychology, 46*, 265–293.

Conger, R. D., Rueter, M. A., & Elder, G. H. (1999). Couple resilience to economic pressure. *Journal of Personality and Social Psychology 76*(1), 54–71.

Cowan, E. L., Wyman, P. A., Work, W. C., & Parker, G. R. (1990). The Rochester Child Resilience Project: Overview and summary of first year findings. *Development and Psychopathology, 2*, 193–212.

Crnic, K. A., Greenberg, M. T., Ragozin, A. S., Robinson, N. M., & Basham, R. B. (1983). Effects of stress and social support on mothers and premature and full-term infants. *Child Development, 54*, 209–217.

Crook, T., & Eliot, J. (1980). Parental death during childhood and adult depression: A critical review of the literature. *Psychological Bulletin, 87*, 252–259.

Deater-Deckard, K., Dodge, K. A., Bates, J. E., & Pettit, G. E. (1998). Multiple risk factors in the development of externalizing behavior problems: Group and individual differences. *Development and Psychopathology, 10*(3), 469–493.

Debold, E., Brown, L. M., Weseen, S., & Brookins, G. K. (1999). Cultivating hardiness zones for adolescent girls: A reconceptualization of resilience in relationships with caring adults. In N. G. Johnson, M. C. Roberts, & J. Worell (Eds.), *Beyond appearance: A new look at adolescent girls* (pp. 181–204). Washington, DC: American Psychological Association.

Delgado, M. (Ed.). (1998). *Alcohol use/abuse among Latinos: Issues and examples of culturally competent service*. New York: Haworth Press.

Demos, V. (1989). Resiliency in infancy. In T. Dagan & R. Coles (Eds.), *The child in our times: Studies in the development of resiliency* (pp. 3–22). New York: Brunner-Mazel.

Denham, S. A., Workman, E., Cole, P. M., Weissbrod, C., Kendziora, K. T., & Zahn-Waxler, C. (2000). Prediction of externalizing behavior problems from early to middle childhood: The role of parental socialization and emotion expression. *Development and Psychopathology, 12*(1), 23–45.

Dishion, T. J., Capaldi, D. M., & Yoerger, K. (1999). Middle childhood antecedents to progressions in male adolescent substance use: An ecological analysis of risk and protection. *Journal of Adolescent Research, 14*(2), 175–205.

Dodge, K. A., Bates, J. E., & Pettit, G. S. (1990). Mechanisms in the cycle of violence. *Science, 250*, 1678–1683.

DuBois, D. L., Holloway, B. E., Valentine, J. C., & Cooper, H. (2002). Effectiveness of mentoring programs for youth: A meta-analytic review. *American Journal of Community Psychology, 30*(2), 157–197.

Duncan, G. J. (1991). The economic environment of childhood. In A. C. Houston (Ed.),

Children in poverty: Child development and public policy (pp. 23–50). New York: Cambridge University Press.

Duncan, G. J., Brooks-Gunn, J., & Klebanov, P. K. (1994). Economic deprivation and early childhood development. *Child Development, 65,* 296–318.

Duncan, G. J., & Raudenbush, S. W. (2001). Neighborhoods and adolescent development: How can we determine the links? In A. Booth & A. C. Crouter (Eds.), *Does it take a village?* (pp. 105–136). Mahwah, NJ: Lawrence Erlbaum.

Eisenberg, N., Fabes, R. A., Guthrie, I. K., & Reiser, M. (2002). The role of emotionality and regulation in children's social competence and adjustment. In L. Pulkkinen & A. Caspi (Eds.), *Path to successful development: Personality in the life course* (pp. 46–70). New York: Cambridge University Press.

Eisenberg, N., Guthrie, I. K., Fabes, R. A., Shepard, S., Losoya, S., Murphy, B. C., Jones, S., Poulin, R., & Reiser, M. (2000). Prediction of elementary school children's externalizing problem behaviors from attentional and behavioral regulation and negative emotionality. *Child Development, 71*(5), 1367–1382.

Elder, G. H., Jr. (1974). *Children of the great depression.* Chicago: University of Chicago Press.

Elder, G. H., Jr., Nguyen, T., & Caspi, A. (1985). Linking family hardship to children's lives. *Child Development, 56,* 361–375.

Elliott, D. S., Wilson, W. J., Huizinga, D., Sampson, R. J., Elliott, A., & Rankin, B. (1996). The effects of neighborhood disadvantage on adolescent development. *Journal of Research in Crime and Delinquency, 33*(4), 389–426.

Emery, R. E., & Forehand, R. (1994). Parental divorce and children's well-being: A focus on resilience. In R. J. Haggerty, L. R. Sherrod, N. Garmezy, & M. Rutter (Eds.), *Stress, risk and resilience in children and adolescents: Processes, mechanisms, and interventions* (pp. 64–99). New York: Cambridge University Press.

Entwisle, D., Alexander, K., & Olson, L. (1997). *Children, schools, and inequality.* Boulder, CO: Westview Press.

Epstein, J. A., Griffin, K. W., & Botvin, G. J. (2002). Positive impact of competence skills and psychological wellness in protecting inner-city adolescents from alcohol use. *Prevention Science, 3*(2), 95–104.

Factor, D. C., & Wolfe, D. A. (1990). Parental psychopathology and high-risk children. In R. T. Ammerman & M. Hersen (Eds.), *Children at risk: An evaluation of factors contributing to child abuse and neglect* (pp. 171–198). New York: Plenum Press.

Farber, E. A., & Egeland, B. (1987). Invulnerability among abused and neglected children. In E. J. Anthony & B. J. Cohler (Eds.), *The invulnerable child* (pp. 253–288). New York: Guilford Press.

Farrington, D. P., Loeber, R., Elliott, D. S., Hawkins, J. D., Kandel, D. B., Klein, M. W., McCord, J., Rowe, D. C., & Tremblay, R. E. (1993). Advancing knowledge about the onset of delinquency and crime. In B. B. Lahey & A. E. Kazdin (Eds.), *Advances in clinical child psychology* (Vol. 13, pp. 283–342). New York: Plenum Press.

Feldman, R., Stiffman, A., & Jung, K. (Eds.). (1987). *Children at risk: In the web of parental mental illness.* New Brunswick, NJ: Rutgers University Press.

Felix-Ortiz, M., & Newcomb, M. D. (1992). Risk and protective factors for drug use among Latino and white adolescents. *Hispanic Journal of Behavioral Sciences, 14,* 291–309.

Felner, R. D., Brand, S., Dubois, D. L., Adan, A. M., Mulhall, P. F., & Evans, E. (1995). Socioeconomic disadvantage, proximal environmental experiences, and socioemotional and academic adjustment in early adolescence: Investigation of a mediated effects model. *Child Development, 66,* 774–792.

Fergusson, D. M., & Lynskey, M. T. (1996). Adolescent resiliency to family adversity. *Journal of Child Psychology and Psychiatry, 37,* 281–292.

Fisher, L., Kokes, R. F., Cole, R. E., Perkins, P. M., & Wynne, L. C. (1987). Competent children at risk: A study of well-functioning offspring of disturbed parents. In E. J. Anthony & B. J. Cohler (Eds.), *The invulnerable child* (pp. 211–228). New York: Guilford Press.

Franz, C., McClelland, D., & Weinberger, J. (1991). Childhood antecedents of conventional social accomplishment in mid-life adults: A 36-year prospective study. *Journal of Personality and Social Psychology, 60*(4), 1–10.

Fraser, M. W., Nash, J. K., Galinsky, M. J., & Darwin, K. E. (2000). *Making choices: Social problem-solving skills for children.* Washington, DC: NASW Press.

Fraser, M. W., Richman, J. M., & Galinsky, M. J. (1999). Risk, protection, and resilience: Toward a conceptual framework for social work practice. *Social Work Research, 23*(3), 131–143.

Furstenberg, F. F., Jr., Cook, T. D., Eccles, J., Elder, G. H., Jr., & Sameroff, A. (1999). *Managing to make it: Urban families and adolescent success.* Chicago: University of Chicago Press.

Garbarino, J. (2001). Making sense of senseless youth violence. In J. M. Richman & M. W. Fraser (Eds.), *The context of youth violence: Resilience, risk, and protection* (pp. 83–95). Westport, CT: Praeger.

Garbarino, J., Kostelny, K., & Dubrown, N. (1991). What children can tell us about living in danger. *American Psychologist, 46,* 376–383.

Garcia Coll, C. T., Sepkoski, C., & Lester, B. M. (1982). Effects of teenage childbearing on neonatal and infant behavior in Puerto Rico. *Infant Behavior and Development, 5,* 227–236.

Garmezy, N. (1971). Vulnerability research and the issue of primary prevention. *American Journal of Orthopsychiatry, 41,* 101–116.

Garmezy, N. (1985). Stress-resistant children: The search for protective factors. In J. E. Stevenson (Ed.), *Recent research in developmental psychopathology* (pp. 213–233). Tarrytown, NY: Pergamon Press.

Garmezy, N. (1993a). Children in poverty: Resilience despite risk. *Psychiatry, 56,* 127–136.

Garmezy, N. (1993b). Vulnerability and resilience. In D. C. Funder, R. D. Parke, C. Tomlinson-Keasey, & K. Widaman (Eds.), *Studying lives through time* (pp. 377–398). Washington, DC: American Psychological Association.

Garmezy, N., & Masten, A. (1991). The protective role of competence indicators in children at risk. In E. M. Cummings (Ed.), *Life span developmental psychology: Perspectives on stress and coping* (pp. 151–176). Hillsdale, NJ: Lawrence Erlbaum.

Gil, A. G., Vega, W. A., & Dimas, J. M. (1994). Acculturative stress and personal adjustment among Hispanic adolescent boys. *Journal of Community Psychology, 22*(1), 43–54.

Gil, A.G., Wagner, E. F., & Vega, W.A. (2000). Acculturation, familism and alcohol use among Latino adolescent males: Longitudinal relations. *Journal of Community Psychology, 28*(4), 443–458.

Gilmartin, B. G. (1987). Peer group antecedents of severe love-shyness in males. *Journal of Personality, 55,* 467–489.

Gottfredson, D. C. (2000). *Schools and delinquency.* New York: Cambridge University Press.

Graham, C. A., & Easterbrooks, M. A. (2000). School-aged children's vulnerability to depressive symptomatology: The role of attachment security, maternal depressive symptomatology, and economic risk. *Development and Psychopathology, 12*(2), 201–213.

Graham, Y. P., Heim, C., Goodman, S. H., Miller, A. H., & Nemeroff, C. B. (1999). The effects of neonatal stress on brain development: Implications for psychopathology. *Development and Psychopathology, 11*(3), 545–565.

Greenberg. M. T., Speltz, M. L., DeKlyen, M., & Jones, K. (2001). Correlates of clinic referral for early conduct problems: Variable- and person-oriented approaches. *Development and Psychopathology, 13,* 255–276.

Grizenko, N., & Fisher, C. (1992). Risk and protective factors for psychopathology in children. *Canadian Journal of Psychiatry, 37,* 711–721.

Grizenko, N., & Pawliuk, N. (1994). Risk and protective factors for disruptive behavior disorders in children. *American Journal of Orthopsychiatry, 64,* 534–544.

Grossman, J. B., & Rhodes, J. E. (2002). The test of time: Predictors and effects of duration in youth mentoring relationships. *American Journal of Community Psychology, 30*(2), 199–219.

Grossman, J. B., & Tierney, J. P. (1998). Does mentoring work? An impact study of the Big Brothers/Big Sisters program. *Evaluation Review, 22,* 403–426.

Hanish, L. D., & Guerra, N. G. (2002). A longitudinal analysis of patterns of adjustment following peer victimization. *Development and Psychopathology, 14,* 69–89.

Hart, B., & Risley, T. R. (1995). *Meaning differences in the everyday experience of young American children.* Baltimore: Paul H. Brookes.

Hartup, W. W. (1983). Peer relations. In P. J. Mussen (Series Ed.) & E. M. Hetherington (Vol. Ed.), *Handbook of child psychology: Vol. 4. Socialization, personality, and social development* (pp. 103–196). New York: John Wiley & Sons.

Hawkins, J. D., Catalano, R. F., & Miller, J. Y. (1992). Risk and protective factors for alcohol and other drug problems in adolescence and early adulthood: Implications for substance abuse prevention. *Psychological Bulletin, 112,* 64–105.

Hazler, R. J. (1996). *Breaking the cycle of violence: Interventions for bullying and victimization.* Washington, DC: Accelerated Development.

Herrenkohl, T. I., Guo, J., Kosterman, R., Hawkins, J. D., Catalano, R. F., & Smith, B. H. (2001). Early adolescent predictors of youth violence as mediators of childhood risks. *Journal of Early Adolescence, 21*(4), 447–469.

Herrenkohl, T. I., Hawkins, J. D., Chung, I., Hill, K. G., & Battin-Pearson, S. (2001). School and community risk factors and interventions. In R. Loeber & D. P. Farrington (Eds.), *Child delinquents: Development, intervention, and service needs* (pp. 211–246). Thousand Oaks, CA: Sage Publications.

Huang, B., Kosterman, R., Catalano, R. F., Hawkins, J. D., & Abbott, R. D. (2001). Modeling mediation in the etiology of violent behavior in adolescence: A test of the Social Development Model. *Criminology, 39*(1), 75–108.

Iacono, W. G., Carlson, S. R., Taylor, J., Elkins, I. J., & McGue, M. (1999). Behavioral disinhibition and the development of substance-use disorders: Findings from the Minnesota Twin Family Study. *Development and Psychopathology, 11*(4), 869–900.

Ingoldsby, E. M., Shaw, D. S., & Garcia, M. M. (2001). Intrafamily conflict in relation to boys adjustment at school. *Development and Psychopathology, 13*(1), 35–52.

Ingram, R. E., & Price, J. M. (2001). The role of vulnerability in understanding psychopathology. In R. E. Ingram & J. M. Price (Eds.), *Vulnerability to psychopathology: Risk across the lifespan* (pp. 3–19). New York: Guilford Press.

Jackson, A. P., Brooks-Gunn, J., Huang, C., & Glassman, M. (2000). Single mothers in low-wage jobs: Financial strain, parenting, and preschoolers' outcomes. *Child Development, 71*(5), 1409–1423.

Jaffee, S., Caspi, A., Moffitt, T. E., Belsky, J., & Silva, P. (2001). Why are children born to teen mothers at risk for adverse outcomes in young adulthood? Results from a 20-year longitudinal study. *Development and Psychopathology, 13*, 377–397.

Jarrett, R. L. (1995). Growing poor: The family experiences of socially mobile youth in low income African-American neighborhoods. *Journal of Adolescent Research, 10*(1), 111–135.

Johnson, N. G., Roberts, M. C., & Worell, J. (Eds.). (1999). *Beyond appearance: A new look at adolescent girls.* Washington, DC: American Psychological Association.

Kaltiala-Heino, R., Rimpela, P. R., & Rimpela, A. (2000). Bullying at school: An indicator of adolescents at risk for mental disorders. *Journal of Adolescence, 23*, 661–674.

Kelley, B., Thornberry, T., & Smith, C. (1997). *In the wake of childhood maltreatment.* Juvenile Justice Bulletin (NCJ No. 165257). Washington, DC: U.S. Department of Justice, Office of Juvenile Justice and Delinquency Prevention.

Kempf-Leonard, K., Chesney-Lind, M., & Hawkins, D. (2001). Ethnicity and gender issues. In R. Loeber & D. P. Farrington (Eds.), *Child delinquents: Development, intervention, and service needs* (pp. 247–269). Thousand Oaks, CA: Sage Publications.

Kline, B. E., & Short, E. B. (1991a). Changes in emotional resilience: Gifted adolescent boys. *Roeper Review, 13*(4), 184–187.

Kline, B. E., & Short, E. B. (1991b). Changes in emotional resilience: Gifted adolescent females. *Roeper Review, 13*(3), 118–121.

Kreiger, N., Rowley, D. L., Herman, A. A., Avery, B., & Phillips, M. T. (1993). Racism, sexism, and social class: Implications for studies of health, disease, and well-being. *American Journal of Preventive Medicine, 9*(Suppl. 6), 82–122.

Kumpulainen, K., & Rasanen, E. (2000). Children involved in bullying at elementary and school age: Their psychiatric symptoms and deviance in adolescence. *Child Abuse and Neglect, 24*, 1567–1577.

Kumpulainen, K., Rasanen, E., & Puura, K. (2001). Psychiatric disorders and the use of mental health services among children involved in bullying. *Aggressive Behavior, 27*, 102–110.

Ladd, G. W., & Burgess, K. B. (2001). Do relational risks and protective factors moderate the linkages between childhood aggression and early psychological and school adjustment? *Child Development, 72*(5), 1579–1601.

LaFromboise, T., Coleman, H. L., & Gerton, J. (1993). Psychological impact of biculturalism: Evidence and theory. *Psychological Bulletin, 114*(3), 395–412.

Lamer, M., & Collins, A. (1996). Poverty in the lives of young children. In E. J. Erwin (Ed.), *Putting children first* (pp. 55–75). Baltimore: Paul H. Brookes.

Lang, J. G., Munoz, R., Bernal, G., & Sorensen, J. (1982). Quality of life and psychological well-being in a bicultural Latino community. *Hispanic Journal of Behavioral Sciences, 4*, 433–450.

Laub, J. H., Nagin, D. S., & Sampson, R. J. (1998). Trajectories of change in criminal offending: Good marriages and the desistance process. *American Sociological Review, 63*, 225–238.

Lengua, L. J. (2002). The contribution of emotionality and self-regulation to the understanding of children's response to multiple risk. *Child Development, 73*(1), 144–161.

Lengua, L. J., Sandler, I. N., West, S. G., Wolchik, S. A., & Curran, P. J. (1999). Emotionality and self-regulation, threat appraisal, and coping in children in divorce. *Development and Psychopathology, 11*(1), 15–37.

Levy, J. E., & Kunitz, S. J. (1987). A suicide prevention program for Hopi youth. *Social Science and Medicine, 25*, 931–940.

Lewis, M., & Ramsay, D. (2002). Cortisol response to embarrassment and shame. *Child Development, 73*(4), 1034–1045.

Lilienfield, A. M., & Lilienfield, D. E. (1980). *Foundations of epidemiology* (2nd ed.). New York: Oxford University Press.

Loeber, R., & Farrington, D. P. (2000). Young children who commit crime: Epidemiology, developmental origins, risk factors, early interventions, and policy implications. *Development and Psychopathology, 12*(4), 737–762.

Loeber, R., Farrington, D. P., Stouthamer-Loeber, M., & Van Kammen, W. B. (1998a). *Antisocial behavior and mental health problems: Explanatory factors in childhood and adolescence*. Mahwah, NJ: Lawrence Erlbaum.

Loeber, R., Farrington, D. P., Stouthamer-Loeber, M., & Van Kammen, W. B. (1998b). Multiple risk factors for multiproblem boys: Co-occurrence of delinquency, substance use, attention deficit, conduct problems, physical aggression, covert behavior, depressed mood, and shy/withdrawn behavior. In R. Jessor (Ed.), *New perspectives on adolescent risk behavior* (pp. 91–149). New York: Cambridge University Press.

Loeber, R., & Stouthamer-Loeber, M. (1996). The development of offending. *Criminal Justice and Behaviour, 23*(1), 12–24.

Lotspeich, L. J. (1998). Genetic, prenatal, and delivery history. In J. D. Noshpitz (Eds.), *Handbook of child and adolescent psychiatry. Vol. 5. Clinical assessment and intervention planning* (pp. 191–198). New York: John Wiley & Sons.

Luthar, S. S. (1991). Vulnerability and resilience: A study of high-risk adolescents. *Child Development, 62*, 600–616.

Luthar, S. S., Cicchetti, D., & Becker, B. (2000). The construct of resilience: A critical evaluation and guidelines for future work. *Child Development, 71*(3), 543–562.

Luthar, S. S., & Cushing, G. (1999). Neighborhood influences and child development: A prospective study of substance abusers' offspring. *Development and Psychopathology, 11*(4), 763–784.

Luthar, S. S., Doernberger, C. H., & Zigler, E. (1993). Resilience is not a unidimensional construct: Insights from a prospective study of inner-city adolescents. *Development and Psychopathology, 5*, 703–717.

Luthar, S, S., & Zigler, E. (1991). Vulnerability and competence: A review of research on resilience in childhood. *American Journal of Orthopsychiatry, 61*, 6–22.

MacKinnon-Lewis, C., Lamb, M. E., Hattie, J., & Baradaran, L. P. (2001). A longitudinal examination of the associations between mothers' and sons' attributions and their aggression. *Development and Psychopathology, 13*(1), 69–81.

Marks, G., Garcia, M., & Solts, J. M. (1990). Health risk behaviors of Hispanics in the United States: Findings from the Hispanic Health and Nutrition Examination Survey (HHANES), 1982–1984. *American Journal of Public Health, 80*(Suppl.), 20–26.

Masten, A. (1987). Resilience in development: Implications of the study of successful adaptation for developmental psychopathology. In D. Cicchetti (Ed.), *The emergence of a discipline: Rochester symposium on developmental psychopathology* (pp. 261–294). Hillsdale, NJ: Lawrence Erlbaum.

Masten, A. (1994). Resilience in individual development: Successful adaptation despite risk and adversity. In M. C. Wang & E. W. Gordon (Eds.), *Educational resilience in inner-city America: Challenges and prospects* (pp. 3–26). Hillsdale, NJ: Lawrence Erlbaum.

Masten, A. (2001). Ordinary magic: Resilience processes in development. *American Psychologist, 56*(3), 227–238.

Masten, A., Best, K. M., & Garmezy, N. (1990). Resilience and development: Contributions from the study of children who overcome adversity. *Development and Psychopathology, 2*, 425–444.

Masten, A. S., & Coatsworth, J. D. (1995). Competence, resilience, and psychopathology. In D. Cicchetti & D. Cohen (Eds.), *Developmental psychopathology: Vol. 2. Risk, disorder, and adaptation* (pp. 715–752). New York: John Wiley & Sons.

Masten, A., & Coatsworth, J. D. (1998). The development of competence in favorable and unfavorable environments: Lessons from research on successful children. *American Psychologist, 53*(2), 205–220.

Masten, A. S., & Curtis, W. J. (2000). Integrating competence and psychopathology: Pathways toward a comprehensive science of adaptation in development. *Development and Psychopathology, 12*(3), 529–550.

Masten, A. S., Hubbard, J. J., Gest, S. D., Tellegen, A., Garmezy, N., & Ramirez, M. (1999). Competence in the contest of adversity: Pathways to resilience and maladaptation from childhood to late adolescence. *Development and Psychopathology, 11*, 143–169.

McAdoo, H. P. (1998). African-American families: Strengths and realities. In H. I. McCubbin, E. A. Thompson, A. I. Thompson, & J. A. Futrell (Eds.), *Resiliency in African-American families* (pp. 17–30). Thousand Oaks, CA: Sage Publications.

McCloskey, L. A., & Stuewig, J. (2001). The quality of peer relationships among children exposed to family violence. *Development and Psychopathology, 13*(1), 83–96.

McCubbin, H. I., McCubbin, M. A., Thompson, A. I., Han, S., & Allen, C. T. (1997). Families under stress: What makes them resilient? *Journal of Family and Consumer Sciences, 89*(3), 2–11.

McGroder, S. M. (2000). Parenting among low-income, African-American single mothers with preschool-age children: Patterns, predictors, and developmental correlates. *Child Development, 71*(3), 752–771.

McLoyd, V. C. (1990). The impact of economic hardship on black families and children: Psychological distress, parenting, and socioemotional development. *Child Development, 61*, 335–343.

McLoyd, V. C. (1998). Socioeconomic disadvantage and child development. *American Psychologist, 53*(2), 185–204.

McMillen, J. C. (1999). Better for it: How people benefit from adversity. *Social Work, 44*(5), 455–467.

Merton, R. K. (1938). *Science, technology, and society in seventeenth century England.* Bruges, Belgium: Saint Catherine Press.

Meyer, J. M., Rutter, M., Silberg, J. L., Maes, H. H., Simonoff, E., Shillady, L. L., Pickles, A., Hewitt, J. K., & Eaves, L. J. (2000). Familial aggregation for conduct disorder symptomatology: The role of genes, marital discord and family adaptability. *Psychological Medicine, 30*(4), 759–774.

Miller-Johnson, S., Coie, J. D., Maumary-Gremaud, A., Bierman, K., & Conduct Problems Prevention Research Group. (2002). Peer rejection and aggression and early starter models of conduct disorder. *Journal of Abnormal Child Psychology, 30*(3), 217–230.

Miranda, A., Estrada, D., & Firpo-Jimenez, M. (2000). Differences in family cohesion, adaptability, and environment among Latino families in dissimilar stages of acculturation. *Family Journal: Counseling and Therapy for Couples and Families, 8*(4), 341–350.

Moffitt, T. E., & Caspi, A. (2001). Childhood predictors differentiate life-course persistent and adolescence-limited antisocial pathways among males and females. *Development and Psychopathology, 13*, 355–375.

Moffitt, T. E., Caspi, A., Rutter, M., & Silva, P. A. (2001). *Sex differences in antisocial behavior.* New York: Cambridge University Press.

Moran, P. B., & Eckenrode, J. (1992). Protective personality characteristics among adolescent victims of maltreatment. *Child Abuse & Neglect, 16*, 743–754.

Morisset, C. E. (1993). Language and emotional milestones on the road to readiness (Report No.18, Center on Families, Communities, Schools and Children's Learning). Arlington, VA: Zero to Three National Center for Clinical Infant Programs.

Mrazek, I. J., & Haggerty, R. J. (Eds.). (1994). *Reducing risks for mental disorders: Frontiers for preventive intervention research.* Washington, DC: National Academy Press.

Munson, J. A., McMahon, R. J., & Spieker, S. J. (2001). Structure and variability in the developmental trajectory of children's externalizing problems: Impact of infant attachment, maternal depressive symptomatology, and child sex. *Development and Psychopathology, 13*, 277–296.

Myers, H. F., Taylor, S., Alvy, K. T., Arrington, A., & Richardson, M. A. (1992). Parental and family predictors of behavior problems in inner-city black children. *American Journal of Community Psychology, 20*, 557–575.

Nansel, T. R., Overpeck, M., Pilla, R. S., Ruan, W. J., Simons-Morton, B., & Scheidt, P. (2001). Bullying behaviors among U.S. youth. *Journal of the American Medical Association, 285*(16), 2094–2100.

Neighbors, B., Forehand, M. S., & McVicar, D. (1993). Resilient adolescents and interparental conflict. *American Journal of Orthopsychiatry, 63*, 462–471.

Nettles, S. M., & Pleck, J. H. (1994). Risk, resilience, and development: The multiple ecologies of black adolescents. In R. J. Haggerty, L. R. Sherrod, N. Garmezy, & M. Rutter (Eds.), *Stress, risk and resilience in children and adolescents: Processes, mechanisms and interventions* (pp. 147–181). New York: Cambridge University Press.

O'Donnell, J., Hawkins, J. D., & Abbott, R. D. (1995). Predicting serious delinquency and substance abuse among aggressive boys. *Journal of Consulting and Clinical Psychology, 63*, 529–537.

O'Dougherty, M., & Wright, F. S. (1990). Children born at medical risk: Factors affecting vulnerability and resilience. In J. Rolf, A. Masten, D. Cicchetti, K. H. Nuechterlein, & S. Weintraub (Eds.), *Risk and protective factors in the development of psychopathology* (pp. 120–140). New York: Cambridge University Press.

Office of Juvenile Justice and Delinquency Prevention. (1995). *Juvenile Justice Bulletin: OJJDP update on programs.* Washington, DC: U.S. Department of Justice, Office of Justice Programs.

O'Keefe, M. (1994). Adjustment of children from maritally violent homes. *Families in Society, 75*, 403–415.

Olweus, D. (1994). Bullying at school: Long-term outcomes for the victims and an effective school-based intervention. In L. R. Huesmann (Ed.), *Aggressive behavior: Current perspectives* (pp. 97–130). New York: Plenum Press.

Olweus, D. (1995). Bullying or peer abuse in school: Fact and intervention. *Current Directions in Psychological Science, 4*, 196–200.

Parker, S., Greer, S., & Zuckerman, B. (1988). Double jeopardy: The impact of poverty on early child development. *Pediatric Clinics of North America, 35*, 1127–1241.

Patterson, G. R. (1982). *Coercive family process.* Eugene, OR: Castalia.

Patterson, G. R., Forgatch, M. S., Yoerger, K. L., & Stoolmiller, M. (1998). Variables that initiate and maintain an early-onset trajectory for juvenile offending. *Development and Psychopathology, 10,* 531–547.

Patterson, G. R., Reid, J. B., & Dishion, T. J. (1992). *Antisocial boys.* Eugene, OR: Castalia.

Pellegrini, D. S. (1990). Psychosocial risk and protective factors in childhood. *Developmental and Behavioral Pediatrics, 11*(4), 201–209.

Pellegrini, D. S., Kosisky, S., Nackman, D., Cytryn, L., McKnew, D. H., Gershon, E., Hamovit, J., & Cammuso, K. (1986). Personal and social resources in children of patients with bipolar affective disorder and children of normal controls. *American Journal of Psychiatry, 143*, 856–861.

Peoples, F., & Loeber, R. (1994). Do individual factors and neighborhood context explain ethnic differences in juvenile delinquency? *Journal of Quantitative Criminology, 10*(2), 141–157.

Pines, M. (1975, December). In praise of "invulnerables." *APA Monitor*, p. 7.

Plomin, R., De Fries, J. C., McClearn, G. E., & Rutter, M. (1997). *Behavioral genetics* (3rd ed.). San Francisco: W. H. Freeman.

Pollard, J. A., Hawkins, J. D., & Arthur, M. W. (1999). Risk and protection: Are both necessary to understand diverse behavioral outcomes in adolescence? *Social Work Research, 23*, 145–158.

Radke-Yarrow, M., & Sherman, T. (1990). Hard growing: Children who survive. In J. Rolf, A. Masten, D. Cicchetti, K. H. Nuechterlein, & S. Weintraub (Eds.),

Risk and protective factors in the development of psychopathology (pp. 97–119). New York: Cambridge University Press.

Rae-Grant, N., Thomas, B. H., Offord, D. R., & Boyle, M. H. (1989). Risk, protective factors, and the prevalence of behavioral and emotional disorders in children and adolescents. *Journal of the American Academy of Child and Adolescent Psychiatry, 28,* 262–268.

Reid, J. B., Patterson, G. R., & Snyder, J. (2002). *Antisocial behavior in children and adolescents.* Washington, DC: American Psychological Association.

Rende, R., & Plomin, R. (1993). Families at risk for psychopathology: Who becomes affected and why? *Development and Psychopathology, 5,* 529–540.

Reynolds, A., Temple, J., Robertson, D., & Mann, E. (2001). Long-term effects of an early childhood intervention on educational achievement and juvenile arrest: A 15-year follow-up of low-income children in public schools. *Journal of the American Medical Association, 285*(18), 2339–2346.

Richman, J. M., & Fraser, M. W. (Eds.). (2001). *The context of youth violence: Resilience, risk, and protection.* Westport, CT: Praeger Publishers.

Roberts, W. B., Jr., & Morotti, A. A. (2000). The bully as victim: Understanding bully behaviors to increase the effectiveness of interventions in the bully-victim dyad. *Professional School Counseling, 4*(2), 148–155.

Rogler, L. H., Cortes, R. S., & Malgadi, R. G. (1991). Acculturation and mental health status among Hispanics. *American Psychologist, 46,* 585–597.

Roosa, M. W. (2000). Some thoughts about resilience versus positive development, main effects versus interactions, and the value of resilience. *Child Development, 71*(3), 567–569.

Rothbart, M. K., & Ahadi, S. A. (1994). Temperament and the development of personality. *Journal of Abnormal Psychology, 103,* 55–66.

Rowe, D. C. (2001). *Biology and crime.* Los Angeles: Roxbury Press.

Roy, P., Rutter, M., & Pickles, A. (2000). Institutional care: Risk from family background or pattern of rearing? *Journal of Child Psychology and Psychiatry and Allied Disciplines, 41*(2), 139–149.

Rutter, M. (1979). Protective factors in children's responses to stress and disadvantage. In J. S. Bruner & A. Garten (Eds.), *Primary prevention of psychopathology* (Vol. 3, pp. 49–74). Hanover, NH: University Press of New England.

Rutter, M. (1983). Statistical and personal interactions: Facets and perspectives. In D. Magnusson & V. L. Allen (Eds.), *Human development: An interactional perspective* (pp. 295–320). New York: Academic Press.

Rutter, M. (1985). Family and school influences on behavioral development. *Journal of Child Psychology and Psychiatry, 26,* 349–368.

Rutter, M. (1987). Psychosocial resilience and protective mechanisms. *American Journal of Orthopsychiatry, 57,* 316–331.

Rutter, M. (1994). Stress research: Accomplishments and tasks ahead. In R. J. Haggerty, L. R. Sherrod, N. Garmezy, & M. Rutter (Eds.), *Stress, risk and resilience in children and adolescents: Processes, mechanisms and interventions* (pp. 354–386). New York: Cambridge University Press.

Rutter, M. (2000a). Psychosocial influences: Critiques, findings, and research needs. *Development and Psychopathology, 12,* 375–405.

Rutter, M. (2000b). Resilience reconsidered: Conceptual considerations, empirical findings, and policy implications. In J. P. Shonkoff & S. J. Meisels (Eds.), *Handbook of early childhood intervention* (2nd ed., pp. 651–682). New York: Cambridge University Press.

Rutter, M. (2001). Psychosocial adversity: Risk, resilience, and recovery. In J. M. Richman & M. W. Fraser (Eds.), *The context of youth violence: Resilience, risk, and protection* (pp. 13–41). Westport, CT: Praeger Publishers.

Rutter, M., Dunn, J., Plomin, P., Simonoff, E., Pickles, A., Maughan, B., Ormel, J., Meyer, J., & Eaves, L. (1997). Integrating nature and nurture: Implications of person-environment correlations and interactions for developmental psychopathology. *Development and Psychopathology, 9,* 335–364.

Rutter, M., Giller, H., & Hagell, A. (1998). *Antisocial behavior in young people.* New York: Cambridge University Press.

Rutter, M., Pickles, A., Murray, R., & Eaves, L. (2001). Testing hypotheses on specific environmental causal effects on behavior. *Psychological Bulletin, 127*(3), 291–324.

Saleebey, D. (1996). The strengths perspective in social work practice: Extensions and cautions. *Social Work, 41,* 296–305.

Saleebey, D. (Ed.). (1997). *The strengths perspective in social work practice: Power in the people* (2nd ed.). White Plains, NY: Longman.

Saleebey, D. (2000). Power in the people: Strengths and hope. *Advances in Social Work, 1*(2), 127–136.

Sameroff, A. (1995). General systems theories and developmental psychopathology. In D. Cicchetti & D. Cohen (Eds.), *Developmental psychopathology: Vol. 1. Theories and methods* (pp. 659–695). New York: John Wiley & Sons.

Sameroff, A. J., Bartko, W. T., Baldwin, A., Baldwin, C., & Seifer, R. (1998). Family and social influences on development of child competence. In M. Lewis & C. Feiring (Eds.), *Families, risk, and competence* (pp. 161–185). Mahwah, NJ: Lawrence Erlbaum.

Sameroff, A. J., & Fiese, B. H. (2000). Transactional regulation: The developmental ecology of early intervention. In J. P. Shonkoff & S. J. Meisels (Eds.), *Handbook of early childhood intervention* (2nd ed., pp. 135–159). New York: Cambridge University Press.

Sameroff, A. J., & Gutman, L. M. (2004). Contributions of risk research to the design of successful interventions. In P. Allen-Meares & M. W. Fraser (Eds.), *Intervention with children and adolescents: An interdisciplinary perspective* (pp. 9–26). Needham Heights, MA: Allyn & Bacon.

Sameroff, A. J., & Seifer, R. (1990). Early contributors to developmental risk. In J. Rolf, A. Masten, D. Cicchetti, K. H. Nuechterlein, & S. Weintraub (Eds.), *Risk and protective factors in the development of psychopathology* (pp. 52–66). New York: Cambridge University Press.

Sampson, R. J. (2001). How do communities undergird or undermine human development? What are the relevant contexts and what mechanisms are at work? In A. Booth & A. C. Crouter (Eds.), *Does it take a village?* (pp. 3–30). Mahwah, NJ: Lawrence Erlbaum.

Sampson, R. J., & Laub, J. H. (1996). Socioeconomic achievement in the life course of disadvantaged men: Military service as a turning point, circa 1940–1965. *American Sociological Review, 61,* 347–367.

Sampson, R. J., Raudenbush, S., & Earls, F. (1997). Neighborhoods and violent crime: A multilevel study of collective efficacy. *Science, 277,* 918–924.

Schteingart, J. S., Molnar, J., Klein, T. P., Lowe, C. B., & Hartman, A. H. (1995). Homeless and child functioning in the context of risk and protective factors moderating child outcomes. *Journal of Clinical Child Psychology, 24*(3), 320–331.

Scott-Jones, D. (1991). Adolescent childbearing: Risks and resilience. *Education and Urban Society, 24*(1), 53–64.

Seidman, E., Yoshikawa, H., Roberts, A., Chesir-Teran, D., Allen, L., Friedman, J. L., & Aber, J. L. (1998). Structural and experiential neighborhood contexts, developmental stage, and antisocial behavior among urban adolescents in poverty. *Development and Psychopathology, 10*(2), 259–281.

Seifer, R., & Sameroff, A. J. (1987). Multiple determinants of risk and invulnerability. In E. J. Anthony & B. J. Cohler (Eds.), *The invulnerable child* (pp. 51–69). New York: Guilford Press.

Seifer, R., Sameroff, A. J., Baldwin, C. P., & Baldwin, A. (1992). Child and family factors that ameliorate risk between 4 and 13 years of age. *Journal of the American Academy of Child and Adolescent Psychiatry, 31,* 893–903.

Shaw, C. R., & McKay, H. D. (1942). *Juvenile delinquency in urban areas.* Chicago: University of Chicago Press.

Shaw, D. S., Vondra, J. I., Hommerding, K. D., Keenan, K., & Dunn, M. (1994). Chronic family adversity and early child behavior problems: A longitudinal study of low-income families. *Journal of Child Psychology and Psychiatry, 35,* 1109–1122.

Shields, A., & Cicchetti, D. (2001). Parental maltreatment and emotional dysregulation as risk factors for bullying and victimization in middle childhood. *Journal of Clinical Child Psychology, 30*(3), 349–363.

Silverthorn, P., & Frick, P. J. (1999). Developmental pathways to antisocial behavior: The delayed-onset pathway in girls. *Development and Psychopathology, 11,* 101–126.

Simeonsson, R. J. (1994). Toward an epidemiology of developmental, educational and social problems of childhood. In R. J. Simeonsson (Ed.), *Risk, resilience, and prevention: Promoting the well-being of all children* (pp. 13–32). Baltimore: Paul H. Brookes.

Smokowski, P., Reynolds, A., & Bezrucko, N. (1999). Resilience and protective factors in adolescence: An autobiographical perspective from disadvantaged youth. *Journal of School Psychology, 37*(4), 425–448.

Sonn, C. C., & Fisher, A. T. (1998). Sense of community: Community resilient responses to oppression and change. *Journal of Community Psychology, 26*(5), 457–472.

Spencer, M. B. (2001). Resiliency and fragility factors associated with the contextual experiences of low resource urban African American male youth and families. In A. Booth & A. C. Crouter (Eds.), *Does it take a village?* (pp. 51–77). Mahwah, NJ: Lawrence Erlbaum.

Sroufe, L. A., Carlson, E. A., Levy, A. K., & Egeland, B. (1999). Implications of attachment theory for developmental psychopathology. *Development and Psychopathology, 11,* 1–13.

Stevenson, H. W., Chen, C., & Lee, S.Y. (1993). Mathematics achievement of Chinese, Japanese, and American children: Ten years later. *Science, 259*, 53–58.

Stouthamer-Loeber, M., Loeber, R., Farrington, D. P., Zhang, Q., van Kammen, W., & Maguin, E. (1993). The double edge of protective and risk factors for delinquency: Interrelations and developmental patterns. *Development and Psychopathology, 5*, 683–701.

Stouthamer-Loeber, M., Loeber, R., Wei, E., Farrington, D. P., & Wikstrom, P. (2002). Risk and promotive effects in the explanation of persistent serious delinquency in boys. *Journal of Consulting and Clinical Psychology, 70*(1), 111–123.

Svanberg, P. (1998). Attachment, resilience, and prevention. *Journal of Mental Health, 7*(6), 543–578.

Szapocznik, J., & Kurtines, W. M. (1980). Acculturation, biculturalism and adjustment among Cuban Americans. In A. Padilla (Ed.), *Acculturation: Theory, models, and some new findings* (pp. 139–159). Boulder, CO: Praeger.

Taylor, R. D. (1994). Risk and resilience: Contextual influences on the development of African-American adolescents. In M. C. Wang & E. W. Gordon (Eds.), *Educational resilience in inner-city America: Challenges and prospects* (pp. 119–130). Hillsdale, NJ: Lawrence Erlbaum.

Thornton, M. C. (1998). Indigenous resources and strategies of resistance: Informal caregiving and racial socialization in black communities. In H. I. McCubbin, E. A. Thompson, A. I. Thompson, & J. A. Futrell (Eds.), *Resiliency in African-American families* (pp. 49–66). Thousand Oaks, CA: Sage.

Torres-Matrullo, C. (1976). Acculturation and psychopathology among Puerto Rican women in mainland United States. *American Journal of Orthopsychiatry, 46*(4), 710–719.

U.S. Census Bureau. (2000, March). *The Hispanic population in the United States* [Online]. Retrieved from http://www.census.gov/population/socdemo/hispanic/p20 -535/p20-535.pdf on September 15, 2003.

U.S. Department of Health and Human Services. (2001). *Youth violence: A report of the surgeon general.* Rockville, MD: U. S. Department of Health and Human Services, Centers for Disease Control and Prevention, National Center for Injury Prevention and Control; Substance Abuse and Mental Health Services Administration, Center for Mental Health Services; and National Institutes of Health, National Institute of Mental Health.

U.S. Department of Health and Human Services, Administration on Children, Youth, and Families. (1999). *Child maltreatment 1997: Reports from the states to the national child abuse and neglect data system.* Washington, DC: U.S. Government Printing Office.

Vance, J. E. (2001). Neurobiological mechanisms of psychosocial resiliency. In J. M. Richman & M. W. Fraser (Eds.), *The context of youth violence: Resilience, risk, and protection* (pp. 43–81). Westport, CT: Praeger.

Vega, W., Kolody, B., Aguilar-Gaxiola, S., Alderete, E., Catalano, R., & Caraveo-Anduaga, J. (1998). Lifetime prevalence of DSM-III-R psychiatric disorders among urban and rural Mexican Americans in California. *Archives of General Psychiatry, 55*(9), 771–778.

Velez, C. N., Johnson, J., & Cohen, P. (1989). A longitudinal analysis of selected risk factors for childhood psychopathology. *Journal of the American Academy of Child and Adolescent Psychiatry, 28*, 861–864.

Vondra, J. I. (1990). Sociological and ecological factors. In R. T. Ammerman & M. Hersen (Eds.), *Children at risk: An evaluation of factors contributing to child abuse and neglect* (pp. 149–170). New York: Plenum Press.

Walsh, F. (1998). *Strengthening family resilience.* New York: Guilford Press.

Wang, M. C., Haertel, G. D., & Walberg, H. J. (1994). Educational resilience in inner cities. In M. C. Wang & E. W. Gordon (Eds.), *Educational resilience in inner-city America: Challenges and prospects* (pp. 45–72). Hillsdale, NJ: Lawrence Erlbaum.

Wangby, M., Bergman, L. R., & Magnusson, D. (1999). Development of adjustment problems in girls: What syndromes emerge? *Child Development, 70*(3), 678–699.

Wekerle, C., & Wolfe, D. A. (1998). The role of child maltreatment and attachment style in adolescent relationship violence. *Development and Psychopathology, 10*(3), 571–586.

Werner, E. E. (1984). Resilient children. *Young Children, 40*(1), 68–72.

Werner, E. E. (1992). The children of Kauai: Resiliency and recovery in adolescence and adulthood. *Journal of Adolescent Health, 13*(4), 262–268.

Werner, E. E. (1993). Risk, resilience, and recovery: Perspectives from the Kauai Longitudinal Study. *Development and Psychopathology, 5*, 503–515.

Werner, E. E., & Smith, R. S. (1977). *Kauai's children come of age.* Honolulu: University of Hawaii Press.

Werner, E. E., & Smith, R. S. (1982). *Vulnerable but invincible: A longitudinal study of resilient children and youth.* New York: Cambridge University Press.

Werner, E. E., & Smith, R. S. (1992). *Overcoming the odds: High risk children from birth to adulthood.* Ithaca, NY: Cornell University Press.

Wicks-Nelson, R., & Israel, A. C. (1997). *Behavioral disorders of childhood* (3rd ed.). Upper Saddle River, NJ: Prentice Hall.

Widom, C. S. (1989). Does violence beget violence? A critical examination of the literature. *Psychological Bulletin, 106*, 3–28.

Widom, C. S. (1999). Childhood victimization, running away, and delinquency. *Journal of Research on Crime and Delinquency, 36*(4), 347–370.

Wikstrom, P. H. (1998). Communities and crime. In M. Tonry (Ed.), *Handbook of crime and punishment* (pp. 241–273). New York: Oxford University Press.

Wikstrom, P. H., & Loeber, R. (2000). Do disadvantaged neighborhoods cause well-adjusted children to become adolescent delinquents? A study of male juvenile serious offending, individual risk, and protective factors, and neighborhood context. *Criminology, 38*(4), 1109–1142.

Wills, T. A., Baccara, D., & McNamara, G. (1992). The role of life events, family support, and competence in adolescent substance use: A test of vulnerability and protective factors. *American Journal of Community Psychology, 20*, 349–374.

Wilson, W. J. (1996). *When work disappears: The world of the new urban poor.* New York: Vintage Books.

Woodward, L. J., & Fergusson, D. M. (1999). Early conduct problems and later risk of teenage pregnancy in girls. *Development and Psychopathology, 11*, 127–141.

Youngblade, L. M., & Belsky, J. (1990). Social and emotional consequences of child maltreatment. In R. T. Ammerman & M. Hersen (Eds.), *Children at risk: An evaluation of factors contributing to child abuse and neglect* (pp. 109–148). New York: Plenum Press.

Zimmerman, M. A., & Bigenheimer, J. B. (2002). Natural mentors and adolescent resiliency: A study with urban youth. *American Journal of Community Psychology, 30*(2), 221–243.

Zubin, J., & Spring, B. (1977). Vulnerability: A new view of schizophrenia. *Journal of Abnormal Psychology, 86*, 103–126.

3

Methods in the Analysis of Risk and Protective Factors: Lessons from Epidemiology

James K. Nash and Karen A. Randolph

An ecological–developmental approach to the study of social and health problems provides a framework for the assessment of risk and protective factors and for the design of effective programs for children and adolescents (Fraser, Richman, & Galinsky, 1999; Garbarino, 1995; Germain & Gitterman, 1995). Central to this approach is the social work concept of person-in-environment, which emphasizes the importance of identifying and assessing the role of multiple individual and environmental protective factors that promote optimal development and the risk factors that lead to and exacerbate social problems. The goal of intervention is to increase the degree of fit between an individual and his or her environment by reducing or removing risk and building protection.

An ecological–developmental perspective has much in common with the discipline of *epidemiology,* which is concerned with identifying and describing patterns of the occurrence of disease and health in human populations. From both ecological and epidemiological perspectives, researchers investigate the roles and interaction of individual and environmental risk and protective factors in producing health and developmental outcomes (Gordis, 2000; U.S. Public Health Service, 2001). Research results provide information about the precursors and correlates of health and social problems. Practitioners seeking to base practice on empirical evidence can use this information to "decrease uncertainty about how to attain a certain outcome" (Gambrill, 1999, p. 340). Consistent with an evidence-based approach to practice, this chapter describes basic epidemiological methods for the analysis and presentation of data on risk and protective factors.

AN EPIDEMIOLOGICAL PERSPECTIVE

Like all social sciences and social work research, epidemiological research aims to generate knowledge that can be put to practical use in prevention and treatment (Gordis, 2000; Hennekens & Buring, 1987). Epidemiological research focuses on identifying patterns and causal agents of diseases, social problems, and health-related states. In addition, it aims to "study the natural history and prognosis of disease . . . [and to] provide the foundations for developing public policy. . . ." (Gordis, 2000, p. 3).

Three important ideas emerge from the epidemiological literature. To understand social and health problems, it is necessary to examine the distribution of wellness and problems in large groups and populations, to identify potential causal agents, and to produce knowledge to guide the design and implementation of policies and services. An epidemiological approach provides a framework for studying how frequently problems occur, for identifying factors that may lead to or exacerbate problems, and for developing strategies to address problems. More important, perhaps, it provides a means for identifying and assessing the importance of factors that promote healthy development and protect children and adolescents from risk.

LARGE GROUPS AND POPULATIONS

Epidemiology focuses on large groups and populations, not on the course of a problem or disorder in an individual. A focus on populations leads to the use of simple analytical techniques to determine whether the presence or absence of individual and environmental factors is associated with the occurrence of health or disease. A key idea in epidemiology is that a large sample size is necessary to establish a reliable association between the existence of a factor and the occurrence of an outcome. Determining that an association exists is often the first step in establishing whether there is a causal relationship between a risk or protective factor and a particular outcome.

CAUSATION

The second element in an epidemiological approach is to identify the causes of a problem or outcome. Social problems and health disorders rarely have single causes (Garbarino, 1995; Gordis, 2000). Rather, multiple environmental and individual factors are usually suspected to cause or increase the likelihood of problems. These factors may interact with one another and affect outcomes in ways that are difficult to observe or to measure.

Distinguishing factors that play a causal role from factors that are simply associated with a particular outcome (that is, *correlates*) is necessary for effective practice. For a causal relationship to exist, a risk factor "must have both a theoretical rationale and a demonstrated ability to predict" an outcome (U.S. Public Health Service, 2001, chapter 4, p. 2). Knowledge of causal processes involving the interaction of multiple risk factors informs effective practice (Fraser et al., 1999). In contrast, knowledge of the correlates—sometimes called "risk markers"—of a problem informs decisions about where to target prevention and intervention, but it does not necessarily indicate which strategy to use. For example, research has shown that male gender is a correlate of youth violence (see, for example, Loeber, Farrington, Stouthamer-Loeber, & Van Kammen, 1998), which suggests that prevention should target males. However, a theoretical perspective that explains why males are prone to use violence and supportive research are necessary to develop interventions.

In this book, we advocate an ecological perspective to evaluate the roles of suspected causal agents. By basing their conclusions on findings from many studies, chapter authors frequently contend that the presence of one or more factors is associated with an increased probability, risk, or odds of a condition or problem. As demonstrated in this chapter, this concept—risk for a social or health outcome—can be expressed mathematically.

PREVENTION, CONTROL, AND TREATMENT

From risk and odds data, researchers, policymakers, and practitioners attempt to develop interventions that will prevent the occurrence or spread of a problem or a condition and that will result in effective treatment. For some conditions—particularly some health problems—researchers can prove causality. They, along with policymakers and practitioners, can develop and implement preventive and treatment strategies accordingly.

However, causality does not need to be proved for preventive and treatment strategies to be developed. It may not be possible to identify all the causes of many problems, and causes may vary by developmental level, gender, and race or ethnicity. Moreover, it is often impractical to obtain the experimental evidence necessary to prove causality for many health and social problems (U.S. Public Health Service, 2001). But once research has demonstrated that the presence of a particular factor increases the risk or odds of the occurrence of a problem, and once an evidence-based theoretical rationale exists for how the factor operates, it is possible to develop strategies for prevention, control, and treatment that target the factor and the conditions associated with it. And when research has identified a protective factor, scholars, policymakers, and practitioners can design and implement strategies aimed at enhancing its effects.

These strategies are then tested. For example, research has shown that a cluster of individual and environmental risk factors is related to aggression and other problems in youths (see Loeber et al., 1998). A framework using ecological–developmental, social learning, family systems, and other theories has shed light on a risk process through which these factors are thought to operate to bring about and maintain aggressive behavior. On the basis of this framework, researchers have designed and tested interventions that target one or more risk factors to interrupt this risk process. An example is multisystemic therapy (MST), which has been tested in multiple rigorous trials (see Henggeler, Schoenwald, Borduin, Rowland, & Cunningham, 1998). Results have shown MST to have positive short- and long-term effects on individual-level symptoms, behavior problems, and family dynamics (U.S. Public Health Service, 2001).

ASSESSING RISK IN LARGE GROUPS AND IN INDIVIDUALS

The concepts of risk and protection are measurable and can be expressed as numbers. By taking accurate measurements on members of a population or large group, researchers (including practitioners) can identify subgroups with and without risk and protective factors and compare the occurrence of desired outcomes or problems across subgroups (Hennekens & Buring, 1987). For example, suppose a school social worker is responsible for several elementary schools and is concerned that student absences seem excessive at two schools, when compared with other elementary schools in the district. In this situation, the social worker can invoke a large-number (that is, epidemiological) approach to measure risk and protection.

To test her idea about absentee rates, the social worker would have to measure the number of students enrolled in all schools and examine attendance records. By comparing attendance rates, she can confirm or reject her suspicion about excessive absences at two schools. If these schools exhibit higher absentee rates, she can use relevant theories and research to identify potential risk and protective factors that are associated with the different rates. In addition, the social worker may draw on other sources of information including practice experience; knowledge about the particular schools and neighborhoods; and interviews with teachers, students, and parents. When the social worker has identified and measured suspected factors, she can compare their occurrence at different schools to determine whether they function as risk or protective factors.

We describe several relatively simple methods for analyzing and presenting data on risk and protection. Each method yields a number expressing the estimated strength and direction of the relationship between a risk or protective factor and an outcome. Use of one or more of these methods can help practitioners target resources and energy more effectively. However, the resulting number expressing estimated risk or protection cannot be generalized or applied to other problems or communities until additional studies produce similar results.

If a practitioner is concerned with developing an individual-focused intervention, assessment of risk and protective factors has a somewhat different meaning. Standardized instruments that measure known individual and environmental risk and protective factors are useful tools in assessment. In other chapters of this book, authors describe instruments designed to identify risk and protective factors for a range of social problems affecting children and adolescents. Of course, standardized instruments represent one of many assessment tools that practitioners should use. An instrument may be excellent for identifying factors that are amenable to intervention and change and for highlighting strengths and resources. But the instrument may also miss factors unique to an individual or situation that contribute to a problem or that might promote a solution. Moreover, individuals perceive their situations idiosyncratically, based on their life experiences, values, and styles of processing information (Zelli & Dodge, 1999). Consumers may view as resources and strengths factors that a practitioner presumes to be risk factors (see, for example, Brodsky, 1996). A comprehensive and ongoing assessment that employs methods such as semistructured interviews is necessary to develop a complete picture of a person in his or her environment.

TERMS FROM EPIDEMIOLOGY

RISK

Epidemiologists distinguish between "risk factor" and "risk." A *risk factor* refers to an attribute of an individual, family, neighborhood, community, or society that is associated with an outcome and that, potentially, affects the outcome in an undesired manner. In contrast, *risk* is simply a number: a population-based rate, proportion, or probability. Risk is specific to an identified, usually undesired, outcome or event, such as dropping out of school. However, the concepts of risk (and protection) are useful for analyzing and presenting data about desired outcomes as well (Nash & Bowen, 2002).

The terms "rate," "proportion," and "probability" are often considered to be synonymous (see, for example, Fleiss, 1981). Proportions and probabilities express the populationwide relative frequency of an event. For example, the dropout risk for a population of high school students is defined as the proportion of students in the population who drop out (that is, the number of students who drop out, divided by the total number of students). In contrast, rates include a temporal component (for example, the number of students who drop out per year, divided by the total number of students enrolled in the same year).

RISK AND PROTECTION

In the linear (or additive) model, as opposed to an interactive one, the concept of risk factor is essentially identical to that of protective factor. As discussed in chapter 2, the distinction lies in the direction of the association between a factor and the nature of an outcome (desired or undesired). For example, a positive association between a factor (for example, survivor of sexual abuse) and an undesired outcome (for example, depression) is evidence that the former acts as a risk factor. A positive association between a factor (for example, positive relationship with an adult) and a desired outcome (for example, completes high school) is evidence that the former acts as a protective, or, perhaps, a "promotive" factor (Sameroff, Bartko, Baldwin, Baldwin, & Seifer, 1998). Methods for analyzing and presenting data on risk and protection are identical. Correct interpretation requires precise specification of the nature of antecedent factors and outcomes.

PREVALENCE AND INCIDENCE RATES

Knowledge of populationwide risk provides information about the overall level of a health or social problem in a population. Two types of rates are commonly reported in epidemiological research: prevalence and incidence rates. Each is interpretable as a populationwide risk.

Prevalence is the rate (that is, the population relative frequency) of an event at a given time. This can be "a specific point in calendar time" or a "fixed point in the course of events that varies in real time from person to person," such as the onset of puberty or graduation from high school (Hennekens & Buring, 1987, p. 57). For example, suppose a hospital emergency room nurse is concerned about the number of young people who possess handguns. He could measure the prevalence of adolescent gun ownership by administering a survey on the first day of June to every adolescent in the neighborhoods served by his hospital. Questions about current gun ownership (that is, "Do you *now* own or have possession of a gun?") would capture information about prevalence. The nurse could also complete the same survey in other neighborhoods and compare the risk of gun ownership by adolescents across neighborhoods. Hypothetical data appear in Table 3-1 under "Year 1." These indicate that the prevalence of gun ownership is higher in neighborhoods served by the hospital where the nurse works.

The nurse could also repeat the survey each year to measure year-to-year changes in the prevalence, or risk, of gun ownership. Hypothetical data appear in Table 3-1 and show that prevalence is increasing in neighborhoods served by his hospital but is stable in other neighborhoods. Results can also be presented graphically (see Figure 3-1). Presentation of risk data can be a powerful aid in demonstrating the scope of a problem and in advocacy efforts.

Table 3-1. Risk (Prevalence) of Gun Ownership, by Neighborhood Using Hypothetical Data

NEIGHBORHOOD	YES	NO	TOTAL	YEAR 1 % YES	YEAR 2 % YES	YEAR 3 % YES	YEAR 4 % YES	YEAR 5 % YES
A[a]	20	180	200	10	15	15	16	18
B[a]	48	352	400	12	14	15	17	20
C	16	384	400	4	5	4	4	4
D	20	980	1,000	2	2	1	2	3
E	10	490	500	2	3	2	2	3
F	10	490	500	2	2	3	3	2
G	6	594	600	1	1	2	2	2

NOTE: These data are hypothetical.
[a]Neighborhoods served by the hospital in which the researcher works.

Incidence is also a rate, but it expresses new occurrences of a problem or condition within an interval of time. Incidence "quantifies the number of new events or cases of disease that develops in a population of individuals at risk during a specified time interval" (Hennekens & Buring, 1987, p. 57). Unlike prevalence, which gives the number of existing cases, incidence expresses the number of new cases. Incidence is calculated over an interval of time, in contrast to prevalence, which is calculated at a specific point in time.

Figure 3-1

Prevalence (Risk) of Gun Ownership by Neighborhood over Five-Year Period Using Hypothetical Data

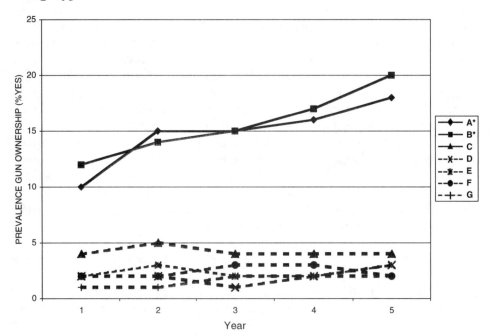

Table 3-2. Monthly Incidence (Risk) of First-Time Gun Ownership, over a One-Year Period

| MONTH | NUMBER OF NEW CASES PER 100 RESPONDENTS | |
	NEIGHBORHOOD A	NEIGHBORHOOD B
January	0	0
February	0	1
March	1	0
April	0	0
May	1	1
June	5	6
July	6	7
August	6	6
September	0	1
October	1	0
November	0	1
December	0	0

NOTE: These data are hypothetical.

One can define incidence of adolescent gun ownership in terms of the number of adolescents who acquire a gun for the first time during a given month. A survey to measure incidence would include a suitably worded item (for example, "Did you buy or come into possession of a gun for the first time during the past 30 days?"). Hypothetical incidence data for two neighborhoods appear in Table 3-2. The table shows monthly incidence rates (that is, new cases) for one year. Note that incidence—the risk of acquiring a gun for the first time—is higher during summer months. This could be useful information for planning intervention. These data could easily be depicted graphically (not shown).

MEASURES OF ASSOCIATION: RELATIVE RISK AND ODDS RATIO

ANALYZING RISK: COMPARING RATES IN SUBGROUPS

Researchers and practitioners are not only interested in the populationwide risk of outcomes. Often, there is interest in comparing risk across two or more population subgroups. A common approach is to compare the rate of an outcome in two subgroups: those with a suspected risk factor and those without the suspected risk factor. A simple extension of this approach involves grouping (or *stratifying*) a population into subpopulations (for example, males and females) before analysis and then completing the risk analysis separately for each subpopulation (*stratum*).

It is usually not feasible to collect data on every member of a population. Rather, researchers and practitioners gather information from a sample of individuals to gain information about populationwide risk. Analysis procedures and interpretation of results vary depending on how the data are collected (that is, the study design). Regardless of design, comparing rates across subgroups yield a single number that serves as an estimate of the magnitude of the risk for those with the factor, relative to the risk for those without the factor.

For example, suppose a counselor in a high school–based health clinic wishes to examine factors associated with students' likelihood of contracting a sexually transmitted disease (STD). On the basis of her knowledge of research and adolescent development, she suspects that older students are at greater risk. However, her practice experience and conversations with students leads her to question whether this is true at her school.

In this example, the suspected risk factor is higher age, and the outcome of interest is contracting an STD. Thus, the counselor must be able to measure both of these attributes. One approach to measuring age would be to use school records to divide the entire student population into two groups: older students (for example, 17 and older) and younger students (for example, 16 and younger). The counselor could measure the presence or absence of any STD by examining clinic records, taking steps to ensure confidentiality. This would be a simple and relatively feasible approach to measurement. Other strategies (for example, interviewing students) might yield more precise information but would increase the complexity of the procedures and, possibly, introduce ethical concerns.

Analysis of the resulting data begins by calculating the rate of contracting any STD for the entire population. Next, analysis of risk by subgroups involves calculating the rate of contracting any STD for older students, calculating the rate for younger students, and comparing these rates. Data from this hypothetical example appear in Table 3-3.

Analysis of data on all students shows, first, that approximately 4.1 percent of all students have contracted any STD (see Table 3-3, part 1). The counselor can com-

Table 3-3. Hypothetical Risk Data on Contracting a Sexually Transmitted Disease (STD) in a High School

| | CONTRACTED STD | | | |
	YES	NO	TOTAL	% YES
	ANALYSIS OF ALL STUDENTS			
Age				
Older	100	1,400	1,500	6.7
Younger	40	1,900	1,940	2.1
Total	140	3,300	3,440	4.1
	ANALYSIS BY GENDER			
Female				
Older	80	800	880	9.1
Younger	10	900	910	1.1
Total	90	1,700	1,790	5.0
Male				
Older	20	600	620	3.2
Younger	30	1,000	1,030	2.9
Total	50	1,600	1,650	3.0

NOTE: These data are hypothetical.

pare this rate with what is known from prior research about STDs among high school students to evaluate the scope of the problem in this school. A higher rate at this school relative to other schools may indicate a need for heightened prevention and treatment efforts.

Next, the counselor examines rates by age groups. Approximately 6.7 percent of older students have contracted any STD, compared with roughly 2.1 percent of younger students. A simple way to compare these rates is to calculate their *ratio*. Ratios are commonly used in epidemiological research to summarize a comparison of two rates. A ratio is one number divided by a second number. Here, 6.7 divided by 2.1 yields 3.2. In this example, the ratio of rates provides evidence that higher age is a risk factor—or at least a risk marker—for contracting any STD. The rate for older students is more than three times that of younger students. This is consistent with what the counselor knows from the literature but contradicts her suspicion about this school.

To gain additional information, the counselor can complete the analysis separately by gender (see Table 3-3, part 2). She finds that, for males, the rate of STDs for older students is slightly higher than 3 percent and for younger students the rate is slightly below 3 percent. The ratio of these two, roughly equal, rates is close to 1. For females, the rate is 9.1 percent for older students and 1.1 percent for younger students. The ratio of these two rates is close to 9—the rate for older females is nine times higher than the rate for younger females. These hypothetical results indicate that higher age may be an important risk factor, or risk marker, for contracting any STD for girls but not for boys.

Calculating subgroup rates and their ratio yields a single number that quantifies the strength and direction of a relationship between a suspected risk or protective factor and an outcome. Such ratios provide information about the importance of a risk or protective factor in a population and in population subgroups. As we describe below, epidemiological research uses two kinds of ratios: the relative risk and, more commonly, the odds ratio. The design of a particular study determines which is appropriate for summarizing the information in the data.

RELATIVE RISK

Direct measurement of risk in population subgroups requires use of a *prospective* design, with data collected on all members of a population. In a prospective design, a researcher or practitioner follows two subgroups over time—one subgroup with a suspected risk factor and a second subgroup without the risk factor—and observes the proportion in each that experiences a particular event or outcome. The risk of the event for the subgroup with the factor is defined as the proportion (that is, rate) of individuals in the subgroup who experience the event during the study period. The risk for the subgroup without the factor is defined similarly.

The *relative risk* (RR) is the ratio of two proportions: the proportion of the subgroup with the risk factor that experiences the event, divided by the proportion of the subgroup without the risk factor that experiences the event (Fleiss, 1981; Nash & Bowen, 2002; Stokes, Davis, & Koch, 1995). If these proportions are equal, then the RR is equal to 1, implying that the factor does not operate as a risk factor. If the RR is greater than 1, then there is evidence that the factor is a risk factor for an (undesired) outcome. If the RR is less than 1, then there is evidence that the factor is a protective factor for an (undesired) outcome. Thus, population RRs different from 1 are usually of interest to researchers and practitioners.

Table 3-4 shows data from a hypothetical prospective study of a population of 100,000 high school students, followed from ages 16 to 19. All students were in school at age 16. The event of interest is whether a student dropped out during the study period. The suspected risk factor is whether a student was retained in an early elementary grade, which is determined by reviewing the student's school record at age 16. Thus, the first subgroup comprised students who were retained in an early grade. The second subgroup comprised students who were not retained in an early grade. Suppose follow-up dropout data were collected at age 19.

As shown in Table 3-4, the risk of dropping out (that is, the dropout rate) for this hypothetical population was 0.021. For students who were retained in an early

Table 3-4. Hypothetical Risk of School Dropout in a Population

RETAINED IN EARLY GRADE	YES	NO	TOTAL	RISK OF DROPPING OUT
Yes	1,000	7,000	8,000	1,000/8,000 = 0.125 (12.5%)
No	1,100	90,900	92,000	1,100/92,000 = 0.012 (1.2%)
Total	2,100	97,900	100,000	2,100/100,000 = 0.021 (2.1%)

Relative Risk (RR) of Dropping Out:

$$RR = \frac{[\text{Risk of Dropping Out (Retained = Yes)}]}{[\text{Risk of Dropping Out (Retained = No)}]} = \frac{0.125}{0.012} = 10.4$$

Odds Ratio (OR):

$$\text{Odds [Dropping Out (Retained = Yes)]} = \frac{0.125}{0.875} = 0.14$$

$$\text{Odds [Dropping Out (Retained = No)]} = \frac{0.012}{0.988} = 0.012$$

$$OR = \frac{\text{Odds [Dropping Out (Retained = Yes)]}}{\text{Odds [Dropping Out (Retained = No)]}} \approx \frac{0.14}{0.012} \approx 11.7^a$$

Calculation using the "cross product"

$$OR = \frac{1,000 \times 90,900}{1,100 \times 7,000} = 11.8^a$$

NOTE: These data are hypothetical.
[a]Difference is due to rounding when calculating the numerator (Retained = Yes) and denominator (Retained = No) of the OR.

grade, the risk was .125. The risk for those not retained was .012. The relative risk of dropout for those retained, compared with those not retained, was 10.4. Thus, risk of dropping out was 10.4 times higher for students who were retained in an early grade, relative to students who were not retained. This provides evidence that being retained in an early grade may be an important risk factor for dropping out of school.

ODDS RATIO

The odds ratio (OR) is commonly used to estimate the magnitude of an association between a suspected risk factor and an outcome. An OR is a ratio of two odds. The *odds* of an event are defined as the probability (that is, risk) that an event occurs divided by the probability that the event does not occur (Fleiss, 1981; Nash & Bowen, 2002; Stokes et al., 1995). For example, as shown in Table 3-4, the probability, or risk, of dropping out of high school for the entire population was 0.021 or 2.1 percent (2,100/100,000). The probability of not dropping out for the population was 0.979 or 97.9 percent (97,900/100,000). Thus, the odds of dropping out for the population were 0.021/0.979, which is approximately equal to 0.021. Note that, in this example, the odds of dropping out and the risk of dropping out are equal (rounded to three decimal places), thus the odds serve as a good estimate of the risk. Also, note that a simple way to calculate the probability that an event does not occur is to subtract the probability that the event does occur from 1. In this example, the probability of not dropping out was 0.979, which is equal to 1 minus 0.021. This is because a probability equal to 1 is defined as "certainty" in probability theory, and the probability that an event does occur and the probability that the event does not occur must always sum to 1.

The OR of interest from these data is the odds of dropping out for the subgroup with the suspected risk factor, divided by the odds of dropping out for the subgroup without the suspected risk factor. As shown in Table 3-4, the odds of dropping out for those who were retained in an early grade were 0.125/0.875, or approximately 0.14. The odds of dropping out for those who were not retained in an early grade were 0.012/0.988, or approximately 0.012. The ratio of the two odds was 0.14/0.012, which is equal to approximately 11.7. Thus, the OR of dropping out for those who were retained in an early grade, relative to those who were not retained, was approximately 11.7. Note that the OR can easily be calculated as the cross product of the cells in Table 3-4; that is: $(1,000 \times 90,900)/(1,100 \times 7,000)$.

INTERPRETING THE ODDS RATIO

Researchers and practitioners often use data from a sample to estimate risk. Unlike RR, which requires a prospective study design on a population, the OR can be used with data from a sample, and its use does not require a prospective design. However, interpretation of the OR depends on the study design and on the populationwide rate of an outcome.

When a design is prospective, as in the school dropout example, the sample OR is a good estimate of RR if the rate of the event for the population is less than 0.10—the rare outcome assumption (Fleiss, 1981; Stokes et al., 1995). In a cross-sectional study in which data on risk and protective factors and on outcomes are collected at the same time, interpretation of the sample OR is somewhat controversial.

Stokes and colleagues argued that the sample OR from a cross-sectional study does not estimate risk, "but (the OR) does give you an idea of the prevalence of a condition in one group compared to another" (p. 29). Fleiss, however, argued that if "one of the two characteristics being studied is antecedent to the other" (p. 61), the sample OR does estimate risk, provided the rare outcome assumption is tenable.

Interpretation is aided by noting that the OR is always nonnegative.

- An OR equal to 1 implies that there is no association between a suspected risk or protective factor and an outcome, that is, that the factor is not an important predictor of the outcome.
- An OR greater than 1 implies that an outcome is more likely to occur when a factor is present. If the outcome is undesired, this can be evidence that a factor is a risk factor.
- An OR between 0 and 1 implies that an outcome is less likely to occur when a factor is present. If the outcome is undesired, this can be evidence that a factor is a protective factor.
- A factor with an OR far from 1 has a stronger relationship with an outcome compared with a factor with an OR close to 1. An OR of 3 implies a stronger relationship than does an OR of 2; similarly, an OR of 0.5 implies a stronger relationship than does an OR of 0.6. ORs of 0.5 and 2 imply relationships of equal strength, but opposite directions (2 is the reciprocal of 0.5).

As noted earlier, the OR is a good estimate of RR only if the underlying rate of an event is 0.10 or less. As the populationwide rate increases, the OR deviates more and more from RR. To see why this is true, take another look at the calculations of the RR and OR in the hypothetical school dropout example (Table 3-4). The RR is the risk (that is, probability) for one subgroup, divided by the risk (that is, probability) for the other subgroup. The OR is the odds for one subgroup, divided by the odds for the other subgroup. For each subgroup, the odds are simply the probability of the event, divided by 1 minus the probability of the event. The latter number, 1 minus the probability of the event, will be close to 1 if the probability of the event is small because subtracting a small number (say 0.05) from 1 results in a number that is close to 1. The subgroup odds will be close to the corresponding subgroup risk because a number divided by 1 is simply that number. In this example, the odds of dropping out for the subgroup of retained students were 0.14, which is close to 0.125, the risk of dropping out for this subgroup. The odds of dropping out for the subgroup of students who were not retained were 0.012, which is equal to the risk of dropping out for this subgroup (rounded to three decimal places). Because subgroup odds are close to the corresponding subgroup risk, the OR will be close to the RR.

Schwartz, Woloshin, and Welch (1999) described a study in which use of ORs resulted in misleading conclusions because the rare outcome assumption was not tenable. Davies, Crombie, and Tavakoli (1998) provided guidelines for determining the extent to which an OR underestimates or overestimates RR when the population-level risk is greater than 0.10.

In summary, the OR is relatively simple to calculate and interpret. It can be used whenever a researcher or practitioner collects data on the presence or absence of suspected risk and protective factors and outcomes. This is a common and feasible approach to measurement in many situations. The OR is a good estimate of RR in some, but not all, situations. However, the OR always provides an estimate of the magnitude of a relationship between one (or more) risk and protective factors and an outcome. Thus, it is widely reported in research studies and is well-suited for use in settings in which practitioners have access to data on large groups of individuals.

SURVIVAL ANALYSIS

The RR and OR are useful in assessing the effects of risk and protective factors after a defined period of observation; however, they do not help us understand *when*, during a period of time, risk or protective factors are likely to influence outcomes. In an earlier example, the OR provided evidence that high school students who dropped out were more likely to have experienced early school retention. However, a practitioner would be unable to draw conclusions from such data about when, during high school, students were most likely to drop out. It would be useful if she could determine whether there is a certain period when a youth is at particularly high risk of dropping out. Similarly, it would be useful to know whether there is a period during which a protective factor has its greatest influence, and whether the positive effects of a protective factor tend to wear off over time. Finally, in designing interventions, it is useful to know whether the potential effects of risk and protective factors change over time. *Survival analysis* is an increasingly common approach for investigating the temporal dimension of risk and protection.

Survival analysis has been applied extensively in medical research to increase understanding about the length of time patients diagnosed with particular conditions or receiving certain treatments survived in good health. Survival analysis is now used to study a variety of phenomena in social work (for example, days in foster care), public health (for example, days not using drugs), and criminology (for example, recidivism). It is sometimes called *event history analysis* (Luke, 1993).

SURVIVAL TIME

A key concept in survival analysis is *survival time*. For individuals under study who experience an event, survival time is the length of time until the event occurs. For individuals who do not experience the event, survival time is the entire time "at risk," sometimes called the *risk period*. For example, consider survival times for experiencing divorce. For a couple that divorces, survival time is the time from marriage until divorce. For a couple that remains married, survival time is the length of the marriage.

Survival times are simple to calculate. Suppose a social worker wishes to examine the data more closely to calculate survival times for dropping out of high school for students who experienced early school retention. First, she establishes that the risk period for dropout coincides with the period during which students are in high school. Next, she divides the risk period into intervals, such as eight semesters. Then, the social worker reviews the records of students who experienced early grade retention to find out whether they dropped out and, if so, in which interval (that is, semester). To illustrate, consider data on 10 at-risk students (Table 3-5). Observing survival

Table 3-5. Survival Times for 10 Students Who Experienced Early School Retention Using Hypothetical Data

STUDENT	DROPPED OUT?	SEMESTER DROPPED OUT	SURVIVAL TIME (SEMESTERS)
1	Yes	6	6
2	Yes	7	7
3	No	NA	8
4	No	NA	8
5	Yes	6	6
6	Yes	6	6
7	No	NA	8
8	Yes	2	2
9	No	NA	8
10	Yes	7	7

NOTE: These data are hypothetical. NA = not applicable.

times, the counselor concludes that, for these students, the period of greatest risk occurred in the latter part of their high school careers.

LIFE TABLES

With a small number of students, displaying data in this format provides a straightforward method for discerning high-risk periods. If the social worker is interested in looking at survival times for large groups, this format becomes cumbersome. It is more efficient to count how many individuals experienced the event during each interval. To do this, a *life table* can be constructed (Norusis, 1993). The first step is to divide the risk period into intervals. Then, for each interval, one counts the number of individuals experiencing the event during that interval. Table 3-6 provides an example of a life table for 60 students who experienced early school retention. The intervals—in this case semesters—are listed in the first column. The second column shows the number of students who were enrolled in school on the first day of a particular semester, and the third column provides the number of students who dropped out during that semester.

The social worker can use the information in Table 3-6 to assess the effect of early grade retention (or any other risk or protective factor) on the probability of dropping out during each interval. The proportion of interest, shown in the last column of Table 3-6, is *the number of students dropping out during and interval* divided by *the total number of students at risk during the interval*. From this information, the social worker sees that, for these students, the periods of highest risk were toward the end of high school, with relatively higher risk in the seventh semester.

PLOTTING RISK

Risk can be plotted on graphs to illustrate when individuals experience problem conditions. We will describe two ways to plot risk: (1) graphs of survival curves and

Table 3-6. Life Table of School Dropout among Youths Who Experienced Early School Retention, Using Hypothetical Data

SEMESTER	STUDENTS IN SCHOOL AT BEGINNING OF SEMESTER	STUDENTS DROPPING OUT DURING SEMESTER	PROBABILITY OF STUDENT DROPPING OUT DURING SEMESTER
1	60	0	0/60 = .00
2	60	5	5/60 = .08
3	55	5	5/55 = .09
4	50	5	5/50 = .10
5	45	10	10/45 = .22
6	35	10	10/35 = .29
7	25	15	15/25 = .60
8	10	0	0/10 = .00

NOTE: These data are hypothetical.

(2) graphs of hazard curves. Survival curves are plots of survival functions. A survival function provides an estimate of the probability of not experiencing an event, usually death in medical research (hence, the term "survival"), beyond a certain point in time. Hazard curves are plots of hazard functions. A hazard function shows how the probability of experiencing an event changes over time at every possible point in time (Allison, 1995). Calculations of survival and hazard functions are relatively complex and will not be discussed in this chapter. Interested readers are referred to relevant textbooks (for example, Allison, 1995; Norusis, 1993). However, it is becoming increasingly common to see survival and hazard curves in social work articles and books. Thus, we provide the following illustration to help readers use this information.

PLOTS OF SURVIVAL CURVES

Survival curves show the proportion of people who do not experience an event over a period of time. For example, survival curves might show the proportion of children remaining in foster care (in which the event of interest is "leaving foster care") or the proportion of patients in a smoking cessation program remaining smoke free. For high school dropouts, a survival curve shows the proportion of students remaining in school over a specified time.

Figure 3-2 is an example of a survival curve for remaining in high school, using information about dropout for an actual group of "at-risk" youths (Orthner et al., 1995). The risk period is the typical length of high school (that is, four years, eight semesters, or 48 months).

The numbers across the bottom of the graph represent the month of school, beginning with the first month of the ninth grade and ending with the last month of the 12th grade. The numbers on the left side of the graph represent the proportion of students remaining in school. The "1" at the top represents 100 percent of the students in school. The first dot on the curve starts at 1 at the first month. This means that none

Figure 3-2

Survival Curve for Completing High School

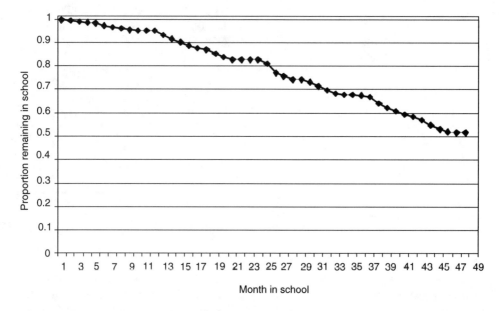

of the students has left school yet. As students drop out, the curve shows the proportion remaining in school.

Examining the survival curve provides insight into the overall level of dropout risk for these students, and how risk changes over time. The final point on the curve indicates that just over 50 percent of these students dropped out before the end of the risk period. The curve also shows that youths were more likely to drop out after the ninth grade because the curve decreases more rapidly after month 12, when youths typically enter the 10th grade.

PLOTS OF HAZARD CURVES

In contrast to a survival curve, which depicts the cumulative proportion of students not experiencing the event during the risk period, a hazard curve shows the dropout rate at each point in time. Figure 3-3 is an example of a hazard curve for the same group of students used in plotting the survival curve (Orthner et al., 1995). The hazard curve is plotted over the same period of time (48 months), as shown across the bottom of the graph. The numbers on the left-hand side of the graph represent the rate at which students drop out at each point in time.

The hazard curve shows precisely the dropout risk at each point in time for these students. First, note the increasing heights of the peaks, which show that the risk of dropout increases over time. The hazard curve also shows that students are at greatest risk of dropping out during the 26th month, or the middle of the first semester of 11th grade. Moreover, these students are at relatively high risk of dropping out when they are in the 12th grade, close to finishing high school. Finally, it appears that the curve jumps dramatically at four different points during the 11th and 12th grades. On

Figure 3-3

Hazard Curve for Leaving High School Prematurely

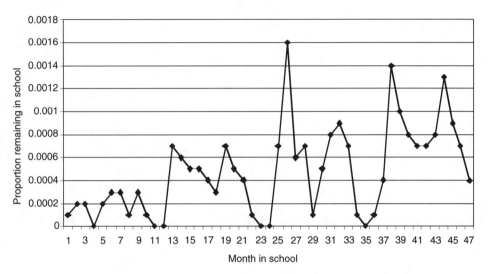

closer examination, these jumps occur immediately after summer and winter breaks. This information might be useful for social workers interested in designing interventions aimed at helping these students maintain attachment to school over breaks.

PLOTS OF SURVIVAL CURVES: ANOTHER USE

One can also use survival curves to show the effect of particular risk or protective factors. Using the example of high school dropouts, suppose the social worker suspects that students in her caseload who participate in extracurricular activities do better in school than those who do not. The social worker can use survival curves to examine the relationship between participating in an extracurricular activity and staying in school for at-risk students. She would begin by identifying two subgroups of at-risk students: those involved in activities and those not involved in activities. For each subgroup, she plots survival functions, thus revealing a difference in the risk of dropout for the two subgroups.

Figure 3-4 provides an example using actual data on at-risk youths as in the prior examples (Orthner et al., 1995). The graph shows the proportion of youths who remain in high school, based on whether they participated in extracurricular activities. The line with the boxes represents the proportion of students remaining in school who were involved in activities. The other line, with the diamonds, represents the proportion of students remaining in school who were not involved in activities.

As shown, the curves diverge early in the risk period and, over time, the gap between the curves becomes larger. The curves start to separate almost immediately, suggesting that, early on, those at-risk youths in activities were more likely to remain in school. The final points on the curves show that over 90 percent of youths in activities finished high school, whereas only about 45 percent of the youths not in activities finished high school. School social workers might use this information to justify offering

Figure 3-4

Survival Status Based on Activity Participation in High School

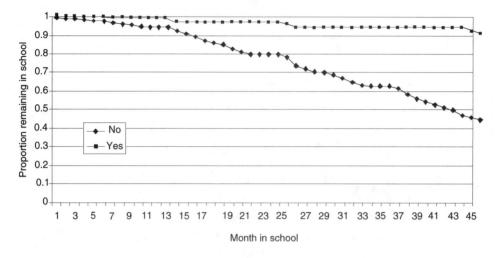

extracurricular activities, or they might identify youths at risk as they enter high school and help to link them to an activity right away.

In summary, the survival and hazard functions describe how probability and risk change over time. Graphs of survival functions can be useful in making risk trends explicit. Graphs of hazard functions illustrate change in risk over time. Both may be used to investigate linear combinations of risk and protective factors, thus expressing the complexities of risk chains. Resulting information can be of great use for providing an evidence base to human services practice (Fraser, Jensen, Kiefer, & Popuang, 1994).

PERSON-ORIENTED ANALYSIS

Calculating an RR, an OR, or a survival function exemplifies analysis methods in which the focus is on relationships among variables (for example, risk factors, and outcomes) in a sample or population of individuals. Such variable-oriented methods aggregate information from individuals to estimate the magnitude of the influence of a risk or protective factor on outcomes. However, these methods shed little light on the unique process of development for a particular individual. As an alternative, researchers sometimes use analysis methods known collectively as a *person-oriented approach* (Cairns, Cairns, & Neckerman, 1989) or a *person-centered approach* (Bates, 2000).

Person-oriented methods focus on patterns of factors, within an individual and in the environment, and how these interact over time to affect outcomes. Examples include case studies and examining subgroups of individuals. A person-oriented approach is useful for social workers, in part, because it examines developmental processes and how these operate in different subgroups of individuals. These include "typical" or "normal" subgroups, but also subgroups that depart from the mainstream, such as children who display chronic and escalating problem behaviors over time or children who overcome the odds and are successful despite high levels of risk (Hill, White, Chung, Hawkins, & Catalano, 2000).

In a person-oriented approach, researchers often divide a sample into subgroups based on shared individual and contextual risk or protective factors. Then they follow the subgroups over time (Cairns, Cairns, Rodkin, & Xie, 1998). For example, in a sample of adolescents, it might be possible to identify subgroups based on dichotomous measures of individual risk (for example, hyperactivity) and contextual protection (for example, positive relationship with an adult mentor). This would result in four subgroups: hyperactive–no mentor; hyperactive–mentor; not hyperactive–no mentor; and not hyperactive–mentor. The focus of a person–oriented analysis might be to track these adolescents over time to assess how outcomes differ for each subgroup. Often, there is interest in studying in detail, perhaps with qualitative methods, individuals in a high-risk subgroup (for example, hyperactive–no mentor) who experience positive outcomes. Such an approach can shed light on resilience.

One example of a person-oriented approach involved a study of 475 seventh graders who were followed until the 11th grade to determine their dropout status (Cairns et al., 1989). Researchers divided the sample into seven subgroups on the basis of behavioral, cognitive, and demographic characteristics. Results showed that 82 percent of one subgroup—boys who displayed aggressive behavior and poor academic performance in the seventh grade—left high school without completing the requirements. In contrast, 36 percent of the boys identified as aggressive in the seventh grade but with average academic performance dropped out. This person-oriented analysis highlighted a unique combination of factors that put youths at greater risk of leaving school prematurely.

Both variable- and person-oriented methods can enhance our understanding of child development and of factors that promote or inhibit positive development. Variable-oriented methods examine relationships among variables, and they are especially useful for identifying variables that may act as keystone risk or protective factors (Bergman & Magnusson, 1997). Analysis procedures, including those discussed in this chapter, are well developed, and many yield results that are readily interpretable. In contrast, person-oriented analysis procedures have emerged relatively recently. There is a need to develop these procedures further, for example, to increase the reliability of results (Bergman & Magnusson, 1997). Nonetheless, person-oriented methods represent a promising approach for understanding how multiple risk and protective factors operate holistically and over time. These methods carry the potential to shed light on developmental pathways that are of special interest to social workers. Together, variable-oriented and person-oriented methods can contribute to a body of evidence upon which to base effective social work practice (Gambrill, 1999).

SUMMARY

This chapter has described methods for analyzing and estimating the magnitude of risk and protection. To analyze risk, practitioners and researchers must be able to measure the presence or absence of a suspected risk or protective factor and the occurrence or nonoccurrence of a particular outcome in a sample or population. By comparing rates of an outcome in subgroups with and without risk or protective factors, practitioners and researchers can calculate numerical values that estimate risk and protection. The chapter provided explanations on using and correctly interpreting odds ratios to assess the importance of risk and protective factors. The chapter described methods for analyzing the strength of risk and protective factors over time using survival analysis and for presenting results graphically. Finally, the chapter provided an overview of a person-oriented approach to analysis.

Quantifying risk and protective factors produces useful information that practitioners, policy makers, and researchers can use to develop interventions targeting specific groups or communities and to advocate for resources to address a specific problem. Knowledge gained from analyzing risk and protection as well as knowledge gained from published research using these methods can also be used to guide comprehensive individualized assessment for practitioners working with a particular child or adolescent.

REFERENCES

Allison, P. D. (1995). *Survival analysis using the SAS system*. Cary, NC: SAS Institute.

Bates, M. (2000). Integrating person-centered and variable-centered approaches in the study of developmental courses and transitions in alcohol use: Introduction to the special section. *Alcoholism: Clinical and Experimental Research, 24*, 878–881.

Bergman, L. R., & Magnusson, D. (1997). A person-oriented approach in research on developmental psychopathology. *Development and Psychopathology, 9*, 291–319.

Brodsky, A. E. (1996). Resilient single mothers in risky neighborhoods: Negative psychological sense of community. *Journal of Community Psychology, 24*, 347–363.

Cairns, R., Cairns, B., & Neckerman, H. (1989). Early school dropout: Configurations and determinants. *Child Development, 60*, 1437–1452.

Cairns, R., Cairns, B., Rodkin, P., & Xie, H. (1998). New directions in developmental research: Models and methods. In R. Jessor (Ed.), *New perspectives on adolescent risk behavior* (pp. 13–40). Cambridge, England: Cambridge University Press.

Davies, H. T., Crombie, I. K., & Tavakoli, M. (1998). When can odds ratios mislead? *British Medical Journal, 316*, 989–991.

Fraser, M. W., Jensen, J. M., Kiefer, D., & Popuang, P. (1994). Statistical methods for the analysis of critical life events. *Social Work Research, 18*, 163–177.

Fraser, M. W., Richman, J. M., & Galinsky, M. J. (1999). Risk, protection, and resilience: Toward a conceptual framework for social work practice. *Social Work Research, 23*, 131–143.

Fleiss, J. (1981). *Statistical methods for rates and proportions* (2nd. ed.). New York: John Wiley & Sons.

Gambrill, E. (1999). Evidence-based practice: An alternative to authority-based practice. *Families in Society: Journal of Contemporary Human Services, 80*, 341–350.

Garbarino, J. (1995). *Raising children in a socially toxic environment*. San Francisco: Jossey-Bass.

Germain, C. B., & Gitterman, A. (1995). Ecological perspective. In R. L. Edwards (Ed.-in-Chief), *Encyclopedia of social work* (19th ed., Vol. 1, pp. 816–824). Washington, DC: NASW Press.

Gordis, L. (2000). *Epidemiology* (2nd ed.). Philadelphia: W. B. Saunders.

Henggeler, S. W., Schoenwald, S. K., Borduin, C. M., Rowland, M. D., & Cunningham, P. B. (1998). *Multisystemic treatment of antisocial behavior in children and adolescents.* New York: Guilford Press.

Hennekens, C. H., & Buring, J. E. (1987). *Epidemiology in medicine.* Boston: Little, Brown.

Hill, K., White, H., Chung, I.-J., Hawkins, J., & Catalano, R. (2000). Early adult outcomes of adolescent binge drinking: Person- and variable-centered analyses of binge drinking trajectories. *Alcoholism: Clinical and Experimental Research, 24,* 892–901.

Loeber, R., Farrington, D. P., Stouthamer-Loeber, M., & Van Kammen, W. B. (1998). *Antisocial behavior and mental health problems: Explanatory factors in childhood and adolescence.* Mahwah, NJ: Lawrence Erlbaum.

Luke, D. (1993). Charting the process of change: A primer on survival analysis. *American Journal of Community Psychology, 21,* 203–246.

Nash, J. K., & Bowen, G. L. (2002). Defining and estimating risk, protection, and resilience: An example from the School Success Profile. *Child and Adolescent Social Work Journal, 19,* 247–262.

Norusis, M. J. (1993). *SPSS for Windows: Advanced statistics* (Version 6.0). Chicago: SPSS.

Orthner, D., Neenan, P., Deang, L., Flair, K., Fergusson, M., Stafford, R., & Ingle, J. (1995). *North Carolina jobs program: Impact evaluation report.* Chapel Hill: University of North Carolina at Chapel Hill, Human Services Research and Design Laboratory.

Sameroff, A. J., Bartko, W. T., Baldwin, A., Baldwin, C., & Seifer, R. (1998). Family and social influences on development of child competence. In M. Lewis & C. Feiring (Eds.), *Families, risk, and competence* (pp. 161–185). Mahwah, NJ: Lawrence Erlbaum.

Schwartz, L. M., Woloshin, S., & Welch, H. G. (1999). Misunderstandings about the effects of race and sex on physicians' referrals for cardiac catheterization. *New England Journal of Medicine, 341,* 279–283.

Stokes, M., Davis, C., & Koch, G. (1995). *Categorical data analysis using the SAS system.* Cary, NC: SAS Institute.

U.S. Public Health Service. (2001). *Youth violence: A report of the U.S. Surgeon General.* [Online]. Retrieved from http://www.surgeongeneral.gov/library/youthviolence/youvioreport.htm on June 9, 2003.

Zelli, A., & Dodge, K. A. (1999). Personality development from the bottom up. In D. Cervone & Y. Shoda (Eds.), *The coherence of personality: Social-cognitive bases of consistency, variability, and organization* (pp. 94–126). New York: Guilford Press.

4

Child Maltreatment: A Risk and Protective Factor Perspective

Barbara Thomlison

C hild maltreatment refers to child abuse, neglect, and sexual abuse. In addition, practitioners and scholars frequently refer to emotional abuse, medical neglect, and educational neglect as subtypes of child maltreatment. Three decades of research have resulted in an expansion of knowledge regarding risk and protective factors associated with child maltreatment. In addition, much more is known about the consequences of maltreatment.

Despite this research, definitions of child maltreatment vary, and there is no consensus definition of the different forms of maltreatment. On balance, child abuse refers to four major types of maltreatment (U.S. Department of Health and Human Services [DHHS], 2001): (1) physical abuse, (2) neglect, (3) emotional or psychological abuse, and (4) sexual abuse. *Physical abuse* commonly refers to the infliction of non-accidental injury (an act of commission) as a result of punching, biting, kicking, shaking, beating, burning, suffocating, poisoning, or otherwise harming a child. The injury is often associated with excessive discipline or inappropriate treatment of a child and it is usually incident specific (Hildyard & Wolfe, 2002). *Neglect*, an act of omission, is the most common form of maltreatment, often characterized by its chronicity. Neglect involves the degree to which parents provide little stimulation or structure or fail to provide minimal standards of nurturing and caregiving in the crucial areas of education, nutrition, supervision, health care, emotional availability, and general safety (Wolfe, 1987). *Emotional abuse* (psychological abuse–verbal abuse–mental injury) or *deprivation* includes acts or omissions by the parents or other caregivers that have caused, or could cause, serious behavioral, cognitive, emotional, or mental disorders. It is the most difficult type of abuse to prove. Exposure to family violence is increasingly included as a form of emotional abuse. *Sexual abuse* refers to the fondling of a child's genitals, intercourse, incest, rape, sodomy, exhibitionism, and commercial exploitation through prostitution or the production of pornographic materials. Many experts believe that sexual abuse is the most underreported form of child maltreatment because secrecy characterizes these situations (Finkelhor, 1994; Finkelhor & Berliner, 1995). Although any of the forms of maltreatment may be found separately, they often occur in combination, and emotional abuse is always present when other forms are identified. For legal purposes, the definitional emphasis of child abuse is increasingly being placed on the circumstances and nature of the act rather than on the consequences to the child.

The risk and resilience model presented in chapter 2 points to the importance of unraveling the ways in which child maltreatment disrupts normal developmental outcomes. Of particular importance, especially with regard to the design of preventive and interventive services, is the need to identify factors that protect against child abuse and neglect or buffer children exposed to maltreatment. Applying a scientific framework to maltreatment holds the potential for the design of more effective services. But the challenge is large. The term "child maltreatment" refers to a multifaceted developmental, relationship-based problem, arising from a myriad of risk and protective factors and occurring in a dynamic social–ecological context that influences children and their parents in complicated ways. Interactions among child, family, and community systems, along with the child's exposure to abuse and neglect, influence outcomes. The chronicity, severity, and age of onset of maltreatment are thought to be of great importance in influencing differential developmental outcomes ranging from mild to catastrophic (Kinard, 1999; Margolin & Gordis, 2000; Veltman & Browne, 2001; Wolfe, 2001).

To be sure, child maltreatment is a major public health problem (Powell et al., 1996). Public education, professional education, environmental improvements for families, and enhanced methods of case identification are common prevention and early identification strategies. These strategies are designed to respond to child abuse and neglect or to conditions that place children at risk of harm (Bross, Miyoshi, Miyoshi, & Krugman, 2000). Reducing the risks and identifying protective strategies for child maltreatment are integral to service delivery. Clearly, a sustainable and focused effort to address the problem of child maltreatment is needed.

To provide a foundation for early intervention and the design of more effective treatment strategies, this chapter

- reviews risk and protective factors related to child maltreatment
- describes methods for assessing risk and protective factors
- posits practice guidelines to assist in the design of interventions that protect children from maltreatment. Particular attention is placed on early intervention strategies geared to buffer or alter cumulative risk.

EFFECT OF CHILD MALTREATMENT ON CHILD DEVELOPMENT

At each stage of child development, child maltreatment appears to have different effects on children. However, infants and young children are at highest risk for lasting damage (Webster-Stratton, 2000, 2001; Wolfe, 2001). The sequelae of maltreatment include delayed language, impaired cognitive development, lower IQ, educational underachievement, and mild to severe behavioral and social–emotional deficits (Ammerman & Hersen, 1999; Veltman & Browne, 2001; Wolfe, 2001). Some of these outcomes result from specific injuries; other outcomes, equally damaging but often less apparent, are the result of the absence of positive interactions between parents and their children and the lack of appropriate responses to a child's basic physical and emotional needs (Chalk, Gibbons, & Scarupa, 2002). For example, children who experience physical abuse tend to be aggressive toward peers and adults and have difficulty empathizing with others (Johnson et al., 2002). In the long run, abused children appear to be at increased risk for the intergenerational transmission of abuse and use of physical coercion in relationships (Osofsky & Thompson, 2000; Wolfe, 2001). Rates of family violence are higher in adults who were physically victimized as children (Corcoran, 2000b; Feerick & Haugaard, 1999).

Curiously, neglect—the most common form of maltreatment—has received the least amount of attention. Somewhat different risk factors appear to distinguish abusive parents from neglectful parents, which suggests that neglect is a different construct than child abuse and needs to be assessed and treated differently (Zuravin & DiBlasio, 1996). Young children who have been severely neglected have numerous ongoing developmental and health problems and often suffer from anxiety, inattention, avoidant behavior, and low academic achievement (Lutzker, Bigelow, Doctor, & Kessler, 1998). According to some estimates, by the end of kindergarten, 65 percent of children who experienced neglect are held back a grade or are referred for special education. Moreover, children who are neglected tend to have lower standardized test scores than nonmaltreated children (Corcoran, 2000a, 2000b; Eckenrode, Laird, & Doris, 1991; Knitzer, 2000; Webster-Stratton, 2000; Zero To Three, 1994). The long-term effects of neglect—of having parents who are psychologically and physically unavailable—are far less visible but can be extremely damaging, often irreparable, and even fatal (Azar, Vera, Lauretti, & Pouquette, 1998; Zuravin & DiBlasio, 1996).

Children who are sexually abused are at increased risk for a variety of externalizing behaviors as well as anxiety, depression, and other internalizing problems. No syndrome or set of symptoms clearly distinguishes a sexually abused child. Some sexually abused children appear asymptomatic, performing normally at school and with peers, while others experience depression, anxiety, low self-esteem, low academic achievement, and somatic problems. Some also engage in age-inappropriate sexual and other self-destructive behaviors (Finkelhor, 1994, 1995; Wolfe, 1994, 1999).

Studies by Lynch and Cicchetti (1998) and Wolfe and McEachran (1997) have found that combinations of different forms of maltreatment compound the damaging effects. For example, neglected and physically abused infants may have multiple impairments such as physical injuries, brain damage, developmental delays, functional problems leading to poor attachment and difficulty forming relationships, learning or cognitive difficulties, aggressive behavior, and chronic low self-esteem (Ayoub, Willett, & Robinson, 1992; Hansen, Sedlar, & Warner-Rogers, 1999; Kazdin, 1992; Kendall-Tackett & Eckenrode, 1996; Wolfe, 2001). School-age children may have impaired social skills, difficulty forming reciprocal and supportive relationships, depression, low levels of academic achievement, and low readiness for demands of adult life (Gershater-Molko & Lutzker, 1999; Wolfe & McGee, 1994). Adolescents who were physically and sexually abused have an increased risk for substance abuse problems, mental illness, aggression, and violence (Veltman & Browne, 2001; Webster-Stratton & Taylor, 2001; Widom, 1989a, 1989b; Wolfe, 2001).

Description of the Problem

Although we all have a common understanding of what is meant by child maltreatment, legal definitions of child abuse and neglect vary across states in terms of specificity, especially in regard to the range of harm considered abusive or neglectful. Maltreatment that results not in discrete injury but in cumulative harm—such as neglect or emotional abuse—is difficult to describe with legal precision; and states vary markedly in how they define neglect, emotional abuse, and medical neglect (Chadwick, 1999). Competing definitions affect incidence and prevalence estimates across the states and shape differential responses by legal and protective service systems. This has a direct effect on the number of officially reported and substantiated cases of child maltreatment, and therefore caution is warranted in comparing state statistics. A good definition of maltreatment must be specific, sensitive to multiple causes, and based on understandings of developmental outcomes (Chadwick, 1999; Portwood, 1999).

The secretive nature of child maltreatment makes it difficult to detect. Children are unlikely to seek help on their own because of their age, developmental circumstances, and dependent status. Normative levels and timing of developmental milestones are varied for children attempting to adapt within their context, and the absence of negative or observable consequences may contribute to continued abuse (Hansen, Sedlar, & Warner-Rogers, 1999). Also, parents often do not want to admit to problems because they fear losing their children or being charged with a crime. Loyalty, apprehension, and affection often coexist with violence and abuse; maltreated children fear dissolution of their families and retribution from perpetrators if abuse is disclosed. Of course, the longer the duration and the greater the severity of maltreatment, the greater the likelihood of detection (Wolfe, 2001).

RATES OF CHILD MALTREATMENT

No single source can be used to estimate the incidence and prevalence of child maltreatment. On balance, two sources of information are used: (1) carefully devised household surveys (in which the same definitions are used across states) and (2) state reports of investigations for different types of maltreatment (in which slightly different definitions may be used across states) and related injuries. The most recent household survey is called the Third National Incidence Study (NIS-3), and because it was completed in 1993, it is becoming somewhat dated. Based on the NIS-3, the total number of children seriously injured and the total number of children considered endangered quadrupled from 1986 to 1993 (Sedlak & Broadhurst, 1996). From 1993 to 1997, the rates of children referred for investigation of maltreatment rose from 39.2 per 1,000 to 42 per 1,000 (DHHS, 2001). The rate of substantiated victimization declined from 15.3 per 1,000 children in the child population in 1993 to 13.8 per 1,000 children in 1997, suggesting that some of the increase in referrals may be due to improvements in surveillance and services. Perhaps reflecting declines in the poverty rate, the victimization rate further declined through 1999 when it reached a decade low of 11.8 per 1,000 children.

About three children die each day from maltreatment, and children under six years of age comprise 86 percent of these deaths (DHHS, 2001, p. 42). Child deaths are perhaps the most reliable indicator of child maltreatment. Child deaths are always investigated, and changes in the child death rate over time may reflect changes in levels of child maltreatment. Approximately 1,500 children died from maltreatment in 1993, yielding a maltreatment fatality rate of 1.62 per 100,000 children (Sedlak & Broadhurst, 1996). Since 1993, this rate has changed little. For example, in 1999, 937 children died from child maltreatment, yielding a maltreatment fatality rate of 1.66 per 100,000 children (DHHS, 2001, p. 42). In 1999 maltreatment deaths were more often associated with neglect (38.2 percent) than with any other type of abuse, and 45 percent of child fatality cases involved very young children from ages 0 to three (Wang & Daro, 1998). Physical abuse alone accounted for 26.1 percent of maltreatment fatalities, and physical abuse plus neglect accounted for 22.7 percent of child maltreatment fatalities. The remaining 13 percent were accounted for by combinations of neglect, abuse, and other factors, including maltreatment deaths in which the cause was unreported (DHHS, 2001).

Overall, neglect is the most frequently reported form of child maltreatment (Chadwick, 1999). Nearly 60 percent of substantiated cases of maltreatment were cases of neglect. Mothers are more likely to be reported for neglect, and fathers are more likely to be reported for physical abuse (DHHS, 2001; Gershater-Molko, & Lutzker, 1999). In 1999, the victimization rate for child neglect (including medical neglect) was 6.9 per 1,000 children; for physical abuse the rate was 2.5 per 1,000 children; and the rate for sexual abuse was 1.3 per 1,000 children (DHHS, 2001, p. 22).

Are rates of child abuse and neglect so high as to constitute an epidemic? Sadler, Chadwick, and Hensler (1999) compared economic investments related to child maltreatment and other diseases and demonstrated that the incidence rate of child abuse is 10 times higher than all forms of cancer. Yet the total federal research commitment for child maltreatment was one nickel for every 100 dollars, while cancer received two dollars for every 100 dollars of estimated annual costs. Although child maltreatment is not viewed as serious a health problem as AIDS or cancer, it is epidemic in scope. It is a major public health problem.

Age and Gender

Rates of child maltreatment vary by both age and gender. As a result of physical abuse, boys have a higher risk for serious injury than girls; and boys have a higher incidence of fatal injuries than girls (Sedlak & Broadhurst, 1996). But girls are overall more likely to be victimized. In 1999, 52 percent of victims were female, and 48 percent were male (DHHS, 2001, p. 23). Regardless of gender, children in the youngest age group (0 to three) have the highest rates of neglect—about 13.9 per 1,000 children (DHHS, 2001, p. 24). Adolescents are only one-third as likely as preschool children to be physically abused by a parent. Rates of physical abuse decline as age increases, probably as a result of the increased ability of children to protect themselves using disclosure, placation, and avoidance (Finkelhor, 1995; DHHS, 2001; Wolfe, 1994).

Differences in gender and age are evident for physical and sexual abuse rates. Females ages 12 to 15 are more likely to be physically abused than younger females. However, younger males ages four to 11 are more likely to be physically abused than either very young or adolescent males. Females are four times more likely to be victims of sexual abuse. Approximately 1.6 females per 1,000 children are sexually abused; males have a lower risk of 0.4 sexual victimizations per 1,000 (DHHS, 2001, p. 28). The incidence of sexual abuse is highest for female preadolescents (ages eight to 11, 1.8 per 1,000) and adolescents (ages 12 to 15, 2.8 per 1,000; DHHS, 2001, p. 28).

Poverty and Neglect

Children from families with incomes below $15,000 per year, as compared with children from families with annual incomes above $30,000 per year, appear more likely to experience maltreatment. In the NIS-3, low-income children were over 22 times more likely to be seriously injured from maltreatment (Sedlak & Broadhurst, 1996). Substantiated neglect reports decrease for older children, but neglect is intricately tied to poverty and income. The poorest of the poor are at highest risk. In the NIS-3, children from the lowest income families were 18 times more likely to be sexually abused and almost 56 times more likely to be educationally neglected (Sedlak & Broadhurst, 1996).

Ethnicity, Race, and Culture

The NIS-3 found no race or ethnicity differences in maltreatment incidences or maltreatment-related injuries, which was a consistent finding in all NIS studies (Sedlak & Broadhurst, 1996). NIS studies identify a broader range of children than those found in the child welfare population, in which a disproportionate number of children of color are often served. Official state reports from child protective services of victimization range from a low of 4.4 Asian/Pacific Islander victims per 1,000 children to a high of 25.2 African American victims per 1,000 children (DHHS, 2001, p. 28). The rate for American Indian/Alaska Natives was 20.1 victims per 1,000 children. The rate for Latino children was 12.6 victims per 1,000 children. The rate for non-Hispanic European American children was 10.6 victims per 1,000 children (DHHS, 2001, pp. 28–30). NIS-3 findings suggest that the differential representation of minorities in the child welfare population does not derive from inherent differences in the rates at which they are abused or neglected. On balance, studies that control for poverty and other factors suggest that race, culture, and ethnicity are not directly related to rates of child maltreatment (Korbin, 1994, p. 195); however, children of color are more likely than others to encounter poverty, violence, crime, and poor schools. Racism and other discriminatory experiences may exacerbate risk factors for abuse and neglect (Chaffin, Kelleher, & Hollenberg, 1996; Kendall-Tackett & Eckenrode, 1996; Pelton, 1994).

Rates for sexual abuse are relatively consistent across race and ethnicity (Korbin, 1994). White, non-Latino girls appear somewhat more vulnerable to sexual abuse in the preschool years, whereas African American girls appear somewhat more vulnerable to sexual abuse in the preteen years (Wyatt, 1985). The lifetime prevalence for sexual abuse has been reported equal for white and African American girls (Finkelhor & Baron, 1986; Wyatt, 1985).

The parenting techniques of some ethnic and racial groups, which are often discussed as a source of bias in official statistics, may differ from those of the dominant culture (Garbarino & Kostelny, 1992). Defining abuse and neglect within a cultural context received significant attention in the 1990s. Although it continues to be a topic of great interest in the media, experts seem to agree that different child-rearing practices should not be construed as good or bad as long as the safety of children is assured. Korbin (2002) suggests that we need to understand more clearly how culture, in an ecological context, is involved in the risk and protective factors of maltreatment and how it can be used in the development of prevention and intervention strategies. It is certainly an important issue and one that has marked implications for practice and policy.

RISK AND PROTECTIVE FACTORS RELATED TO CHILD MALTREATMENT

Risk factors are those characteristics or conditions that, if present for a given child, make it more likely that this child, rather than another child selected from the general population, will experience child maltreatment. Protective factors are those factors that mediate or moderate the effect of the risk factors and result in reducing the risk of child maltreatment (see chapter 2; Pollard, Hawkins, & Arthur, 1999). The exact nature of the interactional processes among risk and protective factors is unclear. However, it is thought that in the absence of mediating factors, situational and predisposing contextual circumstances provide the opportunity for maltreatment to occur. Understanding these risk processes in a practice context is important for enhancing protective factors and devising interventions that produce positive outcomes (Pollard, Hawkins, & Arthur, 1999).

From a multisystemic perspective, the context—that is, the parent-child context and family–community–environment context—acts to influence the course of both child maltreatment and normal child development. From a protective perspective, these same contextual influences can reduce or buffer the impact of stress and create opportunities for positive experiences (Fantuzzo, McDermott, & Lutz, 1999; Rutter, 2000). But what is to one child a surmountable challenge may be to another a serious threat accompanied by high chances for failure (Rutter, 2000). The presence of protective factors promotes successful adaptation—even in the face of high risk (Jensen & Hoagwood, 1997).

Risk and protective factors may be either enduring or transient in nature (see Table 4-1). Enduring influences include psychological, environmental, cultural, or biological factors that affect the odds for maltreatment. (For a discussion of odds and odds ratios, see Nash & Randolph, chapter 3.) Enduring protective factors include a history of good parenting, positive marital support, humor, high intelligence, and employment. Transient risk factors include the effects of an illness, injury, marital discord, unemployment, or other life stressors—both perceived and actual—that may affect a vulnerable parent and elevate the odds for abuse or neglect of a child.

To understand a child's functioning and his or her chances for poor versus normative developmental outcomes, it is essential to take into account spheres of influence in the environment. Each life setting exposes children to risk and protective factors, and levels of risk and protective factors interact with various events at differing times throughout childhood to produce developmental outcomes. One of the more important systems to analyze is the parent–child environment (Fantuzzo, McDermott, & Lutz, 1999). In this context, intervention aims to reduce the number and magnitude of family environment risk factors while increasing protective factors. The child's adaptive or maladaptive response to harmful experiences may then depend on whether the parenting environment has adequate social and economic resources to change childcare patterns. Addressing the specific mechanisms related to child maltreatment involves understanding the child's context before, during, and after maltreatment occurs (Rutter, 2000, p. 670).

PARENTAL RISK AND PROTECTIVE FACTORS

Childhood is expected to be a period of protection and safety wherein parents introduce children to healthy adaptation and prosocial behavior. Recent brain research has demonstrated with unprecedented clarity the importance of early experiences in influencing actual growth and development of neural pathways in the brain (Kotulak, 1996). Caregiver behaviors take on great importance because the early years are a

Table 4-1. Risk and Protective Factors Related to Child Maltreatment

SYSTEM	RISK FACTORS	PROTECTIVE FACTORS
Community environmental conditions	**Social Cultural Environment** • Inaccessible or unaffordable health and child care • High levels of neighborhood crime and violence • Reduced or negative neighboring interactions • Social disintegration or disorganization • Social intolerance or discrimination • Socially impoverished community • Exposure to environmental toxins	**Social Cultural Environment** • Many positive adult and peer role models • Stable and cohesive neighborhood • Strong informal networks of social support • Access to health, education and support services • Safe community • Good schools and teachers
Family and family environmental conditions	**Family Life and Stress** • Inadequate housing • Inadequate material resources • Prolonged economic distress • Employment stress or unemployment • Rapid and stressful life changes • Single parent household • High levels of conflict or violence • Threats of separation/ divorce • Large number of children	**Family Life and Stress** • Supervision, routines, and rituals • Family and marital harmony • Family cohesiveness • Positive and caring family interactions • Economic security • Employment consistency
	Parental Disorder • Parent with substance abuse • Parent with mental disorder/ depression • Parent with antisocial behavior • Poor reasoning and problem-solving skills • Unrealistic expectations • Poor emotional control • Low warmth • Low nurturing skills • High criticism • Use of harsh, inconsistent discipline	**Parental Competencies** • Available in times of stress • History of good parenting • Psychological well-being of parents • Competence in roles and responsibilities • Satisfaction in parenting role • High self-esteem • Provides positive adult model • Provides supervision of child

Table 4-1. (continued)

SYSTEM	RISK FACTORS	PROTECTIVE FACTORS
	Family Social Support • Excessive reliance on others • Isolation • Lack of support from others • Marital/relationship discord **Parental Experiences** • Distorted perception of history of care • Lack of emotional closeness with child • Limited positive family interactions	**Family Social Support** • Emotional closeness with family and friends • Good social skills • Social support network of family and friends • Positive marital support
Child psychosocial and biological conditions	**Early Childhood** • Poor infant attachment to mother • Poor child health/medical disorder • Developmental difficulties • Premature birth or complications • Difficult temperament, behavior, and mood • Cognitive impairment • Low intellect **Child Competencies** • Lack of a healthy adult model • Early educational failure • Negative peer role models • Poor adult supervision • Poor problem-solving skills	**Early Childhood** • Outgoing or easy temperament • Affectionate • Positive or secure attachment to mother • Active and alert • Good nutrition and health care • Quality consistent child care • Low distress • Advanced self-help skills **Child Competencies** • Developmentally competent • Educational achievement • Normal to above average intelligence and language skills • High sociability • High cognitive functioning • Self-efficacy/perception of competence • High self-esteem • Gets along with children and adults • Competent problem-solving skills • Sense of belonging and security • Has external sources of support

particularly sensitive time for that portion of the brain that is used for language acquisition and the facilitation of logical thinking. The quality of the young child's environment has a critical influence on his or her capacity to develop a foundation for learning
and emotional regulation (Osofsky & Thompson, 2000).

Researchers estimate that about 10 percent of American families have generic
risk factors in the living environment, such as exposure to inadequate resources,
parental conflict, alcoholism, and employment stresses, which elevate the odds for
child maltreatment (Ayoub & Jacewitz, 1982). But the presence of one or two risk
factors is not usually sufficient to produce maltreatment. In longitudinal studies, researchers have found that the number of risk factors to which a child is exposed is the
most salient predictor of maltreatment and the negative developmental outcomes with
which it is associated. Moreover, they found that the combination of risk factors had a
greater effect than the sum of effects of each risk factor (Fantuzzo, McDermott, &
Lutz, 1999, p. 12).

Individual Risk Factors

As shown in Table 4-1, psychological distress of the parent–caregiver is the
primary individual risk factor associated with child maltreatment. Included in this set
of risks are

- parental affective disturbances, such as depression, withdrawal, anger, and
  aggression (Ayoub, Jacewitz, Gold, & Milner, 1983; Barth, 1991; Kotch
  et al., 1995)
- low self-esteem, immaturity, rigid or unrealistic expectations
- excessive reliance on others, which places the parent's immediate needs
  in conflict with the child's needs (Faust, Runyan, & Kenny, 1995; Iverson
  & Segal, 1990).

Depressive disorders have a direct and negative influence on parent–child transactions. High anxiety levels, lack of impulse control under stress, and low social supports
are also implicated in the increased risk of maltreatment associated with maternal
depression (Altemeier, O'Connor, Sherrod, & Tucker, 1986; Coohey, 1996; Garbarino,
Dubrow, Kostelney, & Pardo, 1992; Kinard, 1995; Mrazek & Haggerty, 1994; Radke-
Yarrow, & Sherman, 1990; Rutter, 2000).

Parental knowledge, expectations, behavior, and skills are associated with
maltreatment. Rigid and unrealistic parental expectations about home, children, and
self and, in particular, a distorted belief of one's own history of care are risk factors
(Wolfe, 2001). Related factors include poor problem-solving skills in child-rearing situations (Azar, Robinson, Hekimian & Twentyman, 1984), inconsistent discipline, and
harsh or excessive physical punishment (Hansen, Sedlar, & Warner-Rogers, 1999).
Parents who are low on warmth and nurturing qualities and high on criticism in their
response to children are at greater risk of maltreatment. Other child, family, and contextual risk factors are compounded in the presence of parental problems such as alcoholism and antisocial behavior, which influence interactions, perceptions, and other
transactions in the parent–child environment (Smith & Saunders, 1995; Wolfe, 2001).
According to several reports, as many as 80 percent of maltreating parents may have

past or current substance abuse problems (Cohn & Daro, 1987; Dore, Doris, & Wright, 1995; Jaudes, Ekwo, & Van Voorhis, 1995). Regardless of culture, individual parental characteristics increase the risk for maltreatment when accompanied by psychological distress, mental disorder, and a history of childhood maltreatment (English & Pecora, 1995, p. 465).

Parental characteristics and parenting styles often interact with child characteristics and environmental conditions to elevate risk. If parents are harsh and inconsistent and have difficulties monitoring their child's activities, and if the child has a disruptive temperament and is having difficulties with others, parent and child risk factors may interact to elevate risk synergistically. Although parental individual characteristics play a role in placing children at risk, environmental stresses can exacerbate negative outcomes by affecting parenting styles and thereby elevating distress or feelings of low sense of control, anger, and aggression (Kinard, 1995; Wolfe, 1994, 2001). Webster-Stratton and Taylor (2001) found that children who are more impulsive and quick to anger tend to overwhelm parents and raise the risk of parental responses characterized by high arousal, anger, and harsh discipline—all risk factors for maltreatment.

Biological Risk Factors

As indicated in Table 4-1, parental biological problems occurring during pregnancy and delivery or as a result of chronic health conditions have often been linked to increased stress and, subsequently, to an increased risk for abusive and neglectful behavior (Ayoub, Willett, & Robinson, 1992; Barth, 1991; Finkelhor, 1986; Iverson & Segal, 1990; Marks & McDonald, 1989). Ninety percent of the brain's mapping occurs in the first three years of a child's life, placing great importance on parenting skills for the child's earliest emotional, mental, and physical development (Kotulak, 1996; Shonkoff & Marshall, 2000). When a parent cannot provide adequate child care because of serious parental health problems, inattention, and abandonment—though they may not be intentional—are assaults to the brain that can produce serious consequences.

Risk Factors for Types of Maltreatment

Developing understandings of the different etiological pathways associated with different types of maltreatment has only recently been undertaken in large studies. It is clear that no single pathway explains abuse or neglect. Rather, a range of risk factors appears to produce the conditions under which abuse and neglect occur. Notwithstanding, some risk factors appear more predictive of abuse than neglect, and vice versa. Physical abuse, for example, appears to be associated with parents with a childhood history of maltreatment or harsh physical punishment. When they are placed in circumstances involving rapid life changes or high stress, parents who experienced abuse as children are themselves at increased risk for engaging in abusive behavior (Ammerman & Hersen, 1999; Wolfe, 2001). Apart from economic distress, a key risk factor in the etiology of neglect appears to be the lack of a social support system (Gershater-Molko & Lutzker, 1999).

Parental Protective Factors

Three clusters of compensatory protective effects appear to moderate risk for maltreatment. These include factors that lead to reduction of stress and inhibition of aggression (for example, a supportive spouse, socioeconomic stability, success at work and school, social supports, and positive adult role models); to improvement in the management of crises and provocation (for example, parent-focused strategies on coping with stress); and (3) to the abatement of parental patterns of arousal and aggression with family members (for example, improved anger–mood regulation skills; Wolfe, 1999). As shown in Table 4-1, individual parental factors that protect against maltreatment of children include high self-esteem and self-efficacy, an ability to function within normal boundaries on measures of behavior and social competence (Kinard, 1995; Rutter, 1987), and an easygoing temperament that aids the parent in displaying warmth and satisfaction in relationships with others (Runyon et al., 1998). Other common protective factors include economic stability and access to adequate health care, education, and employment (Mrazek & Mrazek, 1987; Wolfe, 2001).

CHILD RISK AND PROTECTIVE FACTORS

Child-related risk and protective factors associated with maltreatment can be thought of as biological and psychosocial attributes or characteristics. As shown in Table 4-1, biological risks include birth or health complications, low intellect, and developmental abnormalities (Kopp & Kaler, 1989). Infant health problems associated with physical abuse and neglect include prematurity (Kotch et al., 1995; Roberts, 1988), congenital physical or developmental disabilities (Iverson & Segal, 1990; Roberts, 1988), and characteristics such as gender or physical features that may be outside of rigid parental expectations and therefore a source of stress (Ayoub et al., 1983; Roberts, 1988). Psychosocial risk factors include a child's temperament, behavior, and mood. Abusive or neglectful parent-child interactions may result when a parent perceives a child's behavior as difficult or stressful (Guterman & Embry, 2004). Distressed infants and those who do not have well-established eating or sleeping patterns are more difficult to care for and are three times more likely to be abused (Ayoub et al., 1983; Barth, 1991; Osofsky & Thompson, 2000). Temperamental, aggressive, and noncompliant child behaviors increase risk for physical abuse and coercive parent–child interactions, particularly when parental beliefs promote harsh corporal punishment (Garbarino et al., 1992; Hansen et al., 1999; Wolfe, 2001).

Child Protective Factors

Research consistently emphasizes parenting competency and knowledge as affording comparatively greater protection against child maltreatment than positive child characteristics (Briere, Berliner, Bulkley, Jenny, & Reid, 1996; Chaffin, Kelleher, & Hollenberg, 1996; Guterman, 2001; Olds & Kitzman, 1993; Osofsky & Thompson, 2000; Veltman & Browne, 2001; Wolfe, 2001). The presence of both biological and psychosocial risks that are immediately apparent during infancy and early childhood and the lack of parental competence may explain—at least in part—why the youngest children are considered more vulnerable to physical abuse and neglect and why children under the age of five are at an overall increased risk of death (DHHS, 2001).

However, children who are socially skilled and cognitively competent are at lower risk (Kinard, 1995, 1999; Werner, 2000). Perceptions of children as being easy-going, cuddly, or affectionate are also protective factors (Garbarino et al., 1992; Garmezy & Tellegen, 1984; Radke-Yarrow & Sherman, 1990; Rutter, 2000). In a review of longitudinal studies of protective factors in high-risk young children, Werner (2000) identified the following protective factors: low distress levels, high sociability, high activeness and alertness, advanced language skills, high intelligence, problem-solving skill, and self-control (see also Herrenkohl, Herrenkohl, & Egolf, 1994; Kinard, 1995, 1999; Mrazek & Haggerty, 1994; Rutter, 1987, 2000).

Attachment is often used as an indicator of parent–child relations. It is a sentinel indicator of the warmth, caring, and safety provided by a child's parents and of the child's capacity to respond to caregiving with warmth, reciprocated care, and behavioral compliance. Compared with children who have weak bonds of attachment, children who have a deep sense of belonging and security are widely known to function more adaptively across settings (Belsky & Vondra, 1989; Crittenden, 1988a, 1988b; Kolko, 1996). From birth, attachments evolve from interactions with a positive, caring parent who is available in times of stress for support (Ainsworth, 1989; Garbarino & Kostelny, 1994; Garbarino et al., 1992; Kopp & Kaler, 1989; Mrazek & Mrazek, 1987; Rutter, 1987; Wekerle & Wolfe, 1993; Widom, 1989b). A predictable and stable environment is central for attachments to develop. Studies by Werner (2000) and Rutter (2000) observed that resilient children with high-risk backgrounds had effective coping skills, were able to detach or distance themselves from high-risk circumstances, and were rewarded for being socially skilled.

Recovery from Maltreatment

Children who attempt to prevail over stress rather than retreat from it also develop confidence, demonstrate higher levels of self-esteem, and appear to recover from maltreatment more quickly (Garbarino & Kostelny, 1994, p. 327; Hillson & Kuiper, 1994; Werner, 2000). Furthermore, the older and more developmentally competent children are when they are exposed to the first maltreatment trauma, the more likely they will cope positively with stressors (Garbarino et al., 1992; Rutter, 2000).

ENVIRONMENTAL FACTORS ASSOCIATED WITH MALTREATMENT

The social networks and community environments in which families are embedded play a contributing role to overall risk and protection for child maltreatment (Coohey, 1996; Guterman & Embry, 2004; Quinton & Rutter, 1988; Tracy, 1988; Tracy & McDonell, 1991). As indicated in Table 4-1, the quality of social and emotional sources of support emerges as a recurrent theme in longitudinal research on children who overcome great odds (Werner, 2000). External support systems, such as those associated with churches, youth groups, and schools, or through affectional ties with friends, relatives, and others, buffer stress. These resources can be thought of as risk-reducing processes that shape responses to adversity and give rise to resilience in the face of a variety of contexts (Rutter, 2000; Werner, 2000; Wolfe, 2001).

Family Environment Risk Factors

The presence of violence, harsh punishment, marital discord, threats of separation, poverty or lack of material resources, unemployment, and a conflictual social support network are associated differentially with all types of maltreatment (Barnard, 1994; Belsky & Vondra, 1989; Emery, 1989; Garbarino et al., 1992; Kolko, 2003; Kotch et al., 1995; Wolfe, 1994). Single-parent households as compared with two-parent households often have higher levels of stress. They are more likely to lack financial resources (Hay & Jones, 1994; Tracy, 1988; Tracy & McDonell, 1991; Wolfe, 1994). Perhaps because of financial pressures, low-income women are almost twice as likely as higher-income women to suffer from depression, and the presence of a depressive disorder is a risk factor for neglect (National Center for Children in Poverty, 2001).

Prolonged economic distress is associated with neglect. Indirect stresses resulting from lack of money, food, and other necessities produce stress, shorten tempers, and contribute to poor parenting. (Garbarino et al., 1992; Garbarino & Kostelny, 1994; Hay & Jones, 1994; Melton & Barry, 1994a; Pelton, 1994; DHHS, 2001). Pelton (1994) observed, "The probability of child abuse and neglect is largely dependent on the extent of one's ability to cope with poverty and its stressors" (p. 153). Most children growing up in poverty are not abused, but poverty elevates the risk of abuse and other forms of maltreatment. It is the combination of risk and protective factors that potentiate maltreatment (Guterman & Embry, 2004).

Family Environment Protective Factors

To date, little research focuses on protective family environmental factors related to child maltreatment; however, much is known about family conditions that promote positive developmental outcomes in general. The availability of caring and emotionally supportive family, friends, siblings, teachers, and neighbors mediates stresses (Finkelhor & Berliner, 1995; Rutter, 2000). Kotch and colleagues (1995) found that in the presence of stressful life events, the odds of child maltreatment decreased as social support increased. When parents are more involved with others in a social network, the stress of daily hassles and of critical life events is moderated (Straus, 1995). In addition, family cohesiveness and marital harmony promote adaptation and coping (Briere et al., 1996). For boys, structure and rules in households appear to be a protective factor; while for girls an emphasis on autonomy with emotional support from parents plays a protective role (Werner, 2000). For both boys and girls, chores and routines requiring helpfulness should be encouraged. The presence of a positive adult role model in children's life settings, as well as the amount of time spent with that role model, is an important influence (Quinton & Rutter, 1988; Werner, 2000; Wolfe, 1994, 2001). In high-risk families, sibling caregiving is not a risk factor if it is supplementary and does not substitute for effective parenting (Anthony & Cohler, 1987; Hegar, 1988; Werner, 2000). These family–environment factors are likely to produce positive developmental outcomes in children and these factors should also reduce the risk of maltreatment, particularly if the factors are present in early childhood. Cicchetti and Lynch (1993) found that the presence of protective factors at any level of the ecology helps to explain why some children display successful adaptation in the face of adversities.

COMMUNITY ENVIRONMENT FACTORS

Social–environmental factors such as inaccessible and unaffordable health and child care, high rates of neighborhood crime and violence, reduced or negative interactions with neighbors, and social–cultural discrimination have been positively correlated with higher incidents of child maltreatment (see Table 4-1; Knitzer, 2000; Rutter, 2000). Socially impoverished communities have many more needs, and stressed and worried families living in settings characterized by a lack of cohesion among neighbors, and where community life is unstable, disorganized, and violent, must compete for limited resources (Coulton, Korbin, Su, & Chow, 1995).

The experience of traumatic events, such as witnessing family or street violence, can interrupt normal developmental processes, affecting the child's ability to make friends, work with others, and sustain relationships (Fantuzzo, Boruch, Beriama, Atkins, & Marcus, 1997; Feerick & Haugaard, 1999; Garbarino & Kostelny, 1994; Korbin, Coulton, Lindstrom-Ufuti, & Spilsbury, 2000; Werner, 2000). Also at the community level, attitudes and behaviors providing covert support for the dynamics of sexual abuse may contribute to rates of maltreatment. These include a stereotype of male dominance in sexual relationships, social tolerance for sexual interest in children, and barriers to women's equality (Hay & Jones, 1994).

Communities with high levels of employment, effective schools, and sufficient resources and services are more likely to have stable and cohesive neighborhoods (Garbarino et al., 1992; Hay & Jones, 1994; Melton & Barry, 1994a, 1994b; Richman & Bowen, 1997). Like other sources of support, these reinforce children's coping and provide opportunities for involvement with positive peer models, supportive neighbors, teachers, and other prosocial adult role models. In neighborhoods with an adequate social and economic infrastructure, there is more positive parenting and social interaction and less abuse and neglect (Pelton, 1994).

RISK ASSESSMENTS FOR CHILD MALTREATMENT

Assessment of risk for the occurrence or reoccurrence of child maltreatment is a critical aspect of child protection work. In child welfare practice, the goal of risk assessment is to estimate the probability that a family will again maltreat a child—that is, to predict future abuse or neglect. Risk and safety assessments have been used since the 1980s as decision-making tools in child protective services. The underlying purpose for applying risk assessment is to improve the consistency and effectiveness of child protective services investigations and case planning for families involved in child abuse and neglect. This is very important, considering that possibly one-third of parents continue to maltreat children after an investigation and during treatment (Cohn & Daro, 1987). At least 76 percent of the states use some form of risk assessment system to aid in the screening of maltreatment reports, to promote a comprehensive assessment of risk, and to tailor case planning to the needs of children and their families (English & Graham, 2000). Nevertheless, predicting which of those children can be safely left at home, can be safely returned to their homes after a temporary out-of-home placement, or must be removed from their homes because of the potential for continued maltreatment has proven difficult. Research studies in medicine, psychology, and social work have shown risk assessment to help in processing large quantities of information and in making case-based judgments (Gambrill & Shlonsky, 2000; Jagannathan & Camasso, 1996). But too often risk assessments are "made under considerable uncertainty in terms of the relationship between the information at hand (predictor variables) and service outcome" (Gambrill & Shlonsky, 2000, p. 814).

To be most useful, risk assessment should inform decision making and the design of intervention strategies. It requires the integration of a great deal of information. One of the practical issues involved in risk assessment is the reluctance of maltreating parents to participate in assessment procedures; therefore, a thorough explanation of the assessment process and procedures with parents is necessary (Hansen, Sedlar, & Warner-Rogers, 1999). Factors that may threaten valid assessments include language barriers, differential meanings to particular constructs, and various perceptions and interpretations of observed behavior. Although research studies have demonstrated the superiority of using risk assessment systems over decision making generated by consensus or prediction based on practice wisdom, risk assessment instruments are far from perfect. They continue to lack predictive validity as well as acceptability from practitioners (Baird & Wagner, 2000; Cash, 2001; Doueck, English, DePanfilis, & Moote, 1993; English & Graham, 2000; English & Pecora, 1994; Gambrill & Shlonsky, 2000; Jagannathan, & Camasso, 1996; Lawlor & Raube, 1995; Marks & McDonald, 1989; Pecora, 1991; Rittner, 2002; Wald & Woolverton, 1990).

Two types of assessment processes are used today: (1) consensus-based systems and (2) actuarial systems. The consensus-based systems assess specific child and family characteristics identified by the consensus judgment of experts (that is, expert opinion and accepted practice wisdom), wherein severity of risk to the child is estimated. Examples of consensus-based models are the California Risk Assessment System (CAS; Johnson & L'Esperance, 1984; Johnson & Scott, 1999) and Washington Risk Assessment Matrix (WRAM; English & Graham, 2000; Miller, Williams, English, & Olmstead, 1987). Other consensus-based instruments are family risk assessment scales in which child, parent, and family functioning are assessed. Examples include the Utah Risk Assessment Scales (Nasuti & Pecora, 1993), the Child Well-Being Scales (Magura & Moses, 1986; Magura, Moses, & Jones, 1987), and the Family Assessment Form (McCroskey & Nelson, 1989), which is similar to a practice protocol. Finally, Child At Risk Field methods (CARF; Holder & Corey, 1986) is an ecological approach, whereby practitioners rate risk influences for the child, parent, family, maltreatment, and the level of intervention needed to address the risk factors is noted. Many of these systems appear to lack predictive and construct validity (Baird & Wagner, 2000; English & Graham, 2000; Gambrill & Shlonsky, 2000). Furthermore, most represent theoretical compromises and give inconsistent weight to individual child, parent, family, community, and sociocultural risk factors. Studies have found no relationship between structured risk assessment implementation and the type of service in child protection, demonstrating clearly that prioritization of cases is not occurring, and there is no relationship between risk level and the amount of effort assigned to cases (Jagannathan & Camasso, 1996; Johnson & L'Esperance, 1984). Risk assessment is more often linked to case-closing decisions (Jagannathan & Camasso, 1996).

The empirical bases of risk assessment continue to improve. Promising findings emerged in a recent validity study comparing two consensus-based models, the CAS and the WRAM with one actuarial model, the Michigan Structured Decision Making

(SDM) model. Findings indicate that, compared with the CAS and WRAM, the SDM is more accurate in estimating the risk of future maltreatment (Baird & Wagner, 2000). Although the SDM shows promise, more work needs to be done to ensure that measures include protective as well as risk factors and are sensitive to different populations and types of maltreatment (Baird & Wagner, 2000; Cash, 2001; English & Graham, 2000; Gambrill & Shlonsky, 2000; Jagannathan, & Camasso, 1996; Rittner, 2002).

In risk assessment, prediction and classification are often used interchangeably, but they denote differences in expectations (Baird & Wagner, 2000). Classification, the act of establishing groups or categories based on risk, is probably a more realistic goal of risk assessment in child protective services. Although accurate prediction would greatly benefit child protective services and society, it has proved difficult. The accuracy of risk assessment is related directly to our knowledge base about the causes of child maltreatment. Given that no single pathway appears to produce child maltreatment, risk assessment may never be error free in distinguishing those families that are likely to reoffend from those that are not likely to reoffend. Experts increasingly agree that the goals of risk assessment should be modest—simply "to assign cases to different categories based on observed rates of behavior" (Baird & Wagner, 2000, p. 851). Resources and services can then be allocated on the basis of risk categories.

ASSESSMENT FOR CLINICAL PRACTICE

After an initial determination of risk and safety, the next objective of practice involving child maltreatment is to assess the child and family in order to develop a case or services plan. As noted earlier in this chapter, a number of issues complicate this task. First, children may suffer from multiple types of maltreatment, some of which are known and some of which may yet be identified. Second, the effects of maltreatment may vary on the basis of a child's age or health and the home environment. These factors must be incorporated into case planning. Separating the effect of abuse and neglect from other risk factors in the child's family and social environment may be extremely difficult if not impossible.

An evidence-based approach is important to service planning and will be especially helpful when the case is under court supervision and child protective services. In addition, information on the clinical needs of child victims and adult perpetrators, availability of specialized services, and prior practices in making decisions regarding similar cases are considered part of the assessment (Guterman, & Embry, 2004). Beyond the assessment of risk for future maltreatment, the practitioner asks, What does the parent understand, believe, know, do, and have the capacity to do? (Lyons, 1998). Assessing parenting knowledge and the potential future behavior of the parent is a central focus of case and service planning.

SOURCES AND DOMAINS OF CLINICAL ASSESSMENT

The goal of clinical assessment is to acquire information and understanding that will protect the child and foster his or her normal development and psychological adjustment. Accurate and comprehensive clinical assessments are not easily obtained. Assessment is difficult because there is no single behavioral syndrome for abuse and neglect, and there are no standardized markers for maltreatment. Furthermore, although it is critical to engage the family in the assessment, this may be difficult (Thomlison, 2002). Families are under many sources of stress (such as unemployment, substance abuse, and poverty), and family engagement is related to how and when families are involved rather than to the particular type of service received (Burns, Hoagwood, & Mrazek, 1999). In this context, assessment is often complicated by the fact that family members are involved with multiple systems and efforts to involve another service may complicate engagement. An integrated, coordinated, culturally sensitive assessment and intervention plan is necessary to promote engagement (Chalk, Gibbons, & Scarupa, 2002).

Plans rely on information obtained directly from children, parents, and others. It is never acceptable to rely on archival case records. Case records are subjective, inconsistent, and unstandardized (Ammerman & Hersen, 1999; Mash & Wolfe, 1991; Thomlison, 2002). Assessment involves gathering family information to develop an individualized family service plan that responds to family and parenting concerns, resources, and priorities of the child (Thomlison, 2002). Child assessment involves evaluation of the effects of the abusive events as well as posttraumatic symptoms and distress. This includes the physical well-being and educational progress of the child. A complete physical examination of the child is needed to provide medical treatment. Collecting such information is also important for possible legal involvement. An assessment of parental factors usually includes an examination of parenting competencies; parental psychopathology; parenting skills and strengths; quality parent-child interactions; parental stress, anger, depression, and physiological arousal; expectations for the child; knowledge of child development and behavior; problem–solving skills; and the social support system. In addition, assessment involves examination of the living environment for the level of cleanliness and the presence of any hazards that may pose harm to the child (Gershater-Molko & Lutzker, 1999). The general consensus among professionals is that victims and perpetrators should be interviewed separately to avoid intimidation by the perpetrator. This usually involves interviews with both children and parents, direct observation of behavior, checklists and standardized measures, and peer and teacher ratings of children's behavior. No single method or measure should be used.

Once a child's safety is guaranteed, emphasis is placed on assessing the potential to improve a child's living environment. This includes evaluating the parent's understanding of his or her child caring competencies and discipline responsibilities; assessing parental understanding of the child's need for continuing care, stimulation, and attachment; and reviewing the actual and perceived sources of support for parenting. In this regard, how parents feel about their strengths and vulnerabilities may be as important as what their strengths and abilities actually are (Wolfe, 2001). The question for assessment, then, is whether there is a "good enough fit" between the needs of the child and the capacities of the parents to both protect the child and create a more positive family environment. Clinical assessment at this point should lead to the identification of structural interventions that may be necessary. These comprise the type and level of supervision needed, including placement out of the home, as well as the initial treatment goals (Saunders, Berliner & Hanson, 2001).

Tasks of assessment to this point include

- separating and interviewing child, parents, siblings, and other caretakers with regard to the maltreatment, the parenting and nurturing capacity of parents, the stability of the home, and the resources of family members
- assessing the parent–child interaction and parent performance to identify family and environmental stress and their contribution to the current problems, including life cycle transitions, cultural issues, and adequacy of resources
- evaluating the type and quality of support available from relatives, friends, and neighbors
- compiling physical evidence, medical assessments, and criminal records, if necessary
- making decisions about the need for court charges, respite care, intervention services, and protective placements.

Many rural and urban communities now provide centralized clinical assessment centers where child and family well-being are evaluated and where highly trained practitioners develop evidential information. Assessment centers offer a range of assessment and treatment services, including integrated case management as well as culture- and language-sensitive investigations.

Structured Clinical Interviews

Clinical assessment is, as a rule, accomplished through the interview method; but this process is of course subject to considerable distortion, bias, and poor recall. When possible, structured interviews consisting of various combinations of existing validated clinical evaluation measures should be used. Because evaluation measures are subject to court review, they must be valid, reliable, applicable, and sensitive to diverse populations. An assessment and planning report usually integrates various kinds of data such as self-report, observation, practice protocols, measures addressing parental competencies, family functioning, marital dynamics, child functioning, and environmental resources. Although some measures are reviewed below, a complete review of valid and reliable measures is beyond the scope of this chapter and the reader is referred to Rittner and Wodarski (1995) for measures used in child abuse and neglect, and Ammerman and Hersen (1999) for specific issues and measures for types of maltreatment. For an example of a structured parent interview and assessment, see the Child Abuse and Neglect Schedule, Revised (CANIS-R). It is designed to identify family problems contributing to maltreatment (Ammerman, Hersen, Van Hasselt, Lubetsky, & Sieck, 1994). The CANIS-R protocol assesses maltreatment risk behaviors such as parental disciplinary practices, child behavior, and corporal punishment and other physically abusive behaviors.

Assessment of Parenting Practices

A number of instruments have been developed to assess parenting attitudes and practices but none assess parenting capacity. Three extensively used measures are (1) the Parent Opinion Questionnaire, (2) the Child Abuse Potential Inventory (CAPI), and (3) the Parenting Stress Index. The Parent Opinion Questionnaire (Azar & Rohrbeck, 1986) is designed for parents to rate the appropriateness of a variety of child behaviors in areas such as self-care, punishment, help and affection for parents, and family responsibility and care of siblings. Parents are assessed for unrealistic expectations about the developmental abilities of their children. Abusive parents' scores are significantly different from those of nonabusive parents (Azar, Robinson, Hekimian, & Twentyman, 1984), so the instrument is reported to distinguish abusive from nonabusive parents. The CAPI (Milner, 1994) is a widely used self-report measure with published validation data and cross-validation information for differentiating parents who are physically abusive. The CAPI measures distress, rigidity, unhappiness, problems with child and self, problems with family, and problems from others. This measure appears to hold promise as a screening tool, but it should not be used alone to predict child abuse. Finally, as its name suggests, the Parenting Stress Index (Abidin, 1995) can be used to assess parent–child relationships and stress associated with parenting.

Assessment of Family Functioning

Practitioners often need to assess the level of family violence, conflict, and stress from marital relationships, family situations, and community factors. There are many family functioning scales, but one specific measure and one general measure of individual and family functioning are commonly used: (1) the Revised Conflict Tactics Scale (Straus, Hamby, Boney-McCoy, & Sugarman, 1996), which attempts to measure three factors related to violence in the family—reasoning, verbal aggression, and physical violence and (2) the Multi-Problem Screening Inventory (MPSI; Hudson, 1992; Hudson & McMurtry, 1997), which assesses 10 common areas of family and marital functioning. These areas include family relationship problems, marital satisfaction, partner abuse, personal stress, and partner or child problems. Some instruments focus more directly on family functioning, with children ages 12 or older. For example, the McMaster Family Assessment Device (FAD; Epstein, Baldwin, & Bishop, 1983) measures six areas of family functioning: problem solving, communication, roles, affective responsiveness, affective involvement, and behavior control. The Self-Report Family Inventory (SFI; Beavers & Hampson, 1990) measures family functioning and has been used in settings with great socioeconomic diversity.

Assessment of Psychopathology and Substance Abuse

Assessing for parental disorders and the ability of parents to engage in services is important. Parental depression and substance abuse have been linked to maltreatment (Olds et al., 1997; Zuravin, 1989). The Beck Depression Inventory (Beck, Steer, & Garbin, 1988) measures symptoms and attitudes of depression in terms of intensity. The Brief Symptom Inventory (Derogatis, 1993) assesses a variety of psychopathology problems and stress. Self-report formats present problems for substance abuse measurement, and collateral information will be needed to assess the severity of these conditions and their role in child maltreatment. Some useful alcohol and drug assessment tools for adults include the short version of the Michigan Alcohol Screening Test (SMAST; Selzer, Moskowitz, Schwartzman, & Ledingham, 1991), the Drug Abuse Screening Test (DAST; Skinner, 1982), and the Addiction Severity Index (ASI, McLellan, Luborsky, Woody, & O'Brien, 1980), which has an abuse history section and can be used as a screen for trauma and posttraumatic stress disorder (Najavits et al., 1998; Rice et al., 2001). Additional assessment measures can be obtained through the National Institute on Alcohol Abuse and Alcoholism (Allen, Columbus, & Fertig, 1995; NIAAA, 2001).

Assessment of Children

Assessing children is complex because different constructs are expressed differently according to the developmental age of the child (Fantuzzo, McDermott, & Lutz, 1999). It therefore becomes necessary to use only those measures that reflect age-appropriate constructs, for example, social competence of preschool children is understood within peer interaction in play. To understand a child's functioning, it is essential to take account of the contextual influences. These often define whether the child's functioning is adaptive or maladaptive (Fantuzzo, McDermott, & Lutz, 1999). A child's behavior should also be examined from the perspective of the culture in which she or he lives. Child management and parent-child interaction skills are contextually and culturally dependent.

Two measures to assess child distress and impairment are (1) the Trauma Symptom Checklist for Children (Briere, 1995), which assesses for posttraumatic symptoms and distress in children using a structured diagnostic interview, and (2) the Child and Adolescent Functional Impairment Scale (Hodges, 1994), which can be used to assess the level of functional impairment or the degree to which children are having difficulties in role-functioning at home, at school, in the community, and in their behavior with others. The Behavioral and Emotional Strengths Scale (Epstein, Quinn, & Cumblad, 1992) assesses children's behavioral strengths on five dimensions: self-control, affective development, family involvement, school performance, and self-confidence. Measuring neglect is difficult, but one rating scale designed to assess essential elements of child care and neglect of young children under age 7 is the Childhood Level of Living Scale (Polansky, Chalmers, Buttenweiser, & Williams, 1981), with which chronicity and severity of caretaking deficits are assessed. Finally, to assess children's internalizing and externalizing behaviors, the Child Behavior Checklist (Achenbach, 1991) is a validated and widely used parent- and teacher-based measure of children's problems.

INTERVENTIONS FOR CHILD ABUSE AND NEGLECT

Prevention of child maltreatment is aimed at intervening *before* maltreatment occurs. In contrast, intervention strategies focus on the prevention of the *reoccurrence* of child maltreatment or avoidance of out-of-home placement, allowing the child to remain safely at home. Child abuse prevention and early intervention are large topics and beyond the scope of this chapter. Nevertheless selected prevention programs—in which clinical trials provide evidence of effectiveness—are described briefly below.

(For a comprehensive review of services research for child abuse and neglect, please see Daro & Cohn Donnelly, 2002b; Gershater-Molko, Lutzker, & Sherman, 2002; Guterman & Embry, 2004; Kolko, 2003; Thomlison, 2003; and Wolfe & Wekerle, 1993.)

Most intervention programs for the treatment of abuse and neglect focus on treating parents; few offer direct therapeutic interventions to children. Home-based interventions have been demonstrated to meet diverse needs of maltreating families and families at risk of maltreating, especially where interventions incorporated a combination of behavioral interventions targeting multiple factors, including family support (Daro & Cohn Donnelly, 2002a, 2002b; Gershater-Molko, Lutzker, & Wesch, 2002; Lutzker, Bigelow, Doctor, & Kessler, 1998; Lutzker & Rice, 1984; Webster-Stratton, 1998a, 1998b). The intervention programs highlighted here are those that have garnered positive empirical support in experimental or quasi-experimental studies. The best empirical support is found for interventions that focus on parent skills and training that teach cognitive, behavioral, and affective competencies, especially when tailored to the family's needs and cultural values (Daro & Cohn Donnelly, 2002a). In terms of the research evidence, the next most promising strategies involve creating collaborative efforts with parents, teachers, and others in the community. On balance, these intervention programs are compatible with the risk and resilience framework and adhere to core principles of effective interventions presented in this book and elsewhere (Cohn Donnelly, 1999; Fraser, Nelson, & Rivard, 1997). Three kinds or levels of intervention that have been tested are (1) child-focused interventions, (2) parent- and family-focused interventions, and (3) ecological- or multisystemic-focused interventions.

CHILD-FOCUSED INTERVENTIONS

Resilient Peer Training Intervention (Fantuzzo, Sutton-Smith, Atkins, & Meyers, 1996; Fantuzzo, Weiss, & Coolahan, 1998) is a preschool, classroom-based intervention developed for maltreated children at higher than average risk for maladaptive social functioning. Children engage in 15 play sessions of activities designed to enhance the development of social competencies. Used in therapeutic preschool or Head Start classroom environments, parent helpers at the beginning of each session orient a resilient peer to the play area activities and identify successful play encounters with the withdrawn (maltreated and poorly functioning) child. Compared with maltreated children in a randomly assigned control group, 46 maltreated children in a resilient peer group showed significant improvements in positive peer interaction, decreases in social isolation, and reductions in aggression at treatment completion and at a two month follow-up (Corcoran, 2000b, 2000c; Fantuzzo, Weiss, & Coolahan, 1998; Webster-Stratton & Taylor, 2001). Intervention techniques included simple instructions, pictorial prompts, task analyses, modeling, rehearsal, role playing, feedback, token economies, behavioral contracting, and positive reinforcement to teach new skills. Positive peer interventions such as Resilient Peer Training appear to promote prosocial behavior, positive self-concepts, and cognitive development.

Early Intervention Foster Care (EIFC; Fisher & Chamberlain, 2000; Fisher, Ellis, & Chamberlain, 1999) is a comprehensive intervention focusing on abused and neglected children (three to seven years old) in protective services custody. The children are placed in foster homes with parents who receive intensive and extensive specialized training and supervision. A parent management training model is used and trained helpers take on a consulting role to the child's parents. The trained helpers establish an alliance with the family that is supportive and constructive before introducing parent-training techniques. In-home practice of skills occurs after office-based treatment sessions. As the parent learns particular skills, supervised visits with the child at the treatment center take place, and then the visits are lengthened and transitioned to the family home. In the treatment foster-care home, concomitant child interventions focus on the development of emotional regulation capabilities and, as needed, other consequences of maltreatment. Foster parents receive extensive support through daily telephone contacts, and the child's behavior and progress are tracked and modified in the foster home. Treatment foster parents engage in weekly support groups as well. The therapist remains in contact with the family up to three months after the child is reunified.

Techniques used in EIFC include intense and close supervision of children, the use of contracts and rewards for prosocial behaviors, behavioral reinforcement, time out, and limit setting (Chamberlain & Reid, 1991; Patterson, Reid, & Dishion, 1992). Services are delivered by a multidisciplinary team, which may include parents, teachers, foster parents, family therapists, and others necessary for the treatment of the child and family.

The pilot study results compared 30 substantiated maltreated children in protective custody in three different parenting environments: specialized foster care, regular foster care, and a comparison community sample. Study hypotheses centered on the mediating role that parenting practices play in determining outcomes. EIFC foster parents showed higher levels of consistent discipline, monitored the child's whereabouts more consistently, and provided greater positive reinforcement than regular foster care, and the children were more similar to the community comparison group. Outcome analyses revealed a positive effect of the specialized foster parents' parenting strategies. Emotional regulation and responses to stress (affected by maltreatment) improved in the EIFC group of children as early as three weeks and throughout the 12-week period, suggesting the possibility of bringing about physiological changes related to emotion regulation through an environmental intervention. A new longitudinal study with 180 maltreated children is currently in progress. It addresses the pilot study limitations of a small number of participants, lack of random assignment to the three comparison groups, absence of subsequent maltreatment rates, and dearth of developmental status outcome variables. Preliminary evidence suggests that EIFC may be an effective approach to the treatment of seriously maltreated children. It holds promise for reducing the cognitive, social, emotional, and developmental delays associated with child maltreatment. Moreover, the program appears to promote the development of stable and safe foster and home placements (Fisher & Chamberlain, 2000; Fisher, Ellis, & Chamberlain, 1999; Guterman & Embry, 2004; Meadowcroft, Thomlison, & Chamberlain, 1994).

PARENT- AND FAMILY-FOCUSED INTERVENTIONS

Parent- and family-focused interventions address both the recurrence of maltreatment and the negative effects of prior maltreatment. Parenting enhancement programs such as parent training are frequently reported in the literature on the subject. Parent training programs vary considerably, but essentially these interventions are based on principles of applied behavior analysis. They involve the use of procedures such as modeling, instruction, practice, feedback, and positive reinforcement to produce significant behavior change (Gershater-Molko, Lutzker, & Sherman, 2002) and target behavior problems in child management and child development. Parent training interventions have been found effective for parents of preschool and school-age children with conduct problems, but there is limited research with abusive (Corcoran, 2000a, 2000b) or neglectful parents (Gershater-Molko, Lutzker, & Sherman, 2002). Most parent training programs include problem-solving and communications skills training using modeling, coaching, and rehearsal techniques, often in individual sessions, before attending parent-group meetings; supervised practice of child management skills using videotape demonstrations and role playing, followed by videotape review and corrective feedback; use of homemakers or home visitors as in-home teachers for child development concerns; and behavioral and skills training with an emphasis on use of immediate, positive reinforcement (Corcoran, 2000a, 2000b; Kolko, 1996; Lyons, 1998;Webster-Stratton, 2001; Wolfe, 1994, 2001).

Cognitive–behavioral approaches using a combination of parenting skills training, anger management, and stress management have shown promise in reducing rates of abuse and neglect (Gershater-Molko, Lutzker, & Sherman, 2002). Studies of parent training based on the combination of cognitive therapy and family therapy suggest both methods reduce parental anger, improve child management, and help to change parental expectations for children. Two studies suggest that cognitive-behavioral intervention reduces the use of harsh physical discipline compared with families receiving regular community services (Kolko, 1996; Webster-Stratton, & Taylor, 2001). Research suggests that, similar to child-focused interventions, parent-training programs need to be intensive and specific to family needs, and they should use in-home visits to support and coach parents in learning new skills (Gershater-Molko, Lutzker, & Sherman, 2002; Wolfe, Edwards, Manion, & Koverola, 1988).

Homebuilders Intervention (English, 1999; Fraser, Pecora, & Haapala, 1991; Kinney, Haapala, & Booth, 1991) is an in-home, family-centered intervention in which the whole family receives services. Designed to prevent out-of-home placement and reduce the risk for child maltreatment, the intervention is intensive and time-limited—sometimes as brief as six weeks. Treatment often focuses on parenting skills and anger management, but treatment goals and activities vary significantly. Corcoran (2000c) reviewed family preservation studies as a group and observed that multisystemic approaches like Homebuilders seem beneficial in improving parent–child relationships. Additionally, Corcoran (2000c) reported modest but statistically significant differences in rates of postservice maltreatment referrals for an in-home services group (21.3 percent) compared with a standard child protective services group (28.5 percent). Findings using home-based family preservation services in juvenile justice are positive, whereas the studies of the effectiveness of in-home family preservation approaches in child welfare population are mixed, suggesting that for younger children services of greater duration may be needed (for a review, see Fraser, Nelson, & Rivard, 1997).

Parent–Child Education Program for Physically Abusive Parents (Wolfe, 1987, 1994, 2001; Wolfe, Edwards, Manion, & Koverola, 1988; Wolfe & Sandler, 1981; Wolfe, Sandler, & Kaufman, 1981) is a parent-training intervention that blends parent-centered training with efforts to teach and provide supportive child-rearing experiences. In a controlled study, 30 mother–child dyads, which were supervised by a child protection agency, were randomly assigned to one of two conditions. A control group received information from the protection agency; a treatment group received the same information plus behavioral parent support training. Parent training was provided in two-hour sessions on a weekly basis for eight weeks. The home-based intervention was designed to establish positive parent–child interactions and improve child-rearing methods. Explicit training was given for parents in positive parenting strategies that are responsive to child situational and developmental changes. The goal was to reduce parental reliance on power assertive methods and verbal and physical abuse. Parents were given demonstrations to promote skill enhancement to teach the use of nonviolent discipline methods, self-control, and ways to access community resources. At the end of one year, the parent training group was associated with reductions in child problems and improved child management skills, and none of the treated families had been reported or suspected of abuse at the one-year follow-up (Lyons, 1998; Wolfe, 1987, 1994). Subsequent maltreatment rates were not reported for the control group (Wolfe, 1987, 1994).

The Incredible Years Training Series (Webster-Stratton, 1990, 1998a, 1998b, 2000, 2001) is a parent training program based on cognitive–behavioral and social learning theories. It is designed for preschool and early school-age children. It focuses on counteracting parent and family risk factors by teaching parents about positive, nonviolent discipline methods and supporting parenting approaches that promote children's self-confidence, prosocial behaviors, and academic success (Webster-Stratton & Taylor, 2001). It has been field tested in six published randomized trials within various settings and in selective prevention programs with Head Start and other diverse and low-income families. The manualized program focuses on children with aggressive behavior and it has been translated into several languages throughout the world (C. Webster-Stratton, personal communication, July 2001). Three components are included in the program series. The BASIC program has been evaluated with over 700 high-risk Head Start families as a prevention program. The Teacher Training Program has been evaluated in two independent, randomized trials with Head Start teachers as well as in studies with teachers of students in kindergarten through third grade. Results indicate that children's problem behaviors decrease while social competence and academic engagement are increased (Webster-Stratton, 1998a, 1998b, 2001).

The program series was designed as both a prevention and intervention strategy for parents and teachers of children three to 12 years old. Parenting strategies for dealing with common child management problems are the focus. There are three components of training. The first is the BASIC Training Program, which is offered to parents in groups to foster support, problem solving, and self-management. The BASIC program includes promoting positive play, helping children learn, using praise and encouragement, providing incentives to motivate children, setting effective limits, and handling misbehavior. There are two versions of the BASIC program, one for parents of young children two to seven years old and one for parents of school-age children five to 12 years old. The second component is the ADVANCE program for parent training with children four to 10 years old. The ADVANCE program is a supplement to BASIC training that addresses other family risk factors such as depression, marital discord, poor coping skills, poor anger management, and lack of support. The EDUCATION parent training program is the third component. It supplements either the early childhood or school-age BASIC program by focusing on ways to foster children's academic competence. It is designed to teach parents to strengthen their children's reading and academic readiness and promote strong connections between home and school.

The EDUCATION curriculum is designed to reduce conduct problems in childhood. This is accomplished by teaching skills for increasing parent and teacher competencies in positive communication, child-directed play, consistent and clear limit setting, and nonviolent discipline strategies. Goals for children include strengthening social and academic competence; reducing behavior problems; and increasing positive interactions with peers, teachers, and parents. Video vignettes provide parents with more than 250 child management situations. Parents attend group sessions and can receive in-home coaching. The child training component resulted in significantly improved social skills and positive conflict management with peers. A randomized study found that combining parent and child training was more effective than parent training alone; both were superior to a control condition (Webster-Stratton & Hammond, 1997). Academic skills also appear to be enhanced for children in the program.

The efficacy of the Incredible Years parent program has been demonstrated as an early intervention for children with conduct problems and verbal or physical aggression. C. Webster-Stratton (personal communication, July 2001; Webster-Stratton & Taylor, 2001) indicated that child maltreatment occurred or was a risk factor for many of the families and children in the studies. Webster-Stratton argued that low school performance and conduct disorders are related and that both arise from the same child and family risk factors for maltreatment discussed earlier in this chapter. As noted in Table 4-1, maltreated children often have comorbid problems of learning delays, attention deficit hyperactivity disorder, and cognitive deficits. It is not clear whether the program prevents child maltreatment, but we know it improves parenting skills, reduces children's aggression with peers and teachers, and decreases conduct problems at home; these are factors that place children at high risk of maltreatment.

Nurse Family Partnership Program (Olds et al., 1997) attempt to improve the environmental contexts of low-income first-time mothers and their babies. Nurses— who provide counseling, family planning, parenting education, nutrition, and substance abuse information—deliver a comprehensive, long-term in-home intervention. Following protocols, nurses visit families weekly during the first month of enrollment and every other week throughout a woman's pregnancy. Then, they visit weekly for the first six weeks postpartum and every other week thereafter through the child's 21st month. In the final three months, they visit monthly until the child reaches age 2. Service begins with teaching mother–child attachment or relational behaviors, consistent feeding and child care, infant–toddler stimulation, and home management (Carnegie Task Force on Meeting the Needs of Young Children, 1994; Wekerle & Wolfe, 1993). Outcomes from two randomized trials and a 15-year follow-up showed that participants in the Nurse Home Visit Program had better family planning (43 percent reduction in subsequent pregnancy), greater self-sufficiency (83 percent increase in the rates of labor force participation by the child's first birthday), and an 80 percent reduction in rates of child maltreatment through the child's second year. In addition, the children whose parents participated in the program had significantly lower rates of delinquency when compared with comparable children whose parents did not participate in the program (Olds et al., 1997, 1999). Such findings suggest that, to prevent child maltreatment, home-based interventions that both monitor parents and provide support and skills training need to be introduced during pregnancy and followed with services in the postpartum period (Kendall-Tackett & Eckenrode, 1996; Kitzman, 1997; Olds, Eckenrode, & Henderson, 1997; Olds & Kitzman, 1993).

MULTISYSTEMIC-FOCUSED INTERVENTIONS

Multisystemic interventions concomitantly focus on individual, family, school, peer, and broader system levels in addressing problem behaviors and the interactions that influence or maintain problems.

Multisystemic Family Treatment (MST) has been found effective for the prevention of juvenile delinquency and drug use and more recently with physically abusive families (Henggeler, Schoenwald, Borduin, Rowland, & Cunningham, 1998). In eight randomized clinical trials, MST appears to improve both parenting practices and change the family environment. In an early study of MST, Brunk, Henggeler, and Whelan (1987) compared group-based parent training with MST to parent training only for 43 families investigated for abuse or neglect and randomly assigned to one of the treatment conditions. MST interventions used reframing, joining, and tasks aimed at family restructuring. In addition, parent education, information about parent–child expectations, marital therapy, advocacy, coaching, and emotional support were delivered in the home. Results indicated reduction in stress and severity of problems and fewer psychiatric symptoms. Parents receiving MST showed greater progress in controlling their child's behavior, greater improvement in parent–child interactions when compared with parents in the parent training–only group. Maltreated children of parents in the MST program exhibited less passive noncompliance, and neglecting parents who received MST became comparatively more responsive to their children's behavior. However, parent training was superior to MST in decreasing social problems associated with social support networks.

In other studies of juvenile delinquents and youths with conduct problems, MST has consistently demonstrated improved family relations and family functioning, improved school attendance, decreased adolescent drug use, and lower rearrest and out-of-home placement rates. MST has become a treatment of choice for working with children and youths who have serious conduct problems. However, in the early trial evaluating the effectiveness of MST versus parent training with abusive and neglectful families, families that received MST had no further incidents of abuse during the study and families with neglect problems became more responsive to their children. Both groups (MST and parent training) showed statistically significant reductions in parent stress and social problems, as well as improved family functioning (Brunk, Henggeler, & Whelan, 1987; Saunders, Berliner, & Hanson, 2001). Although more data are needed, the findings suggest that MST may also be useful in working with abusive families; a study is currently underway with physically abusive parents in South Carolina.

Project 12-Ways (Lutzker et al., 1998) is characterized as an ecobehavioral approach and focuses on enhancing environments and social supports for families. The in-home multifaceted intervention has three elements: (1) child health, (2) home safety, and (3) parent–child interactions. Practical and direct teaching approaches are used to address the specific needs of families and children. Planned activities training (PAT) helps parents learn to structure activities and child care skills. Marital counseling, financial planning, home health, and similar concerns are addressed using paraprofessionals such as neighbors, child-care practitioners, and volunteers to provide help. In a quasi-experimental evaluation (without random assignment) of Project 12-Ways, 352 neglectful families received 12-Ways treatment, and 358 neglectful families received routine services. At the one-year follow-up, families from Project 12-Ways were less likely to be reported for child abuse or neglect. Using official reporting sources out of Illinois, Lutzker and Rice (1987) found a 21.3 percent recidivism rate for the project families, compared with 28.5 percent for comparison families. Project 12-Ways appears to improve family environmental conditions associated with child abuse and neglect. Key elements in the 12-Ways interventions include basis skills training, money management, home safety, drug and alcohol abuse referrals, job training, and parent–child interaction training, stress reduction, self-control, social support, health and nutrition information, and job placement (Lutzker & Rice, 1984).

Project Safecare is an in-home treatment program for parents reported for child abuse and neglect. Based on a systematic replication of Project 12-Ways, it focuses on child health care, parent–child interactions for bonding, and home safety. A matched comparison group design of substantiated child abuse and neglect cases, involving 41 Project Safecare families and 41 Family Preservation families as the comparison group, received services and follow-up for 36 months after intervention began. At 36 months, 85 percent of the Project Safecare families and 54 percent of the Family Preservation group families had no reports of child abuse and neglect (Gershater-Molko, Lutzker, & Wesch, 2002).

Social Support Network Interventions (Gaudin, Wodarski, Arkinson, & Avery, 1990–1991; Lutzker et al., 1998; Webster-Stratton, 1998a, 1998b) focus on reducing social isolation, a keystone risk factor for neglect. The goal is to increase the level of informal social support for families, with the intent of improving personal and social resources for parenting. Strengthening parental and family support networks may reduce stress and isolation and increase control over the environment and provide resources for dealing with children's behavior problems (Bronfenbrenner, 1986; Clark & Clarke, 1996; Garbarino & Kostelny, 1992, 1994; Gaudin et al., 1990–1991). Gaudin and colleagues (1990–1991) randomly assigned a culturally diverse sample of verified neglectful families from the child protective service caseloads to services as usual (36 families) or to a multicomponent intervention group (52 families) consisting of family support networking, a mutual aid group, social skills training, help from volunteers, and neighbor-to-neighbor connections. Services ranged in duration from 10 weeks to 23 months. The intensive social network interventions were successful in strengthening the informal networks and improving parenting adequacy at six- and 12-month follow-up. Nearly 60 percent of the treatment families had their cases closed, and 80 percent of families who received more than nine months of treatment improved significantly on measures of parenting adequacy. Subsequent neglect is not reported in the study.

WHAT DO WE KNOW ABOUT INTERVENTION?

Although the volume of research on child maltreatment is disproportionately small given the magnitude of the child maltreatment problem, a growing number of intervention studies have promising findings. From the collective findings of these studies, we can distill nascent guidelines for practitioners who work in the field of child abuse or neglect. All interventions related to child maltreatment must ensure the safety of the child. To ensure child safety and to promote healthy child development, out-of-home placements are often necessary. It is the responsibility of child welfare practitioners to ensure that these placements are safe. However, it is also their responsibility to ensure safety in the least restrictive environment. Therefore, in this respect, child welfare agencies bear responsibility to provide services that promote family preservation that protect children and strengthen families at risk for maltreatment.

To prevent the initial occurrence of maltreatment or to prevent future maltreatment once it has occurred, services should be configured to intervene early as keystone risk factors can be clearly identified. To the extent that they are malleable, risk factors must be addressed using developmentally appropriate, culturally sensitive intervention techniques. On the basis of the research, these include parenting training (for self-control and child management) and behavior management (to reduce coercive behavior), cognitive-behavioral skills training for children (for assertion and self-control), peer-based skills training (for improved interactions), therapeutic day programs (for behavior problems), abuse-specific individual and family therapy (to reduce coercion), and other services to resolve case-specific problems such as social isolation, parental psychopathology, or the physical inhabitability of the home environment. Because no single pathway leads to child abuse and neglect, services must be based on

- a comprehensive risk and clinical assessment, including a child development, family, and medical assessment. Maltreated children show variability in their clinical symptoms; therefore, individualized assessments are required to identify whether problems are present.
- a treatment plan that is explicitly linked to comprehensive assessment, risk factors for child maltreatment (at individual, family, school, peer, and other ecological levels), and developmentally appropriate interventions that have a high degree of empirical support.
- a collaboration with other efforts to improve fundamental needs related to family members' health, housing, nutrition, and education.

Progress has been made in treatment research, but there continues to be a considerable gap between practice and research. Useful interventions have been identified in various research settings, including community-based settings. However, much of this work must be considered preliminary as researchers and practitioners identify more ways to make these interventions appealing to clinicians and families. Problems of the research include small sample sizes, weak designs (lacking random assignment), and findings that are equivocal or fail to measure child maltreatment as outcomes. Although early intervention programs, such as the Incredible Years and the Nurse Family Partnership interventions, appear to improve the odds for vulnerable children, these interventions are expensive and complex. They need to be delivered by well-trained and knowledgeable personnel. Although it appears that parent training and cognitive–behavioral interventions emerge as programs of choice for child, parent–child, and family-level change, it is far less clear what interventions are effective at the larger environmental system level. Moreover, as suggested by Shonkoff and Phillips (2000,

p. 413), the "prompt provision of an appropriate intervention can improve developmental outcomes. . . . However, not all interventions are effective, when they do work, they are rarely panaceas, and they do not confer a lifetime of protection." Significant challenges remain both in implementing what we already know and in further developing programs for children at risk of maltreatment.

In conclusion, we must embrace research-supported treatment services for maltreated children and their families by providing timely and developmentally appropriate services of sufficient intensity and duration to build safe, stable family environments for children. This requires actively coordinating health, mental health, and education programs so that assessments are shared and a comprehensive yet individualized treatment plan is developed for every child. And, consistent with a risk and resilience perspective, it requires providing services that reduce identified risk factors and promote protection in the least restrictive environment with the least amount of burden on the family. Additionally, "the impact of different protective and risk factors changes at various life phases and an individual who is resilient at one phase is not necessarily resilient in the next phase. Thus future research in this area should be longitudinal and should focus on both the content of risk and protective factors as well as the continuity and discontinuity of these factors over time" (Heller, Larrieu, D'Imperio, & Boris, 1999, p. 335).

FUTURE CHALLENGE

Finally, there is great need for studies to use randomized trials that compare routine child welfare services with new models of service. Child welfare agencies have been reluctant to engage in rigorous research, and they have rarely had resources to fund early intervention. But the outcomes of existing services are sufficiently poor in some states that routine services should not be regarded as a standard for ethical practice. There is need to conduct and pilot interventions in community-based settings The research reviewed here suggests that much can and should be done. Arguably, it may be unethical to fail to engage in developing and testing new services.

This research is suggestive at best. Follow-up data are lacking. Where promising findings exist, there is a need to disentangle the elements of programs that may be more or less effective. Moreover, poverty, substance abuse, and maternal depression remain significant risk factors for child maltreatment, and no intervention studies address these in the context of child welfare services.

Much more work is needed in developing strategies for early intervention to prevent maltreatment in high-risk families and in identifying evidence-based interventions that are acceptable to families and practitioners. The attachment and developmental psychology research literature on early childhood may contribute to the design of innovative early interventions for prevention of maltreatment. The enhancement of parent–child relationships appears to act as one of the more important factors in protecting children from maltreatment and in creating resilience in children who have been victimized. Although caring adults remain critical to children as they reach school age, other processes become important in shaping the child's sense of self-worth. Relationships and their effect on development form a powerful process. Identifying effective interventions for very young children and their families may moderate risk in the early years, but there is a need to understand family and social relationships for school-age and adolescent children who have been victimized. The link between familial, school, and peer relationships is not well understood in terms of the processes that influence recovery from maltreatment. Much remains to be learned about child maltreatment. It appears that abuse and neglect contribute to other disorders and negative developmental outcomes. Studies by Fisher and Chamberlain (2000), Henggeler and colleagues (1998, 1996b), Lutzker and colleagues (1998), and others (Webster-Stratton & Taylor, 2001; Wolfe, 2001) suggest that much better developmental outcomes can be observed when specific parent and child skills training are provided. But these studies are very small, and findings are unconfirmed in large studies in real-life settings in which child-welfare workers are buffeted by hostile media reports, requirements to testify in court, large caseloads, low parental motivation, little training and supervision, and adversarial bureaucracies.

To change outcomes in child welfare, a flowering of both early intervention and treatment studies with high research rigor is needed. Despite the use of mental health services by the child welfare system, the application of evidence-based treatments is very low, with a focus on treatment of sexual abuse (U.S. Public Health Service, 2000). Little attention is given to the damaging effects of neglect, and neglected children often receive no mental health treatment. There is an urgent need to close the gap between research and practice in providing evidence-based services to neglected and abused children. We must provide adequate and appropriate education and training to frontline staff, particularly child welfare practitioners; recognize and manage the range of health and mental health problems related to child maltreatment; and create innovative, more effective prevention and treatment services. These are the challenges.

REFERENCES

Abidin, R. R. (1995). *Parenting Stress Index* (3rd ed.). Odessa, FL: Psychological Assessment Resources.

Achenbach, T. M. (1991). *Manual for the Child Behavior Checklist/4–18 and 1991 profile*. Burlington: University of Vermont.

Ainsworth, M. S. (1989). Attachments beyond infancy. *American Psychologist, 44,* 709–716.

Allen, J. P., Columbus, M., & Fertig, J. (1995). Assessment in alcoholism treatment: An overview. In *Assessing alcohol problems: A guide for clinicians and researchers* (NIAAA Treatment Handbook Series 4, NIH publication No. 95-3745, pp. 1–9). Washington, DC: National Institutes of Health, National Association on Alcohol Abuse and Alcoholism.

Altemeier, W. A., O'Connor, S., Sherrod, K. B., & Tucker, D. (1986). Outcome of abuse during childhood among pregnant low-income women. *Child Abuse & Neglect, 10,* 319–330.

Ammerman, R. T., & Hersen, M. (1999). Current issues in the assessment of family violence: An update. In R. T. Ammerman & M. Hersen (Eds.), *Assessment of family violence. A clinical and legal sourcebook* (2nd ed., pp. 3–10). New York: John Wiley & Sons.

Ammerman, R. T., Hersen, M., Van Hasselt, V. B., Lubetsky, M. J., & Sieck, W. R. (1994). Maltreatment in psychiatrically hospitalized children and adolescents with developmental disabilities: Prevalence and correlates. *Journal of the American Academy of Child and Adolescent Psychiatry, 33*, 567–576.

Anthony, E. J., & Cohler, B. (1987). *The invulnerable child.* New York: Guilford Press.

Ayoub, C., & Jacewitz, J. (1982). Families at risk of poor parenting: A descriptive study of sixty at-risk families in a model prevention program. *Child Abuse & Neglect, 6*, 413–422.

Ayoub, C., Jacewitz, M., Gold, R., & Milner, J. (1983). Assessment of a program's effectiveness in selecting individuals "at risk" for problems in parenting. *Journal of Clinical Psychology, 39*, 334–339.

Ayoub, C., Willett, J., & Robinson, D. (1992). Families at risk of child maltreatment: Entry-level characteristics and growth in family functioning during treatment. *Child Abuse & Neglect, 16*, 495–511.

Azar, S. T., Robinson, D. R., Hekimian, E., & Twentyman, C. T. (1984). Unrealistic expectations and problem-solving ability in maltreating and comparison mothers. *Journal of Consulting and Clinical Psychology, 52*, 687–691.

Azar, S. T., & Rohrbeck, C. A. (1986). Child abuse and unrealistic expectations: Further validation of the Parent Opinion Questionnaire. *Journal of Consulting and Clinical Psychology, 54*, 867–868.

Azar, S. T., Vera, T. Y., Lauretti, A. F., & Pouquette, C. L. (1998) The current status of etiological theories in intrafamilial child maltreatment. In J. R. Lutzker (Ed.), *Handbook of child abuse research ad treatment* (pp. 3–20). New York: Plenum Press.

Baird, C., & Wagner, D. (2000). The relative validity of actuarial- and consensus-based risk assessment systems. *Children and Youth Services, 22*(11/12), 839–871.

Barnard, C. (1994). Resiliency: A shift in our perception? *American Journal of Family Therapy, 22*, 135–144.

Barth, R. P. (1991). An experimental evaluation of in-home child abuse prevention services. *Child Abuse & Neglect, 15*, 363–375.

Beavers, W. R., & Hampson, R. (1990). *Successful families: Assessment and intervention.* New York: W. W. Norton.

Beck, A. T., Steer, R. A., & Garbin, M. G. (1988). Psychometric properties of the Beck Depression Inventory: Twenty-five years of evaluation. *Clinical Psychology Review, 8*, 77–100.

Belsky, J., & Vondra, J. (1989). Lessons from child abuse: The determinants of parenting. In D. Cicchetti & V. Carlson (Eds.), *Child maltreatment: Theory and research on the causes and consequences of child abuse and neglect* (pp. 153–202). Cambridge, England: Cambridge University Press.

Briere, J. (1995). *Trauma Symptom Inventory professional manual.* Odessa, FL: Psychological Assessment Resources.

Briere, J., Berliner, L., Bulkley, J., Jenny, C., & Reid, T. (1996). *The APSAC handbook on child maltreatment.* Thousand Oaks, CA: Sage Publications.

Bronfenbrenner, E. (1986). Ecology of the family as a context for human development research perspectives. *Developmental Psychology, 22*, 723–742.

Bross, B. C., Miyoshi, T. J., Miyoshi, P. K., & Krugman, R. D. (2000). *World perspectives on child abuse: The fourth international resource book*. Denver: Kempe Children's Center and the International Society for Prevention of Child Abuse and Neglect.

Brunk, M., Henggeler, S. W., & Whelan, J. P. (1987). A comparison of multisystemic therapy and parent training in the brief treatment of child abuse and neglect. *Journal of Consulting and Clinical Psychology, 55*, 311–318.

Burns, B. J., Hoagwood, K., & Mrazek, P. J. (1999). Effective treatment for mental disorders in children and adolescents. *Clinical Child and Family Psychology Review, 2*, 199–254.

Carnegie Task Force on Meeting the Needs of Young Children. (1994). *Starting points: Meeting the needs of our youngest children*. New York: Carnegie Corporation of New York.

Cash, S. (2001). Risk assessment in child welfare: The art and science. *Children and Youth Services Review, 23*(11), 811–830.

Chadwick, D. L. (1999) The vision. *Child Abuse & Neglect, 23*, 955–956.

Chaffin, M., Kelleher, K., & Hollenberg, J. (1996). Onset of physical abuse and neglect: Psychiatric, substance abuse, and social risk factors from prospective community data. *Child Abuse & Neglect, 20*, 191–203.

Chalk, R., Gibbons, A., & Scarupa, H. (2002). The multiple dimensions of child abuse and neglect: New insights into an old problem [Online]. *Child Trends Research Brief*. Retrieved from http://www.childtrends.org/MediaAdvisoryMay2302.asp on May 14, 2003.

Chamberlain, P., & Reid, J. B. (1991). Using a specialized foster care treatment model for children and adolescents leaving the state mental hospital. *Journal of Community Psychology, 19*, 266–276.

Cicchetti, D., & Lynch, M. (1993). Toward an ecological/transactional model of community violence and child maltreatment: Consequences for children's development. *Psychiatry: Interpersonal and Biological Processes, 56*, 96–118.

Clark, H. B., & Clarke, R. T. (1996). Research on the wraparound process and individualized services for children with multi-system needs. *Journal of Child and Family Studies, 5*, 1–5.

Cohn, A. H., & Daro, D. (1987). Is treatment too late: What ten years of evaluative research tell us. *Child Abuse & Neglect, 11*, 433–442.

Cohn Donnelly, A. (1999). The practice. *Child Abuse & Neglect, 23*, 987–994.

Coohey, C. (1996). Child maltreatment: Testing the social isolation hypothesis. *Child Abuse & Neglect, 20*, 241–254.

Corcoran, J. (2000a). Family interventions with child physical abuse and neglect: A critical review. *Children and Youth Services Review, 22*, 563–591.

Corcoran, J. (2000b). Family treatment with child abuse and neglect. In J. Corcoran (Ed.), *Evidence-based social work practice with families* (pp. 3–75). New York: Springer Publishing.

Corcoran, J. (2000c). Family treatment with child maltreatment using family preservation approaches. In J. Corcoran (Ed.), *Evidence-based social work practice with families* (pp. 76–123). New York: Springer.

Coulton, C. J., Korbin, J. E., Su, M. & Chow, J. (1995). Community level factors and child maltreatment rates. *Child Development, 66*, 1262–1276.

Crittenden, P. M. (1988a). Families and dyadic patterns of functioning in maltreating families. In K. Browne, C. Davies, & P. Stratton (Eds.), *Early prediction and prevention of child abuse* (pp. 161–189). New York: John Wiley & Sons.

Crittenden, P. M. (1988b). Relationships at risk. In J. Belsky & T. Nezworski (Eds.), *Clinical implications of attachment* (pp.136–174). Hillsdale, NJ: Lawrence Erlbaum Associates.

Daro, D., & Cohn Donnelly, A. (2002a). Charting the waves of prevention: Two steps forward, one step back. *Child Abuse & Neglect, 26,* 731–742.

Daro, D., & Cohn Donnelly, A. (2002b) Child abuse prevention: Accomplishments and challenges. In J. Myers, L. Berliner, J. Briere, T. Hendrix, C. Jenny, & T. Reid (Eds.), *APSAC handbook on child maltreatment* (2nd ed., pp. 431–448). Newbury Park, CA: Sage Publications.

Derogatis, L. (1993). *Brief Symptom Inventory: Administration, scoring, and procedures manual*. Minneapolis: National Computer Systems.

Dore, M. M., Doris, J. M., & Wright, P. (1995). Identifying substance abuse in maltreating families: A child welfare challenge. *Child Abuse & Neglect, 19,* 531–543.

Doueck, H. J., English, D., DePanfilis, D., & Moote, G. T. (1993). Decision-making in child protective services: A comparison of selected risk-assessment systems. *Child Welfare, 72*(5), 441–452.

Eckenrode, J., Laird, M., & Doris, J. (1991). *Maltreatment and social adjustment of school children* (Grant No. 90CA1305). Washington, DC: U.S. Department of Health and Human Services, National Center on Child Abuse and Neglect.

Emery, R. (1989). Family violence. *American Psychologist, 44,* 321–328.

English, D. (1999). *Family preservation services and intensive family preservation services evaluation progress report*. Office of Children's Administration Research, State of Washington, Olympia.

English, D., & Pecora, P. (1994). Risk assessment as a practice method in child protective services [Special issue]. *Child Welfare, 73,* 451–475.

English, D. J., & Graham, J. C. (2000). An examination of relationships between children's protective services social worker assessment of risk and independent LONGSCAN measures of risk constructs. *Children and Youth Services Review, 22*(11/12), 897–933.

Epstein, M., Quinn, K., & Cumblad, C. (1992). *Program initiatives to improve special education services for students with behavior disorders/emotional disorders: Evaluation plans*. DeKalb, IL: Educational Research and Services Center.

Epstein, N., Baldwin, L., & Bishop, D. (1983). The McMaster Family Assessment Device. *Journal of Marital and Family Therapy, 9,* 171–180.

Fantuzzo, J., Boruch, R., Beriama, A., Atkins, M., & Marcus, S. (1997). Domestic violence and children: Prevalence and risk in five major U.S. cities. *Journal of the American Academy of Child and Adolescent Psychiatry, 36,* 116–122.

Fantuzzo, J., McDermott, P., & Lutz, M. (1999). Clinical issues in the assessment of family violence involving children. In R. T. Ammerman & M. Hersen (Eds.), *Assessment of family violence: A clinical and legal sourcebook* (2nd ed., pp. 10–24). New York: John Wiley & Sons.

Fantuzzo, J., Sutton-Smith, B., Atkins, M., & Meyers, R. (1996). Community-based resilient peer treatment of withdrawn maltreated preschool children. *Journal of Consulting and Clinical Consulting Psychology, 64,* 1377–1386.

Fantuzzo, J., Weiss, A., & Coolahan, K. (1998). Community-based partnership-directed research: Actualizing community strengths to treat victims of physical abuse and neglect. In R. J. Lutzker (Ed.), *Child abuse: A handbook of theory, research, and treatment* (pp. 1213–1238). New York: Pergamon Press.

Faust, J., Runyon, M., & Kenny, M. (1995). Family variables associated with the onset and impact of intrafamilial childhood sexual abuse. *Clinical Psychology Review, 15*, 443–456.

Feerick, M. M., & Haugaard, J. J. (1999). Long-term effects of witnessing marital violence for women: The contribution of childhood physical and sexual abuse. *Journal of Family Violence, 14*, 377–398.

Finkelhor, D. (1986). Prevention: A review of programs and research. In D. Finkelhor (Ed.), *A sourcebook on child sexual abuse* (pp. 224–254). Beverly Hills, CA: Sage Publications.

Finkelhor, D. (1994). The international epidemiology of child sexual abuse. *Child Abuse & Neglect, 18*, 409–417.

Finkelhor, D. (1995). The victimization of children: A developmental perspective. *American Journal of Orthopsychiatry, 65*, 177–193.

Finkelhor, D., & Baron, L. (1986). High-risk children. In D. Finkelhor (Ed.), *A sourcebook on child sexual abuse* (pp. 60–88). Beverly Hills, CA: Sage Publications.

Finkelhor, D., & Berliner, L. (1995). Research on the treatment of sexually abused children: A review and recommendations. *Journal of the American Academy of Child and Adolescent Psychiatry, 34*, 1–16.

Fisher, P. A., & Chamberlain, P. (2000). Multidimensional treatment foster care: A program for intensive parenting, family support, and skill building. *Journal of Emotional and Behavioral Disorders, 8*(3), 155–164.

Fisher, P. A., Ellis, B. H., & Chamberlain, P. (1999). Early Intervention Foster Care: A model for preventing risk in young children who have been maltreated. *Children's Services: Social Policy, Research, and Practice, 2*(3), 159–182.

Fraser, M. W., Nelson, K. E., & Rivard, J. C. (1997). Effectiveness of family preservation services. *Social Work Research, 21*, 138–153.

Fraser, M. W., Pecora, P. J., & Haapala, D. A. (1991). *Families in crisis: The impact of intensive family preservation services.* New York: Aldine de Gruyter.

Gambrill, E., & Shlonsky, A. (2000). Risk assessment in context. *Children and Youth Services Review, 22*(11/12), 813–837.

Garbarino, J., Dubrow, N., Kostelney, K., & Pardo, C. (1992). *Children in danger: Coping with the consequences of community violence.* San Francisco: Jossey-Bass.

Garbarino, J., & Kostelny, K. (1992). Child maltreatment as a community problem. *Child Abuse & Neglect, 16*, 455–464.

Garbarino, J., & Kostelny, K. (1994). Neighborhood-based programs. In G. B. Melton & F. D. Barry (Eds.), *Protecting children from abuse and neglect: Foundations for a new national strategy.* New York: Guilford Press.

Garmezy, N., & Tellegan, A. (1984). Studies of stress-resistant children: Methods, variables, and preliminary findings. In F. J. Morrison, G. Lord, & D. P. Keating (Eds.), *Applied developmental psychology* (pp. 231–287). Orlando, FL: Academic Press.

Gaudin, J. M., Wodarski, J. S., Arkinson, M. K., & Avery, L. S. (1990–1991). Remedying child neglect: Effectiveness of social network interventions. *Journal of Applied Social Science, 15*, 97–123.

Gershater-Molko, R. M., & Lutzker, J. (1999). Child neglect. In R. T. Ammerman & M. Hersen (Eds.), *Assessment of family violence: A clinical and legal sourcebook* (2nd ed., pp. 157–183). New York: John Wiley & Sons.

Gershater-Molko, R. M., Lutzker, J., & Sherman, J. (2002). Intervention in child neglect: An applied behavioral perspective. *Aggression and Violent Behavior, 7,* 103–124.

Gershater-Molko, R. M., Lutzker, J., & Wesch, D. (2002). Using recidivism data to evaluate Project Safecare: Teaching bonding, safety, and health care skills to parents. *Child Maltreatment, 7,* 277–285.

Guterman, N. (2001). *Stopping child maltreatment before it starts: Emerging horizons in early home visitation services.* Thousand Oaks, CA: Sage Publications.

Guterman, N. B., & Embry, R. A. (2004). Prevention and treatment strategies targeting physical child abuse and neglect. In P. Allen-Meares & M. W. Fraser (Eds.), *Intervention with children and adolescents: An interdisciplinary perspective* (pp. 130–158). Boston: Allyn & Bacon.

Hansen, D. J., Sedlar, G., & Warner-Rogers, J. E. (1999). Child physical abuse. In R. T. Ammerman & M. Hersen (Eds.), *Assessment of family violence: A clinical and legal sourcebook* (2nd ed., pp. 127–156). New York: John Wiley & Sons.

Hay, T., & Jones, L. (1994). Societal interventions to prevent child abuse and neglect [Special issue]. *Child Welfare, 73,* 379–405.

Hegar, R. L. (1988). Sibling relationships and separations: Implications for child placement. *Social Service Review, 62,* 446–467.

Heller, S. S., Larrieu, J. A., D'Imperio, R., & Boris, N. W. (1999). Research on resilience to child maltreatment: Empirical considerations. *Child Abuse & Neglect, 23,* 321–338.

Henggeler, S. W., Schoenwald, S. K., Borduin, C. M., Rowland, M. D., & Cunningham, P. B. (1998). *Multisystemic treatment of antisocial behavior in children and adolescents.* New York: Guilford Press.

Herrenkohl, E., Herrenkohl, R., & Egolf, B. (1994). Resilient early school-age children from maltreating homes: Outcomes in late adolescence. *American Journal of Orthopsychiatry, 64*(2), 301–309.

Hildyard, K. L., & Wolfe, D. A. (2002). Child neglect: Developmental issues and outcomes. *Child Abuse & Neglect, 26,* 679–695.

Hillson, J., & Kuiper, N. (1994). A stress and coping model of child maltreatment. *Clinical Psychology Review, 14,* 261–285.

Hodges, K. (1994). *Child and Adolescent Functional Assessment Scale.* Ypsilanti: Eastern Michigan University, Department of Psychology.

Holder, W., & Corey, M. (1986). *Child protective services risk management: A decision-making handbook.* Charlotte, NC: ACTION for Child Protection.

Hudson, W. W. (1992). *The WALMYR Assessment Scales scoring manual.* Tempe, AZ: WALMYR Publishing.

Hudson, W. W., & McMurtry, S. (1997). Comprehensive assessment in social work practice: The Multi-Problem Screening Inventory. *Research on Social Work Practice, 7,* 79–98.

Iverson, T. J., & Segal, M. (1990). *Child abuse and neglect: An information and reference guide.* New York: Garland Publishing.

Jagannathan, R., & Camasso, M. (1996). Risk assessment in child protective services: A canonical analysis of the case management function. *Child Abuse & Neglect, 20*(7), 599–612.

Jaudes, P. K., Ekwo, E., & Van Voorhis, J. (1995). Association of drug abuse and child abuse. *Child Abuse & Neglect, 19*, 1065–1075.

Jensen, P. S., & Hoagwood, K. (1997). The book of names: DSM-IV in context. *Development and Psychopathology, 9*, 231–249.

Johnson, R. M., Kotch, J. B., Catellier, D. J., Winsor, J. R., Dufort, V., Hunter, W., & Amaya-Jackson, L. (2002). Adverse behavioral and emotional outcomes from child abuse and witnessed violence. *Child Maltreatment, 7*(3), 179–186.

Johnson, W., & L'Esperance, J. (1984). Predicting the recurrence of child abuse. *Social Work Research and Abstracts, 20*, 21–26.

Johnson, W., & Scott, R. (1999). A description of the California Child Welfare Services structured decision-making project. In American Humane Association, Children's Division & American Public Human Services Association (Eds.), *Twelfth national roundtable on CPS risk assessment: summary of proceedings, July 8–10, 1998, San Francisco* (pp. 37–42). Englewood, CO: American Humane Association, Children's Division.

Kazdin, A. E. (1992). Child and adolescent dysfunction and paths toward maladjustment: Targets for intervention. *Clinical Psychology Review, 12*, 795–817.

Kendall-Tackett, K., & Eckenrode, J. (1996). The effects of neglect on academic achievement and disciplinary problems: A developmental perspective. *Child Abuse & Neglect, 20*, 161–171.

Kinard, E. M. (1995, July). *Assessing resilience in abused children*. Paper presented at the Fourth International Family Violence Research Conference, Durham, NH.

Kinard, E. M. (1999). Psychosocial resources and academic performance in abused children. *Children and Youth Services, 21*, 351–376.

Kinney, J. M., Haapala, D., & Booth, C. L. (1991). *Keeping families together: The Homebuilders Model*. New York: Aldine de Gruyter.

Kitzman, H. (1997). Effects of prenatal and infancy home visitation by nurses on pregnancy outcomes, childhood injuries, and repeated childbearing: A randomized controlled trial. *Journal of the American Medical Association, 278*, 644–652.

Knitzer, J. (2000). Early childhood mental health services: A policy and systems development perspective. In J. P. Shonkoff & S. J. Meisels (Eds.), *Handbook of early childhood intervention* (2nd ed., pp. 416–439). New York: Cambridge University Press.

Kolko, D. J. (1996). Individual cognitive behavioral therapy and family therapy for physically abused children and their offending parents: A comparison of clinical outcomes. *Child Maltreatment, 1*, 322–342.

Kolko, D. J. (2003). Child physical abuse. In J. Myers, L. Berliner, J. Briere, C. T. Hendrix, C. Jenny, & T. Reid, (Eds.), *The APSAC handbook on child maltreatment* (2nd ed., pp. 21–55). Thousand Oaks, CA: Sage Publications.

Kopp, C., & Kaler, S. (1989). Risk in infancy: Origins and implications. *American Psychologist, 44*(2), 224–230.

Korbin, J. (1994). Sociocultural factors in child maltreatment. In G. B. Melton & F. D. Barry (Eds.), *Protecting children from abuse and neglect: Foundations for a new national strategy* (pp. 182–223). New York: Guilford Press.

Korbin, J. (2002). Culture and child maltreatment: Cultural competence and beyond. *Child Abuse & Neglect, 26,* 637–644.

Korbin, J., Coulton, C., Lindstrom-Ufuti, H., & Spilsbury, J. (2000). Neighborhood views on the definition and etiology of child maltreatment. *Child Abuse & Neglect, 24,* 1509–1527.

Kotch, J., Browne, D., Ringwalt, C., Stewart, P., Ruina, E., Holt, K., Lowman, B., & Jung, J. (1995). Risk of abuse or neglect in a cohort of low-income children. *Child Abuse & Neglect, 19,* 1115–1130.

Kotulak, R. (1996). *Inside the brain: Revolutionary discoveries of how the mind works.* Kansas City, MO: Andrews & McNeel.

Lawlor, E., & Raube, K. (1995). Social interventions and outcomes in medical effectiveness research. *Social Service Review, 69,* 383–404.

Lutzker, J. R., Bigelow, K. M., Doctor, R. M., & Kessler, M. L. (1998). Safety, health care, and bonding, within an ecobehavioral approach to treating and preventing child abuse and neglect. *Journal of Family Violence, 13,* 163–185.

Lutzker, J. R., & Rice, J. M. (1984). Project 12-Ways: Measuring outcome of a large in-home service for treatment and prevention of child abuse and neglect. *Child Abuse & Neglect, 8*(4), 519–524.

Lutzker, J. R., & Rice, J. M. (1987). Using recidivism data to evaluate Project 12-Ways: An ecobehavioral approach to the treatment and prevention of child abuse and neglect. *Journal of Family Violence, 2,* 283–290.

Lynch, M. A., & Cicchetti, D. (1998). An ecological-transactional analysis of children and contexts: The longitudinal interplay among child maltreatment, community violence, and children's symptomatology. *Developmental Psychopathology, 10,* 235–257.

Lyons, P. (1998). Child maltreatment. In J. S. Wodarski & B. A. Thyer (Eds.), *Handbook of empirical practice: Social problems and practice issues* (Vol. 2, pp. 33–53). New York: John Wiley & Sons.

Magura, S., & Moses, B. S. (1986). *Outcome measures for child welfare services: Theory and applications.* Washington, DC: Child Welfare League of America.

Magura, S., Moses, B. S., & Jones, M. A. (1987). *Assessing risk and measuring change of families: The family risk scales.* Washington, DC: Child Welfare League of America.

Margolin, G., & Gordis, E. B. (2000). The effects of family and community violence on children. *Annual Review of Psychology, 51,* 445–479.

Marks, J., & McDonald, T. (1989). *Risk assessment in child protective services. 4. Predicting recurrence of child maltreatment.* Portland: University of Southern Maine.

Mash, E. J., & Wolfe, D. A. (1991). Methodological issues in research on physical child abuse. *Criminal Justice and Behavior, 18,* 8–29.

McCroskey, J., & Nelson, J. (1989) Practice-based research in a family support program: The Family Connection Project example. *Child Welfare, 68,* 573–587.

McLellan, A. T., Luborsky, L., Woody, G. E., & O'Brien, C. P. (1980). An improved diagnostic evaluation instrument for substance abuse patients: The Addiction Severity Index. *Journal of Nervous and Mental Disorders, 168,* 26–33.

Meadowcroft, P., Thomlison, B., & Chamberlain, P. (1994). Treatment foster care services: A research agenda for child welfare. *Child Welfare, 73*(5), 565–581.

Melton, G. B., & Barry, F. D. (1994a). Neighbors helping neighbors: The vision of the U.S. Advisory Board on child abuse and neglect. In G. B. Melton & F. D. Barry (Eds.), *Protecting children from abuse and neglect: Foundations for a new national strategy* (pp. 1–14). New York: Guilford Press.

Melton, G. B., & Barry, F. D. (Eds.). (1994b). *Protecting children from abuse and neglect: Foundations for a new national strategy*. New York: Guilford Press.

Miller, J. S., Williams, K. M., English, D. J., & Olmstead, J. (1987). *Risk assessment in child protection: A review of the literature*. Olympia, WA: Department of Social and Health services, Division of Children and Family Services.

Milner, J. S. (1994). Assessing physical child abuse risk: The Child Abuse Potential Inventory. *Clinical Psychology Review, 14*, 547–583.

Mrazek, P. J., & Haggerty, R. J. (Eds.). (1994). *Reducing risks for mental disorders: Frontiers for preventive intervention research*. Washington, DC: National Academy Press.

Mrazek, P. J., & Mrazek, D. A. (1987). Resilience in child maltreatment victims: A conceptual exploration. *Child Abuse & Neglect, 11*, 357–366.

Najavits, L. M., Weiss, R. D., Reif, S., Gastfriend, D. R., Siqueland, L., Barber, J. P., Butler, S. F., Thase, M., & Blaine, J. (1998). The Addiction Severity Index as a screen for trauma and posttraumatic stress disorder. *Journal of Studies on Alcohol, 59*(7), 56–63.

Nasuti, J. P., & Pecora, P. J. (1993). Risk assessment scales in child protection: A test of the internal consistency and interrater reliability of one statewide system. *Social Work Research and Abstracts, 29*(2), 28–33.

National Center for Children in Poverty. (2002, January). *Promoting the emotional well-being of children and families policy paper series*. New York: Columbia University, Mailman School of Public Health.

Olds, D., Eckenrode, J., Henderson, C. R., Kitzman, H., Powers, J., Cole, R., Sidora, K., Morris, P., & Pettit, L. M. (1997). Long-term effects of home visitation on maternal life course and child abuse and neglect: Fifteen-year follow-up of a randomized trial. *Journal of the American Medical Association, 278*, 637–643.

Olds, D., & Kitzman, H. (1993). Review of research on home visits for pregnant women and parents of young children. *The Future of Children, 3*(3), 53–92.

Olds, D. L., Henderson, C. R., Kitzman, H. J., Eckenrode, J. J., Cole, R. E., & Tatelbaum, R. C. (1999). Prenatal and infancy home visitation by nurses: Recent findings. *The Future of Children, 9*(1), 44–65.

Osofsky, J. D., & Thompson, M. D. (2000). Adaptive and maladaptive parenting: Perspectives on risk and protective factors. In J. P. Shonkoff & S. J. Meisels (Eds.), *Handbook of early childhood intervention* (2nd ed., pp. 54–76). New York: Cambridge University Press.

Patterson, G. R., Reid, J. B., & Dishion, T. J. (1992). *A social learning approach. Vol. 4. Antisocial boys*. Eugene, OR: Castalia.

Pecora, P. (1991). Investigating allegations of child maltreatment: The strengths and limitations of current risk assessment systems. *Child and Youth Services, 15*(2), 73–92.

Pelton, L. (1994). The role of material factors in child abuse and neglect. In G. B. Melton

& F. D. Barry (Eds.), *Protecting children from abuse and neglect: Foundations for a new national strategy* (pp. 131–181). New York: Guilford Press.

Polansky, N. A., Chalmers, M. A., Buttenweiser, E., & Williams, B. (1981). *Damaged parents: An anatomy of child neglect*. Chicago: University of Chicago Press.

Pollard, J. A., Hawkins, D. J., & Arthur, M. W. (1999). Risk and protection: Are both necessary to understand diverse behavioral outcomes in adolescence? *Social Work Research, 23*, 145–159.

Portwood, S. (1999). Coming to terms with a consensual definition of child maltreatment. *Child Maltreatment, 4*, 56–68.

Powell, K. E., Dahlberg, L. L., Friday, J., Mercy, J. A., Thornton, T., & Crawford, S. (1996). Prevention of youth violence: Rationale and characteristics of 15 evaluation projects. *American Journal of Preventive Medicine, 12*(5), 3–12.

Quinton, D., & Rutter, M. (1988). *Parenting breakdown: The making and breaking of intergenerational links*. Aldershot, England: Gower.

Radke-Yarrow, M., & Sherman, T. (1990). Hard growing: Children who survive. In J. Rolf, A. S. Masten, D. Cicchetti, K. H. Nuechterlein & S. Weintraub (Eds.), *Risk and protective factors in the development of psychopathology* (pp. 97–119). New York: Cambridge University Press.

Rice, C., Del Boca, F. K., Mattson, M., Mohr, C., Young, L., Brady, K., & Nickless, C. (2001). Self-reports of physical, sexual, and emotional abuse in an alcoholism treatment sample. *Journal of Studies on Alcohol, 61*(1), 114–123.

Richman, J. M., & Bowen, G. L. (1997). School failure: An ecological-interactional-developmental perspective. In M. W. Fraser (Ed.), *Risk and resilience in childhood: An ecological perspective* (pp. 95–117). Washington, DC: NASW Press.

Rittner, B. (2002). The use of risk assessment instruments in child protective services case planning and closures. *Children and Youth Services Review, 24*(3), 189–207.

Rittner, B., & Wodarski, J. S. (1995). Clinical assessment instruments in the treatment of child abuse and neglect. *Early Child Development and Care, 106*, 43–58.

Roberts, J. (1988). Why are some families more vulnerable to child abuse? In K. Browne, C. Davies, & P. Stratton (Eds.), *Early prediction and prevention of child abuse* (pp. 43–56). New York: John Wiley & Sons.

Runyon, D., Hunter, W. M., Socolar, R. R., Amaya-Jackson, L., English, D., Landsverk, J., Dubowitz, H., Brown, D. H., Bangdiwala, S. I., & Mathew, R. M. (1998). Children who prosper in unfavorable environments: The relationship to social capital. *Pediatrics, 101*, 12–18.

Rutter, M. (1987). Psychosocial resilience and protective mechanism. *American Journal of Orthopsychiatry, 57*, 316–330.

Rutter, M. (2000). Resilience reconsidered: Conceptual considerations, empirical findings, and policy implications. In J. P. Shonkoff & S. J. Meisels (Eds.), *Handbook of early childhood intervention* (2nd ed., pp. 651–683). New York: Cambridge University Press.

Sadler, B. L., Chadwick, D. L., & Hensler, D. J. (1999). The summary chapter—the national call to action: Moving ahead. *Child Abuse & Neglect, 23*, 1011–1018.

Sedlak, A. J., & Broadhurst, D. D. (1996). *Third National Incidence Study of Child Abuse and Neglect: Final report*. Washington, DC: U.S. Department of Health and Human Services.

Selzer, M. L., Moskowitz, D. S., Schwartzman, A. E., & Ledingham, J. E. (1991). A self-administered Short Michigan Alcoholism Screening Test. *Journal of Studies on Alcohol, 36,* 117–126.

Saunders, B. E., Berliner, L., & Hanson, R. F. (2001). *Guidelines for the psychosocial treatment of intrafamilial child physical and sexual abuse* (Final Report). Charleston, SC: National Crime Victims Research and Treatment Center and Center for Sexual Assault and Traumatic Stress.

Shonkoff, J. P., & Marshall, P. C. (2000). The biology of developmental vulnerability. In J. P. Shonkoff & S. J. Meisels (Eds.), *Handbook of early childhood intervention* (2nd ed., pp. 35–54). New York: Cambridge University Press.

Shonkoff, J. P., & Phillips, D. A. (Eds.). (2000). *From neurons to neighborhoods: The science of early childhood development.* National Research Council and Institute of Medicine. Washington, DC: National Academy Press.

Skinner, H. A. (1982). The Drug Abuse Screening Test. *Addictive Behaviors, 7,* 363–371.

Smith, D. W., & Saunders, B. E. (1995). Personality characteristics of father/perpetrators and non-offending mothers in incest families: Individual and dyadic analyses. *Child Abuse & Neglect, 19,* 607–617.

Straus, M. A. (1995). Trends in cultural norms and rates of partner violence: An update to 1992. In S. M. Stith & M. A. Straus (Eds.), *Understanding partner violence: Prevalence, causes, consequences, and solutions* (pp. 30–33). Minneapolis: National Council on Family Relations.

Straus, M., Hamby, S., Boney-McCoy, S., & Sugarman, D. (1996). The Revised Conflict Tactics Scales (CTS2). *Journal of Family Issues, 17,* 283–316.

Thomlison, B. (2002). *Family assessment handbook: An introductory practice guide to family assessment and intervention.* Pacific Grove, CA: Brooks/Cole.

Thomlison, B. (2003). Characteristics of evidence-based child maltreatment interventions [Special issue]. *Child Welfare, 82*(5).

Tracy, E. (1988). Social support resources of at-risk families: Implementation of social support assessments in an intensive family preservation program (University Microfilms No. DA8826430). *Dissertation Abstracts International, 49,* 2813-A.

Tracy, E., & McDonell, J. (1991). Home based work with families: The environmental context of family intervention. *Journal of Independent Social Work, 5*(3/4), 93–108.

U.S. Department of Health and Human Services, Administration on Children, Youth, and Families. (2001). *Child maltreatment 1999.* Washington, DC: U.S. Government Printing Office.

U.S. Public Health Service. (2000). *Report of the Surgeon General's Conference on Children's Mental Health: A national action agenda.* Washington, DC: Author.

Veltman, M. W., & Browne, K. D. (2001). Three decades of child maltreatment research: Implications for the school years. *Trauma, Violence, & Abuse: A Review Journal, 2,* 215–240.

Wald, M., & Woolverton, N. (1990). Risk assessment. *Child Welfare, 69*(6), 483–511.

Wang, C., & Daro, D. (1998). *Current trends in child abuse reporting and fatalities: The results of the 1997 Annual Fifty State Survey.* Chicago: Prevent Child Abuse America.

Webster-Stratton, C. (1990). Long-term follow-up with young conduct problem children: From preschool to grade school. *Journal of Clinical Child Psychology, 19,* 144–149.

Webster-Stratton, C. (1998a). Parent training with low-income families: Promoting parental engagement through a collaborative approach. In J. R. Lutzker (Ed.), *Handbook of child abuse research and treatment* (pp. 183–211). New York: Plenum Press.

Webster-Stratton, C. (1998b). Preventing conduct problems in Head Start children: Strengthening parenting competencies. *Journal of Consulting and Clinical Psychology, 66,* 715–730.

Webster-Stratton, C. (2000). The Incredible Years Training Series. *Juvenile Justice Bulletin.* Washington, DC: Office of Juvenile Justice and Delinquency Prevention.

Webster-Stratton, C. (2001, July). *Prevention and treatment for young children with conduct problems: The Incredible Years Training Series.* Paper presented at the Second Biennial Niagara Conference on Evidence-Based Treatments for Childhood and Adolescent Mental Health Problems, Niagara-On-the-Lake, Canada.

Webster-Stratton, C., & Hammond, M. (1997). Treating children with early-onset conduct problems: Comparison of child and parent training interventions. *Journal of Consulting and Clinical Psychology, 65,* 93–109.

Webster-Stratton, C., & Taylor, T. (2001). Nipping early risk factors in the bud: Preventing substance abuse, delinquency, and violence in adolescence through interventions targeted at young children (0–8 years). *Prevention Science, 2,* 165–192.

Wekerle, C., & Wolfe, D. (1993). Prevention of child physical abuse and neglect: Promising new directions. *Clinical Psychology Review, 13,* 501–540.

Werner, E. E. (2000). Protective factors and individual resilience. In J. P. Shonkoff & S. J. Meisels (Eds.), *Handbook of early childhood intervention* (2nd ed., pp. 115–135). New York: Cambridge University Press.

Widom, C. S. (1989a). Child abuse, neglect, and adult behavior: Research design and findings on criminality, violence, and child abuse. *American Journal of Orthopsychiatry, 59,* 355–367.

Widom, C. S. (1989b). Does violence beget violence? A critical examination of the literature. *Psychological Bulletin, 6,* 3–28.

Wolfe, D. A. (1987). *Child abuse: Implications for child development and psychopathology.* Newbury Park, CA: Sage Publications.

Wolfe, D. A. (1994). The role of intervention and treatment services in the prevention of child abuse and neglect. In G. B. Melton & F. D. Barry (Eds.), *Protecting children from abuse and neglect: Foundations for a new national strategy* (pp. 224–304). New York: Guilford Press.

Wolfe, D. A. (1999). *Child abuse: Implications for child development and psychopathology* (2nd ed.). Thousand Oaks, CA: Sage Publications.

Wolfe, D. A. (2001, July). *Interventions for physically abused children and adolescents.* Paper presented at the Second Biennial Niagara Conference on Evidence-Based Treatments for Childhood and Adolescent Mental Health Problems, Niagara-on-the-Lake, Canada.

Wolfe, D. A., Edwards, B., Manion, I., & Koverola, C. (1988). Early intervention for parents at-risk for child abuse and neglect: A preliminary investigation. *Journal of Consulting and Clinical Psychology, 56,* 40–47.

Wolfe, D. A., & McEachran, A. (1997). Child physical abuse and neglect. In E. J. Mash & L. G. Terdal (Eds.), *Assessment of childhood disorders* (3rd ed., pp. 523–568). New York: Guilford Press.

Wolfe, D. A., & McGee, R. (1994). Assessment of emotional status among maltreated children. In R. Starr & D. Wolfe (Eds.), *The effects of child abuse and neglect: Issues and research* (pp. 257–277). New York: Guilford Press.

Wolfe, D. A., & Sandler, J. (1981). Training abusive parents in effective child management. *Behavior Modification, 5,* 320–335.

Wolfe, D. A., Sandler, J., & Kaufman, K. (1981). A competency-based parent training program for child abusers. *Journal of Consulting and Clinical Psychology, 49,* 6333–6340.

Wolfe, D. A., & Wekerle, C. (1993). Treatment strategies for child physical abuse and neglect: A critical progress report. *Clinical Psychology Review, 13,* 473–500.

Wyatt, G. E. (1985). The sexual abuse of Afro-American and White-American women in childhood. *Child Abuse & Neglect, 9,* 507–519.

Zero To Three. (1994). *Diagnostic classification of mental health and developmental disorders of infancy and early childhood.* Washington, DC: Zero To Three: National Center for Infants, Toddlers and Families.

Zuravin, S. (1989). Severity of maternal depression and three types of mother-to-child aggression. *American Journal of Orthopsychiatry, 59,* 377–389.

Zuravin, S. J., & DiBlasio, F. A. (1996). The correlates of child physical abuse and neglect by adolescent mothers. *Journal of Family Violence, 11,* 149–166.

5

School Failure: An Eco-Interactional Developmental Perspective

*Jack M. Richman, Gary L. Bowen, and Michael E. Woolley**

Many students in public schools today experience difficulty adjusting to school and acquiring the social and academic skills necessary for pursuing advanced education and training. As a result, the opportunity for students to function successfully as adults in work and family roles is being jeopardized. With limited means and opportunities to achieve self-sufficiency through employment, many of these young adults are unable either to participate meaningfully in society or to find personal satisfaction and purpose. The rates of unemployment in 1999 were 52 percent higher for high school dropouts than for high school graduates (U.S. Department of Education, 2001). Poverty and welfare dependency become a way of life for many, especially for females and their children; almost half of families on welfare are headed by a school dropout (Bowen, Desimone, & McKay, 1995; Schwartz, 1995). For others, the future is even bleaker; for example, poor academic achievement has been associated with higher mortality rates, higher incidence of suicide, increased criminal behavior, higher incidence of intravenous drug use, and more frequent admissions to state mental hospitals (Kaplan & Peck, 1997; Kasen, Cohen, & Brook, 1998; Mahoney, 2000; Obot, Hubbard, & Anthony, 1999; Rumberger, 2004).

In addition to school dropout, we define school failure as inclusive of poor social and academic performance while a student is in school. Dropout may be the culmination of chronic school failure, but it is also possible that a student may stay in school while failing to display the necessary academic or social school involvement to achieve success. The effect of school failure has consequences for society as well as for the individual, including loss of national income, lower family and individual incomes, higher unemployment, loss of tax revenues, earlier involvement in sexual intercourse, higher risk of sexually transmitted disease, increased likelihood of school-age pregnancy, increased use of and demand for social services, increased crime, reduced political participation, and higher health care costs (Carnahan, 1994; Decker, Rice, Moore, & Rollefson, 1997; Manlove, 1998; U.S. Department of Education, 2001). In addition to these concerns, business leaders have noted that many students either graduate or leave

*The authors would like to thank the John S. and James L. Knight Foundation of Miami, Florida, and the BellSouth Foundation of Atlanta, Georgia, for their support of the development of the School Success Profile. The authors would also like to thank David Sheaves of the H. W. Odum Institute for Research in Social Science at the University of North Carolina at Chapel Hill and Lawrence Rosenfeld, professor in the Department of Communication Studies at the University of North Carolina at Chapel Hill, for their statistical assistance in preparing this chapter.

before graduation without the basic competencies to perform even rudimentary tasks in industry, much less to hold positions requiring more technical ability or knowledge (Slavin, Karweit, & Madden, 1988). Such a waste of human capital places a heavy burden on the U.S. economy and restricts this nation's competitiveness in the world economy. Helping to keep students in school and to promote academic success are critical steps toward promoting greater and more competent adult-role performance. These aims have important implications for children, the family system, the community, the economy, and the general well-being of society.

The heightened interest in school dropout and school success by researchers, politicians, educators, business and community leaders, and consumers comes at a time when dropout rates are declining. In 1900 roughly 4 percent of the population completed high school; by 1950 the school completion rate rose to 50 percent; and as of 1999 the high school completion rate for all adults 18 to 24 years old in the United States stood at approximately 86 percent (Carnahan, 1994; Kaufman, Kwon, Klein, & Chapman, 2000). Kaufman and colleagues (2000) estimated that in 1999 more than three in four students (77 percent) graduated from high school with a diploma while the remainder (23 percent) dropped out of school. Of those 18 to 24 year olds who did drop out, a portion eventually completed a GED or other high school equivalency, and when this group is included in the 1999 total high school completion rate, the 86 percent is reached.

This chapter focuses on the 23 percent of young adults who drop out of high school without receiving a diploma, as well as those who may remain in school but are not functioning adequately. High school completion is only one indicator of school success. Many students graduate from high school without the preparation needed for continuing their education or for successful entry into the job market (Decker et al., 1997; Warburton, Bugarin, Nunez, & Carroll, 2001). These students are not considered to be among the ranks of successful students and therefore are included in the focus of this chapter.

RATIONALE AND CHAPTER FOCUS

Given positive trends in high school completion for the past 100 years, why does school success remain an important concern in America today? As discussed earlier, school failure has severe consequences for individuals and society (Rumberger, 2004). The implications of not acquiring minimal high school competencies in the context of prevailing social and economic realities place young people in much greater jeopardy of failing to achieve the entry-level abilities necessary to function as competent adults in a complex society. Furthermore, school failure seems to affect poor and minority individuals at disproportionately higher rates than economically stable and nonminority populations. We will return to this point in a subsequent section of this chapter.

This chapter considers resiliency as being derived from a composite of protective factors that promote successful adaptation to the challenges and demands faced by children in school, in the family, in the neighborhood, and in the larger social environment. After discussing the concept of school failure and the profile of students most likely to experience difficulty in academic settings, an eco-interactional developmental (EID) perspective is used to explain variations in levels of educational resiliency.

At the center of an EID perspective is the person–environment fit, a dominant viewpoint in a variety of helping professions. Concepts from this perspective are used to discuss social structural experiences that may promote the development of resilience in children, and how these experiences can become the foci of prevention, early intervention, and remedial efforts to reduce school failure. Last, the development and implementation of the School Success Profile (SSP), an assessment instrument for guiding social work interventions for students at risk of school failure, is discussed.

NATURE OF THE PROBLEM

THE CONCEPT OF SCHOOL FAILURE

Although school dropout should not to be overlooked or minimized, it is only one manifestation of school failure. Large numbers of students stay in school but do not or cannot participate in ways that enable them to successfully acquire the requisite skills to function even at basic educational levels. Some researchers have postulated that the number of "academically marginal students" (Alpert & Dunham, 1986) or "interior dropouts" (Martz, 1992) is equal to the number of students who actually drop out of school (Martz, 1992). Alpert and Dunham (1986) define academically marginal students as those youths in school who display low attendance, low grade point average, and low achievement test scores. Therefore, the school failure problem is not only preventing school dropout, but also focusing on the larger issue of maximizing school success. As Wehlage and Rutter (1986) stated, "The problem is not simply to keep educationally at-risk youth from dropping out but, more importantly, to provide them with educationally worthwhile experiences" (p. 375).

Redefining the focus from dropping out to maximizing school success greatly increases the area of concern because it is inclusive of the total population of school-age youths, that is, school dropouts, academically marginal students (interior dropouts), and students who are currently functioning at acceptable educational levels or higher. In addition, the emerging issues surrounding the current emphases on end-of-year testing or high-stakes testing for students at all levels may apply pressure—individual and institutional—for students to leave school rather than to remain as marginal students who may not be promoted. Furthermore, these issues may encourage school administration to reconceptualize this type of "pressured" dropout as a necessary loss in an effort to raise the pass rate of the end-of-the-year test and heighten the academic rating of particular schools (Hauser, Simmons, & Pager, 2000).

Our perspective on school failure encompasses school dropout (physical absence), as well as poor attendance, psychological absence, low achievement, and grade retention. It is possible to construct a simple typology of school failure by treating physical presence and psychological involvement in school as dichotomous variables.[1] Physical school dropout is a dichotomous variable that assesses whether a student is physically enrolled (present) or withdrawn (absent). Poor attendance, low achievement, and grade retention are indicators of psychological investment in school.

This typology reveals four categories of students. The first group includes those students who have both physically and psychologically withdrawn from school.

---

[1]This typology is adapted from the work of Pauline Boss (1988) on boundary ambiguity.

For these students, dropping out of school merely formalized their psychological withdrawal, manifesting in poor attendance, low achievement, and grade retention. For example, data from the National Education Longitudinal Study (NELS) of 1988 suggest that a high percentage of students who leave school drop out, in part, because they are failing and could not keep up with their schoolwork (U.S. Department of Education, 1992). These students may be unlikely to return to a traditional school setting.

The second group involves students who physically drop out of school but who are psychologically invested in their education and who, while attending school, evidenced at least satisfactory academic progress. It is likely that these students drop out of school because of situational circumstances or structural constraints such as pregnancy. For example, a number of females who participated in NELS and who dropped out of school reported a family-related reason for dropping out of school; they became pregnant, became a parent, got married, or had to support the family or care for a family member (U.S. Department of Education, 1992). In the context of social support and encouragement, students in this group are likely either to return to school to complete their education or to pursue alternative educational opportunities.

Martz's (1992) label of "interior dropouts" perhaps best captures the next group of students, those who are physically enrolled in school but who are psychologically withdrawn. It is this group of students who often require the most resourcing by school officials and who, without intervention, are likely to join the first group of students.

The fourth group of students who represent what may be described as school success completes this logical typology—students who are both physically and psychologically involved in school. This cell provides a bridge to move from a pathological model of school failure to a salutogenic or strengths model of school success, which is oriented toward health, well-being, and successful coping (Antonovsky, 1991). An important goal of school-based interventions is to help students move from the first three groups into the fourth group or to move them successfully into alternative educational or career opportunities that will increase their economic prospects.

ASSESSMENT OF VULNERABILITY: A PROFILE OF SCHOOL FAILURE

Although no student is immune to school problems, certain students are more vulnerable to academic problems and poor psychosocial adjustment in school. One may identify specific demographic groups in which membership has been empirically shown to be a risk marker. Racial and ethnic minority youths, youths from lower socioeconomic families, and sexual minority youths experience higher rates of academic failure and dropping out. Students who are members of more than one of these groups may be at even greater risk of school failure due to cumulated risk factors. First, the issues of race and class will be considered.

RACE AND CLASS

Students from racial and ethnic minority groups and lower socioeconomic backgrounds possess two composite group effects that are highly confounded with one another and are related to other predictors of school failure, such as family structure (for example unemployed parents, parental education level, single-headed household, number of children residing in a household; Hauser et al., 2000; Mulkey, Crain, & Harrington, 1992). These contextual variables serve as proxy indicators for more specific situational and behavioral factors that are related to variation in school failure. Each variable is associated with the system of opportunities and constraints that individuals experience in society, as well as the normative system of values and beliefs that informs behavioral choices (Bowen & Pittman, 1995).

Rumberger (2004) summarized two explanations for the achievement gap among racial and ethnic groups: (1) a resource disparity perspective and (2) a sociocultural perspective. The resource disparity perspective holds that the discrepancy of personal and community resources and social capital may explain the higher school failure and dropout rates for racial and ethnic minorities. The sociocultural perspective suggests that variance across a culture, values, attitudes, beliefs, and behaviors concerning education, and a student's and family's role in supporting education can explain the gap in school success and achievement. For African American students, research suggests that racial identity, socialization (Miller & MacIntosh, 1999), and the parents' beliefs about education (Greif, Hrabowski, & Maton, 1998) have a protective effect on students' functioning.

In the following analysis of *Current Population Survey* data from the U.S. Census Bureau, we examine dropout rates as an indicator of school failure across racial or ethnic group and socioeconomic status (U.S. Census Bureau, 2000).[2]

Racial or Ethnic Group

When the percentages of 18 to 24 year olds who completed high school are compared by racial or ethnic group identity in 1979, 1989, and 1999, small increases are evident in the high school graduation rates of white, black, and Hispanic students (see Figure 5-1). Although a higher proportion of white students (91.2 percent) continues to graduate from high school than either black students (83.5 percent) or Hispanic students (63.4 percent), black students have shown the largest percentage gain over the 20-year time period (10.9 percent increase). The comparative increase for white and Hispanic students was 4.6 percent and 4.9 percent, respectively. It should be noted that these high school completion rates include students who graduate from high school with a diploma as well as those youths who pursue alternative methods of completing a high school equivalency (for example, a GED).

Figure 5-2 depicts the rates of high school dropout for all 16 to 24 year olds by race or ethnicity. This measure of dropout is called *status dropout* because it "provides cumulative data on dropouts among all young adults within a specified age range" (Kaufman et al., 2000, p. 2). It is clear from Figure 5-2 that overall minority youth drop

---

[2]Gender is not a major correlate of school failure and therefore is not included in the body of this discussion. There has been a steady upward trend in the past 20 years for both male and female students in grades 10 to 12 to stay in school. Females completed high school at a slightly higher rate in 1999 (87.1 percent vs. 84.8 percent). Female and male students did not differ in their dropout rates (approximately 5 percent event rate) for 1999 (Kaufman, Kwon, Klein, & Chapman, 2000).

Figure 5-1

High School Completion Rates of 18 to 24 Year Olds (Who Are Not Currently Enrolled in School), by Race and Ethnicity

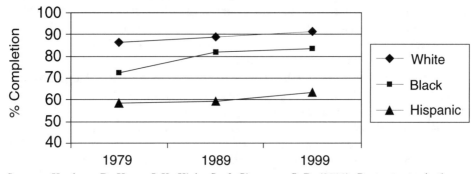

SOURCE: Kaufman, P., Kwon, J. Y., Klein, S., & Chapman, C. D. (2000). *Dropout rates in the United States: 1999.* Washington, DC: U.S. Department of Education.

out in greater percentages than white youths. Over the past 20 years, white and black youth have had lower dropout rates (7.3 percent and 12.6 percent in 1999, respectively) than Hispanic youths (28.6 percent), who continue to drop out at more than twice the rate of black youths and nearly four times the rate of white youths.

In considering the relationship between recent immigration status, language, and school success or failure, Frase (1992) argued that many Hispanic students face special challenges in school that help explain their lower graduation rates. Frase showed that 45 percent of the Hispanic population between the ages of 16 and 24 in 1989 were born outside the United States. In addition, Frase noted that 73.9 percent of Hispanics

Figure 5-2

Rates of High School Dropout for All 16 to 24 Year Olds, by Race and Ethnicity

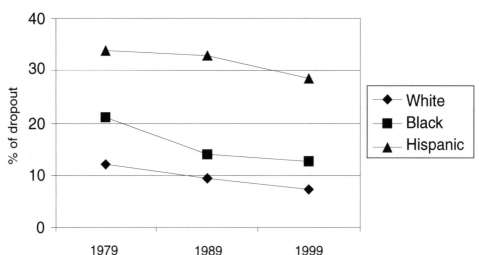

SOURCE: Kaufman, P., Kwon, J. Y., Klein, S., & Chapman, C. D. (2000). *Dropout rates in the United States: 1999.* Washington, DC: U.S. Department of Education.

in the same age range in 1992 reported that Spanish was the language spoken in their homes. Kaufman and colleagues (2000) found that in 1999 the dropout rate for Hispanic youths ages 16 to 24 who were immigrants to the United States was 44.2 percent, and the rate for Hispanic youths born within the United States was 16.1 percent. On balance, the data suggest that race and ethnicity are highly associated with school failure. Progress is being made in closing the achievement gap, with black youths making the greater strides. Although Figures 5-1 and 5-2 suggest that the trends are in a positive direction, much remains to be achieved.

Socioeconomic Status

Figure 5-3 illustrates the association between socioeconomic status (SES) and *event dropout*. Event dropout is "the proportion of students who leave school each year without completing a high school program. This annual measure of recent dropout occurrences provides important information about how effective educators are in keeping students enrolled in school" (Kaufman et al., 2000, p. 2). In Figure 5-3, SES is divided into three categories: (1) low (bottom 20 percent of all family incomes), (2) middle (middle 60 percent of all family incomes), and (3) high (upper 20 percent of all family incomes). Across the four successive cohorts of students (1973, 1983, 1993, and 1999) who were in grades 10 to 12 and between ages 15 and 24, a smaller proportion of low SES students, as compared with their middle and higher SES counterparts, maintained continuous enrollment from the previous October to the subsequent October. Further, Figure 5-3 suggests that while the continuous enrollment differential between the

Figure 5-3

Percentage of Students in Grades 10 to 12, Ages 15 to 24, Enrolled the Previous October Who Were Enrolled Again the Following October, By Family Income

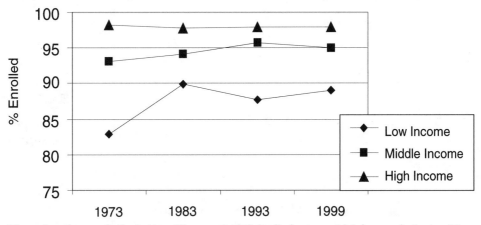

NOTE: Low income is the bottom 20 percent of all family incomes; high income is the top 20 percent of all family incomes; middle income is the 60 percent in-between.

SOURCE: Kaufman, P., Kwon, J. Y., Klein, S., & Chapman, C. D. (2000), *Dropout rate in the United States: 1999.* Washington, DC: U.S. Department of Education.

middle and high family income students is closing, the gap between the middle and high family income students and the low family income students is consistent, in that the low-income students always exhibit a higher rate of dropout.

In 1990 the President of the United States was joined by the governors of the 50 states in issuing educational goals for the United States to meet by the year 2000. Among these goals was a demand to meet a 90 percent standard for graduation rates for all students (U.S. Department of Education, 1990). Although Figure 5-3 suggests that the nation is close to realizing this goal, children and youths who are in the lowest 20 percent family income bracket have not yet reached and maintained this standard. A stable and sufficient family income is likely to provide children with a set of experiences, as well as opportunities and resource bases, that reinforce the importance of education and an orientation toward the future (see chapter 2; U.S. Department of Education, 1995).

In discussing the relationship among racial or ethnic group identity, SES, and school dropout, Wehlage and Rutter (1986) considered the relationship between racial or ethnic group identity and school failure to be spurious, explained by the association between racial or ethnic group identity and SES. After adjusting for SES, they concluded that the relationship between racial or ethnic group identity and school dropout disappeared. From data provided by the U.S. Census Bureau (2000), dropout rates among youth ages 16 to 24 by family income and race or ethnicity were compared, and the results are supportive of Wehlage and Rutter's conclusion. As seen in Figure 5-4, racial or ethnic group differences diminish as family income increases. Dropout rates for white, black, Hispanic, and Asian/Pacific Islander youths from high-income families are 2.1 percent, 2.4 percent, 4.1 percent, and 0 percent, respectively; only 4.1 percent sep-

Figure 5-4

Event Dropout, by Race, Ethnicity, and Family Income

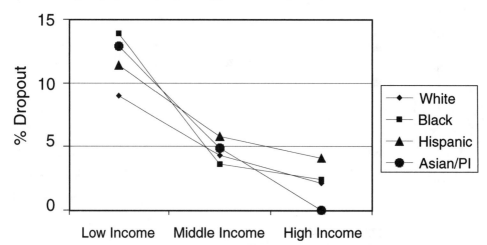

NOTE: Low income is the bottom 20 percent of all family incomes; high income is the top 20 percent of all family incomes; middle income is the 60 percent in-between.

SOURCE: U.S. Census Bureau (2000), *Current population survey*, October 1999. Washington, DC: Author.

arates the lowest from the highest group. For low-income families, the 1999 dropout percentages are shown in Figure 5-4 as 9.0 percent, 13.9 percent, 11.4 percent, and 12.9 percent, respectively. The lowest and highest groups are differentiated by 4.9 percent. The greatest reduction in dropout rates for all racial or ethnic groups was between the low family income categories and the rates for the middle family income groups. Clearly, for white, black, Hispanic, and Asian/Pacific Islander students the higher the income, the lower the dropout rate.

Gay, Lesbian, Bisexual, and Transgender Students

Sexual minority students, or gay, lesbian, bisexual, and transgender (GLBT) youths, comprise a third demographic group in which membership serves as a risk marker. GLBT youths have recently drawn increased attention from researchers and school practitioners as experiencing higher rates of multiple risk factors for school failure. Among the risk factors identified as affecting GLBT youths are harassment, social isolation, stigmatization, violence, family disruption, depression, suicide, substance abuse, homelessness, and general health problems (Lock & Steiner, 1999; Marinoble, 1998; McFarland & Dupuis, 2001). Given this list of risk factors affecting multiple developmental domains—social, psychological, familial, and physical—it is not surprising GLBT students experience a higher rate of school failure.

Many of the risk factors affecting GLBT youths appear to share the common etiology of homophobia and heterosexism. GLBT students often experience the effect of homophobia or heterosexism as conflict with their families and as harassment by peers at school and other settings. Psychological and physical health problems may result when conflict and oppression are internalized.

Although few schools would tolerate hate speech or behavior toward racial, ethnic, or religious minorities, words such as "queer" and "fag" continue to be heard regularly in our nation's schools (Smith & Smith, 1998). A setting that tolerates harassment or worse of GLBT students supports an environment for negative outcomes including school dropout. Several authors describe a pattern in which school personnel ignore, discount, or even participate in the harassment and rejection of GLBT students (Anderson, 1997; Fontaine, 1998; Smith & Smith, 1998). In the context of identifying programs to reduce harassment of GLBT students, Henning-Stout, James, and Macintosh (2000) proposed a three-level definition of harassment, including individual, group, and sociocultural harassment. Individual and group harassment are self-explanatory, and all groups who are marginalized within a setting suffer from this form of harassment, including GLBT students. However, sociocultural harassment occurs in an environment in which "overt and covert . . . negative and harmful stereotypes about homosexual people" (Henning-Stout et al., 2000, p. 182) are left unrecognized or unchecked by those in positions of authority.

RISK FACTORS AND SCHOOL FAILURE

Risk can be broadly defined by "the presence of one or more factors or influences that increase the probability of a negative outcome for a child or youth" (Richman & Fraser, 2001, p. 2). These risk factors may have a biological or ecological etiology or a combined biopsychosocial origin. Therefore, risk may be conceptualized as individual attributes or conditions existing within the environment. At the individual level, conditions include biological factors (for example, attention deficit and hyperactivity disorder, low birthweight) and individual social characteristics (for example, having a risk-taking temperament). Ecological or contextual factors include parental loss (for example, divorce, separation or death) and living in an impoverished neighborhood with a high crime rate (see chapter 2 for a full discussion of risk, protection, and resiliency). Identifying which risk factors or cumulation of factors are correlated with or predictive of negative school outcomes for children and youth is critical to developing effective interventions for impacting school failure (Richman & Fraser, 2001).

One of the more important developments in research examining school-related outcomes is the increasing emphasis by researchers on risk factors in the social context (Nash & Bowen, 1999; Pollard, Hawkins, & Arthur, 1999). This includes risk factors at multiple levels in the ecology of the student, including the family, the peer group, the school, and the neighborhood. When school failure is viewed in context rather than by focusing only on the demographic and personal characteristics of students, the focus shifts from profiling the individual to addressing broader situational concerns.

Recent research examining the relationship between risk factors in the neighborhood and school-related outcomes is a case in point. For example, Bowen and Bowen (1999) found that students' reports of neighborhood danger were associated with their self-reported attendance, trouble avoidance at school, and grades. As reports of neighborhood danger increased, students' difficulties increased. In a subsequent analysis, Bowen, Bowen, and Ware (2002) presented evidence showing that neighborhood social disorganization exerts a direct negative effect on educational behavior and an indirect negative effect through decreasing supportive parenting behavior and educational support from parents.

Research is helping not only to identify aspects of the social environment associated with school failure, but also to determine for whom and under what circumstances these social contextual factors pose more challenge. Bowen and Bowen (1999) noted that students experiencing the highest level of neighborhood and school danger are those of color, those from families who struggle economically, and those who live in urban areas—characteristics that are highly confounded. Continued research is needed to identify the risk profiles of students at highest risk of school failure; the operation and interaction of risk factors over time for specific groups of students, including the operation of complex risk chains; and the protective factors buffering the impacts of specific risk factors on school outcomes.

BEATING THE ODDS

Of course, not all students who may possess one or more of the risk factors related to school failure actually experience school failure. Whatever their respective adversities, the majority of students graduate from high school, including GLBT youth and lower-income Hispanic and black youths. In recent years, there has been increasing attention paid to those students who seem to "beat the odds" (Wang, Haertel, & Walberg, 1994, p. 46). In the search for protective factors that buffer the potential effects of risks and promote the positive adaptation of individuals, the concept of *resilience* has been introduced as a psychological construct (Garmezy, 1993; Wang et al., 1994).

A number of behavioral and social scientists have offered nominal definitions of resiliency. Garmezy (1993) suggested that "the central element in the study of resilience lies in the power of recovery and in the ability to return once again to those patterns of adaptation and competence that characterized the individual prior to the pre-stress period" (p. 129). Vance (2001) defined resiliency as "the ability of a person to rise above significant adversity and have a reasonably successful life course, avoiding serious psychiatric disorder, substance abuse, criminality, or social–relational problems" (p. 44). In some cases, authors have attempted to provide more situation-specific definitions of resiliency. For example, Wang and colleagues (1994) defined educational resilience as "the heightened likelihood of success in school and other life accomplishments, despite environmental adversities brought about by early traits, conditions, and experiences" (p. 46). Perhaps the critical part of many of these perspectives on resilience is that resilience is fashioned and exists in the presence of risk or adversity; this idea is consistent with the broad definition of resilience offered by Richman and Fraser (2001), which states that "Resilience is not necessarily based on individual characteristics; it occurs at the nexus of high risk and exceptional resources, whether these resources are personal or environmental in nature" (p. 7).

TOWARD A NOMINAL DEFINITION OF RESILIENCY

If resiliency is a major discriminator between at-risk students who succeed at school and those who do not, it seems critical for the purposes of intervention to better understand variations in this variable. Clinicians need to be able to identify individual and ecological characteristics that have a high potential for building and supporting resilience. Practitioners can then develop strategies of intervention that target the development and maintenance of these characteristics of resilience.

Resiliency is defined for this review as a general frame of reference through which individuals appraise and react to events and situations in the environment. It allows children and youths, when confronted with stressful situations, to construct socially adverse situations as challenges and opportunities and to access adequate amounts of available individual and environmental resources. Resiliency is demonstrated and becomes observable as youth respond with understanding, confidence, persistence, and resourcefulness in rebounding from the consequences of adversities through environmental mastery and individual adaptation.

As reflected in the work of Benard (1991, p. 2), the elements or characteristics that comprise this resilient frame of reference may include the following: social competence, autonomy, a sense of purpose, contextual factors, and problem-solving skills (Benard, 1991; Wang, Haertel, & Walberg, 1999). Social competence involves individual flexibility as well as the ability to demonstrate empathy, communicate effectively, and express the facility to develop positive relationships with adults and peers. Autonomy includes individual feelings of self-esteem, self-efficacy, and self-discipline. A sense of purpose consists of the ability to be planful, to be goal directed, and to maintain healthy expectations. Contextual factors include perceptions of living in a safe environment—home, school, and neighborhood—and having accessible and supportive peers and adults. Problem-solving skills allow youths to evidence some control over their ecology, exercise planfulness, and develop a variety of potentially successful solutions to various problematic issues. This frame of reference relates to both internal and external factors and realities in the life of a child or youth. The characteristics of resiliency can help focus practitioners as they consider strategies of intervention that will build resilience and support school success.

Our definition of resiliency parallels definitions of similar constructs in the literature, including Antonovsky's (1991) "sense of coherence," Bandura's (1986) "self-efficacy," Kobasa's (1979) "hardiness," and Rotter's (1975) "locus of control" (see Antonovsky, 1991, for a discussion of the similarities and distinctions among these concepts). Each of these related constructs reflects a salutogenic perspective, which focuses attention on explaining health and well-being, as compared with sickness and pathology. Like resiliency, each is best understood in the context of specific stressors that are faced by the individual at particular points in the life span (Rutter, 2001). A sense of coherence, self-efficacy, hardiness, and locus of control may be conceptualized as manifest indicators of resiliency—an approach similar to that used by Benard (1991) in describing the profile of the resilient child. This may be an especially attractive idea because operational measures have been developed for each of these related constructs.

Why are some children more resilient than others when confronted with stressors and risk factors in their environments? Newspapers are filled with stories about children who somehow seem to rise above their problematic situations. However, there are also stories about other children who fail to thrive or fall victim to in even the most advantageous situations. How do we understand such differences in the outcomes that children experience? The following discussion of the EID perspective attempts to address this issue of individual differences.

AN ECO-INTERACTIONAL DEVELOPMENTAL PERSPECTIVE

The study of individual differences has been informed by two rich traditions in the behavioral and social sciences: the "human factors" approach and the "situational" approach. The human factors approach focuses attention on the more or less stable and enduring features of individuals, including needs, values, expectations, beliefs, motives, traits, feelings, abilities, and attitudes (see Chatman, 1989). From this perspective, individual outcomes are best understood as reflecting variations in the internal characteristics of individuals.

From the "situational" perspective, individual differences are understood through viewing persons in the context of the social structures that inform their individual orientations and behavioral choices (Bowen & Pittman, 1995). Such biographic, social, political, economic, and historical forces are typically viewed as more dynamic than individual-level features and, therefore, more open to change and intervention.

Although studies of resiliency reflect both "human factors" and "situational" perspectives, it is increasingly recognized that the development of explanatory models of resiliency requires the study of both the additive and interactive nature of individual and situational variables. In social work and other fields, the interplay between the features of individuals and the features of their situations is often captured from a person-environment fit or interactional perspective.

Yet, to fully comprehend this complex interplay, it is necessary to conceptualize the nature of the situation beyond the immediate environments of the individual (for example, neighborhood, school, friends, and family) to include broader structural and normative influences (Bowen & Richman, 2002). Such a viewpoint is perhaps best seen in the ecological approach (Bronfenbrenner, 1979; Garbarino, 1992; Germain & Gitterman, 1995). Also, the nature of person and environment fit must be conceptualized as dynamic to reflect how the individual and the situation, as well as their interaction, change and evolve over time—a developmental or transactional perspective. Last, an understanding of resilience requires more than an understanding of risk factors. The balancing and moderating influence of assets and protective factors is also an important focus—a salutogenic perspective. Each of these aspects of the EID perspective is discussed below.

AN INTERACTIONAL PERSPECTIVE

An interactional perspective focuses on the "goodness of fit" between the characteristics of individuals and the characteristics of their environments. Goodness of fit is a variable that ranges from favorable to unfavorable, and its evaluation is made in the context of the individual's development and within the broader sociocultural-historical milieu (Germain & Gitterman, 1995). The EID perspective assumes that resiliency is a consequence of favorable goodness of fit over time, which "promotes continued development and satisfying social functioning and sustains or enhances the environment" in the presence of adversity (Germain & Gitterman, 1995, p. 817).

At least two levels of "fit" can be specified: needs–supplies and demands–competencies (Caplan, 1987; French, Caplan, & Harrison, 1982). First, individuals have certain needs related to their physical and psychological survival. For example, Maslow's (1954) hierarchy includes needs that are physiological, social, and affiliative, as well as needs for safety and security, esteem and recognition, and self-actualization. Maslow suggested that individuals are motivated to meet these needs and that needs at a higher level are not motivating until needs at the lower level are satisfied. The first type of fit considers these needs in the context of the opportunities, resources, and supplies available in the environment to meet them: the needs–supplies fit. It is likely, for example, that few children "beat the odds" in environments—such as those living in war-torn countries—that are so chaotic that basic needs for safety and security cannot be guaranteed.

The second type of fit considers the level of congruency between demands and requirements from the environment and a child's competencies, capacities, and skills for meeting these demands: the demands–competencies fit. Like their adult counterparts, children occupy social positions (for example, student) that have associated expectations for performance that tend to become more ambitious as children move across the developmental life span. At the same time, children have certain competencies at particular developmental points that are based on the interplay of heredity, learning, and maturation. A goodness of fit is achieved when children are faced with demands from their environment that are appropriate to their abilities. It is important to note that environments may be both overdemanding as well as underdemanding in the context of a child's abilities. Children who lack the competencies to meet environmental demands may experience feelings of self-doubt, frustration, hopelessness, and despair. However, children who face situations that fail to challenge them and mobilize their skills and capabilities may experience boredom. They may seek out experiences that have negative implications for their development, personal well-being, and social functioning, as well as negative implications for their host communities. In either of these incongruous situations, prevailing over adversity—resilience—is unlikely.

These two types of person–environment fit are not necessarily independent from one another. For example, Kulik, Oldham, and Hackman (1987, p. 179) concluded that "reducing the demands of the environment in order to provide a better match with the person's abilities may result in a lessened capacity of that environment to satisfy the person's needs for growth and development." It is also important to distinguish between the objective reality and the reality as perceived by the child (Caplan, 1987). Children's views of themselves as well as perceptions of their environments may be more or less congruent with assessments by independent observers. Yet, it is the subjective reality to which children respond and which forms the basis for their development of resiliency. Last, the nature of person–environment fit must be seen as dynamic. Both the environment and the child change over time. We can think of child development as the efforts of children and their parents to find the best level of fit between themselves and their environments in the context of developmental tasks (Germain & Gitterman, 1995).

AN ECOLOGICAL PERSPECTIVE

Encompassing the process of mutual adaptation and accommodation that takes place between individuals and their environment, a person–environment fit perspective, by definition, reflects an ecological approach. Bronfenbrenner (1979) conceptualized the environment as a set of four regions, each of which is embedded within the next and defined from the perspective of their proximity to the individual: microsystem, mesosystem, exosystem, and macrosystem. Risks and protective factors operate at each level.

The microsystem is the environment in which the person directly participates and interacts (activities, roles, and relationships), such as neighborhood, school, family, and friends (Bronfenbrenner, 1979). Because children's experiences in the microsystem most directly shape their views of the world and are incorporated into their beliefs about self (Garbarino, 1992), events in the microsystem play a decisive role in contributing to the development of resiliency in children.

The mesosystem represents the connections between the microsystems in which children participate. Bronfenbrenner (1979, p. 25) noted that the mesosystem "comprises the interrelations among two or more settings in which the developing person actively participates." An important mesosystem for adolescents is the relationship between their parents and friends. Strong and positive connections between various microsystems provide a supportive context for the child's development; weak connections or the existence of value conflicts between various microsystems may place the child at a disadvantage to develop those attitudes and behaviors that are associated with developmental success.

The child does not directly participate in the next setting, the exosystem; however, events in the exosystem reverberate to influence situations and circumstances in the microsystem. Bronfenbrenner (1979, p. 25) defined the exosystem as "one or more settings that do not involve the developing person as an active participant, but in which events occur that affect, or are affected by, what happens in the setting containing the developing person." For example, a sibling's experience at school or a parent's experience at work will impact the developing youth even though the child does not directly participate in the specific environment.

The macrosystem is the most distal environment from the developing child and reflects the broad ideological and institutional patterns in society. It is important to underscore that the "environment" goes beyond the immediate environments that individuals inhabit to also include the economic, political, and sociocultural environments (Jessor, 1993). Forces in the environment that limit opportunities for children or weaken the operation of environments at the lower levels (for example, national policies that tolerate families living in poverty) place a child at developmental risk and provide a poor context for the development of resiliency.

A Developmental Perspective

From a developmental perspective, children are not passive agents within their environments. They act, as well as react, in response to their surroundings. The nature of this interaction and its consequences for the individual and society must be understood from a perspective that captures the dynamic interplay between individuals and their environments over time. Masten and colleagues (1999) operationalized resilience as an adaptive response to a threat to healthy development, which involves an interplay between the characteristics of individuals and their environment. This continuous interaction between individual and environmental forces over the course of a child's physical, cognitive, emotional, and social development provides the context and experiences for the development of resiliency.

From a developmental perspective, it is important to focus on the timing as well as the nature of events in a child's life (Rutter, 1989). For example, the ability of children to understand and cope with parental divorce depends in part on their developmental maturity (Richman, Chapman, & Bowen, 1995). Events that happen at nonnormative times, such as pregnancy during the teenage years, may spill over to disrupt progress along parallel trajectories. For example, a pregnancy may lead to a school change or changes in peer relationships.

A developmental perspective focuses attention not only on the present, but also on the past and the anticipated future. Children and youth have a developmental past, a history that informs and constrains their present situation. Children who have been abused or neglected may carry emotional scars into future relationships with adults. Children and youth also have some level of future orientation and anticipation about their lives, which may be imbued with positive or negative expectations. Some students who drop out of school may see little chance of graduating in the context of their current performance. The dynamic pushes and pulls from past experiences and future expectations provide an important context in which children experience the present.

A Salutogenic Perspective

A salutogenic perspective addresses factors that push children toward positive outcomes, like resilience. This perspective, which is similar to the strengths perspective in social work (Cohen, 1999; Delgado, 1997), helps counterbalance a focus on risk factors alone by addressing assets and protective factors that increase the probability that children will experience healthy developmental outcomes. Researchers have devoted a significant amount of attention to identifying and classifying protective factors associated with positive outcomes when children are confronted with risk. As discussed in Chapter 2, these protective factors cluster into three categories: (1) individual temperamental qualities, (2) family affective characteristics, and (3) external support network characteristics (Waller, 2001; Werner, 1990).

Of the many protective factors and processes that have been associated with helping children overcome or avoid negative outcomes associated with exposure to risk, support from adults has been identified across a number of investigations as one of the more important protective factors in the adaptation of children (Nash & Bowen, 1999; Richman, Rosenfeld, & Bowen, 1998). The critical role of parents and adult caregivers in fostering children's development and ability to overcome life's adversities (Steinberg, 2001), the "centrality of the teacher" in supporting student achievement (Rosenfeld, Richman, & Bowen, 2000), and the critical role of neighbors as supportive resources and agents of social control in child development (Bowen, Bowen, & Cook, 2000) affirm an additive model of support and the importance of multiple and diverse adults in the lives of children.

In sum, the EID perspective provides a broad conceptual lens from which to view resiliency as a dynamic construct. It also offers clues about the types of experiences that may promote the development of resiliency in childhood, which is viewed from the perspective of this chapter both as directly associated with school success and as a buffer between individual and situational risk factors and school success.

IMPLICATIONS FOR ASSESSMENT, PREVENTION, AND INTERVENTION

The domains that are regularly identified in the research as capable of promoting educational resilience—if functional and serving as areas of strengths—include the individual, the family, the peer group, the school, and the community (Benard, 1991; Wang, Haertel, & Walberg, 1999). Practitioners interested in intervening with students who are at risk of school failure might find it helpful, from an EID viewpoint, to work mutually with the client to make an assessment of the individual student (addressing values, beliefs, skills, and competencies, for example); his or her interactions within environmental contexts; and his or her developmental stage. The goal is to begin to develop interventions that support and strengthen the student individually and the microsystems in which the student is embedded. The most efficient course for the practitioner is to attempt to intervene in the social environment to effect change in the individual student; that is, the practitioner should work with the family, peer group, school, and community to produce positive change and help promote the development of resiliency. As discussed by Antonovsky (1991), the environment must provide the student with three types of protective conditions—(1) stability, (2) load balance, and (3) participation.

STABILITY

Stable, close, and caring relationships between parent and child, as well as the supportiveness of relationships that children experience with others outside of the family, play a crucial role in the development of resiliency (Wang, Haertel, & Walberg, 1999;

Werner, 1990). Coleman (1988) referred to the strengths and supports that individuals have available from these relationships as *social capital*, a resource that may be accumulated and, if needed, mobilized in meeting internal needs and responding to external demands. Although the parent–child relationship is an important source of social capital for children, social capital may come from sources both within and outside the household environment as well as from linkages that exist between the microsystems in which children are embedded (Coleman, 1988; Rosenfeld, Richman, & Bowen, 2000). Supportive relationships between parents or adult caregivers and other adults in the lives of children hold the potential to provide consistency in norms and experiences, which creates a stable and secure foundation for child development.

LOAD BALANCE

Load balance for children and youths involves determining how well the demands of the environment fit with the capabilities of the individual student (Antonovsky, 1991). On the one hand, the ecosystem in which the student is embedded can provide care and support; on the other hand, it can be a source of risk and stress. Each youth may or may not possess the individual competencies or resources to respond to the stressors presented. For example, parent employment may require that a child be left at home without adult supervision for several hours after school. The concept of load balance has to do with whether or not the child is capable of managing that time alone. Rutter (1987) suggested that one way to achieve a good load balance is to shield children against risk factors in their environment. Other researchers (Chess, 1989) note that in situations where one environment is highly stressful (the family, perhaps) children often cope with this negative circumstance by seeking greater support from the other microsystems (for example, peers, teachers, or community).

PARTICIPATION

Research suggests that educational resiliency is encouraged and developed when children and youths who are at risk have opportunities to participate in and contribute to their environments in a meaningful way. When families, schools, peer groups, and communities communicate the expectation that youth can and will successfully handle their responsibilities and participate in valued ways, the youth respond by developing a sense of autonomy, independence, heightened social competence, and greater resilience (Benard, 1991; Wang et al., 1994). For example, recent research has highlighted the protective value of students' participation in school activities outside of class work (Mahoney, 2000). Werner and Smith (1982) described this sense of involvement and participation as developing and enabling the social relationships that provide meaning for life and a reason for caring.

The three characteristics of person–environment fit that promote positive developmental outcomes in children—(1) stability, (2) load balance, and (3) participation—can also provide keys to planning interventions. Together with a focus on the contextual areas of family, school, peers, and community, ideas of stability, load balance, and participation can help practitioners and educational specialists begin to design intervention strategies that strengthen children's social competencies, autonomy, sense of purpose, and problem-solving skills.

A PRACTICE PLANNING FORM: ASSESSMENT TO INTERVENTION

The Practice Planning Form (see Figure 5-5) can be used to inform the design of interventions to build resilience and to increase school success by promoting the development of protective conditions within multiple ecological contexts. A matrix may be constructed by crossing the four ecological domains (family, school, peer group, and community–neighborhood) with the three protective conditions (stability, load balance, and participation). The practitioner may plan strategies that affect each appropriate intersect and ultimately influence the resilience characteristics listed on the right of the Planning Form, which were adapted and expanded from the work of Benard (1991). For example, in the family-stability intersect the practitioner might plan interventions that attempt to enhance stability and caring within the family. In the school–participation intersect, the worker might intervene in an attempt to increase a student's meaningful participation in school activities. The important practice issue here is that the practitioner assesses the student's environment for areas of strength or potential and then works together with the student to develop practice strategies that target the identified intersect. The intent is to foster positive developmental outcomes for all children at risk to promote greater individual resilience. Examples of such targeted interventions are provided in Figure 5-5, in which each of the intersects is completed with a potential intervention strategy.

The interventions in the Practice Planning Form are provided as examples only. Practitioners, using their professional expertise and judgment, should assess the ecosystem, the client, and the client's developmental stage as appropriate. Mutually acceptable and developed interventions can then be planned and implemented to promote stability, load balance, and participation.

ASSESSING RISK AND PROTECTION: THE SCHOOL SUCCESS PROFILE

Professionals who attempt to intervene with their clients to foster resilience may need to evaluate their progress. Increasing such accountability can be a critical aspect of program planning and development. Assessment often helps to ensure that programs use resources in the most efficient and effective manner. A number of programs and products exist that provide ecological assessments of youths and their families for informing the design of intervention and prevention strategies. For example, Communities That Care (CTC; Hawkins, 1999) offers the CTC Youth Survey, which provides a youth needs assessment report; the report serves as a guide for building strong communities that can support children and families. The Search Institute (2003) also provides a survey for students and uses an asset-building model that results in the Profile of Student Life report, which can be used to develop relevant and appropriate programs and interventions that support students and families. Although many initia-

Figure 5-5

Practice Planning Form

Protective Conditions That Promote Resilience

Ecological Domains	Stability	Load Balance	Participation
Family	**Home Visit**—Intervene with family to develop more positive relationships between student and parent(s) or guardian(s). **Parenting Education**—Offer multifamily parenting skills training classes open to all parents of students. Instruct parents on importance of stability for healthy development.	**Teacher–Parent discussion**—Talk with students and parents about developing reasonable expectations regarding free time versus supervised/academically productive time. Consider negotiating a lower load balance of responsibility if, for example, an adolescent is working more than ten hours a week or is shouldering an exceedingly heavy child care responsibly for younger siblings	**Parent Days**—Organize special events at school that involve parents and their students. Early morning breakfast events like "Donuts with Dad" or "Muffins with Mom." **Home–School Communication**—Send letters home each week to update parents on progress, focusing on the positive academic, social or emotional behaviors.[a]
School	**Teacher and Staff Training**—At least once a year have a staff training day focused on the direct correlation between a student's positive relationship with teachers and staff and school success. Enthusiastically remind teachers and staff what a powerful protective factor they can be.	**Balancing Act**—Great teacher skill is required to assess the level of academic demands on a particular student that will maximize school success. Exceedingly high demands lead to frustration and failure; low demands sell students short of their potential. Students need high yet attainable academic challenges.	**Recognize Every Student Publicly**—Find something each student does well and provide recognition in front of the class or school. Find it, show it off, and give out certificates, awards, or ribbons. Especially useful for the students not ordinarily involved in activities like sports, the school play, or cheerleading.
Peer Group	**Social Support Group**—Organize support groups especially for at-risk kids. Include issues like pregnancy and parenting, GLBT, family stress, divorce, moving (for new kids), ADHD, or academic struggles. A "lunch group" for socially withdrawn kids both connects them socially and relieves the eating alone stress.	**Peer Group Stress Audit**—Work with students in groups to help them look at their peer involvement. What is gained by their current peer involvement (for example, feelings of belonging or support) and what stress might be increased because of current peer group affiliations (for example, exposure to violence, drugs, alcohol, or conflict with parents)?	**Encouraging Words**—Put a box up in the classroom with small forms to fill out. Any student who experiences support or something positive from another student can fill out a form and recognize it. The teacher can open the box on Fridays and read the slips out loud to the class. Kids with slips in the box can get some small reward.[a]
Neighborhood	**Volunteer Program**—Recruit adults from the neighborhood to spend time in the school on a regular basis. They can supervise fun activities, teach about what they do for a living, or engage the kids in public service projects around the school or immediate neighborhood. Mentoring will naturally occur.	**Neighborhood Safety Assessment**—Work with neighborhood leaders and stakeholders like parents, police, public housing administrators, mayor or city manager, churches, and community organizations to develop a list of common safety and neighborhood issues. Use this list to organize a neighborhood task force to generate solutions.	**Neighborhood Student Involvement**—Get students out into the neighborhood volunteering and helping others. Organizations like Habitat for Humanity, homeless shelters, senior citizens homes are great ways for youth to feel good about themselves by giving back and doing positive things for others.

Characteristics of Resiliency

Social Competence and Connectedness
- flexibility
- empathy and caring
- communication skills
- positive adult relationships
- prosocial peers

Autonomy
- sense of power
- self-esteem
- self-efficacy
- impulse control and self-discipline
- adaptive distancing

Sense of Purpose
- future plans
- healthy expectations
- internal locus-of-control
- goal directedness

Contextual Factors
- safe from bullying, teasing and social violence at school
- safe from physical violence in school and neighborhood
- supportive peers
- accessible supportive adults

Problem-Solving Skills
- alternative solutions
- planning
- impulse control

School Success

[a] Adapted with permission from techniques used by Kara A. Rosenfeld, a teacher at Efland-Cheeks Elementary School in Efland, North Carolina, and Mary C. Fletcher, a fifth-grade teacher at North Chatham School in Chapel Hill, North Carolina.

tives in schools continue to function without discernible outcome measures, the SSP (Bowen, Woolley, Richman, & Bowen, 2001) has proved highly useful for informing interventions and monitoring the progress of students over the school year.

In 1992 BellSouth Foundation awarded a grant to the School of Social Work at the University of North Carolina at Chapel Hill to collaborate with Communities-In-Schools (CIS) representatives at the national, state, and local levels to develop and field test assessment instruments that local CIS staff may use to monitor their success in achieving objectives. CIS is the largest private nonprofit network in the United States devoted to promoting high school graduation and success among students at risk of school failure. In 1995 the John S. and James L. Knight Foundation and in 2000 the National Institute for Drug Abuse (NIDA) joined the BellSouth Foundation as a stake-holders in this work. The SSP was developed as one such assessment instrument.

The SSP is a hard-copy, optical scan, survey questionnaire with 220 multiple-choice items designed to inform the process by which comprehensive programs of academic services, social services, and employment and life-skills training are pro-vided to middle school and high school students. The SSP is useful in monitoring changes in program participants over time, developing effective and responsive inter-vention programs, and increasing accountability to the major stakeholders. Although the SSP was designed in partnership with CIS, the survey is currently used in a vari-ety of educational settings. (For a more detailed description of applying the SSP to school intervention, see Bowen, Woolley, Richman, & Bowen, 2001.)

Consistent with an EID perspective, the SSP places emphasis on students' perceptions of their four primary microsystems: (1) neighborhood (35 items), (2) school (55 items), (3) friends (26 items), and (4) family (47 items). In addition, the survey includes modules assessing the demographic profile of students (nine items) and their health and well-being (48 items). Based on their responses, students receive a one-page summary (see Figure 5-6), which includes a Social Environment Profile and an Individual Adaptation Profile. Twenty-two core dimensions are currently assessed on the SSP, which have been associated in the literature with middle school and high school students' outcomes. Each dimension is assessed by a minimum of three sum-mary items.

The 14 social environmental dimensions (see Figure 5-6) are results that can be targeted for intervention and prevention planning as a means to influence student results associated with individual adaptation. Each dimension on the SSP has a positive label (for example, "Neighborhood Support") and scores on each dimension represent a continuum of protection ranging from red (potential risk) to yellow (some caution may be warranted) to green (potential asset). A student's score on a particular dimension is calculated by aggregating his or her answers to the questions in that particular scale. The ordinal, color-coded cutoffs for each dimension were determined based on compar-ison to national norms, criterion analysis, and expert review. Reference information about the school and child is included on the left side of the profile form.

Special care was taken to keep the wording of instructions and survey items and response formats simple, and to avoid highly sensitive subjects and questions that may violate community sensitivities. The SSP includes no questions about illegal behavior, substance abuse, sexual activities, or issues of child abuse that may place students or families in self-incriminating situations. Validity and reliability of the meas-ures on the SSP have been empirically supported across a number of research inves-

Figure 5-6

School Success Profile

Reference Information

Student ID: 1234567
Age: 14
Grade: 9th grade (Freshman)
Gender: Male
Race/Ethnicity African American

School: Sample school
District: Sample county
State: Sample state

Date Processed: May 24, 2002

Key	
●	Risk
○	Caution
◐	Asset

Individual Profile

Social Environment Profile

Neighborhood
Neighborhood support	○	Caution
Neighbor youth behavior	●	Risk
Neighborhood safety	●	Risk

School
School satisfaction	◐	Asset
Teacher satisfaction	●	Risk
School safety	●	Risk

Friends
Friend support	●	Risk
Peer group acceptance	○	Caution
Friend behavior	●	Risk

Family
Family togetherness	●	Risk
Parent support	●	Risk
Home academic environment	◐	Asset
Parent education support	◐	Asset
School behavior expectations	○	Caution

Individual Adaptation Profile

Personal Beliefs and Well-Being
Social support use	○	Caution
Physical health	◐	Asset
Happiness	●	Risk
Personal adjustment	●	Risk
Self-esteem	○	Caution

School Attitudes and Behavior
School engagement	○	Caution
Trouble avoidance	●	Risk

Academic Performance
Grades	◐	Asset

SOURCE: Bowen, G. L., & Richman, J. M. (2001). *School Success Profile.* Chapel Hill, University of North Carolina (Available http://www.uncssp.org/use_sampleindividualprofile.asp).

tigations (see Bowen & Bowen, 1999; Bowen, Bowen, & Cook, 2000; Bowen & Chapman, 1996; Bowen, Richman, Brewster, & Bowen, 1998; Nash, 2002; Nash & Bowen, 1999; Richman, Rosenfeld, & Bowen, 1998). A comprehensive assessment of reliability and validity of the SSP's 22 dimensions is also available (Bowen, Rose, & Bowen, 2003). In this assessment with 16,042 middle and high school students that included a diverse racial and ethnic group mix, 12 of the 22 dimensions had reliability coefficients above .80, demonstrating sufficiently high internal consistency reliability for their use in informing social worker practitioners about individual students. All but one of them had a reliability coefficient above .70. It is this characteristic that sets the SSP apart from other widely used youth assessment surveys.

The SSP is designed to yield both individual student profiles and site-level aggregate profiles, which include both Summary Group Profiles (a composite of Individual Profiles) and Detailed Group Profiles. The Detailed Group Profile provides information on 20 indicators of contextual risks, 20 indicators of social capital, and 20 indicators of internal assets. Summary indicators on the Detailed Group Profile are expressed in percentages (0 percent to 100 percent) and have demonstrated good discriminate validity in prior studies of personal adjustment, school attitudes and behavior, and academic performance. Information from the two group profiles allows practitioners to become aware of areas that may warrant group interventions and to plan change strategies in these areas. Yet, before using any results from the SSP for purposes of planning interventions, school-based practitioners are encouraged to meet with students who completed the SSP to discuss the group findings and their validity. Practitioners who wish to use the SSP must attend training that covers its administration, interpretation, and use for informing practice interventions and monitoring the effectiveness of such interventions.

The results are presented as one potential view into the life of the student, and practitioners are encouraged to carefully establish whether the findings have validity from the student's perspective by discussing the profiles with the student. The SSP is designed to augment the observations and dialogue that practitioners have with students on an ongoing basis. It is not a substitute for this process—it is designed to enhance and support this process. The intervention and monitoring form that accompanies the SSP helps the practitioner develop intervention plans with each student who completes the SSP. The form is designed to inform and monitor intervention activities that are directly connected to the SSP data profiles (contact first author to review a copy of this form).

The SSP may be administrated repeatedly; most often, the SSP is administered to students at the beginning and at the end of the academic year. These repeated administrations make it possible to calculate change scores for both aggregate group and individual profiles. The changes in scores allow practitioners to determine the extent to which their interventions are producing desired effects.

In response to requests from practitioners using the middle school and high school version of the SSP, an elementary school version of the survey (ESSP) is now being developed with funding from the National Institute on Drug Abuse (NIDA). The elementary school version will assess the same major domains as the current SSP, but will include items and language appropriate for third through fifth graders. To enhance its ability to sustain children's interest, the form will be computerized with graphics and audio features. Because of concerns about the reliability and validity of self-report data from young children, some ESSP data will be collected from parents and teachers. The elementary version will be rigorously tested throughout its development. The ESSP will allow school-based practitioners to address risk and protective factors known to be associated with adolescent behavior problems before the problems fully develop.

CONCLUSION

This chapter has attempted to accomplish the following five goals: (1) define the relationship between resiliency and school success, (2) provide a profile of school failure, (3) present the EID perspective as a theoretical viewpoint that helps in understanding individual variation in the level of resiliency as a factor in school success, (4) suggest a salutogenic practice framework that may be useful in developing strategies and interventions that will lead to greater resiliency in students, and (5) discuss the SSP, a comprehensive assessment instrument that has been useful in informing student-level interventions and evaluating and monitoring programs that attempt to promote school success.

Promoting school success for all youth involves developing, supporting, and maintaining safe, caring, and challenging environments in which students can fully participate. Such environments encourage a sense of acceptance and belonging, promote resilience, and help prepare students for adult roles. Unfortunately, many students face serious ecological disadvantages across multiple contexts. Continued efforts are needed to promote a social context in which at-risk students can build resiliency, succeed in school, and move successfully toward assuming adult roles and responsibilities.

REFERENCES

Alpert, G., & Dunham, R. (1986). Keeping academically marginal youths in school. *Youth & Society, 17*(4), 346–361.

Anderson, J. D. (1997). Students need to value diversity. *Education Digest, 63*(1), 20–23.

Antonovsky, A. (1991). The structural sources of salutogenic strengths. In C. L. Cooper & R. Payne (Eds.), *Personality and stress: Individual differences in the stress process* (pp. 67–104). Chichester, England: John Wiley & Sons.

Bandura, A. (1986). *Social foundations of thought and action: A social cognitive theory*. Englewood Cliffs, NJ: Prentice Hall.

Benard, B. (1991). *Fostering resiliency in kids: Protective factors in the family, school, and community*. Portland, OR: Western Center for Drug-Free Schools and Communities.

Bowen, G. L., Bowen, N. K., & Cook, P. G. (2000). Neighborhood characteristics and supportive parenting among single mothers. In G. L. Fox & M. L. Benson (Eds.), *Families, crime and criminal justice* (Vol. 2, pp. 183–206). New York: Elsevier.

Bowen, G. L., & Chapman, M. V. (1996). Poverty, neighborhood danger, social support, and the individual adaptation among at-risk youth in urban areas. *Journal of Family Issues, 17*, 641–666.

Bowen, G. L., Desimone, L. M., & McKay, J. K. (1995). Poverty and the single mother family: A macroeconomic perspective. *Marriage and Family Review, 20*(1/2), 115–142.

Bowen, G. L., & Pittman, J. F. (1995). Introduction. In G. L. Bowen & J. F. Pittman (Eds.), *The work and family interface: Toward a contextual effects perspective* (pp. 1–13). Minneapolis: National Council on Family Relations.

Bowen, G. L., & Richman, J. M. ([1997] 2001). School Success Profile. Chapel Hill: University of North Carolina at Chapel Hill, School of Social Work, Jordan Institute for Families.

Bowen, G. L., & Richman, J. M. (2002). Schools in the context of communities. *Children & Schools, 24*, 67–71.

Bowen, G. L., Richman, J. M., Brewster, A., & Bowen, N. (1998). Sense of school coherence, perceptions of danger at school, and teacher support among youth at risk of school failure. *Child and Adolescent Social Work Journal, 15*, 273–286.

Bowen, G. L., Rose, R. A., & Bowen, N. K. (2003). *The reliability and validity of the School Success Profile*. Chapel Hill: University of North Carolina at Chapel Hill.

Bowen, G. L., Woolley, M. E., Richman, J. M., & Bowen, N. K. (2001). Brief intervention in schools: The School Success Profile. *Brief Treatment and Crisis Intervention, 1*, 43–54.

Bowen, N. K., & Bowen, G. L. (1999). Effects of crime and violence in neighborhoods and schools on the school behavior and performance of adolescents. *Journal of Adolescent Research, 14*, 319–342.

Bowen, N. K., Bowen, G. L., & Ware, W. B. (2002). Neighborhood social disorganization, families, and the educational behavior of adolescents. *Journal of Adolescent Research, 17*, 468–490.

Bronfenbrenner, U. (1979). *The ecology of human development: Experiments by nature and design*. Cambridge, MA: Harvard University Press.

Caplan, R. D. (1987). Person–environment fit theory and organizations: Commensurate dimensions, time perspectives, and mechanisms. *Journal of Vocational Behavior, 31*, 248–267.

Carnahan, S. (1994). Preventing school failure and dropout. In R. J. Simeonsson (Ed.), *Risk, resilience, and prevention: Promoting the well-being of all children* (pp. 103–123). Baltimore: Paul H. Brookes.

Chatman, J. A. (1989). Improving interactional organizational research: A model of person–organization fit. *Academy of Management Review, 14*, 333–349.

Chess, S. (1989). Defying the voice of doom. In T. Dugan & R. Coles (Eds.), *The child in our times* (pp. 179–199). New York: Brunner/Mazel.

Cohen, B. Z. (1999). Intervention and supervision in strengths-based social work practice. *Families in Society, 80*(5), 460–466.

Coleman, J. S. (1988). Social capital in the creation of human capital. *American Journal of Sociology, 94*(Suppl.), S95–S120.

Decker, P. T., Rice, J. K., Moore, M. T., & Rollefson, M. R. (1997). *Education and the economy: An indicators report* (NCES 97-269). Washington, DC: U.S. Department of Education, National Center for Educational Statistics.

Delgado, M. (1997). Strengths-based practice with Puerto Rican adolescents: Lessons from a substance abuse prevention project. *Social Work in Education, 19*(2), 101–112.

Fontaine, J. H. (1998). Evidencing a need: School counselors' experiences with gay and lesbian students. *Professional School Counseling, 1*(3), 8–14.

Frase, M. (1992). *Are high Hispanic dropout rates a result of recent immigration?* Washington, DC: U.S. Department of Education, National Center for Education Statistics.

French, J.R.P., Jr., Caplan, R. D., & Harrison, R. V. (1982). *The mechanisms of job stress and strain*. Chichester, England: John Wiley & Sons.

Garbarino, J. (1992). *Child and families in the social environment*. New York: Aldine de Gruyter.

Garmezy, N. (1993). Children in poverty: Resilience despite risk. *Psychiatry, 56,* 127–136.

Germain, C. B., & Gitterman, A. (1995). Ecological perspective. In R. L. Edwards (Ed.-in-Chief), *Encyclopedia of Social Work* (19th ed., Vol. 1, pp. 816–824). Washington, DC: NASW Press.

Greif, G. L., Hrabowski, F. A., & Maton, K. I. (1998). African American fathers of high-achieving sons: Using outstanding members of an at-risk population to guide intervention. *Families in Society, 79*(1), 45–52.

Hauser, R. M., Simmons S. J., & Pager, D. I. (2000). *High school dropout, race-ethnicity, and social background from the 1970s to the 1990s* [Online]. Retrieved from http://www.ksg.harvard.edu/inequality/Summer/Summer01/papers/Hauser01.pdf on June 24, 2003.

Hawkins, J. D. (1999). Preventing crime and violence through Communities That Care. *European Journal on Criminal Policy and Research, 7,* 443–458.

Henning-Stout, M., James, S., & Macintosh, S. (2000). Reducing harassment of lesbian, gay, bisexual, transgender, and questioning youth in schools. *School Psychology Review, 29*(2), 180–191.

Jessor, R. (1993). Successful adolescent development among youth in high-risk settings. *American Psychologist, 48*(2), 117–126.

Kaplan, D. S., & Peck, B. M. (1997). Decomposing the academic failure-dropout relationship: A longitudinal analysis. *Journal of Educational Research, 90*(6), 331–343.

Kasen, S., Cohen, P., & Brook, J. S. (1998). Adolescent school experiences and dropout, adolescent pregnancy, and young adult deviant behavior. *Journal of Adolescent Research, 13*(1), 49–72.

Kaufman, P., Kwon, J. Y., Klein, S., & Chapman, C. D. (2000). *Dropout rates in the United States* (NCES 2001-022). Washington, DC: U.S. Department of Education, National Center for Education Statistics.

Kobasa, S. (1979). Stressful life events, personality, and health: An inquiry into hardiness. *Journal of Personality and Social Psychology, 37,* 1–11.

Kulik, C. T., Oldham, G. R., & Hackman, J. R. (1987). Work design as an approach to person-environment fit. *Journal of Vocational Behavior, 31,* 278–296.

Lock, J., & Steiner, H. (1999). Gay, lesbian, and bisexual youth risks for emotional, physical, and social problems: Results from a community-based survey. *Journal of the American Academy of Child and Adolescent Psychiatry, 38*(3), 297–304.

Mahoney, J. L. (2000). School extracurricular activity participation as a moderator in the development of antisocial patterns. *Child Development, 71*(2), 502–516.

Manlove, J. (1998). The influence of high school dropout and school engagement on the risk of school-age pregnancy. *Journal of Research on Adolescence, 8*(2), 187–220.

Marinoble, R. M. (1998). Homosexuality: A blind spot in the school mirror. *Professional School Counseling, 1*(3), 4–7.

Martz, L. (1992). *Making schools better*. New York: Times Books.

Maslow, A. (1954). *Motivation and personality*. New York: Harper & Row.

Masten, A. S., Hubbard, J. J., Scott, S. D., Tellegen, A., Garmezy, N., & Ramirez, M. (1999). Competence in the context of adversity: Pathways to resilience and maladaptation from childhood to late adolescence. *Development and Psychopathology, 11*, 143–169.

McFarland, W. P., & Dupuis, M. (2001). The legal duty to protect gay and lesbian students from violence in school. *Professional School Counseling, 4*(3), 171–180.

Miller, D. B., & MacIntosh, R. (1999). Promoting resilience in urban African American adolescents: Racial socialization and identity as protective factors. *Social Work Research, 23*(3), 159–169.

Mulkey, L. M., Crain, R. L., & Harrington, A. J. (1992). One-parent households and achievement: Economic and behavioral explanations of a small effect. *Sociology of Education, 65*, 48–65.

Nash, J. K. (2002). Neighborhood effects on sense of school coherence and educational behavior in students at risk of school failure. *Children & Schools, 24*, 73–89.

Nash, J. K., & Bowen, G. L. (1999). Perceived crime and informal social control in the neighborhood as a context for adolescent behavior: A risk and resilience perspective. *Social Work Research, 23*, 171–186.

Obot, I. S., Hubbard, S., & Anthony, J. C. (1999). Level of education and injecting drug use among African Americans. *Drug and Alcohol Dependence, 55*(1/2), 177–182.

Pollard, J. A., Hawkins, J. D., & Arthur, M. W. (1999). Risk and protection: Are both necessary to understand diverse behavioral outcomes in adolescence? *Social Work Research, 23*, 145–158.

Richman, J. M., Chapman, M. V., & Bowen, G. L. (1995). Recognizing the impact of marital discord and parental depression on children: A family centered approach. In W. L. Coleman & E. H. Taylor (Eds.), *Family focused pediatrics: Issues, challenges, and clinical methods* (pp. 167–180). Philadelphia: W. B. Saunders.

Richman, J. M., & Fraser, M. W. (2001). Resilience in childhood: The role of risk and protection. In J. M. Richman & M. W. Fraser (Eds.), *The context of youth violence: Resilience, risk, and protection* (pp. 1–12). Westport, CT: Praeger.

Richman, J. M., Rosenfeld, L. B., & Bowen, G. L. (1998). Social support for adolescents at risk of school failure. *Social Work, 43*, 309–323.

Rosenfeld, L. B., Richman, J. M., & Bowen, G. L. (2000). Social support networks and school outcomes: The centrality of the teacher. *Child and Adolescent Social Work, 17*, 205–226.

Rotter, J. B. (1975). Some problems and misconceptions related to the construct of internal versus external control of reinforcement. *Journal of Consulting and Clinical Psychology, 43*, 56–67.

Rumberger, R. W. (2004). What can be done to prevent and assist school dropouts? In P. Allen-Meares & M. W. Fraser (Eds.), *Intervention with children and adolescents: An interdisciplinary perspective* (pp. 311–334). Boston: Allyn & Bacon.

Rutter, M. (1987). Psychosocial resilience and protective mechanisms. *American Journal of Orthopsychiatry, 57*, 316–331.

Rutter, M. (1989). Pathways from childhood to adult life. *Journal of Child Psychology and Psychiatry, 30*(1), 23–51.

Rutter, M. (2001). Psychosocial adversity: Risk, resilience, and recovery. In J. M. Richman & M. W. Fraser (Eds.), *The context of youth violence: Resilience, risk, and protection* (pp. 13–43). Westport, CT: Praeger.

Schwartz, W. (1995). *School dropouts: New information about an old problem* (No. 109, ERIC Digest). New York: ERIC Clearinghouse on Urban Education.

The Search Institute. (2003). *The updated profiles of student life: attitudes and behaviors dataset* [Online]. Retrieved from http://www.search-institute.org/research/assets/UpdatedData.html on June 30, 2003.

Slavin, R. E., Karweit, N. L., & Madden, N. A. (1988). *Effective programs for students at risk*. Boston: Allyn & Bacon.

Smith, G. W., & Smith, D. E. (1998). The ideology of "fag": The school experience of gay students. *Sociological Quarterly, 39*(2), 309–335.

Steinberg, L. (2001). We know some things: Parent-adolescent relationships in retrospect and prospect. *Journal of Research on Adolescence, 11*, 1–19.

U.S. Census Bureau (2000, October). *Current population survey October 1999* [Data]. Washington, DC: Author. Retrieved from http://www.bls.census.gov/cps/

U.S. Department of Education, National Center for Education Statistics (1988, 1990, 1992). *National Education Longitudinal Study of 1988, First Followup Survey, 1990, Second Followup Survey, 1992*, unpublished data. Washington, DC: U.S. Government Printing Office.

U.S. Department of Education, National Center for Education Statistics. (1995). In A. M. Livingston & S. Miranda (Eds.), *The condition of education, 1995*. Washington, DC: Author.

U.S. Department of Education, National Center for Education Statistics (2001). *Digest of education statistics, 2000*. Washington, DC: U.S. Government Printing Office.

Vance, J. E. (2001). Neurobiological mechanisms of psychosocial resiliency. In J. M. Richman & M. W. Fraser (Eds.), *The context of youth violence: Resilience, risk, and, protection* (pp. 43–82). Westport, CT: Praeger.

Waller, M. A. (2001). Resilience in ecosystemic context: Evolution of the concept. *American Journal of Orthopsychiatry, 71*, 290–297.

Wang, M. C., Haertel, G. D., & Walberg, H. J. (1994). Educational resilience in inner cities. In M. C. Wang & E. W. Gordon (Eds.), *Educational resilience in inner-city America: Challenges and prospects* (pp. 45–72). Hillsdale, NJ: Lawrence Erlbaum.

Wang, M. C., Haertel, G. D., & Walberg, H. J. (1999). Psychological and educational resilience. In A. J. Reynolds, H. J. Walberg, & R. P.Weissberg (Eds.), *Promoting positive outcomes* (pp. 329–365). Washington, DC: CWLA Press.

Warburton, E. C., Bugarin, R., Nunez, A., & Carroll, C. D. (2001). *Bridging the gap: Postsecondary success of first-generation students* (NCES 2001-153). Washington, DC: U.S. Department of Education, National Center for Education Statistics.

Wehlage, G. G., & Rutter, R. A. (1986). Dropping out: How much do schools contribute to the problem? *Teachers College Record, 87*(3), 374–391.

Werner, E. E. (1990). Protective factors and individual resilience. In S. J. Meisels &
    J. Shonkoff (Eds.), *Handbook of early childhood intervention* (pp. 97–116). New
    York: Cambridge University Press.
Werner, E. E., & Smith, R. S. (1982). *Vulnerable but invincible: A longitudinal study of
    resilient children and youth.* New York: McGraw-Hill.

6

Developmental Vulnerability in Young Children with Disabilities

Irene Nathan Zipper and Rune J. Simeonsson

Efforts to promote the development of children with disabilities are faced with unique challenges. Lack of agreement about definitions of disability, difficulties in assessment, inadequate resources, and limited information about effective interventions, coupled with negative societal attitudes toward those who are different, all contribute to these challenges. Although development is inevitably affected, the extent and nature of the effects of disabilities on children are highly variable. If these children are to achieve their potential, it is critically important to identify the factors that may facilitate or impede their development.

The scope and severity of disabilities vary substantially, as do the definitions of disability (Simeonsson & Rosenthal, 2001). In addition, the conditions attendant with disability, as well as the conditions that occur secondarily, vary as a function of many factors, including some whose effects are not well understood. Thus, by itself, the determination that a child has a disability provides relatively little information about the child's future functioning. The development of children is dependent on complex and interrelated factors. Some of these factors, and their effect on the development of children with disabilities, are outlined below.

Disability is described in different ways based on the child's age and on the criteria for eligibility for services, among other factors. In infancy and in early childhood, definitions of disability typically reflect developmental delay, which is identified through functional assessment. For school-age children, disability is generally defined in categorical terms, such as mental retardation, learning disability, and motor impairment. With the transition from adolescence to adulthood, the term "developmental disability" indicates a variety of conditions associated with mental retardation, autism, cerebral palsy, seizure disorders, and other disabilities originating in the developmental period. Differences in terminology and lack of conceptual clarity about the nature of disability are further complicated by the reality that children develop at individual and variable rates, making it inappropriate to use definitive terminology that might serve to stigmatize them. A functional perspective is needed to guide effective intervention and to facilitate the development of appropriate criteria for determining eligibility for services.

Although documentation of developmental delay or disability in young children has important implications for intervention, it does not by itself predict their development and socialization with typically developing peers. In addition to their unique characteristics, multiple factors in the physical and social environment govern children's development. Child factors such as adaptive skills and behavioral processes, as well as social interactions, availability and use of resources, and relationships between families and service providers are key to understanding children's development (Guralnick, 1999; Kopp & Kaler, 1989). The purpose of this chapter is twofold: (1) to identify and define the factors that place children with atypical development at risk of more severe disabilities and their secondary effects and (2) to examine the factors that protect them against these possibilities.

THE PREVALENCE OF DISABILITY IN CHILDREN AND ADOLESCENTS

Establishing the actual prevalence of childhood disabilities is difficult, in part because no single classification system has been adopted and inconsistent data collection procedures make aggregation of data difficult (Aron, Loprest, & Steuerle, 1996). Available figures suggest that at least 12.2 percent of the students in U.S. schools in 1993 to 1994 had a disability (U.S. Department of Education, 1997). Using population-based data, Hogan, Msall, Rogers, and Avery (1997) estimated that 12.3 percent of American children between five and 17 years old had functional limitations in one of the four areas: (1) mobility, (2) self-care, (3) communication, and (4) learning. The complexity of the problems associated with disabilities is often underestimated because traditional categorical definitions present disabilities as relatively one-dimensional constructs. Children's eligibility for special education, for example, is established by meeting criteria for one of 13 categories of disability (Table 6-1). It is important to note that these figures represent the numbers of children served. Since all states do not use categorical definitions with younger children, they represent estimates of the actual prevalence of disabilities.

Approaches to serving children with disabilities and their families have changed dramatically in recent decades. Medical and technological advances have meant that babies born with congenital disorders or with pre- or perinatal complications are more likely to survive, with subsequent risk for manifesting delays or disabilities as they mature. At the same time, changing attitudes toward disabilities have contributed to the deinstitutionalization movement. As a result, children with complex disabilities are likely to live with their families and continue to reside in the community as adults. Consequently, the need for community-based resources and services has increased, along with public acceptance of the integration of persons with disabilities into the life of the community.

ASSESSMENT

An accurate and reliable assessment of the level of functioning and needs of children with disabilities is a prerequisite for access to promising supports and services. A number of issues need to be considered to ensure an appropriate assessment.

Accurate documentation of developmental disability in young children is a challenge. A child with impairments in one domain may well exhibit delays in other domains, so a broad evaluation of functioning may be more useful in assessing risk and protective factors for purposes of intervention planning. In young children, delayed development in one or more of the major domains of functioning generally serves as a

Table 6-1. Number of Children Served Under IDEA, Part B, by Disability and Age, during the 2001–2002 School Year

DISABILITY	3 YEARS OLD	4 YEARS OLD	5 YEARS OLD	6 YEARS OLD	7 YEARS OLD	8 YEARS OLD	9 YEARS OLD
Specific learning disabilities	2,019	3,910	9,488	29,191	78,151	144,262	214,728
Speech or language impairments	52,316	101,795	159,427	213,742	212,076	188,344	153,578
Mental retardation	4,858	7,076	12,086	17,928	25,955	34,445	42,471
Emotional disturbance	932	1,949	4,138	7,651	14,369	22,440	30,570
Multiple disabilities	1,922	2,842	4,893	7,523	7,750	9,143	10,135
Hearing impairments	1,817	2,453	3,205	4,166	4,851	5,517	5,905
Orthopedic impairments	2,595	3,339	4,171	5,446	5,839	6,180	6,393
Other health impairments	2,840	4,231	6,889	12,364	17,627	24,694	30,958
Visual impairments	884	1,074	1,273	1,551	1,808	2,026	2,234
Autism	3,555	5,395	8,102	10,813	11,121	11,379	11,641
Deafness and blindness	70	73	74	93	109	106	121
Traumatic brain injury	213	307	461	663	881	1,209	1,453
Developmental delay	61,753	87,633	48,137	21,204	14,190	7,749	1,985
All disabilities	135,774	222,077	262,344	332,335	394,727	457,494	512,172

NOTE: Developmental delay is applicable only to children ages 3 through 9.
SOURCE: Data based on the December 1, 2001, count, updated as of August 30, 2002. U.S. Department of Education, Office of Special Education Programs, *Data Analysis System* (DANS).

marker for later developmental disability, but assessment findings obtained in infancy are only weakly predictive of developmental status in later childhood (Shevell, Majnemer, Rosenbaum, & Abrahamowicz, 2001). This apparent inconsistency results both from the dynamic nature of early development and from the difficulty of trying to precisely assess the functioning of young children.

VARIABLE RATE OF DEVELOPMENT

The infant and preschool years account for dramatic accomplishments, as evidenced by the remarkable transition from a newborn with primitive sensory and motor behavior to a young child with significant competencies in social and communicative interaction, motor control, and cognitive readiness for academic skills. The rate at which all children develop in the major domains of cognitive, communicative, motor, social, and behavioral functioning is highly variable. This is evident in children with neurological complications or impairments in visual, motor, and auditory functioning, who may acquire developmental skills at a pace and in a sequence different from the typical pattern. Such variability suggests the need for caution in the diagnosis of disability in very young children, particularly in light of the lowered expectations and stigmatization that frequently accompany diagnosis.

Whether the etiologies are congenital or acquired, the extent of disability reflects the ongoing interaction of the child with the environment. The importance of this interaction is evident in the terms used to describe problems in this phase of development. The significant influence of the environment on child functioning and disability is reflected in the terms "developmental delay" (Schendel et al., 1997), "developmental vulnerability" (Kalter, 1987), and "developmental morbidity" (Rogers, Sills, Cohen, & Seidel, 1990). Each of these terms, as opposed to "developmental disability," emphasizes the dynamic nature of development in young children. This terminology reflects the plasticity of early development and the potential for protection against more severe difficulty. It reflects the fact that many specific conditions are difficult to diagnose at young ages (Simeonsson, 1991a, 1991b) and avoids the additional risks, such as the effects of stigmatization and lowered expectations, that may be imposed on the child by identification as a class member. Postponing the assignment of a categorical label allows time to promote the child's development and protect the child against more severe manifestations of an existing condition. Eligibility criteria for early intervention services in most states thus call for the determination of functional developmental delay in one or more domains of development; a categorical diagnosis that might suggest the likelihood of developmental disability in the future need not be established.

Although some delays in development are readily explained by obvious physical disability, the explanation for delays in other domains may be less apparent. Even children born without obvious congenital anomalies may gradually manifest developmental disabilities if their environment is inadequate. Moreover, existing developmental delays and deviations may be exacerbated by such an environment, as proposed in the transactional model of mediated effects (Sameroff & Chandler, 1975). The transactions that account for development are complex. An important priority is to identify factors that are likely to influence risk for adaptation and developmental progress. Clearly, an adequate model of disability needs to account for interactive factors—the nature of the condition, its severity, other characteristics of the child, and the context within which the child develops over time. The interrelationship of all of these factors contributes to developmental outcome and to the challenges and limitations faced by children with disabilities (see, for example, Sameroff & Fiese, 1990; Shonkoff & Phillips, 2000). Further, it is becoming increasingly apparent that specific developmental delays do not occur in isolation; rather, a delay in one domain of functioning frequently co-occurs with difficulties in functioning in other domains. To be useful, definitions of disability need to reflect this variability accurately.

AN ECOLOGICAL FRAMEWORK OF CHILDHOOD DISABILITY

An ecological perspective views the child in the context of the family and the family in the context of the community and the wider society (Bronfenbrenner, 1979). Consistent with this view, one must look beyond the child to identify risk and protective factors for children with developmental disabilities. It is now widely acknowledged that children's development is influenced by their interactions with their environment (see, for example, Hartup, 1989; Landesman & Ramey, 1989; Luthar, 1999; Sameroff & Fiese, 1990), but the complex interaction of biological and environmental factors makes it difficult to discern cause from effect in these transactions (Sameroff & Chandler, 1975). Nonetheless, it is clear that conditions both within the child and in the environment can place a child at risk of more pronounced childhood disabilities; likewise, some individual and environmental factors can protect the child against more severe manifestations of an existing impairment.

Educational programs set up to provide "normalizing" experiences for children with disabilities illustrate the complexity of transactions between child and environment. The Individuals with Disabilities Education Act (IDEA) mandates that children with disabilities be placed within inclusive environments so that they can be educated with their typically developing peers and benefit from the everyday social interactions of school life. The extent to which children with disabilities benefit from inclusion, however, may depend as much on aspects of the environment as on the child. Such placements promote children's achievement and well-being when school policies give priority to placing children with disabilities with skilled, enthusiastic teachers; allow for gradual transition into the regular classroom; and maintain relatively small class sizes. In this context, the child's temperament and readiness to interact with other children may protect against social difficulties. Moreover, a child may acquire other individual, unique coping strategies in this setting—protective factors—that reduce vulnerability and facilitate development in multiple domains. No single factor can protect the child from further disability, but in a transactional framework, everyone can help promote the child's optimal development.

In growth and development, children experience both demands that challenge their functioning and conditions that support their development. For infants, a caregiving environment that elicits and reinforces early communication, provides opportunities for object manipulation and play, and contributes to an awareness of cause and effect is crucial for fostering development. For toddlers and preschool children, socialization experiences in the form of small-group activities, opportunities for incidental learning, and exposure to readiness skills are key elements for developmental mastery.

Factors that are effective for typically developing children are also effective for children with disabilities. However, children whose primary impairments may restrict their functioning are at risk for complications and secondary conditions (Simeonsson & Leskinen, 1999). Secondary conditions reflect situations in which inadequate environments contribute to or exacerbate the effect of a primary condition. Such secondary conditions may take the form of physical effects, such as pressure sores for a child with cerebral palsy, or psychological effects, such as loneliness and a sense of rejection for a child with mental retardation. Secondary conditions may also be expressed in dependency on others through the lack of encouragement to become increasingly independent along with typically developing peers. The nature and severity of the disability may increase with age, with the possibility of developing further secondary conditions. The extent to which such outcomes can be prevented depends on a number of complex and interrelated factors. To prevent disability or to ameliorate its effects, we need to identify those factors that place a child at risk and those that contribute to a child's resilience so that interventions may promote children's optimal development.

RISK AND PROTECTIVE FACTORS RELEVANT TO CHILDREN WITH DISABILITIES

Young children's relationships with others are influenced by a variety of factors and these factors, if malleable, can be focal points in the design of potentially more effective interventions. For example, a child's social interactions and affective responses to others form the basis for framing interventions to prevent the development of psychopathology in young children (Holinger, 2000). Given that the ability of young children with disabilities to display emotion or respond to stimuli may be limited, it would be especially helpful to understand the role of affect in their lives. This seems particularly important in light of longitudinal studies of typically developing children that indicate that the quality of engagement with others constitutes a protective factor for children at risk (Werner, 2000). Investigating the role of affect in the development of children with disabilities would further our ability to identify resiliency and to promote optimal psychological development.

Although longitudinal research on the development of young children with disabilities has been sparse (Shonkoff, Hauser-Cram, Krauss, & Upshur, 1992), efforts are underway to establish the empirical foundation for a discussion of risk and protection for children with disabilities. Some of the factors that influence children's development are described below.

GENDER

A number of studies have found that child gender is differentially associated with factors that increase children's risk and promote their resilience (Werner 1990; Werner & Smith, 1982). These studies do not specifically focus on developmental disability; yet, their findings have implications for understanding protective factors for children with disabilities. In longitudinal studies carried out in Kauai, Werner and colleagues found that resilient girls seemed to come from households that provided consistent emotional support for the child and emphasized risk taking and independence.

Resilient boys, however, were from homes in which emotional expressiveness was encouraged, in which greater structure and supervision were provided, and in which a male role model was available for the child (Werner, 1990).

PRENATAL AND PERINATAL COMPLICATIONS

Children with congenital anomalies and children who have experienced prenatal or perinatal complications are at risk of secondary conditions that vary according to the nature and severity of the primary impairment. In a yearlong study of 190 infants and toddlers who were receiving early intervention services, Shonkoff and colleagues (1992) found that children with seizure disorders or relatively severe psychomotor impairments were slower to develop in cognitive and social domains than children without other conditions. The authors noted that psychomotor development in the first two years of life is relatively predictable regardless of the child's environment. However, it is not possible to know whether the delayed development of these children was a symptom of the underlying condition, a result of their neurological condition, or a secondary condition resulting from the effects of the medications used to control seizures.

SECONDARY CONDITIONS

As described above, children are vulnerable to secondary effects of their disabilities. These may be physical, social, or psychological (Simeonsson, McMillen, & Huntington, 2002). For example, difficulties in peer interactions may result from a sense of self that is grounded in difference, from limitations on the ability to participate in certain activities, from the unrealistic or inappropriate expectations of others, and from lack of information or understanding on the part of peers about the effects of a child's disability and its implications. The likelihood that children with developmental delays and disabilities will develop positive social behaviors is increased when they are included in normal daily activities. In addition to facilitating their interaction with typically developing peers, their inclusion offers the opportunity to increase public sensitivity to the challenges they face and to enhance recognition of their potential contributions (Guralnick, 2001).

FAMILY FACTORS

Relationship with the Primary Caregiver

Within a transactional framework of development, risk factors associated with a child's disability may be exacerbated or ameliorated by family and other environmental conditions. For example, a premature infant of low birthweight in a neonatal intensive care unit (NICU) is likely to be at risk for a variety of developmental disabilities. The risk may be increased, as observed by McFadyen (1994), if the emotional state of the infant's parents—who may feel confused, anxious, and helpless—makes it hard for them to relate to their new baby. Parents under such stress may distance themselves and limit the kinds of interactions that promote optimal development. In a study of couples with children in NICUs, mothers reported greater levels of emotional disturbance than fathers (Affleck, Tennen, & Rowe, 1990), suggesting that a strong and positive relationship between the mother and infant may be particularly jeopardized during this stressful time.

Ramey and colleagues have hypothesized that behavioral interactions with adults are the most important influence on the infant's cognitive development (Ramey, Bryant, Sparling, & Wasik, 1984; Ramey et al., 1992). Certainly, parents' problem-solving abilities, coping skills, and self-esteem are critical to their children's development (American Academy of Pediatrics, 2003). The nature of the relationship between the child and primary caregiver is affected by a variety of factors, including poverty, substance abuse, parental physical and mental illness, exposure to violence, job instability, and violence in the home (Eamon, 2001; Osofsky & Thompson, 2000; Tannen, 2000). These conditions frequently co-occur, placing children in such circumstances at developmental risk. Regardless of other environmental circumstances, a strong, consistent relationship between the primary caregiver and the child may well provide the most effective protection against the development of more severe disability. Hartup (1989) hypothesized that mothers who have good relationships with their children are more likely to engage them and support their problem-solving attempts. Children in these relationships may be more open to maternal assistance and more likely to use their mothers as a stable emotional base from which to explore the wider world. Because disabilities may increase a child's dependency on others (Wolery, 2000), the child's relationships with sensitive family members who are able to anticipate needs may constitute an important aspect of protection for the child. Children's efforts to explore and to interact with the environment may be particularly critical for development when a disabling condition limits or modifies the way in which they incorporate newly learned information. Thus, a strong and secure attachment between the child with a developmental delay and the child's primary caregiver may serve to moderate the effects of disability.

Families with children with disabilities face special challenges. It is important to recognize, however, that these challenges do not necessarily translate into severe forms of distress. In their study of 190 infants and their families, Shonkoff and colleagues (1992) found that the child's condition did not necessarily lead to maladaptive family functioning. In fact, mothers reported no greater stress as parents than did mothers of typically developing children. It is likely, however, that parents who are facing other adverse conditions—who do not have access to adequate resources, who have little support from family and friends, or who are coping with their own physical or mental illness—will have difficulty with the additional challenges involved in raising a child with disabilities.

Parental Substance Abuse

Parental substance use by itself places the child's development at risk because abusing parents frequently have accompanying physical, psychological, and social problems that may render them incapable of meeting the child's basic needs. It is likely that these children face inconsistent caregiving, untrained caregivers, and poor attachment (Vincent, Poulsen, Cole, Woodruff, & Griffith, 1991), which put them at increased risk. Further, the extent of that risk depends on the duration of use, the nature of the substance, and the likelihood of polydrug use (Coles, 1995).

Adequacy of Resources Available to the Family

Poverty, with its attendant conditions, places children at significant risk for maladjustment, and for developmental delay and disability (Farran, 2000; Kamerman & Kahn, 1995; Luthar, 1999; Wacharasin, Barnard, & Spieker, 2003); moreover, risk factors for many conditions occur far more frequently among children living in poverty (Eamon, 2001; Ohlson, 1998; Schorr, 1988). Poor nutrition, medical complications of pregnancy, lack of access to medical care, and inadequate housing all arise from low socioeconomic status (Bryant & Ramey, 1987). Each of these conditions increases the likelihood that the child's needs will go unmet, and the cumulative effects make it very difficult to provide an environment in which the child can thrive. Children's health is related to their economic circumstances. In 1998 although 87 percent of children in families living at or above the poverty line were in very good or excellent health, the same was true for only 70 percent of children living in poverty (Federal Interagency Forum on Child and Family Statistics, 2001). Furthermore, living under adverse conditions such as poverty directly influences the relationships between children and their primary caregivers. The stress that results from such conditions may make it impossible for parents to engage in the positive, nurturant interactions that facilitate children's optimal development.

Parents who have access to financial resources, information, and support in raising their child are far more likely to be able to provide an environment in which the child's health and development will be optimized than will parents who lack such resources. Dunst, Leet, and Trivette (1988) found that the adequacy of resources available to the child's mother closely correlated with both her sense of well-being and an avowed commitment to carrying out professionally prescribed educational and therapeutic interventions with the child. Their findings suggest that when resources are inadequate, families are less likely to participate actively in intervention activities that might promote the child's development.

Given the influence of the child's earliest years on later development, recent poverty data (see chapter 1) suggest that a substantial number of children in this country are at risk of developmental delay or disability. The role of this critical risk factor is disproportionate by racial and ethnic status, in that African American and Hispanic children are much more likely to be raised in conditions of poverty (Kamerman & Kahn, 1995). Although the nature and extent of the effects may vary, poverty constitutes a significant risk factor for effective functioning of the family and optimal development for children with developmental disabilities. Conversely, it is likely that the availability of adequate resources constitutes a protective factor for the child.

Race and Ethnicity

Relatively little is known about the relationship between developmental delay and race or ethnicity, although some studies have focused on the relationships among race or ethnicity, parental attitudes, and involvement with the human services system. For example, in a study examining how 60 African American, Hispanic, and white mothers reacted to having a child with mental retardation, Mary (1990) found no significant differences in reports of negative feelings. However, Mary also found that Hispanic mothers reported a greater sense of self-sacrifice and were more likely to say they experienced loneliness. Such findings suggest that race and ethnicity may affect children indirectly through their parents' beliefs, values, and support.

Participation in educational and other services also appears to be related to race or ethnicity. Research findings indicate that parents of color want to be involved actively in their children's education, but they tend to be less involved in special education programs (Chavkin & Garza-Lubeck, 1990; Harry, 1992). In a study of more than 500 families with young children with special needs, Sontag & Schacht (1994) found that American Indian and Hispanic parents reported a greater need for information about services than did white parents, and white parents were more likely to report that they helped make decisions about their children's programs and that they coordinated services for their children. These differences suggest that some families are not gaining information and access to resources through collaborative relationships with service providers.

A disproportionately high rate of placement of students of color in special education programs has been noted, suggesting that placement in special education is not dependent on disability status alone (Harry, 1992). Information on race and ethnicity became a new component of the child count for all programs under IDEA in 1998, providing additional information about this issue. According to the 22nd annual report to Congress on the implementation of IDEA (2000), the racial and ethnic composition of infants and toddlers served through Part C of IDEA was comparable with that of the general population. Because this is the first time this information was requested, it should be interpreted with caution (U.S. Department of Education, 2000).

Parents' Sense of Efficacy

The beliefs and values of the child's primary caregivers play a subtle but critical role in the child's development. Parents who believe in their own efficacy expect to have a positive influence on their child's development, even if the process is slow and tentative. These parents are more likely to refuse to accept results of a diagnostic assessment with which they disagree and to insist on validation of the original findings in an effort to get accurate information about the child's condition and prognosis. The relationships that they develop and maintain with service providers reflect their own decision-making authority vis-à-vis their child, and they take an active role in the planning and implementation of services. Thus, parents who believe in their own ability to shape their circumstances may provide critical protection against the development of more severe disability.

Type of Disability and Family Functioning

Although there is little empirical information about the differential effect of children's disabilities on their families, Shonkoff and colleagues (1992) found that parents of children with motor impairments reported greater stress than parents of children with other disabilities. Moreover, parents of children with motor impairments reported decreasing social support over time, presumably because the nature of their child's condition made it difficult for them to participate in routine school and community activities. Such findings suggest that children with motor impairments may be at increased risk for difficulties resulting from parental stress and isolation.

CUMULATIVE RISK AND PROMOTIVE FACTORS

Each risk factor increases the odds that the development of a child with disabilities will be compromised. The constellation of risk factors places the child's development in jeopardy. Their additive effects place the child's development in even greater jeopardy and increase the likelihood of negative outcomes (Dunst, 1993; Sameroff, Bartko, Baldwin, Baldwin, & Seifer, 1998; Schorr, 1997). Thus, it is extremely difficult and perhaps even meaningless to attempt to establish the differential impact of individual risk factors on development. As an example, a young family with a child with a developmental delay would benefit from complete information about the child's condition and ways to promote the child's development. The family might also need educational opportunities, housing assistance, and food stamps. When long waiting lists, complicated eligibility requirements, and language barriers impede the family's access to needed services and resources, the likelihood that the child's development will be further compromised is increased.

The mere absence of risk factors does not guarantee the child's optimal development, however. Dunst (1993) has hypothesized that optimal development is more likely to occur in the presence of multiple opportunity factors, just as the likelihood of negative outcomes increases when multiple risk factors are present.

In the situation described above, a well-coordinated, culturally competent service system that responds to the needs of children and families by providing information about services and convenient access to services and resources can do much to support the family in protecting the child against further disability. Such factors, which may serve to protect the child against further disability when they are present in their positive form, have been defined as *promotive factors* (Sameroff et al., 1998).

ASSESSING RISK AND RESILIENCE

Research in the field of developmental disabilities has focused on risk. Knowledge about the factors that place a child at risk of developmental disability has therefore been growing, but understanding of the factors that protect children against disability has been limited. Consistent with chapter 2, the transactional model implies that assessment should address multiple risk and protective factors and encompass the child, the family, and the broader environment (Wachs, 2000). An important area for further exploration is the definition and measurement of opportunity factors (Dunst, 1993). The development of indices to profile the specific risk and protective factors affecting individual children would be helpful in tailoring services to enhance resilience and promote development of children in a wide range of community settings.

An important implication of an ecological perspective is that families should be directly involved in the process of assessing the child's development and relevant risk and protective factors. The significant role that families can play in assessment has been recognized by Bloch and Sietz (1989) and has emerged as a major trend in intervention efforts for infants and young children in the context of effective partnerships between parents and professionals (Stonestreet, Johnson, & Acton, 1991). Even when the opportunity for participation is provided, the level of family involvement may vary substantially as a function of family preference and availability, as well as the nature and focus of the assessment.

The emphasis on involvement of families and other caregivers in the assessment process coincides with a growing interest in functional assessment, which emphasizes documentation of functional ability. These converging trends promote a more comprehensive approach to assessment of risk and protective factors, one in which the perspectives and experiences of families complement those of evaluation specialists. With information gathered through questionnaires, observations by families and service providers, and interaction between parents and professionals, risk as well as protective factors can be identified. Data obtained in this manner can include documentation of child characteristics, such as the nature and severity of the disability (Bailey, Simeonsson, Buysse, & Smith, 1993). Together with information about the child's behavioral style or temperament (Huntington & Simeonsson, 1993), these data provide initial information about the additional demands placed on the family by the child's condition. Further assessment of factors that affect the child's development involves learning about the family's priorities and expectations (Simeonsson et al., 1996). Their expectations are particularly important because these are grounded in the context of the family's resources, as described by Dunst, Trivette, & Deal (1988). With this information, the likelihood that services will be provided in a manner consistent with family priorities is increased.

The data derived through these means can be used to help determine eligibility or to plan interventions at the level of individuals or populations. A good example of such integration of data is provided by a report by Sinclair (1993) that described children with special needs in Head Start programs. Child characteristics, medical and developmental history, family background, and behavioral and academic functioning served as the basis for profiling children. Cluster analysis of the profiles yielded three distinct groups of children who were certified as having special needs. Different combinations of risk and protective factors in terms of family context, developmental and medical history, and current functioning defined the clusters. The differentiation of the groups along these variables was paralleled by differential rates of recommendation for special education placement in kindergarten. This approach represents a useful model for applying knowledge of risk and protective factors in prevention efforts.

IMPLICATIONS FOR PREVENTION AND EARLY INTERVENTION

A major intervention challenge is to gather information about factors that place children at risk for disability, about the differential effects of risk factors on development, and about their interactive effects. The complexity of the issues suggests that both individual and contextual factors should be examined, in order to understand how risk and protective factors operate to influence developmental outcomes among children with disabilities (Sameroff, Bartko, Baldwin, Baldwin, & Seifer, 1998). Thus, a broad research agenda is needed to better understand how to optimize development of young children. The information gained from these studies should guide early intervention efforts that focus on the development of additional protective factors and on enhancing their salience.

The complex and interrelated factors that affect children's development call for a broad-based, coherent prevention agenda framed within an array of initiatives to support families early in the life of their child (Chamberlin, 1994; Osofsky & Thompson, 2000). Efforts to reduce risk and increase protection in young children must include programs that enhance the context in which children develop and are consistent with current understandings of the role of environment in child development. Secondary prevention programs, ranging from hospital-based stimulation programs for low birthweight infants born prematurely to home-based parent support services, have been assigned increasing priority. In the past two decades, recognition of factors that place children at risk have framed efforts to protect against further developmental delay or disability. These efforts have focused on policy initiatives, community-based approaches, integration of services, and family support.

POLICY INITIATIVES

The passage of P.L. 99-457 formalized a prevention agenda for the states, focusing on enhancing the developmental context for young children with disabilities (Florian, 1995). This governmental mandate can play an important role in increasing the resilience of young children and protecting them against some of the effects of developmental disability. Enhancement of the development of infants and toddlers with disabilities by providing support to their families, both directly and indirectly, is the central premise of Part C of IDEA (1997). It gives strong legislative direction for family-centered services, promoting active participation on the part of parents, and authorizing them to make decisions about early intervention services for their children. Its specific mandates define how services are provided at the local level, and include guidelines for the involvement of family members. The legislation outlines a process for the development of an "individualized family service plan" as a means by which the family's concerns, resources, and priorities guide the planning and provision of services. By assuring that services address parents' priorities, the legislation focuses on enhancing the family's ability to foster the optimal development of the young child.

Legislative efforts such as the Americans with Disabilities Act (1990) and IDEA have been key to increasing public sensitivity to the rights and needs of young children with disabilities, and they have created a climate conducive to development of services and programs dedicated to inclusion of children with disabilities in normalized settings. Such programs are intended to increase sensitivity to the needs of children with disabilities while establishing an environment that helps to protect them against further disability. Curricula and programs have been developed to promote effective relationships between children with disabilities and their typically developing peers and to guide teachers in providing factual information to typically developing children about their peers with disabilities (Sapon-Shevin, 1999; Snell & Janney, 2000; Staub, 1998). These programs can facilitate the participation of children with disabilities in daily activities with their typically developing peers, and make these peers more knowledgeable about and sensitive to the challenges faced by children with disabilities. The relationships that can be established in this context are valuable to the child with a disability as well as his or her typically developing peers, and they increase the likelihood that positive outcomes will result from the inclusion of children with disabilities in activities and environments that are shared by all children.

Weiss (1990) argued that nurturing children is the shared responsibility of the family, the state, the voluntary community, and the private sector. Efforts to create the conditions under which parents are able to protect their children against developmental delay, then, must be comprehensive and integrated. Perhaps most basic is addressing the poverty that limits the ability of parents to provide adequately for their children (Farran, 2000; Knitzer & Aber, 1995; Schorr, 1997). It is obvious that access to medical care, appropriate housing, and adequate nutrition are essential for family well-being and children's optimal development. Services need to be readily accessible with supports provided in the context of collaboration among families, and medical and other services.

In addition to limited and inadequate access to services and supports, political agendas often contribute to the vulnerability of families, including those with children with disabilities. Passage of the Personal Responsibility and Work Opportunity Reconciliation Act of 1996, for example, ended the assurance that children and families living in poverty would receive federal aid, and its implementation may create particular difficulties for families with children with disabilities (Meisels & Shonkoff, 2000). Its provisions include a requirement that families receiving financial aid engage in work activities, necessitating that families find skilled and affordable child care for their children with disabilities. It narrows eligibility for Supplemental Security Income, which has been a major source of financial support for families with children with disabilities; and it limits the amount of federal child care funding available to states, which serves to limit the availability of child care for all children. There are concerns that such legislation will have unforeseen negative consequences for children with disabilities, for their families, and for the service system.

COMMUNITY-BASED APPROACHES

Continued efforts are needed to increase public knowledge about the nature of developmental disabilities and the factors that can foster the development of children and support their families. The public needs to know much more about genetic factors associated with developmental disabilities, the importance of prenatal care, the ways in which optimal development in infancy is promoted, and the rights of children with disabilities and their families.

The mandate to provide community-based services for children with disabilities implies a greater level of public responsibility for the well-being of children with disabilities and for their families. Because opportunities for these children are enhanced when they are able to develop in an environment that is as normal as possible, the community context is critical for the development of circumstances and characteristics that protect the child from the negative effects of disability. Inclusion of children in environments shared by typically developing peers protects against isolation and a self-image grounded in difference. The provisions of IDEA reflect a commitment to promoting protective factors in the community. The mandate that children be served in the "least restrictive environment" possible is intended to enhance the educational process for children with disabilities and to protect them against the effects of segregation from their peers.

INTEGRATED SERVICES

The complex needs of children with disabilities and their families may warrant the involvement of multiple service providers operating in different agencies. The services they provide are often fragmented and uncoordinated, creating additional stress for family members as they attempt to negotiate an increasingly complicated service system. Frequent changes in personnel, agency, and service setting—which can lead to service gaps and inconsistencies—threaten the child's optimal development (Dokecki & Heflinger, 1989). A coherent, well-integrated service system that allows for close collaboration among service providers can facilitate continuity of services for the child and family, and enhance their effectiveness. The service coordinator mandated under Part C of IDEA may protect against some of the inconsistent policies and procedures that can result from such categorically organized services by serving as an intermediary between the family and the service system (Roberts, Akers, & Behl, 1996; Zipper, 1996). By facilitating collaboration among service providers, the service coordinator increases the likelihood that the family will be able to access services that are coordinated and well-integrated.

FAMILY SUPPORT

Service providers and advocates need to work to ensure that legislative agendas are implemented in ways that are as supportive as possible of families (Ohlson, 1998). Early intervention service providers come from many academic disciplines, such as social work, education, psychology, and medicine, which vary in their approaches to intervention and expectations of family involvement (Bailey, Palsha, & Simeonsson, 1991; Nash, Rounds, & Bowen, 1992). There is general agreement that service providers need to respect the family's decision-making role and their values and priorities and collaborate skillfully with both family members and service providers. They need to understand the role of the environment, including the community, in the development of young children, and they need skills in planning and effecting change at community and population levels (Simeonsson & Thomas, 1994; Zipper, Weil, & Rounds, 1993).

Although all parents benefit from understanding their child's development and from access to supportive services, families with children with disabilities require additional community resources and supports to promote their child's optimum development (Rounds, Zipper, & Green, 1997). Parents need specific information about the child's condition, prognosis, and available services and resources. Parent-to-parent programs pair trained, experienced parents with parents who are still learning about their child's special needs, so that they may provide emotional and informational support. Recent studies have demonstrated that such programs are valuable in providing information, reducing isolation, and increasing adaptation (Santelli, Turnbull, Marquis, & Lerner, 2000; Singer et al., 1999).

Mutually respectful relationships between family members and service providers require that service providers take time to build rapport with the family and find out about their concerns and priorities, as well as their expectations (Simeonsson, Edmondson, Smith, Carnahan, & Bucy, 1995; Zipper, Weil, & Rounds, 1993). When families and service providers collaborate to arrive at treatment goals and decisions about the course of treatment for the child, the likelihood that the family will follow prescribed medical regimens is greatly increased (Christophersen & Mortweet, 2001).

To be able to make the best use of the service system, family members need to believe that service providers understand and respect their values and priorities. In the absence of such trusting relationships, family members may misunderstand service providers' recommendations or choose to ignore them, as described by Fadiman (1997) with reference to Hmong immigrants. Policies that support the recruitment and hiring of professionals from diverse cultural and ethnic backgrounds are needed, as well as opportunities for staff development aimed at understanding the implications of difference and promoting cultural competence (Lynch & Hanson, 1992; McCollum, Ree, & Chen, 2000).

All parents, and particularly those with young children with disabilities, benefit from increased support in carrying out their caregiving responsibilities. Kamerman and Kahn (1995) have suggested a policy strategy that includes paid leaves for parents. Such extended parental leave when a child is born and for several months afterward would allow parents to be available to their young children when the protection they provide may have the greatest effect on the child's future. The Family and Medical Leave Act of 1993 (P.L. 103-3) established the right to parental leave under certain conditions, but the actual impact of this legislation has been limited. Although it calls for protection of the employee's employment and benefit rights, the act does not apply to all employees, and it does not provide for payment for employees on leave.

The critical importance of the environment during the first years of life supports the value of programs that target young prospective parents by providing them with information about risk and protective factors even before a child is born. With such information, young parents can learn how to create an environment in which their newborn infants thrive. The growth and development of infants and young children may be promoted by programs that support their families in providing positive, nurturing experiences for their children. Such efforts should be grounded in a thorough understanding of the factors that place children at risk, as well as those that promote their optimal development.

REFERENCES

Affleck, G., Tennen, H., & Rowe, J. (1990). Mothers, fathers, and the crisis of newborn intensive care. *Infant Mental Health Journal, 11*(1), 12–25.

American Academy of Pediatrics. (2003). Family pediatrics. *Pediatrics, 111* (6 Suppl.).

Americans with Disabilities Act of 1990, P.L. 101-336.

Aron, L. Y., Loprest, P. J., & Steuerle, C. E. (1996). *Serving children with disabilities: A systematic look at the programs.* Washington, DC: Urban Institute Press.

Bailey, D. B., Palsha, S. A., & Simeonsson, R. J. (1991). Professional skills, concerns, and perceived importance of work with families in early intervention. *Exceptional Children, 58*(2), 156–165.

Bailey, D. B., Simeonsson, R. J., Buysse, V., & Smith, T. M. (1993). Reliability of an index of child characteristics. *Developmental Medicine and Child Neurology, 35,* 806–815.

Bloch, J., & Seitz, M. (1989). Parents as assessors of children: A collaborative approach to helping. *Social Work in Education, 11*(4), 226–244.

Bronfenbrenner, U. (1979). *The ecology of human development.* Cambridge, MA: Harvard University Press.

Bryant, D. M., & Ramey, C. T. (1987). An analysis of the effectiveness of early intervention programs for environmentally at-risk children. In M. J. Guralnick & F. C. Bennett (Eds.), *The effectiveness of early intervention for at-risk and handicapped children* (pp. 33–78). Orlando, FL: Academic Press.

Chamberlin, R. W. (1994). Primary prevention: The missing piece in child development legislation. In R. J. Simeonsson (Ed.), *Risk, resilience, and prevention: Promoting the well-being of all children.* (pp. 33–52). Baltimore: Paul H. Brookes.

Chavkin, N. F., & Garza-Lubeck, M. (1990). Multicultural approaches to parent involvement: Research and practice. *Social Work in Education, 13*(1), 22–33.

Christophersen, E. R., & Mortweet, S. L. (2001). *Treatments that work with children: Empirically supported strategies for managing childhood problems.* Washington, DC: American Psychological Association.

Coles, C. D. (1995). Children of parents who abuse drugs and alcohol. In G. H. Smith, C. D. Coles, M. K. Poulsen, & C. K. Cole (Eds.), *Children, families, and substance abuse: Challenges for changing educational and social outcomes* (pp. 3–24). Baltimore: Paul H. Brookes.

Dokecki, P. R., & Heflinger, C. A. (1989). Strengthening families of young children with handicapping conditions: Mapping backward from the "street level." In S. J. Meisels & J. P. Shonkoff (Ed.), *Handbook of early childhood intervention* (pp. 59–84). Cambridge, England: Cambridge University Press.

Dunst, C. J. (1993). Implications of risk and opportunity factors for assessment and intervention practices. *Topics in Early Childhood Special Education, 13*(2), 143–153.

Dunst, C. J., Leet, H. E., & Trivette, C. M. (1988). Family resources, personal well-being, and early intervention. *Journal of Special Education, 22*(1), 108–116.

Dunst, C. J., Trivette, C. M., & Deal, A. (1988). *Enabling and empowering families: Principles and guidelines for practice.* Cambridge, MA: Brookline Books.

Eamon, M. K. (2001). The effects of poverty on children's socioemotional development: An ecological systems analysis. *Social Work, 46*(3), 256–266.

Fadiman, A. (1997). *The spirit catches you and you fall down: A Hmong child, her American doctors, and the collision of two cultures.* New York: Farrar, Straus, & Giroux.

Family and Medical Leave Act of 1993, P.L. 103-3.

Farran, D. (2000). Another decade of intervention for children who are low income or disabled: What do we know now? In J. P. Shonkoff & S. J. Meisels (Eds.), *Handbook of early childhood intervention* (2nd ed., pp. 510–548). Cambridge, England: Cambridge University Press.

Federal Interagency Forum on Child and Family Statistics. (2001). *America's children: Key national indicators of well-being, 2001.* Washington, DC: U.S. Government Printing Office.

Florian, L. (1995). Part H early intervention programs: Legislative history and intent of the law. *Journal of Early Intervention, 15*(3), 247–262.

Guralnick, M. J. (1999). The nature and meaning of social integration for young children with mild developmental delays in inclusive settings. *Journal of Early Intervention, 22*(1), 70–86.

Guralnick, M. J. (Ed.). (2001). *Early childhood inclusion: Focus on change.* Baltimore: Paul H. Brookes.

Harry, B. (1992). *Cultural diversity, families, and the special education system.* New York: Teachers College Press.

Hartup, W. W. (1989). Social relationships and their developmental significance. *American Psychologist, 44*(2), 120–126.

Hogan, D. P., Msall, M. E., Rogers, M. L., & Avery, R. C. (1997). Improved disability population estimates of functional limitation among American children aged 5–17. *Maternal and Child Health Journal, 1*(4), 203–213.

Holinger, P. C. (2000). Early intervention and prevention of psychopathology: The potential role of affect. *Clinical Social Work Journal, 28*(1), 23–41.

Huntington, G. S., & Simeonsson, R. J. (1993). Temperament and adaptation in young handicapped children. *Infant Mental Health Journal, 14*(1), 49–60.

Individuals with Disabilities Education Act of 1997, P.L. 105-17.

Kalter, N. (1987). Long-term effects of divorce on children: A developmental vulnerability model. *American Journal of Orthopsychiatry, 57,* 587–600.

Kamerman, S. B., & Kahn, A. J. (1995). *Starting right: How America neglects its youngest children and what we can do about it.* New York: Oxford University Press.

Knitzer, J., & Aber, J. L. (1995). Young children in poverty: Facing the facts. *American Journal of Orthopsychiatry, 65*(2), 174–176.

Kopp, C. B., & Kaler, S. R. (1989). Risk in infancy: Origins and implications. *American Psychologist, 44*(2), 224–230.

Landesman, S., & Ramey, C. (1989). Developmental psychology and mental retardation: Integrating scientific principles with treatment practice. *American Psychologist, 44*(2), 409–415.

Luthar, S. S. (1999). *Poverty and children's adjustment.* Thousand Oaks, CA: Sage Publications.

Lynch, E. W., & Hanson, M. J. (1992). Steps in the right direction: Implications for interventionists. In E. W. Lynch & M. J. Hanson (Eds.), *Developing cross-cultural competence: A guide for working with young children and their families* (pp. 353–370). Baltimore: Paul H. Brookes.

Mary, N. L. (1990). Reactions of black, Hispanic, and white mothers to having a child with handicaps. *Mental Retardation, 28*(1), 1–5.

McCollum, J., Ree, Y., & Chen, Y. (2000). Interpreting parent-infant interactions: Cross-cultural lessons. *Infants & Young Children, 12*(4), 22–33.

McFadyen, A. (1994). *Special care babies and their developing relationships.* London: Routledge.

Meisels, S. J., & Shonkoff, J. P. (2000). Early childhood intervention: A continuing evolution. In J. P. Shonkoff & S. J. Meisels (Eds.), *Handbook of early childhood intervention* (2nd ed., pp. 3–31). Cambridge, England: Cambridge University Press.

Nash, J., Rounds, K. A., & Bowen, G. L. (1992). Level of parental involvement on early childhood intervention teams. *Families in Society, 73,* 93–99.

Ohlson, C. (1998). Welfare reform: Implications for young children with disabilities, their families, and service providers. *Journal of Early Intervention, 21*(3), 191–206.

Osofsky, J. D., & Thompson, D. (2000). Adaptive and maladaptive parenting: Perspectives on risk and protective factors. In J. P. Shonkoff & S. J. Meisels (Eds.), *Handbook of early childhood intervention* (2nd ed., pp. 54–75). Cambridge, England: Cambridge University Press.

Personal Responsibility and Work Opportunity Reconciliation Act of 1996, P.L. 104-193.

Ramey, C. T., Bryant, D. M., Sparling, J. J., & Wasik, B. (1984). A biosocial systems perspective on environmental interventions for low birth weight infants. *Clinical Obstetrical Gynecology, 27,* 672–692.

Ramey, C. T., Bryant, D. M., Wasik, B. H., Sparling, J. J., Fendt, K. H., & LaVange, L. M. (1992). Infant health and development program for low birth weight, premature infants: Program elements, family participation, and child intelligence. *Pediatrics, 3,* 454–465.

Roberts, R. N., Akers, A. L., & Behl, D. B. (1996). Family-level service coordination within home visiting programs. *Topics in Early Childhood Special Education, 16*(3), 279–301.

Rogers, B., Sills, I., Cohen, M., & Seidel, G. (1990). Neurologic collapse during treatment followed by severe developmental morbidity. *Clinical Pediatrics, 29,* 451–456.

Rounds, K. A., Zipper, I. N., & Green, T. (1997). Social work practice in early intervention: Child service coordination in a rural health department. In T. S. Kerson (Ed.), *Social work in health settings: Practice in context* (2nd ed., pp. 111–130). New York: Haworth Press.

Sameroff, A., Bartko, W. T., Baldwin, A., Baldwin, C., & Seifer, R. (1998). Family and social influences on the development of child competence. In M. Lewis & C. Feiring (Eds.), *Families, risk, and competence* (pp. 161–186). Mahwah, NJ: Lawrence Erlbaum.

Sameroff, A. J., & Chandler, M. J. (1975). Reproductive risk and the continuum of caretaking casualty. In F. D. Horowitz (Ed.), *Review of Child Development Research* (Vol. 4). Chicago: University of Chicago Press.

Sameroff, A. J., & Fiese, B. H. (1990). Transactional regulation and early intervention. In S. J. Meisels & J. P. Shonkoff (Ed.), *Handbook of early childhood intervention* (pp. 119–149). Cambridge, England: Cambridge University Press.

Santelli, B., Turnbull, A., Marquis, J., & Lerner, E. (2000). Statewide parent-to-parent programs: Partners in early intervention, *Infants and Young Children, 13*(1), 74-88.

Sapon-Shevin, M. (1999). *Because we can change the world: A practical guide to building cooperative, inclusive classroom communities.* Boston: Allyn & Bacon.

Schendel, D. E., Stockbauer, J. W., Hoffman, H. J., Herman, A. A., Berg, C. J., Schramm, W. F. (1997). Relation between very low birth weight and developmental delay among preschool children without disabilities. *American Journal of Epidemiology, 146,* 740–749.

Schorr, L. B. (1988). *Within our reach: Breaking the cycle of disadvantage.* New York: Doubleday.

Schorr, L. B. (1997). *Common purpose: Strengthening families and neighborhoods to rebuild America.* New York: Doubleday.

Shevell, M. I., Majnemer, A., Rosenbaum, P., & Abrahamowicz, M. (2001). Profile of referrals for early childhood developmental delay to ambulatory subspecialty clinics. *Journal of Child Neurology, 16,* 645–650.

Shonkoff, J. P., Hauser-Cram, P., Krauss, M. W., & Upshur, C. C. (1992). Development of infants with disabilities and their families. *Monographs of the Society for Research in Child Development, 57*(6, Serial No. 230).

Shonkoff, J. P., & Phillips, D.A. (Eds.). (2000). *From neurons to neighborhoods: The science of early childhood development.* Washington, DC: National Academy Press.

Simeonsson, R. J. (1991a). Early intervention eligibility: A prevention perspective. *Infants and Young Children, 3*(4), 48–55.

Simeonsson, R. J. (1991b). Early prevention of childhood disability in developing countries. *International Journal of Rehabilitation Research, 14,* 1–12.

Simeonsson, R. J., Edmondson R., Smith, T., Carnahan, S., & Bucy, J. (1995). Family involvement in multidisciplinary team evaluation: Professional and parent perspectives. *Child: Care, Health, and Development, 21*(30), 199–215.

Simeonsson, R. J., Huntington, G. S., McMillen, J. S., Haugh-Dodds, A. E., Halperin, D., Zipper, I. N., et al. (1996). Services for young children and families: Evaluating early intervention cycles. *Infants and Young Children, 9*(2), 31–42.

Simeonsson, R. J., & Leskinen, M. (1999). Disability, secondary conditions, and quality of life: Conceptual issues. In R. J. Simeonsson & L. McDevitt (Eds.), *Issues in disability and health: The role of secondary conditions and quality of life* (51–72). Chapel Hill: University of North Carolina Press.

Simeonsson, R. J., McMillen, J., & Huntington, G. S. (2002). Secondary conditions in children with disabilities: Spina bifida as a case example. *Research in Mental Retardation and Developmental Disabilities, 8*(3), 198–205.

Simeonsson, R. J., & Rosenthal, S. L. (Eds.). (2001). *Psychological and Developmental Assessment.* New York: Guilford Press.

Simeonsson, R. J., & Thomas, D. (1994). Promoting children's well-being: Priorities and principles. In R. J. Simeonsson (Ed.), *Risk, resilience, and prevention: Promoting the well-being of all children* (pp. 321–343). Baltimore: Paul H. Brookes.

Sinclair, E. (1993). Early identification of preschoolers with special needs in Head Start. *Topics in Early Childhood Special Education, 13*(2), 184–201.

Singer, G.H.S., Marquis, J., Powers, L. K., Blanchard, L., Divenere, N., Santelli, B., Ainbinder, J. G., & Sharp, M. (1999). A multi-site evaluation of parent to parent programs for parents of children with disabilities. *Journal of Early Intervention, 22*(3), 217–229.

Snell, M. E., & Janney, R. (2000). *Social relationships and peer support.* Baltimore: Paul H. Brookes.

Sontag, J. C., & Schacht, R. (1994). An ethnic comparison of parent participation and information needs in early intervention. *Exceptional Children, 60*(5), 422–433.

Staub, D. (1998). *Delicate threads: Friendships between children with and without special needs in inclusive settings.* Bethesda: Woodbine House.

Stonestreet, R. H., Johnson, R. G., & Acton, S. J. (1991). Guidelines for real partnerships with parents. *Infant–Toddler Intervention: Transdisciplinary Journal, 1*(1), 37–46.

Tannen, N. (2000). *The impact of parental illness on the child and family: Implications for systems change.* Washington, DC: Georgetown University Child Development Center.

U.S. Department of Education. (2000). *To assure the free appropriate public education of all children with disabilities: Twenty-second annual report to Congress on the implementation of the Individuals with Disabilities Education Act.* Washington DC: Author. Retrieved from http://www.ed.gov/offices/OSERS/OSEP/Products/OSEP2000AnlRpt/ on October 29, 2001.

U.S. Department of Education. (2002). *Data Analysis System (DANS)*. Washington, DC: Office of Special Education Programs.

U.S. Department of Education National Institute on Disability and Rehabilitation Research (1997). *Disabilities among children* (Disability Statistics Abstract No. 19). Washington, DC: Author.

Vincent, L. J., Poulsen, M. K., Cole, C. K., Woodruff, G., & Griffith, D. R. (1991). *Born substance exposed, educationally vulnerable*. Reston, VA: Council for Exceptional Children.

Wacharasin, C., Barnard, K. E., & Spieker, S. J. (2003). Factors affecting toddler cognitive development in low-income families. *Infants and Young Children, 16*(2), 175–181.

Wachs, T. D. (2000). *Necessary but not sufficient: The respective roles of single and multiple influences on individual development*. Washington, DC: American Psychological Association.

Weiss, H. B. (1990). Beyond *parens patriae*: Building policies and programs to care for our own and others' children. *Children and Youth Services Review, 12*, 269–284.

Werner, E. E. (1990). Protective factors and individual resilience. In S. J. Meisels & J. P. Shonkoff (Eds.), *Handbook of early childhood intervention* (pp. 97–116). Cambridge, England: Cambridge University Press.

Werner, E. E. (2000). Protective factors and individual resilience. In J. P. Shonkoff & S. J. Meisels (Eds.), *Handbook of early childhood intervention* (2nd ed., pp. 115–132). Cambridge, England: Cambridge University Press.

Werner, E. E, & Smith, R. (1982). *Vulnerable but invincible: A study of resilient children*. New York: McGraw-Hill.

Wolery, M. (2000). Behavioral and educational approaches to early intervention. In J. P. Shonkoff & S. J. Meisels (Eds.), *Handbook of early childhood intervention* (2nd ed., pp. 179–203). Cambridge, England: Cambridge University Press.

Zipper, I. N. (1996). *Parent perspectives on service coordination in early intervention*. Unpublished doctoral dissertation, University of North Carolina at Chapel Hill.

Zipper, I. N., Weil, M., & Rounds, K. (1993). *Service coordination for early intervention: Parents and professionals*. Cambridge, MA: Brookline Books.

7

Risk and Protective Factors for Alcohol and Other Drug Use in Childhood and Adolescence

Jeffrey M. Jenson

M ore and more American youths grow up in life circumstances that place them at risk of developing alcohol and other drug problems. Identifying factors that decrease risk and protect against alcohol and drug abuse is a critical step in preventing adolescent drug abuse.

SCOPE OF THE PROBLEM

Most data about the prevalence of alcohol and drug use among American youths comes from the Monitoring the Future Study (Johnston, O'Malley, & Bachman, 2003) sponsored by the National Institute on Drug Abuse and the University of Michigan. The study is an annual assessment of alcohol and drug use in a random sample of approximately 16,000 public high school students. In-school surveys with nationally representative samples of high school seniors have been conducted since 1975. Eighth- and 10th-grade students have been surveyed since 1991.[1]

12TH-GRADE STUDENTS

Lifetime illicit drug use peaked among seniors in 1981.[2] Sixty-six percent of 12th graders in 1981 used an illicit drug at least once in their lives; 43 percent used an illicit drug other than marijuana. Lifetime use of illicit drugs reached its lowest point in 1992; only 41 percent of seniors used any illicit drug and 25 percent used an illicit drug other than marijuana. In 1993, seniors reversed a decade-long pattern of declining illicit drug use; 43 percent used an illicit drug and 27 percent used an illicit drug other than marijuana. Rates of illicit drug use rose to 54 percent by 1997 and

---

[1]The Monitoring the Future study may underestimate the magnitude of substance use among high school seniors in the United States because it does not include school dropouts (an estimated 15 percent to 20 percent of students in this age group), a group at high risk for alcohol and drug use. Estimates of drug and alcohol use among minority groups may be particularly affected because more American Indian and Hispanic high school seniors drop out of school than African American, Asian American, or white seniors (Johnston et al., 2003).

[2]Illicit drug use includes any use of marijuana; hallucinogens; cocaine; heroin or other opiates; and stimulants, barbiturates, or tranquilizers that are not under a doctor's order.

Figure 7-1

Lifetime Prevalence of Illicit Drug Use by 12th Graders, 1975–2002

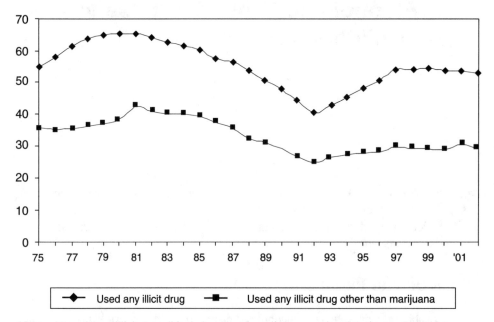

NOTE: Use of "any illicit drugs" includes use of marijuana, cocaine, heroin or other opiates, stimulants, barbiturates, or tranquilizers not prescribed by a doctor.

SOURCE: Data are from the Monitoring the Future Study conducted annually by the University of Michigan and the National Institute on Drug Abuse (Johnston, O'Malley, & Bachman, 2003).

have changed very little since 1998. Use of illicit drugs other than marijuana increased to 30 percent by 1997 and remained at similar levels through 2002. Figure 7-1 shows the lifetime prevalence of illicit drug use for 12th graders between 1975 and 2002.

Lifetime alcohol and tobacco use by seniors reached its highest level in the late 1970s and early 1980s. Approximately 93 percent of seniors reported lifetime alcohol use in the nine consecutive years between 1977 and 1985. Lifetime prevalence of alcohol use decreased moderately between 1985 and 1993; 87 percent of students in the class of 1993 used alcohol. In 2002, 72 percent of seniors reported lifetime alcohol use.[3] Lifetime cigarette smoking peaked in 1977; 76 percent of seniors smoked cigarettes that year compared with 57 percent of seniors in 2002.

In 2002, 72 percent of seniors reported drinking alcohol during the past 12 months. Twenty-two percent used marijuana and 2 percent used hallucinogens in the past month.

---

[3]This reduction, however, may be an artifact of a change in item wording pertaining to alcohol use initiated by Johnston and colleagues in the Monitoring the Future surveys following 1993. The question for lifetime alcohol use was changed in 1993 to mean drinks of "more than a few sips." Before 1993, lifetime use included any amount of alcohol (Johnston et al., 2003).

Figure 7-2

Lifetime Prevalence of Use of Various Drugs by Eighth Graders, 1991–2002

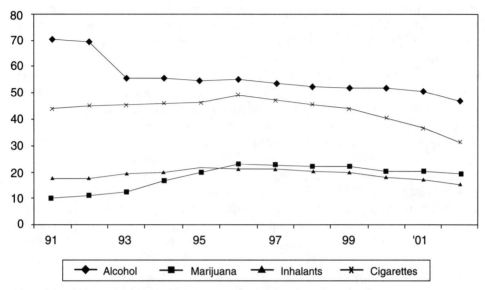

NOTE: Alcohol use was changed in 1993 to mean "more than a few sips."

SOURCE: Data are from the Monitoring the Future Study conducted annually by the University of Michigan and the National Institute on Drug Abuse (Johnston, O'Malley, & Bachman, 2003).

EIGHTH-GRADE STUDENTS

Knowledge of drug use prevalence among eighth-grade students is important to practitioners because alcohol and drug use by young adolescents may be a precursor of drug use trends among future high school students. Awareness of drug use prevalence among eighth graders may also inform the content and direction of prevention and treatment programs.

Forty-seven percent of adolescents used alcohol by the eighth grade in 2002. Thirty-one percent had used cigarettes, 15 percent tried inhalants, and 19 percent smoked marijuana. Lifetime prevalence of marijuana use increased from 13 percent in 1993 to 17 percent in 1994, rising to a high of 23 percent by 1996 (Figure 7-2).

Eight percent of eighth graders used marijuana in the past month during 2002. Four percent used inhalants, 20 percent drank alcohol, and 11 percent smoked cigarettes in the past 30 days. These data suggest that use of gateway drugs such as alcohol, cigarettes, inhalants, and marijuana is common among youths 13 and 14 years old. Longitudinal studies of drug use prevalence among children and youths indicate that many youths who experiment with gateway drugs proceed further to such drugs as hallucinogens, cocaine, amphetamines, and heroin (Clark, Kirisci, & Moss, 1998; Kandel, Simcha-Fagan, & Davies, 1986; Loeber, 1990). Such findings suggest that a substantial number of eighth graders are already at risk for continued drug use.

DIFFERENCES BY GENDER AND ETHNICITY

Early studies of alcohol and other drug use among adolescents indicated that substance use was more prevalent among males than among females (Johnston, O'Malley, & Bachman, 1985). Males continue to use most drugs at higher rates than females. However, recent results from Monitoring the Future surveys show a decrease with regard to gender differences in drug use. For example, 59 percent of boys and 49 percent of girls reported lifetime illicit drug use in 1978. By 2002, the difference in illicit drug use between boys and girls was only five percentage points; 44 percent of boys compared with 39 percent of girls used an illicit drug in 2002. Historically, females have used amphetamines at a slightly higher rate than males, while males have been more involved in heavy drinking and drunk driving than females. These trends continued in 2002 (Johnston et al., 2003).

Survey results indicate that alcohol and drug use are more prevalent among white high school seniors than among African American or Hispanic high school seniors (Johnston et al., 2003). In 2002, annual prevalence of marijuana use ranged from 28 percent in African American students to 39 percent for white students. Twenty-eight percent of Hispanic seniors used marijuana during the past year in 2002. White teenagers had the highest 30-day prevalence of alcohol use at 54 percent; 48 percent of Hispanics and 30 percent of African Americans used alcohol in the past month. White high school seniors were also more likely to drink five or more drinks in a row in the past two weeks; 34 percent reported doing so. Twenty-six percent of Hispanics, and 12 percent of African Americans reported binge drinking.

Long-term trends in cigarette smoking reveal interesting differences by ethnicity. White, Hispanic, and African American seniors had similar daily smoking rates in the late 1970s; 29 percent of white students, 25 percent of African American students, and 23 percent of Hispanic students smoked daily in 1977. All three groups showed declines between 1977 and 1981. Between 1981 and 1993, African Americans and Hispanics showed a consistent decline while smoking rates changed little for white youths. Daily cigarette use increased for all groups beginning in 1994. By 2002, 22 percent of white students, 9 percent of Hispanic students, and six percent of African American students smoked cigarettes daily.

Differences between ethnic groups with regard to rates of alcohol and drug use should be interpreted with caution. African American and Hispanic inner-city youth, particularly males, are often underrepresented in national surveys. Other sources reveal that African American men account for one-third of admissions to emergency rooms for drug-related episodes (Institute of Medicine, 1990) and that substance use rates are highest among Hispanic men (Anthony, 1991). Evidence also indicates that American Indian youths, a group not included in annual Monitoring the Future surveys, consume alcohol and use drugs at higher levels than all other racial or ethnic groups (Institute of Medicine, 1990; Potthoff et al., 1998).

SUMMARY OF PREVALENCE STUDIES

Results of the above studies reflect important trends and long-term patterns in adolescent alcohol and drug use. First, national surveys of youths enrolled in school showed a decrease in the prevalence of most drug use between 1981 and 1992 (Johnston et al., 2003). These results suggest that prevention efforts and social norms favoring drug abstinence during the 1980s may have helped curb adolescent alcohol and drug use. Second, increases in illicit drug use between 1993 and 2002 signal a reversal of a decade-long pattern of decreasing drug use among the nation's youths. Noteworthy in the past decade has been the use of *designer* and *club* drugs by adolescents. Eleven percent of seniors used the club drug ecstasy, a synthetic compound with stimulant and hallucinogenic properties, at least once in their lifetime in 2001. This represented an increase of nearly five percent from 1996. These findings should remind policy makers that drug abuse is a recurring problem that must be addressed over the long run. Despite the improvements of the 1980s, secondary school students in 2002 showed a level of drug involvement exceeding that of any other industrialized nation (Johnston et al., 2003). Third, disparities in alcohol and drug use between males and females have decreased in the past decade. Finally, substance use appears to be more prevalent among white and American Indian youths than among Hispanic and African American youths.

RISK AND PROTECTIVE FACTORS FOR ADOLESCENT ALCOHOL AND DRUG ABUSE

Knowledge generated by investigations examining the relationship between risk and protective factors and drug use has led to significant advancements in understanding the etiology, assessment, and prevention of drug abuse (for a review of such investigations, see Belcher & Shinitzky, 1998; Hawkins, Catalano, & Miller, 1992; Hawkins, Kosterman, Maguin, Catalano, & Arthur, 1997; Jessor, 1992; Patton, 1995; Weinberg, Rahdert, Colliver, & Glantz, 1998). Yet definitions and practice applications underlying concepts of risk and protection are clouded with controversy. Most researchers, practitioners, and public health specialists agree that specific risk factors for adolescent drug use can be empirically identified. There is less agreement about the concept and definition of protective factors. Some authors (Luthar, 1991; Sameroff, Bartko, Baldwin, Baldwin, & Seifer, 1998) assert that risk and protective factors act as polar opposites of one another. Other investigators (Rossa, 2000; Rutter, 2000) argue that protective factors are characteristics and conditions that moderate or mediate levels of risk for problem behaviors like drug abuse. The discussion of protective factors in this chapter, consistent with the interpretation presented in chapter 2, is based on the view that protective factors are traits, conditions, and characteristics that influence or modify risk for drug abuse.

RISK FACTORS FOR ALCOHOL AND DRUG ABUSE

A multisystems framework, which offers a way both to understand etiological factors of drug abuse and to inform assessment strategies for identifying drug problems, is used below to classify risk factors for adolescent drug abuse at environmental, interpersonal, social, and individual levels. Risk factors for alcohol and other drug abuse are summarized in Table 7-1.

Environmental Risk Factors for Drug Abuse

Community laws and norms that favor drug use, such as low legal drinking ages and low taxes on alcoholic beverages, increase the risk of drug use during adolescence

Table 7-1. Risk Factors for Adolescent Alcohol and Drug Abuse

ENVIRONMENTAL FACTORS	INTERPERSONAL AND SOCIAL FACTORS	INDIVIDUAL FACTORS
Laws and Norms	**Family Factors**	**Psychosocial and**
• Taxation of alcohol and drugs	• Family conflict	**Biological Factors**
• Regulation of alcohol and drugs	• Poor parent–child bonding	• Family history of alcoholism
• Criminal laws for alcohol and drug use	• Poor family management practices	• Sensation-seeking orientation
• Cultural and social norms about alcohol and drug use	• Family communication	• Poor impulse control
	• Family alcohol and drug use	• Attention deficits
Availability of Alcohol and Drugs		• Hyperactivity
	School Factors	
Poverty and Economic Deprivation	• School failure	
	• Low commitment to school	
Low Economic Opportunity		
	Peer Factors	
Neighborhood Factors	• Rejection by conforming peer groups	
• Neighborhood disorganization	• Association with drug-using peers	
• Low neighborhood attachment		
• Residential mobility		
• High population density		
• High rates of adult criminality		

(Joksch, 1988). Studies examining the relationship between legal age for drinking and adolescent drinking and driving have shown that lowering the drinking age increases underage drinking and teen traffic fatalities (Joksch, 1988; Saffer & Grossman, 1987). Laws and norms that express intolerance for use of alcohol and illicit drugs by adolescents are associated with a lower prevalence of drug use (Johnston, 1991).

In 1995, 14 million children lived in poor families; five million of these children were less than six years old (Behrman, 1997). Poverty is associated with many adolescent outcomes, including conduct problems, delinquency, and unwanted pregnancy (Farrington, Gallagher, Morley, St. Leger, & West, 1988). Interestingly, research on social class and drug use has produced conflicting results about the association between poverty and drug use prevalence. Several studies report a negative relationship between extreme poverty and alcohol and drug use (Murray, Richards, Luepker, & Johnson, 1987; Robins & Ratcliff, 1979), suggesting that children who are raised in poor households and neighborhoods are at increased risk for adolescent drug abuse. Other studies indicate that adolescents from nonpoor families use drugs more often than youths from poor families (Adams, Blanken, Ferguson, & Kopstein, 1990). Poverty may also have an indirect effect on adolescent drug use. Family income is associated with many other risk factors for drug use (for example, parenting practices and academic difficulties); low family income may affect drug use indirectly through such risk factors. Additional studies are necessary to understand better the complex relationship between social class and drug use.

Low neighborhood attachment, school transitions, and residential mobility are associated with drug and alcohol abuse (Felner, Primavera, & Cauce, 1981; Murray, 1983). Neighborhoods with high population density and high rates of adult crime also have high rates of adolescent crime and drug use (Simcha-Fagan & Schwartz, 1986). Neighborhood disorganization may also indirectly affect risk for drug abuse by eroding the ability of parents to supervise and control their children.

Interpersonal and Social Risk Factors for Drug Abuse

Interpersonal and social risk factors for adolescent drug abuse occur in family, school, and peer settings. Children whose parents or siblings engage in serious alcohol or illicit drug use are themselves at greater risk for these behaviors (Biederman, Faraone, Monuteaux, & Feighner, 2000; Brook, Whiteman, Gordon, & Brook, 1988; Hill, Shen, Lowers, & Locke, 2000). Children who are raised in families with lax supervision, excessively severe or inconsistent disciplinary practices, and little communication and involvement between parents and children are also at high risk for later drug abuse (Baumrind, 1983). Similarly, studies have shown that parental conflict is related to subsequent alcohol or drug use by adolescent family members (DeMarsh & Kumpfer, 1986).

School failure, low degree of commitment to education, and lack of attachment to school have been identified as school-related factors that increase the risk of drug abuse during adolescence (Fleming, Kellam, & Brown, 1982; Holmberg, 1985). In addition, adolescent drug users are more likely to skip classes, be absent from school, and perform poorly than nondrug users (Gottfredson, 1981; Kim, 1979).

Associating with friends who use drugs is among the strongest predictors of adolescent alcohol or drug abuse (Barnes & Welte, 1986; Elliott, Huizinga, & Ageton, 1985; Fergusson & Horwood, 1999; Jenson & Howard, 1999a; Reinherz, Giaconia, Carmola Hauf, Wasserman, & Paradis, 2000). Peer rejection in elementary grades is associated with school problems and delinquency (Coie, 1990; Kupersmidt, Coie, & Dodge, 1990), which in turn are also risk factors for drug abuse (Hawkins, Jenson, Catalano, & Lishner, 1988). Some investigators hypothesize that rejected children form friendships with other rejected children and that such groups become delinquent during adolescence (Hartup, 1983; Tremblay, 1988). This hypothesis has not been adequately tested for adolescent drug use outcome measures.

Individual Risk Factors for Drug Abuse

Psychosocial and biological factors are related to drug and alcohol abuse during adolescence. For example, evidence from adoption, twin, and half-sibling studies supports the notion that alcoholism is an inherited disorder (Cadoret, Cain, & Grove, 1980). Several investigators have found that a sensation-seeking orientation predicts initiation and continued use of alcohol and other drugs (Cicchetti & Rogosch, 1999; Cloninger, Sigvardsson, & Bohman, 1988; Sussman, Dent, & Galaif, 1997). Research also indicates that attention deficit disorders, hyperactivity, and poor impulse control before the age of 12 predict the age of onset of drinking and drug use (Shelder & Block, 1990).

In recent longitudinal investigations, Jenson and Potter (2003) and Potter and Jenson (2003) found three distinct patterns of co-occurring mental health and substance use patterns among a sample of 154 detained youths. Adolescents who were most likely to abuse alcohol and other drugs also had high levels of self-reported depression, paranoia, hostility, and suicidal ideation. This and other investigations (Loeber, Farrington, Stouthamer-Loeber, & Van Kammen, 1998a, 1999b; Teplin, 2001; Timmons-Mitchell et al., 1997) suggest that mental health problems may play an important role in a youth's decision to experiment and use alcohol or other drugs.

SUMMARY OF RISK FACTORS

Current knowledge of drug abuse risk factors is correlational, not causal. It is important to note that the presence of risk factors only increases the likelihood that an adolescent may develop problem alcohol or drug use. The interaction and overlap of risk factors during adolescence are not well understood (Blum, 1997; Hawkins, Catalano, & Miller, 1992; Kraemer, Stice, Kazdin, Offord, & Kupfer, 2001), and some investigators even argue that such factors may be consequences of drug abuse rather than characteristics that increase risk for drug use (Macdonald, 1989). Despite these limitations, several conclusions about risk factors for alcohol and drug abuse can be drawn.

First, risk factors have been shown to be stable in the past 25 years. The factors summarized above consistently predict alcohol and drug use even though social norms about the acceptability of substance use changed several times during this period. Second, research indicates that the more risk factors are present, the greater the risk a child will have for alcohol or drug problems (Bry, McKeon, & Pandina, 1982; Pollard, Hawkins, & Arthur, 1999; Vega, Zimmerman, Warheit, Apospori, & Gil, 1993). These findings suggest that prevention programs should target risk factors at multiple levels, including differential vulnerability, child-rearing practices, school achievement, social influences, social learning, and broad social norms. Third, early initiation of drug and alcohol use is a key factor in the development of drug abuse problems. The early onset of any drug increases the subsequent frequency of drug use and the probability of involvement in deviant activities such as selling drugs (Myers, Brown, & Mott, 1995).

PROTECTIVE FACTORS AGAINST ALCOHOL AND DRUG ABUSE

Many adolescents develop healthy relationships and succeed in school and in the community despite their exposure to multiple risk factors. Empirical research devoted to identifying individual and environmental characteristics that protect youths from drug abuse has lagged behind similar efforts aimed at identifying risk factors for drug use. However, an increasing number of investigators have begun to examine the relationship between protective factors and drug use in recent years (Johnson et al., 1998; Pollard et al., 1999; Rutter, 2000; Stouthamer-Loeber et al., 1993; Tolan, Guerra, & Kendall, 1995; Werner, 1994). When identified in children and adolescents, protective factors can be manipulated or enhanced to reduce risks for drug abuse. Protective factors for alcohol and other drug use are summarized below and in Table 7-2.

Table 7-2. Protective Factors against Adolescent Alcohol and Drug Abuse

ENVIRONMENTAL, INTERPERSONAL, AND SOCIAL FACTORS	INDIVIDUAL FACTORS
Family Factors • Being a firstborn child • Being raised in a small family • Experiencing low parental conflict • Caring relationships with siblings • Caring relationships with extended family • Attachment to parents Social Support from Nonfamily Members Commitment to School Involvement in Conventional Activities Belief in Prosocial Norms and Values	Social and Problem-Solving Skills Positive Attitude Temperament High Intelligence Low Childhood Stress

Environmental, Interpersonal, and Social Protective Factors against Drug Abuse

Environmental, interpersonal, and social protective factors are attributes that buffer community, neighborhood, family, school, and peer risk factors. Werner and colleagues have conducted the most comprehensive study of protective factors among children. Werner and Smith (1989) began following a cohort of high-risk children in Kauai, Hawaii, in 1955. Analysis of the children's outcomes as adolescents and adults has contributed to knowledge about factors that prevent youths from abusing alcohol and other drugs.

Werner (1994) found that being raised in a family with four or fewer children experiencing low parental conflict and being a firstborn child reduce the effects of poverty and other risk factors for drug abuse. Children who abstained from drug use during adolescence and early adulthood had positive parent–child relationships in early childhood and caring relationships with siblings and grandparents. Children abstaining from alcohol and other drugs also received social support and frequent counsel from teachers, ministers, and neighbors (Werner, 1994).

A positive family milieu and community supports are protective factors for drug abuse among children exposed to multiple risk factors. Garmezy (1985) found low childhood stress among high-risk children living in supportive family environments and in adolescents who had strong external support systems. Because stress increases risk for drug use in later adolescence and early adulthood (Rutter, 1985), such findings have implications for preventing childhood and early adolescent drug abuse.

Strong social bonds to parents, to teachers, and to prosocial peers are significant factors in children's resistance to drug use (Berrueta-Clement, Schweinhart, Barnett, Epstein, & Weikhard, 1984; Hawkins, Catalano, & Associates, 1992). Four elements of the social bond have been found to be inversely related to adolescent drug abuse: (1) strong attachments to parents (Brook, Brook, Gordon, Whiteman, & Cohen, 1990); (2) commitment to school (Friedman, 1983); (3) involvement in prosocial activities such as church or community organizations (Gottfredson, 1981; Miller, Davies, & Greenwald, 2000); and (4) belief in the generalized norms and values of society (Jenson & Howard, 1999a; Krohn & Massey, 1980).

Understanding the processes by which strong social bonds develop is necessary to develop strategies that increase healthy bonding in high-risk youths. Social
learning (Bandura, 1986) and social development (Hawkins, Catalano, & Associates,
1992) theorists indicate that three conditions are critical to the formation of strong
social bonds: (1) opportunities for involvement in prosocial activities, (2) possession of
the requisite behavioral and cognitive skills necessary to achieve success in such activities, and (3) rewards or recognition for positive behaviors. To promote healthy bonds,
practitioners should use intervention strategies that provide opportunities, enhance
skills, and offer rewards to high-risk youths.

Individual Protective Factors against Drug Abuse

Individual protective factors are psychosocial and biomedical characteristics
that inhibit drug use. Competence in social and problem-solving situations is associated with abstinence and reductions in teenage drug use and delinquency (Fraser,
1996; Jenson & Howard, 1990). In a sample of high-risk urban children, Rutter (1985)
found that problem-solving skills and strong self-efficacy were associated with successful adolescent outcomes. Youths who possessed adequate problem-solving skill
and the ability to use them were less likely to engage in drug use and delinquency.
Jenson and colleagues (1993) found that strong self-efficacy decreased the likelihood of
drug use six months following drug treatment among adjudicated delinquents. These
findings suggest that social and problem-solving skills moderate the effects of multiple
risk factors for drug abuse and other adolescent outcomes.

Attitude and temperament are protective factors for drug abuse; positive social
orientation and positive temperament reduce the likelihood of adolescent drug abuse in
several studies of high-risk youths (see for example, Jenson & Howard, 1999a). Low
intelligence (Werner, 1994) is also related to drug use.

SUMMARY OF PROTECTIVE FACTORS

A limited number of studies have been conducted in an effort to understand
better the reciprocal nature of risk and protective factors. These investigations typically viewed protective factors as characteristics that affect individual responses to a
given amount of exposure to risk. This interpretation provides an opportunity to test
the mediating and moderating effects of protective factors on risk and to examine nonlinear and interactive relationships among risk and protective factors. Additional research is needed to increase our understanding of risk and protective factors and of the
multiple pathways to teenage substance abuse.

DIFFERENCES IN RISK AND PROTECTIVE FACTORS BY AGE, GENDER, AND RACE OR ETHNICITY

Few etiological studies of adolescent drug abuse devote attention to characteristics
such as age, gender, and race or ethnicity (Feldman & Elliott, 1990; Vega, Gil, &

Associates, 1998). Most of what is known about risk and protective factors for adolescent drug abuse has been drawn from studies of white junior and senior high school students residing in middle-class neighborhoods. Prevention and treatment programs often assume that risk and protective factors related to alcohol and drug use are the same for different adolescent populations. However, age, gender, and ethnic minority status are central issues in the developmental process of children and adolescents and warrant additional research attention.

AGE

Different risk and protective factors are salient at different stages in a child's development (Coie et al., 1993; Hawkins, Catalano, & Miller, 1992). For example, aggressiveness in children as young as five predicts later drug use (Kellam & Brown, 1982), while association with deviant peers in early adolescence is strongly related to drug use in later adolescence and early adulthood (Dishion, 1990). Poor parenting and family management practices are related to drug use during childhood and adolescence (Kendziora & O'Leary, 1993). Community supports and extended family members are protective factors against drug abuse for older adolescents (Werner, 1994).

Knowledge of developmental differences in the saliency of risk and protective factors must be considered in prevention and treatment efforts. Factors that are predictive of drug use in early childhood differ considerably from factors that are most important during later stages of adolescence, so practitioners must be familiar with the saliency of risk and protective factors across all developmental stages. Predictions of problem behaviors such as drug abuse are generally best made from proximal or situational risk factors (Coie et al., 1993).

GENDER

Most studies of risk and protective factors associated with alcohol and other drug use have been conducted with male or mixed-gender samples. The few investigations that have examined the relationship between gender and risk and protective factors have identified surprisingly few differences between boys and girls (see, for example, Fishbein & Perez, 2000; Kempf-Leonard, Chesney-Lind, & Hawkins, 2001; Khoury, 1998).

Girls do evidence higher rates of prior abuse and victimization than boys, two risk factors that are significantly related to drug abuse in many studies (Boyd, 2000; Widom, 1999). Evidence suggests that girls are at greater risk for mental health disorders than boys (Johnson, Roberts, & Worell, 1999; Timmons-Mitchell et al., 1997); as noted earlier, mental health problems may in turn increase the likelihood of drug abuse during adolescence and early adulthood. Investigators have also speculated that differential patterns of adolescent development between boys and girls, including pubertal changes, gender role characteristics, and self-esteem, are related to problem behaviors such as drug use and delinquency (Gilligan & Mikel-Brown, 1992; Khoury, 1998). Aggression, particularly relational aggressive behavior (Crick, 1996), is also associated with drug abuse among girls.

RACE OR ETHNICITY

Adolescents in the United States receive differential exposure to risk based on racial and ethnic characteristics. Youths of color are overrepresented in persistent poverty (Sawhill, 1992) and are more likely than white youths to be incarcerated (Hsisa & Hamparian, 1997; Pope & Feyerherm, 1993). Youths of color are also more likely to be victims of violent crime (Jenson & Howard, 1999b; U.S. Department of Health and Human Services, 2001) and to be raised in single-parent households (National Research Council, 1993) than white youths. Differential exposure to predisposing factors because of race or ethnicity may increase the risk for alcohol and drug abuse among youths of color.

The Social Development Research Group examined racial differences in individual (Gillmore et al., 1990; Wells et al., 1992) and family (Catalano, Hawkins, Krenz, Gillmore, & Morrison, 1993; Catalano et al., 1992) risk factors related to drug use among white, African American, and Asian American adolescents. Data were drawn from a longitudinal study of drug use and delinquency among public schoolchildren in Seattle between 1981 and 1986. Subjects were in the fifth grade at the time of analysis. Tobacco and alcohol use were highest among white students at 23 percent; 19 percent of African Americans and 9 percent of Asian Americans used tobacco by the fifth grade. Forty-nine percent of white youths, 40 percent of African American youths, and 17 percent of Asian American youths drank alcohol (Gillmore et al., 1990).

Differences in family factors related to drug use were found for the three groups; white and African American children reported significantly better family communication than Asian Americans, while African Americans reported a significantly higher proportion of deviant siblings than the other two groups (Catalano et al., 1992). Asian American children had the lowest, and African Americans the highest, involvement in family work and activities (Catalano et al., 1992). White youths reported less use of proactive family management practices by their parents than youths in the other two groups (Catalano et al., 1993). These findings suggest that families of different racial groups do not always influence their children in the same way.

Wells and colleagues (1992) examined the relationship between antisocial behaviors and attitudes and early initiation of drug use for white, African American, and Asian American students. Self-reported antisocial behaviors and attitudes were the strongest predictors of drug use for fifth-grade Asian American children. Teacher ratings of antisocial behavior were significantly related to drug use for white students but not for African American or Asian American students. Teachers perceived African American youths as more aggressive than other students; however, this perception was not related to self-reported initiation of tobacco, alcohol, or marijuana.

Gillmore and colleagues (1990) examined exposure to risk factors for white, African American, and Asian American fifth graders. Caucasians reported the greatest access to marijuana, greatest parental tolerance of drug use, and greatest intentions to use drugs in the future. No racial differences were found in the number of peers who used alcohol or other drugs.

Differences between risk and protective factors for Hispanic and non-Hispanic adolescents have been examined. Jenson (1993) found that strong family bonds among Hispanic families acted as a buffer for drug use among adjudicated delinquents. Parent involvement and family communication were significantly higher among delinquents of Hispanic origin than among non-Hispanic delinquent youths.

At least one study examined the relationship between the number of risk factors and drug use by racial or ethnic groups. Vega and colleagues (1993) examined risk factors for drug use among sixth- and seventh-grade Cuban, Other Hispanic, African American, and white youths. African Americans were the least likely to have no risk factors and the most likely to have three to six risk factors; African Americans also had the highest mean number of risk factors across groups. Low self-esteem and delinquency were related to drug use among Other Hispanics. Depression symptoms predicted alcohol use among white youths, while parental drug use was a strong predictor of drug use among African American youths. Low family pride and willingness to engage in antisocial behaviors were related to alcohol use in all groups.

These findings suggest that prevention and treatment programs may need to be tailored when applied to different racial or ethnic groups. For example, parent bonding and family communication appear to be salient protective factors against drug abuse for Hispanic children and youths (Gilbert, 1989; Jenson, 1993). Hispanic youths at risk of drug abuse may benefit from family-based programs that enhance family strengths. Poor parent modeling of alcohol use in some African American families may place youths at high risk for drug abuse (Institute of Medicine, 1990). Prevention efforts aimed at African American youths might include intervention strategies that address appropriate modeling practices for alcohol use. These and other racial or ethnic differences in risk factors should be systematically included in intervention strategies for high-risk youths.

Research is only beginning to address racial or ethnic differences in risk and protective factors. Additional studies are needed to provide the empirical base necessary to design culturally sensitive prevention and treatment programs.

Assessing Risk and Protective Factors

Assessing the prevalence of risk and protective factors among children and youths at risk of drug abuse is an essential part of targeting and designing prevention and treatment programs. Screening instruments and comprehensive diagnostic inventories that assess actual levels of drug use are also helpful in evaluating risk and protective factors for drug abuse.

Screening Instruments

Screening instruments offer practitioners and clients the opportunity to assess the likelihood of a drug abuse problem. Such instruments are short, are easy to administer, and provide clinical criteria that identify clients who may benefit from a comprehensive diagnostic evaluation (Martin & Winters, 1998). Screening tools provide information about levels of risk and protection experienced by youths.

Winters (1992) developed the Personal Experience Screening Questionnaire (PESQ) to meet the need for a quick adolescent drug abuse screening tool. The PESQ is also useful in determining the need for a comprehensive assessment of risk and protective factors associated with drug use. Psychometric properties have been established for an 18- and a 38-item PESQ (Winters, 1992; Winters, Weller, & Meland, 1993).

The PESQ is a paper-and-pencil screening tool written at the fourth-grade reading level. The test is scored for problem severity, drug use history, and psychological problems. The total score for problem severity gets either a green or a red flag; the red flag score suggests the need for further assessment. Discriminant function analyses were used to identify a score that maximized the correct classification of adolescents into relevant criterion groups (need for a comprehensive assessment vs. no need for a comprehensive assessment; Winters, 1992).

The Problem Oriented Screening Instrument for Teenagers (POSIT) is designed to identify risk and protective factors for drug abuse that may require additional assessment (Radhert, 1991). The POSIT is intended to operate as a first screen for drug use problems. Ten functional areas incorporating many of the risk and protective factors discussed in this chapter are assessed in the POSIT, including substance use and abuse, physical health, mental health, family relationships, peers, educational status, vocational status, social skills, leisure and recreation, and aggressive behavior. Scores exceeding an established cutoff point for each area may indicate that a drug use problem exists. The POSIT scoring system is based on expert clinical judgment and has been widely used in juvenile justice settings (for example, Dembo, Schmeidler, Borden, Chin Sue, & Manning, 1997).

The Substance Abuse Subtle Screening Inventory (SASSI; Miller, 1985) is an 85-item instrument that evaluates risk and protective factors associated with alcohol and other drug problems. The instrument yields clinically relevant scores for drug and alcohol history. Risberg, Stevens, and Graybill (1995) found that SASSI scores corresponded well to subsequent diagnoses of alcohol and drug use disorders among a sample of adolescents referred for residential drug treatment.

DIAGNOSTIC INVENTORIES

Diagnostic inventories provide an in-depth examination of actual drug use and of risk and protective factors associated with use. Diagnostic tools are typically used with youths who exceed problem levels on the previously described screening instruments.

The Personal Experience Inventory (PEI) is a self-report inventory that measures psychosocial risk factors associated with adolescent drug involvement (Winters, Latimer, Stinchfield, & Henly, 1999; Winters, Stinchfield, & Henly, 1993). The inventory includes five scales that assess (1) personal involvement with drug use, (2) effects of drug use, (3) social benefits of drug use, (4) personal consequences of drug use, and (5) polydrug use. Each of the five scales has a range of eight to 29 items; all have demonstrated reliability and validity. Studies of the PEI indicate that the scales are significantly related to the *Diagnostic and Statistical Manual of Mental Disorders, Fourth Edition* (DSM-IV) criteria for substance use disorders and treatment recommendations (Henly & Winters, 1988; Winters et al., 1993). The PEI has also successfully classified high-risk adolescents into outpatient or inpatient treatment referral subgroups. A parent version of the PEI has demonstrated high reliability and validity (Winters, Anderson, Bengston, Stinchfield, & Latimer, 2000).

The Adolescent Diagnostic Interview (ADI; Winters & Henly, 1993) assesses symptoms of alcohol and drug use disorders as defined by the DSM-IV. The ADI evaluates a host of risk and protective traits associated with drug use, including psychosocial functioning, mental health symptoms, and family relationships. Practitioners working in environments that use the DSM-IV may find the ADI to be particularly helpful in assessing risk and protective factors for drug abuse (Winters, Latimer, & Stinchfield, 1999).

Dennis and colleagues (Dennis, 1999; Dennis, Rourke, & Caddell, 1993) developed the Global Appraisal of Individual Needs (GAIN) to assess drug use and factors associated with drug use in high-risk adolescents. The instrument is divided into eight areas that include detailed questions about drug use, physical health, mental and emotional health, environmental influences, interpersonal relationships, and legal and vocational status. Administration time for the GAIN varies from one to two hours depending on the extent of drug use history.

Farrell and colleagues (Farrell, 1993; Farrell, Anchors, Danish, & Howard, 1992; Farrell, Danish, & Howard, 1992) created a risk factor index for youth ages 12 to 17 based on a subset of nine risk factors for drug abuse: (1) is home alone after school, (2) has friends who approve of drug use, (3) has friends who use drugs, (4) knows adults who use drugs, (5) feels pressure to use drugs, (6) has a history of trouble with the police, (7) displays delinquent behavior, (8) has intentions to use drugs, and (9) has inadequate coping and social skills. Self-report interviews in which adolescents respond to questions assessing each of the above risk factors are used to determine a subject's risk for drug abuse. Farrell has demonstrated the predictive validity of the index in studies of rural (Farrell, Anchors, et al., 1992) and urban (Farrell, Danish, et al., 1992) adolescents.

SPECIALIZED INSTRUMENTS

Many instruments available to practitioners are designed to assess single or, in some cases, sets of risk or protective factors (for example, peer or family factors). These inventories can be administered with the screening and diagnostic measures identified above as part of a comprehensive strategy to evaluate risk and protective factors.

Social skills and self-efficacy, critical to the development of prosocial behavior, have been used as indicators of risk for drug abuse by several investigators (Hawkins, Jenson, Catalano, & Wells, 1991; Winters, 1999). The Social Skills Rating System (SSRS) is a checklist that provides student, parent, and teacher ratings of cooperation, assertion, responsibility, empathy, and self-control skills (Elliot, Gresham, Freeman, & McCloskey, 1988). Elementary and secondary school versions of the SSRS have been standardized on 4,000 youths between three and 18 years old.

The Adolescent Problem Situation Inventory is an audiotaped skills inventory that evaluates social, behavioral, and cognitive abilities (Wells, Jenson, Hurwitz, Catalano, & Hawkins, 1988). Subjects listen and respond to 31 role-play situations that place youths at risk for drug use or delinquency; responses are scored by two or more raters to assess a youth's skill level. The instrument has been used to accurately identify skill deficits in delinquent and drug-abusing youths (Hawkins et al., 1991; Jenson et al., 1993).

The importance of family factors in the onset and persistent use of alcohol and other drugs was noted earlier. The Family Crisis Oriented Personal Evaluation Scales (F-COPES; McCubbin, Thompson, & McCubbin, 1996) evaluates how families cope with external difficulties. Coping responses to internal problems and conflicts between family members are also assessed. Results from the F-COPES can be used to understand the strength of family members' abilities to cope with stressful situations that are present in the home and social environment.

Hodges (1999) developed the Children and Adolescent Functional Assessment Scale (CAFAS) to rate functional impairment in adolescents. The instrument includes a substance use scale and assesses many known risk and protective factors including school performance, family relationships, behavior toward others, thinking processes, and mood. Although it is not designed exclusively for drug abuse assessment, results of the CAFAS may help practitioners understand the factors that contribute to drug use among adolescents. Reliability and validity for the CAFAS are in the acceptable range. See Hodges (1999) for a review of the instrument's psychometric properties and additional information about the application of this measure to adolescent drug use.

Dembo and colleagues (Dembo & Pacheco, 1999; Dembo et al., 1996) created the Prototype Screening and Triage Form for youths placed in juvenile detention and other correctional settings. The instrument is used to evaluate a youth's delinquent background and to assess substance use, home environment, family history, and mental health status. Dembo has successfully used the measure to describe the characteristics of juvenile detainees and to assess risk for future offending (Dembo et al. 1996).

Summary of Screening and Diagnostic Measures

Using information about risk and protective factors to predict subsequent involvement in drug abuse is complex. Many predictions are false positive—not all children who are at risk of drug abuse actually engage in drug use during adolescence (Kraemer et al., 1997). Teachers and community members may treat youths who are labeled "high risk" differently from other youths, and this may have a negative effect on a young person's behavior. Conversely, some predictions are false negative— some children do not exhibit patterns of drug use until late in their development, precluding early intervention efforts. To decrease the likelihood of inaccurate predictions, practitioners should use multiple sources to assess risk and protective factors. For a comprehensive review of these and other assessment instruments, see Martin and Winters (1998).

Implications for Prevention, Early Intervention, and Treatment

This chapter establishes that there is empirical evidence of the stability of risk and protective factors for drug abuse. Knowledge gained from these factors should be put to work in prevention and treatment programs. To implement programs or strategies based on risk and protective factors, practitioners should use systematic screening and diagnostic tools to identify youths at risk for drug abuse, focus prevention efforts on known risk and protective factors before drug use problems stabilize or become serious, adjust intervention efforts according to developmental stages of childhood and adolescence, be sensitive to gender and racial and ethnic differences, and select and implement empirically supported treatment approaches for drug-abusing adolescents.

PRACTICE GUIDELINES AND INTERVENTION CHALLENGES

Clinical practice and research in adolescent drug abuse has largely been descriptive or correlational in nature. Historically, research has most often focused on identifying factors associated with onset or relapse of drug use, rather than on the effectiveness or efficacy of prevention and treatment efforts (Jenson & Howard, 2001). This has led to a lack of information about interventions and services that are most effective in preventing or treating adolescent drug abuse.

The use of a public health framework—a model that incorporates principles of risk and protection—has been a welcome contribution to efforts aimed at evaluating interventions for high-risk and drug-abusing youths (Hawkins, Catalano, & Associates, 1992; Kraemer et al., 1997). A particularly encouraging development is found in the application of risk and protection to the field of drug abuse prevention. Evaluations of prevention programs have increased rapidly in recent years. A number of effective programs have been identified; most are based on tenants of social learning and cognitive–behavioral theories and seek to enhance young peoples' social and cognitive abilities (see Hawkins et al., 1997, for a review of promising and effective prevention programs). We have also learned that large, resource-rich strategies do not necessarily ensure a program's effectiveness. Recent evaluations of the Drug Abuse Resistance Education Program (DARE), a joint national effort between law enforcement and education to reduce drug use, have shown the program to be ineffective in preventing the onset of alcohol and other drug use (Lyman et al., 1999). Practitioners should be informed of empirically supported prevention programs and be encouraged to implement such strategies whenever possible.

Less is known about the effects of adolescent drug abuse treatment. Four intervention models—12-step programs based on principles of Alcoholics Anonymous, family therapy, therapeutic community programs, and cognitive–behavioral training—have dominated the field of adolescent drug abuse treatment (Jenson & Howard, 2001; Winters, 1999). While cognitive–behavioral training and family therapy have yielded the largest number of effective evaluations, there is little evidence to suggest that one treatment modality is superior to any other (Jenson & Howard, 2001).

The lack of empirical evidence to support specific treatment approaches is a deterrent to developing practice guidelines that identify and describe effective strategies for adolescent drug abuse treatment. Practice guidelines are empirically supported statements that offer practitioners tested and validated intervention strategies for client problems such as drug abuse (Chambless & Hollon, 1998; Howard & Jenson, 1999; Kazdin & Weisz, 1998; Kendall, 1998). The creation of practice guidelines is therefore dependent on the quality and amount of empirical evidence that is available to support the effectiveness of a particular intervention strategy.

There is considerable interest in developing practice guidelines for adolescent drug abuse treatment (Jenson & Howard, 2001; Winters, 1999). Unfortunately, the absence of empirical evidence to support the effectiveness of adolescent drug abuse treatment strategies renders the creation of specific and detailed treatment guidelines premature. Existing guidelines have been limited to statements that offer treatment suggestions based on client information about drug use history and chronicity across a continuum of primary prevention, early intervention, outpatient treatment, residential care, and hospitalization (Winters, 1999). This step represents a beginning phase in the development of practice guidelines for adolescent drug abuse treatment, but much remains to be accomplished. Several social work investigators have recently called for an increase in intervention-based research studies as a way to increase the lack of clinically relevant information about drug treatment and other outcome data that is available to practitioners (Fraser, 2000; Jenson & Howard, 2001; Rosen, Proctor, & Staudt, 1999). Practitioners and researchers should initiate new and rigorous investigations to assess the effectiveness of adolescent drug abuse treatment. Social workers should increase their involvement and visibility in addressing this important social problem.

CONCLUSION

Risk, protection, and resiliency in childhood and adolescence are key components of assessment techniques and interventions for high-risk youths. Strategies that practitioners in schools, clinics, the community, and other settings use in prevention and treatment programs for youths at risk of drug abuse need to be based on those factors that mitigate risk and promote resilience. Multicomponent strategies can delay the initiation of alcohol and drug use among high-risk children and reduce substance use among adolescents who already engage in drug use. No one strategy can be applied successfully in every instance—approaches should be tried in various combinations and evaluated for their efficacy in preventing the initiation and continuance of alcohol and drug use. Information derived from such studies should be used to inform and develop practice guidelines aimed at preventing or treating adolescent drug abuse.

REFERENCES

Adams, E. H., Blanken, A. J., Ferguson, L. D., & Kopstein, A. (1990). *Overview of selected drug trends*. Rockville, MD: National Institute on Drug Abuse.

Anthony, J. C. (1991). The epidemiology of drug addiction. In N. S. Miller (Ed.), *Comprehensive handbook of drug and alcohol addiction* (pp. 55–86). New York: Marcel-Dekker.

Bandura, A. (1986). *Social foundations of thought and action: A social-cognitive view.* Englewood Cliffs, NJ: Prentice Hall.

Barnes, G. M., & Welte, J. W. (1986). Patterns and predictors of alcohol use among 7–12th grade students in New York State. *Journal of Studies on Alcohol, 47,* 53–62.

Baumrind, D. (1983, October). *Why adolescents take chances—and why they don't.* Paper presented at the National Institute for Child Health and Human Development, Bethesda, MD.

Belcher, H. M., & Shinitzky, H. E. (1998). Substance abuse in children: Prediction, protection, and prevention. *Archives of Pediatrics and Adolescent Medicine, 152,* 952–960.

Berhman, R. E. (1997). Children and poverty. *The Future of Children, 7*(2, Whole).

Berrueta-Clement, J. R., Schweinhart, L. J., Barnett, W. S., Epstein, A. S., & Weikhard, D. P. (1984). *Changed lives: The effects of the Perry Preschool Program on youths through age 19*. Ypsilanti, MI: High/Scope Press.

Biederman, J., Faraone, S. V., Monuteaux, M. C., & Feighner, J. A. (2000). Patterns of alcohol and drug use in adolescents can be predicted by parental substance use disorders. *Pediatrics, 106,* 792–797.

Blum, R. W. (1997). Adolescent substance use and abuse. *Archives of Pediatric Adolescent Medicine, 151,* 805–808.

Boyd, M. R. (2000). Predicting substance abuse and comorbidity in rural women. *Archives of Psychiatric Nursing, 14,* 64–72.

Brook, J. S., Brook, D. W., Gordon, A. S., Whiteman, M., & Cohen, P. (1990). The psychosocial etiology of adolescent drug use: A family interactional approach. *Genetic, Social and General Psychology Monographs,* No. 116. (Whole No. 2).

Brook, J. S., Whiteman, M., Gordon, A. S., & Brook, D. W. (1988). The role of older brothers in younger brothers' drug use viewed in the context of parent and peer influences. *Journal of Genetic Psychology, 151,* 59–75.

Bry, B. H., McKeon, P., & Pandina, R. J. (1982). Extent of drug use as a function of number of risk factors. *Journal of Abnormal Psychology, 91,* 273–279.

Cadoret, R. J., Cain, C. A., & Grove, W. M. (1980). Development of alcoholism in adoptees raised apart from alcoholic biologic relatives. *Archives of General Psychiatry, 37,* 561–563.

Catalano, R. F., Hawkins, J. D., Krenz, C., Gillmore, M. R., & Morrison, D. M. (1993). Using research to guide culturally appropriate drug abuse prevention. *Journal of Consulting and Clinical Psychology, 61,* 804–811.

Catalano, R. F., Morrison, D. M., Wells, E. A., Gillmore, M. R., Iritani, B., & Hawkins, J. D. (1992). Ethnic differences in family factors related to early drug initiation. *Journal of Studies on Alcohol, 53*(3), 208–217.

Chambless, D. L., & Hollon, S. D. (1998). Defining empirically supported therapies. *Journal of Consulting and Clinical Psychology, 66,* 7–18.

Cicchetti, D., & Rogosch, F. A. (1999). Psychopathology as risk for adolescent substance use disorders: A developmental psychopathology perspective. *Journal of Clinical Child Psychology, 28,* 355–365.

Clark, D. B., Kirisci, L., & Moss, H. B. (1998). Early adolescent gateway drug use in sons of fathers with substance use disorders. *Addictive Behaviors, 23,* 561–566.

Cloninger, C. R., Sigvardsson, S., & Bohman, M. (1988). Childhood personality predicts alcohol abuse in young adults. *Alcoholism: Clinical and Experimental Research, 12,* 494–503.

Coie, J. D. (1990). Towards a theory of peer rejection. In S. R. Asher & J. D. Coie (Eds.), *Peer rejection in childhood* (pp. 365–398). New York: Cambridge University Press.

Coie, J. D., Watt, N. F., West, S. G., Hawkins, J. D., Asarnow, J. R., Markman, H. J., Ramey, S. L., Shure, M. B., & Long, B. (1993). The science of prevention: A conceptual framework and some directions for a national research program. *American Psychologist, 48*(10), 1013–1022.

Crick, N. R. (1996). The role of overt aggression, relational aggression, aggression and prosocial behavior in the prediction of children's future social adjustments. *Child Development, 67,* 2317–2327.

DeMarsh, J., & Kumpfer, K. L. (1986). Family-oriented interventions for the prevention of chemical dependency in children and adolescents. In S. Griswold-Ezekoye, K. L. Kumpfer, & W. Bukoski (Eds.), *Childhood and chemical abuse: Prevention and intervention* (pp. 117–151). New York: Haworth Press.

Dembo, R., & Pacheco, K. (1999). Criminal justice response to adolescent substance abuse. In R. T. Ammerman & P. J. Ott (Eds.), *Prevention and societal impact of drug and alcohol abuse* (185–199). Mahwah, NJ: Lawrence Erlbaum.

Dembo, R., Schmeidler, J., Borden, P., Chin Sue, C., & Manning, D. (1997). Use of the POSIT among arrested youths entering a juvenile assessment center: A replication and update. *Journal of Child and Adolescent Substance Abuse, 6,* 19–42.

Dembo, R., Turner, G., Schmeidler, J., Sue, C. C., Borden, P., & Manning, D. (1996). Development and evaluation of a classification of high risk youths entering a juvenile assessment center. *Substance Use and Misuse, 31,* 301–322.

Dennis, M. L. (1999). *Overview of the Global Appraisal of Individual Needs: Summary.* Bloomington, IL: Chestnut Health Systems.

Dennis, M. L., Rourke, K. M., & Caddell, J. M. (1993). *Global Appraisal of Individual Needs: Administration manual.* Research Triangle Park, NC: Research Triangle Institute.

Dishion, T. J. (1990). The peer context of troublesome behavior in children and adolescents. In P. Leone (Ed.), *Understanding troubled and troublesome youth* (pp. 128–153). Beverly Hills, CA: Sage Publications.

Elliott, D. S., Huizinga, D., & Ageton, S. A. (1985). *Explaining delinquency and drug use.* Beverly Hills, CA: Sage Publications.

Elliott, S. N., Gresham, F. M., Freeman, T., & McCloskey, G. (1988). Teachers and observers ratings of children's social skills. *Journal of Psychoeducational Assessment, 6,* 225–235.

Farrell, A. D. (1993). Risk factors for drug use in urban adolescents: A three-wave longitudinal study. *Journal of Drug Issues, 23,* 443–462.

Farrell, A. D., Anchors, D. M., Danish, S. J., & Howard, C. W. (1992). Risk factors for drug use in rural adolescents. *Journal of Drug Education, 22,* 313–328.

Farrell, A. D., Danish, S. J., & Howard, C. W. (1992). Risk factors for drug use in urban adolescents: Identification and cross-validation. *American Journal of Community Psychology, 20,* 263–275.

Farrington, D. P., Gallagher, B., Morley, L., St. Leger, R., & West, D. (1988). Are there any successful men from criminogenic backgrounds? *Psychiatry, 51,* 116–130.

Feldman, S. S., & Elliott, G. R. (1990). *At the threshold: The developing adolescent.* Cambridge, MA: Harvard University Press.

Felner, R. D., Primavera, J., & Cauce, A. M. (1981). The impact of school transitions: A focus for preventive efforts. *American Journal of Community Psychology, 9,* 449–459.

Fergusson, D. M., & Horwood, L. J. (1999). Prospective childhood predictors of deviant peer affiliations in adolescence. *Journal of Child Psychology and Psychiatry and Allied Disciplines, 40,* 581–592.

Fishbein, D. H., & Perez, D. M. (2000). A regional study of risk factors for drug abuse and delinquency: Sex and racial differences. *Journal of Child and Family Studies, 9,* 461–479.

Fleming, J. P., Kellam, S. G., & Brown, C. H. (1982). Early predictors of age at first use of alcohol, marijuana, and cigarettes. *Drug and Alcohol Dependence, 9,* 285–303.

Fraser, M. W. (1996). Cognitive problem-solving and aggressive behavior among children. *Families in Society, 77,* 19–32.

Fraser, M. W. (2000, May 4). *Intervention research in social work: A basis for evidence-*

based practice? Paper presented at the Developing Practice Guidelines for Social Work Interventions Conference, George Warren Brown School of Social Work, Washington University, St. Louis.

Friedman, A. S. (1983). High school drug abuse clients. In *Clinical research notes*. Rockville, MD: National Institute on Drug Abuse.

Garmezy, N. (1985). Stress-resistant children: The search for protective factors. In J. E. Stevenson (Ed.), *Recent research in developmental psychology* (pp. 213–233). Oxford, England: Pergamon Press.

Gilbert, M. J. (1989). Alcohol use among Latino adolescents: What we know and what we need to know. *Perspectives on adolescent drug use*. Binghamton, NY: Haworth Press.

Gilligan, C., & Mikel-Brown, L. (1992). *Meeting at the crossroads: Women's psychology and girls' development*. Cambridge, MA: Harvard University Press.

Gillmore, M. R., Catalano, R. F., Morrison, D. M., Wells, E. A., Iritani, B., & Hawkins, J. D. (1990). Racial differences in acceptability and availability of drugs and early initiation of substance use. *American Journal of Drug and Alcohol Abuse, 16,* 185–206.

Gottfredson, G. D. (1981). Schooling and delinquency. In S. E. Martin, L. B. Sechrest, & R. Redner (Eds.), *New directions in the rehabilitation of criminal offenders* (pp. 421–469). Washington, DC: National Academy Press.

Hartup, W. W. (1983). Peer relations. In P. H. Mussed (Ed.), *Handbook of child psychology: Vol. 4. Socialization, personality, and social development* (pp. 103–196). New York: John Wiley & Sons.

Hawkins, J. D., Catalano, R. F., & Associates. (1992). *Communities that care: Action for drug abuse prevention*. San Francisco: Jossey-Bass.

Hawkins, J. D., Catalano, R. F., & Miller, J. Y. (1992). Risk and protective factors for alcohol and other drug problems in adolescence and early adulthood: Implications for substance abuse prevention. *Psychological Bulletin, 112,* 64–105.

Hawkins, J. D., Jenson, J. M., Catalano, R. F., & Lishner, D. L. (1988). Delinquency and drug abuse: Implications for social services. *Social Service Review, 62,* 258–284.

Hawkins, J. D., Jenson, J. M., Catalano, R. F., & Wells, E. A. (1991). Effects of skills training intervention with juvenile delinquents. *Research on Social Work Practice, 1,* 107–121.

Hawkins, J. D., Kosterman, R., Maguin, E., Catalano, R. F., & Arthur, M. W. (1997). Substance use and abuse. In R. T. Ammerman & M. Hersen (Eds.), *Handbook of prevention and treatment with children and adolescents: Intervention in the real world context* (pp. 203–237). New York: John Wiley & Sons.

Henly, G. A., & Winters, K. C. (1988). Development of problem severity scales for the assessment of adolescent alcohol and drug abuse. *International Journal of the Addictions, 23,* 65–85.

Hill, S. Y., Shen, S., Lowers, L., & Locke, J. (2000). Factors predicting the onset of adolescent drinking in families at high risk for developing alcoholism. *Biological Psychiatry, 48,* 265–275.

Hodges, K. (1999). Child and adolescent functional assessment scale. In M. E. Maruish (Ed.), *The use of psychological testing for treatment planning and outcomes assessment* (2nd ed., pp. 631–664). Mahwah, NJ: Lawrence Erlbaum.

Holmberg, M. B. (1985). Longitudinal studies of drug abuse in a fifteen year old population: 1. Drug career. *Acta Psychiatrica Scandanavia, 71,* 67–79.

Howard, M. O., & Jenson, J. M. (1999). Clinical practice guidelines: Should social work develop them? *Research on Social Work Practice, 9,* 283–301.

Hsisa, H. M., & Hamparian, D. (1997, September). Disproportionate minority confinement: 1997 update. *Juvenile Justice Bulletin.* Washington, DC: Office of Juvenile Justice and Delinquency Prevention.

Institute of Medicine. (1990). *Broadening the base of treatment for alcohol problems.* Washington, DC: National Academy Press.

Jenson, J. M. (1993, November). *Factors related to gang membership among juvenile probationers.* Presentation at the Annual Meeting of the American Society of Criminology, Phoenix, AZ.

Jenson, J. M., & Howard, M. O. (1990). Skills deficits, skills training, and delinquency. *Children and Youth Services Review, 12,* 213–238.

Jenson, J. M., & Howard, M. O. (1999a). Hallucinogen use among juvenile probationers: Prevalence and characteristics. *Criminal Justice and Behavior, 26,* 357–372.

Jenson, J. M., & Howard, M. O. (Eds.). (1999b). *Youth violence: Current research and recent practice innovations.* Washington, DC: NASW Press.

Jenson, J. M., & Howard, M. O. (2001, January 20). *Toward guidelines for social work intervention in substance abuse.* Presentation at the Annual Meeting of the Society for Social Work and Research, Atlanta.

Jenson, J. M., & Potter, C. C. (2003). The effects of cross-system collaboration on mental health and substance abuse problems of detained youths. *Research on Social Work Practice, 13,* 588–607.

Jenson, J. M., Wells, E. A., Plotnick, R. D., Hawkins, J. D., & Catalano, R. F. (1993). The effects of skills and intentions to use drugs on posttreatment drug use of adolescents. *American Journal of Drug and Alcohol Abuse, 19,* 1–17.

Jessor, R. (1992). Risk behavior in adolescence: A psychosocial framework for understanding and action. In D. E. Rogers & E. Ginzburg (Eds.), *Adolescents at risk: Medical and social perspectives* (pp. 19–34). Boulder, CO: Westview Press.

Johnson, K., Bryant, D. D., Collins, D. A., Noe, T. D., Strader, T. N., & Berbaum, M. (1998). Preventing and reducing alcohol and other drug use among high-risk youths by increasing family resilience. *Social Work, 43,* 297–308.

Johnson, N. G., Roberts, M. C., & Worell, J. (Eds.). (1999). *Beyond appearance: A new look at adolescent girls.* Washington DC: American Psychological Association.

Johnston, L. D. (1991). Toward a theory of drug epidemics. In L. Donohew, H. E. Sypher, & W. J. Bukoski (Eds.), *Pervasive communication and drug abuse prevention* (pp. 93–131). Hillsdale, NJ: Lawrence Erlbaum.

Johnston, L. D., O'Malley, P. M., & Bachman, J. G. (1985). *Drug use, drinking, and smoking: National survey results from high school, college, and young adult populations.* Washington, DC: U.S. Government Printing Office.

Johnston, L. D., O'Malley, P. M., & Bachman, J. G. (2003). *Drug use, drinking, and smoking: National survey results from high school, college, and young adult populations.* Washington, DC: U.S. Government Printing Office.

Joksch, H. C. (1988). *The impact of severe penalties on drinking and driving.* Washington, DC: AAA Foundation for Traffic Safety.

Kandel, D., Simcha-Fagan, O., & Davies, M. (1986). Risk factors for delinquency and illicit drug use from adolescence to young adulthood. *Journal of Drug Issues, 60,* 67–90.

Kazdin, A. E., & Weisz, J. R. (1998). Identifying and developing empirically supported child and adolescent treatments. *Journal of Consulting and Clinical Psychology, 66,* 19–36.

Kellam, S. G., & Brown, H. (1982, December 3–4). *Social adaptational and psychological antecedents of adolescent psychopathology ten years later.* Paper presented at a research workshop on prevention aspects of suicide and affective disorders among adolescents and young males, Harvard School of Public Health and Harvard School of Medicine, Boston.

Kempf-Leonard, K., Chesney-Lind, M., & Hawkins, D. (2001). Ethnicity and gender issues. In R. Loeber & D. P. Farrington (Eds.), *Child delinquents: Development, intervention, and service needs* (pp. 247–269). Thousand Oaks, CA: Sage Publications.

Kendall, P. C. (1998). Empirically supported psychological therapies. *Journal of Consulting and Clinical Psychology, 66,* 3–6.

Kendziora, K. T., & O'Leary, S. G. (1993). Dysfunctional parenting as a focus for prevention and treatment of child behavior problems. In T. H. Ollendick & R. J. Prinz (Eds.), *Advances in clinical child psychology* (Vol. 15). New York: Plenum Press.

Khoury, E. L. (1998). Are girls different? A developmental perspective on gender differences in risk factors for substance use among adolescents. In W. A. Vega, A. G. Gil, & Associates (Eds.), *Drug use and ethnicity in early adolescence.* New York: Plenum Press.

Kim, S. (1979). *An evaluation of Ombudsman Primary Prevention program on student drug abuse.* Charlotte, NC: Charlotte Drug Education Center.

Kraemer, H. C., Kazdin, A. E., Offord, D. R., Kessler, R.C., Jensen, P. S., & Kupfer, D. J. (1997). Coming to terms with the terms of risk. *Archives of General Psychiatry, 54,* 337–343.

Kraemer, H. C., Stice, E., Kazdin, A., Offord, D., & Kupfer, D. (2001). How do risk factors work together? Mediators, moderators, and independent, overlapping, and proxy risk factors. *American Journal of Psychiatry, 158,* 848–856.

Krohn, M. D., & Massey, J. L. (1980). Social control and delinquent behavior: An examination of the elements of the social bond. *Developmental Psychology, 18,* 359–368.

Kupersmidt, J. B., Coie, J. D., & Dodge, K. A. (1990). The role of poor peer relationships in the development of disorder. In S. R. Asher & J. D. Coie (Eds.), *Peer rejection in childhood* (pp. 274–305). New York: Cambridge University Press.

Loeber, R. (1990). Development and risk factors of juvenile antisocial behavior and delinquency. *Clinical Psychology Review, 10,* 1–41.

Loeber, R., Farrington, D. P., Stouthamer-Loeber, M., & Van Kammen, W. B. (1998a). *Antisocial behavior and mental health problems: Explanatory factors in childhood and adolescence.* Mahwah, NJ: Lawrence Erlbaum.

Loeber, R., Farrington, D. P., Stouthamer-Loeber, M., & Van Kammen, W. B. (1998b). Multiple risk factors for multiproblem boys: Co-occurrence of delinquency, substance use, attention deficit, conduct problems, physical aggression, covert behavior, depressed mood, and shy/withdrawn behavior. In R. Jessor (Ed.), *New perspectives on adolescent risk behavior* (pp. 91–149). New York: Cambridge University Press.

Luthar, S. S. (1991). Vulnerability and resilience: A study of high-risk adolescents. *Child Development, 62,* 600–616.

Lyman, D. R., Milich, R., Zimmerman, R., Novak, S. P., Logan, T. K., Matin, C., Leukefeld, C., & Clayton, R. (1999). Project DARE: No effects at 10-year follow-up. *Journal of Consulting and Clinical Psychology, 67,* 590–593.

Macdonald, D. I. (1989). *Drugs, drinking, and adolescents* (2nd ed.). Chicago: Year Book Medical Publishers.

Martin, C. S., & Winters, K. C. (1998). Diagnosis and assessment of alcohol use disorders among adolescents. *Alcohol, Health, and Research World, 22,* 95–105.

McCubbin, H. I., Thompson, A. I., & McCubbin, M. A. (1996). *Family assessment, resiliency coping and adaptation: Inventories for research and practice.* Madison: University of Wisconsin Press.

Miller, G. (1985). *The Substance Abuse Subtle Screening Inventory—Adolescent version.* Bloomington, IN: SASSI Institute.

Miller, L., Davies, M., & Greenwald, S. (2000). Religiosity and substance use and abuse among adolescents in the National Comorbidity Survey. *Journal of the American Academy of Child and Adolescent Psychiatry, 39,* 1190–1197.

Murray, C. A. (1983). The physical environment and community control of crime. In J. Q. Wilson (Ed.), *Crime and public policy.* San Francisco: Institute for Contemporary Studies.

Murray, D. M., Richards, P. S., Luepker, R. V., & Johnson, C. A. (1987). The prevention of cigarette smoking in children: Two- and three-year follow-up comparisons of four prevention strategies. *Journal of Behavioral Medicine, 10,* 595–611.

Myers, M. G., Brown, S. A., & Mott, M. A. (1995). Preadolescent conduct disorder behaviors predict relapse and progression of addiction for adolescent alcohol and drug abusers. *Alcoholism: Clinical and Experimental Research, 19,* 1528–1536.

National Research Council (1993). *Losing generations: Adolescents in high-risk settings.* Washington, DC: National Academy Press.

Patton, L. H. (1995). Adolescent substance abuse: Risk factors and protective factors. *Pediatric Clinics of North America, 42,* 283–293.

Pollard, J. A., Hawkins, J. D., & Arthur, M. W. (1999). Risk and protection: Are both necessary to understand diverse behavioral outcomes in adolescence? *Social Work Research, 23,* 145–158.

Pope, C., & Feyerherm, W. (1993). *Minorities in the juvenile justice system.* Washington, DC: Office of Juvenile Justice and Delinquency Prevention.

Potter, C. C., & Jenson, J. M. (2003). The co-occurrence of mental health problem symptoms and substance abuse among delinquent youth. *Criminal Justice and Behavior, 30,* 230–250.

Potthoff, S. J., Bearinger, L. H., Skay, C. L., Cassuto, N., Blum, R. W., & Resnick, M. D. (1998). Dimensions of risk behaviors among American Indian youth. *Archives of Pediatrics and Adolescent Medicine, 152,* 157–163.

Rahdert, E. R. (1991). *The adolescent assessment/referral system manual.* Washington, DC: Alcohol, Drug Abuse, and Mental Health Administration.

Reinherz, H. Z., Giaconia, R. M., Carmola Hauf, A. M., Wasserman, M. S., & Paradis, A. D. (2000). General and specific childhood risk factors for depression and drug disorders by early adulthood. *Journal of the American Academy of Child and Adolescent Psychiatry, 39,* 223–231.

Risberg, R. A., Stevens, M. J., & Graybill, D. F. (1995). Validating the adolescent form of the Substance Abuse Subtle Screening Inventory. *Journal of Child and Adolescent Substance Abuse, 4,* 25–41.

Robins, L. N., & Ratcliff, K. S. (1979). Continuation of antisocial behavior into adulthood. *International Journal of Mental Health, 7,* 96–116.

Rosen, A., Proctor, E. K., & Staudt, M. (1999). Social work research and the quest for effective practice. *Social Work Research, 23,* 3–14.

Rossa, M. W. (2000). Some thoughts about resilience versus positive development, main effects versus interactions, and the value of resilience. *Child Development, 71,* 567–569.

Rutter, M. (1985). Resilience in the face of adversity: Protective factors and resistance to psychiatric disorder. *British Journal of Psychiatry, 147,* 598–611.

Rutter, M. (2000). Psychosocial influences: Critiques, findings, and research needs. *Development and Psychopathology, 12,* 375–405.

Saffer, H., & Grossman, M. (1987). Beer taxes, the legal drinking age, and youth motor vehicle fatalities. *Journal of Legal Studies, 16,* 351–374.

Sameroff, A. J., Bartko, W. T., Baldwin, A., Baldwin, C., & Seifer, R. (1998). Family and social influences on development of child competence. In M. Lewis & C. Feiring (Eds.), *Families, risk, and competence* (pp. 161–185). Mahwah, NJ: Lawrence Erlbaum.

Sawhill, I. (1992). Young children and families. In H. J. Aaron & C. L. Schultze (Eds.), *Setting domestic priorities: What can governments do?* (pp. 97–136). Washington, DC: Brookings Institution.

Shedler, J., & Block, J. (1990). Adolescent drug use and psychological health: A longitudinal inquiry. *American Psychologist, 45,* 612–630.

Simcha-Fagan, O., & Schwartz, J. E. (1986). Neighborhood and delinquency: An assessment of contextual effects. *Criminology, 24,* 667–703.

Stouthamer-Loeber, M., Loeber, R., Farrington, D. P., Zhang, Q., Van Kammen, W., & Maguin, E. (1993). The double edge of protective and risk factors for delinquency: Interrelations and developmental patterns. *Development and Psychopathology, 5,* 683–701.

Sussman, S., Dent, C. W., & Galaif, E. R. (1997). The correlates of substance abuse and dependence among adolescents at high risk for drug abuse. *Journal of Substance Abuse, 9,* 241–255.

Teplin, L. (2001). Assessing alcohol, drug, and mental disorders in juvenile detainees (Fact Sheet No. 2). Washington, DC: U.S. Department of Justice, Office of Juvenile Justice and Delinquency Prevention.

Timmons-Mitchell, J., Brown, C., Schulz, S. C., Webster, S. E., Underwood, L. A., & Semple, W. E. (1997). Comparing the mental health needs of female and male incarcerated juvenile delinquents. *Behavioral Sciences and the Law, 15,* 195–202.

Tolan, P. H., Guerra, N. G., & Kendall, P. C. (1995). A developmental–ecological perspective on antisocial behavior in children and adolescents: Toward a unified risk and intervention framework. *Journal of Consulting and Clinical Psychology, 63,* 579–584.

Tremblay, R. (1988). *Peers and the onset of delinquency.* Paper prepared for the Onset Working Group Program on Human Development and Criminal Behavior, Castine, ME.

U.S. Department of Health and Human Services. (2001). *Youth violence: A report of the surgeon general.* Rockville, MD: U.S. Department of Health and Human

Services, Centers for Disease Control and Prevention, National Center for Injury Prevention and Control, Substance Abuse and Mental Health Services Administration, Center for Mental Health Services, and National Institutes of Health and Mental Health.

Vega, W. A., Gil, A. G., & Associates. (1998). *Drug use and ethnicity in early adolescence*. New York: Plenum Press.

Vega, W. A., Zimmerman, R. S., Warheit, G. J., Apospori, E., & Gil, A. G. (1993). Risk factors for early adolescent drug use in four ethnic and racial groups. *American Journal of Public Health, 83,* 185–189.

Weinberg, N. Z., Rahdert, E., Colliver, J. D., & Glantz, M. D. (1998). Adolescent substance abuse: A review of the past 10 years. *Journal of the American Academy of Child and Adolescent Psychiatry, 37,* 252–261.

Wells, E. A., Jenson, J. M., Hurwitz, H. A., Catalano, R. F., & Hawkins, J. D. (1988). *The Adolescent Problem Situation Inventory*. Seattle: University of Washington, Center for Social Welfare Research.

Wells, E. A., Morrison, D. M., Gillmore, M. R., Catalano, R. F., Iritani, B., & Hawkins, J. D. (1992). Race differences in antisocial behaviors and attitudes and early initiation of substance use. *Journal of Drug Education, 22,* 115–130.

Werner, E. E. (1994). Overcoming the odds. *Developmental and Behavioral Pediatrics, 15,* 131–136.

Werner, E. E., & Smith, R. S. (1989). *Vulnerable but invincible: A longitudinal study of resilient children and youth*. New York: Adams, Bannister, & Cox.

Widom, C. S. (1999). Childhood victimization, running away, and delinquency. *Journal of Research on Crime and Delinquency, 36,* 347–370.

Winters, K. C. (1992). Development of an adolescent alcohol and other drug abuse screening scale: Personal experience screening questionnaire. *Addictive Behaviors, 17,* 479–490.

Winters, K. C. (1999). *Screening and assessing adolescents for substance use disorders: Treatment improvement Protocol Series*. Washington, DC: Substance Abuse and Mental Health Services Administration, Center for Substance Abuse Treatment.

Winters, K. C., Anderson, N., Bengston, P., Stinchfield, R. D., & Latimer, W. W. (2000). Development of a parent questionnaire for use in assessing adolescent drug abuse. *Journal of Psychoactive Drugs, 32,* 3–13.

Winters, K. C., & Henly, G. A. (1993). *Adolescent Diagnostic Interview administration booklet*. Los Angeles: Western Psychological Services.

Winters, K. C., Latimer, W., & Stinchfield, R. D. (1999). The DSM-IV criteria for adolescent alcohol and cannabis use disorders. *Journal of Studies on Alcohol, 60,* 337–344.

Winters, K. C., Latimer, W., Stinchfield, R. D., & Henly, G. (1999). Assessing adolescent drug use with the Personal Experience Inventory. In M. E. Maruish (Ed.), *The use of psychological testing for treatment planning and outcomes assessment* (2nd ed., pp. 599–630). Mahwah, NJ: Lawrence Erlbaum.

Winters, K. A., Stinchfield, R. D., & Henly, G. A. (1993). Further validation of new scales measuring adolescent alcohol and other drug abuse. *Journal of Studies on Alcohol, 54,* 534–541.

Winters, K. A., Weller, C. L., & Meland, J. A. (1993). Extent of drug abuse among juvenile offenders. *Journal of Drug Issues, 23,* 515–524.

8

Risk and Protective Factors in the Development of Delinquency and Conduct Disorder

James Herbert Williams, Charles D. Ayers, Richard A. Van Dorn, and Michael W. Arthur

T he end of the 20th century brought good and bad news about juvenile delinquency and conduct disorder, particularly violent behavior. On the one hand, these behaviors continue to plague America and are major social problems that the American public wants solved. On the other hand, the 20th century ended with arrests for both the juvenile violent crime index and the property crime index at the lowest rates for the decade.

By 2000 the tide of delinquency had been reduced due to various intervention strategies. However, throughout the late 1980s and the 1990s, a consensus was building regarding the direction of prevention and intervention efforts. In addition, a risk and protective factor perspective took hold in such organizations as the Institute of Medicine (IOM, 1994) and the Office of Juvenile Justice and Delinquency Prevention (OJJDP). In some arenas, this perspective has also embraced the concept of developmental assets. Only time will tell whether these approaches to delinquency and conduct disorder will be a watershed movement.

As suggested in chapter 2, a risk–protective strategy implies that certain individual and social characteristics, variables, and hazards (risk factors) present in an individual's life make it more likely than others to engage in delinquent activity or develop mental health disorders (conduct disorders). Other characteristics and variables (protective factors) are known to reduce an individual's risk level or to buffer an individual from the effects of risk. Risk and protective factors for juvenile delinquency and conduct disorder are known to exist in all domains of a youth's life, including family, school, community, and peer group, as well as within the youth's biological makeup. Consequently, the risk–protective factor perspective is consistent with ecological theory and provides a conceptual framework for prevention, intervention, and treatment based on the person-in-environment model.

This chapter reviews the research literature on risk and protective factors of juvenile delinquency and conduct disorder and discusses their implications for prevention, intervention, and treatment efforts. To provide context, this chapter defines juvenile delinquency and conduct disorder, putting these terms in a sociological context by reviewing recent behavioral trends, purported developmental pathways of delinquent behavior, and critical life periods. Risk factors are then presented by social domain—community, family, school, and peer group—and by genetic and biological factors. Protective factors also are reviewed and, when appropriate, associated with the idea of developmental assets. The chapter concludes with a review of some risk and protective factor assessment strategies and a discussion of the implications of the risk–protective strategy for the prevention, intervention, and treatment of juvenile delinquency and conduct disorder.

NATURE OF THE PROBLEM

Juvenile delinquency is defined as illegal acts committed by persons under 18 years of age, including some acts that, if committed by someone 18 or older, would not be illegal (status offenses; Federal Bureau of Investigation [FBI], 2000). The FBI classifies delinquent acts into three categories based on the severity of the offense. The most serious of the three categories is violent index crimes—forcible rape, robbery, aggravated assault, murder, and nonnegligent manslaughter. Property index crimes, the second-most serious offense level, include burglary, larceny (theft), motor vehicle theft, and arson. All other delinquent acts are categorized as nonindex offenses. Nonindex offenses include forgery, vandalism, gambling, driving under the influence, drunkenness, disorderly conduct, vagrancy, and status offenses, such as running away and violating curfew.

Conduct disorder is a clinical mental health diagnosis. It subsumes delinquent behavior, but not all delinquency constitutes conduct disorder. The essential feature of conduct disorder is a "repetitive and persistent pattern of behavior in which the basic rights of others or the major age-appropriate societal norms or rules are violated" (American Psychiatric Association [APA], 1994, p. 85). Such behaviors are classified into four groups: (1) aggressive behavior that causes or threatens physical harm to other people or animals, (2) nonaggressive behavior that causes property loss or damage, (3) deceitfulness or theft, and (4) serious violations of rules.

A clinical diagnosis of conduct disorder is made when children or adolescents under the age 18 have exhibited three or more characteristic behaviors during the preceding 12 months, with at least one behavior having occurred in the preceding six months. Consequently, even though all delinquent acts are classified in the behavioral grouping of conduct disorder, not all individuals engaging in delinquent activities meet clinical criteria for conduct disorder. The specific guidelines for a clinical diagnosis of conduct disorder, as defined in *Diagnostic and Statistical Manual of Mental Disorders, Fourth Edition* (DSM–IV; APA, 1994), are detailed in Table 8-1.

GENERAL TRENDS

The good news–bad news story of juvenile delinquency and conduct disorder at the close of the 20th century in this country is evident in official arrest data. In 2000 U.S. law enforcement agencies made approximately 2.5 million juvenile arrests—accounting for 17 percent of all arrests and 16 percent of all violent crime arrests that year (OJJDP, 2000a; Snyder, 2002). More than 103,900 of these arrests were for violent index crimes. Another 541,500 were for property index crimes (FBI, 2000). This is the bad news.

Table 8-1. DSM-IV Diagnostic Criteria for Conduct Disorder

- initiate frequent physical fights
- use a weapon that can cause physical harm (for example, a bat, brick, broken bottle, knife, or gun)
- physically cruel to people or animals
- steal while confronting a victim (for example, mugging, purse snatching, extortion, or armed robbery)
- force someone into sexual activity
- physical violence (for example, rape, assault, and, in rare cases, homicide)
- fire setting
- deliberate destruction of other people's property
- deceitfulness or theft (for example, breaking and entering, car vandalism, or burglary)
- frequent lying (for example, "conning" other people)
- stealing items of nontrivial value without confronting the victim (for example, shoplifting, forgery)
- running away from home, staying out late despite parental prohibitions

Criteria for Severity of Conduct Disorder

Mild: Few if any conduct problems in excess of those required to make the diagnosis are present, and conduct problems cause relatively minor harm to others (for example, lying, truancy, staying out after dark without permission).

Moderate: The number of conduct problems and the effect on others are intermediate between "mild" and "severe" (for example, stealing without confronting a victim, or vandalism).

Severe: Many conduct problems in excess of those required to make the diagnosis are present, or conduct problems cause considerable harm to others (for example, forced sex, physical cruelty, use of a weapon, stealing while confronting a victim, breaking and entering).

SOURCE: Reprinted with permission from American Psychiatric Association. (1994). *Diagnostic and statistical manual of mental disorder* (4th ed., pp. 90–91). Washington, DC: Author.

The good news is that in 2000 the juvenile arrest rate for property crime index offenses was at its lowest level since at least 1980 (Figure 8-1). Moreover, the juvenile violent crime index arrest rate that year was at its lowest level since 1988. In fact in 2000 the latter had dropped 36 percent from its peak in 1994 (Figure 8-2). Over the 10-year period from 1990 to 2000, juvenile arrests for six of eight crimes comprising the property and violent crime indexes fell. Most notably, arrests for murder and non-negligent manslaughter fell 55 percent! From 1995 to 2000, juvenile arrests for all eight index offenses declined substantially—from a low of 11 percent for forcible rape to a high of 56 percent for murder and nonnegligent manslaughter (Figure 8-3). From 1993 to 2000, the number of arrests declined in every violent crime category despite an 8 percent growth in the juvenile population (OJJDP, 2000a; Snyder, 2002).

As for nonindex offenses, juvenile arrests for 11 of 21 crimes fell over the 10-year period from 1990 to 2000. Of the 10 crimes for which arrests increased, at least half may have been an artifact of increased law enforcement rather than actual engagement by youths. These include "other" assaults, drug abuse violations, offenses against the family and children, disorderly conduct, and curfew violations and loitering. During

Figure 8-1

Property Crimes Arrests per 100,000 Juveniles, Ages 10 to 17

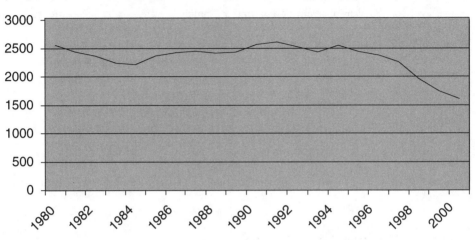

- The FBI assesses trends in the volume of property crimes by monitoring four offenses that are consistently reported by law enforcement agencies nationwide and are pervasive in all geographical areas of the country.
- In 2000, for every 100,000 youths in the United States ages 10 through 17, there were 1,615 arrests of juveniles for Property Crime Index offenses.
- Compared with the arrest rate for Violent Crime Index offenses, the juvenile arrest rate for Property Crime Index offenses changed relatively little between 1980 and 2000.
- Between 1980 and 1997, the juvenile Property Crime Index arrest rate reached its highest level in 1991 (2,612) and its lowest level in 1984 (2,221). Between 1997 and 2000, however, the rate declined 29 percent and fell to its lowest level in a generation.

SOURCE: Adapted from Snyder, H. (2002). Juvenile arrests 2000. Washington, DC: Office of Juvenile Justice and Delinquency Prevention. Retrieved from http://ojjdp.ncjrs.org/ojstatbb/asp/JAR_Display.asp?ID=qa2206012002 on January 20, 2002.

the five-year period from 1995 to 2000, arrests for all five of these offenses leveled off (OJJDP, 2000b; Snyder, 2002).

Although sobering, these official statistics fail to portray the full extent of childhood and adolescent delinquency and conduct disorder. According to self-report data, a majority of America's youths will commit at least one delinquent act by the time they reach adulthood (Elliott, 1994a, 1994b; Elliott, Huizinga, & Ageton, 1985; Farrington, Loeber, Stouthamer-Loeber, Van Kammen, & Schmidt, 1996). Furthermore, the rate of conduct disorder in the general child and adolescent population runs about 6 percent to 16 percent for boys and 2 percent to 9 percent for girls (APA, 1994), accounting for the majority of all child and adolescent clinical referrals (Barlow & Stewart-Brown, 2000; Kazdin & Wassell, 1999). This prevalence of criminal involvement not only makes juvenile delinquency statistically normative, but it also makes juveniles one of the most criminal segments of the U.S. population.

Of course, most of the youths accounting for the high prevalence of delinquency and conduct disorder have committed relatively minor offenses and have committed them infrequently. Furthermore, the vast majority will terminate their

Figure 8-2

Violent Crimes Arrests per 100,000 Juveniles, Ages 10 to 17

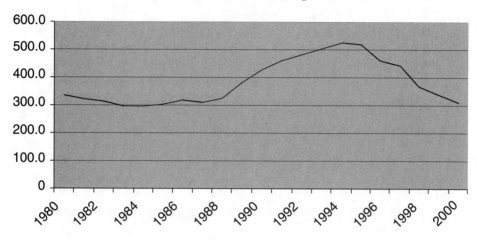

- Between 1994 and 2000, the juvenile arrest rate for Violent Crime Index offenses dropped 41 percent, to 309 arrests for every 100,000 persons ages 10 to 17.
- The growth in the juvenile Violent Crime Index arrest rate that began in the latter part of the 1980s was erased by 2000.
- If each of these arrests involved a different juvenile (that is, if each juvenile arrested in 2000 for a Violent Crime Index offense was arrested only once that year, which is unlikely), then no more than 1 in every 320 persons ages 10 through 17 in the United States was arrested for a Violent Crime Index offense in 2000. This means that about one-third of 1 percent of juveniles ages 10 to 17 were arrested for a violent crime in 2000.

SOURCE: Adapted from Snyder, H. (2002). Juvenile arrests 2000. Washington, DC: Office of Juvenile Justice and Delinquency Prevention. Retrieved from http://ojjdp.ncjrs.org/ojstatbb/asp/ JAR_Display.asp?ID=qa2201012002 on January 20, 2002.

criminal careers during the normal course of adolescent development. In this sense, delinquency represents a transient response to adolescence, a response that most youths will outgrow (Elliott, Huizinga, & Menard, 1989; Moffitt & Caspi, 2001). However, between 7 percent and 25 percent of adolescents engage in frequent and serious offending. This subpopulation accounts for a substantial amount of the total incidence of juvenile offending as well as the bulk of all serious and violent offenses committed by youths (Farrington & West, 1993; Thornberry, Huizinga, & Loeber, 1995).

In the National Youth Survey (NYS) study, serious juvenile offenders made up fewer than 5 percent of the study sample in 1980; yet, they accounted for 83 percent of all index offenses committed and half of all offenses reported (Elliott, 1994b). Wolfgang, Figlio, and Sellin's (1972) seminal study found that although "chronic offenders" (five or more police contacts) constituted only 6 percent of their study's 1945 birth cohort and 18 percent of the delinquents, they were responsible for 52 percent of all offenses committed and about two-thirds of all violent offenses. Other studies have found similar results (Farrington, 1983; Farrington & West, 1990, 1993; Hamparian, Schuster, Dinitz, & Conrad, 1978; Huizinga, Loeber, & Thornberry, 1993; Shannon, 1988, 1991; Tracy, Wolfgang, & Figlio, 1990).

Figure 8-3

Arrests for All Crimes per 100,000 Juveniles, Ages 10 to 17

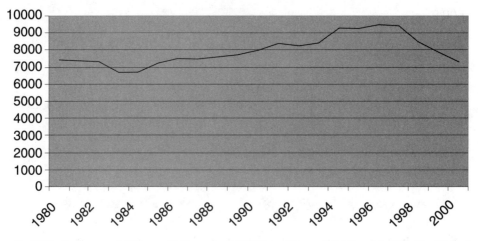

- In 2000, there were 7,327 arrests for every 100,000 youths ages 10 through 17 in the United States.
- The overall juvenile arrest rate was lower in 2000 than in 1980.

SOURCE: Adapted from Snyder, H. (2002). Juvenile arrests 2000. Washington, DC: Office of Juvenile Justice and Delinquency Prevention. Retrieved from http://ojjdp.ncjrs.org/ojstatbb/asp/JAR_Display.asp?ID=qa2200012002 on January 20, 2002.

DEMOGRAPHICS OF DELINQUENCY AND CONDUCT DISORDER

Regardless of the data source, either official arrest statistics or self-reports, the prevalence of delinquent involvement and conduct disorder is much greater among males than females (Anderson, Holmes, & Ostresh, 1999; OJJDP, 2000b; Piquero & Chung, 2001; Snyder, 2002). This is especially true for more serious offenses. For instance, in 2000 males represented 73 percent of all juveniles arrested but 83 percent of arrests for violent index crimes—including 92 percent of arrests for murder and nonnegligent manslaughter, 98 percent of arrests for forcible rape, and 91 percent of arrests for robbery (OJJDP, 2000a; Snyder, 2002). However, criminal propensity is not restricted to males. Over the past several decades, dramatic increases in antisocial behavior have been noted for females (Cote, Zoccolillo, Tremblay, Nagin, & Vitaro, 2001; Jenson, Potter, & Howard, 2001; Loeber, Burke, Lahey, Winters, & Zera, 2000; Piquero, 2000). In fact, between 1990 and 1999, arrests of juvenile females generally increased more (or decreased less) than arrests of males in most offense categories (Figure 8-4; FBI, 2000; OJJDP, 2000c; Snyder, 2002). For example, although arrests of males declined 5 percent for aggravated assault, 24 percent for larceny (theft), 13 percent for vandalism, and 7 percent for weapons charges during this period, arrests for females increased 57 percent, 6 percent, 28 percent, and 44 percent, respectively, for the same offenses.

Unlike delinquency data regarding gender, involvement in delinquency across ethnic or racial groups varies according to the data source. On the one hand, official arrest data indicate that African American youths are overrepresented in juvenile crime arrests—particularly arrests for violent crimes. In 2000, 15 percent of the U.S.

Figure 8-4

Arrests per 100,000 Juveniles, Males and Females, Ages 10 to 17

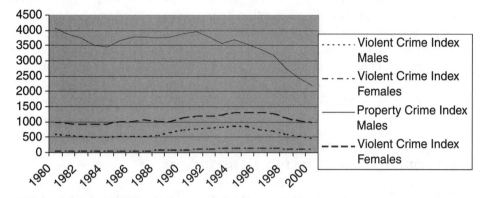

- Trends in the overall arrest rate followed similar patterns for female and male juveniles. For both groups, the rates increased between 1983 and 1997 and then declined through 2000. Since 1983, the female rate increased more (72 percent versus 30 percent) and then declined less (18 percent versus 24 percent) than the male rate. In 2000, the male rate had returned to its 1983 low point while the female rate was still 42 percent above its 1983 level.
- Between 1987 and 1994, the Violent Crime Index arrest rate more than doubled for females and increased 64 percent for males. However, declines since the mid-1990s have brought the rate in 2000 below the 1980 rate for males, but not for females. The 2000 arrest rate for females (117) remained 66 percent above the 1980 rate (70). The 2000 rate for males (492) was 16 percent below the 1980 rate (587).
- Between 1980 and 2000, the male juvenile Property Crime Index arrest rate declined 46 percent and the rate for females increased 3 percent.
- Property Crime Index arrest rates dropped from 1994 to 2000 for both male and female juveniles. The decline was smaller for females (25 percent) than for males (41 percent).

SOURCE: Adapted from Snyder, H. (2002). *Juvenile arrests 2000.* Washington, DC: Office of Juvenile Justice and Delinquency Prevention. Retrieved from http://ojjdp.ncjrs.org/ojstatbb/asp/ JAR_Display.asp?ID=qa2301031502 on March 15, 2002.

juvenile population was African American (79 percent was Caucasian, with most Hispanics/Latinos classified as Caucasian, and 5 percent other ethnic groups or races); yet, African Americans accounted for 41 percent of all juvenile arrests for violent crimes and 27 percent of all juvenile arrests for property crimes. For Caucasians, those figures were 57 percent and 69 percent, respectively (OJJDP, 2000c; Snyder, 2002).

On the other hand, Huizinga and colleagues (1993) reported no racial or ethnic differences in analyses of self-reports of criminal involvement. In fact, with the exception of higher prevalence rates for serious offenses, such as felony assault, robbery, and total index offenses for African Americans, most self-report studies have not found significant racial differences in illegal behavior (Elliott et al., 1989). Peeples and Loeber (1994) found that racial or ethnic differences disappeared in one study when residence in "underclass" neighborhoods was controlled. These results suggest that racial differences in officially reported arrest data might actually be indicators of other social processes and conditions, such as socioeconomic status and system response bias. Research by Pope and Feyerherm (1990a, 1990b, 1993) supports this conclusion, suggesting that the juvenile justice system is not racially neutral because youths of color are more likely than other youths to become involved with the system, to stay involved longer, and to receive harsher sentences.

As for conduct disorder, it is the most common disorder seen in child mental health clinics (IOM, 1994). The six-month and one-year prevalence rates obtained from clinic populations range from 1.5 percent to 11.9 percent. Boys are diagnosed more frequently with conduct disorder than girls. Conduct disorder frequently occurs in conjunction with other disorders, such as attention deficit hyperactivity disorder (ADHD), and it can persist into late adolescence and adulthood (Gresham, Lane, & Lambros, 2000; Jensen, Martin, & Cantwell, 1997; Molina & Pelham, 2001).

DEVELOPMENTAL PATHWAYS, CRITICAL PERIODS OF DELINQUENCY, AND CONDUCT DISORDER

Over the past decade, various schemes and typologies have been developed to classify juvenile offenders and to project the likelihood of their involvement in delinquent behavior over time. For example, Shelden and Chesney-Lind (1993) used court referral data to classify one-time offenders, nonchronic recidivist offenders, and chronic offenders, while Loeber and colleagues (1991) proposed a longitudinal classification scheme based on youths' self-reports and parental surveys. Differences in some schemes and typologies may exist because of the data on which they are based.

From their study, Loeber and colleagues posited that whether overt (aggressive), covert (concealed), or both, the delinquent activities of most youths follows a common pattern of initiation, escalation, de-escalation, and desistance. Furthermore, they suggested that less serious behaviors generally preceded more moderate, problematic, and illegal behaviors (Loeber, Farrington, Stouthamer-Loeber, & Van Kammen, 1998). It is uncertain, however, whether a single behavioral pathway encompassing both types of behavior (overt and covert) explains this pattern of involvement or whether the pattern of involvement differs for each behavioral type.

Reviewing the literature, Loeber and colleagues (Loeber, Farrington, Stouthamer-Loeber, Moffitt, & Caspi, 1998; Loeber & Hay, 1997; Loeber, Wei, Stouthamer-Loeber, Huizinga, & Thornberry, 1999) concluded that evidence supported a dual pathway model with an aggressive–versatile pathway (aggressive and concealing behavior) and a nonaggressive–antisocial pathway (nonaggressive, covert behavior only). However, empirical support for three pathways in the development of delinquency and conduct disorder has also been reported (Loeber & Stouthamer-Loeber, 1993). These pathways include:

- authority conflict (stubborn behavior, defiance, and authority avoidance)
- covert behaviors (minor covert behaviors such as lying, shoplifting, property damage, and moderate to serious delinquency)
- overt behaviors (aggression, physical fighting, and violence).

Membership in one pathway does not exclude membership in another—in fact, dual and triple pathway membership was not uncommon.

Loeber (1996) pioneered the notion that individuals experience "stacking" of problem behaviors. The "stacking" model suggests that engagement in early disruptive behaviors, such as aggressive behaviors at home and at school, predict subsequent involvement in delinquent activities. Those youths who act out early and often in their lives are likely to be those who engage in more frequent and serious behaviors later in their lives (Loeber, 1996)—thus the idea of behavioral stacking. Farrington (1986) posited the "stepping stones" model, which delineated episodes and conditions leading to criminality as a long-term prediction framework. He identified a range of factors, measured at different points in relation to chronological aging to predict adult criminality.

Historically, the peak age for the onset of delinquency has been decreasing. The peak age of onset for the cohort panel in studies by Wolfgang and colleagues (1972) and Wolfgang, Thornberry, and Figlio (1987) was 16 years. Elliott and colleagues (1986) found the peak age for their panel to be 13 to 15 years. More recent studies have found that most youths engaging in delinquent behavior begin their delinquency around ages 12 and 13 (Ayers et al., 1999; OJJDP, 2000a; Thornberry, 1996; Wilson & Herrnstein, 1985). However, for many youths the onset of delinquent activity occurs even before the teenage years. Sixty percent of 11 year olds in the NYS reported participating in general delinquency, and 20 percent reported participating in index offenses (Elliott et al., 1989).

Self-report studies suggest that initiation of serious violent offending generally occurs between ages 14 and 17, with the highest risk of initiation between ages 15 and 16. The risk of initiating serious violent offending decreases to nearly zero after age 20 (Elliott, 1994a; Williams, Ayers, Outlaw, Abbott, & Hawkins 2001; Williams, Van Dorn, Hawkins, Abbott, & Catalano, 2001). Both prevalence and offending rates for general delinquent involvement tend to peak around mid- to late adolescence, or ages 15 to 17 (Hirschi, 1969; Thornberry, 1996; Wilson & Herrnstein, 1985). Elliott (1994a) reported that the prevalence of self-reported violent behavior peaks at age 17 for males and at around ages 15 to 16 for females.

Half of the youths in the NYS who had been involved in delinquent activity before age 18 discontinued those activities for one or more years while still under age 18; they had not resumed general offending by ages 18, 19, or 20, depending on the study cohort (Elliott et al., 1989). More than 50 percent of the sample was not involved in general delinquency by age 18, and more than 90 percent either terminated or did not initiate index offending by age 17. Elliott (1994a) found peak termination to occur between ages 18 and 19. A steeper decline in involvement was noted for females. Elliott reported that, in the NYS, involvement differentials between males and females increased from 2:1 at age 12, to 3:1 at age 18, to 4:1 at age 21. After age 17, participation rates dropped dramatically for both males and females. Eighty percent of those who had engaged in serious violent offending had not done so again by age 21 (Elliott, 1994a).

RISK FACTORS FOR DELINQUENCY AND CONDUCT DISORDER

Risk factors predict the increased probability of a subsequent undesirable outcome (Barnes & Farrell, 1992; Elliott et al., 1989; Farrington & West, 1993; Gillmore, Hawkins, Catalano, Day, & Abbott, 1991; Hawkins, Catalano, & Miller, 1992; Hawkins, Jenson, Catalano, & Lishner, 1988; IOM, 1994; Stouthamer-Loeber, Loeber, & Farrington, 1993). Extensive research has identified risk factors for delinquency and conduct disorder (Forehand, Wierson, Frame, Kempton, & Armistead, 1991; Hawkins, Catalano, Morrison, & et al., 1992; J. D.

Hawkins et al., 1998; Robins, 1966; Williams, Ayers, Abbott, Hawkins, & Catalano, 1999; Williams & Van Dorn, 1999; Yoshikawa, 1994).

These factors can be divided into two categories: (1) contextual or community risk factors (2) and interpersonal or individual risk factors. Contextual factors are associated with the structure and values within the individual's social environment and peer group. Risk factors that exist in the social context include cultural or community norms or laws that foster delinquency, availability of drugs or weapons, poverty, and neighborhood disorganization (Alexander, Massey, Gibbs, & Altekruse, 1985; Garbarino, DuBrow, Kostelny, & Pardo, 1992; Hawkins, Catalano, Morrison, et al., 1992; Loftin, McDowell, & Wiersema, 1993; Loftin, McDowell, Wiersema, & Cottey, 1991; Sampson, 1986; Yoshikawa, 1994). Individual risk factors are associated with the adolescent's personal environment—including family, peers, school, and genetic factors (Cadoret, Cain, & Crowe, 1983; Cairns, Cairns, Neckerman, Ferguson, & Gariepy, 1989; Farrington, 1991; McCord, 1988). Among the risk factors for an adolescent are family management problems, family conflict, early onset of problem behavior, academic failure, low commitment to school, association with antisocial peers, alienation, rebelliousness, favorable attitudes toward delinquent behavior, physiological abnormalities, temperamental behavior, cognitive and neuropsychological deficits, and hyperactivity (Costello et al., 1996; Earls, 1981; Hawkins, Catalano, & Miller, 1992; IOM, 1994; Kandel, Simcha-Fagan, & Davies, 1986; Lahey et al., 1995; Loeber, Green, Keenan, & Lahey, 1995; Rutter & Giller, 1983; White, Moffitt, & Silva, 1989; Yoshikawa, 1994).

Risk factors for delinquency and conduct disorder have been identified in many longitudinal studies (for example, Hawkins, Catalano, & Miller, 1992; Kandel et al., 1986; Lahey et al., 1995; Loeber et al., 1995; Tolan & Guerra, 1994; Yoshikawa, 1994). Unfortunately, contemporary research has given far too little attention to comparative study of the factors influencing delinquency and conduct disorder across racial groups, in part because adequate multiethnic samples are lacking. Many of the studies have concluded that African American delinquency rates are affected by the same sociostructural factors as white delinquency rates (Hawkins, Laub, & Lauritsen, 1998; Williams et al., 1999). These studies suggest that the causes of violence and delinquency appear to be similar across racial groups. However, because African American and Caucasian children often live in physically separate environments, it becomes necessary to understand the community contexts in which African American and white youths are reared. Additional multilevel studies are needed to differentiate individual and community contexts. Antisocial behaviors among white youths are considered to have a strong correlation with emotional or psychological dysfunction, whereas social risk factors are more prevalent among African Americans (Dembo, Williams, & Schmeidler, 1994).

COMMUNITY RISK FACTORS

Community norms and levels of crime in a neighborhood help determine whether youths will thrive or whether they will develop antisocial behaviors (Garbarino et al., 1992; Williams, Stiffman, & O'Neal, 1998). Community norms—the attitudes and policies a community holds concerning crime and violence—are communicated through formal means (such as laws or written policies) and informal means (such as social practices or community expectations; Alexander et al., 1985; National Research Council, 1993). Chronic community violence can have a long-term effect on children's development and levels of functioning (Garbarino et al., 1992). Poverty is also an important risk factor for delinquency and conduct disorder (Lahey et al., 1995; Simcha-Fagan & Schwartz, 1986). Adolescents who live in economically deprived neighborhoods characterized by extreme poverty, poor living conditions, and high unemployment rates are more likely to engage in delinquent behavior than adolescents living in less-deprived neighborhoods (Peeples & Loeber, 1994; Yoshikawa, 1994). The quality of housing in these communities is often poor and the levels of violence and crime are often high. Access to health care, social services, and good schools is often limited for people who live in poverty (Yoshikawa, 1994). Statistics for arrest, mortality, and morbidity have long suggested that ethnic minority youths have higher rates of delinquent behavior, but racial differences tend to vanish when poverty is controlled (National Research Council, 1993). Because researchers have found it difficult to separate the influences of race and community from those of poverty, it has been a challenge for them to make a strong argument for the relationship between poverty and delinquency (National Research Council, 1993).

Neighborhood characteristics such as high population density and mobility (families frequently moving in and out), physical deterioration, low resident attachment to the community, high crime rates, and the lack of social cohesion are related to juvenile participation in delinquent behavior (Bursik & Webb, 1982; Farrington et al., 1990; Sampson, Raudenbush, & Earls, 1997). Neighborhoods with high residential mobility usually have higher rates of juvenile crime (Wilson & Herrnstein, 1985), and when neighborhoods undergo rapid residential shifts, victimization and crime rates increase (Sampson, 1986). Research has shown that children who reside in disorganized communities with high population density, physical deterioration, and low levels of attachment to the neighborhood are at higher risk of delinquent behavior than those who do not live in such communities (Laub & Sampson, 1988; Sampson & Laub, 1994).

FAMILY RISK FACTORS

The influence of family is another correlate of antisocial behavior. Family management problems, family conflict, family history of high-risk behaviors, and parents' modeling of inappropriate and illicit behavior (including attitudes and involvement in problem behaviors) are associated with delinquent behavior and conduct disorder. Poor family management practices include unspecified expectations for behavior, inadequate supervision and monitoring, and excessively severe or inconsistent punishment. Children exposed to poor family management practices are at high risk of developing conduct disorder and engaging in delinquent behavior than those who are not (Farrington, 1991; Lahey et al., 1995; Patterson & Dishion, 1985; Thornberry, 1994). Lack of parental monitoring and supervision also increases the likelihood that a child will develop aggressive and violent patterns of behavior during adolescence and early adulthood (Farrington, 1991). A comprehensive review of parenting behavior by Loeber and Stouthamer-Loeber (1986) found that two of the strongest correlates of conduct disorder in children were (1) poor parental supervision and (2) lack of parental involvement in their child's activities. Lahey and colleagues (1995) identified parental antisocial personality disorder as a significant correlate of conduct disorder. Other studies of delinquent children have supported these findings (Cernkovich & Giordano, 1987; Voorhis, Cullen, Mathers, & Garner, 1988). Harsh, abusive discipline and inconsistent discipline also have been linked to severe conduct problems (Lahey et al., 1995; Patterson, 1982; Patterson & Stouthamer-Loeber, 1984; Robins, 1991; Voorhis et al., 1988).

Parental conflict and coercive family interaction create a situation that reinforces aggressiveness and coercive behavior (Farrington, 1991; Loeber & Dishion, 1984; Patterson & Dishion, 1985). Furthermore, Loeber and Dishion found that domestic violence increases the likelihood of an adolescent's involvement in violent behavior. In their study, boys who lived in homes characterized by parental conflict or marital discord had a high predilection for fighting.

Adolescents who experience family instability because of divorce also have higher rates of delinquent behavior (Rutter & Giller, 1983; Williams et al., 1998). Divorce can create disruption and conflict, of course, but the major life transitions necessitated by a divorce are perhaps more consequential. Divorce can reduce risk that is attributable to family conflict, but risk caused by the major transitions in the child's life might be heightened. If resolving family conflict by some means other than divorce is an option, then that route should be considered. If such a solution is not feasible, however, removing the conflict through divorce is preferable to letting the conflict remain. Even though family management problems are a risk factor for conduct disorder and delinquency, family structure is not. Although it may be harder for a single parent to manage the family unit, the children of single parents are at no greater risk than those of two-parent families based solely on family composition. Risk factors for delinquency may increase over time—often the outcome of divorce is poverty, and poverty exerts a direct contextual influence on children and their families. All else being equal, however, the children of divorce may be at less risk than those who remain in households experiencing parental conflict.

Other risk factors in the family domain include favorable parental attitudes toward antisocial behavior, parental involvement in problem behavior, and parental psychopathology. Favorable parental norms and attitudes toward crime and antisocial behavior influence the behavior of children (Hawkins & Weis, 1985). Children of parents with histories of criminal behavior, substance-abusing behavior, or both are at increased risk of conduct disorder (Rutter, 1985). According to Robins (1991), the risk factor of parental criminal or substance-using behavior is a more striking indicator when the mother rather than the father is affected. Finally, children (especially boys) who display aggressive and antisocial behavior have been found to be more likely to come from families in which the parents are suffering from depression (Biederman, Munir, & Knee, 1987; Frick et al., 1992; Robins, 1991).

SCHOOL-RELATED RISK FACTORS

Early and persistent antisocial behavior, academic failure in elementary school, and a low degree of commitment to school are risk factors within the school domain that are predictors of adolescent delinquent behavior. Studies have found that individuals who exhibit aggressive behavior, negative moods, and temper tantrums in early childhood are more likely to have problems with aggressive behavior in adolescence and early adulthood (Cairns & Cairns, 1991; Farrington, 1991; IOM, 1994; Loeber, 1988; Robins, 1978). Farrington (1991) found that 57 percent of boys identified as aggressive between the ages of 12 and 14 had been convicted of a violent crime by age 32. Pisecco and colleagues (2001) found that students' academic self-concept of abilities was strongly related to the presence of ADHD and delinquent behavior in early adolescence. Low academic and social skills are significant predictors of delinquency across racial groups (Ayers et al., 1999; Williams et al., 1999).

School failure and poor academic performance, whether they are the caused by learning disabilities, boredom, or a poor teacher–student match, are common risk factors in children diagnosed with conduct disorder and in the prevalence and onset of delinquency (Lahey et al., 1995; Maguin & Loeber, 1996; Robins, 1991). Maguin and Loeber (1996) found that 35 percent of academically low-performing children became delinquent, but only 21 percent of high-performing children did so. They also found that the relationship between academic performance and delinquent behavior was stronger for white students than for African American students and stronger for males than for females. Farrington (1991) found that boys who were low achievers in school or who had low levels of intelligence had an increased chance of developing aggressive behavior. Beginning at grade 4, academic achievement is a stable predictor of later behavior problems (Hawkins, Catalano, & Brewer, 1995; Yoshikawa, 1994).

The level of an individual's commitment to education is considered one of the best predictors of delinquent behavior for adolescents (Gottfredson, 1986). Children who have discipline problems and who display a lack of commitment to school (as defined by a lack of motivation to achieve) were more likely than other children to develop problem behavior (Farrington, 1991). Cairns and colleagues (1989) found that both boys and girls who were rated as aggressive and who had academic problems were much more likely than others to drop out of school.

INDIVIDUAL AND PEER GROUP RISK FACTORS

Research indicates that adolescents with favorable attitudes toward delinquent behaviors and who associate with delinquent peers are more likely than adolescents who disapprove of delinquent behaviors and who do not associate with delinquent peers to engage in delinquent behaviors themselves (Cairns et al., 1989; Elliott et al., 1989; Farrington, 1991; Hawkins, Catalano, & Miller, 1992; Huang, Kosterman, Catalano, Hawkins, & Abbott, 2001; Williams et al., 1998, 1999). The socialization perspective of learned behavior and acquired values and beliefs posits that peer affiliation provides the environment for learning and reinforcing delinquent behaviors and antisocial attitudes and beliefs. Delinquent peers are strongly correlated with delinquent behavior because they create a fertile environment for the onset of and the continued engagement in delinquent behavior (Elliott et al., 1985; Matsueda, 1982; Thornberry, Lizotte, Krohn, Farnworth, & Jang, 1994). Furthermore, attitudes and beliefs that favor deviance and impulsiveness are risk factors for violent offending behavior (Elliott, 1994b; Van Dorn & Williams, 2003).

Research has shown that peer influence, including friendship and group affiliation, has a significant effect on delinquent behaviors (Cairns et al., 1989; Matsueda & Heimer, 1987; Thornberry et al., 1994; Williams et al., 1999). Peers serve an important role in the socialization and social development of adolescents. Furthermore, research demonstrates that adolescents tend to associate with peers with similar backgrounds, in terms of age, gender, and socioeconomic status, and with peers whose values concerning delinquent behavior are similar to their own (Cairns et al., l989; Elliott et al., 1985). Studies by Agnew (1991) and Elliott and colleagues (1985) using data from

NYS found a strong association between delinquent peers and delinquent behavior. However, the strength of this association may vary by race and ethnicity. Matsueda and Heimer (1987) found that delinquent peers had a greater effect on Caucasian youths than on African American youths. More research is needed on racial and gender differences, but it is clear that frequent engagement in delinquent behavior is strongly correlated with associating with delinquent friends (Menard & Elliott, 1994).

GENETIC OR BIOLOGICAL RISK FACTORS

Research literature suggests that biological and congenital predispositions for delinquent behavior exist. In her study of families, Robins (1966) found that one of the best predictors of antisocial behavior in boys was the criminal arrest of their fathers. Other methods of studying genetic influences have also shown promising results. In comparing identical, or monozygotic (MZ), twins with fraternal, or dizygotic (DZ), twins, Mednick and Volavka (1980) found that MZ twins had a much higher concordance rate for delinquent behavior than did DZ twins. In an effort to isolate the effects of hereditary and environmental influences, Mednick, Gabrielli, and Hutchings (1984) studied a cohort of 14,427 nonfamilial children adopted in Denmark between 1924 and 1947. They found that the correlation of criminal conviction rates for biological fathers and their adopted-away sons was much higher than those for the adoptive fathers and their adopted sons.

Other genetic and biological factors related to delinquency include perinatal trauma, neurotoxins, and alcohol and drug use by the mother during pregnancy (Hawkins, Catalano, & Miller, 1992; IOM, 1994). Antecedent factors associated with hyperactive and impulsive children include exposure to neurotoxins, such as lead, early malnutrition, low birthweight, and the mother's substance use during pregnancy (Breslau, Klein, & Allen, 1988; Needleman, 1982); these children are also at greater risk of engaging in antisocial behaviors (Loeber, 1990). (For a further review of biological and genetic risk factors for antisocial behaviors, see Farrington, 1994.)

Research continues to link the relationship between genetics and biology and the development of conduct disorder. Some studies show a significant link, but the data are often inconsistent, inconclusive, and methodologically flawed. Conduct disorder is a relatively new diagnosis—it appeared in the DSM for the first time in 1968—and practitioners are not always consistent in their assessment of the diagnosis. Despite these limitations, some research studies have found both genetic and environmental predictors of individuals' involvement in antisocial behavior (Cadoret et al., 1983; Earls & Jung, 1987; Offord et al., 1987). In two studies—one on adopted children (Cadoret et al., 1983) and one on biological fathers and male adoptees (Mednick, Moffit, Gabrielli, & Hutchings, 1983)—researchers concluded that there is a genetic predisposition to conduct disorder.

Conduct disorder occurs at a much higher rate in boys than in girls (Robins, 1991), and this rate difference has remained stable over time. In the Ontario Child Health Study, Offord and colleagues (1987) found that, among children ages six to 11, boys had a rate of conduct disorder that was six times that of girls. These gender differences were not as pronounced in older adolescents (Offord & Waters, 1983). It is not clear whether the differences for gender are caused by behavioral influences or by differences in socialization that result in different expectations for boys and girls (IOM, 1994).

Results of the investigation of racial differences in the prevalence of conduct disorder have been mixed. Rutter (1978) found racial differences in the prevalence of conduct disorder among 10-year-old children in London. In the United States, studies have shown no differences in the proportions of African American and white youths who reported three or more symptoms of conduct disorder before age 15 (Robins, 1991). Although African Americans are overrepresented in the criminal justice system as juvenile delinquents, data collected on self-reported delinquent acts have shown no differences in involvement across racial groups (Elliott et al., 1985; Elliott et al., 1986).

Other risk factors that are common in children who are diagnosed with conduct disorder include ADHD, difficult temperament, poor physical coordination and motor skills, developmental delays, and low IQ (Lahey et al., 1995; Offord et al., 1992; Robins, 1991). The literature shows a significant relationship between ADHD and conduct disorder: In the Ontario Child Health Study, 40 percent of the children with an initial diagnosis of ADHD had symptoms of conduct disorder four years later (Offord et al., 1992). Although Rutter and Quinton (1984) found that children with difficult temperaments were more likely to develop later behavioral problems, overall research on childhood temperament as a risk factor for conduct disorder has been inconclusive. Other possible antecedents to conduct disorder identified in the research literature include difficulty with language, neurological impairment, and low birthweight (Breslau et al., 1988; Lahey et al., 1995; Loeber, 1990; Robins, 1991; White et al., 1989).

PROTECTIVE FACTORS, RESILIENCY, AND YOUTH ASSETS FOR EFFECTIVE RISK REDUCTION

Criminologists and others have researched the implications of protective factors associated with preventing and treating delinquent behavior and conduct disorder (Farrington & Hawkins, 1991; Farrington & West, 1993; Hawkins, Catalano, Kosterman, Abbott, & Hill, 1999; Minde, 1992; Rutter, 1985; Stouthamer-Loeber et al., 1993; Werner & Smith, 1992). Research data from the causes and correlates of juvenile delinquency studies in Denver, Colorado, Rochester, New York, and Pittsburgh, Pennsylvania, indicate that delinquency risk factors are not simply additive but that they interact to produce higher levels of risk burden. Protective factors are related to the concept of resilience and associated with successful adaptation to stressful life situations (Kaplan, 1999; Rutter, 1985, 1990).

Over the past two decades, the major focus in delinquency prevention research and program development has been on identifying risk factors and high-risk youths. This research has informed practitioners with a strong knowledge base of the various causal factors that are predictive of delinquent behavior and the group of youths who seems to have most of those causal factors. For some time, a small group of researchers has been focusing on what keeps some high-risk individuals from engaging in delinquent behavior. This research has focused on what is known as "protective factors." Other researchers have studied resilient individuals who have defied multiple risk factors and survived daunting and overwhelming obstacles and problems. The resiliency research has offered important profundities to the research on delinquency and conduct disorder. According to Kaplan (1999), two varieties of risk factors were preponderate in the resilience-related literature. The first risk factors defined the at-risk status of a population (such as having a drug-using parent or delinquent friends). The second factors distinguished between more or less positive outcomes among youths at primary risk or among groups that have no specific risk (Kaplan, 1999).

Protective factors can be conceptualized in different ways (Cowen & Work, 1988; Rutter, 1985; Werner, 1989). One might think of them as the opposite of risk factors. Poor parental supervision would be considered a risk factor, whereas proactive family management would be a protective factor. Some might consider protective factors to be freestanding, with no corresponding risk factor. Finally, protective factors may be viewed as variables that interact or buffer the effect of risk factors. Some have theorized that protective factors are processes that inhibit the onset of antisocial behavior (Rutter, 1990; Werner, 1989). It is also posited that risk factors are moderated by protective factors in the family and in the youth's environment, and by internal resiliency factors or processes (Thornberry et al., 1994, 1995; Williams & Van Dorn, 1999; Williams et al., 1999).

The protective factors that reduce the chance that a child at risk—or any child for that matter—will become involved in delinquent behavior include female gender, strong attachment to prosocial parents, resilient or positive temperament or disposition, ability to adjust and recover, strong external support system that reinforces children's coping efforts, prosocial beliefs, prosocial orientation (easygoing disposition and enjoyment of social interaction), and social problem-solving skills (Farrington, 1994; Hawkins, Catalano, & Brewer, 1995; Hawkins, Catalano, Morrison, et al., 1992; Hawkins et al., 1999).

Research from various longitudinal studies has identified four major types of protective family factors. These are (1) supportive parent–child relationships and family environment, (2) positive discipline techniques, (3) monitoring and supervision, and (4) family advocacy, seeking information and support for the benefit of their children (Brook, 1993; Catalano et al., 1993; Huizinga et al., 1993; Nye, Zucker, & Fitzgerald, 1995). Family strength researchers have found distinct factors among African American families that serve as protective mechanisms for children. These factors include a strong economic base, a strong orientation to achievement, strong spiritual values, racial pride, extended family bonds, community involvement, and commitment to family (Gonzales, Cauce, Friedman, & Mason, 1996; Williams et al., 1999).

The literature highlights some protective factors that reduce the chances that an at-risk child will develop conduct disorder. These include moderate intelligence, easygoing disposition, strong social skills, strong bond with parents, prosocial peer group, academic success, and self-discipline (Lahey et al., 1995; Minde, 1992; Robins, 1991; Rutter, 1979; Werner & Smith, 1992).

The research conducted by the Search Institute on the influence of developmental assets on youths' behaviors has expanded on the resiliency and protective factor knowledge base (Benson, Leffert, Scales, & Blyth, 1998; Leffert et al., 1998). In conducting numerous studies of sixth- to 12th-grade students over a five-year period, the Search Institute posited a framework of 40 developmental assets (Search Institute, 1998). These assets are both internal and external and protect youths against involvement in delinquent behavior (Leffert et al., 1998). External assets are more environmental (for example, support, empowerment, boundaries and expectations, and constructive use of time), whereas internal assets are more intrapersonal or behavioral (for example, commitment to learning, positive values, social competencies, and positive identity; Search Institute, 1998). It is important to note that, although the developmental assets–approach provides an additional method of conceptualizing and defining resiliency and protective factors, much of the research for this approach has been conducted on samples nonnationally representative in that they generally overrepresent Caucasian youths from small Midwestern towns whose parents have a higher-than-average level of education (Search Institute, 2001). Recently, many practitioners, program developers, and service providers have begun incorporating concepts of resiliency—in conjunction with protective factors—into their standards for developing new prevention and treatment programs. However, additional research is needed to understand how developmental assets are contextualized within communities of color.

ASSESSING RISK AND PROTECTIVE FACTORS FOR DELINQUENCY AND CONDUCT DISORDER

ASSESSMENT STRATEGIES

The choice of strategy for assessing risk and protective factors for delinquency and conduct disorder depends on the purpose of the assessment and the age of the target population. For example, conduct disorder can have an early onset marked by aggressive and disruptive behavior in the preschool years, or it can develop in late childhood or during adolescence as a pattern of delinquent behavior or substance abuse (IOM, 1994). Purposes of the assessment might be, among other things, to assess the clinical intake of children or the risk and protective factors in a population (for epidemiological studies or for decision making in the judicial system, for example) or to test etiological theory (Achenbach & Edelbrock, 1983; Loeber & Stouthamer-Loeber, 1986, 1987; OJJDP, 1995). Assessment procedures can follow either a clinical or an empirical approach; both approaches predict the likelihood of conduct problems based on current levels of risk and protective factors. This chapter explores three different empirically based assessment instruments used for different purposes.

THE CHILD BEHAVIOR CHECKLIST

One widely used instrument for assessing children's conduct problems and competencies is the Child Behavior Checklist (CBCL) developed by Achenbach and Edelbrock (1983). The original form, designed to be completed by a parent in about 15 minutes, consists of 118 items describing problematic child behaviors and four items asking about behavioral competencies (Achenbach & Edelbrock, 1983). Empirical analyses of CBCL responses concerning children assessed at intake for clinical services were used to construct scales for rating problem behavior at different ages for both genders. Three competence scales (activities, school, and social) reflecting the content of the items were also developed. All scales were normed on nonclinical samples and subjected to extensive validation analyses. Two more versions of the CBCL have been developed more recently, one reporting teacher responses and the other reporting responses from youths (see, for example, Achenbach, 1991; Achenbach & Edelbrock, 1986).

The CBCL is noteworthy because of the extensive empirical work that has gone into its development and because of its widespread use for assessing conduct problems in young children, some as young as four years old. It is useful for clinicians assessing children referred for treatment, for research into behavior problems, and for epidemiological assessments of the prevalence of problem behaviors in children. It has been used to assess the risk factor of early and persistent behavior problems and the protective factor of social competence in studies predicting delinquency (Atkins & Stoff, 1993; Edelbrock, 1986; Hawkins, Catalano, & Miller, 1992). It is easy for parents, teachers, and youths to complete, and the evidence that it reveals is reliable and valid for different age, gender, racial, and socioeconomic groups (Achenbach, 1991; Achenbach & Edelbrock, 1983). Lizotte and colleagues (1992) used data from the Pittsburgh and Rochester Youth Studies to investigate a shortened version of the CBCL for delinquency studies. The reduced version produced scales that were highly correlated with the full scales maintained the original meaning and produced high reliabilities in predicting delinquent behavior.

Because the CBCL focuses entirely on the youths' behavior, however, its use as an ecological assessment of risk and protective factors has thus far been limited. The CBCL reflects the historical focus on the individual in the prevention and treatment of conduct disorder and delinquency. Within an ecological approach to problem behaviors, the CBCL is best considered only a small part of a comprehensive assessment of risk and protection. Nevertheless, the CBCL is useful for the construction of a standardized profile of a youth's behavior that can be compared with normative data. This can be a valuable, albeit incomplete, part of an assessment of risk and protective factors.

JUVENILE PROBATION AND AFTERCARE ASSESSMENT OF RISK

Unlike the CBCL, which offers an extensive assessment of behavior, risk assessment instruments used in the juvenile justice system typically supply only cursory information. The purpose of justice system assessments depends on the stage of processing and the primary concerns of that stage (OJJDP, 1995). For example, the Juvenile Probation and Aftercare Assessment of Risk (Baird, 1984) seeks to classify offenders into one of three levels of risk for reoffending so that the appropriate level of supervision can be determined for probationers or parolees. The instrument includes eight items shown by empirical research to predict recidivism: (1) age at first adjudication, (2) prior criminal behavior, (3) prior institutional placements, (4) drug use, (5) alcohol use, (6) inadequate parental control, (7) school disciplinary problems, and (8) problematic peer relationships. A similar instrument developed for the state of Michigan successfully discriminated between high-, medium-, and low-risk offenders in Wayne County, Michigan. The recidivism rate among the high-risk group was 76 percent, among the medium-risk group 39 percent, and among the low-risk group 19 percent (OJJDP, 1995).

Other empirical instruments are also beginning to be widely used in the juvenile justice system. In placement and custody dispositions, for example, decisions made must consider the appropriate sanctions for the juvenile's offense as well as the chances that the juvenile will commit other offenses. Assessment tools designed to inform placement and custody decisions typically give more weight to the seriousness of the current offense than would be justified by the weak relationship between offense seriousness and reoffending risk. Instruments for needs assessment, which typically present a complete array of risk and protective factors related to potential areas of intervention (such as family relationships, parental problems and skills, levels of academic achievement, school problems, peer relationships, or life and vocational skills), are also being used in the juvenile justice system to guide case planning and workload decisions (OJJDP, 1995). In contrast, risk screening for detention decisions focuses on the relative likelihood that an offender will represent a threat to the community or will run away during the period between arrest and adjudication. Risk screening in decisions concerning placement includes assessment of the seriousness of the offense, risk of reoffending, and risk of behavior problems during placement.

In each instance, however, the primary focus of these measures is on assessment of the individual offender's behavior and a few characteristics of his or her immediate social environment. Although these measures offer a broader view of the risk and protective factor ecology than do behavioral assessment tools, such as the CBCL, they still provide a fairly limited picture of the ecology of risk and protection. They are useful for classifying individuals within certain defined levels of risk and need, which is valuable for both treatment and policy decision making. However, they are less useful for planning ecologically based delinquency prevention strategies for populations whose members have not yet exhibited conduct problems. Given the apparent effectiveness of prevention strategies that are environment and population focused—they reduce risk for delinquency, violence, and substance abuse (see, for example, Brewer, Hawkins, Catalano, & Neckerman, 1995; Hawkins, Arthur, & Catalano, 1995)—methods for assessing a broader array of risk and protective factors should be used by communities, juvenile justice personnel, and others concerned with the prevention of delinquency and interventions for conduct disorders.

STUDENT SURVEY OF RISK AND PROTECTIVE FACTORS AND ADOLESCENT ANTISOCIAL BEHAVIOR

The Center for Substance Abuse Prevention (CSAP) continues to fund efforts to develop and validate an epidemiological assessment tool designed to cover a comprehensive array of risk and protective factors for delinquency and substance abuse, such as the Six State Student Survey (Pollard, Hawkins, Catalano, & Arthur, 1995). This self-report instrument contains 129 items measuring 22 risk factors and 11 protective factors in the community, school, family, peer, and individual domains. It is designed for 10- to 18-year-old youths and can be completed by most students in school during one class period (45 to 50 minutes). The instrument was developed, pretested, pilot tested, and administered to statewide samples of students in grades 6 through 12 in six states under a contract with CSAP (Pollard et al., 1995). The survey scales have been validated for the samples within and across states, and work is proceeding to test the reliability and validity of the scales and constructs within various demographic subgroups within the total sample. (A copy of the six-state student survey is available from the Social Development Research Group, School of Social Work, University of Washington, Seattle.)

This instrument differs markedly in both content and purpose from the others discussed in this chapter because it focuses on the epidemiological assessment of risk and protective factors in a group or population; it does not assess individuals' characteristics to predict behavior. Much of the content of survey items reflects respondents' ratings of community, school, family, and peer-group environments. Such assessments are useful in identifying specific populations at high risk of the development of conduct problems, including delinquency and substance abuse, and for identifying specific risk and protective factors that are either elevated or depressed in the assessed populations. This information can be used to direct more prevention services to high-risk populations and to select prevention strategies that focus on the risk or protective factors identified as priorities. Thus, this instrument is particularly useful in designing interventions that address population-level, rather than individual-level, needs.

ISSUES IN ASSESSMENT OF RISK AND PROTECTIVE FACTORS

Several important issues should be considered before assessing risk and protective factors for behavior problems. First, it should be understood that risk and protective factors are probabilistic, not perfect, predictors of conduct disorder and delinquency. The accurate prediction of a specific individual's conduct problems is typically problematic, characterized by high false-positive rates along with false-negative rates (Loeber & Stouthamer-Loeber, 1987). That is, many youths whose current risk and protective status would indicate high risk of behavior problems do not develop conduct problems, whereas some low-risk youths do develop serious behavior problems. The implications of this fact are serious indeed: prevention and treatment programs that target individuals based on assessments of risk and protective factors might exclude low-risk youths who need intervention, and high-risk youths who otherwise would have avoided conduct problems but who might not do so because of the iatrogenic effects of labeling and net widening.

Additional issues related to measuring risk factors, protective factors, and resiliency is the lack of a unifying conceptual framework to accommodate the integration of findings across disciplines (Winkle, 1999)—a range of characteristics that are present in an individual's personality or environment to define risk factors. This diversity in risk factors presents challenges for evaluating protective factors and resiliency. To better evaluate the processes of protective factors and resiliency, a more-encompassing framework may facilitate better comparisons across studies to improve the findings across disciplines (Luthar & Cushing, 1999).

MULTIPLE GATING

One advocated method for reducing errors in prediction is multiple gating (Loeber, 1988; Loeber, Dishion, & Patterson, 1984; Loeber & Hay, 1994; Loeber et al., 1991). This stepwise assessment procedure uses an inexpensive, broad assessment (a school or teacher survey, for example) as the first gate. Individuals identified at the first gate as potentially at risk for conduct problems are then reassessed some time later through a more intensive assessment procedure (for example, a parent survey). The youths passing through the second gate who are still classified as high risk can be assessed again through an even more intensive process (interview with the parent or child, or both) to determine the need for intervention to reduce risk for conduct problems. Loeber and colleagues (1984) demonstrated that such procedures could improve the accuracy of prediction and minimize the costs of risk assessment.

POPULATION-LEVEL PROGRAMS

Another approach to the issue of imperfect prediction is to focus the assessments for risk and protective factors at the population level rather than the individual level. Universal programs can still address specific factors that the assessment identified within the population as particularly elevated (risk) or depressed (protection; Hawkins, Catalano, Morrison, et al., 1992). This is consistent with an ecological approach to prevention and promotion of well-being, wherein the focus of programs is on reducing risk and enhancing protection in the physical and social environment, not on changing the individual person. This approach minimizes the potential for labeling and for any problems associated with net widening because the goal of the intervention is to protect and promote health in the entire population.

METHODOLOGICAL LIMITATIONS

A third issue concerns the validity of instruments for assessing risk and protective factors across demographic groups. Gottfredson and colleagues (1995) noted in their assessment of promising instruments for measuring risk and protective factors for adolescent drug abuse that only a few of the instruments had been validated with different racial and ethnic groups. Questions about how differences in age and socioeconomic status affect the validity and appropriateness of assessment tools also need to be answered. Current research by Gottfredson and Koper (1993), the six-state consortium (Pollard et al., 1995), and others should soon shed light on these issues.

IMPLICATIONS FOR PREVENTION, EARLY INTERVENTION, AND TREATMENT

Recent advances in knowledge about risk factors for delinquency and conduct disorder have important implications for intervention and prevention. Risk factors are found all across the social ecology of childhood in the domains of the individual, family, school, peers, and community. Moreover, the greater the number of risks in an individual's life, the greater the probability of involvement in delinquent behavior (IOM, 1994). Thus, to be most effective, prevention and treatment interventions must focus on a comprehensive approach that includes individual, family, school, peer, and community risk factors. Program development should emphasize the reduction of risk factors and, at the same time, the enhancement of identified protective factors.

Current strategies use three approaches for implementing intervention and prevention programs. The first approach is universal preventive interventions. Universal interventions are targeted at a whole population group that has not been identified on the basis of individual risk (IOM, 1994). Universal interventions are desirable when their per person cost is low and the risk of negative effects from the intervention is minimal. These interventions are good for everyone in the population. Risk factors such as poverty, exposure to toxins, problematic laws and norms, poor family management practices, and inadequate parenting skills can be lessened through a broad approach. Programs focused on providing training in parenting and social skills can universally enhance protective factors without targeting a specific population (IOM, 1994). Other programs and policies targeted toward decreasing poverty, improving policing strategies, developing more effective educational systems, limiting exposure to neurotoxins, and reducing the availability of handguns and drugs are considered to be universal precautions (Loftin et al., 1991; Loftin et al., 1993).

The second approach, or selective preventive interventions, uses programs primarily focused on at-risk populations. Selective interventions are targeted at individuals or groups whose risk of becoming delinquent or having conduct disorder is higher than average. These programs also use intervention, with the ultimate goal of minimizing risks and enhancing or increasing protective factors.

The third approach, or indicated preventive interventions, is targeted at high-risk individuals thought to have a predisposition for delinquency or conduct disorder. Indicated interventions are targeted at individuals whose symptoms appear early but who have not initiated delinquent acts or who do not meet the diagnostic criteria for conduct disorder. Indicated interventions have historically been referred to as "early interventions." The underpinnings of universal, selected, and indicated prevention interventions are identified risk factors. Several researchers have reviewed well-designed evaluations of preventive interventions targeting delinquent behavior (Hawkins & Catalano, 1992; Hawkins, Catalano, Morrison, et al., 1992; Howell, Krisberg, Hawkins, & Wilson, 1995; IOM, 1994).

Reducing delinquency and conduct disorder requires a multifaceted, coordinated approach; early intervention is a critical step. Although strategies for delinquency prevention or intervention focus on all social domains, strategies for conduct disorder intervention focus primarily on the individual and the family. However, because conduct disorder and delinquency exhibit common risk factors (including aggressive behavior, school failure, poor family management, and family conflict) and because behaviors are similar and overlapping in the two disorders, intervention strategies within the individual and family domains overlap.

In the following sections, we will discuss numerous preventive interventions currently being implemented and evaluated in the individual, family, peer, educational, and community domains to ameliorate delinquency and conduct disorder. Many of these strategies have excellent outcomes that have been documented. We have highlighted four such programs as exemplary in their strategic approach and outcomes and will address them later in this chapter. These programs include (1) the Incredible Years Training Series (Webster-Stratton, 2000), (2) the Strengthening Families Program (SFP; Kumpfer & Tait, 2000), (3) the Brief Strategic Family Therapy (BSFT; Robbins & Szapocznik, 2000), and (4) the Intensive Aftercare Program (IAP; Altschuler, Armstrong, & MacKenzie, 1999).

INDIVIDUAL AND FAMILY INTERVENTIONS

Programs for prenatal and perinatal health and parent education provide health and parenting education, job and education counseling, and emotional and social support during and after pregnancy (Olds, Henderson, Tatelbaum, & Chamberlin, 1986b). The main goal of prenatal and parenting education programs is to minimize biological or genetic risk factors and to increase protective factors such as parenting and job skills. Evaluations of prenatal programs have been favorable. Results from program participation include decreased perinatal difficulties and fewer referrals for child abuse or neglect as well as higher birthweight and increased parent employment (Greenwood, Model, Rydell, & Chiesa, 1996; Olds, Henderson, Tatelbaum, & Chamberlin, 1986a).

Intensive family preservation services are short-term crisis interventions for families whose children are at risk of out-of-home placement. These programs address the risk factors of poor family management practices and family conflict as they simultaneously enhance family bonding and social supports (Bergquist, Szwejda, & Pope, 1993; Henggeler & Borduin, 1990; Henggeler, Melton, & Smith, 1992). Interventions such as intensive family preservation services have been shown to be effective for reducing family conflict and children's antisocial behavior and for improving family management practices (Dumas, 1989; Henggeler & Borduin, 1990; Henggeler et al., 1992; Rossi, 1992; Shadish, 1992). Other interventions include marital and family services and training to improve parent–child interaction by minimizing the risk factors of family conflict, poor family management practices, and family instability (Dumas, 1989; Strayhorn & Weidman, 1991).

Peer Cluster Interventions

Interventions specifically targeted at peer-group relationships should build social skills, acceptable techniques for conflict resolution, and skills for avoiding problem behavior (Wasserman & Miller, 1998). Sound conflict-resolution and violence-prevention curriculums attempt to minimize early aggressive behavior and association with delinquent peers and to enhance the protective factors for skills in childhood social problem solving and anger management. Many such curriculums have been extensively evaluated. Results from these evaluation studies indicate some effectiveness, but more studies are needed to address possible interaction effects and cultural relevancy.

Empowering Children to Survive and Succeed (ECSS; Brennan, 1992) and Second Step (Committee for Children, 1992) are two curriculums that target elementary school children. Both programs emphasize interpersonal problem solving, appropriate social behavior, and self-control and self-confidence. The evaluation of ECSS showed mixed results, whereas the evaluation of the Second Step program showed improvement for students who received the structured lessons (Brennan, 1992; Committee for Children, 1988, 1992).

Think First and Fighting Fair are two programs developed for students in middle school. They focus on mediation, negotiation, anger and aggression control, problem solving, and school attendance incentives (Larson, 1992; Marvel, Moreda, & Cook, 1993). Both programs were effective in decreasing problem behaviors within the school settings where they were administered (Larson, 1992; Marvel et al., 1993). Positive Adolescents Choices Training (PACT) is a violence-prevention program specifically designed for African American youths in middle school (Hammond & Yung, 1991, 1993). PACT uses African American role models and culturally relevant vignettes to help youths develop social skills for resisting peer pressure and for problem solving and negotiating. Evaluation studies showed decreases in physical and verbal aggression and lower rates of juvenile court-recorded offenses for program participants (Hammond & Yung, 1993).

Dealing with Conflict and Violence Prevention are two curriculums specifically targeted at high school students. Activities in these curriculums build participant trust, group cohesion, and ability to identify and articulate consequences and alternatives to violence (Bretherton, Collins, & Ferretti, 1993; Wasserman & Miller, 1998; Webster, 1993). Student participants in both curriculums had significantly decreased self-reported violent behavior and fighting in comparison with a control group (Bretherton et al., 1993; Webster, 1993). Both curriculums showed promising results, but concerns about methodology require more extensive evaluation studies.

Peer mediation programs and peer counseling are two other programs used to address problem-solving abilities and peer culture (Gottfredson, 1987). Such programs are often carried out in conjunction with programs for conflict resolution and violence prevention. Peer mediation programs address risk factors of early and persistent anti-social behavior and association with antisocial peers (Lam, 1989); peer counseling addresses risk factors of favorable attitudes toward delinquency, alienation, rebelliousness, and association with delinquent peers (Gottfredson, 1987). Protective factors, including problem solving to resolve conflicts, healthy beliefs, and clear expectations for behavior, are the enhancement goals of peer mediation and peer counseling programs; peer counseling also seeks to enhance opportunities and skills to communicate. Lam's (1989) review of 14 peer mediation programs suggested that they had positive effects on knowledge, attitudes, and behaviors. The research on peer counseling has produced mixed results (Gottfredson, 1987).

INTERVENTIONS IN EDUCATIONAL SETTINGS

Intervention strategies in the school domain—classroom organization, classroom management, and instructional strategies, for instance—promote the protective factors of bonding to school, opportunities for achievement, and involvement with prosocial peers (Hawkins et al., 1999). These strategies seek to reduce the risk factors of academic failure, low commitment to school, and early antisocial behavior (Hawkins et al., 1999; Hawkins, Catalano, Morrison, et al., 1992; Slavin, 1994). The "good behavior game," which uses motivational tools to decrease aggressive behavior and reward learning and prosocial behavior, has been introduced to children in elementary school (Kellam, Rebok, Ialongo, & Mayer, 1994). The good behavior game is an example of an educational program that seeks to advance cognitive and social development in younger children. Kellam and colleagues (1994) found that children enrolled in classes using this program showed significantly less aggressive behavior than the control group. The Seattle Social Development Project (SSDP), a longitudinal study developed to prevent delinquency, used a multicomponent prevention program in selected elementary school classrooms (Hawkins & Lam, 1987). The strategies of the program included cooperative learning, proactive classroom management, and interactive teaching. Results indicate that the SSDP produced significant effects in various areas, including a reduction in aggressive behavior; moreover, longitudinal analysis revealed that children in the classrooms using the program were less likely to have reported self involvement in violent behaviors, heavy drinking, and sexual intercourse (Hawkins et al., 1999; Hawkins, Catalano, Morrison, et al., 1992; Huang et al., 2001).

There are many other research studies on prevention strategies within the educational setting—too many, in fact, to allow extensive coverage in this chapter. In brief, other strategies shown to be effective include behavioral monitoring, attendance reinforcement, special education placements, and graduation incentives (Brooks, 1975; Bry, 1982; Hahn, Leavitt, & Aaron, 1994; Safer, 1990; Taggart, 1995).

COMMUNITY STRATEGIES

Strategies developed for use in the community domain attempt to address the risk factors of community disorganization, low neighborhood attachment, and crime-tolerant norms. These strategies include regulations restricting the carrying, sale, and transfer of firearms; mandatory sentencing; community mobilization; and new, innovative policing strategies. Regulations and restrictions regarding firearms and mandatory sentencing are universal. Policing strategies and community mobilization are often implemented in high-risk communities, when the goals are to enhance opportunities for involvement and bonding with police and to promote the prosocial skills needed to monitor and influence the neighborhood. Community policing and neighborhood block watch programs are currently being implemented in high-risk communities to decrease delinquent behavior. Evaluations of community policing programs show mixed results for effectiveness (Rosenbaum, Yeh, & Wilkinson, 1994; Thurman, Giacomazzi, & Bogen, 1993). Neighborhood block watch programs have been shown to be effective in decreasing victimization rates of burglary and vandalism (Lindsay & McGillis, 1986).

EXEMPLARY PROGRAMS

Although advances have been made in the identification of multiple risk and protective factors, there have also been advances in programmatic efforts aimed at risk reduction and protection enhancement. Specifically, multiple universal, selective, and indicated interventions have been evaluated as effective in the reduction of social problems of youths; the four programs described below are examples.

INCREDIBLE YEARS TRAINING SERIES

The Incredible Years Training Series consists of multiple interventions designed to reduce or prevent conduct problems in children and to promote social, emotional, and academic competencies (Webster-Stratton, 2000). Furthermore, the Incredible Years program attempts to promote parental competencies and to strengthen families. In the school context, the program addresses teacher competencies and classroom management techniques and strengthens the school–home connection.

The series is designed for, and has been evaluated on, children between ages two and 10. Adhering to the tenor of this chapter, and other chapters in this volume, the Incredible Years program targets specific risk factors (for example, deficient social skills, negative attributions, and family conflict) and attempts to strengthen protective factors (for example, conflict management, problem solving, and family support; Webster-Stratton, 1990).

The BASIC Parent program is designed for parents with children between ages two and seven. The two-week program teaches parents interactive play and reinforcement skills, nonviolent discipline techniques, logical and natural consequences, and problem-solving strategies through a series of videotaped vignettes. The School-

Age BASIC program is similar to the BASIC Parent program; however, it is designed for children ages five to 12 and contains a multicultural program with an increased focus on monitoring children's behavior and family problem solving. There is also a 12-week ADVANCE Parent curriculum that addresses specific family risk factors, including parental conflict, family management, and poor parental skills. The EDUCATION Parent Training Program is a supplement to any of the Parent programs and addresses ways in which parents can foster academic competence by strengthening academic readiness. Finally, the Teacher Training component addresses classroom management skills, such as encouraging and motivating students, increasing social competence, and decreasing inappropriate behaviors.

Multiple evaluations over the past decade have found the Incredible Years program to be effective in reducing risk factors and in enhancing protective factors in various domains. Specifically, positive effects were shown immediately postintervention, and in many cases between one and four years posttreatment (Webster-Stratton, 1990, 1994; Webster-Stratton & Hammond, 1997). Finally, the Incredible Years Training Series is available in multiple languages and has demonstrated efficacy with multiple ethnic groups.

STRENGTHENING FAMILIES PROGRAM

The SFP consists of 14 consecutive weekly sessions, each approximately two hours long. SFP's goals are to reduce risk factors associated with alcohol, tobacco, other drug use, and delinquency and to enhance protective factors in the family domain (Kumpfer & Tait, 2000). SFP's two versions are targeted at elementary school-age children and their families and 10- to 14-year-old youths and their families. Each version includes skills training for children, parents, and families. SFP has separate training manuals that have been designed for African American families; recent versions of SFP have been developed for English-speaking Australian families and French- and English-speaking families in Canada.

Similar to the Incredible Years program, SFP has undergone multiple evaluations that have proved its efficacy both immediately after intervention and up to and five years postintervention. Furthermore, some of the follow-up examinations of the SFP program have been conducted with minority families in both urban and rural areas (Aktan, Kumpfer, & Turner, 1996; Kameoka & Lecar, 1996; Molgaard, Kumpfer, & Spoth, 1994).

BRIEF STRATEGIC FAMILY THERAPY

Brief Strategic Family Therapy (BSFT) has been used as a targeted, as well as a preventive, intervention addressing conduct and substance-abuse problems displayed by Hispanic/Latino and African American youths. The premise behind BSFT, which is based on the family therapy principles of Haley (1976), Madanes (1981), and Minuchin (1974), is that the family is the foundation of child development. As such, the program attempts to address family risk factors that are correlated with social problems of youths. However, other risk factors in the community and the school are also addressed, as are peer-risk factors; at the same time familial protective factors are enhanced (for example, a strong extended family is created; Szapocznik et al., 1985; Szapocznik et al., 1989).

BSFT is designed for children between ages eight and 17. The intervention focuses on the family system. Attending to these leverage points allows for a strategic intervention that is practical, focused, and well planned. The length of the intervention typically ranges between 12 and 15 weeks (Robbins & Szapocznik, 2000). BSFT was shown to be more effective than both group treatment and individual treatment in retaining clients, increasing family functioning, and decreasing various problems, including aggression (Santisteban et al., 1996).

INTENSIVE AFTERCARE PROGRAM

The IAP is designed to address risk factors associated with recidivism. Based on social learning, strain, and social control theories, IAP is a model of community-based reintegration that attempts to address youths' social, academic, vocational, health, and family needs (Altschuler & Armstrong, 1996). The premise behind IAP is to provide both treatment and supervision as prior research supports the notion that recidivism only declines when both factors are in place (Gendreau, 1996).

The necessary components of IAP include continuous risk assessment, individual case planning incorporating both the family and the community context, and a balance between incentives and graduated sanctions. With regard to the risk assessment, the IAP model stresses addressing criminogenic, nonstatic risk factors. Finally, the IAP model proposes that services delivered in institutions be similar to those delivered in the community, thus creating a consistent transition between institutional and community treatment (Altschuler, Armstrong, & MacKenzie, 1999).

Four recent evaluations of IAP have produced mixed results. However, programs that showed nonsignificant findings generally experienced problems with implementation and high rates of staff turnover. Having said that, a recent report to the U.S. Congress, *Preventing Crime: What Works, What Doesn't, What's Promising*, shows that IAP models which are appropriately implemented show promise in reducing recidivism of youths (MacKenzie, 1997).

CONCLUSION

Whether the good news–bad news pendulum of juvenile delinquency and conduct disorder continues to swing as it has over the past several decades, and in what direction, is unknown. Variables likely to influence its movements include economic resources targeted toward the behaviors, public attitudes, legislation, policing, and other juvenile justice system policy and practices (for example, levels of arrest, detention, and incarceration) and the effectiveness of prevention and intervention practices. In terms of the latter variables, many evaluation studies have noted positive program effects. However, it is apparent that more research will be needed to determine the preventive effectiveness of our intervention efforts. Previous research indicates the various domains in which interventions will be useful, but more work is necessary to learn what will facilitate more effective approaches and when gaps might exist in our knowledge base. For instance, few studies have investigated the relationship of race and gender to delinquent behavior and the effectiveness of prevention interventions across racial or cultural groups and across gender. Critical issues of racial disparities in delinquency require more research using a risk factor approach. Studies are also needed to investigate causal factors that may explain racial and gender differences in the prevalence of and participation in delinquent behavior. Notwithstanding the need for further research, the effectiveness of programs reviewed here and elsewhere warrants their continued use by practitioners who work to mitigate risk factors and enhance protective factors for children.

REFERENCES

Achenbach, T. M. (1991). *Manual for the Teacher's Report Form and 1991 Profile.* Burlington: University of Vermont, Department of Psychiatry.

Achenbach, T. M., & Edelbrock, C. (1983). *Manual for the Child Behavior Checklist and revised Child Behavior Profile.* Burlington, VT: University Associates in Psychiatry.

Achenbach, T. M., & Edelbrock, C. (1986). *Manual for the Teacher's Report Form and teacher's version of the Child Behavior Profile.* Burlington, VT: University Associates in Psychiatry.

Agnew, R. (1991). A longitudinal test of social control theory and delinquency. *Journal of Research in Crime and Delinquency, 28*(2), 126–156.

Aktan, G., Kumpfer, K. L., & Turner, C. (1996). Effectiveness of a family skills training program for substance use prevention with inner city African American families. *Substance Use and Misuse, 31*(2), 157–175.

Alexander, G. R., Massey, R. M., Gibbs, T., & Altekruse, J. M. (1985). Firearm-related fatalities: An epidemiological assessment of violent death. *American Journal of Public Health, 75,* 165–168.

Altschuler, D. M., & Armstrong, T. L. (1996). Aftercare not afterthought: Testing the IAP model. *Juvenile Justice, 3*(1), 15–22.

Altschuler, D. M., Armstrong, T. L., & MacKenzie, D. L. (1999). *Reintegration, supervised release, and intensive aftercare.* Washington, DC: Office of Juvenile Justice and Delinquency Prevention.

American Psychiatric Association. (1994). *Diagnostic and statistical manual of mental disorders* (4th ed.). Washington, DC: Author.

Anderson, B. J., Holmes, M. D., & Ostresh, E. (1999). Male and female delinquents' attachments and effects of attachments on severity of self-reported delinquency. *Criminal Justice and Behavior, 26*(4), 435–452.

Atkins, M. S., & Stoff, D. M. (1993). Instrumental and hostile aggression in childhood disruptive behavior disorders. *Journal of Abnormal Child Psychology, 21,* 165–178.

Ayers, C. D., Williams, J. H., Hawkins, J. D., Peterson, P. L., Catalano, R. F., & Abbott, R. D. (1999). Assessing correlates of onset, escalation, deescalation, and desistence of delinquent behavior. *Journal of Quantitative Criminology, 15*(3), 277–306.

Baird, S. C. (1984). *Classification of juveniles in corrections: A model systems approach.* Madison, WI: National Council on Crime and Delinquency.

Barlow, J., & Stewart-Brown, S. (2000). Behavior problems and group-based parent education programs. *Journal of Developmental and Behavioral Pediatrics, 21*(5), 356–370.

Barnes, G. M., & Farrell, M. P. (1992). Parental support and control as predictors of adolescent drinking, delinquency and related problem behaviors. *Journal of Marriage and the Family, 54,* 763–776.

Benson, P. L., Leffert, N., Scales, P. C., & Blyth, D. A. (1998). Beyond the "village" rhetoric: Creating healthy communities for children and adolescents. *Applied Developmental Science, 2*(3), 138–159.

Bergquist, C., Szwejda, D., & Pope, G. (1993). *Evaluation of Michigan's Families First Program: Summary report.* Lansing: Michigan Department of Social Services.

Biederman, J., Munir, K., & Knee, D. (1987). Conduct and oppositional disorder in clinically referred children with attention deficit disorder: A controlled family study. *Journal of the American Academy of Child and Adolescent Psychiatry, 26,* 724–727.

Brennan, T. (1992). Project evaluation: ECSS program of the Lesson One Foundation beginners' curriculum prekindergarten to third grade. Boston: Lesson One Foundation.

Breslau, N., Klein, N., & Allen, L. (1988). Very low birth weight: Behavioral sequelae at nine years of age. *Journal of the American Academy of Child and Adolescent Psychiatry, 67,* 605–612.

Bretherton, D. L., Collins, L., & Ferretti, C. (1993). Dealing with conflict: Assessment of a course for secondary school students. *Australian Psychologist, 28,* 105–111.

Brewer, D. D., Hawkins, J. D., Catalano, R. F., & Neckerman, H. J. (1995). Preventing serious, violent, and chronic juvenile offending: A review of evaluations of selected strategies in childhood, adolescence, and the community. In J. C. Howell, B. Krisberg, J. D. Hawkins, & J. J. Wilson (Eds.), *Sourcebook on serious, violent, & chronic juvenile offenders* (pp. 61–142). Thousand Oaks, CA: Sage Publications.

Brook, J. S. (1993). Interactional theory: Its utility in explaining drug use behavior among African-American and Puerto Rican youth. In M. R. De La Rosa & J.L.R. Adrados (Eds.), *Drug abuse among minority youth: Advances in research methodology* (National Institute on Drug Abuse Research Monograph No. 130, NIH Pub. No. 93-3479, pp. 79–101). Washington, DC: U.S. Government Printing Office.

Brooks, B. D. (1975). Contingency management as a means of reducing school truancy. *Education, 95,* 206–211.

Bry, B. H. (1982). Reducing the incidence of adolescent problems through preventive intervention: One- and five-year follow-up. *American Journal of Community Psychology, 10,* 265–276.

Bursik, R. J., Jr., & Webb, J. (1982). Community change and patterns of delinquency. *American Journal of Sociology, 88,* 24–42.

Cadoret, R. J., Cain, C. A., & Crowe, R. R. (1983). Evidence for gene–environment interaction in the development of adolescent antisocial behavior. *Behavior Genetics, 13,* 301–310.

Cairns, R. B., & Cairns, B. D. (1991). Social cognition and social networks: A developmental perspective. In D. Pepler & K. H. Rubin (Eds.), *The development and treatment of childhood aggression* (pp. 249–278). Hillsdale, NJ: Lawrence Erlbaum.

Cairns, R. B., Cairns, B. D., Neckerman, H. J., Ferguson, L. L., & Gariepy, J. L. (1989). Growth and aggression: Childhood to early adolescence. *Developmental Psychology, 25,* 320–330.

Catalano, R. F., Hawkins, J. D., Krenz, C., Gillmore, M., Morrison, D., Wells, E., & Abbott, R. (1993). Using research to guide culturally appropriated drug abuse prevention. *Journal of Consulting and Clinical Psychology, 61,* 804–811.

Cernkovich, S. A., & Giordano, P. C. (1987). Family relationships and delinquency. *Criminology, 25,* 295–319.

Committee for Children. (1988). *Second Step, grades 1–3, pilot project 1987–88: Summary report.* Seattle: Author.

Committee for Children. (1992). *Evaluation of Second Step, preschool–kindergarten: A violence prevention curriculum kit.* Seattle: Author.

Costello, E. J., Angold, A., Burns, B. J., Erkanli, A., Stangl, D. K., & Tweed, D. L. (1996). The Great Smoky Mountains Study of Youth: Functional impairment and serious emotional disturbance. *Archives of General Psychiatry, 53,* 1137–1143.

Cote, S., Zoccolillo, M., Tremblay, R. E., Nagin, D., & Vitaro, F. (2001). Predicting girls' conduct disorder in adolescence from childhood trajectories of disruptive behaviors. *Journal of the American Academy of Child and Adolescent Psychiatry, 40*(6), 678–684.

Cowen, E., & Work, W. (1988). Resilient children, psychological wellness, and primary prevention. *American Journal of Community Psychology, 16,* 591–607.

Dembo, R., Williams, L., & Schmeidler, J. (1994). Psychosocial, alcohol/other drug use, and delinquency differences between urban black and white male high risk youth. *International Journal of Addictions, 29,* 461–483.

Dumas, J. E. (1989). Treating antisocial behavior in children: Child and family approaches. *Clinical Psychology Review, 9,* 197–222.

Earls, F. (1981). Temperament characteristics and behavior problems in three-year-old children. *Journal of Nervous and Mental Disease, 169,* 367–373.

Earls, F., & Jung, K. (1987). Temperament and home environment characteristics as causal factors in the early development of childhood psychopathology. *Journal of the American Academy of Child and Adolescent Psychiatry, 26,* 491–498.

Edelbrock, C. (1986). Behavioral rating of children diagnosed for attention deficit disorder. *Psychiatric Annals, 16,* 36–40.

Elliott, D. S. (1994a). Serious violent offenders: Onset, developmental course and termination—The American Society of Criminology 1993 presidential address. *Criminology, 32,* 1–21.

Elliott, D. S. (1994b). *Youth violence: An overview.* Boulder: University of Colorado, Center for the Study and Prevention of Violence.

Elliott, D. S., Huizinga, D., & Ageton, S. (1985). *Explaining delinquency and drug use.* Beverly Hills, CA: Sage Publications.

Elliott, D. S., Huizinga, D., & Menard, S. (1989). *Multiple problem youth: Delinquency, substance, and mental health problems.* New York: Springer-Verlag.

Elliott, D. S., Huizinga, D., & Morse, B. (1986). Self-reported violent offending: A descriptive analysis of juvenile violent offenders and their offending careers. *Journal of Interpersonal Violence, 1,* 472–514.

Farrington, D. P. (1983). Offending from 10 to 25 years of age. In K. T. Van Dusen & S. A. Mednick (Eds.), *Prospective studies of crime and delinquency* (pp. 17–37). Boston: Kluwer-Nijhoff.

Farrington, D. P. (1986). Stepping stones to adult criminal careers. In D. Olweus, J.

Block, & M. R. Yarrow (Eds.), *Development of antisocial and prosocial behavior* (pp. 359–384). New York: Academic Press.

Farrington, D. P. (1991). Childhood aggression and adult violence. In D. Pepler & K. H. Rubin (Eds.), *The development and treatment of childhood aggression* (pp. 2–29). Hillsdale, NJ: Lawrence Erlbaum.

Farrington, D. P. (1994). Early developmental prevention of juvenile delinquency. *Criminal Behaviour and Mental Health, 4,* 209–227.

Farrington, D. P., & Hawkins, J. D. (1991). Predicting participation, early onset, and later persistence in officially recorded offending. *Criminal Behaviour and Mental Health, 1,* 1–33.

Farrington, D. P., Loeber, R., Elliott, D. S., Hawkins, J. D., Kandel, D. B., Klein, M. W., McCord, J., Rowe, D. C., & Tremblay, R. E. (1990). Advancing knowledge about the onset of delinquency and crime. In B. B. Lahey & A. E. Kazdin (Eds.), *Advances in clinical child psychology* (Vol. 13, pp. 283–342). New York: Plenum Press.

Farrington, D. P., Loeber, R., Stouthamer-Loeber, M., Van Kammen, W. B., & Schmidt, L. (1996). Self-reported delinquency and a combined delinquency seriousness scale based on boys, mothers, and teachers: Concurrent and predictive validity for African-Americans and Caucasians. *Criminology, 34,* 501–525.

Farrington, D. P., & West, D. J. (1990). The Cambridge Study in delinquent development. In H. J. Kerner & G. Kaiser (Eds.), *Criminality: Personality, behavior and life history* (pp. 115–138). Berlin: Springer-Verlag.

Farrington, D. P., & West, D. J. (1993). Criminal, penal, and life histories of chronic offenders: Risk and protective factors in early identification. *Criminal Behaviour and Mental Health, 3,* 492–523.

Federal Bureau of Investigation. (2000). *Crime in the United States 1999.* Washington, DC: U.S. Government Printing Office.

Forehand, R., Wierson, M., Frame, C., Kempton, T., & Armistead, L. (1991). Juvenile delinquency entry and persistence: Do attention problems contribute to conduct problems? *Journal of Behavior Therapy & Experimental Psychiatry, 22*(4), 261–264.

Frick, P. J., Lahey, B. B., Loeber, R., Stouthamer-Loeber, M., Christ, M. G., & Hanson, K. (1992). Familial risk factors to oppositional defiant disorder and conduct disorder: Parental psychopathology and maternal parenting. *Journal of Consulting and Clinical Psychology, 60,* 49–55.

Garbarino, J., DuBrow, N., Kostelny, K., & Pardo, C. (1992). *Children in danger: Coping with the consequences of community violence.* San Francisco: Jossey-Bass.

Gendreau, P. (1996). The principles of effective intervention with offenders. In A. Harland (Ed.), *Choosing correctional options that work* (pp. 117–130). Thousand Oaks, CA: Sage Publications.

Gillmore, M. R., Hawkins, J. D., Catalano, R. F., Day, L. E., & Abbott, R. D. (1991). Structure of problem behaviors in preadolescence. *Journal of Consulting and Clinical Psychology, 59,* 499–506.

Gonzales, N., Cauce, A. M., Friedman, R. J., & Mason, C. A. (1996). Family, peer, and neighborhood influences on academic achievement among African-American adolescents: One-year prospective effects. *American Journal of Community Psychology, 24*(3), 365–387.

Gottfredson, D. C. (1986). An empirical test of school-based environmental and individual intervention to reduce the risk of delinquent behavior. *Criminology, 24,* 705–731.

Gottfredson, D. C. (1987). An evaluation of an organization development approach to reducing school disorder. *Evaluation Review, 2,* 739–763.

Gottfredson, D. C., Harmon, M. A., Gottfredson, G. D., Jones, E. M., & Celestin, J. A. (1995). *ATOD prevention program outcomes and instrument selection system (CSAP draft).* Rockville, MD: National Center for the Advancement of Prevention.

Gottfredson, D. C., & Koper, C. S. (1993). *Race and sex differences in the measurement of risk for delinquency and substance abuse.* Paper presented at the annual meeting of the American Society of Criminology, Phoenix, AZ.

Greenwood, P. W., Model, K. E., Rydell, C. P., & Chiesa, J. (1996). *Diverting children from a life of crime: Measuring costs and benefits.* Santa Monica, CA: Rand Corporation.

Gresham, F. M., Lane, K. L., & Lambros, K. M. (2000). Comorbidity of conduct problems and ADHD: Identification of "fledgling psychopaths." *Journal of Emotional and Behavioral Disorders, 8*(2), 83–93.

Hahn, A., Leavitt, T., & Aaron, P. (1994). Evaluation of the Quantum Opportunities Program (QOP): Did the program work? A report on the postsecondary outcomes and cost-effectiveness of the QOP program (1989–1993). Waltham, MA: Brandeis University.

Haley, J. (1976). *Problem-solving therapy.* San Francisco: Jossey-Bass.

Hammond, W. R., & Yung, B. R. (1991). Preventing violence in at-risk African American youth. *Journal of Health Care for the Poor and Underserved, 2,* 359–373.

Hammond, W. R., & Yung, B. R. (1993). *Evaluation and activity report: Positive Adolescents Choice Training (PACT) program.* Dayton, OH: Wright State University, School of Professional Psychology.

Hamparian, D., Schuster, R., Dinitz, S., & Conrad, J. (1978). *The violent few: A study of dangerous juvenile offenders.* Lexington, MA: Lexington Books.

Hawkins, D. F., Laub, J. H., & Lauritsen, J. L. (1998). Race, ethnicity, and serious juvenile offending. In R. Loeber & D. P. Farrington (Eds.), *Serious and violent juvenile offenders: Risk factors and successful interventions* (pp. 30–47). Thousand Oaks, CA: Sage Publications.

Hawkins, J. D., Arthur, M. W., & Catalano, R. F. (1995). Prevention of substance abuse. In M. Tonry & D. Farrington (Eds.), *Crime and justice: An annual review of research* (Vol. 18). Chicago: University of Chicago Press.

Hawkins, J. D. , & Catalano, R. F. (1992). *Communities that care: Action for drug abuse prevention.* San Francisco: Jossey-Bass.

Hawkins, J. D., Catalano, R. F., & Brewer, D. D. (1995). Preventing serious, violent, and chronic juvenile offending: Effective strategies from conception to age 6. In J. C. Howell, B. Krisberg, J. D. Hawkins, & J. J. Wilson (Eds.), *Sourcebook on serious, violent, and chronic juvenile offenders* (pp. 47–61). Thousand Oaks, CA: Sage Publications.

Hawkins, J. D., Catalano, R. F., Kosterman, R., Abbott, R., & Hill, K. G. (1999).

Preventing adolescent health-risk behaviors by strengthening protection during childhood. *Archives of Pediatric and Adolescent Medicine, 153*. 226–234.

Hawkins, J. D., Catalano, R. F., & Miller, J. Y. (1992). Risk and protective factors for alcohol and other drug problems in adolescence and early adulthood: Implication for substance abuse prevention. *Psychological Bulletin, 112*, 64–105.

Hawkins, J. D., Catalano, R. F., Morrison, D. M., O'Donnell, J., Abbott, R. D., & Day, L. E. (1992). The Seattle Social Development Project: Effects of the first four years on protective factors and problem behaviors. In J. McCord & R. Tremblay (Eds.), *The prevention of antisocial behavior in children* (pp. 139–161). New York: Guilford Press.

Hawkins, J. D., Herrenkohl, T., Farrington, D. P., Brewer, D., Catalano, R. F., & Harachi, T. W. (1998). A review of predictors of youth violence. In R. Loeber & D. P. Farrington (Eds.), *Serious and violent juvenile offenders: Risk factors and successful interventions* (pp. 106–166). Thousand Oaks, CA: Sage Publications.

Hawkins, J. D., Jenson, J. M., Catalano, R. F., & Lishner, D. M. (1988). Delinquency and drug use: Implications for social services. *Social Service Review, 62*, 258–284.

Hawkins, J. D., & Lam, T. (1987). Teacher practices, social development, and delinquency. In J. D. Burchard & S. N. Burchard (Eds.), *Prevention of delinquent behavior*. Newbury Park, CA: Sage Publications.

Hawkins, J. D., & Weis, J. G. (1985). The social development model: An integrated approach to delinquency prevention. *Journal of Primary Prevention, 6*(2), 73–97.

Henggeler, S. W., & Borduin, C. M. (1990). Family therapy and beyond: A multisystemic approach to treating the behavior problems of children and adolescents. Pacific Grove, CA: Brooks/Cole.

Henggeler, S. W., Melton, G. B., & Smith, L. A. (1992). Family preservation using multisystemic therapy: An effective alternative to incarcerating serious juvenile offenders. *Journal of Consulting and Clinical Psychology, 60*, 953–961.

Hirschi, T. (1969). *Causes of delinquency*. Berkeley: University of California Press.

Howell, J. C., Krisberg, B., Hawkins, J. D., & Wilson, J. J. (Eds.). (1995). *Sourcebook on serious, violent and chronic juvenile offenders*. Thousand Oaks, CA: Sage Publications.

Huang, B., Kosterman, R., Catalano, R. F., Hawkins, J. D., & Abbott, R. D. (2001). Modeling mediation in the etiology of violent behavior in adolescence: A test of the social development model. *Criminology, 39*(1), 75–108.

Huizinga, D., Loeber, R., & Thornberry, T. (1993). *Urban delinquency and substance abuse: Initial findings*. Washington, DC: Office of Juvenile Justice and Delinquency Prevention.

Institute of Medicine. (1994). Reducing risks for mental disorders: Frontiers for preventive intervention research. Washington, DC: National Academy Press.

Jensen, P. S., Martin, D., & Cantwell, D. P. (1997). Comorbidity in ADHD: Implications for research, practice, and *DSM-V*. *Journal of the American Academy of Child and Adolescent Psychiatry, 36*(8), 1065–1079.

Jenson, J. M., Potter, C. C., & Howard, M. O. (2001). American juvenile justice: Recent trends and issues in youth offending. *Social Policy & Administration, 35*(1), 48–68.

Kameoka, V. A., & Lecar, S. (1996). *The effects of a family-focused intervention on reducing risk for substance abuse among Asian and Pacific Island youths and families: Evaluation of the Strengthening Hawaii's Families Project.* Honolulu: University of Hawaii, Social Welfare Evaluation and Research Unit.

Kandel, D., Simcha-Fagan, O., & Davies, M. (1986). Risk factors for delinquency and illicit drug use from adolescence to young adulthood. *Journal of Drug Issues, 16,* 67–90.

Kaplan, H. B. (1999). Toward an understanding of resilience: A critical review of definitions and models. In M. D. Glantz & J. L. Johnson (Eds.), *Resilience and development: Positive life adaptations* (pp. 17–84). New York: Kluwer Academic/Plenum.

Kazdin, A. E., & Wassell, G. (1999). Barriers to treatment participation and therapeutic change among children referred for conduct disorder. *Journal of Clinical Child Psychology, 28*(2), 160–172.

Kellam, S. G., Rebok, G. W., Ialongo, N., & Mayer, L. S. (1994). The course and malleability of aggressive behavior from early first grade into middle school: Results of a developmental epidemiologically based preventive trial. *Journal of Child Psychology and Psychiatry, 35,* 259–281.

Kumpfer, K. L., & Tait, C. M. (2000). *Family skills training for parents and children.* Washington, DC: Office of Juvenile Justice and Delinquency Prevention.

Lahey, B. B., Loeber, R., Hart, E. L., Frick, P. J., Applegate, B., Zhang, Q., Green, S. M., & Russo, M. F. (1995). Four-year longitudinal study of conduct disorder in boys: Patterns and predictors of persistence. *Journal of Abnormal Psychology, 104*(1), 83–93.

Lam, J. A. (1989). *The impact of conflict resolution programs on schools: A review and synthesis of the evidence.* Amherst, MA: National Association for Mediation in Education.

Larson, J. D. (1992). Anger and aggression management techniques through the Think First Curriculum. *Journal of Offender Rehabilitation, 18,* 101–117.

Laub, J. H., & Sampson, R. J. (1988). Unraveling families and delinquency: A reanalysis of the Gluecks' data. *Criminology, 26,* 355–380.

Leffert, N., Benson, P. L., Scales, P. C., Sharma, A., Drake, D., & Blyth, D. A. (1998). Developmental assets: Measurement and prediction of risk behaviors among adolescents. *Applied Developmental Science, 2*(4), 209–230.

Lindsay, B., & McGillis, D. (1986). Citywide community crime prevention: An assessment of the Seattle program. In D. P. Rosenbaum (Ed.), *Community crime prevention: Does it work?* (pp. 46–67). Beverly Hills, CA: Sage Publications.

Lizotte, A. J., Chard-Wierschem, D. J., Loeber, R., & Stern, S. B. (1992). A shortened Child Behavior Checklist for delinquency studies. *Journal of Quantitative Criminology, 8,* 233–245.

Loeber, R. (1988). Natural histories of conduct problems, delinquency, and associated substance use: Evidence for developmental progressions. In B. B. Lahey & A. E. Kazdin (Eds.), *Advances in clinical child psychology* (Vol. 11, pp. 73–124). New York: Plenum Press.

Loeber, R. (1990). Development and risk factors of juvenile antisocial behavior and delinquency. *Clinical Psychology Review, 10,* 1–41.

Loeber, R. (1996). Developmental continuity, change, and pathways in male juvenile problem behaviors and delinquency. In J. D. Hawkins (Ed.), *Delinquency and crime: Current theories* (pp. 1–27). New York: Cambridge University Press.

Loeber, R., Burke, J. D., Lahey, B. B., Winters, A., & Zera, M. (2000). Oppositional defiant and conduct disorder: A review of the past 10 years, part 1. *Journal of the American Academy of Child and Adolescent Psychiatry, 39*(12), 1468–1484.

Loeber, R., & Dishion, T. J. (1984). Boys who fight at home and school: Family conditions influencing cross-setting consistency. *Journal of Consulting and Clinical Psychology, 52,* 759–768.

Loeber, R., Dishion, T. J., & Patterson, G. R. (1984). Multiple gating: A multistage assessment procedure for identifying youths at risk for delinquency. *Journal of Research on Crime and Delinquency, 24,* 7–32.

Loeber, R., Farrington, D. P., Stouthamer-Loeber, M., Moffitt, T. E., & Caspi, A. (1998). The development of male offending: Key findings from the first decade of the Pittsburgh Youth Study. *Studies on Crime and Crime Prevention, 7*(2), 141–171.

Loeber, R., Farrington, D. P., Stouthamer-Loeber M., & Van Kammen, W. B. (1998). *Antisocial behavior and mental health problems: Explanatory factors in childhood and adolescence.* Mahwah, NJ: Lawrence Erlbaum.

Loeber, R., Green, S. M., Keenan, K., & Lahey, B. B. (1995). Which boys fare worse? Early predictors of the onset of conduct disorder in a six-year longitudinal study. *Journal of American Academy of Child and Adolescent Psychiatry, 34*(4), 499–509.

Loeber, R., & Hay, D. F. (1994). Developmental approaches to aggression and conduct problems. In M. Rutter & D. F. Hay (Eds.), *Development through life: A handbook for clinicians* (pp. 488–516). Oxford, England: Blackwell Scientific.

Loeber, R., & Hay, D. F. (1997). Key issues in the development of aggression and violence from childhood to early adulthood. *Annual Review of Psychology, 48,* 371–410.

Loeber, R., & Stouthamer-Loeber, M. (1986). Family factors as correlates and predictors of juvenile conduct disorder and delinquency. In M. Tonry & N. Morris (Eds.), *Crime and justice* (Vol. 7, pp. 29–149). Chicago: University of Chicago Press.

Loeber, R., & Stouthamer-Loeber, M. (1987). The prediction of delinquency. In H. C. Quay (Ed.), *Handbook of juvenile delinquency* (pp. 325–382). New York: John Wiley & Sons.

Loeber, R., & Stouthamer-Loeber, M. S. (1993). Developmental progressions. In D. Huizinga, R. Loeber, & T. Thornberry (Eds.), *Urban delinquency and substance abuse: Technical report.* Washington, DC: Office of Juvenile Justice and Delinquency Prevention.

Loeber, R., Stouthamer-Loeber, M. S., Van Kammen, W., & Farrington, D. P. (1991). Initiation, escalation, and desistance in juvenile offending and their correlates. *Journal of Criminal Law and Criminology, 82,* 36–82.

Loeber, R., Wei, E., Stouthamer-Loeber, M., Huizinga, D., & Thornberry, T. P. (1999). Behavioral antecedents to serious and violent offending: Joint analyses from the Denver Youth Survey, Pittsburgh Youth Study and the Rochester Youth Development Study. *Studies on Crime and Crime Prevention, 8*(2), 245–263.

Loftin, C., McDowell, D., & Wiersema, B. (1993). Evaluating effects of changes in gun laws. American *Journal of Preventive Medicine, 9*(Suppl.), 39–43.

Loftin, C., McDowell, D., Wiersema, B., & Cottey, T. J. (1991). Effects of restrictive licensing of handguns on homicide and suicide in the District of Columbia. *New England Journal of Medicine, 23,* 1615–1620.

Luthar, S. S., & Cushing, G. (1999). Measurement issues in the empirical study of resilience. In M. D. Glantz, & J. L. Johnson (Eds.), *Resilience and development: Positive life adaptations* (pp. 129–160). New York: Kluwer Academic/ Plenum.

MacKenzie, D. L. (1997). Criminal justice and crime prevention. In L. W. Sherman, D. Gottfredson, D. L. MacKenzie, J. Eck, P. Reuter, & S. Bushway (Eds.), *Preventing crime: What works, what doesn't, and what's promising*. Washington, DC: National Institute of Justice.

Madanes, C. (1981). *Strategic family therapy*. San Francisco: Jossey-Bass.

Maguin, E., & Loeber, R. (1996). Academic performance and delinquency. In M. Tonry (Ed.), *Crime and justice: Vol. 20. A review of research* (pp. 145–264). Chicago: University of Chicago Press.

Marvel, J., Moreda, I., & Cook, I. (1993). Developing conflict resolution skills in students: A study of the Fighting Fair model. Miami: Peace Education Foundation.

Matsueda, R. L. (1982). Testing control theory and differential association: A causal modeling approach. *American Sociological Review, 47,* 489–504.

Matsueda, R. L., & Heimer, K. (1987). Race, family structure, and delinquency: A test of differential association and social control theories. *American Sociological Review, 52,* 826–840.

McCord, J. (1988). Parental behavior in the cycle of aggression. *Psychiatry, 51,* 14–23.

Mednick, S., Moffitt, T., Gabrielli, W. F., Jr., & Hutchings, B. (1983). Genetic influence in criminal behavior: Evidence from an adoption cohort. In K. T. Van Dusen & S. A. Mednick (Eds.), *Prospective studies of crime and delinquency* (pp. 39–56). Boston: Kluwer-Nijhoff.

Mednick, S. A., Gabrielli, W. F., & Hutchings, B. (1984). Genetic influences in criminal convictions: Evidence from an adoption cohort. *Science, 224,* 891–894.

Mednick, S. A., & Volavka, J. (1980). Biology and crime. In N. Morris & M. Tonry (Eds.), *Crime and justice: An annual review of research* (Vol. 2, pp. 85–158). Chicago: University of Chicago Press.

Menard, S., & Elliott, D. S. (1994). Delinquent bonding, moral beliefs, and illegal behavior: A three-wave panel model. *Justice Quarterly, 1,* 173–188.

Minde, K. (1992). Aggression in preschoolers: Its relation to socialization. *Journal of the American Academy of Child and Adolescent Psychiatry, 31,* 853–862.

Minuchin, S. (1974). *Families and family therapy*. Cambridge, MA: Harvard University Press.

Moffitt, T. E., & Caspi, A. (2001). Childhood predictors differentiate life-course persistent and adolescence-limited antisocial pathways among males and females. *Development and Psychopathology, 13*(2), 355–375.

Molgaard, V., Kumpfer, K. L., & Spoth, R. (1994). *The Iowa Strengthening Families Program for pre- and early-teens*. Ames: Iowa State University.

Molina, B.S.G., & Pelham, W. E. (2001). Substance use, substance abuse, and LD among adolescents with a childhood history of ADHD. *Journal of Learning Disabilities, 34*(4), 333–342.

National Research Council. (1993). *Losing generations: Adolescents in high-risk settings.* Washington, DC: National Academy Press.

Needleman, H. L. (1982). The neuropsychiatric implications of low level exposure to lead. *Psychological Medicine, 12,* 461–463.

Nye, C., Zucker, R., & Fitzgerald, H. (1995). Early intervention in the path to alcohol problems through conduct problems: Treatment involvement and child behavior change. *Journal of Consulting and Clinical Psychology, 63,* 831–840.

Office of Juvenile Justice and Delinquency Prevention. (1995). *Guide for implementing the comprehensive strategy for serious, violent, and chronic juvenile offenders.* Washington, DC: U.S. Department of Justice.

Office of Juvenile Justice and Delinquency Prevention. (2000a). *Juvenile arrests 1999.* Washington, DC: U.S. Department of Justice.

Office of Juvenile Justice and Delinquency Prevention. (2000b). *Statistical briefing book* [Online]. Washington, DC. Retrieved from http://ojjdp.ncjrs.org/ojstatbb/html/qa253.html on October 12, 2001.

Office of Juvenile Justice and Delinquency Prevention. (2000c). *Statistical briefing book* [Online]. Washington, DC. Retrieved from http://ojjdp.ncjrs.org/ojstatbb/html/qa254.html on October 12, 2001.

Offord, D. R., Boyle, M. H., Racine, Y. A., Fleming, J. E., Cadman, D. T., Blum, H. M., Byrne, C., Links, P. S., Lipman, E. L., & Macmillan, H. L. (1992). Outcome, prognosis and risk in a longitudinal follow-up study. *Journal of the American Academy of Child and Adolescent Psychiatry, 31,* 916–923.

Offord, D. R., Boyle, M. H., Szatmari, P., Rae Grant, N. I., Links, P. S., Cadman, D. T., Byles, J. A., Crawford, J. W., Blum, H. M., Byrne, C., Thomas, H., & Woodward, C. A. (1987). Ontario Child Health Study: Six month prevalence of disorder and rates of service utilization. *Archives of General Psychiatry, 44,* 832–836.

Offord, D. R., & Waters, B. G. (1983). Socialization and its failure. In M. D. Levine, W. B. Carey, A. C. Crocker, & R. T. Gross (Eds.), *Developmental–behavioral pediatrics* (pp. 650–682). Philadelphia: W. B. Saunders.

Olds, D. L., Henderson, C. R., Jr., Chamberlin, R., & Tatelbaum, R. (1986a). Preventing child abuse and neglect: A randomized trial of nurse home visitation. *Pediatrics, 78,* 65–78.

Olds, D. L., Henderson, C. R., J. L., Tatelbaum, R., & Chamberlin, R. (1986b). Improving the delivery of pre-natal care and outcomes of pregnancy: A randomized trial of nurse home visitation. *Pediatrics, 77,* 16–27.

Patterson, G. R. (1982). *Coercive family process.* Eugene, OR: Castalia.

Patterson, G. R., & Dishion, T. J. (1985). Contributions of families and peers to delinquency. *Criminology, 23,* 63–77.

Patterson, G. R., & Stouthamer-Loeber, M. (1984). The correlation of family management practices and delinquency. *Child Development, 55,* 1299–1307.

Peeples, F., & Loeber, R. (1994). Do individual factors and neighborhood context explain ethnic differences in juvenile delinquency? *Journal of Quantitative Criminology, 10,* 141–158.

Piquero, A. R. (2000). Assessing the relationships between gender, chronicity, seriousness, and offense skewness in criminal offending. *Journal of Criminal Justice, 28*(2), 103–115.

Piquero, A. R., & Chung, H. L. (2001). On the relationships between gender, early onset, and the seriousness of offending. *Journal of Criminal Justice, 29*(3), 189–206.

Pisecco, S., Wrister, K., Swank, P., Silva, P. A., & Baker, D. B. (2001). The effect of academic self-concept on ADHD and antisocial behaviors in early adolescence. *Journal of Learning Disabilities, 35*(4), 450–461.

Pollard, J. A., Hawkins, J. D., Catalano, R. F., & Arthur, M. W. (1995). *Development of a school-based survey measuring risk and protective factors predictive of substance abuse in adolescent populations.* Unpublished manuscript, University of Washington, Social Development Research Group, Seattle.

Pope, C. E., & Feyerherm, W. (1990a). Minority status and juvenile justice processing: 1. An assessment of the research literature. *Criminal Justice Abstracts, 22,* 327–336.

Pope, C. E., & Feyerherm, W. (1990b). Minority status and juvenile justice processing: 2. An assessment of the research literature. *Criminal Justice Abstracts, 22,* 527–542.

Pope, C. E., & Feyerherm, W. (1993). *Minorities and the juvenile justice system.* Washington, DC: Office of Juvenile Justice and Delinquency Prevention.

Robbins, M. S., & Szapocznik, J. (2000). *Brief strategic family therapy.* Washington, DC: Office of Juvenile Justice and Delinquency Prevention.

Robins, L. N. (1966). Deviant children grown up: A sociological and psychiatric study of sociopathic personality. Baltimore: Williams & Wilkins.

Robins, L. N. (1978). Sturdy childhood predictors of adult anti-social behavior: Replications from longitudinal studies. *Psychological Medicine, 8,* 611–622.

Robins, L. N. (1991). Conduct disorder. *Journal of Child Psychology and Psychiatry and Allied Disciplines, 32,* 193–212.

Rosenbaum, D. P., Yeh, S., & Wilkinson, D. L. (1994). Impact of community policing on police personnel: A quasi-experimental test. *Crime & Delinquency, 40,* 331–353.

Rossi, P. H. (1992). Assessing family preservation programs. *Children and Youth Services Review, 14,* 77–97.

Rutter, M. (1978). Family, area, and school influences in the genesis of conduct disorders. In L. A. Hersov & M. Berger (Eds.), *Aggression and antisocial behaviour in childhood and adolescence.* (pp. 95–114). London: Pergamon Press.

Rutter, M. (1979). Protective factors in children's responses to stress and disadvantage. In M. W. Kent & J. E. Rolf (Eds.), *Primary prevention of psychopathology: Vol. 3. Social competence in children* (pp. 49–74). Hanover, NH: University Press of New England.

Rutter, M. (1985). Resilience in the face of adversity: Protective factors and resistance to psychiatric disorders. *British Journal of Psychiatry, 147,* 598–611.

Rutter, M. (1990). Psychosocial resilience and protective mechanisms. In J. Rolf (Ed.), *Risk and protective factors in the development of psychopathology* (pp. 181–214). Cambridge, England: Cambridge University Press.

Rutter, M., & Giller, H. (1983). *Juvenile delinquency: Trends and perspectives.* New York: Penguin Books.

Rutter, M., & Quinton, D. (1984). Parental psychiatric disorders: Effects on children. *Psychological Medicine, 14,* 853–880.

Safer, D. J. (1990). A school intervention for aggressive adolescents. In L. J. Hertzberg, G. F. Ostrum, & J. R. Field (Eds.), *Violent behavior: Vol. 1. Assessment and intervention.* Great Neck, NY: PMA Publishing.

Sampson, R. J. (1986). Crimes in cities: The effects of formal and informal social control. In A. J. Reiss & M. Tonry (Eds.), *Crime and justice: An annual review of research: Vol. 8. Communities and crime* (pp. 271–311). Chicago: University of Chicago Press.

Sampson, R. J., & Laub, J. H. (1994). Urban poverty and the family context of delinquency: A new look at structure and process in a classic study. *Child Development, 65,* 523–540.

Sampson, R. J., Raudenbush, S. W., & Earls, F. (1997). Neighborhoods and violent crime: A multilevel study of collective efficacy. *Science, 277,* 918–924.

Santisteban, D. A., Szapocznik, J., Perez-Vidal, A., Kurtines, W. M., Murray, E. J., & LaPierre, A. (1996). Engaging behavior problem drug abusing youth and their families in treatment: An investigation of the efficacy of specialized engagement interventions and factors that contribute to differential effectiveness. *Journal of Family Psychology, 10,* 35–44.

Search Institute. (1998). *Healthy Communities: Healthy Youth Tool Kit.* Minneapolis: Search Institute.

Search Institute. (2001). *The current data on which Search Institute publications are based* [Online]. Search Institute, Minneapolis. Retrieved from http://www.search-institute.org/research/assets/currentdata.html on October 1, 2001.

Shadish, W. R., Jr. (1992). Do family and marital psychotherapies change what people do? A meta-analysis of behavioral outcomes. In T. D. Cook, H. Cooper, D. S. Cordray, H. Hartmann, L. V. Hedges, R. J. Light, T. A. Louis, & F. Mosteller (Eds.), *Meta-analysis for explanation: A casebook* (pp. 129–208). New York: Russell Sage Foundation.

Shannon, L. W. (1988). *Criminal career continuity: Its social context.* New York: Human Sciences Press.

Shannon, L. W. (1991). *Changing patterns in delinquency and crime: A longitudinal study in Racine.* Boulder, CO: Westview Press.

Shelden, R. G., & Chesney-Lind, M. (1993). Gender and race differences in delinquent careers. *Juvenile and Family Court Journal, 44,* 73–90.

Simcha-Fagan, O., & Schwartz, J. E. (1986). Neighborhood and delinquency: An assessment of contextual effects. *Criminology, 24,* 667–703.

Slavin, R. E. (1994). School and classroom organization in beginning reading: Class size, aides, and instructional grouping. In R. E. Slavin, N. L. Karweit, & B. A. Wasik (Eds.), *Preventing early school failure: Research, policy, and practice* (pp. 122–142). Boston: Allyn & Bacon.

Snyder, H. (2002). *Juvenile Arrest 2000.* Washington DC: Office of Juvenile Justice and Delinquency Prevention.

Stouthamer-Loeber, M., Loeber, R., & Farrington, D. P. (1993). The double edge of protective and risk factors for delinquency: Interrelations and developmental patterns. *Development & Psychopathology, 5,* 683–690.

Strayhorn, J. M., & Weidman, C. S. (1991). Follow-up one year after Parent-Child Interaction Training: Effects on behavior of preschool children. *Journal of American Academy of Child and Adolescent Psychiatry, 30,* 138–143.

Szapocznik, J., Perez-Vidal, A., Brickman, A., Foote, F. H., Santisteban, D., Hervis, O., & Webster-Stratton, C. (1985). Predictors of treatment outcome in parent training for conduct-disordered children. *Behavior Therapy, 16,* 223–243.

Szapocznik, J., Rio, A., Murray, E., Cohen, R., Scopetta, M., Rivas-Vazquez, A., Hervis, O., Posada, V., & Kurtines, W. (1989). Structural family versus psychodynamic child therapy for problematic Hispanic boys. *Journal of Consulting and Clinical Psychology, 57,* 571–578.

Taggart, R. (1995). *Quantam Opportunity Program.* Philadelphia: Opportunities Industrialization Centers of America.

Thornberry, T. P. (1994). *Violent families and youth violence* (Fact Sheet 21). Washington, DC: Office of Juvenile Justice and Delinquency Prevention.

Thornberry, T. P. (1996). Empirical support for interactional theory: A review of the literature. In J. D. Hawkins (Ed.), *Delinquency and crime: Current theories* (pp. 198–236). New York: Cambridge University Press.

Thornberry, T. P., Huizinga, D., & Loeber, R. (1995). The prevention of serious delinquency and violence: Implication from the Program of Research on the Causes and Correlates of Delinquency. In J. C. Howell, B. Krisberg, J. D. Hawkins, & J. J. Wilson (Eds.), *Sourcebook on serious, violent, and chronic juvenile offenders* (pp 213–237). Thousand Oaks, CA: Sage Publications.

Thornberry, T. P., Lizotte, A. J., Krohn, M. D., Farnworth, M., & Jang, S. J. (1994). Delinquent peers, beliefs, and delinquent behavior: A longitudinal test of interactional theory. *Criminology, 32,* 47–83.

Thurman, Q. C., Giacomazzi, A., & Bogen, P. (1993). Research note: Cops, kids, and community policing: An assessment of a community policing demonstration project. *Crime and Delinquency, 39,* 554–564.

Tolan, P., & Guerra, N. (1994). *What works in reducing adolescent violence: An empirical review of the field* (Report submitted to the Center for the Study and Prevention of Violence). Chicago: University of Illinois at Chicago.

Tracy, P. E., Wolfgang, M. E., & Figlio, R. M. (1990). *Delinquency in two birth cohorts.* Washington, DC: National Institute of Juvenile Justice and Delinquency Prevention.

Van Dorn, R. A., & Williams, J. H. (2003). Correlates associated with escalation of delinquent behavior in incarcerated youths. *Social Work, 48,* 523–531.

Voorhis, P. V., Cullen, F. T., Mathers, R. A., & Garner, C. C. (1988). The impact of family structure and quality on delinquency: A comparative assessment of structural and functional factors. *Criminology, 26,* 235–248.

Wasserman, G. A., & Miller, L. S. (1998). The prevention of serious and violent juvenile offending. In R. Loeber & D. P. Farrington (Eds.), *Serious & violent offenders: Risk factors and successful interventions* (pp. 197–247). Thousand Oaks, CA: Sage Publications.

Webster, D. W. (1993). The unconvincing case for school-based conflict resolution programs for adolescents. *Health Affairs, 12,* 126–141.

Webster-Stratton, C. (1990). Long-term follow up of families with young conduct problem children: From preschool to grade school. *Journal of Clinical Child Psychology, 19*(2), 144–149.

Webster-Stratton, C. (1994). Advancing videotape parent training: A comparison study. *Journal of Consulting and Clinical Psychology, 62*(3), 583–593.

Webster-Stratton, C. (2000). *The Incredible Years Training Series.* Washington, DC: Office of Juvenile Justice and Delinquency Prevention.

Webster-Stratton, C., & Hammond, M. (1997). Treating children with early-onset conduct problems: A comparison of child and parent training interventions. *Journal of Consulting and Clinical Psychology, 65*(1), 93–109.

Werner, E. E. (1989). High risk children in young adulthood: A longitudinal study from birth to 32 years. *American Journal of Orthopsychiatry, 59,* 72–81.

Werner, E. E., & Smith, R. S. (1992). *Overcoming the odds: High risk children from birth to adulthood.* Ithaca, NY: Cornell University Press.

White, J. L., Moffitt, T. E., & Silva, P. A. (1989). A prospective replication of the protective effects of IQ in subjects at high risk for juvenile delinquency. *Journal of Clinical and Consulting Psychology, 57,* 719–724.

Williams, J. H., Ayers, C. D., Abbott, R. D., Hawkins, J. D., & Catalano, R. F. (1999). Racial differences in risk factors for delinquency and substance use among adolescents. *Social Work Research, 23*(4), 241–257.

Williams, J. H., Ayers, C. D., Outlaw, W. S., Abbott, R. D., & Hawkins, J. D. (2001). The effects of race in juvenile justice system: Investigating early stage processes. *Journal for Juvenile Justice & Detention Services, 16*(2), 77–91.

Williams, J. H., Stiffman, A. R., & O'Neal, J. L. (1998). Environmental and behavioral factors associated with violence among urban African American youths. *Social Work Research, 24*(1), 3–13.

Williams, J. H., & Van Dorn, R. A. (1999). Delinquency, gangs, and youth violence. In J. M. Jenson & M. O. Howard (Eds.), *Prevention and treatment in violence in children and youth: Etiology, assessment, and recent practice innovations* (pp. 199–225). Washington, DC: NASW Press.

Williams, J. H., Van Dorn, R. A., Hawkins, J. D., Abbott, R. D., & Catalano, R. F. (2001). Correlates contributing to involvement in violent behaviors among young adults. *Violence and Victims, 16*(4), 371–388.

Wilson, J. Q., & Herrnstein, R. J. (1985). *Crime and human nature.* New York: Simon & Schuster.

Winkle, M. (1999). Critical conceptual and measurement issues in the study of resilience. In M. D. Glantz & J. L. Johnson (Eds.), *Resilience and development: Positive life adaptations* (pp. 161–178). New York: Kluwer Academic/Plenum.

Wolfgang, M. E., Figlio, R. F., & Sellin, T. (1972). *Delinquency in a birth cohort.* Chicago: University of Chicago Press.

Wolfgang, M. E., Thornberry, T. P., & Figlio, R. M. (1987). *From boy to man, from delinquency to crime: Follow up to the Philadelphia birth cohort of 1945.* Chicago: University of Chicago Press.

Yoshikawa, H. (1994). Prevention as cumulative protection: Effects of early family support and education on chronic delinquency and its risks. *Psychological Bulletin, 115,* 28–54.

9

Preventing Sexually Transmitted Infections among Adolescents

Kathleen A. Rounds

Sexually transmitted infections (STIs), also referred to as sexually transmitted diseases (STDs), are a major health problem for adolescents. Three million adolescents are affected with an STI each year, accounting for one-fourth of the 15.3 million new STI cases each year (Centers for Disease Control and Prevention [CDC], 2000c). Every year, about one in four sexually active teens becomes infected with an STI (Cates & American Social Health Association [ASHA] Panel, 1999; Alan Guttmacher Institute, 1999). For various biological, developmental, psychological, and social reasons, sexually active adolescents are at higher risk than adults for contracting STIs. Furthermore, adolescent girls are at higher risk than adolescent boys; the anatomy of adolescent girls makes them more susceptible to STIs, makes them less likely to experience symptoms, and makes their STIs more difficult to diagnose (Institute of Medicine [IOM], 1997). The more severe consequences of STIs for adolescents—again, especially for adolescent girls, whose fertility, pregnancy, and offspring may be jeopardized—may not become apparent until they reach young adulthood.

This chapter describes the nature of the adolescent STI epidemic, details the risk and protective factors associated with adolescents' risky sexual behavior; examines differences in these factors by age, gender, and race or ethnicity; suggests guidelines for the assessment of risky behavior; and addresses implications for practice. For the purposes of this chapter, HIV will be regarded as an STI because the major route of transmission of HIV for adolescents is through sexual activity.

THE STI EPIDEMIC AMONG ADOLESCENTS

According to Cates and Rauh (1985), it was not until the 1970s that public health and medical clinicians realized that STIs had reached epidemic levels among adolescents and began to understand the true magnitude of STIs among adolescents. The HIV epidemic in the 1980s and 1990s further heightened awareness of the magnitude of the STI problem. Adolescents who are sexually active are at higher risk for contracting nearly all STIs than any other age group (Rosenthal, Cohen, & Biro, 1994). In a survey of adolescents and adults, three out of 10 adolescents noted that they knew another adolescent with an STI (ASHA, 1996b).

Because of the variability in reporting across states and within states, accurate, complete statistics on the incidence and prevalence of STIs among adolescents are difficult to obtain. Syphilis, gonorrhea, and chlamydia are the only STIs that are reported by all 50 states to the CDC (IOM, 1997). Common STIs, such as genital herpes, are not systematically tracked in all states. Furthermore, screening for STIs varies considerably among states, depending on the availability of laboratory testing facilities and federal and state funding for screening (AHSA, 1996a). Another factor that influences the accuracy of STI statistics is the differential reporting between public and private providers. Because private providers do not report every case they diagnose, data from these providers may underestimate the STI incidence by as much as 50 percent, as well as skew the demographic characteristics of reported cases (Anderson, McCormick, & Fichtner, 1994). Moreover, many cases of STIs are asymptomatic, so many infected adolescents do not seek health care because they are not experiencing symptoms, and those who do have symptoms may not have access to care. Statistics on the number of HIV cases among adolescents illustrates this problem: Because most adolescents who contract HIV will not develop symptoms that would lead to testing until young adulthood, the number of adolescents infected with HIV is much higher than reported (DiClemente, 1992).

Multiple syndromes and more than 20 organisms are currently known to be transmitted sexually. The most common STIs reported among adolescents include two bacterial infections: neisseria gonorrhea and chlamydia trachomatis. Syphilis, another bacterial STI, is less common but is clearly on the rise in the adolescent population. Although bacterial STIs, if detected, can usually be treated and cured with antibiotics, the most common bacterial STIs—gonorrhea and chlamydia—are often asymptomatic and thus go undetected. Because of the growing problem of antibiotic-resistant strains, especially of gonorrhea, in some cases treatment has become more challenging (CDC, 1999b). Common viral STIs among sexually active adolescents include genital herpes (herpes simplex virus or HSV type 2) and genital warts (human papillomavirus or HPV). Viral STIs are infections for which there is no known cure (IOM, 1997). HIV, although estimated to be less common than other viral STIs among adolescents, obviously has the most serious consequences.

The rates for the most common bacterial and viral STIs are reported below. These rates, unless otherwise noted, are from the *1999 Sexually Transmitted Disease Surveillance Report* (CDC, 2000a), which compiles data from national surveys and the CDC's STD surveillance system. Compared with national rates among adolescents, the rates for STIs are much higher for certain subgroups of the adolescent population—youths in the juvenile justice system, adolescents who reside where the STI prevalence is high among the general population, adolescents who exchange sex for drugs or other perceived benefits, adolescents who are runaways or homeless, and youths who live where the prevalence of IV drug use is high (CDC, 2000a; Kelly, Bair, Baillargeon, & German, 2000).

BACTERIAL STIS

Neisseria Gonorrhea

Although gonorrhea rates declined by 72 percent from 1975 to 1997, the rates increased from 1997 to 1999. The 1999 gonorrhea rate for youths ages 15 to 19 years old was 534 per 100,000 and remains higher than for other age groups. The rate for adolescent females (738.1 per 100,000) was higher than for males (341.1 per 100,000). Adolescent females ages 15 to 19 have the highest age-specific reported gonorrhea rate among females.

Chlamydia Trachomatis

Chlamydia is the fastest-spreading STI in the United States. The reported rate for females is much higher than for males; in 1999 the rate for females nationwide (405.5 per 100,000) for all ages was more than four times higher than the rate for males (94.7 per 100,000). The highest age-specific reported rates of chlamydia in 1999 occurred among youths ages 15 to 19 years old—2,483.8 per 100,000. The substantial difference in rates between male and female adolescents may reflect the fact that females are more likely to be screened for chlamydia than males. Reported cases among males may increase as programs target males for screening.

Syphilis

Syphilis is a genital ulcerative disease that, if left untreated, can lead to major health problems and eventually to death. The number of syphilis cases reported in 1999 is the lowest since 1957. The rates are higher among men than women, which is perhaps associated with male-to-male sex (CDC, 1999a). Syphilis rates also differ across geographic areas. The rate for 1999 was higher in the South than in any other region (Northeast, Midwest, and West) in the country. Counties in the South reported 65 percent of the cases reported at the county level in 1999.

VIRAL STIS

Herpes Simplex Virus

Herpes is not a reportable STI, and thus exact prevalence rates are not available. Like chlamydia, herpes simplex virus (HSV) can be asymptomatic and thus go undetected. The ASHA estimates that 90 percent of infected individuals do not know that they have herpes (ASHA, 2001). Most genital herpes infections may be spread by asymptomatic individuals who are unaware that they are infected (Mertz, Benedetti, Ashley, Selke, & Corey, 1992). National surveys conducted in the 1970s and 1990s indicated that the rates of HSV increased the fastest among white American teens ages 12 to 19—the rates were five times greater in the 1990s than in the 1970s (Fleming et al., 1997). It is estimated that by the time the current cohort of youths reach adulthood 15 percent to 20 percent of them will be infected with HSV (Fleming et al., 1997).

Human Papilloma Virus

Human papilloma virus (HPV), which commonly presents as genital warts, concerns public health officials because it has been found to be associated with genital and anal cancers (IOM, 1997). HPV, too, can be asymptomatic and go undetected. The prevalence of HPV among adolescents is not known precisely.

HIV and AIDS

As a result of varying reporting standards across the United States, the actual number of youths who are infected with HIV and who have AIDS is not known. It is estimated that youths ages 13 to 24 years old comprise 3 percent of people currently living with AIDS (CDC, 2001). However, because the period between HIV infection and clinical diagnosis of AIDS is lengthy—from eight to 10 years—these prevalence estimates for AIDS cases truly underestimate the prevalence of HIV infection among adolescents. Public health officials analyzed surveillance data from 25 states with integrated HIV and AIDS reporting systems for the period between January 1996 and June 1999. They estimated that half of the approximately 40,000 new HIV infections each year are diagnosed in youths between ages 13 and 24. A disproportionate percentage (64 percent) of the newly reported HIV infections in these youths were among females. African Americans accounted for 56 percent of all HIV cases ever reported in this age group in these 25 states (Office of National AIDS Policy, 2000).

CONSEQUENCES OF STIS FOR ADOLESCENTS

Adolescents may not experience the consequences of STI infections until they reach young adulthood. HIV infection clearly results in the most severe long-term consequences (including chronic illness with bouts of opportunistic infections, disability, and death). The consequences for other STIs include cervical cancer, heart disease, blindness, reproductive problems, increased risk for contracting and transmitting other STIs (particularly HIV), and affected offspring (CDC, 2000c). For example, untreated gonorrhea and chlamydia in females can lead to pelvic inflammatory disease (PID), which puts women at risk of reproductive loss (through ectopic pregnancy, for example) and infertility (IOM, 1997). It is estimated that 50 percent to 75 percent of ectopic pregnancy cases are related to a history of gonorrhea or chlamydia (Yarber & Parrillo, 1992). A more immediate consequence of many STIs (gonorrhea, syphilis, or HSV, for example) is that they can facilitate the transmission of HIV (Cohen et al., 1997; Fleming & Wasserheit, 1999).

STIs also affect pregnancy and offspring. If a pregnant adolescent is infected, some STIs can be transmitted to the fetus in utero or at birth, with the following possible results: stillbirth (syphilis), premature birth (chlamydia, gonorrhea, syphilis, or genital herpes), fetal malformations, brain damage, and severe mental retardation (genital herpes), wart-like tumors of the larynx (HPV), conjunctivitis and blindness (gonorrhea), pneumonia (chlamydia), congenital syphilis, and pediatric AIDS (IOM, 1997).

Pregnancy loss, death of an infant, or having a child with chronic health problems or developmental disabilities all have profound short- and long-term implications for adolescent girls and their families (Rosenthal, Cohen, & Biro, 1994).

The literature describing the consequences of STIs focuses almost exclusively on medical and reproductive health issues. Although some researchers have examined the psychosocial consequences of STIs (in particular HSV and HIV), few researchers have focused on these consequences for adolescents in particular (Rosenthal, Cohen, & Biro, 1994). The stigmas associated with having an STI can be damaging. Examining the psychological impact of STIs on adolescent females with a history of infections, Rosenthal and Biro (1991) found that 82 percent of the study respondents reported that receiving an STI diagnosis would be the "worst thing that could happen" or "a major upset."

RISKY SEXUAL BEHAVIORS AMONG ADOLESCENTS

The primary risky sexual behaviors that increase the likelihood of transmitting and contracting STIs include early initiation of sexual intercourse, unprotected sex (that is, vaginal or anal intercourse without the proper use of a condom and unprotected oral sex), frequent sexual intercourse, and having multiple sexual partners (concurrent or sequential; Santelli, Lindberg, Abma, McNeely, & Resnick, 2000). Having multiple partners increases risk because the "number of potentially infectious exposures is greater." Moreover, it indicates the lack of a "selective partner recruitment strategy," which increases the chances of selecting an infected partner (Seidman, Mosher, & Aral, 1994, p. 127). Other factors that increase the risk of STIs for sexually active adolescents—even those who do not necessarily engage in risky behavior—include the immunological and physiological immaturity of the urogenital tract in young adolescent females, the presence of another STI, and high STI prevalence rates among an adolescent's sexual partners.

As background to this discussion on risky sexual behaviors, it is critical to keep in mind that, although risky sexual behavior clearly can have negative consequences, adolescent sexual behavior in itself is not necessarily negative and may serve many developmental functions. Jessor (1992) argued that adolescent risk behaviors are "functional, purposive, instrumental, and goal-directed" and that "the goals involved are often those that are central in normal adolescent development" (p. 24). For example, by engaging in sex with others, adolescents may seek to enhance their sense of intimacy and connection with others, elevate their status in their peer group, and challenge authority or assert their autonomy. Moreover, adolescents may believe that the initiation of intercourse marks their transition to adulthood.

National efforts to monitor and to understand adolescent sexual behavior rely on data from four surveys: the Youth Risk Behavior Survey (YRBS), the National Survey of Adolescent Males, the National Longitudinal Study of Adolescent Health (Add Health), and the National Survey of Family Growth (NSFG). (For a detailed comparison of these surveys and their findings see Santelli et al., 2000.) The data reported in this chapter are from the CDC's Youth Risk Behavior Surveillance System (YRBSS). In 1990, the CDC began surveying high school students about health-risk behaviors (CDC, 1995b). The CDC's YRBSS monitors six categories of health-risk be-haviors among adolescents and young adults; one of these categories is "sexual behaviors." Some YRBS questions specific to sexual behavior include: Have you ever had sexual intercourse? During your life, with how many people have you had sexual intercourse? During the past three months, with how many people did you have sexual intercourse? The last time you had sexual intercourse, did you or your partner use a condom? During your life, have you ever injected ("shot up") any illegal drug? (CDC, 1995a; Morris, Warren, & Aral, 1993). (For more detailed information about this surveillance system see Kann et al., 1995.)

Results from the 1999 survey (Table 9-1) indicate that 49.9 percent of high school students had engaged in sexual intercourse (52.2 percent males and 47.7 percent

Table 9-1. Percentage of High School Students Who Engaged in Sexual Behaviors, by Sex, by Race and Ethnicity, and by Grade—United States, Youth Risk Behavior Survey, 1999

CATEGORY	EVER HAD SEXUAL INTERCOURSE			FIRST SEXUAL INTERCOURSE BEFORE AGE 13			FOUR OR MORE SEX PARTNERS DURING LIFETIME			CURRENTLY SEXUALLY ACTIVE[a]			CURRENTLY ABSTINENT[b]		
	FEMALE	MALE	TOTAL	FEMALE	MALE	TOTAL	FEMALE	MALE	TOTAL	FEMALE	MALE	TOTAL	FEMALE	MALE	TOTAL
Race or Ethnicity															
White American[c]	44.8 (±4.5)[d]	45.4 (±4.6)	45.1 (±4.2)	3.5 (±0.7)	7.5 (±1.1)	5.5 (±0.8)	12.7 (±2.4)	12.1 (±2.9)	12.4 (±2.2)	34.7 (±4.6)	31.3 (±4.2)	33.0 (±3.5)	22.4 (±4.0)	31.3 (±4.9)	27.0 (±2.5)
African American[c]	66.9 (±11.3)	75.7 (±6.5)	71.2 (±8.2)	11.4 (±5.4)	29.9 (±5.9)	20.5 (±4.8)	21.3 (±8.8)	48.1 (±12.8)	34.4 (±10.4)	50.3 (±9.1)	55.8 (±10.1)	53.0 (±9.0)	24.9 (±5.0)	25.8 (±9.6)	25.3 (±5.9)
Hispanic American	45.5 (±6.2)	62.9 (±5.5)	54.1 (±5.0)	4.4 (±1.5)	14.2 (±2.6)	9.2 (±1.5)	10.5 (±3.7)	23.0 (±6.4)	16.6 (±4.5)	34.0 (±4.7)	38.5 (±6.2)	36.3 (±4.4)	25.3 (±4.2)	38.4 (±7.4)	32.7 (±5.0)
Grade															
9	32.5 (±7.6)	44.5 (±6.1)	38.6 (±6.2)	5.5 (±1.7)	17.7 (±3.1)	11.7 (±1.8)	7.9 (±2.3)	15.6 (±3.4)	11.8 (±2.4)	24.0 (±7.2)	29.1 (±5.2)	26.6 (±5.8)	26.7 (±7.2)	34.7 (±6.8)	31.3 (±6.1)
10	42.6 (±5.0)	51.1 (±7.6)	46.8 (±5.8)	5.1 (±2.5)	13.9 (±3.9)	9.4 (±3.0)	10.1 (±2.7)	21.4 (±8.1)	15.6 (±5.1)	32.0 (±4.9)	33.9 (±7.9)	33.0 (±5.2)	24.8 (±4.8)	33.1 (±7.9)	29.2 (±4.0)
11	53.8 (±4.5)	51.4 (±5.8)	52.5 (±4.3)	4.5 (±2.4)	7.8 (±2.1)	6.2 (±1.6)	15.1 (±4.7)	19.4 (±5.5)	17.3 (±4.3)	39.5 (±3.8)	35.4 (±5.2)	37.5 (±3.7)	26.5 (±3.8)	30.9 (±6.0)	28.6 (±3.5)
12	65.8 (±7.6)	63.9 (±6.3)	64.9 (±5.0)	2.1 (±1.6)	7.6 (±2.3)	4.8 (±1.2)	20.6 (±5.4)	20.6 (±3.9)	20.6 (±3.0)	53.0 (±8.6)	48.1 (±5.7)	50.6 (±5.2)	19.5 (±5.6)	24.6 (±4.1)	22.0 (±3.8)
Total	47.7 (±4.2)	52.2 (±4.5)	49.9 (±4.0)	4.4 (±1.1)	12.2 (±1.9)	8.3 (±1.3)	13.1 (±2.3)	19.3 (±3.8)	16.2 (±2.8)	36.3 (±4.2)	36.2 (±4.1)	36.3 (±3.7)	23.9 (±3.0)	30.5 (±3.5)	27.3 (±2.4)

[a]Sexual intercourse during the three months preceding the survey.
[b]Among those who have ever had sexual intercourse, no sexual intercourse during the three months preceding the survey.
[c]Non-Hispanic Americans.
[d]Ninety-five percent confidence interval.

SOURCE: Centers for Disease Control and Prevention. (June 9, 2000). MMWR Surveillance Summaries, 49 (SS05), 1–96.

females); 8.3 percent had first sexual intercourse before age 13 (12.2 percent males and 4.4 percent females); 36.3 percent were currently sexually active, meaning that they had had sexual intercourse during the past three months (36.2 percent males and 36.3 percent females); and 16.2 percent had had sexual intercourse with four or more people during their lifetime (19.3 percent males and 13.1 percent females). The highest percentages in all of these categories were among African American males (CDC, 2000c).

Since 1991 there have been significantly decreasing linear trends ($p < .05$) in the percentage of students who had ever had sexual intercourse, had sexual intercourse before age 13, or had sexual intercourse with more than four partners. Between 1991 and 1999, significant increasing linear trends were found for condom use (CDC, 2000c).

One limitation of the YRBS and other national surveys of school-based populations is that they do not include subpopulations of adolescents who may be engaging in risky sexual behavior at much higher rates, such as adolescents who have dropped out of school, are at risk for dropping out, are homeless or runaway youths, or are incarcerated youths. Also, the term "sexual intercourse" as used in the YRBS may not collect data on other sexual behaviors that transmit STIs, such as anal and oral sex. The terminology used in survey questions about sexual behavior is critical. Anecdotal reports in the media and by clinicians suggest that adolescents, particularly young adolescents, may be increasingly engaging in oral sex as a way to protect themselves from pregnancy and STIs. Remez (2000) reported personal communication with researchers who were conducting small-scale evaluations of abstinence education programs. These researchers had discovered a much higher rate of oral sex among young adolescents than expected. To monitor and understand adolescent sexual behavior fully, surveys need to use terminology that the adolescents themselves use to ask about a full range of sexual behaviors.

RISK FACTORS FOR ADOLESCENT INVOLVEMENT IN RISKY SEXUAL BEHAVIOR

In earlier chapters, risk factors were said to be influences that increase the probability of onset, digression to a more serious state, or maintenance of a problem condition. For the purposes of this discussion of STIs, the problem condition is defined as engaging in risky sexual behavior that increases the likelihood of contracting an STI. Risk factors that are associated with adolescents' engagement in risky sexual behaviors are listed in Table 9-2 along two dimensions: (1) proximity to engaging in risky sexual behaviors (proximal and distal) and (2) the system level at which these risk factors occur (individual, psychosocial, and biological; family; and the broader environment and context including neighborhood, school, and peers). These various system levels all influence adolescent sexual behaviors at different developmental stages. The following discussion covers selected risk factors discussed in the empirical literature on adolescent sexuality. The focus is on factors that are associated with risky sexual behavior, not on factors that make adolescents more susceptible to infection (being female, for example, or being a young adolescent, having another STI, or living in a community with high rates of STIs).

Table 9-2. Risk Factor Framework for Adolescents' Risky Sexual Behaviors for Sexually Transmitted Infections

	PROXIMITY TO ENGAGING IN RISKY SEXUAL BEHAVIORS	
SYSTEM LEVEL	PREDISPOSING OR DISTAL FACTOR	SITUATIONAL OR PROXIMAL RISK
Environmental and contextual conditions, including neighborhood, school, and peers	Lack of universal access to health care Lack of emphasis on prevention Societal ambivalence about sexuality and sexuality education Lack of economic and educational opportunities for adolescents Media that sexualize women and promote unsafe sexual practices Risky neighborhood environment (violence, substance abuse, poverty) Limited opportunities for sexuality education Neighborhood and peer norms that accept early initiation of sexual intercourse and multiple partners	Poor access to STI prevention, screening, medical care, and counseling Limited sexuality education Environments or activities that provide opportunities for sexual activity Environments or activities where alcohol and drugs are used Peer pressure Forced sex
Family conditions	Family norms that accept early initiation of sexual intercourse and multiple partners Poor parent-youth relationship and communication Older siblings who are sexually active	Poor parental monitoring
Individual, psychosocial, and biological factors	Lack of acceptance of one's sexuality Incomplete cognitive development Intention to initiate intercourse Early initiation of sexual activity Inaccurate perception of adult rules and attitudes Lack of knowledge about sexuality and safer sex practices Sense of invulnerability Low self-efficacy about safer sex Inadequate communication skills Having been sexually abused Early puberty	Lack of access to condoms Inability to say "no" or to negotiate safer sex Denial regarding one's own sexual behaviors Poor impulse control Inability to use condoms properly Inaccurate perception of risk Having a "steady" romantic partner Lack of partner support for using condoms Substance abuse Negative attitudes, beliefs, and intentions about safer sex practices

NOTE: STI = sexually transmitted infection.

INDIVIDUAL PSYCHOSOCIAL AND BIOLOGICAL RISK CHARACTERISTICS

Biological

Biological theory argues that adrogenic hormones begin to multiply at puberty, thus spurring the disposition to become sexually active (Udry, 1988). The "timing of pubertal maturation" and initiation of sexual intercourse are associated—adolescents who mature earlier are more likely to initiate sexual intercourse earlier (Irwin & Shafer, 1992). Recent studies have found that the age of pubertal onset for females (as measured by the onset on menarche) has gone down during the last century (Herman-Giddens, Slora, & Wasserman, 1997; Kaplowitz & Oberfield, 1999). This early pubertal maturation creates problems for adolescent females.

Early maturing adolescent females may reach other developmental stages earlier (for example, a desire for independence and more interest in sexual activities), thus they tend to interact in social networks composed primarily of older adolescents (Irwin & Millstein, 1986). Involvement in these social networks increases peer pressure on young adolescent girls to be sexually involved with older boys at a time when they are not developmentally mature enough to understand the consequences of sexual activity or to assert their wishes effectively. For example, Abma, Driscoll, and Moore (1998) found that young adolescent girls reported that when their partner was significantly older, they were less likely to use condoms at first intercourse and that the intercourse was more likely to be involuntary. Ford, Sohn, and Lepkowski (2001) conducted a study of adolescents using data from the Add Health, and found that, when the partner was more than two years older or in a higher school grade, adolescents were less likely to use condoms or other forms of birth control. Age and grade differences may reflect differences in power or in the ability to communicate, making it more difficult for the younger partner to engage in protective sexual behavior.

Thus, early pubertal maturation creates an asynchrony between biological, psychological, cognitive, and social development, which may predispose adolescents to engage in risky sexual behaviors (Hine, 1999; Sieving et al., 1997). Further research must be done to determine how environmental factors such as community, cultural, and family norms and parental monitoring mediate the relationship between early onset of puberty and age at first sexual intercourse (Perry, 2000).

Cognitive Development

To practice safer sex the individual must accept and acknowledge that he or she is sexually active and vulnerable to STIs and must be capable of planning for sex (Pestrak & Martin, 1985). Yet most youths do not attain formal operational thinking—the stage of development in which abstract concepts can be comprehended (and consequences foreseen)—until they are older. Individuals in early and middle adolescence are limited in their abilities to translate their knowledge about STI prevention (assuming that they have some knowledge) into actual behavior. They also may construct a "personal fable" that they are immune to STIs (Pestrak & Martin, 1985).

Attitudes, Beliefs, and Intentions

The Theory of Reasoned Action (TRA; Fishbein & Ajzen, 1975) has been used to examine the relationships between attitudes, beliefs, and intentions and adolescent sexual behavior. For example, Gillmore (2004) found that attitudes and beliefs of sexually inexperienced and sexually experienced adolescents predicted their intentions to engage in sex. Gillmore and colleagues have also found that high-risk teens' attitudes about condom use and beliefs about the consequences of using condoms were predictors of condom use (Gillmore, Morrison, Lowery, & Baker, 1994; Gillmore et al., 1997). In a meta-analysis of 121 empirical studies of psychosocial correlates of heterosexual condom use, Sheeran, Abraham, and Orbell (1999) found that attitudes toward condom use, intentions to use condoms, and communication about condoms were the most important predictors of condom use.

Early Sexual Activity

Early onset of sexual intercourse increases an adolescent's risk for exposure to STIs because it may be associated with increased opportunity (the span of time spent sexually active could be longer, and the number of partners greater; Rosenthal, Biro, Succop, Bernstein, & Stanberry, 1997). In addition, young adolescents who are sexually active may be less likely than older adolescents to seek treatment for STI symptoms (Irwin & Shafer, 1992) and, as discussed above, they may be less knowledgeable and less able to negotiate safer sexual practices.

Many other variables are associated with age of onset of first intercourse. Race and gender, for example, are associated with early initiation of sexual activity. In general, African American males begin sexual activity earlier than Hispanic/Latino males, who begin earlier than white males; and males initiate sexual intercourse at an earlier age than females (Blum et al., 2000; Gates & Sonenstein, 2000; Santelli et al., 2000). Other variables associated with early onset of intercourse that have been listed in the empirical literature include

- maternal education, the adolescent's degree of religious affiliation, age at menarche, and family stability when the adolescent is age 14 (Cates, 1991)
- sexual behavior of an older sibling (East, 1996; Widmer, 1997)
- poor school performance or dropping out of school (Santelli & Beilenson, 1992)
- drug and alcohol use (Fergusson & Lynskey, 1996; Halpern-Felsher, Millstein, & Ellen, 1996; Strunin, 1994).

Family structure has also been associated with early onset of intercourse; adolescents from nonintact families tend to initiate earlier sexual intercourse than adolescents from intact families (Irwin & Shafer, 1992). Family structure may be related to parental monitoring (discussed later in this chapter). Parents in single-parent households may monitor their adolescents to a lesser degree than parents in dual-parent households monitor their adolescents.

Perception of peer, and specifically friends', sexual behaviors seems to play a role in early initiation of sexual intercourse (Irwin & Shafer, 1992). In a prospective cohort study of 1,389 sixth-grade students in an urban public school district, researchers found that the strongest predictor of sexual initiation in sixth grade was having high intention to do so at the beginning of the school year. The strongest predictor of high intention is the belief that most of one's friends have already had sexual intercourse (Kinsman, Romer, Furstenberg, & Schwarz, 1998; Meschke, Bartholomae, & Zentall, 2000).

Substance Use

Adolescents may use alcohol and drugs to cope with their feelings about their sexuality or they may use them to be less inhibited about engaging in sex. In either event, alcohol and drug use reduce the likelihood that adolescents will take precautions to prevent contracting STIs (Hingson, Strunin, Berlin, & Heeren, 1990). In a study examining the association between STI and HIV risk behaviors and crack use among African American adolescents, Fullilove and colleagues (1993) found that ado-lescents who used crack were twice as likely to engage in HIV–STI risk behaviors as nonusers ($p < .001$). Similarly, adolescents who had relatives who used drugs were twice as likely to engage in risky sexual behavior ($p > .01$) as those who had nonusing relatives. Investigators postulate that the increase in gonorrhea rates among African American adolescent males in urban areas is associated with the onset of crack cocaine use in those same urban areas (Shafer & Moscicki, 1991). In a study of 985 ethnically or racially diverse ninth-grade urban high school students, use of alcohol and drugs was significantly associated with sexual risk behaviors (Boyer & Tschann, 1999). Although studies have consistently shown an association between substance use and risky sexual behavior, Gillmore (2004) argued that the "jury is out" on whether substance use causes adolescents to engage in risky sexual behavior. She noted that most studies examining this relationship are correlational, and few have ensured temporal ordering: substance use and risky sexual behavior occurred at the same time. Most studies have not controlled for other variables such as perceived peer norms or pressure that might explain both behaviors—substance use and risky sexual behavior.

Sexual Abuse

First, sexually abused adolescents are at risk of STIs transmitted by their abusers. It is estimated that 104,000 children are sexually abused each year (U.S. Department of Health and Human Services, 2000). Second, adolescents who have been abused are more likely than others to engage subsequently in behaviors that put them at risk of STIs (such as earlier age at first intercourse, multiple partners, and substance use). In a multivariate analysis of data from the 1987 National Survey of Children, researchers found that forced sexual intercourse significantly predicted age at first voluntary sexual intercourse (Miller, Monson, & Norton, 1995). Researchers using data from an anonymous self-report survey of 3,448 eighth- and 10th-grade students found that victims of forced sex (conservatively defined as intercourse) reported significantly higher levels of risky sexual behavior. These adolescents were disproportionately African American females who were more likely than the other students to reside in single-parent households (Nagy, Adcock, & Nagy, 1994). In a study of 4,163 female ninth- through 12th-grade students, Silverman and colleagues (2001) found that approximately one out of every five female students reported being physically or sexually abused by a dating partner and that this violence was associated with increased risk of first intercourse before age 15.

FAMILY CONDITIONS

Increased attention has been focused recently on the role of family environmental factors on adolescent health behavior (Jessor, Turbin, & Costa, 1998). Researchers examining this relationship often classify family variables into two categories: family structural variables (including family income, maternal education, maternal marital status) and family process variables (including parental monitoring; parent–adolescent communication in general, and communication specific to sexuality communication; and the context for monitoring and communication—the parent–adolescent relationship; Meschke et al., 2000; Miller, Forehand, & Kotchick, 1999). Research findings on the association between family factors and adolescent sexual behavior are mixed and depend in part on the outcome variable measured (including onset of intercourse, frequency, number of partners, and condom use). Research does suggest, however, that family process variables are stronger predictors of adolescent sexual behavior than family structural variables (Blum et al., 2000; Miller et al., 1999). Thus, the following discussion focuses on family process variables rather than family structural variables.

PARENTAL MONITORING

Parental monitoring seems to be consistently related to later onset of intercourse and less risky sexual behavior in adolescents (fewer sexual partners, less frequency of intercourse, for example; Meschke et al., 2000). In their study of 907 Hispanic/Latino and African American families, Miller and colleagues (1999) found that increases in parental monitoring predicted less sexual behavior across genders and ethnic groups. DiClemente and associates (2001) examined the association between adolescents' perceived levels of parental monitoring and a range of health-risk behaviors in a study of 522 African American females between the ages of 14 and 18. They found a consistent pattern of association between health-risk behaviors and less perceived parental monitoring. With regard to sexual behaviors, the results from logistic regression analyses, controlling for observed covariates, indicated that adolescents who perceived less parental monitoring were more likely to test positive for a sexually transmitted disease (odds ratio [OR]: 1.7), to report not using a condom at last sexual intercourse (OR: 1.7), to have multiple sexual partners in the past six months (OR: 2.0), to have risky sex partners (OR: 1.5), and to have had a new sex partner in the past 30 days (OR: 3.0).

PARENT–ADOLESCENT COMMUNICATION AND RELATIONSHIPS

Although the findings about the relationship between parental communication about sexuality and adolescent sexual behavior are somewhat mixed, overall positive and frequent communication has been found to be associated with less risky sexual behavior (that is, later onset, fewer partners, less-frequent sexual activity; Meschke et al., 2000). In a study of 405 predominately African American 13 to 15 year olds and their mothers, DiIorio, Kelly, and Hockenberry-Eaton (1999) found that an adolescent who talked more with his or her mother about sexual issues than with friends was less likely to initiate sexual intercourse and more likely to hold conservative values about sexual behavior. It is critical, however, to examine the quality and context of communication because it may be a proxy measure for the quality of the parent–adolescent relationship (Miller et al., 1999). For example, in a study of parent–adolescent communication about sexuality in white American and African American families, Kahn (1994) found that when parents talked with adolescents about sexuality, adolescents recalled fewer discussions on sexuality with parents than their parents did. Furthermore, adolescent boys had relatively less recall of conversations about sexuality with parents than did adolescent girls. However, the degree of closeness of parent–adolescent ties was the strongest predictor of teens' recall of the number of sexual topics that they had discussed with their parents (Kahn, 1994). It appears that the quality (warmth and closeness, for example) of the parent–adolescent relationship may mediate the association of both parent–adolescent communication about sexuality and parent monitoring with adolescent sexual behavior (Meschke et al., 2000).

BROAD ENVIRONMENTAL CONDITIONS INCLUDING PEER GROUP, COMMUNITY, AND NEIGHBORHOOD

PEER GROUP ATTITUDES

Peer groups play a critical role in adolescent development and behavior. As individuals reach early and middle adolescence, peer pressure to engage in sex increases (Udry, 1988). For example, in a large prospective cohort study of 1,389 sixth-grade students Kinsman and colleagues (1998), found that students who had initiated sexual intercourse were more likely than students who had not initiated to perceive a high prevalence of sexual initiation among peers, social gains associated with early sexual intercourse, and younger age of peers' sexual initiation. In their description of hip-hop culture, McLaurin and Juzang (1993) discussed how the intense emphasis on peer approval, rejection of mainstream norms and values, and encouragement of risky behaviors such as substance abuse and sexual promiscuity put African American inner-city adolescents at high risk for STIs. Many would argue that sexual intercourse among adolescents, particularly young adolescents, is a violation of social norms, but in many adolescent subcultures, early initiation of sexual behavior is the norm. Other authors (Mann, 1994; Pipher, 1994) have addressed the issue of peer pressure on adolescent girls to become sexually active at increasingly younger ages and the difficulty that young adolescent girls have in dealing with this pressure. Studies have also found a positive association between more condom use among adolescent girls and their perception of condom use among their friends (Brown, DiClemente, & Park, 1992; Sheeran, Abraham, & Orbell, 1999; Shrier, Goodman, & Emans, 1999; Shrier et al., 2001). The distinction between influence of perceived peer behavior and perceived friends' behavior is one that needs more research and has important implications for the design of safer-sex intervention programs.

COMMUNITY AND NEIGHBORHOOD

Researchers use the term "ecology of risk" to suggest an association between the likelihood of an individual engaging in a risky behavior and a high prevalence of such behavior in his or her environment (Andrews, 1985). Research by Brewster, Billy, and Grady (1993) found that timing of first intercourse and use of contraception at that time were shaped by the normative environment and the local opportunity structure. Community social disintegration, low socioeconomic status, and a lack of employment opportunities were found to be important influences on adolescent female sexual behavior. This study examined these relationships in the light of pregnancy prevention. However, because unprotected intercourse is the route to both pregnancy and STI transmission, the findings should be applicable also to STI prevention. In a study specifically examining sexual activity by youths, and using longitudinal data from the National Survey of Children, researchers found significant positive effects of community socioeconomic disadvantage on the frequency of intercourse, the number of different sex partners, and the likelihood of engaging in unprotected intercourse (Baumer & South, 2001). Santelli and colleagues (2000), in their analysis of 1992 YRBS data, suggested that lack of access to treatment services, a community factor that has not been carefully examined, may contribute to higher rates of STIs in communities. When left untreated, STIs increase the number of infected persons in the pool of potential sexual partners, thus increasing the likelihood that infections will be transmitted to others in the community.

LACK OF PUBLIC AWARENESS ABOUT STIS

The IOM referred to the epidemic of STIs as "the hidden epidemic" because "the scope, impact, and consequences of STDs are underrecognized by the public and health care professionals" (IOM, 1997, p. 1). Former Surgeon General David Satcher argued that the epidemic of STIs in this country is the result of "continued or selective silence" about sexuality and responsible sexual behavior (Office of the Surgeon General, 2001). This silence contributes to the public's lack of awareness about the prevalence and the likelihood of contracting STIs. Both the ASHA and the Kaiser Family Foundation have conducted surveys on the level of knowledge about STIs. Forty-two percent of adolescents and 26 percent of adults could not name an STI other than HIV/AIDS (ASHA, 1996b). When asked to estimate how many Americans will get an STI in their lifetimes, close to 76 percent of adolescents thought that the rate was one in 10 or fewer (Kaiser Family Foundation/*Glamour*, 1998). However, the rate calculated by the Alan Guttmacher Institute (AGI) based on CDC incidence data and estimates is one in four people (ASHA, 1998). In a survey that assessed the knowledge level of 661 13 to 15 year olds in seven U.S. cities, Carrera, Kaye, Philliber, and West (2000) found the average score on the STI items to be 53 percent correct. Only 51 percent knew that STIs "do not go away on their own." This lack of awareness about the

STIs in the United States makes it difficult to institute policies and implement programs that effectively address the problem.

INADEQUATE ACCESS TO CULTURALLY AND DEVELOPMENTALLY SENSITIVE SEXUALITY EDUCATION AND PREVENTIVE, SCREENING, AND TREATMENT SERVICES

Health insurance is a critical determinant of adolescents' access to and use of health care services (Newacheck, Brindis, Cart, Marchi, & Irwin, 1999). In 1997, 17 percent of adolescents had no health care coverage and one-third of adolescents with incomes below the poverty line were uninsured. The percentage of adolescents who had not had a health care visit in the past year was 2.6 times higher for those without health insurance than those with health insurance (MacKay, Flingerhut, & Duran, 2000).

Access to confidential health care services is important to adolescents, especially when the services deal with sexual health (Roberts, Boker, Oh, & DiClemente, 2000). However, many confidential services may not be available or adolescents may not know how and where to access such services. In a random digit-dialed survey of 14- to 19-year-old adolescents ($N = 259$) in Upstate New York, researchers found that nearly half of all youths surveyed did not know where to go for confidential health services. They were least likely to know where to obtain mental health, substance abuse, and reproductive health services (Klein, McNulty, & Flatau, 1998).

Adolescents' use of services is in part determined by their perceptions of the degree to which health care providers are culturally and developmentally sensitive, particularly related to sexual health issues. Although medical schools have increased training on sexual health in their curriculums, close to one-third of medical schools do not provide content on taking a sexual history (Dunn & Alarie, 1997). Youths often find it difficult to bring up sexuality concerns with health care providers. It is thus incumbent upon providers to ask about sexual health and behaviors. Communication with health care providers about sexuality may be particularly difficult for gay, lesbian, and transgender youths (Garofalo & Katz, 2001). In a nationally representative sample of 8,728 youths in fifth through 12th grades who completed the Commonwealth Fund Survey, most youths indicated that it would be embarrassing to discuss sensitive topics with a health provider (such as doctors or nurses, including school nurses). Although 61 percent said that they wanted health care providers to discuss STIs with them, they reported that only 26 percent of the providers did so (Ackard & Neumark-Sztainer, 2001). In a study using the Young Adult Health Care Survey with 4,060 adolescents enrolled in managed care organizations—a reliable and valid method for assessing adherence to Guidelines for Adolescent Preventive Services (GAPS)—researchers found that the average preventive counseling and screening score for discussing risky behavior topics including sexual behaviors was 18.2 percent. Older adolescents and females were more likely to report counseling and screening regarding topics related to sex (Bethell, Klein, & Peck, 2001).

The importance of increasing health insurance coverage for adolescents, providing confidential health care services, partnering with adolescents in their treatment, and targeting outreach should not be underestimated. These strategies may increase the likelihood that adolescents will seek screening and treatment for STIs (Gold & Sonfield, 2001; Klein et al., 1998; Milne & Chesson, 2000; Roberts et al., 2000).

PROTECTIVE FACTORS

Protective factors are those factors that decrease exposure to risk, buffer the negative effects of risks, mediate the relationship between exposure to risk and negative outcomes, or increase an individual's resilience. The empirical literature on factors that protect adolescents from engaging in risky sexual behavior is very sparse; the literature has focused almost exclusively on an examination of risk factors. One protective factor that consistently appears in the literature is having a positive attitude toward condom use. Other factors such as religiosity (attending religious services and being affiliated with a religious organization, for example) received attention in earlier studies (Santelli & Beilenson, 1992; Seidman et al., 1994), but not in more recent studies. Factors such as the existence of caring and supportive parent–adolescent relationships and communication, as well as appropriate parental monitoring, could be seen as protective factors. In this chapter, poor quality of, or the lack of, parent–adolescent relationships, parent–adolescent communication, and parent monitoring are listed under risk factors. More research is needed on protective factors related to adolescent risky sexual behavior for the purposes of developing effective interventions.

POSITIVE ATTITUDES AND SOCIAL NORMS TOWARD CONDOM USE AND INTENTIONS TO USE CONDOMS

Positive attitudes by the individual and his or her partner toward condom use may act as a protective factor. In a meta-analysis of 121 empirical studies of the relationship between psychosocial variables and self-reported condom use, Sheeran and colleagues (1999) found positive attitudes toward condom use were a reliable predictor of condom use. This study also found condom use to be strongly correlated to social norms regarding condom use and intentions to use condoms. With regard to social norms, the individual's perception that his or her friends and peer group used condoms was more strongly related to condom use than if the individual believed his or her partner had a positive attitude toward condom use.

An environmental factor that supports the link between positive attitudes, norms, and intentions and actual condom use is the availability of condoms. This meta-analysis (Sheeran et al., 1999) also found preparatory behaviors (carrying a condom, having one available before intercourse, and communication with one's partner about using a condom) to be strongly correlated with condom use. In a recent study comparing condom use between students in New York City schools (where condom availability is mandated) with a matched sample of students in Chicago schools (where condoms are not available), Guttmacher and colleagues (1997) found that the students in the New York schools were more likely to have used a condom during last intercourse than students in the Chicago schools.

ASSESSING RISK AND PROTECTIVE BEHAVIORS

Jessor (1992) distinguished between two stages of being at risk. The first stage referred to an adolescent's risk of engaging in the behavior (in this case, risky sexual behavior); the second stage, which applies to adolescents who are already engaging in the behavior, referred to "the degree of risk associated with the engagement in risk behaviors" (p. 30). The focus of assessment is different for each stage.

Assessment of risk for adolescents who are not yet sexually active should focus on the salient risk and protective factors listed in Table 9-2. For example, the assessment should assess community, peer, and family norms about sexuality; the adolescent's sexual orientation, knowledge and attitudes about sexuality and safer sex practices, intent to initiate sexual intercourse, and perception of his or her friends' sexual behavior; whether the adolescent has ever been or is currently being sexually abused; whether the adolescent is currently in a "romantic relationship"; and at what age the adolescent's older siblings became sexually active. Because adolescents' relationships and communication with parents and perceptions of parental monitoring are strongly associated with sexual behavior, any assessment should include questions covering these areas. As described in chapter 2, risky behavior is often seen in clusters, or bundles, so it is critical to determine whether an adolescent is involved in other risky behavior, particularly drug or alcohol use (see also Jessor, 1992).

For adolescents already involved in risky sexual behavior, the assessment should focus on four areas: (1) degree or intensity of involvement (the overall pattern of risky sexual behavior and the degree to which the pattern is established); (2) the number of risky behaviors (such as multiple partners, frequency of unprotected sex [vaginal, anal, oral], or having sex while using substances); (3) age of onset of sexual intercourse and length of time the adolescent has been sexually active; and (4) the degree to which the adolescent engages in protective sexual behaviors (Jessor, 1992). In this type of assessment, the practitioner would ask about when the adolescent first started having sex, how many partners he or she has had since first initiating sex, if he or she uses condoms and how consistently, and the extent to which he or she uses substances in conjunction with having sex. Protective factors that should be assessed include the adolescent's access to culturally and developmentally sensitive STI screening and treatment services, to prevention education and counseling, and to condoms; the extent to which the adolescent can demonstrate the ability to negotiate safer sex and to use a condom properly; and the degree to which he or she has positive attitudes about condom use, and the intent to use condoms consistently. This assessment should be conducted in the context of understanding the adolescent's sexual orientation and cultural and family norms about sexuality.

Baumer and South (2001) also stress the need in any assessment to recognize the role of the social environment in influencing behavior. That is, not only is risky sexual behavior accepted more in some adolescent social environments than in others, but risk behaviors produce more adverse outcomes in some social environments, such as those with high STI rates.

A theoretical model that has been used to explain adolescent risky sexual behavior and to design risk reduction interventions such as the Theory of Reasoned Action (TRA) could be adapted for assessment purposes (Gillmore, 2004) for a discussion of theoretical approaches to understanding adolescent risky sexual behavior). The TRA (Fishbein, 1998; Fishbein & Ajzen, 1975) is similar to the Health Belief Model (HBM; Becker, 1974; Strecher & Rosenstock, 1997) in that it assumes individuals make decisions about behavior based on their expectations of outcomes. However, unlike the HBM, the TRA hypoth-esizes that the best predictor of a specific behavior is an individual's intention to engage in the behavior. Intention is influenced by the individual's attitudes about the behavior and perception of social norms (such as beliefs of friends, parents, and siblings). Self-efficacy about performing the behavior and beliefs about the likelihood and benefit of achieving the desired outcome influence the individual's attitudes about performing the behavior.

IMPLICATIONS FOR PRACTICE

Epidemiologists use the term "web of causation" to refer to the complex models that explain causes of chronic diseases (MacMahon, Pugh, & Ipsen, 1960, p. 18). The term could also describe the many factors that explain or predict the epidemiology of STIs among adolescents. The immediate behavioral cause is well understood (engaging in unprotected sex with an infected partner), but frameworks to explain both the proximal and distal factors associated with engaging in risky sexual behavior are much more complex. Of the numerous risk and protective factors associated with adolescent risky sexual behaviors a few could be considered keystone factors—factors most likely to lead to or prevent risky sexual behavior (see chapter 2). In reviewing the risk and protective factors presented earlier in this chapter, the factors that appear to be keystone factors are

- early sexual initiation
- attitudes, intentions, and perception of norms about sexual behavior
- quality of the parent–adolescent relationship and communication and parental monitoring
- access to developmentally and culturally appropriate preventive and treatment services.

As discussed in chapter 13, evidence-based practice using a risk and resilience perspective requires that interventions target malleable and empirically validated keystone risk and protective factors. In addition, knowledge of intervention effectiveness and "local" knowledge of what works programmatically and clinically with certain individuals, population groups, and communities should guide the design, implementation, and evaluation of interventions (see chapter 2). Practitioners, community informants, adolescents, and persons who play key roles in the day-to-day lives of adolescents—parents, teachers, and mentors—can provide local knowledge about unique characteristics in their environments and how these might affect intervention processes and outcomes.

Because sexuality and sexual behavior are integral parts of adolescent development, the focus of interventions should be on making sexual behavior and the exploration of one's sexuality less risky. Interventions also need to be sensitive to the different developmental processes and needs of early, middle, and late adolescence. For example, for youths in the early and middle stages of adolescent development, interventions should help them delay the onset of sexual intercourse. For adolescents who are already engaging in intercourse, interventions should focus on helping them use safer sex methods consistently and appropriately, and helping them reduce the number of sexual partners. Helping adolescents of all ages access culturally and developmentally sensitive preventive and treatment services should be a universal focus of STI interventions.

To be effective, in addition to responding to adolescent developmental differences, STI interventions need to address cultural and community differences in how sexuality is viewed and practiced (Sonenstein, 2000). Strunin (1994) emphasized the need to understand the patterns of risk behavior among racial and ethnic groups, as well as the diversity of norms, values, and behavioral patterns within groups. Knowing how individuals in various cultural groups interpret information and translate it into behavior is critical to the design of culturally competent interventions. McLaurin and Juzang (1993) in their focus groups on HIV education with inner-city African American youths, found that participants wanted concrete messages about skills—ones that fit with their peer culture, "Don't tell us what to do, tell us how to do it, step by step, without losing the approval of our peers" (p. 3). They also noted that urban African American youths were very sophisticated consumers of media programming and that they had their own communication style and beliefs about the role of communication, which differed markedly from those of the mainstream culture.

During the past two decades, the interest in and development of practice guidelines have grown (Howard & Jenson, 1999). Moreover, researchers are increasingly interested in intervention design issues and the development of practice guidelines to inform the design of interventions to allow for comparison and replication studies (Stanton, Kim, Galbraith, & Parrott, 1996). In the specific case of preventing risky sexual behavior in adolescence, practice guidelines—for interventions at the individual and programmatic level—should include the following:

- *Use theories of behavioral change to target attitudes, perception of norms, and intentions about initiating intercourse and practicing safer sex.* Interventions to prevent STIs, especially HIV, are increasingly focusing on changing adolescents' attitudes, perceptions of norms about sexual behavior, and intentions. These interventions respond to the identified need for theory-based interventions (Fishbein, 1998; Office of the Surgeon General, 2001; Stanton et al., 1996) and are informed by recent studies of psychosocial risk factors (Sheeran et al., 1999, for example) and TRA (Fishbein, 1998; Fishbein & Ajzen, 1975) and cognitive behavioral theories (Bandura, 1986; Bandura, 1994). These two behavioral change theories, in particular, have been guiding the design, implementation, and evaluation of an increasing number of interventions. Gillmore (2004) provided a comprehensive review of interventions based on these theories. In a quantitative review of the effectiveness of 40 adolescent AIDS-risk reduction interventions, Kim, Stanton, Li, Dickersin, and Galbraith (1997) concluded that interventions that were theory based were more likely to demonstrate an increase in knowledge and behavioral intention to use a condom. Overall, interventions improved adolescents' attitudes and behavioral intentions about safer sex practices and reduced risk practices.

Most interventions to prevent or to reduce adolescent risky sexual behavior target individual behavioral change. However, because positive attitudes toward safer sex practices and perception of peer norms play such a key role in adolescent sexual behavior, to promote and maintain individual level change, interventions at the neighborhood, school, and community levels are needed to promote perceptions of social norms that discourage risky sexual behavior and promote safer sex practices (Chesney, 1994). Through social marketing and diffusion of innovation strategies, programs can create a "social milieu" in which risk-reduction behavior becomes the norm among groups (Rosenthal, Cohen, & Biro, 1994, p. 255).

- *Include parents in interventions to strengthen the quality of parent–adolescent relationships and communication and promote developmentally appropriate parental monitoring.* Most interventions to prevent and change adolescent risky sexual behavior target adolescents. This is as it should be. However, interventions often miss opportunities to make adolescents' family environments more supportive of delayed onset of intercourse and safer sexual behavior by involving parents. Parenting interventions should focus on building warm, supportive relationships between parents and teens, improving communication, and helping parents understand the protective value of monitoring their adolescent's behaviors and how to monitor in a manner that is sensitive to adolescents' developmental needs for increased independence and autonomy. Open and sensitive communication between teens and parents and parental-appropriate monitoring of teens are most feasible and effective in the context of a warm, supportive relationship (Meschke et al., 2000).

Meschke and colleagues (2000) reviewed 19 interventions with a parent component. Sixteen of the 19 programs targeted youths ages 10 to 14. The programs differed considerably in focus (although the programs focused on sex education, increasing communication, and pregnancy prevention, none had a primary focus on STI prevention), longevity, parent participation (in some parent programs participation was optional), format (number of sessions or delivery site, for example), and evaluation. Knowledge of the effectiveness of these programs was limited in that only six programs had conducted outcome evaluations (only four were external evaluations and not all included an evaluation of the parent component). The evaluation results for the parent component have only been published for FACTS and Feelings (Miller et al., 1993), Parent–Child Sex Education (Kirby, 1985), and Project Taking Charge (Jorgenson, 1991). Overall, evaluations of these programs found an increase in parent–adolescent communication and adolescent and parental knowledge about sex. (See Meschke et al., 2000, for a complete discussion of the limitations of these evaluations.)

The strongest body of literature on the effectiveness of parenting and family interventions to prevent or reduce risky adolescent behavior is in the drug abuse–prevention field. A review of this literature found that behavioral parent training, family therapy, and family skills training approaches have demonstrated effectiveness in reducing risk factors and increasing protective factors for drug use and in decreasing drug use (Center for Substance Abuse Prevention, 1998). Research is needed to assess whether these intervention models can be adapted to prevent risky sexual behaviors among adolescents.

- *Increase access to developmentally and culturally appropriate STI prevention and treatment services.* Access to developmentally and culturally sensitive prevention and treatment services is critical to reducing the epidemic of STIs among adolescents (Office of the Surgeon General, 2001; Sonenstein, 2000). The delivery of clinical preventive services, which is one component of broad-based prevention efforts, shows promise: these services are designed to provide prevention as well as treatment services. They focus on preventing or delaying the onset of health and mental health problems or providing early treatment to reduce the effect of STIs (Park et al., 2001). For example, providers (physicians, nurses, health educators, and social workers) may screen for risk factors and provide education and counseling to adolescents to delay onset of first intercourse. In the case of adolescents who are already sexually active, providers should screen for STIs and educate and counsel them about safer sexual behavior so they can prevent contracting or transmitting STIs. The goal of clinical preventive services for adolescents who have contracted an STI is to prevent further morbidity and to change their risky sexual behaviors so that they will not infect others or acquire other STIs. Unlike most medical care, clinical preventive services for adolescents also address the psychosocial factors underlying risky behavior and effects of having an STI through counseling and other interventions (Park et al., 2001).

Clinical preventive health services are delivered in clinical settings such as school-based–school-linked health centers (SBHCs–SLHCs), teen clinics, medical offices, or community health centers. SBHCs–SLHCs have increased in number from 150 in 1990 to more than 1,300 in 2000 and have proved to be effective in providing primary, preventive, and acute care to adolescents, particularly underserved adolescents (Morone, Kilberth, & Langwell, 2001). Research conducted in Colorado suggests that by increasing adolescents' access to preventive services such as screening, these SBHCs–SLHCs prevent costly episodes of care (Kaplan, Calonge, Guernsey, & Hanrahan, 1998). For example, chlamydia screening in urban high schools where the prevalence rate of chlamydia is high has been successful in reducing the prevalence in these schools (Cohen, Nsumami, Martin, & Farley, 1999). Teen clinics operate under various auspices, such as medical centers or county governments, rather than school systems. Researchers have found that teen clinics screen teens more extensively for risks—such as risky sexual behavior and substance abuse—than community family practice, private family practice, or private pediatric settings (Blum, Beuhring, Wunderlich, & Resnick, 1996). In addition, teen clinics can offer clinical preventive services to meet the complex needs of adolescents who are at highest risk for STIs (for example, adolescents who have dropped out of school, run away from home, or are homeless).

Conclusion

A risk and resilience framework reveals many factors, both individual and environmental, that increase the likelihood that adolescents will engage in sexual behaviors that increase the chances of contracting and transmitting STIs. Factors that protect adolescents from engaging in risky sexual behaviors have also been discussed in this chapter, but only briefly, because research on protective factors is only beginning to emerge. Some of these protective factors are the absence or opposite of a specific risk factor; others are at one end of a continuum, with risk factors at the other. Clearly, more needs to be done to conceptualize and identify both individual and environmental protective factors that decrease the likelihood that adolescents will engage in risky sexual behaviors.

Interventions to reduce the incidence and prevalence of STIs among adolescents will be more effective when they are grounded in an ecological framework. That is, interventions should be designed to simultaneously influence keystone risk and protective factors at various levels in the ecology. For example, interventions at the level of the individual often focus on adolescents' acquisition of specific knowledge, attitudes, intentions, and behaviors to postpone sexual activity or to engage in safer sexual practices. To initiate and maintain these behaviors, however, adolescents need considerable support from their peer group, families, schools, communities, and the larger social system. In many cases, support will not be forthcoming without changes in the adolescent's environment.

Thus, interventions also need to target the larger context of adolescent life and the systems within that context to meet the ultimate goal of helping adolescents take care of themselves and their peers. Interventions must have several targets: teaching parents how to develop caring, supportive relationships and communication with adolescents and appropriate monitoring of behavior after-school and on weekends; ensuring personal, school, and community safety; making health care and prevention programs accessible; and increasing opportunities for adolescents' education, employment, recreation, healthy development, and achievement. The development and implementation of these interventions will require coordinated and integrated efforts among adolescents, families, schools, religious organizations, health and community agencies, the media, and governmental policy makers (Office of National AIDS Policy, 2000; Office of the Surgeon General, 2001; Park et al., 2001; Sonenstein, 2000). All of these interventions give adolescents the message that they are valued and that their health and well-being are important.

REFERENCES

Abma, J., Driscoll, A., & Moore, K. (1998). Young women's degree of control over first intercourse: An exploratory analysis. *Family Planning Perspectives, 30*(1), 12–18.

Ackard, D. M., & Neumark-Sztainer, D. (2001). Health care information sources for adolescents: Age and gender differences on use, concerns, and needs. *Journal of Adolescent Health, 29*(3), 170–176.

Alan Guttmacher Institute. (1999). *Facts in brief: Teen sex and pregnancy* [Online]. Retrieved from http://www.agi.usa.org/pubs/fb_teen_sex.html on October 27, 2000.

Anderson, J. E., McCormick, L., & Fichtner, R. (1994). Factors associated with self-reported STDs: Data from a national survey. *Sexually Transmitted Diseases, 21,* 303–308.

Andrews, H. (1985). The ecology of risk and the geography of intervention: From research to practice for the health and well-being of urban children. *Annals of the Association of American Geographers, 75,* 375–382.

American Social Health Association. (1996a). Decrease in lab testing may mask STD problem. *STD News, 3*(2), 4.

American Social Health Association. (1996b). Teenagers know more than adults about STDs, but knowledge among both groups is low. *STD News, 3*(2), 1–5.

American Social Health Association. (1998). *Sexually transmitted diseases in America: How many cases and at what cost?* Prepared for the Kaiser Family Foundation by the American Social Health Association. Retrieved from http://www.ashastd. org on November 20, 2001.

American Social Health Association. (2001). *Herpes fact sheet.* Retrieved from http://www.ashastd.org/pdfs/heguide.htm on November 24, 2000.

Bandura, A. (1986). *Social foundations of thought and action: A social cognitive theory.* Englewood Cliffs, NJ: Prentice Hall.

Bandura, A. (1994). Social cognitive theory and exercise of control over HIV infection. In R. DiClemente, & J. Peterson (Eds.) *Preventing AIDS: Theories and methods of behavioral interventions* (pp. 25–60). New York: Plenum Press.

Baumer, E. P., & South, S. J. (2001). Community effects on youth sexual activity. *Journal of Marriage and the Family, 63*(2), 540–554.

Becker, M. H. (Ed.). (1974). The Health Belief Model and personal health behavior. *Health Education Monographs, 2,* 324–473.

Bethell, C., Klein, J., & Peck, C. (2001). Assessing health system provision of adolescent preventive services: The Young Adult Health Care Survey. *Medical Care, 39*(5), 478–490.

Blum, R. W., Beuhring, T., Shew, M. L., Bearing, L. H., Sieving, R. E., & Resnick, M. D. (2000). The effects of race/ethnicity, income and family structure on adolescent risk behaviors. *American Journal of Public Health, 90*(12), 1879–1884.

Blum, R. W., Beuhring, T., Wunderlich, M., & Resnick, M. D. (1996). Don't ask, they won't tell: The quality of adolescent health screening in five practice settings. *American Journal of Public Health, 86*(12), 1767–1772.

Boyer, C. B., & Tschann, J. M. (1999). Predictors of risk for sexually transmitted disease in ninth grade urban high school students. *Journal of Adolescent Research, 14*(4), 448–446.

Brewster, K. L., Billy, J.O.G., & Grady, W. R. (1993). Social context and adolescent behavior: The impact of community on the transition to sexual activity. *Social Forces, 71*(3), 713–740.

Brown, L. K., DiClemente, R. J., & Park, T. (1992). Predictors of condom use in sexually active adolescents. *Journal of Adolescent Health, 13*(8), 651–657.

Carrera, M., Kaye, J. W., Philliber, S., & West, E. (2000). Knowledge about reproduction, contraception, and sexually transmitted infections among young adolescents in American cities. *Social Policy, 30*(3), 41–51.

Cates, W., Jr. (1991). Teenagers and sexual risk taking: The best of times and the worst of times. *Journal of Adolescent Health, 12*(2), 84–94.

Cates, W., Jr., & American Social Health Association Panel. (1999). Estimates of the incidence and prevalence of sexually transmitted diseases in the United States. *Sexually Transmitted Diseases, 26*(Suppl.), S2–S7.

Cates, W., Jr., & Rauh, J. L. (1985). Adolescents and sexually transmitted diseases: An expanding problem. *Journal of Adolescent Health, 6*(4), 257–261.

Center for Substance Abuse Prevention. (1998). *Prevention enhancement protocol system (PEPS)* (DHHS Publication No. [SMA] 3224-FY98). Washington, DC: U.S. Department of Health and Human Services, Substance Abuse and Mental Health Services Administration.

Centers for Disease Control and Prevention. (1995a). *Adolescent health: State of the nation—pregnancy, sexually transmitted diseases, and related risk behaviors among U.S. adolescents* (Monograph Series No. 2, DHHS Publication No. CDC 099-4630). Atlanta: U.S. Department of Health and Human Services.

Centers for Disease Control and Prevention. (1995b). Trends in sexual risk behavior among high school students—United States, 1990, 1991, and 1993. *Morbidity and Mortality Weekly Reports, 44*(7), 124–133.

Centers for Disease Control and Prevention. (1999a). Resurgent bacterial sexually transmitted disease among men who have sex with men—King County, Washington, 1997–1999. *Morbidity and Mortality Weekly Reports, 48,* 773–777.

Centers for Disease Control and Prevention. (1999b). *Sexually transmitted disease surveillance* (1999 Supplement: Gonococcal Isolate Surveillance Project (GISP) Annual Report—1999). Atlanta, Author.

Centers for Disease Control and Prevention. (2000a). *Sexually transmitted disease surveillance, 1999.* Atlanta: Author.

Centers for Disease Control and Prevention. (2000b). Surveillance summaries. *Morbidity and Mortality Weekly Reports, 49*(SS05), 1–96.

Centers for Disease Control and Prevention. (2000c). *Tracking the hidden epidemics: Trends in STDs in the United States, 2000.* Atlanta: Author.

Centers for Disease Control and Prevention. (2001). *Young people at risk: HIV/AIDS among America's youth.* Atlanta: Author.

Chesney, M. A. (1994). Prevention of HIV and STD infections. *Preventive Medicine, 23*(5), 655–660.

Cohen, D. A., Nsumami, M., Martin, D. H., & Farley, T. A. (1999). Repeated school-based screening for sexually transmitted diseases: a feasible strategy for reaching adolescents. *Pediatrics, 104*(6), 1281–1285.

Cohen, M. S., Hoffman, I. F., Royce, R. A., Kazembe, P., Dyer, J. R., Daly, C. C., Zimba, D., Vernazza, P. L., Maida, M., Fiscus, S. A., Eron, J. J., Jr., & the AIDSCAP Malawi Research Group. (1997). Reduction of concentration of HIV-1 in semen after treatment of urethritis: Implications for prevention of sexual transmission of HIV-1. *Lancet, 349,* 1868–1873.

DiClemente, R. J. (1992). Epidemiology of AIDS, HIV prevalence, and HIV incidence among adolescents. *Journal of School Health, 62*(7), 325–330.

DiClemente, R. J., Wingood, G. M., Crosby, R., Sionean, C., Cobb, B. K., Harrington, K., Davies, S., Hook, E.W., & Oh, M. K. (2001). Parental monitoring: Association with adolescents' risk behaviors. *Pediatrics, 107*(6), 1363–1368.

DiIorio, C., Kelly, M., & Hockenberry-Eaton, M. (1999). Communication about sexual issues: Mothers, fathers, and friends. *Journal of Adolescent Health, 24*(3), 181–189.

Dunn, M. E., & Alarie, P. (1997). Trends in sexuality education in United States and Canadian medical schools. *Journal of Psychology and Human Sexuality, 9,* 175–184.

East, P. L. (1996). The younger sisters of childbearing adolescents: Their attitudes, expectations and behaviors. *Child Development, 67,* 267–282.

Fergusson, D. M., & Lynskey, M. T. (1996). Alcohol misuse and adolescent sexual behaviors and risk taking. *Pediatrics, 98*(1), 91–96.

Fishbein, M. (1998). Changing behavior to prevent STDs/AIDS. *International Journal of Gynecology & Obstetrics, 63,* S175–S181.

Fishbein, M., & Ajzen, I. (1975). *Belief, attitude, intention and behavior: An introduction to theory and research.* Reading, MA: Addison-Wesley Press.

Fleming, D. T., McQuillian, G. M., Johnson, R. E., Nahmias, A. J., Aral, S. O., Lee, F. K., & St. Louis, M. E. (1997). Herpes Simplex Virus Type 2 in the United States, 1976 to 1994. *New England Journal of Medicine, 337*(16), 1105–1111.

Fleming, D. T., & Wasserheit, J. N. (1999). From epidemiological synergy to public health policy and practice: The contribution of other sexually transmitted diseases to sexual transmission of HIV infection. *Sexually Transmitted Infections, 75*(1), 3–17.

Ford, K., Sohn, W., & Lepkowski, J. (2001). Characteristics of adolescents' sexual partners and their association with use of condoms and other contraceptive methods. *Family Planning Perspectives, 33*(3), 100–105.

Fullilove, M. T., Golden, E., Fullilove, R. E., III., Lennon, R., Porterfield, D., Schwarcz, S., & Bolan, G. (1993). Crack cocaine use and high-risk behaviors among sexually active black adolescents. *Journal of Adolescent Health, 14*(4), 295–300.

Garofalo, R., & Katz, E. (2001). Health care issues of gay and lesbian youth. *Current Opinion in Pediatrics, 13*(4), 298–302.

Gates, G. & Sonenstein, F. (2000). Adolescent genital sexual activity among adolescent males: 1988–1995. *Family Planning Perspectives, 32*(6), 295–297, 304.

Gillmore, M. R. (2004). AIDS/STD prevention among U.S. adolescents. In P. Allen-Meares & M. W. Fraser (Eds.). *Intervention with children and adolescents: An interdisciplinary perspective.* Needham Heights, MA: Allyn & Bacon.

Gillmore, M. R., Morrison, D. M., Lowery, C. & Baker, S. (1994). Beliefs about condoms and their association with intentions to use condoms among youths in detention. *Journal of Adolescent Health, 15*(3), 228–237.

Gillmore, M. R., Morrison, D. M., Richey, C. A., Balassone, M. L., Gutierrez, L., & Farris, M. (1997). Effects of a skill-based intervention to encourage condom use among high risk heterosexually active adolescents. *AIDS Education and Prevention, 9,* 22–47.

Gold, R. B., & Sonfield, A. (2001). Reproductive health services for adolescents under the state Children's Health Insurance Program. *Family Planning Perspectives, 33*(2), 81–87.

Guttmacher, S., Liberman, L., Ward, D., Freudenberg, N., Radosh, A., & Des Jarlais, D. (1997). Condom availability in New York City public high schools: Relationship to condom use and sexual behavior. *American Journal of Public Health, 87*(9), 1427–1433.

Halpern-Felsher, B. L., Millstein, S. G., & Ellen, J. M. (1996). Relationship of alcohol use and risky sexual behavior: A review and analysis of findings. *Journal of Adolescent Health, 19*(5), 331–336.

Herman-Giddens, M. E., Slora, E. J., & Wasserman, R. C. (1997). Secondary sexual characteristics and menses in young girls seen in office practice: A study from the pediatric research in office setting network. *Pediatrics, 99*(5), 505–512.

Hine, T. (1999). *The rise and fall of the American teenager.* New York: Avon Books.

Hingson, R., Strunin, L., Berlin, B. M., Heeren, T. (1990). Beliefs about AIDS, use of alcohol and drugs and unprotected sex among Massachusetts adolescents. *American Journal of Public Health, 80,* 295–299.

Howard, M. O., & Jenson, J. M. (1999). Clinical practice guidelines: Should social work develop them? *Research on Social Work Practice, 9*(3), 283–301.

Institute of Medicine. (1997). *The hidden epidemic: Confronting sexually transmitted diseases.* Washington, DC: National Academy Press.

Irwin, C. E., Jr., & Millstein, S. G. (1986). Biopsychosocial correlates of risk-taking behaviors during adolescence: Can the physician intervene? *Journal of Adolescent Health, 7*(65), 825–965.

Irwin, C. E., Jr., & Shafer, M. A. (1992). Adolescent sexuality: Negative outcomes of a normative behavior. In D. Rogers & E. Ginsberg (Eds.), *Adolescents at risk: Medical and social perspectives* (pp. 35–79). Boulder, CO: Westview Press.

Jessor, R. (1992). Risk behavior in adolescence: A psychosocial framework for understanding and action. In D. Rogers & E. Ginsberg (Eds.), *Adolescents at risk: Medical and social perspectives* (pp. 19–34). Boulder, CO: Westview Press.

Jessor, R., Turbin, M. S., & Costa, F. M. (1998). Protective factors in adolescent health behavior. *Journal of Personality and Social Psychology, 75*(3), 788–800.

Jorgensen, S. R. (1991). Project taking charge: An evaluation of an adolescent pregnancy prevention program. *Family Relations, 40,* 373–380.

Kahn, J. R. (1994). Speaking across cultures within your own family. In J. M. Irvine (Ed.), *Sexual cultures and the construction of adolescent identities* (pp. 285–309). Philadelphia: Temple University Press.

Kaiser Family Foundation/*Glamour*. (1998). *1998 survey of men and women on sexually transmitted diseases*. Menlo Park, CA.

Kann, L., Warren, C. W., Harris, W. A., Collins, J. L., Douglas, K. A., Collins, M. E., Williams, B. I., Ross, J. G., & Kolbe, L. J. (1995). Youth risk behavior surveillance—United States, 1993. *Morbidity and Mortality Weekly Report, 44*(SS-1).

Kaplan, D. W., Calonge, B. N., Guernsey, B. P., & Hanrahan, M. B. (1998). Managed care and school-based health centers: Use of health services. *Archives of Pediatrics and Adolescent Medicine, 152,* 1, 25–33.

Kaplowitz, P. B., & Oberfield, S. E. (1999). Reexamination of the age limit for defining when puberty is precocious in girls in the United States: Implications for evaluation and treatment. *Pediatrics, 104*(4), 936–941.

Kelly, P. J., Bair, R. M., Baillargeon, J., & German, V. (2000). Risk behaviors and the prevalence of chlamydia in a juvenile detention facility. *Clinical Pediatrics, 39*(9), 521–528.

Kim, N., Stanton, B., Li, X., Dickersin, K., & Galbraith, J. (1997). Effectiveness of the 40 adolescent AIDS-risk reduction interventions: A quantitative review. *Journal of Adolescent Health, 20,* 204–215.

Kinsman, S., Romer, D., Furstenberg, & Schwarz, D. (1998). Early sexual initiation: The role of peer norms. *Pediatrics, 102*(5), 1185–1192.

Kirby, D. (1985). The effects of selected sexuality education programs: Toward a more realistic view. *Journal of Sex Education and Therapy, 112,* 28–37.

Klein, J. D., McNulty, M., & Flatau, C. N. (1998). Adolescents' access to care—Teenagers' self-reported use of services and perceived access to confidential care. *Archives of Pediatrics and Adolescent Medicine, 152*(7), 676–682.

MacKay, A. P., Flingerhut, L. A., & Duran, C. R. (2000). *Adolescent health chartbook*. Hyattsville, MD: National Center for Health Statistics.

MacMahon, B., Pugh, T. F., & Ipsen, J. (1960). *Epidemiological methods*. Boston: Little, Brown.

Mann, J. (1994). *The difference: Growing up female in America*. New York: Warner Books.

McLaurin, P. & Juzang, I. (1993). Reaching the hip-hop generation. *Focus: A guide to AIDS research and counseling, 8*(3), 1–4.

Mertz, G. J., Benedetti, J., Ashley, R., Selke, S. A., Corey, L. (1992). Risk factors for the sexual transmission of genital herpes. *Annuals of Internal Medicine, 116*(3), 197–202.

Meschke, L. L., Bartholomae, S., & Zentall, S. R. (2000). Adolescent sexuality and parent-adolescent processes: Promoting healthy teen choices. *Family Relations, 49*(2), 143–155.

Miller, B. C., Monson, B. H., & Norton, M. C. (1995). The effects of forced sexual intercourse on white female adolescents. *Child Abuse and Neglect, 19*(10), 1289–1301.

Miller, B. C., Norton, M. C., Jenson, G. O., Lee, T. R., Christopherson, C., & King, P. K. (1993). Impact evaluation of facts and feelings: A home-based video sex education curriculum. *Family Relations, 42*, 392–400.

Miller, K. S., Forehand, R., & Kotchick, B. A. (1999). Adolescent sexual behavior in two ethnic minority samples: The role of family variables. *Journal of Marriage and the Family, 61*(1), 85–99.

Milne, A. C., & Chesson, R. (2000). Health services can be cool: Partnership with adolescents in primary care. *Family Practice, 17*(4), 305–308.

Morone, J. A., Kilberth, E. H., & Langwell, K. M. (2001). Back to school: A health strategy for youth. *Health Affairs, 20*, 1, 122–136.

Morris, L., Warren, C. W., & Aral, S. O. (1993). Measuring adolescent sexual behaviors and related health outcomes. *Public Health Reports, 108*(3, Suppl. 1), 31–36.

Nagy, S., Adcock, A. G., & Nagy, M. C. (1994). A comparison of risky health behaviors of sexually active, sexually abused, and abstaining adolescents. *Pediatrics, 93*(4), 570–575.

Newacheck, P. W., Brindis, C. D., Cart, C. U., Marchi, K., & Irwin, C. E. (1999). Adolescent health insurance coverage: Recent changes and access to care. *Pediatrics, 104*(2), 195–202.

Office of National AIDS Policy. (2000). *Youth and HIV/AIDS 2000: A New American agenda* [Online]. Retrieved from http://www.thebody.org/whitehouse/youth report/contents.html on November 21, 2001.

Office of the Surgeon General. (2001). *The surgeon general's call to action to promote sexual health and responsible sexual behavior* [Online]. Retrieved from http//: www.sg.gov/library/sexualhealth/default.htm on November 24, 2000.

Park, M. J., Macdonald, T. M., Ozer, E. M., Burg, S. J., Millstein, S. G., Brindis, C. D., & Irwin, C. E. (2001). *Investing in clinical preventive health services for adolescents.* San Francisco: University of California, Policy Information and Analysis Center for Middle Childhood and Adolescence, & National Adolescent Health Information Center.

Perry, C. (2000). Preadolescent and adolescent influences on health. In B. Smedley, & S. Syme (Eds.), *Promoting health: Intervention strategies from social and behavioral research* (pp. 217–253). Washington, DC: National Academy Press.

Pestrak, V. A., & Martin, D. (1985). Cognitive development and aspects of adolescent sexuality. *Adolescence, 20*(80), 981–987.

Pipher, M. (1994). *Reviving Ophelia: Saving the selves of adolescent girls.* New York: Ballantine Books.

Remez, L. (2000). Oral sex among adolescents: Is it sex or is it abstinence? *Family Planning Perspectives, 32*(6), 298–304.

Roberts, J., Boker, J. R., Oh, M. K., & DiClemente, R. J. (2000). Health care service use and sexual communication: Past experience and future intention of high-risk male adolescents. *Journal of Adolescent Health, 27*(5), 298–301.

Rosenthal, S. L., & Biro, F. M. (1991). A preliminary investigation of psychological impact of sexually transmitted diseases in adolescent females. *Adolescent and Pediatric Gynecology, 4,* 198–201.

Rosenthal, S. L., Biro, F. M., Succop, P. A., Bernstein, D. I., & Stanberry, L. R. (1997). Impact of demographics, sexual history, and psychological functioning on the acquisition of STDs in adolescents. *Adolescence, 32*(128), 757–769.

Rosenthal, S. L., Cohen, S. S., & Biro, F. M. (1994). Sexually transmitted diseases: A paradigm for risk taking teens. In R. J. Simeonsson, (Ed.), *Risk resilience and prevention: Promoting the well-being of children* (pp. 239–264). Baltimore: Paul H. Brookes.

Santelli, J. S., & Beilenson, P. (1992). Risk factors for adolescent sexual behavior, fertility, and sexually transmitted diseases. *Journal of School Health, 62*(7), 271–279.

Santelli, J. S., Lindberg, L. D., Abma, J., McNeely, C. S., & Resnick, M. (2000). Adolescent sexual behavior: Estimates and trends from four nationally representative surveys. *Family Planning Perspectives, 32*(4), 156–167.

Seidman, S. N., Mosher, W. D., & Aral, S. O. (1994). Predictors of high-risk behavior in unmarried American women: Adolescent environment as risk factor. *Journal of Adolescent Health, 15*(2), 126–132.

Sieving, R., Resnick, M. D., Bearinger, L., Remafedi, G., Taylor, B. A., & Harmon, B. (1997). Cognitive and behavioral predictors of sexually transmitted disease risk behavior among sexually active adolescents. *Archives of Pediatric and Adolescent Medicine, 151,* 243–251.

Shafer, M. B., & Moscicki, A. B. (1991). Sexually transmitted diseases. In W. R. Hendee (Ed.), *The health of adolescents* (pp. 211–249). San Francisco: Jossey-Bass.

Sheeran, P., Abraham, C., & Orbell, S. (1999). Psychosocial correlates of heterosexual condom use: A meta-analysis. *Psychological Bulletin, 125,* 90–132.

Shrier, L. S., Goodman, E., & Emans, S. J. (1999). Partner condom use among adolescent girls with sexually transmitted diseases. *Journal of Adolescent Health, 24*(5), 357–361.

Shrier, L. A., Ancheta, R., Goodman, E., Chiou, V. M., Lyden, M. R., & Emans, S. J. (2001). Randomized controlled trial of a safer sex intervention for high-risk adolescent girls. *Archives of Pediatrics and Adolescent Medicine, 155,* 1, 73–79.

Silverman, J. G., Raj, A., Mucci, L. A., & Hathaway, J. E. (2001). Dating violence against adolescent girls and associated substance use, unhealthy weight control, sexual risk behavior, pregnancy, and suicidality. *Journal of the American Medical Association, 286,* 572–579.

Sonenstein, F. L. (Ed.). (2000). *Young men's sexual and reproductive health: Toward a national strategy.* Washington, DC: Urban Institute.

Stanton, B., Kim, N., Galbraith, J., & Parrott, M. (1996). Design issues addressed in published evaluations of adolescent HIV-risk reduction interventions: A review. *Journal of Adolescent Health, 18,* 387–396.

Strecher, V. J., & Rosenstock, I. M. (1997). The health belief model. In K. Glanz, F. M. Lewis, & B. K. Rimer (Eds.). *Health behavior and health education: Theory, research, and practice* (2nd ed, pp. 41–59) San Francisco: Jossey-Bass.

Strunin, L. (1994). Culture, context, and HIV infection: Research on risk taking among adolescents. In J.M. Irvine (Ed.), *Sexual cultures and the construction of adolescent identities* (pp. 71–87). Philadelphia: Temple University Press.

Udry, J. R. (1988). Biological predispositions and social control in adolescent sexual behavior. *American Sociological Review, 53*(5), 709–722.

U.S. Department of Health and Human Services. (2000). *Child maltreatment 1998: Reports from the states to the National Child Abuse and Neglect Data System.* Washington, DC: U.S. Government Printing Office.

Widmer, E. D. (1997). Influence of older siblings on initiation of sexual intercourse. *Journal of Marriage and the Family, 59*(4), 928–938.

Yarber, W. L., & Parrillo, A. V. (1992). Adolescents and sexually transmitted diseases. *Journal of School Health, 62*(7), 331–338.

10

Risk and Protective Factors for Adolescent Pregnancy: Bases for Effective Intervention

Cynthia Franklin, Jacqueline Corcoran, and Mary Beth Harris

This chapter presents a summary of current statistics and social concerns associated with adolescent pregnancy, followed by a summary of the risk and protective factors associated with adolescent pregnancy. Risk and protective factors interplay, acting together to either increase or modify the risk of an adolescent becoming pregnant, or the resilience they demonstrate if they are pregnant, or parenting a child. Measures that may be helpful in assessing progress in intervention programs, along with several prevention and intervention strategies that target critical risk factors, are also highlighted in this chapter.

DESCRIPTION OF THE PROBLEM

Most researchers who have investigated the predictors and consequences of adolescent pregnancy do not identify risk, protective factors, or resilience as their underlying frameworks, with the notable exceptions of Franklin, Corcoran, and Ayers-Lopez, (1997), Kalil and Kunz (1999), and Smith (1994). The frameworks of risk, protective factors, and resilience have primarily developed in the context of research on developmental psychopathology. Researchers want to be able to better predict, understand, and intervene with psychiatric diagnoses, delinquency, violent behaviors, and substance use disorders. Pregnancy, however, is not a disorder. Rather, bearing a child is a normal condition for females of childbearing age who are sexually active and who do not use contraceptives. The "problem" of pregnancy is primarily a socially constructed problem that happens because a woman's pregnancy occurs in a certain social and developmental context that produces harmful or unwanted outcomes for herself and others. The social and developmental context of adolescent pregnancy is usually accompanied by negative and adverse, health, social, and economic consequences for the young woman and her child. Many of these consequences are intricately intertwined with the social and economic circumstances of adolescent women who are poor and who are single parents (that is, who bear children outside of marriage). It is important to study protective factors that lead to adolescents delaying pregnancy or having more favorable outcomes if they do choose the path of early childbearing in order to be familiar with interventions that practitioners may use in assisting adolescents who are at risk for early pregnancy.

CURRENT STATISTICS AND CONTEXT OF ADOLESCENT PREGNANCY

Since 1991 there has been a steady decline in the birth rate for adolescents. According to a recent report from the Centers for Disease Control and Prevention (CDC; Marlin, Hamilton, & Ventura, 2001) the birth rate for adolescent women in the United States has declined to a record low. Statistical data, based on recorded birth certificates from state vital statistic offices, show that in 2000 the birth rate for adolescent women ages 15 to 17 was 29 percent lower than it was in 1991. Birth rates declined most for African American women (31 percent) and the least for Hispanic American women (12 percent), who have the highest pregnancy rates among adolescent groups. Data from this report also indicate that the birth rate for younger adolescents, who are believed to be the most at risk for negative consequences, has remained stable at 0.9 percent for 1,000 women.

Even though these statistics indicate progress on preventing adolescent pregnancy, births to unmarried adolescents still remain higher in the United States than in other developing countries (Henshaw & Feivelson, 2000). Henshaw and Feivelson reported that 10 percent of women ages 15 to 19 in the United States became pregnant and had a birth, an abortion, or a miscarriage. Recent data from Child Trends (1999) indicated that 494,456 births occurred to teenagers in 1998. The majority (79 percent) of these births occurred outside of marriage. Twenty-two percent of births to adolescents were repeat (second or subsequent) childbirths.

SOCIAL, POLITICAL, AND MORAL DIMENSIONS OF ADOLESCENT PREGNANCY

Concerns for adolescent pregnancy prevention have focused mainly on unmarried, adolescent mothers, and fall along moral and economic positions against childbearing among unwed, economically dependent adolescent women. Unmarried women who bear children, however, are a part of a larger societal trend for women of all ages. The number of births to unmarried women increased 3 percent in 2000 to 1,345,917—the highest number ever reported for the United States. Consistent with the declining trend for adolescent pregnancy, however, the number of births to unmarried adolescents declined (Marlin et al., 2001).

Public concerns about premarital sex, use of contraception by adolescents, the availability of abortion, and most recently, economic dependence (Kelly, 1996; Rhode, 1993) have remained at the core of social, moral, and political debates around preventing adolescent pregnancy (see, for example, Boyer & Fine, 1992; Rhode, 1993; Vinovskis, 1992). As the incidence of adolescent pregnancy continued to rise throughout the 1980s, economic dependency brought unmarried adolescent mothers into the welfare debate (Hamburg & Dixon, 1992); during that period they were identified as a violation of the traditional two-parent family and a drain on the economy (Kelly, 1996). By the late 1980s, unwed, pregnant adolescent mothers were at the center of the welfare debate and a primary target of the 1988 Family Development Act. This legislation was the first of several federal policies that foretold the country's expectations for economic self-sufficiency in this population. To qualify for benefits, however, the adolescent mother and her baby had to live with her parents and had to go to work when her child turned three, whether or not she had finished high school (Gibbs, 1992; Testa, 1992).

The 1996 Temporary Assistance to Needy Families (TANF) policy provided adolescent female welfare recipients with essentially the same restrictions as adult welfare recipients but with the added conditions that the adolescent women must live with their parents and attend school to receive benefits (Rains, Davies, & McKinnon, 1998). Other than child care assistance, TANF does not address nor provide for support services of any kind to assist adolescent mothers (Kelly, 1996; Rains et al., 1998). Thus, because of the societal context and current sociopolitical climate that demands economic independence of adolescent mothers, it is more important than ever to diligently address protective factors that help adolescent women and men delay parenthood until they have economic viability. When adolescents choose the path of early parenthood, it is equally important to help them find the resources to modify risk factors.

DESCRIPTION OF RISK AND PROTECTIVE FACTORS

Chapter 2 defined risk and protective factors in different ways. Differing definitions of risk in research studies have blurred the understanding of what is meant by this term. Risk, for example, may be defined as the probability that adolescent pregnancy will occur. It can be understood as a condition that is associated with the outcome of adolescent pregnancy or events that precede the outcome of a girl becoming pregnant. Risk may be viewed as a cause of the condition of adolescent pregnancy, or as a factor, that if it were changed, would prevent the adolescent from becoming pregnant (Kraemer, Stice, Kazdin, Offord, & Kupfer, 2001). For the social problem of adolescent pregnancy, risk might be best understood as the context in and circumstances under which adolescent pregnancy occurs and becomes a societal problem. Risk, therefore, is understood as a chain of causal events or as a set of risk factors that mediate and modify one another in such as way that not one of these risk factors can be understood except in the context of all the other risk factors involved (Kraemer et al., 2001).

In this chapter, protective factors are broadly defined as those influences and situations that modify risk. Smith and Carlson (1997) pointed out that a large group of interdisciplinary researchers have confirmed "three domains of protective or modifying influences: individual attributes of the child, or adolescent, the climate and resources within the family, and support systems within the wider environment" (p. 14). For the social problem of adolescent pregnancy, a protective factor is any modification to the context and circumstances within these three domains that are associated with adolescent pregnancy and its undesirable consequences. Table 10-1 describes the risk and protective factors for adolescent pregnancy across these domains.

Research has provided volumes of information on the high-risk conditions that are associated with adolescent pregnancy and the modifying influences that appear to work, but causal or explanatory models are not as forthcoming. Table 10-1 shows that there are no simple paths to understanding all the risk factors that lead to an adolescent becoming pregnant nor to understanding the protective factors that prevent pregnancy or ameliorate its undesirable consequences. Similar to other types of human behavior, the risk and protective factors for adolescent pregnancy are complex, interrelated, and bound by context to a high degree. In fact, a review of this chapter quickly informs the reader that many of the risk factors associated with adolescent pregnancy are also risk factors for other childhood problems. For example, low socioeconomic status (SES) and

Table 10-1. Risk and Protective Factors for Adolescent Pregnancy

	RISK FACTORS	PROTECTIVE FACTORS
Wider social environment	• Poverty/low SES • Inadequate social welfare, health, and educational system for adolescents	• Adolescent health services (such as school-based clinics) • Asset-based welfare system • Alternative schools and educational programs for pregnant and parenting teens • Education completion • Job and career placement • Child care and other social support systems
Immediate social environment of family	• Lack of educational achievement/ or being a dropout • Low job skills • Unmarried childbirth or being a single parent • Family structure of parents: single parent, chaotic, low SES, permissive sexual attitudes • Physical abuse and living in high-risk environment	• High educational achievement and staying in school • Job training and advanced education • Marriage or two-earner household • Two-parent family background: parents with higher SES and education • Open family communication • Closeness to parents, especially mother • Parental control of dating and supervision • Father involvement
Immediate social environment of neighborhood and community	• Peers who are sexually active, do not use contraceptives effectively, or have borne a child • Lack of family and community supports	• Religious affiliation and attendance • Prosocial peers who delay sex or use contraceptives • Social support from family, friends, and community • Pregnancy prevention programs
Individual attributes	• Younger age at pregnancy (14 or younger) • Substance use and abuse • Sexual abuse • Lack of knowledge or resistance to the use of contraceptives • Low motivation toward academic achievement and career orientation • Hopeless attitude toward future • Repeat pregnancies and multiple childbirths in a short period of time	• Academic achievement • Delaying sex or pregnancy to 18 or older • Normal development, lack of substance use and other behaviors indicative of behavioral disorders • Effective use of contraceptives • Goal directed, high educational aspiration and career goals • Hopeful future goals and plans beyond parenthood • Delaying repeat pregnancy
Health risks	• Health risks (toxemia, anemia, cephalopelvic disproportion, hypertension) • Low birth weight • Infant mortality • Deficits to maternal and child nutrition • Obesity • Stunted growth of mother	• Older at pregnancy (16 or older) • Prenatal and perinatal care

lack of parental monitoring are risk factors for other, more serious, behavioral disorders. In a similar manner, the protective factors that modify risk are similar for many childhood disorders. In general, protective factors follow themes associated with good child development coupled with an enriching, nurturing, and caring social environment.

Protective factors for youths and adolescents, including those who are at risk for early pregnancy, appear to occur in the immediate social environments of family, peer, and community settings, whereas key contextual and wider system variables (such as discrimination, poverty, and low SES) are believed to exert moderating influences on these other areas (Resnick et al., 1997; Wallace, 1999). For example, being from a single-parent family with little parental oversight may be a risk factor for pregnancy, but if the family is a member of an ethnic minority and has a low SES, these factors moderate and greatly increase risk: Ethnic minorities are disproportionately socially and economically disadvantaged.

RISK AND PROTECTIVE FACTORS ASSOCIATED WITH THE WIDER SOCIAL ENVIRONMENT

High SES serves as a protective factor, whereas low SES is a prominent risk factor for early pregnancy and childbearing (Abrahamse, Morrison, & Waite, 1988; Barnett, Papini, & Gbur, 1991; Corcoran, Franklin, & Bennett, 2000; Hanson, Myers, & Ginsburg 1987; Kalil & Kunz, 1999; Mayfield-Brown, 1989; Robbins, Kaplan, & Martin, 1985; Shah & Zelnik, 1981). For higher-income youth, the costs associated with adolescent parenting (such as lack of educational achievement and limited career potential) seem very high, and adolescent parenting is seen as having negative consequences. For low-income adolescents, however, childbearing may seem more attractive and may even be viewed as a way to achieve personal fulfillment (Luker, 1996). For instance, a survey of 42 adolescent fathers compared with demographically similar young men who were not parents found that the fathers believed that parenthood would not interfere with their futures. Fathers were also less likely to have developed a concrete five-year plan (Gohel, Diamond, & Chambers, 1997).

A substantial proportion (40 percent) of adolescents at risk for pregnancy live in poverty and will continue to live in poverty into their 20s if they choose the path of early childbearing (Moore et al., 1993). The majority of pregnant and parenting adolescents (80 percent) have received public assistance—almost half (44 percent) have received it for more than five years (Maynard, 1995). A protective factor, gleaned from longitudinal data, is that initial dependence on public assistance may offer benefits for the adolescent parent so that she can graduate from high school (Harris 1991).

Public Attitudes and Policies

Societal attitudes and policies against adolescent pregnancy may inadvertently act as a risk factor by spurring on the formulation of faulty policies and public programs that delimit services that can modify risk for adolescents. Wilson (2000) reported in a 1999 survey of public school district superintendents, for example, that although school district policies on sexuality education are widespread (two in three districts), only 14 percent of these districts had comprehensive policies that built a knowledge of both abstinence and contraceptives. More than half of the surveyed districts (51 percent) had abstinence as the preferred option for instruction, when contraception was also discussed. Just over one-third (35 percent) had abstinence as the only basis for instruction, with discussion of contraception forbidden. This approach is highly political and is driven by parents and advocates who object to adolescents participating in sex and who further believe that contraceptive knowledge increases the likelihood of pregnancy. Abstinence as the focal approach, however, runs contrary to the research evidence, which suggests that contraceptive knowledge building and distribution is the best method for reducing pregnancy in sexually active adolescents (Franklin, Grant, Corcoran, O'Dell, & Bultman, 1997).

RISK AND PROTECTIVE FACTORS ASSOCIATED WITH THE IMMEDIATE SOCIAL ENVIRONMENT OF THE FAMILY

In research studies, several aspects of family life have been found to serve as risk and protective factors for adolescent pregnancy: family conflict (Barth, Schinke, & Maxwell, 1983); family stress (Robbins et al., 1985); family strengths (Barnett et al., 1991); family problem solving, family communication, roles, affective responsiveness, affective involvement, and behavior control (Corcoran et al., 2000); and adaptability and cohesion (Barnett et al., 1991). An effective family support system has been found to be one of the most critical factors related to successful adjustment of adolescent mothers (Cutrona & Russell, 1990).

The presence of high family conflict and stress has been demonstrated to have a negative affect on the adolescent mother and her child. Researchers have identified the baby's father as a possible alternative source of support in the absence of a supportive family environment (Kalil, Spencer, Spieker, & Gilchrist, 1998; Wasserman, Brunelli, & Rauh, 1990). Some studies on social support and personal networks for adolescent mothers, however, omit fathers altogether (for example, Richardson, Barbour, & Bubenzer, 1995). Other studies on these issues include the baby's father when he has been identified by mothers as an important source of support (de Anda & Becerra, 1984; Wasserman et al., 1990).

Findings are mixed regarding these fathers' level of involvement with their children. Rhein and colleagues (1997) found that 93 percent of adolescent mothers believed that the fathers should provide financial support and participate in raising the child, whereas only 58 percent of the fathers believed they should do so. Studies have validated that most adolescent fathers provide some financial support and sustain contact with the mother and their child (Miller, 1997). Because there is evidence that a large percentage of young mothers perceive the father of their baby as an important source of support, the potential for this relationship to act as a protective factor is strong.

There is much public discourse on risk factors associated with coming from a single-parent family. Adolescents from single-parent homes are sexually active at earlier ages than are those from two-parent families (see Corcoran, 2000, for a review) and are at increased risk for early pregnancy and parenting (Gohel et al., 1997; Kalil & Kunz, 1999; Robbins et al., 1985).

Several mechanisms may affect this process. First, single-parent status tends to be confounded with low SES (McAnarney & Hendee, 1989a), a chief variable associated with both early sexual activity and childbearing. A role modeling effect may also take place, in which single parents may date and be sexually active themselves. Whereas in two-parent families, two adults can provide financial security, guidance, and emotional support (Young, Jensen, Olsen, & Cundick, 1991), single parents are more likely to work full time and, therefore, not be as available for supervising, monitoring, or spending time with their child (Newcomer & Udry, 1987).

Researchers have found that parental supervision and monitoring of dating assumes a protective function for preventing adolescent pregnancy (Hanson et al., 1987; Perkins, Luster, Villarruel, & Small, 1998; Santelli & Beilenson, 1992). So does explicit disapproval of sexual activity from parents (McAnarney & Hendee, 1989a), especially in the context of a close mother–daughter relationship (Jaccard, Dittus, & Gordon, 1996). Parental communication about sexuality that occurs in an open and skilled manner serves as a protective factor against early pregnancies and also increases condom use (Whitaker, Miller, May, & Levin, 1999).

Lack of parental monitoring and general family dysfunction leave adolescents without guidance, supervision, and clear rules and norms for behavior. This allows adolescents to go unchecked and increases risky behaviors, such as drug and alcohol use and participation with multiple sexual partners.

Lack of parental monitoring also opens opportunities for the adolescent to be sexually exploited by others. Recent studies indicate that over half of the fathers of babies born to adolescent mothers are five or more years older than the mother and that many are well into adulthood (Rhein et al., 1997). Compared with teenagers whose first partner had been roughly their age, adolescents with a partner at least three years older than themselves were younger at first intercourse (13.8 years versus 14.6 years), less likely to use a condom both at first and most recent intercourse, used condoms less consistently, and were more likely to become pregnant (38 percent versus 12 percent; Miller, Clark, & Moore, 1997).

RISK AND PROTECTIVE FACTORS ASSOCIATED WITH THE IMMEDIATE SOCIAL ENVIRONMENT OF NEIGHBORHOOD AND COMMUNITY

Social support from an adolescent's immediate social environment of neighborhood and community includes peers, school, religious institutions, and health care systems. Each has the potential to offer protective factors against early pregnancy and to support positive outcomes for pregnant and parenting adolescents. Several risk factors for adolescent pregnancy have been shown in studies to be positively affected by providing adequate social support to adolescents. These factors include: birthweight (Oakley, 1985), maternal adjustment (Barth & Schinke, 1983; Causby, Nixon, & Bright, 1991; Rhodes & Woods, 1995; Schilmoeller, Baranowski, & Higgins, 1991; Unger & Wandersman, 1988), parenting behavior (Colletta & Lee, 1983; Reis & Herz, 1987; Schilmoeller & Baranowski, 1985), child development knowledge (Schilmoeller & Baranowski, 1985), infant health outcomes (Turner, Grindstaff, & Phillips, 1990), family relationships (Causby et al., 1991), and maternal satisfaction with pregnancy and prenatal and postpartum health care (Giblin, Poland, & Sachs, 1987).

Neighborhood and Community

The risk of adolescent pregnancy is elevated for adolescents living in an urban area where there is a high percentage of female-headed households (Kalil & Kunz, 1999). In such communities, social support for prosocial, future-oriented behaviors are not consistently provided, and sanctions against early childbearing may be lacking. The adolescent may also perceive very few opportunities for a bright future.

Peers

Peers of both genders have an affect on an adolescent's decision to become sexually active. According to a summary of a survey released by the National Campaign to Prevent Teen Pregnancy (1997), a large majority of girls said that they received pressure from boys and other girls to be sexually active. Many girls reported fear of losing their boyfriends if they refused to have sex.

Peer group attitudes and behaviors further influence an adolescent's likelihood of parenting at a young age. A best friend who has been pregnant is implicated in adolescent repeat pregnancies (Gillmore, Lewis, Lohr, Spencer, & White, 1997). Male teens who believed their peers viewed early childbearing as favorable were more likely to be fathers (Gohel et al., 1997). Adolescents from families with problematic relationships might be more susceptible to negative influences by peers (Yamaguchi & Kandel, 1987), demonstrating interaction effects between factors.

School

Academic achievement and positive school experiences act as protective factors to prevent pregnancy. Research has shown that career and academic development are linked to the prevention of pregnancy (see, for example, Kirby, 2001).

Supportive school environments that help pregnant and parenting adolescents finish high school are essential protective factors that affect a variety of other life outcomes. An essential protective factor for pregnant and parenting adolescents is for them to attain more education before and after the pregnancy. Research suggests that adolescent mothers who are attending school do better in adolescent pregnancy programs and have more successful long-term outcomes (Seitz & Apfel, 1999). A multivariate study by Sandfort and Hill (1996) concluded that a woman's income increases $917 annually for every year of education that she receives.

Religious Institutions

Religious institutions play an important role in the resilience of adolescents (Smith, 1994). Most of the research indicates that commitment to a religion acts as a protective factor against early sexual activity (for example, Bingham, Miller, & Adams, 1990; DiBlasio & Benda, 1990; Flewelling & Bauman, 1990; Forste & Heaton, 1988; Thornton & Camburn, 1989). Placing a high importance on religion and prayer and attendance at parochial schools appear to serve as protective factors against the early onset of sexual intercourse (Resnick et al., 1997).

Health Care Systems

It is extremely important for pregnant and parenting adolescents to receive excellent prenatal and postnatal care. Because many pregnant adolescents are poor they may not have access to adequate health care resources, which greatly increases their risk of health problems. Obstetric health risks to adolescent mothers include such conditions as toxemia, anemia, cephalopelvic disproportion, and hypertension. Adverse health risks to the child include low birthweight, prematurity, and infant mortality. These conditions are probably overattributed in the early literature to the physiologic immaturity of the adolescent. It is now recognized, however, that sociodemographic factors, such as low SES or single status, actually confound these variables.

When adolescents receive good medical care their risk for negative health outcomes substantially decreases (McAnarney & Hendee, 1989a; Stevens-Simon & Beach, 1992; Turner et al., 1990). Ongoing relationships with health professionals, such as visiting nurses, have also been shown to reduce repeat pregnancies of adolescents and to produce overall favorable affects on the adolescent mother's adaptation and outcomes (Seitz & Apfel, 1999).

There is modest, inconclusive research on the relationship between adolescent childbearing and long-term health consequences. Although direct risk factors from childbearing have not been demonstrated, adolescent childbearing appears to be related to obesity and hypertension (Stevens-Simon & Beach, 1992). Stevens-Simon and Beach cited additional evidence, although it is inconclusive, that lactation in adolescent mothers might result in a greater likelihood of bone demineralization. Furthermore, depletion of nutrient reserves could contribute to the greater likelihood of neonatal risk in subsequent pregnancies. The evidence is mixed about whether infants of adolescents suffer from higher mortality rates. Some reviews suggest that infants of adolescent mothers have a greater mortality rate in the first 28 days of life (McAnarney & Hendee, 1989b).

RISK AND PROTECTIVE FACTORS ASSOCIATED WITH INDIVIDUAL ATTRIBUTES

Developmental psychopathology and behavioral disorders can increase the risk for early sexual behavior in adolescents (Franklin & Corcoran, 1999), but overall individual psychological attributes, such as self-esteem, do not predict pregnancy or other social and contextual situations. Substance use, sexual abuse, repeat pregnancies, and lack of academic achievement are the individual attributes most associated with risk. Personal distress, developmental crisis, depression, and role conflicts are also evident in pregnant and parenting adolescents.

Substance Use

Substance use is associated with one-third of adolescents' unplanned pregnancies (Flanigan, Mclean, Hall, & Propp, 1990). Numerous studies link substance use and sexuality (Elliott & Morse, 1989; Mott & Haurin, 1988; Perkins et al., 1998; Zabin, Hardy, Smith, & Hirsch, 1986). Substance use contributes to pregnancy by increasing teens' susceptibility to acting on sexual impulses without considering possible consequences. Because of substance use, teenagers may make poor partner choices, have unprotected sex, and forget sexual experiences (Franklin & Corcoran, 1999).

Physical and Sexual Abuse

Some pregnant and parenting adolescents have experienced a history of physical abuse and neglect that also may contribute to their participation in risk-taking behaviors such as drug abuse and early sexual activity. Their abuse history puts pregnant and parenting adolescents at further risk for maltreatment of their own children. Maltreatment researchers, however, have done little systematic examination of child maltreatment by adolescent mothers (Zuravin & DiBlasio, 1996).

Zuravin and DiBlasio (1996) were the first to identify discriminating characteristics between adolescent mothers with maltreated children and adolescent mothers whose children were not maltreated. The results showed less difference between abusive and nonabusive mothers than between neglectful and nonneglectful mothers. Abusers were more likely than nonabusers to have had a mother with emotional problems, to have been "loners" as children, to have lived in a family that received Aid to Families with Dependent Children, and to have been unattached to their mother figure. Neglectors were more likely than nonneglectors to have been sexually abused, to have run away from home, to have been in trouble with the law, and to have lived with multiple caretakers. Neglectors were also more likely to have had a miscarriage or abortion before their first childbirth, to have had their first child at a younger age, and to have had a premature or low-birthweight first child. Neglectors also completed fewer grades in school than nonabusive and abusive mothers. We concluded that the correlates of maltreatment—physical abuse and neglect by adolescent mothers—were similar to correlates identified in older mothers.

Adolescents who are pregnant and parenting also have high rates of sexual abuse (see, for example, Luster & Small, 1997; Stock, Bell, Boyer, & Connell, 1997). Large-scale surveys indicate that teens who have been sexually abused have had sex by age 15 (Raj, Silverman, & Amaro, 2000; Stock et al., 1997), have had more partners (Luster & Small, 1997; Raj et al., 2000; Stock et al., 1997), have failed to use birth control at last intercourse (Stock et al., 1997), and were more likely to have been pregnant or to have caused a pregnancy (Raj et al., 2000).

Lack of Academic Achievement

Adolescents with poor school performance and failure are at risk for early sexual experience and childbearing (Abrahamse et al., 1988; Beutel, 2000; Hofferth, 1987; Perkins et al., 1998; Robbins et al., 1985; Santelli & Beilenson, 1992) and may see early parenting as a viable alternative (DeBolt, Pasley, & Kreutzer, 1990). Rauch-Elnekave (1994) suggested that some adolescents may choose childbearing as a life path as a result of academic difficulties and the general social acceptance they find in early parenting.

Pregnant and parenting adolescents are at significant risk for high school dropout. Dropping out of high school not only affects the young mother's immediate goals and options but it is also a major factor in subsequent underemployment and the increased probability that she and her child will live in poverty (Card & Wise, 1978; Martin, Hill, & Welch, 1998).

Within the pregnant and parenting adolescent population, reasons for dropping out of school can be grouped into the three categories: institutional, personal, and familial (DeBolt et al., 1990; Kissman, 1998). School-related factors that have been shown to influence dropout rates in pregnant and parenting adolescents are rigid school requirements for attendance, minimal encouragement from school staff to continue in school, and lack of individual considerations (Black & DeBlassie, 1985; Fine, 1986; Kissman, 1998). Being below grade level and having low educational goals characterized by high absenteeism have also been found to significantly decrease the likelihood of staying in school for pregnant or parenting adolescents (DeBolt et al., 1990; Furstenberg, Brooks-Gunn, & Morgan, 1987; Roosa, 1986; Wehlage & Rutter, 1986; Weidman & Friedman, 1984).

Repeat Pregnancies

Seitz and Apfel (1999) reported, in a comprehensive review of the research literature, that mothers who did not postpone childbearing were more likely to maintain long-term welfare dependency and were less likely to complete their educations or to have children with higher achievement. Delaying repeat pregnancy serves as a protective factor for adolescent parents. A 20-year follow-up of 121 African American adolescent parents found that success—which was defined as either being employed or being supported by a spouse, and having a high school education—was associated with having only one or two children after the first childbirth (Horwitz, Klerman, Kuo, & Jekel, 1991). Preventing rapid, repeat childbearing also appears to be a protective factor for the children of adolescent parents.

Experimental studies have indicated that brief prenatal and postnatal interventions and prolonged contacts and education with mothers after childbirth had substantive impacts on rapid, repeat childbearing. Interventions, such as nurse visitation in the home and ongoing educational classes, were found to be effective for decreasing rapid, repeat childbearing (Seitz & Apfel, 1999).

Developmental and Emotional Crisis

Adolescent pregnancy and parenting present developmental and emotional crises for adolescents (Martin et al., 1998; Osofsky, Osofsky, & Diamond, 1988; Pines, 1988; Trad, 1994), and the demands of parenting create considerable distress and psychological turmoil for parenting teens (Corcoran et al., 2000). Role conflicts, stress, depression, and a lack of coping skills have been associated with pregnancy and parenting for adolescents. Whereas a young woman is trying to develop autonomy and self-identity by becoming pregnant, she is thrust into a premature parental role, requiring problem solving, parenting skills, and socioeconomic roles and other adult competencies that she has not yet acquired (de Anda et al., 1992).

RISK AND PROTECTIVE FACTORS ASSOCIATED WITH AGE, GENDER, AND RACE OR ETHNICITY

Age

Results of a meta-analysis on pregnancy prevention programs indicate that older adolescents (ages 15 to 19) perform better on contraceptive-use measures than women 14 and younger (Franklin et al., 1997). In addition, younger females use less effective methods (for example, condoms and withdrawal) and use contraception less consistently (Alan Guttmacher Institute, 1996), suggesting that adolescents are more at risk for pregnancy if they engage in sex at a younger age. Younger adolescents are also at risk for complications in pregnancy, because they may deny or conceal their condition, thus delaying optimal prenatal care (Brooks-Gunn & Furstenberg, 1986).

Age of the adolescent at the time of pregnancy appears to be an important factor in whether or not the adolescent drops out of school. Studying retrospective data from 6,288 women between ages 14 and 22, Mott and Marsiglio (1985) reported that 55 percent of 15-year-old pregnant adolescents, and 70 percent of those younger than 15, had dropped out of school. Thus, the conclusion that younger mothers are less likely to complete high school than those over age 15 is well-supported (DeBolt et al., 1990; Moore & Wertheimier, 1982; Trussel, 1984; Waite & Moore, 1978). Furthermore, younger age at first pregnancy may affect adolescents' abilities to get off welfare (Harris, 1991; Rudd, McKenry, & Nah, 1990).

Gender

Pregnancy has been defined and framed by our society as a female problem, perhaps reflecting the double standard that still operates concerning differing sexual responsibilities and roles of males and females. This, unfortunately, has led to the neglect of the father's role in adolescent pregnancy and parenting, even though several of these fathers offer social support and financial resources to the mother and child (Miller, 1997).

Race and Ethnicity

"Women of color are the most adversely affected by early pregnancies and undereducation, and lack of marketable skills, which reduce the chances for economic self-sufficiency not only for themselves but also for their children" (Aguilar, 1995, p. 146). Poor women from ethnic minority groups not only face the risks usually associated with adolescent pregnancy but also discrimination, stigmas, and recrimination by their cultural identification groups who may also disapprove of their behavior.

Adolescents of ethnic minority groups are at greater risk for pregnancies than white American and non-Hispanic American groups. African American adolescent females have a birth rate of 91.4 per 1,000; Hispanic American adolescents have the highest birth rate among adolescents, with a rate of 101.8 per 1,000 (Alan Guttmacher Institute, 1998).

African American adolescents tend to initiate substance use at younger ages with a commensurate risk for early pregnancy (see, for example, Elliott & Morse,

1989). When African Americans become parents, they are at increased risk for welfare dependence and for longer duration than their white American counterparts, in large part because they are more likely to remain single parents (Rudd et al., 1990). At 10 years after teenage pregnancy, 50 percent of African American mothers are living in poverty and two-thirds are welfare dependent (Maynard, 1996). There are also particular risks to the children of African American parents in terms of cognitive deficits, which first appear during the preschool years (Brooks-Gunn & Furstenberg, 1986; Corcoran, 1998).

Hispanic American females have the highest pregnancy and dropout rates of the other groups. The status dropout rates for Hispanic American youths born outside the United States, for example, are an astounding 44.2 percent. Studies within group variations indicate that the dropout rates for Hispanic Americans differ, with most of the risk being associated with Mexican Americans and Puerto Ricans. Little attention has been paid to the particular risk and protective factors for Hispanic Americans despite these high prevalence rates.

Some authors perceive that within the Hispanic American culture marriage is the accepted mode of support for women, and there is a strong emphasis on traditional family roles (Forste & Tienda, 1992; Jarrett, 1990). In an examination of data from the National Survey of Families and Households, Forste and Tienda identified several questions that support these generalizations. Of all ethnic groups in the data, Hispanic American women expressed the greatest disapproval of mothers working and were in most agreement that family comes before self and that divorce should be avoided.

A study by Uno, Florsheim, and Uchino (1998) suggested that a variety of stressors are associated with being an ethnic minority. Sociocultural stressors not commonly experienced by the dominant American culture are seen as factors in both early pregnancy and school dropout for women of color. For example, nearly half the sample in a study of 84 Mexican American college freshmen in southern Texas reported double standards in their families between support for their education and support for their brothers' education. Outside the family, they reported encountering negative cultural biases, such as teachers assuming they would drop out of school, and intolerance for their use of Spanish and their other cultural attitudes and behaviors (Aguilar, 1995).

The acculturation process has also been found to have an impact on adolescent pregnancy. Acculturation factors are crucial to understanding the unique stressors that adolescents of diverse race and ethnic identities experience (de Anda et al., 1992; de Anda & Becerra, 1984; Szapocznik, & Kurtines, 1993). For example, in a study by Del Rio (1999), on the relationship between acculturation and the occurrence of pregnancy among Mexican American adolescents, pregnant participants had made more cultural shifts than nonpregnant participants, and were clearly more acculturated. Pregnant adolescents identified themselves more with the dominant American culture than did their nonpregnant counterparts.

Balcazar, Peterson, and Cobas (1996) also found that their sample of highly acculturated pregnant Mexican American adolescents demonstrated higher stress levels associated with the cultural assimilation process. On the protective side, however, this study, as well as a subsequent similar study (Balcazar, Peterson, & Krull, 1997), found that highly acculturated Mexican women had also developed higher degrees of social support and a more diverse group of coping mechanisms for dealing with cultural transitions.

From a study of the interaction of acculturation and family cohesion, Balcazar and colleagues (1997) suggested that effective intervention strategies for highly acculturated pregnant women with low family cohesion should reflect an individualistic, rather than a familistic orientation. They suggested that the behaviors of this group were more likely to be influenced by peer rather than family relationships, and that these women would be more receptive to standard forms of medical care than American women with low family cohesion (Balcazar et al., 1997). This suggests that interventions with emphasis on individual skills and strengths, emphasizing dominant cultural values, and presented through standard treatment modalities, can be most effective with this group. The research also suggested that mainstream practices may serve as protective factors for more acculturated groups, whereas more culturally relevant programs must be used in situations in which individuals are less acculturated.

Assessment Measures

In this section, we describe two measures that assess adolescent problem solving and coping. In addition, we discuss one measure that assesses family relationships and one measure that assesses social support. Finally, we describe a measure that assesses global characteristics with relation to the behavioral functioning of adolescents. Practitioners may use these measures to assess risk and protective factors in adolescents and to monitor the effectiveness of intervention programs.

The Social Problem–Solving Inventory–Revised, Short Form

Rational problem solving (RPS), as assessed by this measure, is defined as the rational, deliberate, systematic, and skillful application of effective or adaptive problem-solving principles and techniques. The RPS subscale of the Short Form is comprised of five items that measure four problem-solving skills identified in D'Zurilla and Nezu's (1982) social problem-solving model: (1) problem definition and formulation, (2) generation of alternative solutions, (3) decision making, and (4) solution implementation and verification. Examples of items in the RPS subscale are "Before I try to solve a problem, I set a specific goal so that I know exactly what I want to accomplish" and "When I am trying to solve a problem, I think of as many options as possible until I cannot come up with any more ideas."

The Short Form of the RPS scale consists of five items taken directly from the 20-item RPS Long Form, with one or two items from each construct in the subscale (D'Zurilla, Nezu, & Maydeu-Olivares, 1996, cited in Harris & Franklin, 2001). In a norming sample of 601 college students, the RPS Short Form and Long Form correlated at .92. The Long Form contains 20 items on the RPS, for a possible score of 80. The Short Form contains five items for a possible score of 20. Given the high correlation on the RPS between the two forms, the means of norming samples for both the Short Form and the Long Form were used in examining the current sample. In six normal samples tested with the Long Form, means on the RPS converted as described ranged from 10.30 (SD = 12.90) to 11.98 (SD = 15.07). With four psychiatric or distressed samples group means ranged from 7.02 (SD = 16.98) to 9.04 (SD = 14.75). In a sample of 601 college students tested on the Short Form RPS, the mean was 10.88 (SD = 3.73). Concurrent validity was assessed by examining the correlations between the SPSI-R scale and the Problem-Solving Inventory (PSI), another well-known problem-solving inventory. The RPS subscale correlated significantly with the total PSI at 58 and significantly at 63 with the AAS, a comparable subscale in the PSI. Correlations between the SPSI-R Short Form and several external measures of psychological distress and well-being demonstrate good convergent and discriminant validity. In a test of discriminant validity, the RPS correlated significantly with anxiety at 18. In testing convergent validity, the correlation between RPS and life satisfaction was statistically significant at .20. Correlations with other overlapping and independent constructs were similar to these. Internal consistency reliability alpha on the RPS Short Form was .77 with a sample of 601, and .85 with a sample of 582. RPS test–retest reliability over a three-week period was .74.

ADOLESCENT COPING ORIENTATION FOR PROBLEM EXPERIENCES

Problem-focused coping was measured using the Adolescent Coping Orientation for Problem Experiences (A-COPE; Harris & Franklin, 2001). The A-COPE is a 54-item instrument designed to measure the behaviors that adolescents use in managing problems or difficult situations. Although avoidance and denial are identified among 12 factors of the instrument, this study was interested in measuring only problem-focused behaviors. The three factors, or subscales, used in the current study, comprised 18 items, were subscale 1, developing self-reliance and optimism; subscale 2, developing social support; and subscale 3, solving family problems.

Although clinical cutoff points are not available for the A-COPE, the instrument appears to be acceptable for research purposes. Normative data for the subscales used in this study for nonclinical adolescent females (N = 241) give a mean score of 60.19 with a standard deviation of 4.20 (Patterson & McCubbin, 1983). The subscales used in this study have good internal consistency reliability, with alphas ranging from .69 to .75. Test–retest data are not available, although reliability data from the Young Adult COPE, a slightly modified variation of A-COPE, show an overall alpha of .82 and a test–retest correlation of .83. Tests for concurrent validity yielded moderate correlations ranging from .09 to .25 between reported coping patterns and actual behaviors.

Both problem solving and coping have been shown to be protective factors in adolescents; these measures may be used by practitioners to monitor progress on ascertaining these skills in intervention programs.

FAMILY ENVIRONMENT SCALES

The Family Environment Scales (FES) evolved from research on social climates—that is, the unique personality or attributes of social environments (Moos, 1989). The FES is a 90-item, true–false, self-report measure that assesses whole family functioning, and is compatible with social and ecological-systems theory. It has 10 subscales that assess three construct dimensions: (1) relationship, (2) personal growth, (3) systems maintenance (organizational structure) of the family.

The 10 subscales for the dimensions are as follows: *relationship dimensions*—(1) cohesion, (2) expressiveness, (3) conflict; *personal growth dimensions*—(4) independence, (5) achievement orientation, (6) intellectual cultural orientation, (7) active recreational orientation, (8) moral religious emphasis; and *systems maintenance dimensions*—(9) organization and (10) control.

The FES has been widely used in both clinical research and practice and has been demonstrated to be an effective outcome measure.

The FES has excellent psychometric characteristics. The 10 subscales have demonstrated adequate internal consistency reliability ranging from .61 to .78. Test–retest reliability coefficients range from .68 to .86. The FES was constructed using factor analysis and the construct validity of the measure has been examined in over 200 studies. One limitation of this measure, however, is that it has not been widely normed on low SES families. (See Grotevant and Carlson, 1989, for a more detailed exploration of the psychometric studies on the FES.)

The FES offers a global assessment of family functioning than the FACES III described above. The first construct dimension of relationships comprised of cohesion, conflict, and expressiveness (reverse scored) have been used as a unitary measure of family support, and could be used this way in working with adolescents at risk for pregnancy because adolescents' perception of family support are important protective factors. (See Jordan and Franklin, 1995, for other reviews of measures of family functioning that may be helpful in assessing family risk and protective factors associated with adolescent pregnancy.)

SOCIAL SUPPORT BEHAVIORS

The Social Support Behaviors (SSB) was developed by Allen Vaux to measure five types of social support: emotional, socializing, practical assistance, financial assistance, and advice and guidance (Vaux, 1988). The SSB is a 45-item self-report, paper and pencil measure that asks adolescents to indicate, on the basis of past experiences, how likely a friend or a family member is to perform a supportive behavior. Because social support has been found to be a protective factor to pregnant and parenting adolescents, it is particularly important to know what types of supportive behaviors (for example emotional support versus financial assistance) that an adolescent is receiving from family and friends. The SSB was developed along with two other social support measures: the Social Support Resources (SSR) and the Social Support Appraisal Scale (SSA; Vaux, 1988). These measures were developed from differing conceptualizations of social support.

Several studies have provided evidence for the good psychometric characteristics of the SSB. Internal consistency reliability was tested on several samples of college students and found to be good, with alphas of .85. There is also evidence for the content, concurrent, predictive, and construct validity of the measure. Factor analysis supported the factor structure of the measure. (See Streeter and Franklin, 1992, for a review of eight other social support measures that may be used in clinical practice.)

HILSON ADOLESCENT PROFILE

The Hilson Adolescent Profile (HAP) is a standardized behavioral assessment instrument developed specifically to provide a behaviorally oriented assessment for troubled youth. It was designed as a screening tool to assess the presence and extent of adolescent behavior patterns and problems. In short, the purpose of the HAP is to help mental-health practitioners, school personnel, and professionals in the juvenile justice system identify adolescents at risk. The HAP is a 310-item self-report, true or false instrument. A shorter version of the measure is currently being developed. Scoring is based on a *t*-score distribution with a mean of 50 and a standard deviation of 10 (Inwald, Brobst, & Morrissey, 1987).

The HAP contains 16 subscales that fall along four construct dimensions: (1) validity measures, (2) "acting out" behaviors, (3) interpersonal adjustment measures, and (4) internalized conflict measures. The 16 subscales for the construct dimensions are as follows: *validity measure*—(1) guarded responses; *"acting out" behaviors*—(2) alcohol use, (3) drug use, (4) educational adjustment difficulties, (5) law violations, (6) frustration tolerance, (7) antisocial risk taking, (8) rigidity or obsessiveness; *interpersonal adjustment measures*—(9) interpersonal or assertiveness difficulties, (10) home life conflicts, (11) social sexual adjustment; *internalized conflict measures*—(12) health concerns, (13) anxiety phobic avoidance, (14) depression or suicide potential, (15) suspicious temperament, and (16) unusual responses.

Several of these subscales have relevance for assessing risk and protective factors associated with adolescent pregnancy. For example, the "alcohol use" and "drug use" subscales help clinicians identify youth with substance abuse problems, the "homelife conflicts" subscale has items that screen for sexual abuse, and the "educational adjustment difficulties" identifies youths with school and academic achievement problems that may serve as a risk factor for early childbearing.

The HAP has been shown to have good internal construct validity and external criterion–related validity. It has also been shown to have fair-to-good internal consistency reliability with KR20 coefficients ranging from .67 to .90. Most scales show reliability coefficients of .80 or better. Preliminary data on test–retest reliability showed Pearson correlation coefficients between the HAP scales at two periods ranged from .76 to .998, with 11 of the 16 scales having correlations of .95 or greater (Inwald et al., 1987).

IMPLICATIONS FOR PREVENTION AND INTERVENTION

The focus of this section is on effective treatments for working with adolescent pregnancy. Multicomponent interventions and cognitive–behavioral skills-building programs appear to be the most effective interventions. These types of programs have the most success in modifying the numerous risk factors that are associated with adolescent pregnancy and parenting.

INTERVENTIONS FOR PREGNANCY PREVENTION

Multicomponent programs offered in combination with schools and community agencies appear to be the most effective approaches to pregnancy prevention. A recent review by Kirby (2001), for example, discussed several interventions for the primary prevention of adolescent pregnancy, including comprehensive programs targeting both sexuality and development activities for youths. For example, Kirby (2001) recommended the multicomponent program offered by the Children's Aid Society known as the Carrera Program. This program was shown to reduce pregnancies for as long as three years. Carrera is an expensive, comprehensive program that includes five types of interventions that are offered in combination with one another over time: (1) family-life and sex education, (2) individual academic assessment and preparation for standardized tests and college prep exams, (3) tutoring, (4) self-expression activities through the use of the arts, and (5) comprehensive health and mental-health care.

Certain other types of service learning programs which require youths to volunteer in the community and participate in journaling, group reflections, classroom activities and discussions also show a great deal of promise for interventions of a non-sexual nature that have a substantial effect on pregnancy prevention. According to a recent survey, 32 percent of school districts, and close to 50 percent of high schools, used service learning in their curriculums (Westat & Chapman, 1999).

Service learning has been defined in various ways. Service learning can be defined as "curriculum based community service that integrates classroom instruction with community service activities" (Westat & Chapman, 1999, p. 3). The community service must be organized in relation to a class, and there must be clearly stated objectives and classroom goals. Authors usually differentiate service learning from community service alone, but not all school districts offer service learning instruction in the same manner; in some cases these activities may not be developed in ways that have been found to be effective in pregnancy studies. Practitioners can work with schools to increase the amount of service learning offered in high schools and to ensure that service-learning courses are offered in the most effective ways possible.

Fortunately, several evidenced-based curriculums for preventing adolescent pregnancy are also available for practitioners to use with adolescent groups. These curriculums have clearly written manuals and materials and have been found to be effective in one or more experimental and quasi-experimental studies on pregnancy prevention. Some of the curriculums have been widely tested in numerous studies and found to be effective. The Postponing Sexual Involvement curriculum, for example falls into this category (Kirby, 2001). Clinical practitioners working with pregnancy prevention in schools and community organizations should offer these types of evidenced-based curriculums. (See Corcoran and Franklin, 2002, and Franklin and Corcoran, 1999, for a summary of the respective curriculums and for more information on obtaining these materials.)

INTERVENTIONS FOR PREGNANT AND PARENTING ADOLESCENTS

According to Harris and Franklin (2001) adolescent parents face challenges in four domains that predict their economic and social well-being as adults: (1) education, (2) employment, (3) social relationships, and (4) parenting. Of these, the most immediate and well-researched predictor of long-term economic status is education. Enhancing education is perhaps the most protective intervention factor for adolescents who become pregnant. Research suggests a need for offering interventions to adolescent mothers in the very beginning of their roles as mothers, and several authors have also emphasized the benefit of offering the programs in a school setting to mothers who are still attending school (for example Fischer, 1997; Seitz & Apfel, 1999) Studies related to school achievement identify regular attendance and the maintenance of a reasonably age-appropriate grade level as the most important predictors of high school graduation. The importance of school interventions cannot be overstated in designing effective programs for pregnant and parenting adolescents.

Discussion of school achievement, usually focused on retention and dropout, is found abundantly in the education literature (Beck, 1991; Burdell, 1998; Fine; 1986; Steinberg, Blinde, & Chan, 1984, for example) as well as that of the other social sciences (Arons & Schwartz, 1993; Franklin, McNeil, & Wright, 1991; Pearson & Banerji, 1993; Srebnik & Elias, 1993, for example). Intervention related to dropout prevention and recovery is supported by a sizable group of outcome studies (Pearson & Banerji, 1993; Rodriguez, 1995; Vallerand, Fortier, & Guay, 1997), although these interventions were tested over a brief period and follow-up studies were not located that determine long-term outcome.

The dominant prevention strategy for all dropouts, including pregnant and parenting populations, is the alternative school model that has become increasingly common in school systems across the country since the mid-1970s. Although social workers, as well as nurses or public health staff, are usually part of the professional teams in these settings, the programs are structured academically, providing such special courses as sex education, and health, life planning, parenting, and job training (Griffin, 1998; Zellman, 1981), and are primarily administered and staffed by special education and regular high school teachers.

The type of alternative school that appears to work for dropout prevention and retrieval for a large number of diverse youths in urban school districts, including pregnant and parenting adolescents is a small school of choice. The school of choice offers short, flexible schedules, individualized, self-paced learning, and ongoing help with removing the social, psychological, and educational barriers to learning and achievement (Franklin, 1996). (See Figure 10-1 for examples of educational interventions used in alternative schools to prevent dropout among pregnant and parenting adolescents, and Seitz and Apfel, 1999, for other interventions for pregnant and parenting adolescents.)

COGNITIVE–BEHAVIORAL SKILLS–BUILDING PROGRAMS FOR ADOLESCENT PREGNANCY PREVENTION

In a review of programs and practices for adolescent pregnancy prevention, Franklin and Corcoran (1999) identified cognitive–behavioral skills building as an important component for pregnancy prevention programs, using the examples of mastery experiences and processing of logical consequences found frequently in current cognitive behavioral interventions with adolescents. Cognitive–behavioral skills-building programs are gaining wide support in the literature as effective methods for helping adolescents with a wide range of problems. Effective interventions using a cognitive–behavioral skills-building approach have been reported for the primary pregnancy prevention of adolescent pregnancy; with Mexican American adolescent mothers; and for

Figure 10-1

Examples of Effective Educational Programs and Practices Used in Alternative Schools to Prevent Dropout among Pregnant and Parenting Adolescents

High-tech learning modules and enterprise learning. Students have access to computers and computer-based instruction. Computer-based, self-paced instruction is integrated with enterprise learning. Enterprise learning uses hands-on learning experiences in the community where the youth can also earn money and run a business. For example, students have an opportunity to learn horticulture as a part of their science classes. They also participate in landscape design, gardening, and landscaping activities where as a class they bid, win the bid, and carry out projects in the community.

Service learning. Youths volunteer in the community and participate in journaling, group reflections, classroom activities, and discussions. Service learning uses curriculum-based community service that integrates classroom instruction with community service activities. The community service is organized in relation to a class such as science or math and there are clearly stated objectives and classroom goals for learning.

Work and career preparation. Hands-on life skills preparation courses on topics such as career exploration, learning styles, communication skills, goal setting, and workplace skills. Employers are brought on to campus for meetings and workshops. Students are placed in businesses for service learning opportunities. There are numerous opportunities for taking classes at the local junior college and preparing for additional education and training.

Special curriculums and support groups for pregnant and parenting students. Youths who become pregnant or are already parenting and stay in school have better life outcomes, including less welfare dependency, than those who leave school prematurely. Alternative schools offer specialized curricula such as "The Taking Charge Curriculum" to its pregnant and parenting adolescent women. This curriculum was developed by Mary Beth Harris, PhD, and Cynthia Franklin, PhD, at the School of Social Work at the University of Texas at Austin and was first tested on the border in El Paso, Texas, with impoverished Mexican Americans. Compared with a control group, the curriculum was found to be successful in helping adolescent women stay in school and to maintain their grades (Harris & Franklin, 2001).

Early childhood development, lab and parenting learning experiences. Alternative schools operate a day care and preschool program for the children of their pregnant and parenting students. Some schools provide pregnant and parenting teens opportunities to observe and work with college-trained child care professionals and skilled parent leaders so that they can more effectively learn how to be exceptional parents.

Mentoring as an intervention strategy. Zippay's (1995) exploratory study and Rubenstein, Panzarine, and Lanning's (1990) one-group preexperimental study on the impact of mentors for employment skills and social support with pregnant and parenting adolescents suggest positive potential for the mentoring relationship with school dropouts, employment skills, social support, and mother–child health. Although design flaws leave room for doubt about their specific results, studies show that individual

Figure 10-1

(continued)

---

attention and mentoring show promise for modifying risk in pregnant or parenting adolescents (Flynn, 1999; Rubenstein et al., 1990; Seitz & Apfel, 1999).

Brief treatment models: School-based programs more often limit pregnant and parenting adolescents to much shorter periods during which they may continue in special programs following the birth of their baby (for example, Seitz & Apfel, 1993). Schools tend to use short-term interventions. Some research supports the effectiveness of this approach. Dupper's (1998) intervention for dropout prevention and de Anda's (1998) intervention for stress management found significant results within 10 weeks, for example.

Home visitation and outreach teams. Nurse home visiting extended from seven weeks to three years postpartum are effective in terms of preventing repeat childbearing and child maltreatment, reducing welfare dependence and criminal activity, compared with those who did not receive such services (Seitz & Apfel, 1999). School social workers make home visits to retrieve dropout youths and assist the youths in making application to the school of choice. School social workers also work with youths and families to provide information, referral, and psychoeducation and to enable youths to resolve the psychosocial barriers that prevents their school success.

Health, mental health, and social services: Many alternative schools offer a variety of support services to help adolescents who are distressed and who have social problems to finish their education. Case management and individual, group, and family counseling may be available; also available may be a wide variety of health services, such as family planning services (Franklin, 1996; Griffin, 1998).

---

school dropout, drug and alcohol addiction, antisocial behavior, childhood sexual abuse, and depression (Barth, 1985, 1989; Clarke, 1992; Forman, Linney, & Brondino, 1990; Franklin & Corcoran, 1999; Harris & Franklin, 2001; Hogue & Liddle, 1999; Long & Sherer, 1984; McWhirter & Page, 1999; Schinke, Blythe, & Gilchrist, 1981). Other adolescent issues such as problem school behavior (Dupper, 1998), stress and anxiety associated with being an adolescent parent (de Anda et al., 1992), and anger management (St. Lawrence, Crosby, Belcher, Yazdani, & Brasfield, 1999) have also been shown to be positively affected when practitioners used a cognitive–behavioral skills-training approach.

Cognitive–behavioral programs strengthen individual protective factors such as coping with stress, goal setting, and problem solving (Dupper, 1998; Forman et al., 1990; Rice & Meyer, 1994). Enhancing locus of control—a cognitive concept theoretically bound to coping and problem-solving skills—is frequently a goal of these programs. Locus of control has also been used as an outcome variable in studies of skills-building interventions (McWhirter & Page, 1999; Rice & Meyer, 1994). Some interventions also include strategies for mastery of new behaviors associated with education, employment, social relationships, and health (Griffin, 1998; Jemmont, Jemmont, Fong, & McCaffree, 1999). These types of behaviors have also been shown to be protective factors for adolescent pregnancy prevention and have been associated in research studies as potential modifers for the negative outcomes associated with being a pregnant and parenting adolescent.

CORE INTERVENTIONS USED IN COGNITIVE– BEHAVIORAL PROGRAMS

Common to all cognitive–behavioral skills-based approaches with adolescents is a set of four specific steps that has been found to be effective in the acquisition of new skills: (1) practitioner modeling the skill, (2) clients role playing and practicing new skills in session, (3) clients being assigned homework to continue practicing the skills in their daily lives, and (4) practitioner gaining feedback from clients about their successes in learning the skills and adjusting the training to accommodate individual differences that may be encountered in learning (Hogue & Liddle, 1999).

Skills training programs appear to be most effective when they promote a sense of social support, social competence, and self-efficacy, which are believed to also represent important protective factors for adolescent pregnancy prevention. Role playing and in-session, task-related work and homework assignments also appear to be effective tools for learning, as are group-based, peer-support, and positive reinforcement for the skills that adolescents master.

The same cognitive behavioral skills as those identified with other adolescent groups—coping skills, goal setting, problem solving, and mastery experiences—also show promise for pregnant and parenting adolescents.

COPING SKILLS

Adolescents, in general, use a range of coping and adaptation responses, identified as problem-focused (active) strategies, emotional adjustment and acceptance, and passive responses characterized by avoidance (Stern & Alvarez, 1992; Stern & Zevon, 1990; Tolor & Fehon, 1987). Factors such as age and gender appear to be moderating factors for the type of coping used. For example, adolescents younger than 18 have been shown to use emotion-focused and avoidance strategies more than older adolescents (Stern & Zevon, 1990), whereas girls throughout adolescence tend to use emotion-focused strategies more than boys do (Fickova, 1998; Halstead, Johnson, & Cunningham, 1993; Olah, 1995).

Zeidner and Hammer's (1990) study with adolescents suggested that type of coping response may be a more important moderating factor as a determinant of outcome than the frequency or severity of the stressor. Of the three types, emotion-focused coping and avoidance have been associated with negative outcomes for adjustment (Compas, Malcame, & Fondacaro, 1988), whereas problem-focused coping has been associated with positive outcomes for adjustment involving life changes and increased role demands (Aldwin & Revenson, 1987; Aspinwall & Taylor, 1992; de Anda et al., 1992).

A substantial proportion of the existing research on pregnant and parenting adolescents involves the association of stress and coping with the issue of adjustment (for example Barth & Schinke, 1984; Passino et al., 1993; Stern & Alvarez, 1992). How an adolescent copes with the stressful changes and demands that she faces in pregnancy and with the initial stages of parenting can have an impact on her life quality, not only during this time but throughout childrearing (Colletta & Gregg, 1981; Phoenix, 1993). The literature has repeatedly associated a tendency to use active problem-solving strategies over avoidant- or emotion-focused coping behaviors with positive outcomes for young mothers. Colletta and Gregg reported that the level of emotional stress experienced by adolescent mothers was less for those with more direct, active coping styles. Mondell and Tyler (1981) found that young parents with active coping styles reflected higher levels of acceptance, warmth, and helpfulness, and lower levels of disapproval in parent-child interactions.

The Passino and colleagues (1993) study comparing pregnant adolescents to nonpregnant adolescents and to pregnant adults found that not only did pregnant adolescents experience more stress than pregnant adults but their coping and overall adjustment was less than both nonpregnant adolescents and pregnant adults. In Codega, Pasley, and Kreutzer's (1990) comparison of Mexican American and Anglo American adolescent mothers, both groups identified avoidant- or emotion-focused coping strategies as their eight most frequently reported coping activities.

SOCIAL PROBLEM–SOLVING SKILLS

Studies suggest that pregnant and parenting adolescents are less skilled in problem solving than their nonpregnant peers and their older counterparts (Passino et al., 1993). Social problem-solving skills are defined as a set of relatively specific attitudes, behaviors, and skills directed toward successfully solving a particular real-life problem in a social context (D'Zurilla, 1986). They include the tasks of defining and formulating the problem, generating a list of alternative solutions, making a decision, implementing the solution, and evaluating the outcome. According to Bandura (1997), effective social problem-solving skills enhance a sense of self-agency and are important to the development of self-efficacy and a general sense of mastery over one's environment. A sense of mastery over a difficult environment is especially important for adolescents if they are to avoid the risk factors of early pregnancy and negative outcomes associated with adolescent pregnancy.

USE OF GROUP MODALITY

With few exceptions, outcome studies that have a skills-building core in the current literature use the group intervention modality. In fact, across the adolescent literature, group intervention dominates as the modality of choice (Glodich & Allen, 1998). Although there are fewer studies available on group outcomes with pregnant and parenting adolescents than with other teen populations, multivariate studies have identified characteristics associated with adolescent pregnancy and parenting, such as situational loneliness (Klein, 1998) and need for peer support (de Anda & Becerra, 1984), that also suggest the benefits of group interventions.

CONCLUSION

Adolescent pregnancy in the United States, although currently declining, is still higher than in other industrial countries. Adolescent pregnancy is a socially constructed problem that has several risk factors that predispose adolescents to a life of economic dependency and that place their children at significant risk. This chapter investigated a number of these risk factors. Fortunately, research also points to a number of protective factors and effective interventions that can help adolescents prevent pregnancy or avoid the adverse affects if they do become pregnant. This chapter identified several protective factors—from wider social environment and immediate social environments of family, neighborhood, and community to individual attributes that protect adolescents from the risks associated with pregnancy. Age, gender, and race were also considered. Finally, several effective interventions for pregnancy prevention and for pregnant and parenting adolescents were summarized.

REFERENCES

Abrahamse, A. F., Morrison, P. A., & Waite, L. J. (1988). Teenagers willing to consider single parenthood: Who is at greatest risk? *Family Planning Perspectives, 20,* 13–18.

Aguilar, M. A. (1995). Promoting the educational achievement of Mexican American young women. *Social Work, 18*(3), 145–156.

Alan Guttmacher Institute. (1996). *Facts in brief: Teen sex and pregnancy.* Washington, DC: Author.

Alan Guttmacher Institute. (1998). *Guttmacher report.* Washington, DC: Author. Retrieved from http://www.guttmacher.org/journals/tgr_archive.html on August 7, 2003.

Aldwin, C. M., & Revenson, T. T. (1987). Does coping help? A reexamination of the relation between coping and mental health. *Journal of Personality and Social Psychology, 53,* 337–348.

Arons, R. D., & Schwartz, F. S. (1993). Interdisciplinary coleadership of high school groups for dropout prevention: Practice issues. *Social Work, 38*(1), 9–14.

Aspinwall, L. G., & Taylor, S. E. (1992). Modeling cognitive adaptation: A longitudinal investigation of the impact of individual differences and coping on college adjustment and performance. *Journal of Personality and Social Psychology, 63,* 989–1003.

Balcazar, H., Peterson, G., & Cobas, J. (1996). Acculturation and health-related risk behaviors among Mexican American pregnant youth. *American Journal of Health Behavior, 20,* 425–433.

Balcazar, H., Peterson, G., & Krull, J. L. (1997). Acculturation and family cohesiveness in Mexican American pregnant women: Social and health implications. *Family Community Health, 20,* 16–31.

Bandura, A. (1997). *Self efficacy: The exercise of control.* Englewood Cliffs, NJ: Prentice-Hall.

Barnett, J. K., Papini, D. R., & Gbur, E. (1991). Familial correlates of sexually active pregnant and nonpregnant adolescents. *Adolescence, 26,* 457–472.

Barth, R. P. (1985). Beating the blues: Cognitive-behavioral treatment for depression in child-maltreating young mothers. *Clinical Social Work Journal, 13*(4), 317–328.

Barth, R. P. (1989). *Reducing the risk: Building skills to prevent pregnancy.* Santa Cruz, CA: ETR Associates/Network Publications.

Barth, R. P., & Schinke, S. P. (1983). Coping with daily strain among pregnant and parenting adolescents. *Journal of Social Service Research, 7,* 51–63.

Barth, R. P., & Schinke, S. P. (1984). Enhancing the social supports of teenage mothers. *Social Casework, 65,* 523–531.

Barth, R. P., Schinke, S. P., & Maxwell, J. S. (1983). Psychological correlates of teenage motherhood. *Journal of Youth and Adolescence, 12,* 471–487.

Beck, M. S. (1991). *Increasing school completion: Strategies that work* (Monographs in Education No. 13). Athens: University of Georgia, College of Education.

Beutel, A. M. (2000). The relationship between adolescent nonmarital childbearing and educational expectations: A cohort and period comparison. *Sociological Quarterly, 41*(2), 297–314.

Bingham, C. R., Miller, B. C., & Adams, G. R. (1990). Correlates of age at first intercourse in a national sample of young women. *Journal of Adolescent Research, 5,* 18–33.

Black, C., & DeBlassie, E. R. (1985). Adolescent pregnancy: Contributing factors: Consequences, treatment, and plausible solutions. *Adolescence, 20,* 281–290.

Boyer, D., & Fine, D. (1992). Sexual abuse as a factor in adolescent pregnancy and child maltreatment. *Family Planning Perspectives, 24,* 4–11.

Brooks-Gunn, J., & Furstenberg, F. F., Jr. (1986). The children of adolescent mothers: Physical, academic, and psychological outcomes. *Developmental Review, 6,* 224–251.

Burdell, P. (1998). Young mothers as high school students: Moving toward a new century. *Education and Urban Society, 30*(2), 202–223.

Card, J. J., & Wise, L. L. (1978). Teenage mothers and teenage fathers: The impact of early childbearing on the parents' personal and professional lives. *Family Planning Perspectives, 10*(4), 199–205.

Causby, V., Nixon, C., & Bright, J. M. (1991). Influences on adolescent mother-infant interactions. *Adolescence, 26,* 619–630.

Child Trends. (1999). *Facts at a glance, 12/99 overview.* Retrieved from http://www.cdc.gov/ncbddd/folicacid/Ataglance/folicag.htm on August 1, 2003.

Clarke, G. (1992). Cognitive–behavioral group treatment of adolescent depression: Prediction of outcome. *Behavior Therapy, 23,* 341–354.

Codega, S. A., Pasley, B. K., & Kreutzer, J. (1990). Coping behaviors of adolescent mothers: An exploratory study and comparison of Mexican-Americans and Anglos. *Journal of Adolescent Research, 5*(1), 34–53.

Colletta, N. D., & Gregg, C. H. (1981). Adolescent mothers' vulnerability to stress. *Journal of Nervous and Mental Disorders, 169,* 50–54.

Colletta, N. D., & Lee, D. (1983). The impact of support for black adolescent mothers. *Journal of Family Issues, 4,* 127–143.

Compas, B., Malcame, V. L., & Fondacaro, K. M. (1988). Coping with stressful events in older children and young adolescents. *Journal of Consulting and Clinical Psychology, 56*(3), 405–411.

Corcoran, J. (1998). Consequences of adolescent pregnancy/parenting: A review of the literature. *Social Work in Health Care, 27*(2), 49–67.

Corcoran, J. (2000). Ecological factors associated with adolescent sexual activity. *Social Work in Health Care, 30,* 547–588.

Corcoran, J. & Franklin, C. (2002). Multi-systemic risk factors predicting depression, self-esteem, and stress in low SES and culturally diverse adolescents. *Journal of Human Behavior in the Social Environment, 5*(2), 61–76.

Corcoran, J., Franklin, C., & Bennett, P. (2000). Ecological factors associated with adolescent pregnancy and parenting. *Social Work Research, 24,* 29–39.

Cutrona, C. E., & Russell, D. W. (1990). Type of social support and specific stress: Toward a theory of optimal matching. In B. R. Sarason, I. G. Srason, & G. R. Pierce (Eds.), *Social support: An interactional view* (pp. 319–366). New York: John Wiley & Sons.

de Anda, D. (1998). The evaluation of a stress management program for middle school adolescents. *Child and Adolescent Social Work Journal, 15*(1), 73–85.

de Anda, D., & Becerra, R. M. (1984). Social networks for adolescent mothers. *Social Casework: The Journal of Contemporary Social Work, 65,* 172–181.

de Anda, D., Darroch, P., Davidson, M., Gilly, J., Javidi, M., Jefford, S., Komorowski, R., & Morejon-Schrobsdorf, A. (1992). Stress and coping among pregnant adolescents. *Journal of Adolescent Research, 7*(1), 94–100.

DeBolt, M. E., Pasley, B. K., & Kreutzer, J. (1990). Factors affecting the probability of school dropout: A study of pregnant and parenting adolescent females. *Journal of Adolescent Research, 5*(3), 190–205.

Del Rio, S. R. (1999). *The influence of acculturation on Chicana adolescent pregnancy.* Berkeley: California School of Professional Psychology Berkeley/Alameda.

DiBlasio, F. A., & Benda, B. B. (1990). Adolescent sexual behavior: Multivariate analysis of a social learning model. *Journal of Adolescent Research, 5,* 449–466.

Dupper, D. R. (1998). An alternative to suspension for middle school youths with behavior problems: Findings from a "school survival" group. *Research on Social Work Practice, 8*(3), 354–366.

D'Zurilla, T. J. (1986). *Problem-solving therapy: A social competence approach to clinical intervention.* New York: Springer.

D'Zurilla, T. J., & Nezu, A. (1982). Social problem-solving in adults. In P. C. Kendall (Ed.), *Advances in cognitive-behavioral research and therapy* (pp. 202–269). New York: Academic Press.

Elliott, D. S., & Morse, B. J. (1989). Delinquency and drug use as risk factors in teenage sexual activity. *Youth & Society, 21,* 32–60.

Fickova, E. (1998). Interaction of self-concept and coping strategies in adolescents. *Studia Psychologica, 40*(4), 297–302.

Fine, M. (1986). Why urban adolescents drop into and out of public high school. *Teachers College Record, 87,* 392–409.

Fischer, R. L. (1997). Evaluating the delivery of a teen pregnancy and parenting program across two settings. *Research on Social Work Practice, 7*(3), 350–369.

Flanigan, B., Mclean, A., Hall, C., & Propp, V. (1990). Alcohol use as a situational influence on young women's pregnancy risk-taking behaviors. *Adolescence, 25,* 205–214.

Flewelling, R. L., & Bauman, K. E. (1990). Family structure as a predictor of initial substance use and sexual intercourse in early adolescence. *Journal of Marriage and the Family, 52,* 171–180.

Flynn, L. (1999). The adolescent parenting program: Improving outcomes through mentorship. *Public Health Nursing, 16*(3), 182–189.

Forman, S. G., Linney, J. A., & Brondino, M. J. (1990). Effects of coping skills training on adolescents at risk for substance abuse. *Psychology of Addictive Behaviors, 4*(2), 67–76.

Forste, R., & Tienda, M. (1992). Race and ethnic variation in the schooling consequences of female adolescent sexual activity. *Social Science Quarterly, 73,* 12–30.

Forste, R. T., & Heaton, T. B. (1988). Initiation of sexual activity among female adolescents. *Youth & Society, 19,* 250–268.

Franklin, C. (1996). Learning to teach qualitative research: Reflections of a quantitative researcher. In M. B. Sussman & J. F. Gilgun (Eds.), *The methods and methodologies of qualitative family research.* New York: Haworth Press. (Reprint from *Marriage and Family Review*)

Franklin, C., & Corcoran, J. (1999). Preventing adolescent pregnancy: A review of programs and practices. *Social Work in Health Care, 45*(1), 40–52.

Franklin, C., Corcoran, J., & Ayers-Lopez, S. (1997). Adolescent pregnancy prevention: Multisystemic risk and protective factors. In M. W. Fraser (Ed.), *Risk and resilience in childhood* (pp. 195–219). Washington, DC: NASW Press.

Franklin, C., Grant, D., Corcoran, J., O'Dell, P., & Bultman, L. (1997). Effectiveness of prevention programs for adolescent pregnancy: A meta-analysis. *Journal of Marriage and the Family, 59*(3), 551–567.

Franklin, C., McNeil, J. A., & Wright, R. (1991). The effectiveness of social work in an alternative school for high school dropouts. *Social Work with Groups, 14*(2), 59–73.

Furstenberg, F. F., Brooks-Gunn, J., & Morgan, S. P. (1987). *Adolescent mothers in later life.* Cambridge, England: Cambridge University Press.

Gibbs, J. T. (1992). The social context of teenage pregnancy and parenting in the black community: Implications for public policy. In M. K. Rosenheim & M. F. Testa (Eds.), *Early parenthood and coming of age in the 1990s.* New Brunswick, NJ: Rutgers University Press.

Giblin, P. T., Poland, M. L., & Sachs, B. A. (1987). Effects of social supports on attitudes and health behaviors of pregnant adolescents. *Journal of Adolescent Health Care, 8,* 273–279.

Gillmore, M. R., Lewis, S. M., Lohr, M. J., Spencer, M. S., & White, R. D. (1997). Repeat pregnancies among adolescent mothers. *Journal of Marriage and the Family, 59*(3), 536–550.

Glodich, A., & Allen, J. G. (1998). Adolescents exposed to violence and abuse: A review of the group therapy literature with an emphasis on preventing trauma reenactment. *Journal of Child and Adolescent Group Therapy, 8*(3), 135–153.

Gohel, M., Diamond, J. J., & Chambers, C. V. (1997). Attitudes toward sexual responsibility and parenting: An exploratory study of young urban males. *Family Planning Perspectives, 29*(6), 280–283.

Griffin, N. C. (1998). Cultivating self-efficacy in adolescent mothers: A collaborative approach. *Professional School Counseling, 1*(4), 53–58.

Grotevant, H. D., & Carlson, C. I. (1989). *Family assessment: A guide to methods and measures.* New York: Guilford Press.

Halstead, M., Johnson, S. B., & Cunningham, W. (1993). Measuring coping in adolescents; An application of the Ways of Coping Checklist. *Journal of Clinical Child Psychology, 23*(3), 337–344.

Hamburg, B. A., & Dixon, S. L. (1992). Adolescent pregnancy and parenthood. In M. K. Rosenheim, & M. F. Testa (Eds.), *Early parenthood and coming of age in the 1990s* (pp. 17–33). New Brunswick, NJ: Rutgers University Press.

Hanson, S. L., Myers, D. E., & Ginsburg, A. L. (1987). The role of responsibility and knowledge in reducing teenage out-of-wedlock childbearing. *Journal of Marriage and the Family, 49,* 241–256.

Harris, K. M. (1991). Teenage mothers and welfare dependency: Working off welfare. *Journal of Family Issues, 12,* 492–518.

Harris, M. B., & Franklin, C. (2001). Effects of a cognitive-behavioral, school-based, group intervention with Mexican-American pregnant and parenting mothers. *Social Work Research, 27*(2), 71–83.

Henshaw, S. K., & Feivelson, D. (2000). Teenage abortion and pregnancy statistics by state, 1996. *Family Planning Perspectives, 32*(6), 272–280.

Hofferth, S. L. (1987). Social and economic consequences of teenage childbearing. In S. L. Hofferth & C. D. Hayes (Eds.), *Risking the future: Adolescent sexuality, pregnancy, and childbearing* (Vol. 2, pp. 123–144). Washington, D.C.: National Academy Press.

Hogue, A., & Liddle, H. A. (1999). Family-based preventive intervention: An approach to preventing substance abuse and antisocial behavior. *American Journal of Orthopsychiatry, 69,* 275–293.

Horwitz, S. M., Klerman, L. V., Kuo, H. S., & Jekel, J. F. (1991). School-age mothers: Predictors of long-term educational and economic outcomes. *Pediatrics, 87,* 862–868.

Inwald, R. E., Brobst, K. E., & Morrissey, R. F. (1987). *Hilson adolescent profile.* Kew Gardens, NY: Hilson Research.

Jaccard, J., Dittus, P., & Gordon, V. (1996). Maternal correlates of adolescent sexual and contraceptive behavior. *Family Planning Perspectives, 28,* 159–165.

Jarrett, R. (1990). *A comparative examination of socialization patterns among low-income African Americans, Chicanos, Puerto Ricans and Whites: A review of the ethnographic literature* (Report to the Social Science Research Council). Chicago: Loyola University.

Jemmont, J. B., Jemmont, L. S., Fong, G. T., & McCaffree, K. (1999). Reducing HIV risk-associated sexual behavior among African American adolescents: Testing the generality of intervention effects. *American Journal of Community Psychology, 27*(2), 161–187.

Jordan, C., & Franklin, C. (1995). *Clinical assessment for social workers: Quantitative and qualitative methods.* Chicago: Lyceum/Nelson Hall Press.

Kalil, A., & Kunz, J. (1999). First births among adolescent girls: Risk and protective factors. *Social Work Research, 23*(3), 197–208.

Kalil, A., Spencer, M. S., Spieker, S. J., & Gilchrist, L. D. (1998). Effects of grandmother coresidence and quality of family relationships on depressive symptoms in adolescent mothers. *Family Relations: Interdisciplinary Journal of Applied Family Studies, 47*(4), 433–441.

Kelly, D. M. (1996). Stigma stories: Four discourses about teen mothers, welfare, and poverty. *Youth & Society, 27*(4), 421–449.

Kirby, D. (2001). *Emerging answers: Research findings on programs to reduce teenage pregnancies*. Washington, DC: National Campaign to Prevent Teenage Pregnancy.

Kissman, K. (1998). High risk behaviour among adolescent mothers. *International Journal of Adolescence & Youth, 7*(3), 179–191.

Klein, T. M. (1998). Adolescent pregnancy and loneliness. *Public Health Nursing, 15*(5), 338–347.

Kraemer, H.C., Stice, E., Kazdin, A., Offord, D., & Kupfer, D. (2001). How do risk factors work together? Mediators, moderators, and independent, overlapping, proxy risk factors. *American Journal of Psychiatry, 158,* 848–856.

Long, S. J., & Sherer, M. (1984). Social skills training with juvenile offenders. *Child and Family Behavior Therapy, 6*(4), 1–11.

Luker, K. (1996). *Dubious conceptions: The politics of teenage pregnancy*. Cambridge, MA: Harvard University Press.

Luster, T., & Small, S. (1997). Sexual abuse history and number of sex partners among female adolescents. *Family Planning Perspectives, 29,* 204–211.

Marlin, J. A., Hamilton, B. E., Ventura, S. J. (2001). *Preliminary data for 2000* (National Vital Statistics Report, Vol. 495). Hyattsville, MD: Centers for Disease Control and Prevention.

Martin, C. A., Hill, K. K., & Welch, R. (1998). Adolescent pregnancy, a stressful life event: Cause and consequence. In T. Miller (Ed.), *Children of trauma: Stressful life events and their effects on children and adolescents*. Madison, CT: International Universities Press.

Mayfield-Brown, L. (1989). Family status of low-income adolescent mothers. *Journal of Adolescent Research, 4,* 202–213.

Maynard, R. (1995). Teenage childbearing and welfare reform: Lessons from a decade of demonstration and evaluation research. *Children and Youth Services Review, 17,* 309–332.

Maynard, R. (Ed.). (1996). *Kids having kids: A Robin Hood Foundation special report on the costs of adolescent childbearing*. New York: Robin Hood Foundation.

McAnarney, E. R., & Hendee, W. R. (1989a). Adolescent pregnancy and its consequences. *Journal of the American Medical Association, 262,* 74–77.

McAnarney, E. R., & Hendee, W. R. (1989b). The prevention of adolescent pregnancy. *Journal of the American Medical Association, 262*(1), 78–82.

McWhirter, B. T., & Page, G. L. (1999). Effects of anger management and goal setting group interventions on state-trait anger and self-efficacy beliefs among high risk adolescents. *Current Psychology: Developmental, Learning, Personality, Social, 18*(2), 223–237.

Miller, D. B. (1997). Influences on parental involvement of African American adolescent fathers. *Child and Adolescent Social Work, 11*(5), 363–378.

Miller, K., Clark, L., & Moore, J. (1997). Sexual initiation with older male partners and subsequent HIV risk behavior among female adolescents. *Family Planning Perspectives, 29,* 212–214.

Mondell, S., & Tyler, F. (1981). Parental competence and styles of problem-solving/play behavior with children. *Developmental Psychology, 17,* 73–78.

Moore, K. A., Myers, D. E., Morrison, D. R., Nord, C. W., Brown, B. V., & Edmonston, B. (1993). Age of first childbirth and later poverty. *Journal of Research on Adolescence, 3*(4), 393–422.

Moore, K. A., & Wertheimer, R. (1982). *Teenage childbearing: Public sector costs*. Washington, DC: Urban Institute.

Moos, R. H. (1989). *Family environment scale (FES) dimensions and subscales*. Palo Alto, CA: Consulting Psychologist Press.

Mott, F. L., & Haurin, R. J. (1988). Linkages between sexual activity and alcohol and drug use among American adolescents. *Family Planning Perspectives, 20,* 128–136.

Mott, F. L., & Marsiglio, W. (1985). Early childbearing and completion of high school. *Family Planning Perspectives, 17*(5), 234–237.

National Campaign to Prevent Teenage Pregnancy. (April, 1997). *What the polling data tell us: A summary of past surveys*. Washington, DC.

Newcomer, S., & Udry, J. (1987). Parent-child communication and adolescent sexual behavior. *Family Planning Perspectives, 17,* 169–174.

Oakley, A. (1985). Social support and the outcome in pregnancy: The soft way to increase birth weight? *Social Science and Medicine, 21,* 1259–1268.

Olah, A. (1995). Coping strategies among adolescents: A cross-cultural study. *Journal of Adolescence, 18*(4), 491–512.

Osofsky, J. D., Osofsky, H. J., & Diamond, M. O. (1988). The transition to parenthood: Special tasks and risk factors for adolescent parents. In G. Y. Michaels & W. A. Goldberg (Eds.), *The transition to parenthood: Current theory and research* (pp. 209–232). New York: Cambridge University Press.

Passino, A. W., Whitman, T. L., Borkowski, J. G., Schellenbach, C. J., Maxwell, S. E., Keogh, D., & Rellinger, E. (1993). Personal adjustment during pregnancy and adolescent parenting. *Adolescence, 28*(109), 97–123.

Patterson, J. M., & McCubbin, H. (1983). *Adolescent coping orientation for problem experiences (A-COPE)*. Madison: Family Stress, Coping, and Health Project, University of Wisconsin—Madison.

Pearson, L. C., & Banerji, M. (1993). Effects of a ninth-grade dropout prevention program on student academic achievement, school attendance, and dropout rate. *Journal of Experimental Education, 61*(Spring), 247–256.

Perkins, D. F., Luster, T., Villarruel, F. A., & Small, S. (1998). An ecological, risk-factor examination of adolescents' sexual activity in three ethnic groups. *Journal of Marriage and the Family, 60,* 660–673.

Phoenix, A. (1993). Children having children: Teenage pregnancy and public policy from the woman's perspective. In A. Lawson & D. L. Rhode (Eds.), *The politics of pregnancy: Adolescent sexuality and public policy* (pp. 74–97). New Haven, CT: Yale University Press.

Pines, D. (1988). Adolescent pregnancy and motherhood: A psychoanalytical perspective. *Psychoanalytic Inquiry, 8*(2), 234–251.

Rains, P., Davies, L., & McKinnon, M. (1998). Taking responsibility: An insider view of teen motherhood. *Families in Society: The Journal of Contemporary Human Services,* May/June, 308–319.

Raj, A., Silverman, J. G., & Amaro, H. (2000). The relationship between sexual abuse and sexual risk among high school students: Findings from the 1997 Massachusetts Youth Risk Behavior Survey. *Maternal and Child Health Journal, 4*(2), 125–134.

Rauch-Elnekave, H. (1994). Teenage motherhood: Its relationship to undetected learning problems. *Adolescence, 29*(113), 91–103.

Reis, J. S., & Herz, E. J. (1987). Correlates of adolescent parenting. *Adolescence, 22,* 599–609.

Resnick, M. D., Bearman, P. S., Blum, R. W., Bauman, K. E., Harris, K. M., Jones, J., Tabor, J., Beuhring, T., Sieving, R. E., Shew, M., Ireland, M., Bearinger, L. H., Udry, J. R. (1997). Protecting adolescent from harm: Findings from the national longitudinal study on adolescent health. *Journal of the American Medical Association, 278*(10), 823–832.

Rhein, L. M., Ginsburgh, K. R., Schwarz, D. F., Pinto-Martin, J. A., Zhao, H., Morgan, A. P., & Slap, G. B. (1997). Teen father participation in child rearing: Family perspectives. *Journal of Adolescent Health, 21,* 244–252.

Rhode, D. L. (1993). Adolescent pregnancy and public policy. *Political Science Quarterly, 108*(4), 635–670.

Rhodes, J. E., & Woods, M. (1995). Comfort and conflict in the relationships of pregnant, minority adolescents: Social support as a moderator of social strain. *Journal of Community Psychology, 23,* 74–84.

Rice, K. G., & Meyer, A. L. (1994). Preventing depression among young adolescents: Preliminary process results of a psycho-educational intervention program. *Journal of Counseling & Development, 73,* 145–152.

Richardson, R. A., Barbour, N. E., & Bubenzer, D. L. (1995). Peer relationships as a source of support for adolescent mothers. *Journal of Adolescent Research, 10*(2), 278–290.

Robbins, C., Kaplan, H. B., & Martin, S. S. (1985). Antecedents of pregnancy among unmarried adolescents. *Journal of Marriage and the Family, 43,* 339–348.

Rodriguez, R. (1995). Latino educators devise sure-fire K–12 dropout prevention programs. *Black Issues in Higher Education, 12,* 35–37.

Roosa, M. (1986). Adolescent mothers, school drop-outs, and school-based intervention programs. *Family Relations: Interdisciplinary Journal of Applied Family Studies, 35,* 313–317.

Rubenstein, E., Panzarine, S., & Lanning, P. (1990). Peer counselling with adolescent mothers: A pilot program. *Families in Society: Journal of Contemporary Human Services, 71*(3), 136–141.

Rudd, N. M., McKenry, P. C., & Nah, M. (1990). Welfare recipient among black and white adolescent mothers: A longitudinal perspective. *Journal of Family Issues, 11,* 334–352.

Sandfort, J. R., & Hill, M. S. (1996). Assisting young unmarried mothers to become self-sufficient. The effects of different types of early economic support. *Journal of Marriage and the Family, 58*(2), 311–326.

Santelli, J. S., & Beilensen, P. (1992). Risk factors for adolescent sexual behavior, fertility, and sexually transmitted diseases. *Journal of School Health, 62,* 271–279.

Schilmoeller, G. L., & Baranowski, M. D. (1985). Child rearing of firstborns by adolescent and older mothers. *Adolescence, 20,* 805–822.

Schilmoeller, G. L., Baranowski, M. D., & Higgins, B. S. (1991). Long-term support and personal adjustment of adolescent and older mothers. *Adolescence, 26,* 787–797.

Schinke, S. P., Blythe, B. J., & Gilchrist, L. D. (1981). Cognitive–behavioral prevention of adolescent pregnancy. *Journal of Counseling Psychology, 28,* 451–454.

Seitz, V., & Apfel, N. H. (1999). Effective interventions for adolescent mothers. *Clinical Psychology: Science and Practice, 6,* 50–66.

Shah, F., & Zelnik, M. (1981). Parent and peer influence on sexual behavior, contraceptive use, and pregnancy experience of young women. *Journal of Marriage and the Family, 43,* 339–348.

Smith, T. (1994). Adolescent pregnancy. In R. J. Simeonsson (Ed.), *Risk, resilience and prevention: Promoting the well being of all children* (pp. 125–149). Baltimore: Paul H. Brookes.

Smith, C., & Carlson, B.E. (1997). Stress, coping, and resilience in children and youth. *Social Service Review, 71,* 231–256.

Srebnik, D., & Elias, M. J. (1993). An ecological interpersonal skills approach to dropout prevention. *American Journal of Orthopsychiatry, 63*(4), 526–535.

Steinberg, L., Blinde, P., & Chan, K. (1984). Dropping out among language minority youth. *Review of Educational Research, 113*–132.

Stern, M., & Alvarez, A. (1992). Pregnant and parenting adolescents: A comparative analysis of coping response and psychosocial adjustment. *Journal of Adolescent Research, 7*(4), 469–493.

Stern, M., & Zevon, M. A. (1990). Stress, coping, and family environment: The adolescents' response to naturally occurring stressors. *Journal of Adolescent Research, 5,* 290–305.

Stevens-Simon, C., & Beach, R. K. (1992). School-based prenatal and postpartum care: Strategies for meeting the medical and educational needs of pregnant and parenting students. *Journal of School Health, 62,* 304–309.

St. Lawrence, J. S., Crosby, R. A., Belcher, L., Yazdani, N., & Brasfield, T. L. (1999). Sexual risk reduction and anger management interventions for incarcerated male adolescents: A randomized controlled trial of two interventions. *Journal of Sex Education & Therapy, 24*(1/2), 9–17.

Stock, J. L., Bell, M. A., Boyer, D. K., & Connell, F. A. (1997). Adolescent pregnancy and sexual risk-taking among sexually abused girls. *Family Planning Perspectives, 29*(4), 200–203, 227.

Szapocznik, J., & Kurtines, W. M. (1993). Family psychology and cultural diversity: Opportunities for theory, research, and application. *American Psychologist, 48*(4), 400–407.

Streeter, C. L., & Franklin, C. (1992). Defining and measuring social support: Guidelines for social work practioners. *Research on Social Work Practice, 2*(1), 81–98.

Testa, M. F. (1992). Teenage parenthood: Policies and perspectives. In M. K. Rosenheim & M. F. Testa (Eds.), *Early parenthood and coming of age in the 1990s* (pp. 113–135). New Brunswick, NJ: Rutgers University Press.

Thornton, A., & Camburn, D. (1989). Religious participation and adolescent sexual behavior and attitudes. *Journal of Marriage and the Family, 51,* 641–652.

Tolor, A., & Fehon, D. (1987). Coping with stress: A study of male adolescents' coping strategies to adjustment. *Journal of Adolescent Research, 2,* 33–42.

Trad, P. V. (1994). Adolescent pregnancy: An intervention challenge. *Child Psychiatry & Human Development, 24*(2), 99–113.

Trussel, T. J. (1984). Economic consequences of teenage childbearing. *Family Planning Perspectives, 8*(4), 184–190.

Turner, R. J., Grindstaff, C. F., & Phillips, N. (1990). Social support and outcome in teenage pregnancy. *Journal of Health and Social Behavior, 31,* 43–57.

Unger, D. G., & Wandersman, L. P. (1988). The relation of family and partner support to the adjustment of adolescent mothers. *Child Development, 59,* 1056–1060.

Uno, D., Florsheim, P., & Uchino, B. N. (1998). Psychosocial mechanisms underlying quality of parenting among Mexican-American and White adolescent mothers. *Journal of Youth and Adolescence, 27*(5), 585–605.

Vallerand, R. J., Fortier, M. S., & Guay, F. (1997). Self-determination and persistence in a real-life setting: Toward a motivational model of high school dropout. *Journal of Personality and Social Psychology, 72*(5), 1161–1176.

Vaux, A. (1988). *Social support: Theory, research, and intervention.* New York: Praeger.

Vinovskis, M. A. (1992). Historical perspectives on adolescent pregnancy. In M. K. Rosenheim & M. F. Testa (Eds.), *Early parenthood and coming of age in the 1990s.* New Brunswick, NJ: Rutgers University Press.

Waite, L. J., & Moore, K. A. (1978). The impact of early first birth on young women's educational attainment. *Social Forces, 56,* 845–865.

Wallace, J. M. (1999). The social ecology of addiction: Race, risk and resilience. *Pediatrics, 103,* 1122–1127.

Wasserman, G. A., Brunelli, S. A., & Rauh, V. A. (1990). Social supports and living arrangements of adolescent and adult mothers. *Journal of Adolescent Research, 5*(1), 54–66.

Wehlage, G. G., & Rutter, R. A. (1986). Dropping out: How much do schools contribute to the problem? *Teachers College Record, 87,* 375–389.

Weidman, J., & Friedman, R. (1984). The school to work transition for high school dropouts. *Urban Review, 16,* 25–42.

Westat, R. S., & Chapman, C. (1999). *Service learning and community service in K–12 public schools.* Washington, DC: National Center for Education Statistics.

Whitaker, D., Miller, K., May, D., & Levin, M. (1999). Teenage partners' communication about sexual risk and condom use: The importance of parent-teenager discussions. *Family Planning Perspectives, 31,* 117–121.

Wilson, S. (2000). Sexuality education: Our current status, and an agenda for 2010. *Family Planning Perspectives, 32*(5), 252–254.

Yamaguchi, K., & Kandel, D. (1987). Drug use and other determinants of premarital pregnancy and its outcome: A dynamic analysis of competing life events. *Journal of Marriage and the Family, 49,* 257–270.

Young, E. W., Jensen, L. C., Olsen, J. A., & Cundick, B. P. (1991). The effects of family structure on the sexual behavior of adolescents. *Adolescence, 26,* 977–986.

Zabin, L. S., Hardy, J. B., Smith, E. A., & Hirsh, M. B. (1986). Substance use and its relation to sexual activity among inner-city adolescents. *Journal of Adolescent Health Care, 7,* 320–331.

Zeidner, M., & Hammer, A. L. (1990). Life events and coping resources as predictors of stress symptoms in adolescents. *Personality and Individual Differences, 11,* 693–703.

Zellman, G. L. (1981). *The response of the schools to teenage pregnancy and parenthood.* Santa Monica, CA: The Rand Corporation.

Zippay, A. (1995). Expanding employment skills and social networks among teen mothers: Case study of a mentor program. *Child and Adolescent Social Work Journal, 12,* 51–69.

Zuravin, S. J., & DiBlasio, F. A. (1996). The correlates of child physical abuse and neglect by adolescent mothers. *Journal of Family Violence, 11*(2), 149–166.

11

Childhood Depression: A Risk Factor Perspective

M. Carlean Gilbert

S ad affect, withdrawal, sleep disorders, appetite disturbances, hyperactivity, aggressiveness, somatic complaints, school underachievement or failure, and difficulties in peer and family relationships are among the symptoms of children at risk for depression. Of these symptoms, parents, teachers, and practitioners tend to be more responsive, typically, to behavioral manifestations such as hyperactivity, teasing, and losing control. They may fail to recognize that both interpersonal difficulties and less disruptive behaviors, such as social isolation, can also be indicators of childhood depression. In addition, some symptoms can be masked: diminished energy, for example, can be hidden under bursts of hypomanic excitement (Lieberman, 1979).

For decades, researchers and practitioners have puzzled over depression in children, asking, Can children be depressed? If the answer to that question is yes, other questions follow: Are their symptoms identical to adults' symptoms, and are they thus diagnosable by the same criteria? Is childhood depression part of a more complex mental disorder yet unidentified? Do children have prodromal depressions that are harbingers of adult mood disorders? What are the risk and protective factors associated with childhood mood disorders?

The purpose of this chapter is to examine the nature of childhood depression, identify risk and protective factors associated with it, review assessment techniques, and discuss implications for prevention, early intervention, and treatment of childhood depression.

Like research on other disorders in health and mental health, research regarding the assessment, diagnosis, and treatment of children with depression has lagged behind that of adults with depression. This delay is due to several factors. First, more adults suffer from depression, and thus the scope of the problem and its effect on resources are greater for adults than for children. Second, the long-held belief that children do not suffer from depression has been a significant barrier to the designation of research funds for the diagnosis and treatment of childhood depression. Third, disparate views about diagnostic categories and assessment measures have rendered findings of many studies incomparable. In the next section, a brief review of influential and controversial contributions to knowledge about childhood depression provides a backdrop for understanding current issues regarding depressive disorders in youths.

Controversy over Childhood Depression

Early attempts to understand depression, particularly in children, were sparse. Initially, Freud attempted to explain normal and abnormal melancholia, or depression, in *Mourning and Melancholia* (Freud, 1917/1957). His psychodynamic explanation of depression was based on the assumption that people with depression appear to respond to psychological loss with anger turned inward. In 1946, Spitz coined the term "anaclitic depression" to describe the weight loss, psychomotor retardation, withdrawal, and sleep disturbances of infants and children who had been institutionalized (Spitz, 1946). Bowlby (1960) later developed the stages of protest, despair, and detachment secondary to maternal deprivation, especially during hospitalization; he employed the term "mourning" to describe these stages.

In the 1950s and 1960s, a new group of psychoanalytic theorists (Mahler, 1961; Rie, 1966; Rochlin, 1959) challenged the view that children suffered from depression. This community of analysts asserted that because of adolescence children had neither a stable self-concept nor internalized superego, both of which were necessary for punitiveness. They concluded that children lacked the personality structure to experience the ego versus superego conflicts that resulted in depression. As a consequence of this highly influential psychoanalytic stance, many rejected the concept of childhood depression (Carlson & Garber, 1986).

In a controversial article, Toolan (1962) asserted that children and adolescents do experience depression. Advancing the concept of "masked depression," Toolan later argued that before midadolescence childhood depression is disguised by behavioral disorders such as runaway episodes, temper tantrums, academic failure, boredom, and fatigue (Toolan, 1974). Some also considered delinquency and criminal behavior to be indicators of underlying depression (Chwast, 1974). Other researchers later challenged the usefulness of this concept because the symptoms that allegedly "masked" depression spanned almost the entire range of child mental disorders. Researchers never adequately established criteria for differentiating between depression and masking disorders established (Carlson & Cantwell, 1979; Carlson & Garber, 1986). Subsequently, support for the concept of masked depression diminished (Hynd & Hooper, 1992).

Since the 1970s, there has been a significant increase in attempts to classify, to assess, and to treat childhood depression (Hammen & Rudolph, 2003; Kazdin, 1990; Kovacs, Feinberg, Crouse-Novak, Paulauskas, & Finkelstein, 1984; Rutter, 1986). In the early 1970s, Weinberg, Rutman, Sullivan, Penick, and Dietz (1973) proposed diagnostic criteria based on the assumption that children had manifestations of depression similar to those of adults. Acknowledging the ecology of childhood, they argued that a child's diminished academic performance and interest in school were equivalent to an adult's diminished work performance and interest in work. At about the same time, researchers studying depression developed the Feighner Criteria (Feighner et al., 1972) and the Research Diagnostic Criteria (Spitzer, Endicott, & Robins, 1978). These three sets of criteria are precise and exclusive. Consequently, they tend to identify fewer cases of "true" childhood depression than do clinically oriented diagnostic criteria such as those presented in the *Diagnostic and Statistical Manual of Mental Disorders—Third Edition* (DSM–III; Newman & Garfinkel, 1992) and later editions. Conflicting classificatory criteria continue to complicate the study of childhood depression and render research findings incommensurable. A valid and reliable classification system is a prerequisite for studies of prevalence, development of assessment instruments, and measurement of intervention outcomes; this classification system is still emerging.

THE NATURE OF DEPRESSION IN CHILDREN

Current thinking accepts that children experience depression, that childhood depression can be classified, and that there are, in addition to depression, other mood disorders of childhood. Although this chapter focuses on depression, these other mood disorders are of great importance. They include bipolar (manic–depressive) disorders, adjustment disorder with depressed mood (reactive depression), mood disorders due to a medical condition, and substance-induced mood disorders. Discussion of depression remains challenging because both the popular and professional literatures use the term "depression." We must distinguish among depression as a *sign* (for example, a child's observed psychomotor agitation), a *symptom* (for example, a child's self-report of feeling grouchy), or a *syndrome* (for example, a constellation of signs and symptoms that meet specific diagnostic criteria such as *Diagnostic and Statistical Manual of Mental Disorders, Fourth Edition Revised* (DSM–IV–TR; American Psychiatric Association [APA], 2000; Hammen & Rudolph, 1996; Kaplan & Sadock, 2003).

In the United States, researchers and practitioners have used the DSM–IV–TR and its earlier versions widely to define and diagnose childhood depression. The DSM–IV–TR today identifies depressive disorders as one of four major categories of mood disorders. The DSM–IV–TR groups depressive disorders into major depressive disorder (MDD), which is debilitating, and dysthymic disorder (DD), which is milder but more likely to be chronic. Although many researchers and practitioners continue to question the application of adult criteria to children's depression, the DSM–IV–TR uses the same diagnostic criteria with minor modifications for children (APA, 2000; Hammen & Rudolph, 1996; Rutter, 1986; Ryan et al., 1987). This usage probably excludes some cases of childhood depression by failing to incorporate the age-related influences of cognitive, emotional, behavioral, and social development on symptom expression (Cicchetti & Schneider-Rosen, 1986; Hammen & Rudolph, 1996; Kazdin, 1988).

Major Depressive Disorder (MMD)

The criteria for major depressive disorder (MDD) are either a depressed or, for children, irritable mood, or a diminished interest or pleasure in activities. Children must also demonstrate four or more symptoms that include significant weight increase, weight loss, or failure to make expected developmental gains; almost daily sleep disturbance; almost daily psychomotor agitation or retardation; almost daily loss of energy or fatigue; feelings of worthlessness or inappropriate guilt; diminished ability to think or concentrate; and recurrent thoughts of death.

For MDD to be present, symptoms must coexist for two weeks and produce significant functional changes (APA, 2000; Kaplan & Sadock, 1998). Sadness, appetite loss, sleep disturbance, and fatigue are the most common symptoms in children under age six (Kashani & Carlson, 1987). Prepubertal children often exhibit or experience sad affect, exaggerated somatic complaints, psychomotor agitation, separation anxiety, fears, hallucinations, irritability, uncooperativeness, and disinterest (Kashani, Holcomb, & Orvaschel, 1986; Ryan et al., 1987). A few children experience hypersomnia (Kovacs,

1996) or weight loss (Ryan et al., 1987). The median duration for MDD in the pre-adolescent, clinical population is a considerably longer 9.94 months, in contrast to community populations (Kovacs, Obrosky, Gatsonis, & Richards, 1997). Adolescents experience a loss of interest in activities, feelings of hopelessness, hypersomnia, weight changes, use of illicit substances, or suicidal ideation and attempts (Ryan et al., 1987). Most clinical and epidemiological studies of children and adolescents have reported mean durations of MDD episodes to range from six to nine months (Kovacs, Feinberg, Crouse-Novak, Paulauskas, & Finkelstein, 1984; Kovacs et al., 1997; Lewinsohn, Clarke, Seeley, & Rohde, 1994; McCauley et al., 1993). The median duration of first-episode MDD of clinic children, however, may be several times longer than community participants (Kovacs et al., 1997).

Dysthymic Disorder (DD)

Criteria for DD in children require a depressed or irritable mood most of the day, for most days, and over a period longer than one year. Children must also have three of the following symptoms: sleep disturbances, low energy or fatigue, loss of interest in activities, hopelessness or pessimism, social withdrawal, feelings of guilt, low self-esteem, appetite changes, or poor mentation (concentration, memory, and problem solving; APA, 2000).

In clinical populations, DD can last a long time, with a reported median duration of 3.5 to 3.9 years (Kaplan & Sadock, 2003; Kovacs, Feinberg, Crouse-Novak, Paulauskas, & Finkelstein, 1984; Kovacs et al., 1997). Because of its chronicity, DD may result in the greatest psychosocial impairment; adolescents with DD demonstrate significantly lower social support than adolescents with MDD (Klein, Lewinsohn, & Seeley, 1997).

PREVALENCE OF DEPRESSION IN CHILDREN

Hammen and Rudolph (2003) collapsed data from eight epidemiological surveys of children that were completed between 1987 and 1993 and found overall rates for MDD to be between 6 percent and 8 percent. Rates of depression increase with age. For pre-school children, rates are low: they range from 0.3 percent in community samples (Fleming & Offord, 1990; Kaplan & Sadock, 2003) to 0.9 percent in a clinic sample (Kashani & Carlson, 1987) to 0.3 percent in community samples (Fleming & Offord, 1990; Kaplan & Sadock, 2003). The literature reports that between 2 percent and 3 percent of six- to 11-year-old youths have MDD and that between 3 percent and 8 percent of adolescents have MDD (Cohen et al., 1993; Fleming & Offord, 1990; Garrison et al., 1997; Lewinsohn, Hops, Roberts, Seeley, & Andrews, 1993). Dysthymia occurs in 8 percent of teenage boys and 5 percent of teenage girls (Garrison, Addy, Jackson, McKeown, & Waller, 1992). Birth cohort studies provide some evidence that prevalence rates of depression are increasing (Hammen & Rudolph, 2003).

Gender

The prevalence of depression appears to vary by gender; however, gender-related differences in prevalence rates are somewhat controversial. Some studies of prepubertal children find that boys and girls have equal rates of depression (Fleming, Offord, & Boyle, 1989; Silberg et al., 1999), while others find that boys have higher rates of depression (Costello et al., 1988). Most studies conclude that adolescent girls are more frequently depressed than are adolescent boys (Hammen & Rudolph, 1996; Silberg et al., 1999). Pubertal status, however, may be a more distinguishing marker than age. Silberg and colleagues found that the effect of life events (for example, quarreling with parents, breaking up with a boyfriend) on the occurrence of depression was significantly greater in the pubertal girls than prepubescent girls, regardless of age. The lifetime risk for MDD is known to vary from 10 percent to 25 percent for women, and half that prevalence rate for men (Kaplan & Sadock, 2003).

Suicide

Suicide attempts are not only diagnostic criteria and outcomes of depressive disorders, but also risk factors for future episodes of depression. Overall prevalence rates for suicide increase with age. Under the age of 14, the frequency of suicide is low, at approximately two per 100,000 children in the United States. Between the ages of 15 and 19, suicide rates are 9.5 per 100,000; in this age group, boys are almost four times as likely (13.6 per 100,000) than girls (3.6 per 100,000) to commit suicide successfully (Centers for Disease Control and Prevention [CDC], 2001; Kaplan & Sadock, 2003). Over the past few decades, the rate of suicide generally has increased, especially among prepubertal, African American, and ethnically diverse youths. Between 1980 and 1997, the rate of suicide increased 109 percent among youths ages 10 through 14 and 11 percent among teenagers ages 15 through 19. The rate of suicide for 15- to 19-year-old African American males increased from 7.1 per 100,000 in 1986 to 11.4 per 100,000 in 1997. From 1979 to 1992, the suicide rates for 15- to 24-year-old Native American males was 64 percent of all suicides by Native Americans, whose overall rate is about 1.5 times the national rate (CDC, 2001; Wallace, Calhoun, Powell, O'Neil, & James, 1996).

Suicidal ideation and attempts are higher among children with depression than among children in the general population, and it was reported by 60 percent of 187 children ages six to 18 who were recruited from a psychiatric clinic and who met the criteria for MDD (Ryan et al., 1987). Moreover, prepubertal and adolescent children reported similar levels of seriousness of suicidal ideation and intent. Suicide attempts had occurred in 25 percent of prepubertal children and 34 percent of adolescent children; however, the lethality of the methods—firearms or hanging (CDC, 2001)—used in suicide attempts was significantly higher for teenagers. In addition, the rates of suicide ideation, intent, lethality, and attempt were significantly higher for adolescents whose MDD exceeded two years than for those whose episodes of MDD were shorter than that period (see chapter 12). Although researchers have aimed to develop instruments to predict suicide, Shaffer (1996) concluded that measures currently lack predictive validity and advocated that "our goal must be to identify depression and other problems and treat them. When we do that we will almost certainly save a small number of very precious lives but, even more importantly, we will have made a large number of lives more tolerable, productive, and fulfilling" (p. 173).

SUMMARY

In summary, recent attempts to estimate the prevalence of childhood depression are compromised by classification differences that fail to distinguish between the symptoms of the themselves (Goodman, Schwab-Stone, Lahey, Shaffer, & Jensen, 2000); the wide variation in assessment methods, such as self-report, structured or semistructured diagnostic interviews, and epidemiological surveys; incomparable age groupings; and clinic versus community samples. Different sources and methods produce widely disparate estimates of the severity, duration, and frequency of depression (Hammen & Rudolph, 1996). Thus, pending findings from large epidemiological studies of childhood depression (with representative national samples), caution is warranted in discussing the precise extent and seriousness of this disorder in childhood. It is clear, however, that many children experience depression, and many become so seriously ill that they injure themselves.

RISK FACTORS FOR CHILDHOOD DEPRESSION

The ecological perspective is based on a conceptualization of interactions that continuously inform and bind person and environment (Germain & Gitterman, 1995). Coupled with a strengths perspective (see chapter 13), ecological theory emphasizes coping with stress, adapting to adversity, and modifying hostile conditions in the environment. To assess the "goodness of fit" between person and environment, one must examine the risk and protective factors that affect the onset, severity, and duration of childhood problems such as depression. As stated in chapter 2, risk factors are defined as "any influences that increase the chances for harm or, more specifically, influences that increase the probability of onset, digression to a more serious state, or maintenance of a problem condition." Protective factors are defined "as both internal and external resources that modify risk." These risk and protective factors may be classified as broad environmental conditions; family, school, and neighborhood conditions; and individual biopsychosocial conditions.

BROAD ENVIRONMENTAL RISK FACTORS

Findings on poverty as a risk factor for childhood depression are equivocal. Most epidemiological studies have found modest correlations between symptoms of depression and lower socioeconomic status (SES; Hammen & Rudolph, 2003; Kaplan & Sadock, 2003; Mrazek & Haggerty, 1994). At least one investigation reported, however, that poverty, gender, and race combined to increase significantly the risk of MDD in mothers who received public welfare (Siefert, Bowman, Heflin, Danziger, & Williams, 2000). Risk factors such as history of childhood abuse; health-related physical limitations; food insufficiency; caring for a child with an activity-limiting physical, learning, or mental health condition; and stressful life situations were among those factors associated with increased frequency of MDD. A significant association also existed between cumulative risk factors and MDD; for example, 28.5 percent of the mothers in Siefert and colleagues' (2000) investigation had three or more risk factors but accounted for 48.1 percent of the total depressed women. Poor white women were more likely to have MDD than poor African American females. Another study found that divorced, single, low-income mothers with minor children appear to experience more depression compared with divorced, single, high-income mothers with minor children (Garvin, Kalter, & Hansell, 1993). In summary, research indicates that many children live with parents who have depressive symptomatology, if not full-blown MDD, that is associated with the cumulative effects of impoverished environmental and social conditions.

FAMILY, SCHOOL, AND NEIGHBORHOOD RISK FACTORS

Family Relationships

A growing body of research suggests that some family interactions increase the risk for the maintenance, if not development, of childhood depression. Various studies suggest that the emotional climate in families with depressed children is less cohesive, less emotionally expressive, more hostile, more critical, less accepting, more conflictual, and more disorganized than in families without depressed children (DuRant, Cadenhead, Pendergrast, Slavens, & Linder, 1994; Hammen & Rudolph, 2003; Puig-Antich et al., 1993). Analysis of parents' audiotaped speeches about their clinically depressed children, for example, found that parental criticism is significantly higher in families of depressed children than in control families. Depressed children with comorbid behavior disorders received the higher levels of parental criticism (Asarnow, Tompson, Hamilton, Goldstein, & Guthrie, 1994). Children ages seven to 16 with MDD perceived both parents as providing significantly less care and their mothers as being significantly more overprotective than did children in the control group. When the mother was actively depressed, the child reported the mother to be overprotective and the father to be less caring (Stein et al., 2000). Although these findings are intriguing, much research is needed to distinguish further those family conditions that cause depression in children from those family conditions that result from depression in children.

Parental Depression

In many cases, adults who are depressed have spent their formative years with a depressed caregiver, usually a depressed mother (Ollendick & Yule, 1990). First-degree relatives of a community sample of teenagers with MDD had significantly elevated rates of MDD, DD, or substance-related disorders (Klein, Lewinsohn, Seeley, & Rohde, 2001). Women are twice as likely as men to suffer from MDD. The average age of onset is the mid-20s, an age when many adults are parents. And untreated episodes can last from six to 13 months, whereas treated episodes typically last three months (APA, 2000; Kaplan & Sadock, 2003).

Mothers and fathers suffering from MDD may be especially challenged to fulfill parental roles because they are withdrawn, irritable, preoccupied, fatigued, and disorganized. The synergism of the onset, severity, and type of the parent's depression with children's developmental stages and temperaments will alter risk and resiliency factors (Kendler et al., 1994). When a reciprocal relationship is necessary for attachment, during infancy and toddlerhood (Bowlby, 1960), depressed parents may have difficulty bonding, responding to infants' cues, and protecting young children from accidents and trauma. Recently, psychiatrist Daniel Stern contended that the strongest influence on emotional development is "attunement," which is parental mirroring of a child's emotional expressions. When the emotion is "played back" *repeatedly*, Stern argues that the electrical and chemical signals that created it are positively reinforced. If the child's emotional expressions are ignored or punished these circuits are thought to atrophy. Much of this critical "wiring" appears to occur between 10 and 18 months (Begley, 1996). Depressed parents of older children may be unable to act playful, help with homework, assist with grooming, or maintain a home where playmates are welcome—all factors that may promote academic achievement and social development.

It should be no surprise, then, that parental depression is often found to be linked to symptoms of childhood depression. Of nine preschoolers diagnosed with MDD, for example, mothers of six were found to be depressed (Kashani & Carlson, 1987). In their review of the literature, Hammen and Rudolph (2003) found that infants and toddlers of depressed mothers had symptoms of depression, such as negative facial expressions, decreased verbalizations, decreased playfulness, increased inhibition, and anxiety with peers. In one prospective study, negative affective quality and low task involvement by mothers predicted later child affective disorder (Burge & Hammen, 1991). In a later study, severity of maternal depression appeared to contribute to children's risk for depression more so than chronicity (Hammen & Brennan, 2003). Although parental depression is a major risk factor for childhood depression (Beardslee, Versage, & Gladstone, 1998), the interactions of the timing, duration, and severity of parental depression with phases of child development warrant further investigation. The combined biological and social mechanisms that place children at risk are not fully delineated.

Child Abuse and Neglect

Young children with MDD are often found to have a history of child abuse and neglect (Kaplan & Sadock, 2003). In a study of nine preschool children with MDD, a history of physical abuse and neglect was found in each child (Kashani & Carlson, 1987). In a larger study, depression was correlated with severity of corporal punishment among 225 African American adolescents (DuRant et al., 1994). Severe childhood physical abuse has been found to be significantly associated with comorbid DD in a sample of 76 women ages 18 to 70 who suffered from MDD (Harkness & Wildes, 2002). Such findings regarding both short- and long-term effects of abuse are particularly alarming because the numbers of physically abused and neglected children in the United States have risen dramatically in recent years (More Children Being Abused and Neglected, 1996).

School-Related Problems

Researchers generally find that interpersonal problems with teachers and peers are developmental risk factors for depression (Hammen & Rudolph, 2003) and difficulties with peer relationships and academic performance were more likely when their were strains in family relationships (Puig-Antich et al., 1993). Since many of the studies are cross-sectional, however, it is unclear whether interpersonal difficulties lead to depression, or vice versa.

Neighborhood Violence

The few studies that examine the association between depression and neighborhoods, particularly violent neighborhoods, indicate that an unsafe neighborhood can be a risk factor for childhood depression. Among 221 urban African American children, ages seven to 18, being the victim of violence was associated with symptoms of depression (Fitzpatrick, 1993). In a sample of 225 African American youths ages 11 to 19 who lived in or around urban housing projects, depression was significantly correlated with having witnessed or participated in violent activity (DuRant, Getts, Cadenhead, Emans, & Woods, 1995; DuRant et al., 1994). Witnessing or being a part of a violent event elevates the risk of depression.

INDIVIDUAL BIOPSYCHOSOCIAL RISK FACTORS

Academic Performance

Difficulties in academic performance often plague children with depression—like other school-related problems, though, whether these difficulties are antecedents, concomitants, or consequences of depression disorder is unclear. Academic performance and grades often are negatively affected by childhood depression, but findings suggest that these declines are secondary to anhedonia and difficulties with concentration rather than actual intellectual impairments (Kovacs & Goldston, 1991).

Neurobiological Vulnerabilities

Neurotransmitters, the chemicals that carry impulses between neurons (nerve cells), have been strongly implicated in the etiology of depression. In this regard, the two most studied neurotransmitters are norepinephrine (NE) and serotonin (5-HT). Following its release from the axon terminal of one neuron, NE crosses a minute pathway called the synaptic cleft and is received by the dendrites of an adjacent neuron. This process generates an electrical impulse. The transmitting neuron has NE receptor sites that indicate when NE production should stop. Some of the unused NE is then reabsorbed by the first neuron, and the rest is metabolized. When a child is depressed, NE is not well regulated. The receptors become either oversensitized or undersensitized and, as levels of NE fluctuate, respond too much or even not at all. Both *excesses* and *deficiencies* in the breakdown products of NE found in urine are associated with symptoms of depression (Bentley & Walsh, 1996; Grinspoon & Bakalar, 1995; Kazdin, 1988; Riddle & Cho, 1989). Unusually high levels of 5-HT, which is thought to affect mood and bodily functions, such as sleep, appetite, sexual behavior, and circadian rhythms, have been found in many depressed patients. However, the explanation for the correlation between low 5-HT and depression is elusive (Bentley & Walsh, 1996; Grinspoon & Bakalar, 1995). The intricate pathways of these billions of neurons and their relationships to depression remain the focus of much research.

Neuroendocrine dysfunctions also are implicated in the etiology of depression. Disturbances along the hypothalamic–pituitary–adrenal (HPA) axis where cortisol is produced are associated with depression. Hypersecretion of cortisol and disruption in its 24-hour cycle are found in a substantial number of adults with MDD (Grinspoon &

Bakalar, 1995). This phenomenon of high blood levels of cortisol in depressed adults is less well studied in children. Compared with control groups, neither prepubertal children (Puig-Antich et al., 1989) nor adolescents with MDD (Dahl et al., 1989) have demonstrated significant differences in hypersecretion. However, Dahl and colleagues did find that one suicidal teenager had significantly elevated cortisol levels at the onset of sleep. Clearly, more research is needed in this area.

Research has also suggested that disturbances along the hypothylamic–pituitary–thyroid axis are risk factors for depression. The thyroid gland produces hormones that control the basal metabolic rate of the body; abnormally low levels of thyroid hormones result in fatigue, listlessness, and other symptoms of depression. Between 25 percent and 70 percent of persons suffering from MDD have a poor response to an experimental injection of a thyroid-releasing hormone (TRH), which normally is secreted by the hypothalamus to stimulate the pituitary gland to produce thyroid-stimulating hormone (TSH). The TSH in turn promotes the release of thyroid hormones (Grinspoon & Bakalar, 1995). When a person has a blunted, delayed response to the injection of TRH, it suggests a dysfunction at the hypothylamic level. Whether the disturbances on the HPT axis precede, coexist with, or follow depressive illness is an area of contention.

In summary, research on neurotransmitters and neuroendocrine systems, which are decidedly interdependent, has contributed in large part to an understanding of the neurobiological characteristics of depression. Additional areas of research include studies of the relationship of depression to sleep disorders and growth hormone. It is significant that there is considerable "chicken or egg" controversy over findings because it is not clear whether depression causes changes in a child's neurobiology or vice versa.

Genetic Factors

Although few studies of children have been conducted, studies with adult probands suggest that vulnerability to depression is inherited. Gershon, Targum, Kessler, Mazure, and Bunney (1977) found the heritability of an affective disorder in monozygotic twins to be about 65 percent. Using two sources to acquire a sample of more than 15,000 adult twins and their relatives, Kendler and colleagues (1994) found a correlation of depressive symptoms in 30 percent to 37 percent of monozygotic twins. The concordance among dizygotic twins was half that for monozygotic twins, which suggests a clear genetic effect.

Although genetic studies consistently show familial trends toward depression, especially MDD, neither a single gene, a constellation of genes, nor a genetic marker directly correlated with depression has been identified. The diathesis-stress model posits that although the origins of depression may be due to genetics, the course of the disorder is affected by the interplay among biological and environmental factors such as stress and social support (Bentley & Walsh, 1996; Hammen & Rudolph, 2003; Lazarus & Folkman, 1984). Although replication is needed, Caspi and colleagues (2003) provide evidence for a gene-by-environment interaction that increases vulnerability to depression. A prospective–longitudinal study found that 43 percent of adults who had experienced multiple stressful life events (for example, employment, financial, housing, health, and relationship difficulties) within the past five years, also had met criteria for MDD within the past year. The normal variant of the serotonin transporter gene in these study participants was "short" and made less protein. This short gene resulted in increased levels of serotonin in the synaptic cleft, prolonged binding of neurotransmitters to postsynaptic neurons, and decreased cellular ability to block unwanted messages. Only 17 percent of persons with the "long" gene, which may be a protective factor, experienced depression after suffering multiple stressful life events (Caspi et al., 2003). These findings support the search for linkages between genetic vulnerability for depression and environmental factors.

Comorbidity with Other Childhood Mental Disorders

Although it is debatable whether other mental disorders precede, coexist, or follow childhood depression, their co-occurrence is not debatable. A review of six epidemiological studies indicated that the existence of childhood depression increases the likelihood of other disorders 20-fold (Angold & Costello, 1993). Whether comorbidity is due to overlapping risk factors, variations of the same underlying disorder, distinct syndromes, or the creation of risk factors by an initial depressive disorder remains a focus of investigation (Caron & Rutter, 1991; Goodman et al., 2000).

Anxiety disorders are the most prevalent comorbid conditions with childhood depression (Kovacs, Gatsonis, Paulauskas, & Richards, 1989; Ollendick & Yule, 1990). In her review, Kovacs (1990) concluded that 30 percent to 75 percent of depressed children experienced a coexisting anxiety disorder. Kovacs, Paulauskas, Gatsonis, & Richards (1988) reported that in two-thirds of the children with MDD, symptoms of anxiety disorder preceded those of depression by more than two months. Moreover, the anxiety disorder tended to persist after recovery from MDD.

Although MDD and DD are sharply contrasted in terms of acuity and duration, the common clinical symptoms often contribute to a "double depression." Kovacs, Feinberg, Crouse-Novak, Paulauskas, Pollock, & Finkelstein (1984) first report of the comorbidity of MDD and DD in children was validated by Lewinsohn, Rohde, Seeley, and Hops (1991). Dysthymia is a risk factor for the occurrence of MDD (Akiskal, 1994); in one study, 76 percent of clinically referred children with DD later developed MDD (Kovacs, Akiskal, Gatsonis, & Parrone, 1994). Pre-existing DD also was a risk factor that predicted a lengthy median duration (nine months) for clinic patients with MDD (Kovacs et al., 1997).

Depression also co-occurs frequently with conduct disorder (CD). CD was present in 38 percent of prepubertal children and 25 percent of adolescents with MDD, according to Ryan and colleagues (1987). Puig-Antich (1982) found that approximately one-third of prepubertal males with MDD also met criteria for CD. That CD symptoms sometimes decrease when children receive antidepressants caused researchers to raise the question of whether a single disorder may underlie both conditions (Kovacs et al., 1989). They reported that 23 percent of latency-aged children had both MDD and CD; the estimated risk of having both increased to 36 percent by age 19. Like anxiety disorders, CD also commonly preceded depression (Puig-Antich, 1982; Sack, Beiser, Phillips, & Baker-Brown, 1993) and remained after recovery from depression (Kovacs et al., 1988) Aggressive behavior, one of the criteria for CD, is prevalent in depressed children and adolescents. Athough future research may clarify whether aggression occurs only during depressive episodes, one-fourth of 13- to 17-year-old clinic youths with MDD reported significant, chronic aggressive behaviors (Knox, King, Hanna, Logan, & Ghaziuddin, 2000). Only participants with higher levels of aggression had diagnosed comorbid CD or oppositional defiant disorder.

Studies of antisocial behavior often have used all-male populations; this practice has hindered the identification of gender-specific risk factors for externalizing disorders in girls. Antisocial behaviors among adolescent girls may be associated with an underlying depression that predisposes them to delinquency. Findings from a longitudinal study of patterns of adjustment problems in girls suggest a shift from internalizing problems (somatic complaints and timidity) at age 10 to externalizing problems (aggression and CD) by age 13 (Wangby, Bergman, & Magnusson, 1999). Other researchers compared 12- and 15-year-old girls with mild to moderate depressive symptomatology with their nondepressed counterparts. The depressed girls were approximately twice as likely to engage in crimes against others, one and one-half times as likely to commit property crimes, and four times as likely to engage in aggressive behavior (Obeidallah & Earls, 1999). Obeidallah and Earls hypothesized that the antisocial behaviors stemmed from underlying depression that resulted in low self-esteem, diminished concern for personal safety, and withdrawal from schools and other prosocial institutions. Comorbidity with conduct or other externalizing behavior disorders was associated with an increased duration of two-and-one-half years of DD in male and female clinic children (Kovacs et al., 1997).

Having MDD or DD increases the risk of having initial, repeated, or more severe MDD. Sequentially sampling from a clinic-based population of eight- to 13-year-old children, Kovacs, Feinberg, Crouse-Novak, Paulauskas, Finkelstein (1984) found that 50 percent of children with dysthymia later developed MDD; this comorbidity of MDD and DD in 30 percent to 70 percent of children has been validated by others (Kovacs et al., 1994; Kovacs et al., 1997; Lewinsohn et al., 1991). The median time for the onset of MDD was 3.3 years following the diagnosis of DD. The cohort of children with MDD had a cumulative 26 percent risk of a second episode within a year and 72 percent risk within five years. Although DD is not considered a prodrome to MDD, it is thought to increase a child's vulnerability to it (Akiskal, 1994). Overall studies find that 24 percent to 76 percent of children with DD progress to have MDD. This pattern of MDD superimposed on DD is sometimes described as "double depression" (APA, 2000; Keller et al., 1988; Kovacs et al., 1994). Preexisting DD also was a risk factor that predicted a lengthy median duration (nine months) for clinic patients with MDD (Kovacs et al., 1997).

Mental disorders reviewed in earlier chapters also co-occur with depression. Researchers studying clinical populations of substance-abusing youths have found comorbid rates of depression ranging from 16 percent to 50 percent; community samples have found adolescent users of illicit drugs to have more depressed moods than nonusers (Buckstein, 1995). DD preceded substance abuse with a majority of hospitalized teenagers and thus may be a risk factor for substance abuse (Hovens, Cantwell, & Kiriakos, 1994). Comorbidity rates between depression and attention deficit hyperactivity disorder (ADHD) have ranged from chance levels to 70 percent. Some controversial findings suggest that subgroups of children with ADHD have coexisting MDD or DD. Furthermore, CD co-occurs frequently with both depression and ADHD, which suggests possible linkages among them (Biederman, Newcorn, & Sprich, 1991; Fleming & Offord, 1990; Hinshaw, 1994). Thus, the "unmasking" of childhood depression by identifying comorbid disorders heightens awareness of risk factors that may exponentially increase a child's biopsychosocial vulnerability to multiple disorders.

Comorbidity with Chronic Illness

Somatic presentations in children have long been considered manifestations of depression in children, presumably because children lack cognitive and verbal skills to communicate their emotional pain. A meta-analysis of 60 studies found that 9 percent to 14 percent of children with a chronic medical condition have an increased risk for *symptoms* of depression (Bennett, 1994). Bennett reported that children with asthma, sickle-cell disease (SCD), and recurrent abdominal pain appear to be at greater risk for depression than children with other medical conditions, but studies are equivocal. Children with asthma were rated significantly higher on measures of depression by their parents, but self-reports were not statistically significant when compared with healthy children and those with diabetes or cancer (Padur et al., 1995). Children with SCD had higher scores on the Depression Rating Scale (revised) than a healthy control group; however, clinical interviews with a child psychiatrist found fewer subjects with SCD to be depressed (Yang, Cepeda, Price, Shah, & Mankad, 1994). Generally, children with chronic illness appear to have more internalizing than externalizing responses to chronic illness, but the precise relationship between chronic illness and depression is poorly understood (Bennett, 1994). Perhaps related to internalizing tendencies of children with physical limitations, Kashani, Cantwell, Shekim, and Reid (1982) reported that children with depression and somatic complaints did not have CD, and, conversely, children with depression and CD rarely manifested somatic complaints.

Cognitive Styles

Several cognitive styles of perceiving the world are correlated with depression. The influential "learned helplessness" model (Seligman, 1975), which posited that depression results from uncontrollable and aversive events, was reformulated to a causal attribution model (Abramson, Seligman, & Teasdale, 1978). This revision introduced the concept of attributional style, the way in which one perceives events and interprets outcomes. A depressive attributional style is the tendency to expect negative outcomes and to attribute them to the combination of three factors: (1) individual *internal* attributes, (2) *global* and largely uncontrollable forces, and (3) *stability* of hostile attributes over time (Alloy, Peterson, Abramson, & Seligman, 1984). Positive outcomes, in contrast, are attributed to external, specific, and unstable factors. A number of cross-sectional and longitudinal studies have linked children's depression with a depressive attributional style (Hammen & Rudolph, 2003).

Cognitive models of depression, notably those of Beck, emphasize three aspects of cognitive functioning: (1) negative *core beliefs*, fundamental beliefs about oneself; (2) negative *intermediate beliefs*, one's basic assumptions, attitudes, and rules; and (3) negative *automatic thoughts,* one's distorted interpretations of situations and events (Beck, 1995; Beck, Rush, Shaw, & Emery, 1979). Negative perceptions of self, the world, and the future comprise the "negative cognitive triad," a distorted style of thinking that appears to be highly correlated with depression.

Protective Factors in Childhood Depression

Like risks, protective factors are distinguished as broad environmental conditions; family, school, and neighborhood conditions; and individual biopsychosocial conditions. Unfortunately, this is an area of developing knowledge, and there is limited information on protective factors for childhood depression.

Broad Environmental Protective Factors

Mothers living in poverty who felt a sense of mastery regarding their lives (self-efficacy) and social support, that is, knew someone who would baby-sit, were less likely to have MDD than mothers who did not satisfy those two conditions (Siefert et al., 2000).

Family, School, and Neighborhood Protective Factors

Parental education, employment, and health appear to protect children who live in poor, high-crime, urban neighborhoods from depression (DuRant et al., 1994; DuRant et al., 1995). DuRant and colleagues compared African American adolescents who reported lower levels of hopelessness, higher scores on purpose in life, and greater belief that they would be alive at age 25 with depressed teenagers experiencing feelings of hopelessness. Teenagers who lived in households headed by persons with higher education reported fewer feelings of depression and hopelessness. Parental employment was correlated with higher scores on purpose in life. In turn, these more optimistic adolescents were less likely to engage in the violent behavior, which—as discussed earlier in "Family, School, and Neighborhood Risk Factors: Neighborhood Violence"—has been reported as a risk factor for depression. A rise in depression for urban, poor African Americans ages nine to 15 were associated with increased parent–child conflict and decreased parental monitoring (Sagrestano, Paikoff, Holmbeck, & Fendrich, 2003). Sagrestano's group also found that parental depression was associated with increased conflict and decreased positive parenting behaviors, such as support, warmth, and intimacy. Garrison and colleagues (1997) concluded that children's *perceived* family support and cohesion may have been of equal or greater value in the decreased incidence of MDD than actual family structure. An earlier study revealed that support from a male partner significantly decreased depression in adolescent African American women who were new mothers (Thompson & Peebles-Wilkins, 1992). Another study found that social support from an infant's grandmother or father was associated with significantly lower rates of depression among pregnant and postpartum African American teenagers (Barnet, Joffe, Duggan, Wilson, & Repke, 1996). Compared with offspring in single-parent families in which the parent had bipolar disorder, offspring in two-parent families, in which an ill parent was maintained with medications and psychotherapy in an outpatient clinic, had a comparatively lower incidence of depression (Laroche, 1986). The mere presence of a husband or partner, however, was not a significant protective factor for depressed women (Siefert et al., 2000). Although one would likely expect that children from low-income and impoverished neighborhoods would be vulnerable to depression, these studies suggest that their positive perceptions of family and environmental context are protective.

RISK AND PROTECTIVE FACTORS BY AGE, GENDER, RACE, AND ETHNICITY

Age

Studies over the past decade indicate that early onset is a risk factor for increased duration of depressive illness. Onset of MDD in younger school-age children, particularly in children under 11 years of age, is significantly associated with slower recovery (Kovacs, Feinberg, Crouse-Novak, Paulauskas, & Finkelstein, 1984). Researchers report that, in 14- to 18-year-old high school students, early onset—defined as before 15.5 years of age—is correlated with increased duration and suicidal ideation (Lewinsohn et al., 1994). One study found that rates for the onset of depression after exposure to violence were significantly higher in younger children, ages seven to 10 than the rates for older children, ages 11 to 19 (Fitzpatrick, 1993).

Gender

The lifetime prevalence for depression is significantly higher for females than for males. Once MDD occurs, females are almost twice as likely (29 percent) to develop a second MDD episode as males (16 percent); however, the mean time to recurrence, 28.4 months for females and 21.1 months for males, does not appear to differ significantly (Lewinsohn et al., 1994). Gender (female) was found to predict early onset MDD and to be correlated with higher rates of depressive disorder in 14- to 15-year-old adolescents (Rutter, Graham, Chadwick, & Yule, 1976).

Compared with males, females appear to be more susceptible to depressive reactions. Decreased self-esteem and stressful events are more highly correlated with depression in ninth- through 12-grade girls than in boys (Allgood-Merten & Lewinsohn, 1990). Among pregnant teenagers, nearly half (42 percent) have reported depressive symptoms. In addition, one-third report depressive symptoms at two and four months postpartum (Barnet et al., 1996). These rates are higher than the overall rate for postpartum depression, excluding the short-lived "baby blues" of new mothers reported by O'Hara and Zekowski (1988).

Violence, too, appears to affect boys and girls differently. In a study that examined the combined effects of exposure to violence and low income, females, ages seven to 19, had a statistically significant increase in symptoms of depression compared with males exposed to similar conditions (Fitzpatrick, 1993).

Ethnicity, Race, and Culture

The study of depression among minority youths is much neglected by researchers, and there is considerable controversy about the affect of language, cultural values, and norms on diagnostic methods and findings. In one epidemiological study, Roberts and Chen (1995) found that Mexican American middle-school students reported significantly more depression than their Anglo American counterparts. Female Mexican Americans experienced the highest rate of depressive symptoms. Mexican American students also reported significantly more suicide ideation. Suggesting that the concomitants of minority ethnic status rather than ethnic status per se increase the risk for depression, researchers found the strongest associations with depression to be loneliness and a limited ability to speak English.

Too few studies have examined childhood depression among African American children, and the results to date are equivocal. Sampling 550 suburban middle-school children, researchers found higher rates of depression among African American than white children in grade 7; in a later sampling of the same students in grade 9, they reported that only African American females showed a greater prevalence rate over white students (Garrison, Jackson, Marsteller, McKeown, & Addy, 1990). No difference in prevalence rates of depression between African American and white participants was found in a clinical sample of 300 children ages seven to 11 (Costello et al., 1988).

Racial and ethnic influences may contribute to differences in the severity of depressive symptoms reported by sexually abused girls. In a study of 134 females ages six to 18, the 38 Latina girls of primarily Mexican American origin who had experienced penetration tended to be more depressed than African American or white females who experienced penetration and Latina females who had not experienced penetration. The importance of chastity and virginity in the Latin culture may account for the increased level of distress and contribute to depressive symptoms (Mennen, 1995).

ASSESSMENT OF CHILDHOOD DEPRESSION

As suggested by the risk factors, assessment of childhood depression must use complementary types of evaluative methods, screen for comorbid disorders, and evaluate the social context. A comprehensive assessment must include a physical examination by a pediatrician, child neurologist, or psychiatrist and should include a review of educational records, administration of a battery of psychological tests, observation in multiple settings, and reports from parents, teachers, coaches, guidance counselors, friends, clergy, and significant others. To provide a thorough assessment, two sources of information from children, family members, or significant others are recommended: (1) self-report and (2) structured or semistructured interviews. Because perceptions of informants may be discordant, no source can be regarded as singularly valid. For example, researchers found poor correspondence between parental and adolescent reports of aggression, especially when it occurred outside the home or among females (Knox et al., 2000). A triangulation of data is needed to increase the likelihood of making an accurate diagnosis and developing a comprehensive treatment plan.

SELF-REPORT

The majority of measures used to assess childhood depression are self-reports. Self-reports are especially important to the assessment of depression because many of the key criteria—feelings of sadness, guilt, and worthlessness—are subjective. The number of measures has increased greatly in the past 20 years, and they vary in their goals (for example, clinical diagnosis versus assessment of symptom severity; Kazdin, 1988; Mash & Terdal, 1988). Self-report assessments generally take the form of paper-and-pencil tests and structured or semistructured clinical interviews. Paper-and-pencil instruments are useful measures of symptom severity but are inadequately discriminatory to make a diagnosis. Several measures use pictures cued with questions to enhance mental processing of children with verbal or cognitive limitations due to such attributes as youth, inattention, or underdeveloped language skills. Pictorial instruments that assess depression include the Dominic-R (Valla, Bergeron, Bidaut-Russell, St-Georges, & Gaudet, 1997; Valla, Bergeron, & Smolla, 2000), which is also available as an interactive computer program, the Preschool Symptom Self-Report (PRESS; Martini, Strayhorn, & Puig-Antich, 1990), and the Pictorial Instrument for Children and Adolescents (PICA-III-R; Ernst, Cookus, & Moravec, 2000; Ernst, Godfrey, Silva, Pouget, & Welkowitz, 1994). Although pictorial approaches are recent and lack extensive studies of their validity and reliability, they offer a promising addition to the assessment repertoire.

Diagnostic interviews provide broad indicators for the presence or absence of disorders. Interviews require considerable time, however, and careful staff training to minimize practitioner biases such as selective data collection to confirm a diagnosis or inattention to information that rules out diagnoses. Angold (McClellan & Werry, 2000) makes the distinction between respondent-based interviews such as the Diagnostic Interview Schedule for Children (DISC), Children's Interview for Psychiatric Syndromes (ChIPS; Weller, Weller, Fristad, Rooney, & Schecter, 2000), and Diagnostic Interview for Children and Adolescents (DICA) that capture informants' responses and interviewer-based instruments. Interview-based measures such as the Schedule for Affective Disorders and Schizophrenia for School-Age Children (K-SADS), the Interview Schedule for Children and Adolescents (ISCA), and the Child and Adolescent Psychiatric Assessment (CAPA) require clinical decisions—paraphrasing and probing—and interpretations (McClellan & Werry, 2000). Most of the following diagnostic tools not only assess for depression, but also for comorbid disorders.

DIAGNOSTIC INTERVIEW SCHEDULE FOR CHILDREN (DISC)

The National Institute of Mental Health (NIMH)-DISC-IV revision of the DISC-Y and its parallel version for parents (DISC-P) were released in 1997; they are highly structured interviews that are particularly useful in assessing for depression. The DISC-Y can be administered to nine- to 17-year-old youths by lay interviewers who have completed two or three days of training. Administered in approximately 75 minutes to both children and parents, the DISC-IV explores the onset, duration, and severity of depressive symptoms. As a result of DSM–IV and related criteria, DISC-IV is a substantially field-tested measure and provides scores regarding 30 psychiatric disorders, including affective and comorbid disorders. This version of the DISC is available in English and Spanish; a computer-assisted program for interviewers is also available (McClellan & Werry, 2000; Shaffer, Fisher, Lucas, Dulcan, & Schwab-Stone, 2000).

DIAGNOSTIC INTERVIEW FOR CHILDREN AND ADOLESCENTS (DICA)

The fifth version of the DICA became available in 1997 and is compatible with DSM–IV. Although historically classified as a structured interview, DICA authors categorize it as a semistructured interview because it requires clinical judgment to follow specifically patterned probes. The administration time ranges between one and two hours for both parent and child interviews. The DICA targets children from ages six to 17 and assesses for MDD, DD, and comorbid disorders. Some questions are designed to assess factors of risk (for example, parental drug use) and protection (for example, after-school activities). Two to four weeks of extensive training, for example, working with the younger children, are required. A computerized version is available for interviewers (Reich, 2000).

SCHEDULE FOR AFFECTIVE DISORDERS AND SCHIZOPHRENIA FOR SCHOOL-AGE CHILDREN (K-SADS)

The K-SADS-P, a semistructured interview, was created in 1978 by Puig-Antich and Chambers (Puig-Antich, Blau, Marx, Greenhill, & Chambers, 1978) and was last updated in 1996 by Ambrosini and Dixon (Ambrosini, 2000). The current clinical version, K-SADS-PIVR, is used to assess current and the previous 12 months of psychiatric symptoms and their severity. Designed for compatibility with the DSM–IV, the K-SADS-PIVR is often employed to identify children with mood disorders. The same clinician administers an analogous 90-minute interview, first to the parents and then to children ages six to 18. The first part of the interview is unstructured, and the informant identifies a wide range of symptoms; the second part of the interview is structured and elicits information on onset, severity, and duration of identified symptoms (Costello, 1991; Kazdin, 1988). Because there is considerable latitude in adapting questions and probes to the respondents, interviewers must receive substantive training to accomplish reliability of administration (Ambrosini, 2000).

INTERVIEW SCHEDULE FOR CHILDREN AND ADOLESCENTS (ISCA)

Originally called the Interview Schedule for Children (ISC; Kovacs, 1985b), the ISCA and its versions is another widely used semistructured, symptom-oriented interview; it was developed for children ages eight to 17. Liked for its flowing design, severity rating scales, flexibility, and usefulness in research on childhood depression, ISCA is administered to both children and parents. A two-hour to two and one-half hour initial parent interview is followed by a 45- to 90-minute child intake with the same clinician; shorter, follow-up versions of ISCA are used to monitor functioning. The ISCA specifically assesses mood, anxiety, conduct, and other comorbid disorders, and is compatible with DSM–IV. The interviewer must be knowledgeable of DSM-related criteria and have advanced clinical skills. The intake version is available in English and Spanish (Costello, 1991; Kazdin, 1988; Sherrill & Kovacs, 2000).

THE CHILD AND ADOLESCENT PSYCHIATRIC ASSESSMENT (CAPA)

The CAPA collects data on intensity, frequency, duration, and onset of MDD and DD, as well as comorbid externalizing and anxiety disorders. Interviewing nine- to 17-year-old children and their parents, the clinician is guided by a detailed series of probes to ascertain levels of symptom severity and functional impairment. The diagnostic section takes approximately 45 minutes each for parent and child. The CAPA is in modular form, and additional sections assess family functioning, psychosocial impairment, and life events. Only certified CAPA trainees may administer the interview after completing one to two weeks each of didactic and clinical training. The CAPA uses DSM–IV criteria and is available in English and Spanish (Angold & Costello, 2000).

CHILDREN'S DEPRESSION INVENTORY (CDI)

The CDI is a frequently used and well-researched measure of depression in children between ages seven and 17 (Kovacs, 1985a; Kovacs & Beck, 1977). The CDI includes 27 items that measure cognitive, affective, and behavioral signs of depression. Reviewing a number of studies using the CBI, Kazdin (1988) concluded that the CDI has high internal consistency and moderate test–retest reliability. It is correlated in expected directions with self-esteem, negative cognitions, hopelessness, and other constructs, but because it was designed to measure severity, it does not always discriminate depression from other disorders.

IMPLICATIONS FOR PREVENTION, EARLY INTERVENTION, AND TREATMENT OF CHILDHOOD DEPRESSION

With growing evidence that childhood depression is explained—at least in part—by biological factors that may be influenced by contextual risks, the enhancement of protective factors holds enormous potential, both as prevention and as intervention strategies. Individual, family, neighborhood, school, health, and environmental risk factors must be affected in order to reduce the severity and duration of childhood depression. Although they may have little or no effect on middle-income children, environmental conditions may both cause and exacerbate depression in low-income or minority children. Some minority youths lack English-language skills, which are essential for academic and social success in English-speaking settings and promote resilience among at-risk children. For others, access to adequate health and mental health care may be limited, or service providers may be insensitive to cultural differences that affect depression. Because of advances in the treatment of depression in adults and because parental depression is a risk factor for childhood depression, the degree to which a community is successful in developing accessible mental health services may be viewed as a protective factor for childhood depression.

PREVENTION AND EARLY INTERVENTION

Community settings and schools can provide primary prevention at three levels: (1) universal, (2) selected, or (3) indicated (Bucy, 1994). *Universal* programs are offered to all children in an effort to develop awareness of feelings and to build social skills in managing anger, sadness, and other affect. An example is Developing Understanding of Self and Others by Dinkmeyer (cited in Bucy, 1994), a program that uses such activities as storytelling, puppetry, and role-playing to improve self-esteem and positive self-images among school-age children.

Selected programs target children who are members of a group considered to be at risk for internalizing disorders such as depression. The Children of Divorce Intervention Program, by Alpert-Gillis, Pedro-Carroll, and Cowen (cited in Bucy, 1994), attempts to increase children's self-awareness about divorce, to develop a mutually supportive network, to increase problem-solving abilities, and to highlight positive qualities in themselves and their families. Similar programs have been developed for groups of youths who are exposed to violence, are pregnant, or are experiencing significant losses and, as a result, may be at risk of depression.

Indicated primary prevention is designed to help children who are at risk because of particular individual characteristics that are linked with depression. The evidence for increased comorbidity of depression with CD, ADHD, anxiety disorders, substance-abuse disorders, and possibly some chronic illnesses requires that practitioners screen for underlying depression when these other disorders are present.

Practitioners must be mindful of biases that inform their assessment and treatment of childhood depression. Using vignettes that were illustrative of adolescent depression, social workers were asked to identify the problem and to recommend a treatment plan (Kovacs & Goldston, 1991). Respondents with a psychodynamic–psychoanalytic orientation were significantly more likely—while behaviorists were less likely—to recognize depression in an alcoholic family; practitioners younger than 30 were significantly more likely to diagnose depression in a female with school problems and a male with felony charges. Social workers who specialized in mental health, children, and youths, or who have a generalist practice were more likely to address the depression than were family or criminal justice specialists. Although we acknowledge study limitations, important questions about the distorting effects of the practitioner's specialization, theory base, and age on recognition and treatment of childhood depression remain.

TREATMENT

Treatment of Parental Depression

Studies indicate that parents with mood disorders are at risk for impaired role functioning as partners, parents, and employees. Children appear to be protected from depression when, as LaRoche (1986) noted, parents with mood disorders receive adequate treatment and subsequently fulfill parental and other roles. Mounting evidence demonstrates that psychopharmacological, cognitive–behavioral (CBT), psychodynamic, and interpersonal therapies can reduce the severity, duration, and frequency of depression in adults.

A meta-analysis of the use of cognitive therapy with adults suffering from MDD demonstrates its efficacy (Dobson, 1989). The Sheffield Psychotherapy Project found that CBT and psychodynamic–interpersonal therapies were equally effective treatments for depression (Miser, 1996). Severely depressed patients had significantly better outcomes when randomized to the 16-week rather than eight-week trial, a finding that supports lengthier treatment for severely ill persons (Riddle & Cho, 1989). Many practitioners used combined psychotherapeutic and psychopharmacological approaches.

Psychopharmacological treatment is widely viewed as effective in shortening the duration of illness, lessening the severity of symptoms, and preventing relapse in adults with severe MDD. Since the 1950s, two classes of medications have been standard treatment for depressive disorders. Tricyclic antidepressants (TCAs) such as imipramine

(Tofranil), amitriptyline (Elavil), desipramine (Norpramin), and doxepin (Sinequan) block the reabsorption of NE by receptors and thus enhance its effects. Clinical trials report that between 65 percent and 85 percent of persons with depression improve on tricyclics, contrasted with 20 percent to 40 percent of control groups taking a placebo (Grinspoon & Bakalar, 1995). Unpleasant side effects include dry mouth, drowsiness, blurred vision, sexual dysfunction, weight gain, elevated blood pressure, and, rarely, death from cardiovascular complications. Monoamine oxidase inhibitors (MAOIs) comprise the other traditional class of antidepressant medications. The MAOIs such as phenelzine (Nardil) or isocarboxazid (Marplan) block the actions of an enzyme that results in the breakdown of dopamine, NE, and 5-HT (Gelenberg, Bassuk, & Schoonover, 1991; Grinspoon & Bakalar, 1995). The MAOIs are used less because of the side effects such as hypotension, dry mouth, insomnia, drowsiness, fatigue, impotence, edema, and weight gain. The newest class of antidepressants includes the serotonin-reuptake inhibitors (SSRIs), which include fluoxetine (Prozac), sertraline (Zoloft), paroxetine (Paxil), and fluvoxamine (Luvox). The SSRIs, introduced in the 1980s, are increasingly preferred because they generally have fewer side effects than other antidepressants, target specific neurotransmitters, and are safer in overdose (Bentley & Walsh, 1996). Other recent nontricyclic antidepressants include venlafaxine (Effexor), nefazodone (Serzone), trazodone (Desyrel), and mirtazapine (Remeron). Clinical trials have established the efficacy of TCAs, MAOIs, SSRIs, and nontrycylics in adults, wherein choice of a particular medication generally is based on minimization of negative side effects.

In summary, a variety of therapies including psychopharmacological and psychotherapeutic approaches based on cognitive, interpersonal, and psychodynamic theories may reduce adult depression. Assessment and treatment, however, particularly for mothers who suffer from depression, must examine parenting in the interactive social, economic, cultural, and developmental contexts of both parent and child (Kendler et al., 1994). We hope that treatment of parental depression will alter and perhaps even "untrigger" biological and social risk factors for children and render parents more capable of promoting resiliency in their children.

Treatment of Childhood Depression

Because depression has only recently been recognized as a serious disorder in childhood, few empirical studies with adequate samples have examined psychosocial interventions for children. One study found that CBT improved functional status in adolescents (Brent et al., 1998). And implicating again the importance of parental functioning in lowering rates of depression, Lewinsohn and colleagues reported that the greatest therapeutic gains were observed when there was a combination of adolescent and parent CBT groups rather than teenage-only groups (cited in Craighead, Curry, & McMillan, 1994). Gender-specific, integrative programs that address risk and resiliency factors such as poverty, ethnicity, academic performance, victimization, and health and mental health issues, specifically for girls who are likely at risk for depression, are available through the Office of Juvenile Justice and Delinquency Prevention (OJJDP; Gershon et al., 1977). To improve the treatment of youths with depression, the NIMH has launched a multisite clinical trial, the Treatment for Adolescents with Depression Study, to evaluate the effectiveness of treatment for 12- to 17-year-old adolescents with depression (NIMH, 2001).

Because adult-type symptoms of depression occur in children, a dramatic increase in the use of the same antidepressants prescribed for adults with children has occurred (Jensen et al., 1999). Rapidly changing differences in physiological growth, however, can affect the extent and rate of drug absorption, drug distribution in the body, renal functions, and drug response in children and adolescents (Paxton & Dragunow, 1999). Emerging as the drugs of choice for depressed children and adolescents, the SSRIs and nontrycylics are the focus of a number of clinical trials. In general, they have relatively few negative side effects, protect against overdosage, and are often efficacious both with depression and comorbid conditions such as anxiety disorders (Viesselman, 1999). Paroxetine (Keller et al., 2001) and fluoxetine (Emslie et al., 1997; Emslie, et al., 2002; Strober et al., 1999), for example, are effective and well tolerated by adolescents, and—in Emslie's trials—by children as young as seven who suffer from MDD.

Because social workers often have more frequent, in-depth contact with families and children than do physicians, it is critical that they understand the pharmacological actions and side effects of antidepressants. In addition to screening for adverse effects and misuse of medications, practitioners must attend to the meanings associated with psychotropic usage such as parental guilt for being the cause of a genetic disorder, relief at confirming a diagnosis, denial of the disorder, or parent–child conflict regarding autonomy (Dahl et al., 1989). Parents suffering from depression may benefit from suggestions for coping with their own lethargy and disorganization in order to administer the child's medications appropriately.

THE FUTURE

It is critical to develop longitudinal research to further examine the individual, family, school, and other risk and protective factors that contribute to childhood depression. We need prevention trials based on an improved understanding of risk and resilience. For example, if children with CDs were routinely evaluated and subsequently treated for early symptoms of depression, would depression be reduced in frequency, severity, and duration? Studies must examine transactional models of interpersonal functioning among children with depression and family members, who may themselves be suffering from depression; this increases the difficulty of the research. Culturally sensitive interventions must be provided for African American, Hispanic American, Native American, and other children whose rates of depression may be adversely affected by environmental conditions and limited access to services. Finally, studies to develop effective psychological and pharmacological treatments for children are needed.

CONCLUSION

So to ask again the question raised by psychoanalytic theorists from an earlier era: Do children experience depression? Clearly, yes. Moreover, etiological models of childhood depression suggest that the origins of depression are biopsychosocial. Although there is strong evidence for neurobiological contributors to childhood depression, the effect of psychosocial factors remains an essential part of the etiology, and the directionality of the biological and psychosocial conditions that appear to cause depression is unclear. Are biological factors triggered by social and other factors? Or are psychosocial risks the direct manifestation of neurobiological conditions? Although the studies reviewed here represent significant gains in the knowledge base regarding childhood depression, far deeper examinations of the combined and cumulative effects of genetics, social, and environmental factors that produce and that protect against childhood depression are needed.

REFERENCES

Abramson, L. Y., Seligman, M. E., & Teasdale, J. D. (1978). Learned helplessness in humans: Critique and reformulation. *Journal of Abnormal Psychology, 87*(1), 49–74.

Akiskal, H. S. (1994). Dysthymia: Clinical and external validity. *Acta Psychiatrica Scandinavica, 89*(Suppl. 383), 19–23.

Allgood-Merten, B., & Lewinsohn, P. M. (1990). Sex differences and adolescent depression. *Journal of Abnormal Psychology, 99*(1), 55–63.

Alloy, L. B., Peterson, C., Abramson, L. Y., & Seligman, M. E. (1984). Attributional style and the generality of learned helplessness. *Journal of Personality and Social Psychology, 46*(3), 681–687.

Ambrosini, P. J. (2000). Historical development and present status of the Schedule for Affective Disorders and Schizophrenia for School-Age Children (K-SADS). *Journal of the American Academy of Child and Adolescent Psychiatry, 39*(1), 49–58.

American Psychiatric Association. (2000). *Diagnostic and statistical manual of mental disorders* (4th ed.). Washington, DC: Author.

Angold, A., & Costello, E. J. (1993). Depressive comorbidity in children and adolescents: Empirical, theoretical, and methodological issues. *American Journal of Psychiatry, 150*(12), 1779–1791.

Angold, A., & Costello, E. J. (2000). The Child and Adolescent Psychiatric Assessment (CAPA). *Journal of the American Academy of Child and Adolescent Psychiatry, 39*(1), 39–48.

Asarnow, J. R., Tompson, M., Hamilton, E. B., Goldstein, M. J., & Guthrie, D. (1994). Family-expressed emotion, childhood-onset depression, and childhood-onset schizophrenia spectrum disorders: Is expressed emotion a nonspecific correlate of child psychopathology or a specific risk factor for depression? *Journal of Abnormal Child Psychology, 22*(2), 129–147.

Barnet, B., Joffe, A., Duggan, A. K., Wilson, M. D., & Repke, J. T. (1996). Depressive symptoms, stress, and social support in pregnant and postpartum adolescents. *Archives of Pediatrics & Adolescent Medicine, 150*(1), 64–69.

Beardslee, W. R., Versage, E. M., & Gladstone, T. R. (1998). Children of affectively ill parents: A review of the past 10 years. *Journal of the American Academy of Child and Adolescent Psychiatry, 37*(11), 1134–1141.

Beck, A. T., Rush, A. J., Shaw, B. F., & Emery, G. (1979). *Cognitive theory of depression.* New York: Guilford Press.

Beck, J. S. (1995). *Cognitive therapy: Basics and beyond.* New York: Guilford Press.

Begley, S. (1996, February 19). Your child's brain. *Newsweek,* pp. 54–61.

Bennett, D. S. (1994). Depression among children with chronic medical problems: A meta-analysis. *Journal of Pediatric Psychology, 19*(2), 149–169.

Bentley, K. J., & Walsh, J. (1996). *The social worker and psychotropic medication.* Pacific Grove, CA: Brooks/Cole.

Biederman, J., Newcorn, J., & Sprich, S. (1991). Comorbidity of attention deficit hyperactivity disorder with conduct, depressive, anxiety, and other disorders. *American Journal of Psychiatry, 148*(5), 564–577.

Bowlby, J. (1960). Grief and mourning in infancy and early childhood. *Psychoanalytic Study of the Child, 15,* 9–52.

Brent, D. A., Kolko, D. J., Birmaher, B., Baugher, M., Bridge, J., Roth, C., & Holder, D. (1998). Predictors of treatment efficacy in a clinical trial of three psychosocial treatments for adolescent depression. *Journal of the American Academy of Child & Adolescent Psychiatry, 37*(9), 906–914.

Buckstein, O. G. (1995). *Adolescent substance abuse: Assessment, prevention, and treatment.* New York: John Wiley & Sons.

Bucy, J. E. (1994). Internalizing affective disorders. In R. J. Simeonsson (Ed.), *Risk, resilience, and prevention: Promoting the well-being of all children.* Baltimore: Paul H. Brookes.

Burge, D., & Hammen, C. (1991). Maternal communication: Predictors of outcome at follow-up in a sample of children at high and low risk for depression. *Journal of Abnormal Psychology, 100*(2), 174–180.

Carlson, G. A., & Cantwell, D. P. (1979). Unmasking masked depression in children and adolescents. *American Journal of Psychiatry, 137*(4), 445–449.

Carlson, G. A., & Garber, J. (1986). Developmental issues in the classification of depression in children. In M. Rutter, C. E. Izard, & P. B. Read (Eds.), *Depression in young people* (pp. 399–434). New York: Guilford Press.

Caron, C., & Rutter, M. (1991). Comorbidity in child psychopathology: Concepts, issues and research strategies. *Journal of Child Psychology and Psychiatry, 32*(7), 1063–1080.

Caspi, A., Sugden, K., Moffitt, T. E., Taylor, A., Craig, I. W., Harrington, H., McClay, J., Mill, J., Martin, J., Braithwaite, A., & Poulton, R. (2003, July 18). Influence of life stress on depression: Moderation by a polymorphism in the 5-HTT gene. *Science, 301,* 386–389.

Centers for Disease Control and Prevention. 2001. [Unpublished data]. Retrieved from http://www.cdc.gov on August 13, 2001.

Chwast, J. (1974). Delinquency and criminal behavior as depressive equivalents in adolescents. In S. Lesse (Ed.), *Masked depression* (pp. 219–235). New York: Jason Aronson.

Cicchetti, D., & Schneider-Rosen, K. (1986). An organizational approach to childhood depression. In M. Rutter, C. E. Izard, & P. B. Read (Eds.), *Depression in young people* (pp. 71–134). New York: Guilford Press.

Cohen, P., Cohen, J., Kasen, S., Velez, C. N., Hartmark, C., Johnson, J., Rojas, M., Brook, J., & Streuning, E. L. (1993). An epidemiological study of disorders in late childhood and adolescence: 1. Age- and gender-specific prevalence. *Journal of Child Psychology and Psychiatry, 34*(6), 851–867.

Costello, A. J. (1991). Structured interviewing. In M. Lewis (Ed.), *Child and adolescent psychiatry: A comprehensive textbook* (pp. 463–472). Baltimore: Williams & Wilkins.

Costello, E. J., Costello, A. J., Edelbrock, C., Burns, B. J., Dulcan, M. K., Brent, D., & Janiszewski, S. (1988). Psychiatric disorders in pediatric primary care. *Archives of General Psychiatry, 45*(12), 1107–1116.

Craighead, W. E., Curry, J. F., & McMillan, D. K. (1994). Childhood and adolescent depression. In L. W. Craighead, W. E. Craighead, A. E. Kazdin, & M. J. Mahoney (Eds.), *Cognitive and behavioral interventions: An empirical approach to mental health problems* (pp. 301–312). Boston: Allyn & Bacon.

Dahl, R., Puig-Antich, J., Ryan, N., Nelson, B., Novacenko, H., Twomey, J., Williamson, D., Goetz, R., & Ambrosini, P. J. (1989). Cortisol secretion in adolescents with major depressive disorder. *Acta Psychiatrica Scandanavia, 80,* 18–26.

Dobson, K. S. (1989). A meta-analysis of the efficacy of cognitive therapy for depression. *Journal of Consulting and Clinical Psychology, 57*(3), 414–419.

DuRant, R. H., Cadenhead, C., Pendergrast, R. A., Slavens, G., & Linder, C. W. (1994). Factors associated with the use of violence among urban black adolescents. *American Journal of Public Health, 84*(4), 612–617.

DuRant, R. H., Getts, A., Cadenhead, C., Emans, S. J., & Woods, E. R. (1995). Exposure to violence and victimization and depression, hopelessness, and purpose in life among adolescents living in and around public housing. *Developmental and Behavioral Pediatrics, 16*(4), 233–237.

Emslie, G. J., Heiligenstein, J. H., Wagner, K. D., Hoog, S. L., Ernest, D. E., Brown, E., Nilsson, M., & Jacobson, J. G. (2002). Fluoxetine for acute treatment of depression in children and adolescents: A placebo-controlled, randomized clinical trial. *Journal of the American Academy of Child & Adolescent Psychiatry, 41*(10), 1205–1215.

Emslie, G. J., Rush, A. J., Weinberg, W. A., Kowatch, R.O.A., Hughes, C. W., Carmody, T., & Rintelmann, J. (1997). A double-blind, randomized, placebo-controlled trial of fluoxetine in children and adolescents with depression. *Archives of General Psychiatry, 54*(11), 1031–1037.

Ernst, M., Cookus, B. A., & Moravec, B. C. (2000). Pictorial Instrument for Children and Adolescents (PICA-III-R). *Journal of the American Academy of Child and Adolescent Psychiatry, 39*(1), 94–99.

Ernst, M., Godfrey, K. A., Silva, R. R., Pouget, E. R., & Welkowitz, J. (1994). A new pictorial instrument for child and adolescent psychiatry: A pilot study. *Psychiatry Resident, 51,* 87–104.

Feighner, J. P., Robins, E., Guze, S. B., Woodruff, R. A., Winokur, G., & Munoz, R. (1972). Diagnostic criteria for use in psychiatric research. *Archives of General Psychiatry, 26*(1), 57–63.

Fitzpatrick, K. M. (1993). Exposure to violence and presence of depression among low-income African-American youth. *Journal of Counseling and Clinical Psychology, 61*(3), 528–531.

Fleming, J. E., & Offord, D. R. (1990). Epidemiology of childhood depressive disorders: A critical review. *Journal of the American Academy of Child and Adolescent Psychiatry, 29*(4), 571–580.

Fleming, J. E., Offord, D. R., & Boyle, M. H. (1989). The Ontario Child Health Study: Prevalence of childhood and adolescent depression in the community. *British Journal of Psychiatry, 155,* 647–654.

Freud, S. (1957). Mourning and melancholia. In J. Strachey (Ed. and Trans.), *The standard edition of the complete psychological works of Sigmund Freud* (Vol. 19, pp. 243–250). London: Hogarth Press. (Original work published in 1917).

Garrison, C. Z., Addy, C. L., Jackson, K. L., McKeown, R. E., & Waller, J. L. (1992). Major depressive disorder and dysthymia in young adolescents. *American Journal of Epidemiology, 135*(7), 792–802.

Garrison, C. Z., Jackson, K. L., Marsteller, F., McKeown, R., & Addy, C. (1990). A longitudinal study of depressive symptomatology in young adolescents. *Journal of the American Academy of Child and Adolescent Psychiatry, 29*(4), 581–585.

Garrison, C. Z., Waller, J. L., Cuffe, S. P., McKeown, R. E., Addy, C. L., & Jackson, K. L. (1997). Incidence of major depressive disorder and dysthymia in young adolescents. *Journal of the American Academy of Child and Adolescent Psychiatry, 36*(4), 458–466.

Garvin, V., Kalter, N., & Hansell, J. (1993). Divorced women: Individual differences in stressors, mediating factors, and adjustment outcome. *American Journal of Orthopsychiatry, 63*(2), 232–240.

Gelenberg, A. J., Bassuk, E. L., & Schoonover, S. C. (1991). Depression. In A. J. Gelenberg, E. L. Bassuk, & S. C. Schoonover (Eds.), *The practitioner's guide to psychoactive drugs* (3rd ed., pp. 23–89). New York: Plenum Medical Book.

Germain, C. B., & Gitterman, A. (1995). Ecological perspective. In R. L. Edwards (Ed.-in-Chief), *Encyclopedia of social work* (19th ed., Vol. 1, pp. 816–824). Washington, DC: NASW Press.

Gershon, E. S., Targum, S. D., Kessler, L. R., Mazure, C. M., & Bunney, W. E., Jr. (1977). Genetic studies and biological strategies in the affective disorders. *Progress in Medical Genetics, 2*(3), 101–164.

Goodman, S. L., Schwab-Stone, M., Lahey, B. B., Shaffer, D., & Jensen, P. S. (2000). Major depression and dysthymia in children and adolescents: Discriminant validity and differential consequences in a community sample. *Journal of the American Academy of Child and Adolescent Psychiatry, 39*(6), 761–770.

Grinspoon, L., & Bakalar, J. B. (1995). Depression and other mood disorders. *Harvard Medical School Mental Health Review 4.*

Hammen, C., & Brennan, P. A. (2003). Severity, chronicity, and timing of maternal depression and risk for adolescent offspring diagnoses in a community sample. *Archives of General Psychiatry, 60*(3), 253–258.

Hammen, C., & Rudolph, K. D. (2003). Childhood mood disorders. In E. J. Mash & R. A. Barkley (Eds.), *Child psychopathology* (2nd ed., pp. 233–278). New York: Guilford Press.

Harkness, K. L., & Wildes, J. E. (2002). Childhood adversity and anxiety versus dysthymia co-morbidity in major depression. *Psychological Medicine, 32*(7), 1239–1249.

Hinshaw, S. P. (1994). *Attention deficits and hyperactivity in children.* Thousand Oaks, CA: Sage Publications.

Hovens, J. G., Cantwell, D. P., & Kiriakos, R. (1994). Psychiatric comorbidity in hospitalized adolescent substance abusers. *Journal of the American Academy of Child and Adolescent Psychiatry, 33*(4), 476–483.

Hynd, G. W., & Hooper, S. R. (1992). *Neurological basis of childhood psychopathology.* Newbury Park, CA: Sage Publications.

Jensen, P. S., Bhatara, V. S., Vitiello, B., Hoagwood, K., Feil, M., & Burke, L. (1999). Psychoactive medication practices for U.S. children: Gaps between research and clinical practice. *Journal of the American Academy of Child and Adolescent Psychiatry, 38,* 557–565.

Kaplan, H. I., & Sadock, B. J. (2003). *Kaplan and Sadock's synopsis of psychiatry: Behavioral sciences/clinical psychiatry* (9th ed.). Philadelphia: Williams & Wilkins.

Kashani, J. H., Cantwell, D. P., Shekim, W. O., & Reid, J. C. (1982). Major depressive disorder in children admitted to an inpatient community mental health center. *American Journal of Psychiatry, 139*(5), 671–672.

Kashani, J. H., & Carlson, G. A. (1987). Seriously depressed preschoolers. *American Journal of Psychiatry, 144*(3), 348–350.

Kashani, J. H., Holcomb, W. R., & Orvaschel, H. (1986). Depression and depressive symptoms in preschool children from the general population. *American Journal of Psychiatry, 143*(9), 1138–1143.

Kazdin, A. E. (1988). Childhood depression. In E. J. Mash & L. G. Terdal (Eds.), *Behavioral assessment of childhood disorders* (2nd ed., pp. 157–195). New York: Guilford Press.

Kazdin, A. E. (1990). Childhood depression. *Journal of Child Psychology and Psychiatry and Allied Disciplines, 31*(1), 121–160.

Keller, M. B., Beardslee, W., Lavori, P. W., Wunder, J., Dorer, D. L., & Samuelson, H. (1988). Course of major depression in nonreferred adolescents: A retrospective study. *Journal of Affective Disorders, 15,* 235–243.

Keller, M. B., Ryan, N. D., Strober, M., Klein, R. G., Kutcher, S. P., Birmaher, B., Hagino, O. R., Koplewicz, H., Carlson, G. A., Clarke, G. N., Emslie, G. J., Feinberg, D., Geller, B., Kusumaker, V., Papatheodoru, G., Sack, W. H., Sweeney, M., Wagner, K. D., Weller, E. B., Winters, N. X., Oakes, R., & McCafferty, J. P. (2001). Efficacy of paroxetine in the treatment of adolescent depression: A randomized, controlled trial. *Journal of the American Academy of Child and Adolescent Psychiatry, 40*(7), 762–772.

Kendler, K. S., Walters, E. E., Truett, K. R., Heath, A. C., Neale, M. C., Martin, N. G., & Eaves, L. J. (1994). Source of individual differences in depressive symptoms: Analysis of two samples of twins and their families. *American Journal of Psychiatry, 151,* 1605–1614.

Klein, D. N., Lewinsohn, P. M., & Seeley, J. R. (1997). Psychosocial characteristics of adolescents with a past history of dysthymic disorder: Comparison with adolescents of past histories of major depression and nonaffective disorders, and never mentally ill controls. *Journal of Affective Disorders, 42*(2/3), 127–135.

Klein, D. N., Lewinsohn, P. M., Seeley, J. R., & Rohde, P. (2001). A family study of major depressive disorder in a community sample of adolescents. *Archives of General Psychiatry, 58*(1), 13–20.

Knox, M., King, C., Hanna, G. L., Logan, D., & Ghaziuddin, N. (2000). Aggressive behavior in the clinically depressed adolescents. *Journal of the American Academy of Child and Adolescent Psychiatry, 39*(15), 611–618.

Kovacs, M. (1985a). The Children's Depression Inventory (CDI). *Psychopharmacology Bulletin, 21*(4), 995–998.

Kovacs, M. (1985b). The Interview Schedule for Children (ISC). *Psychopharmacology Bulletin, 21*(4), 991–994.

Kovacs, M. (1990). Comorbid anxiety disorders in childhood-onset depressions. In J. D. Maser & C. R. Cloninger (Eds.), *Comorbidity of mood and anxiety disorders* (pp. 272–281). Washington, DC: American Psychiatric Press.

Kovacs, M. (1996). Presentation and course of major depressive disorder during childhood and later years of the life span. *Journal of the American Academy of Child and Adolescent Psychiatry, 35*(6), 705–715.

Kovacs, M., Akiskal, H. S., Gatsonis, C., & Parrone, P. L. (1994). Childhood-onset dysthymic disorder: Clinical features and prospective naturalistic outcome. *Archives of General Psychiatry, 51*(5), 365–373.

Kovacs, M., & Beck, A. T. (1977). The wish to die and the wish to live in attempted suicides. *Journal of Clinical Psychology, 33*(2), 361–365.

Kovacs, M., Feinberg, T. L., Crouse-Novak, M. A., Paulauskas, S. L., & Finkelstein, R. (1984). Depressive disorders in childhood: 1. A longitudinal prospective study of characteristics and recovery. *Archives of General Psychiatry, 41*(7), 229–237.

Kovacs, M., Feinberg, T. L., Crouse-Novak, M., Paulauskas, S. L., Pollock, M., & Finkelstein, R. (1984). Depressive disorders in childhood: 2. A longitudinal study of the risk for a subsequent major depression. *Archives of General Psychiatry, 41*(7), 643–649.

Kovacs, M., Gatsonis, C., Paulauskas, S. L., & Richards, C. (1989). Depressive disorders in childhood: 4. A longitudinal study of comorbidity with and risk for anxiety disorders. *Archives of General Psychiatry, 46*(9), 776–782.

Kovacs, M., & Goldston, D. (1991). Cognitive and social cognitive development of depressed children and adolescents. *Journal of the American Academy of Child and Adolescent Psychiatry, 30*(3), 388–392.

Kovacs, M., Obrosky, D. S., Gatsonis, C., & Richards, C. (1997). First-episode major depressive and dysthymic disorder in childhood: Clinical and sociodemographic factors in recovery. *Journal of the American Academy of Child and Adolescent Psychiatry, 36*(6), 777–785.

Kovacs, M., Paulauskas, S., Gatsonis, C., & Richards, C. (1988). Depressive disorders in childhood: 3. A longitudinal study of comorbidity with and risk for conduct disorders. *Journal of Affective Disorders, 15*(3), 205–217.

Laroche, C. (1986). Prevention in high risk children of depressed parents. *Canadian Journal of Psychiatry, 31*(2), 161–165.

Lazarus, R. S., & Folkman, S. (1984). *Stress, appraisal, and coping.* New York: Springer.

Lewinsohn, P. M., Clarke, G. N., Seeley, J. R., & Rohde, P. (1994). Major depression in community adolescents: Age at onset, episode duration, and time to recurrence. *Journal of the American Academy of Child and Adolescent Psychiatry, 33*(6), 809–818.

Lewinsohn, P. M., Hops, H., Roberts, R. E., Seeley, J. R., & Andrews, J. A. (1993). Adolescent psychopathology: 1. Prevalence of depression and other DSM-III-R disorders in high school students. *Journal of Abnormal Psychology, 102,* 133–144.

Lewinsohn, P. M., Rohde, P., Seeley, J. R., & Hops, H. (1991). Comorbidity of unipolar depression: 1. Major depression with dysthymia. *Journal of Abnormal Psychology, 100,* 205–213.

Lieberman, F. (1979). *Social work with children.* New York: Human Sciences Press.

Mahler, M. (1961). On sadness and grief in infancy and childhood: Loss and restoration of the symbiotic love object. *Psychoanalytic Study of the Child, 16,* 332–351.

Martini, D. R., Strayhorn, J. M., & Puig-Antich, J. (1990). A symptom self-report measure for preschool children. *Journal of the American Academy of Child and Adolescent Psychiatry, 29,* 594–600.

Mash, E. J., & Terdal, L. G. (1988). Behavioral assessment of child and family disturbance. In E. J. Mash & L. G. Terdal (Eds.), *Behavioral assessment of childhood disorders* (2nd ed.). New York: Guilford Press.

McCauley, E., Myers, K., Mitchel, J., Calderon, R., Schloredt, K., & Treder, R. (1993). Depression in young people: Initial presentation and clinical course. *Journal of the American Academy of Child and Adolescent Psychiatry, 32*(4), 714–722.

McClellan, J. M., & Werry, J. S. (2000). Introduction—Research psychiatric diagnostic interviews for children and adolescents. *Journal of the American Academy of Child and Adolescent Psychiatry, 39*(1), 17–19.

Mennen, F. E. (1995). The relationship of race/ethnicity to symptoms in childhood sexual abuse. *Child Abuse & Neglect, 19*(1), 115–124.

Miser, M. D. (1996). Specializations and clinical judgments of social workers in cases involving acting-out female adolescents. *Family and Community Health, 19*(3), 1–13.

More children being abused and neglected, U. S. says. (1996, September 19). *News & Observer,* p. 13A.

Mrazek, P. J., & Haggerty, R. J. (Eds.). (1994). *Reducing risks for mental disorders: Frontiers for preventive intervention research* (pp. 127–214). Washington, DC: National Academy Press.

National Institute of Mental Health. (2001). *Treatment for Adolescents with Depression Study (TADS).* Retrieved from http://www.nimh.nih.gov/studies/tads.cfm on August 12, 2001.

Newman, J. P., & Garfinkel, B. D. (1992). Major depression in childhood and adolescence. In S. R. Hooper, G. W. Hynd, & R. W. Mattison (Eds.), *Child psychopathology: Diagnostic criteria and clinical assessment* (pp. 65–105). Hillsdale, NJ: Lawrence Erlbaum.

O'Hara, M. W., & Zekowski, E. M. (1988). Postpartum depression: A comprehensive review. In R. Kumar & I. F. Brockington (Eds.), *Motherhood and mental illness: Vol. 2. Caregivers and consequences* (pp. 17–63). London: Wright.

Obeidallah, D. A., & Earls, F. J. (1999) *Adolescent girls: The role of depression in the development of delinquency.* Retrieved from http://www.ojp.usdoj.gov/nij on August 14, 2001.

Ollendick, T. H., & Yule, W. (1990). Depression in British and American children and its relation to anxiety and fear. *Journal of Counseling and Clinical Psychology, 58*, 126–129.

Padur, J. S., Rapoff, M. A., Houston, B. K., Barnard, M., Danovsky, M., Olson, N. Y., Moore, W. V., Vats, T. S., & Lieberman, B. (1995). Psychosocial adjustment and the role of functional status for children with asthma. *Journal of Asthma, 32*(5), 345–353.

Paxton, J. W., & Dragunow, M. (1999). Pharmacology. In J. S. Werry & M. G. Aman (Eds.), *Practitioner's guide to psychoactive drugs for children and adolescents* (2nd ed., pp. 23–50). New York: Plenum Medical Book.

Puig-Antich, J. (1982). Major depression and conduct disorder in prepuberty. *Journal of the American Academy of Child and Adolescent Psychiatry, 21*(2), 118–128.

Puig-Antich, J., Blau, S., Marx, N., Greenhill, L., & Chambers, W. J. (1978). Prepubertal major depressive disorders: A pilot study. *Journal of the American Academy of Child Psychiatry, 17*(4), 695–707.

Puig-Antich, J., Dahl, R., Ryan, N., Novacenko, H., Goetz, D., Goetz, R., Twomey, J., & Klepper, T. (1989). Cortisol secretion in prepubertal children with major depressive disorder. *Archives of General Psychiatry, 46*(9), 801–809.

Puig-Antich, J., Kaufman, J., Ryan, N. D., Williamson, D. E., Dahl, R. E., Lukens, E., Todak, G., Ambrosini, P., Rabinovich, H., & Nelson, B. (1993). The psychosocial functioning and family environment of depressed adolescents. *Journal of the American Academy of Child and Adolescent Psychiatry, 32*(2), 244–253.

Reich, W. (2000). Diagnostic Interview for Children and Adolescents (DICA). *Journal of the American Academy of Child and Adolescent Psychiatry, 39*(1), 59–66.

Riddle, M. A., & Cho, S. C. (1989). Biological aspects of adolescent depression. In G. R. Adams, R. Montemayor, & T. P. Gullotta (Eds.), *Biology of adolescent behavior and development* (pp. 223–246). Newbury Park, CA: Sage Publications.

Rie, H. E. (1966). Depression in childhood. *Journal of the American Academy of Child Psychiatry, 5*(4), 653–685.

Roberts, R. E., & Chen, Y.-W. (1995). Depressive symptoms and suicidal ideation among Mexican-origin and Anglo adolescents. *Journal of the American Academy of Child and Adolescent Psychiatry, 34*(1), 81–90.

Rochlin, G. (1959). The loss complex. *Journal of the American Psychiatric Association, 7*(2), 299–316.

Rutter, M. (1986). The developmental psychopathology of depression: Issues and perspectives. In M. Rutter, C. E. Izard, & P. B. Read (Eds.), *Depression in young people* (pp. 3–30). New York: Guilford Press.

Rutter, M., Graham, P., Chadwick, O., & Yule, W. (1976). Adolescent turmoil: Fact or fiction? *Journal of Child Psychology and Psychiatry, 17*(1), 35–56.

Ryan, N. D., Puig-Antich, J., Ambrosini, P., Rabinovich, H., Robinson, D., Nelson, B., Iyengar, S., & Twomey, J. (1987). The clinical picture of major depression in children and adolescents. *Archives of General Psychiatry, 14*(10), 854–861.

Sack, W. H., Beiser, M., Phillips, N., & Baker-Brown, G. (1993). Co-morbid symptoms of depression and conduct disorder in First Nations Children: Some finding from the Flower of Two Soils Project. *Culture, Medicine and Psychiatry, 16*(4), 471–486.

Sagrestano, L. M., Paikoff, R. L., Holmbeck, G. N., & Fendrich, M. (2003). A longitudinal examination of familial risk factors for depression among inner-city African American adolescents. *Journal of Family Psychology, 17*(1), 108–120.

Seligman, M. E. (1975). *Helplessness: On depression, development and death.* San Francisco: W. H. Freeman.

Shaffer, D. (1996). Discussion of "Predictive validity of the Suicide Probability Scale among adolescents in group home treatment." *Journal of the American Academy of Child and Adolescent Psychiatry, 35*(2), 172–173.

Shaffer, D., Fisher, P., Lucas, C. P., Dulcan, M. K., & Schwab-Stone, M. E. (2000). NIMH Diagnostic Interview Schedule for Children Version IV (NIMH DISC–IV): Description, differences from previous versions, and reliability of some common diagnoses. *Journal of the American Academy of Child and Adolescent Psychiatry, 39*(1), 28–38.

Sherrill, J. T., & Kovacs, M. (2000). Interview Schedule for Children and Adolescents (ISCA). *Journal of the American Academy of Child and Adolescent Psychiatry, 39*(1), 67–75.

Siefert, K., Bowman, P. J., Heflin, C. J., Danziger, S., & Williams, D. R. (2000). Social and environmental predictors of depression in current and recent welfare recipients. *American Journal of Orthopsychiatry, 70*(4), 510–522.

Silberg, J., Pickles, A., Rutter, M., Hewitt, J., Simonoff, E., Maes, H., Carbonneau, R., Murrelle, L., Foley, D., & Eaves, L. (1999). The influence of genetic factors and life stress on depression among adolescent girls. *Archives of General Psychiatry, 56*(3), 225–232.

Spitz, R. (1946). Anaclitic depression: An inquiry into the genesis of psychiatric conditions in early childhood. *Psychoanalytic Study of the Child, 2,* 313–342.

Spitzer, R. L., Endicott, J., & Robins, E. (1978). Research diagnostic criteria: Rationale and reliability. *Archives of General Psychiatry, 35*(6), 773–782.

Stein, D., Williamson, D. E., Birmaher, B., Brent, D. A., Kaufman, J., Dahl, R. E., Perel, J. M., & Ryan, N. D. (2000). Parent-bonding and family functioning in depressed children and children at high risk and low risk for future depression. *Journal of the American Academy of Child and Adolescent Psychiatry, 39*(11), 1387–1395.

Strober, M., DeAntonio, M., Schmidt-Lackner, S., Pataki, C., Freeman, R., Rigali, J., & Rao, U. (1999). The pharmacotherapy of depressive illness in adolescents: An open-label comparison of fluoxetine with imipramine historical controls. *Journal of Clinical Psychiatry, 60*(3), 164–169.

Thompson, M. S., & Peebles-Wilkins, W. (1992). The impact of formal, informal, and societal support networks on the psychological well-being of black adolescent mothers. *Social Work, 37*(4), 322–328.

Toolan, J. M. (1962). Depression in children and adolescents. *American Journal of Orthopsychiatry, 32*(3), 404–415.

Toolan, J. M. (1974). Masked depression in children and adolescents. In S. Lesse (Ed.), *Masked depression* (pp. 141–164). New York: Jason Aronson.

Valla, J. P., Bergeron, L., Bidaut-Russell, M., St-Georges, M., & Gaudet, N. (1997). Reliability of the Dominic-R: A young child mental health questionnaire combining visual and auditory stimuli. *Journal of Child Psychology and Psychiatry, 38,* 717–724.

Valla, J.-P., Bergeron, L., & Smolla, N. (2000). The Dominic-R: A pictorial interview for 6- to 11-year-old children. *Journal of the American Academy of Child and Adolescent Psychiatry, 39*(1), 85–93.

Viesselman, J. O. (1999). Antidepressant and antimanic drugs. In J. S. Werry & M. G. Aman (Eds.), *Practitioner's guide to psychoactive drugs for children and adolescents* (2nd ed., pp. 249–296). New York: Plenum Medical Book.

Wallace, L. J. D., Calhoun, A. D., Powell, K. E., O'Neil, J., & James, S. P. (1996). *Homicide and suicide among Native Americans, 1979–1992.* Atlanta: Centers for Disease Control and Prevention, National Center for Injury Prevention and Control.

Wangby, M., Bergman, L. R., & Magnusson, D. (1999). Development of adjustment problems in girls: What syndromes emerge? *Child Development, 70*(3), 678–699.

Weinberg, W. A., Rutman, J., Sullivan, L., Pencik, E. C., & Dietz, S. G. (1973). Depression in children referred to an educational diagnostic center. *Journal of Pediatrics, 83*(6), 1065–1072.

Weller, E. B., Weller, R. A., Fristad, M. A., Rooney, M. T., & Schecter, J. (2000). Children's Interview for Psychiatric Symptoms (ChIPS). *Journal of the American Academy of Child and Adolescent Psychiatry, 39*(1), 76–84.

Yang, Y. M., Cepeda, M., Price, C., Shah, A., & Mankad, V. (1994). Depression in children and adolescents with sickle-cell disease. *Archives of Pediatric and Adolescent Medicine, 148*(5), 457–469.

12

Suicidality among Youths

Mark J. Macgowan

In the shadows, I can sleep without dreams of
despair and deception.
In the shadows, I am home.
Brian Head, suicide, age 15 (2001)

uicide is a leading cause of death among youths in the United States. In 1998 suicide ranked as the third leading cause of death among young people ages 10 to
19 (National Center for Health Statistics, 2000). The suicide rate has been climb-
ing since 1996 among the younger group of adolescents (10 to 14 years old) in contrast
to the rates for other ages. Suicide is also often a factor behind multiple murders committed by youths. In a nationwide examination of 37 shootings at schools where the
attackers were current or recent students, the Secret Service National Threat Assessment Center found that more than three-quarters of the attackers had either threat-
ened to kill themselves, made suicidal gestures, or tried to kill themselves (Vossekuil,
Reddy, Fein, Borum, & Modzeleski, 2000).

Over the past 30 years, research on suicide has expanded significantly. In
1969 the literature yielded approximately 200 citations (Holinger, Offer, Barter, &
Bell, 1994). Ten years later, that number had almost doubled. A recent review of materials published from 1980 until 2000 yielded over 20,000 citations (American Academy
of Child and Adolescent Psychiatry, 2001). Suicide is now recognized as a substantial
public health problem, as reflected by the landmark national strategy for suicide prevention (U.S. Department of Health and Human Services, 2001).

This chapter describes youth suicide from a public health perspective. It presents a four-stage problem-response continuum: (1) defining the problem, (2) identifying risk and protective factors, (3) evaluating interventions, and (4) implementing
interventions (Potter, Powell, & Kachur, 1995). This chapter will emphasize the first
two areas, providing a review of epidemiology and risk and protective factors in youth
suicide. Because few suicides involve children younger than 10, this chapter focuses
on youths ages 10 to 17. This chapter does not provide detailed clinical guidelines for
working with suicidal clients; there are other such sources (for example, American
Academy of Child and Adolescent Psychiatry, 2001; Jacobs, Brewer, & Klein-Benheim,
1999). Instead, it reviews the research and offers an evidence base for understanding
the etiology, assessment, prevention, and treatment of suicidality among youths.

DESCRIPTION OF THE PROBLEM

It is difficult to describe the extent of childhood suicide without consensus on how to
define and measure suicidality. Suicidality is generally classified as suicide, attempted
suicide, and suicidal ideation, but there is wide variation in how these terms are further

defined. For example, ideation could include thoughts that are general, such as "I wish I were dead," to thoughts that are detailed, sometimes including written plans to commit suicide (King, 1997). Definitions of attempted suicide get tangled up in establishing suicidal intent, which is a crucial variable. For example, "when casual suggestive comments are made to others of suicidal intent, followed by an 'accidental' self-harmful and perhaps lethal incident, related to reckless driving or drug overdose, was the incident a suicidal one?" (King, 1997, p. 63). Intent is often difficult to assess in completed suicides. Self-destructive behavior leading to death may be clearly suicidal, but could be classified as an accident or homicide. Furthermore, intent may be particularly difficult to determine in suicides involving African Americans, among whom the expression of suicidal intent is generally taboo; suicidal communication is often expressed as self-destructive behavior within that community (Poussaint & Alexander, 2001).

To clear up the confusion, O'Carroll and colleagues (1996) proposed a standard nomenclature defining suicide, suicide attempts with injuries, suicide attempts without injuries, instrumental suicide-related behaviors, suicide threats, and suicide ideation. The classification takes into account both lethality and intent. For example, thoughts of death or wanting to die without specific thoughts of killing oneself are not suicidal, according to O'Carroll and colleagues. However, suicidal behaviors are "highly heterogeneous in medical lethality and intent" (King, 1997, p. 63) and often defy even expanded classifications. In this chapter, the general term "suicidality" refers to both suicidal behaviors (attempts and completions) and suicidal ideation (thoughts and plans of suicide).

This section reviews the prevalence and incidence of suicide mortality (completed suicides) and morbidity (ideation and attempts). Suicide mortality data are primarily from the National Center for Health Statistics and are based on death certificates reported by each state. Morbidity data are from multiple sources.

SUICIDE MORTALITY

Within the United States, suicide is the third leading cause of death among youths ages 10 to 19 (National Center for Health Statistics, 2000). For older youths ages 15 to 19, the rates are higher; although they have declined since peaking in 1990, they remain high (Figure 12-1). Fewer adolescents ages 10 to 14 commit suicide; however, except for a decline in the late 1980s, the number and rate have been generally increasing since 1981 (Figure 12-2). A recent temporal analysis found that suicides on or near school property occur most frequently in the spring (Centers for Disease Control and Prevention [CDC], 2001a).

Gender

Suicide rates are much higher for boys than for girls. The rates overall have been declining, particularly among boys, but are steadily increasing among 10 to 14 year olds, particularly among boys (National Center for Injury Prevention and Control, 2001).

Race and Ethnicity

Among the several races, the highest suicidal mortality rate for youths ages 10 to 19 is among American Indian and Alaskan Native youths (Figure 12-3). The rate shows

Figure 12-1

Number of Suicides and Suicide Rates per 100,000, Ages 15 to 19: 1981 to 1998

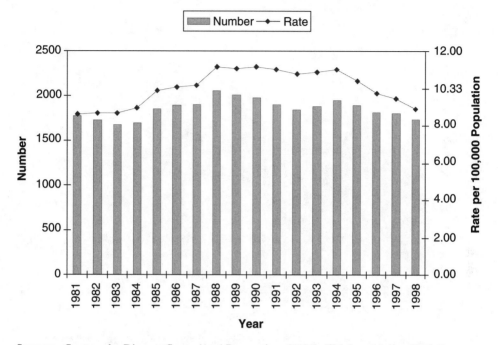

SOURCE: Centers for Disease Control and Prevention. (2002). *Web-based Injury Statistics Query and Reporting System (WISQARS)* [Online]. National Center for Injury Prevention and Control, Centers for Disease Control and Prevention (producer). Retrieved from: http://webapp. cdc.gov/sasweb/ncipc/mortrate.html on January 24, 2002.

wide variability and is on a general increase. White youths have the next highest mortality rate; that rate has been gradually decreasing since 1993 but remains slightly higher than it was in 1981. The suicide rates among African American and Asian and Pacific Islander youths appear to follow similar courses, narrowing the gap between the rates for these groups and the rate for whites. The rate among African American youths increased 300 percent from 1981 to 1994, resulting in a larger net increase in suicides among African Americans than whites. The rate has since declined, but it remains almost double that of 1981. The rate among Asian/Pacific Islanders has declined since peaking in 1992 but remains higher than the rate in 1981. The factors that contribute to these data, and the differences among groups, will be discussed when reviewing the risk and protective factors in the section "Description of Risk and Protective Factors."

Mortality data on Hispanic Americans (or Latinos) have been available only since 1990 for most states and since 1997 for all states. The accuracy of the reporting is limited by the problems with forced-choice ethnic and racial categories, as well as the fact that persons of Hispanic origin may be of any race. Thus, comparisons with other groups become problematic. Because there were too few youths identified as nonwhite Hispanic Americans in the data, Figure 12-4 includes data only concerning white Hispanic Americans. The rates peaked in 1993 and have since declined overall.

Figure 12-2

Number of Suicides and Suicide Rates per 100,000, Ages 10 to 14: 1981 to 1998

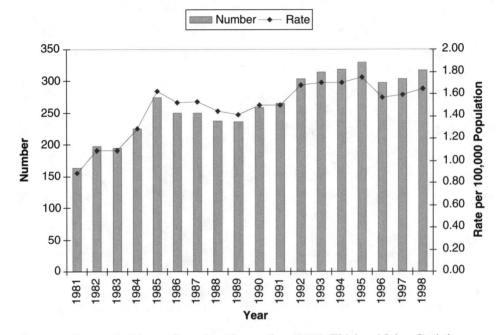

SOURCE : Centers for Disease Control and Prevention. (2002). *Web-based Injury Statistics Query and Reporting System* (*WISQARS*) [Online]. National Center for Injury Prevention and Control, Centers for Disease Control and Prevention (producer). Retrieved from http://webapp.cdc.gov/sasweb/ncipc/mortrate.html on January 24, 2002.

Gay, Lesbian, and Bisexual Youths

No official data exist on suicide among gay, lesbian, and bisexual (GLB) adolescents. Anecdotal reports, however, suggest that the suicide rates are much higher for GLB youths than for their non-GLB counterparts (Remafedi, Farrow, & Deisher, 1993), as much as two to three times higher (U.S. Public Health Service, 1999).

SUICIDE MORBIDITY

We define suicide morbidity broadly as ranging from thoughts and fantasies about suicide (ideation) to suicide attempts that require medical attention. Morbidity data are troubled by definitional and measurement problems (McIntosh, 2000). For example, there is no widely adopted definition of suicide "attempt" that includes both lethality and intent (Móscicki, 1999). In addition, most data are based on self-reports.

An important national source for morbidity data is the biennial Youth Risk Behavior Surveillance System (YRBSS; CDC, 2000). Since 1991 the YRBSS has included data on the prevalence of health risk behavior, including suicide ideation and attempts, among high school students. We draw most of the data for this section from the nationally representative YRBSS, although we use other sources to give perspective on sui-

Figure 12-3

Suicides and Rates per 100,000, Ages 10 to 19, by Race: 1981 to 1998

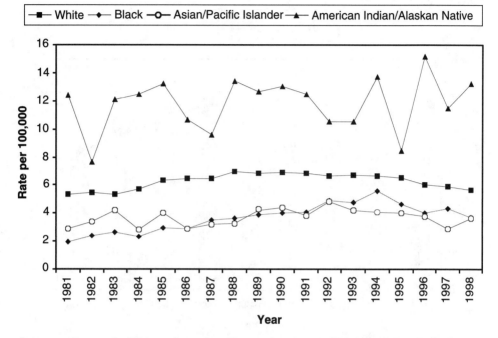

SOURCE : Centers for Disease Control and Prevention. (2002). *Web-based Injury Statistics Query and Reporting System* (*WISQARS*) [Online]. National Center for Injury Prevention and Control, Centers for Disease Control and Prevention (producer). Retrieved from http://webapp. cdc.gov/sasweb/ncipc/mortrate.html on March 14, 2002.

cide morbidity among special populations not identified by the YRBSS. The following section reports data on serious suicidal ideation, plans, and attempts from the 1999 survey, the latest data as of this writing.

The YRBSS revealed that 19.3 percent of students had seriously considered attempting suicide during the previous 12 months (CDC, 2000). The rates of students' attempts or plans in the 12 months preceding the survey were as follows: 14.5 percent had made a specific plan to attempt suicide, 8.3 percent had attempted suicide at least once, and 2.6 percent had made a suicide attempt that resulted in medical treatment.

Suicide morbidity since 1991 peaked in 1993. Suicide ideation declined over the years, but the number of students reporting attempts has remained constant or increased slightly since 1997 (CDC, 2001b). The percentage of students who made an injurious attempt increased significantly from 1991 to 1997 (Brener, Krug, & Simon, 2000).

Gender

In contrast with the data on completed suicides, females are much more likely than males to think about or attempt suicide (CDC, 2001b). According to the YRBSS, females were significantly more likely than males to have seriously considered attempting

Figure 12-4

Suicides and Suicide Rates per 100,000, Ages 10 to 19, by Whites of Hispanic Origin: 1990 to 1998

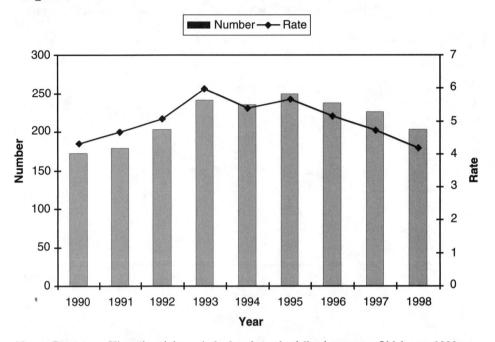

NOTE: Reports on Hispanic origin exclude data from the following states: Oklahoma, 1990 to 1996; New Hampshire, 1990 to 1992; Louisiana, 1990 to 1991. Nonwhite Hispanics are excluded from the figure because there were 10 or fewer deaths reported every year (rates based on 20 or less are considered unstable).

SOURCE: Centers for Disease Control and Prevention. *Web-based Injury Statistics Query and Reporting System (WISQARS)* [Online]. (2002). National Center for Injury Prevention and Control, Centers for Disease Control and Prevention (producer). Retrieved from: http://webapp. cdc.gov/sasweb/ncipc/mortrate.html on March 14, 2002.

suicide (at 24.9 percent and 13.7 percent, respectively), a difference that held across racial and ethnic subgroups. Females were significantly more likely than males to have made a plan to attempt suicide within the preceding 12 months (18.3 percent and 10.9 percent, respectively), and females were significantly more likely than males to have attempted suicide within the preceding 12 months (10.9 percent and 5.7 percent, respectively; CDC, 2001b).

Race and Ethnicity

Hispanic American youths have the highest percentage of suicide ideation and attempts among all racial or ethnic subgroups. According to the 1999 YRBSS (CDC, 2001b), almost one-fifth (19.9 percent) of Hispanic American youths had seriously considered committing suicide in the past year. Over 17 percent (17.6 percent) of white youths and 15.3 percent of African American youths had seriously considered committing suicide within the past year. Hispanic American youths (17.7 percent) were significantly more likely than white and African American youths (12.4 percent and 11.7 percent, respectively) to have made a suicide plan. Hispanic American youths (12.8 percent) were significantly more likely than white and African American youths (6.7 percent and 7.3 percent, respectively) to have attempted suicide at least once within the past year. Among those who had made a suicide attempt requiring medical attention within the past year, Hispanic American youths and African American youths had similar percentages, followed by that of whites (3 percent, 2.9 percent, and 1.9 percent, respectively).

Hispanic females (Latinas) are a particularly vulnerable subgroup. Significantly more Latinas (26.1 percent) had seriously considered suicide than had African American females (18.8 percent), according to the 1999 YRBS (CDC, 2000). These youths were significantly more likely than their white and African American counterparts to have attempted suicide (18.9 percent, 9 percent, and 7.5 percent, respectively). Latinas were significantly more likely than white and African American females to have made a suicide plan (23.3 percent, 15.5 percent, and 13.7 percent, respectively).

GLB Youths

Substantial methodological problems affect data collection on suicide morbidity among GLB youths. These include inconsistencies in defining sexual orientation, uncertain psychometrics of measures for these terms, unrepresentative samples, and the lack of control groups for appropriate comparisons (Muehrer, 1995). Furthermore, there are no systematic, nationally representative prevalence studies of suicide morbidity among GLB youths. However, research involving sizable community samples suggests high rates of ideation and attempts among GLB adolescents. Anhalt and Morris (1998) reported the prevalence rates for past suicide attempts among GLB youths ranged from 11 percent to 42 percent, with most ranging from 30 percent to 42 percent. In a study, Grossman and Kerner (1998a) examined sex differences among gay and lesbian youths; of the 30 percent who reported at least one previous suicide attempt, 38 percent were females and 26 percent were males. Other studies have noted that GLB youths are significantly more likely than their non-GLB peers to have had suicidal ideation and attempts (Garofalo, Wolf, Kessel, Palfrey, & DuRant, 1998; McDaniel, Purcell, & D'Augelli, 2001).

Description of Risk and Protective Factors

Researchers have spent more effort on identifying and reporting risk factors than they have on protective factors. As a result, few studies include detection of protective factors, and fewer still include examination of protective factors exclusively.

Risk Factors

A risk factor is "a measurable characteristic, variable, or hazard that increases the likelihood of development of an adverse outcome" (Móscicki, 1999, p. 44). In a strict sense, a risk factor should precede the outcome in time (Kraemer et al., 1997), but studies do not always make the distinction between causality and correlation. Indeed, most studies are correlational and not causal. As described in chapter 2, risk factors may also be viewed as "proximal" and "distal." Proximal risk factors are triggers or precipitants to suicide but are neither necessary nor sufficient to that outcome (Móscicki, 1999). Distal factors are the foundation for suicide and are a necessary condition to that outcome (Móscicki, 1999). Furthermore, one or two proximal or distal risk factors alone do not elevate risk. Rather, it is their "co-occurrence and interaction among a variety of risk factors that can result in the necessary and sufficient conditions for attempted or completed suicide" (Móscicki, 1999, p. 44). Table 12-1 includes the risk factors from environmental, interpersonal, and individual perspectives.

BROAD ENVIRONMENTAL CONDITIONS

The environment is perhaps the least-studied variable in the subject of youth suicide. A few factors may be noted. Long-term demographic and economic data yield suggestions about suicide risk factors. In the United States, suicide rates are positively related to the proportion of adolescents (Holinger et al., 1994), where an increase in the proportion of adolescents is accompanied by an increase in the youth suicide rates. Researchers believe this population change influences economic conditions. Suicides increase in years of rising unemployment and economic downturns (Holinger et al., 1994). A higher number of adolescents means more competition for resources in an overburdened system: "In these instances, the psychologically vulnerable children are increasingly at risk as the environment is less and less able to provide the external sources of self-esteem, treatment opportunities, and other needs that might aid in preventing a suicidal or homicidal outcome" (Holinger et al., 1994, pp. 79–80).

Another broad environmental risk factor appears to be culture. Countries that are highly goal directed and competitive, such as the United States, are more vulnerable to suicidality than are less-competitive countries (Jilek-Aall, as cited in Goldman & Beardslee, 1999). In addition, cultures that undergo major changes in family and social norms are vulnerable to higher rates of suicide (Goldman & Beardslee, 1999).

The minimal legal drinking age is another environmental risk factor. One study estimated that "reducing the drinking age from 21 to 18 years old in all states could increase the number of suicides in the 18- to 20-year-old population by approximately 125 each year" (Birckmayer & Hemenway, 1999, p. 1365). However, the researchers found little evidence that the drinking age was related to suicides among 15 to 17 year olds.

FAMILY, PEER, SCHOOL, AND NEIGHBORHOOD CONDITIONS

Psychiatric disorders among family members are risk factors for suicidality among youths (Brent et al., 1988; Gould, Fisher, Parides, Flory, & Shaffer, 1996; Grossman & Kruesi, 2000; King et al., 2001). Specifically, children of depressed parents are more likely to report suicidal thoughts or behaviors (Brent, Perper, et al., 1994; Klimes-Dougan et al., 1999). A suicide attempt by the mother and substance abuse of mothers and fathers are factors that are significantly more prevalent among adolescents who have attempted suicide (Brent, Perper, et al., 1994; Pfeffer, Normandin, & Kakuma, 1998). Additional evidence supports the link between suicide

Table 12-1. Risk and Protective Factors for Youth Suicide

SYSTEM LEVEL	RISK FACTORS	PROTECTIVE FACTORS
Broad environmental conditions	• Increase in proportion of adolescents in U.S., competition for services among psychologically vulnerable children • High unemployment • Major changes in family and social norms • Lowering the legal drinking age (for ages affected)	• Opportunities for services • Availability and quality of mental health services (ideation)
Family, peer, school, and neighborhood conditions Family	• Family psychopathology (suicidal history; distal): Depressed parents (ideation, behaviors); suicide attempt by mother, substance abuse by parents (attempts) • Physical/sexual abuse (attempts; risk chains) • Family conflict (proximal; suicide, attempts, ideation) • Living apart from a parent (suicide, attempts) • Low parental monitoring (attempts, ideation) • Poor communication between youth and parents (risk of suicide): Poor communication and divorce (risk of suicide)	• Perceived parent and family support (attempts, ideation) • Harmonious and supportive family relationships
Peer	• Loss/disruption of a romantic relationship (suicidal behaviors)	
School	• Poor school performance (suicide, attempts)	
Neighborhood/ community	• Suicide imitation (proximal; suicide) • Access to lethal means (proximal; suicide)	• Restriction to lethal means (suicide)
Individual characteristics	• Older (suicide) • Male (suicide), female (attempts) • Genetics (suicide, attempts) • Possible reduced neurobiological functioning (suicide, attempts) • Epilepsy (suicide) • Mood disorder, particularly depression (suicide) • Hopelessness (suicide) • Cognitive deficits (poor problem-solving, negative attribution, self-criticism) • AOD use (suicide) • Violence, impulsive aggression (attempts, ideation) • Conduct disorder (suicide) • Previous suicide attempt and suicide ideation (suicide) • Suicidal communication (suicide) • Reluctance to seek help	• Younger (suicide) • Reason for living, survival and coping beliefs (among attempters) • Separation anxiety disorder, among younger youth (attempts) • Connection with responsible adults

NOTE: Terms in parentheses indicate whether the risk is associated with suicide, attempted suicide, or suicidal ideation, if known. AOD = alcohol and other drugs.

in families and the risk for adolescent suicidal behavior (Brent, Bridge, Johnson, & Connolly, 1996; Gould et al., 1996; Johnson, Brent, Bridge, & Connolly, 1998; Kaplan, Pelcovitz, Salzinger, Mandel, & Weiner, 1997).

There is a link between child maltreatment and suicidality. The rates for suicidal behaviors are significantly related to physical or sexual abuse, or both, in studies involving clinical (Shaunesey, Cohen, Plummer, & Berman, 1993) and nonclinical samples (Hibbard, Brack, Rauch, & Orr, 1988). Other research has also noted a link between physical and sexual abuse and suicide attempts (Fergusson, Horwood, & Lynskey, 1996; Wagner, Cole, & Schwartzman, 1995).

Other evidence related to child maltreatment provides evidence for risk chains. A study comparing youths who had been physically abused with nonabused community controls found that

> the abused adolescents carried a significantly greater cumulative burden of risk factors for suicide (such as family disintegration, diagnoses of depression, disruptive behavior disorders, and substance abuse and dependence) than did the nonabused adolescents. This suggests a continuing danger that such adolescents will eventually make an attempt. (Kaplan et al., 1997, p. 805)

Family risk factors are typically considered distal (Móscicki, 1999), but interpersonal conflict can be a trigger to suicide (Marttunen, Aro, & Lonnqvist, 1993). Family problems and parent–child conflict have been identified as risk factors in a number of studies. In a case-control study (Brent, Perper, Moritz, Baugher, Roth, et al., 1993), youths who had committed suicide had experienced a number of stressful life events, including family conflict, within the year before their deaths. Family conflict is a significant factor in other research on suicidality (de Anda & Smith, 1993; Hollis, 1996; Pfeffer et al., 1998; Shagle & Barber, 1995). Low parental monitoring, along with risk behaviors, such as smoking, alcohol use, physical fighting, and sexual activity, have been found to be independently associated with increased suicide ideation and attempts (King et al., 2001). Other evidence has also found that suicide victims are less likely to have lived with both biological parents and are more likely to have been exposed to parent–child conflict, physical abuse, and residential instability (Brent, Perper, et al., 1994). Divorce or separation has had little affect on increased suicide risk, but poor communication between the parents and child, coupled with divorce, increased the risk of suicide (Gould, Shaffer, Fisher, & Garfinkel, 1998).

Peer Factors

Family and peer factors are interpersonal stressors that place youths at risk of suicidal behaviors (Goldman & Beardslee, 1999). Loss of a girlfriend or boyfriend or disruption of a romantic relationship has been a significant factor in several studies of adolescent suicidal behaviors (Brent, Perper, Moritz, Baugher, Roth, et al., 1993; de Anda & Smith, 1993; Marttunen et al., 1993).

School Factors

Poor school performance is a risk factor for suicidal behaviors (Borowsky, Ireland, & Resnick, 2001; Garnefski, Diekstra, & de Heus, 1992; Spirito, Overholser, &

Stark, 1989; Vannatta, 1997; Weinberger, Sreenivasan, Sathyavagiswaran, & Markowitz, 2001). However, capacity for learning is not a risk factor (Carlson & Cantwell, 1982).

Suicide Imitation

Exposure to real or fictional accounts of suicide increases risk for suicide among vulnerable youths (American Academy of Child and Adolescent Psychiatry, 2001; Gould, 2001; Gould, Petrie, Kleinman, & Wallenstein, 1994; O'Carroll & Potter, 1994; Phillips & Carstensen, 1988; Range, Goggin, & Steede, 1988). Suicide contagion is defined as "a phenomenon whereby susceptible persons are influenced toward suicidal behavior through knowledge of another person's suicidal acts" (U.S. Department of Health and Human Services, 2001, p. 197) and may be considered a proximal risk factor. Contagion is more common among youths than adults (Gould, Wallenstein, Kleinman, O'Carroll, & Mercy, 1990; Phillips & Carstensen, 1988) and accounts for 1 percent to 5 percent of youth suicides (Gould, Wallenstein, & Kleinman, 1990; Gould, Wallenstein, Kleinman, O'Carroll, & Mercy, 1990). The mechanisms of spreading are unclear, but identification with the victim, modeling, and notoriety are possible factors (Goldman & Beardslee, 1999). The effect lasts up to about 10 days (Bollen & Philips, 1982), is higher in the location where the suicide occurred, and is proportionate to the amount of publicity the suicide receives (Phillips & Carstensen, 1988; Schmidtke & Schaller, 1998).

Access to Lethal Means

Access to lethal means, another proximal risk factor, is a significant risk factor in many studies of adolescent suicide. Recent data (1998) indicate that the primary means of suicide among older teens ages 15 to 19 is firearm (62.6 percent), followed by suffocation (25.4 percent; National Center for Health Statistics, 2000). Among 10- to 14-year-old youths, the primary means of suicide is firearm (48.3 percent), closely followed by suffocation (46.7 percent). Having a firearm in the home is a significant risk factor for suicide (Brent et al., 1991; Brent, Perper, Moritz, Baugher, & Allman, 1993; Brent, Perper, Moritz, Baugher, Schweers, et al., 1993; Shah, Hoffman, Wake, & Marine, 2000). Grossman and Kruesi (2000) noted that "the risk of suicide was anywhere from two to almost five times greater when a gun was in the house" (p. 172). The presence of firearms in the home of a youth with comorbid problems adds additional risk (further discussed in the section "Risk Clusters: Co-occurrence of Risk Factors").

INDIVIDUAL CHARACTERISTICS

The most commonly examined risk factors are individual. This section describes individual characteristics of youth suicide.

Genetics–Biology

In determining whether suicide is transmitted, research must assess whether the genetic transmission of suicide is independent of the transmission of related psychiatric illness. In a study that controlled for differences in the familial rates of psychiatric problems, Brent and colleagues (1996) found that suicidal behavior (attempts and completions) was higher among families with adolescent suicide victims. In contrast, suicidal ideation was explained by increased family psychopathology. The study concluded that suicidal behavior may be transmitted in the family as a trait, independent of family psychiatric disorders.

Reviews of the neurobiological evidence involving adults have noted reduced serotonergic and noradrenergic functioning in the brains of suicide victims and reduced serotonergic functioning among both suicide victims and those who have attempted suicide (Mann & Arango, 1999). In view of this evidence, "there may be a serotonergic trait marker that will identify the person at risk for suicide" (Mann & Arango, 1999, p. 114). How these findings relate to young persons is speculative: "To date, the demonstration of a primary biochemical abnormality in suicidal youths has not appeared in the literature" (Goldman & Beardslee, 1999, p. 423).

Epilepsy has been associated with increased suicide risk (Brent, 1986; Ettinger, Devinsky, Weisbrot, Ramakrishna, & Goyal, 1999; Nilsson, Tomson, Farahmand, Diwan, & Persson, 1997). Adolescent females with chronic illnesses reported having more suicidal thoughts than controls (Suris, Parera, & Puig, 1996).

Depression

Over 90 percent of adolescents who have committed suicide had at least one of the Axis I diagnoses, primarily depression (Grossman & Kruesi, 2000; Shaffer et al., 1996). The presence of a mood disorder, particularly depression, is a significant risk factor for suicide (Brent et al., 1988; Brent, Perper, Moritz, Allman, et al., 1993; Culp, Clyman, & Culp, 1995; Fritsch, Donaldson, Spirito, & Plummer, 2000; Grossman & Kruesi, 2000; Kelly, Lynch, Donovan, & Clark, 2001; Lewinsohn, Rohde, Seeley, & Baldwin, 2001; Shaffer et al., 1996). Early onset of major depression tends to increase risk (Kovacs, Goldston, & Gatsonis, 1993). When coupled with other risk factors, described in "Risk Clusters: Co-occurrence of Risk Factors" below, depression becomes a robust predictor for suicide. Although it is an important risk factor, depression alone does not always predict suicide, particularly among at-risk youths. For example, there is a subgroup of youths with conduct problems who are not depressed but who are suicidal (Feldman & Wilson, 1997).

Hopelessness

The cognitive state of hopelessness is a strong risk factor, particularly among clinical samples. Adolescents hospitalized for suicide attempts have higher levels of hopelessness than controls (Spirito, Williams, Stark, & Hart, 1988; Swedo et al., 1991; Topol & Reznikiff, 1982). Hopelessness predicted suicide attempts among youths with a history of suicidal behavior (Goldston et al., 2001) and, along with suicidal ideation, correctly classified 93 percent of youths who attempted suicide (Swedo et al., 1991). Among psychiatric inpatients, hopelessness—not depression—was a more important gauge of suicidal ideation (Kumar & Steer, 1995). Other research has also supported the link between hopelessness and serious suicidal behaviors among youths (Beautrais, Joyce, & Mulder, 1999; Hendin, 1991).

Other Cognitive Factors

Investigators have examined the link between thinking patterns and youths' suicidality. Cognitive inflexibility, distortions, and limited problem-solving abilities have been linked to suicidal behaviors among youths (Orbach, Rosenheim, & Hary, 1987; Patsiokas, Clum, & Luscomb, 1979; Rotheram-Borus, Trautman, Dopkins, & Shrout, 1990). Cognitive deficits appeared as a mediating variable in one study of suicidal behavior (Yang & Clum, 2000). Attributional style has also been considered a risk factor for suicidal ideation among youths in psychiatric hospitals (Wagner, Rouleau, & Joiner, 2000) and has been closely associated with depression (Schwartz, Kaslow, Seeley, & Lewinsohn, 2000). Self-criticism, considered a depressive cognitive variable, has been closely related to hopelessness among adolescents who have attempted suicide (Donaldson, Spirito, & Farnett, 2000).

Alcohol and Other Drugs

In a number of studies, the use of alcohol and other drugs (AOD) has been a risk factor in suicides. AOD use is a leading risk factor in studies of completed suicides (Brent, Perper, Moritz, Allman, et al., 1993; Fowler, Rich, & Young, 1986). In a study involving a community sample, lifetime marijuana use and having been drunk in the past six months were independently and significantly associated with suicidality (that is, ideation or attempt in the past six months; Flisher et al., 2000). Other studies involving representative school samples support a significant association between suicide attempts and substance use in general (Woods et al., 1997) and cocaine use in particular (Burge, Felts, Chenier, & Parrillo, 1995).

Studies involving clinical or residential samples provide similar evidence. Among males with delinquency and AOD problems, AOD use was significantly related to suicide attempt histories (Young et al., 1995). AOD abuse, dependence, or both was associated with greater risk for attempted suicide among physically abused adolescents (Kaplan et al., 1997). Among youths in long-term foster care who had attempted suicide, a history of AOD abuse was more prevalent among those who had never communicated about an attempted suicide than among those who did (65 percent and 23 percent, respectively; Handwerk, Larzelere, Friman, & Mitchell, 1998). The strongest associations are seen when AOD co-occurs with other problems, discussed in the section "Risk Clusters: Co-occurrence of Risk Factors."

Violence and Aggression

Aggressive and violent behaviors are often associated with suicidality in adolescents (Brent, Johnson, et al., 1994; Flisher et al., 2000; Garrison, McKeown, Valois, & Vincent, 1993). In one study, physical fighting within the past year was associated with youths ever having attempted suicide (Woods et al., 1997). In a federal report of health risk behaviors in middle school and high school students, fighting was reported in 44 percent and 52 percent, respectively, of students who reported suicidal thoughts and attempts (U.S. Department of Health and Human Services, 2000).

Among males, physical fighting in the past year and carrying a gun in the past month predicted suicide attempts (Vannatta, 1997). In that study, more aggressive behavior among males increased the likelihood of reported suicidal behavior (Vannatta, 1997). Furthermore, the study reported that the principal factor that increased the likelihood of males reporting suicidal behavior was perpetrating forcible sex. Another study found that youths who had attempted suicide had significantly more mood regulation deficits (for example, anger control problems) and higher levels of aggressive impulsivity than the comparison group (Velting, Rathus, & Miller, 2000).

In another study, dangerously violent females (that is, those who reported attacking someone with a knife or shooting someone within the past year) had significantly higher levels of suicidal ideation than matched controls (Flannery, Singer, & Wester, 2001). Flannery and colleagues concluded that "students who have been known to commit violent acts should be adequately assessed for violence exposure and symptoms of psychological trauma, with special attention given to the suicide potential of violent females" (Flannery et al., 2001, p. 435).

Conduct Problems

One study found that conduct disorder (CD) was one of the most significant risk factors for suicide (Brent, Perper, Moritz, Allman, et al., 1993). In another study, CD was an independent risk factor for firearm suicide (Shah et al., 2000). Among hospitalized inpatients in one study, adolescents with CD had the highest suicidal behavior scores. Those youths were significantly more violent than youths with depression, and violence was correlated with suicidal behaviors but not depression (Apter et al., 1995). Other research supports the finding that youths with CDs may be suicidal but not depressed (Feldman & Wilson, 1997). Although there is an association between suicide and CD, there is a stronger association between suicide and legal or disciplinary problems (Brent, Perper, Moritz, Baugher, & Allman, 1993; Brent, Perper, Moritz, Baugher, Roth, et al., 1993). The risk is further heightened with co-occurring substance abuse disorders and legal or disciplinary problems (Shaffer et al., 1996), described in "Risk Clusters: Co-occurrence of Risk Factors."

Suicide Attempts and Ideation

A previous suicide attempt increases the risk of a subsequent completed suicide (Brent, Baugher, Bridge, Chen, & Chiappetta, 1999; Brent, Perper, Moritz, Allman, et al., 1993; Shaffer, 1988; Shaffer et al., 1996). For suicidal ideation, it is not the fleeting thought of suicide, but the prolonged desire to be dead that establishes risk, particularly among older adolescents (Levy & Deykin, 1989). In addition, the co-occurrence of this intense form of ideation with major depression and AOD use places these youths at substantial risk (Levy & Deykin, 1989). Thus, ideation alone does not appear to predict subsequent serious suicidal behavior (Marcenko, Fishman, & Friedman, 1999). However, youths with no apparent psychopathology commit suicide (Brent, Perper, Moritz, Baugher, & Allman, 1993), so caregivers and practitioners should take any form of ideation seriously. Among adolescents in psychiatric inpatient treatment, a history of attempts and thoughts of suicide in prepuberty has been a significant risk factor (Pfeffer, 2000, p. 163).

Suicidal Communication

The evidence suggests that, while most adolescents who attempt suicide make a suicidal communication, many do not. In one study, approximately 20 percent had made no previous suicidal communication and an additional 20 percent had made only one communication (Handwerk et al., 1998). Of concern is that among those who made fewer suicidal communications, more lethal methods were used (Handwerk et al., 1998). In addition, youths who had made two or more suicidal communications before their attempt had significantly lower lethality in their attempts (Handwerk et al., 1998).

Youths may also use an indirect form of suicidal communication. Self-destructive behavior may mask suicidal behavior, a phenomenon known as "covert suicide" (Molin, 1986). This form of communication occurs within the African American community, which generally considers direct suicidal communications taboo (Poussaint & Alexander, 2001).

The evidence strongly suggests that most suicidal youths confide their concerns to peers rather than to adults (see Kalafat, 2000, for a review). Other risk factors are the inaccessibility of adults and the youth's reluctance to seek help (Kalafat, 2000).

RISK CLUSTERS: CO-OCCURRENCE OF RISK FACTORS

Due to their high base rates, the presence of any one of the risk factors in Table 12-1 is generally insufficient for suicide among youths with normal functioning. However, risk heightens when factors accumulate. Moreover, certain risks may combine to form clusters representing significant and substantial risk for suicidal behaviors.

A combination of mood disorders, AOD use, and conduct problems (for example, aggression or delinquency) appears to substantially heighten risk for both suicide (Shaffer et al., 1996) and attempted suicide (Kovacs et al., 1993). The specific evidence bears this out, with little variation. Affective disorder and AOD use increase risk for suicide (Brent et al., 1999; Brent, Perper, Moritz, Allman et al., 1993; Kovacs et al., 1993), as does the presence of a firearm in the home (Brent et al., 1988). The combination of depression, aggression, and AOD use significantly elevates risk for attempts (Andrews & Lewinsohn, 1992; Garrison et al., 1993). Adding delinquency to these factors represents a considerable risk cluster (Young et al., 1995). Youths with CD or AOD problems, and who are facing legal or disciplinary events, are at high risk for suicide (Brent, Perper, Moritz, Baugher, Roth, et al., 1993). The co-occurrence of AOD with physical fighting and gun possession carries a substantially increased risk for suicide attempts (Woods et al., 1997). Youths with disruptive disorders, AOD use, and a history of suicide attempts are at elevated risk for suicide (Renaud, Brent, Birmaher, Chiappetta, & Bridge, 1999). This risk increases if the adolescents have been physically abused and if their parents have AOD abuse and mood disorders (Renaud et al., 1999). The combination of depression, AOD use, and a history of sexual abuse were strongly related to suicidal thoughts and attempts in one study (Garnefski et al., 1992).

A second cluster is the co-occurrence of interpersonal conflict with conduct problems. In one study, youths who attempted suicide reported more problems with family and police than did youths who had not attempted suicide (Wagner et al., 1995). In other research, conflict with parents and with boyfriends or girlfriends, disruption of a romantic attachment, and legal or disciplinary problems were more likely to be associated with youths who had committed suicide than with controls (Brent, Perper, Moritz, Baugher, Roth, et al., 1993). Family problems alone represent a risk factor (see the evidence above under "Family, Peer, School, and Neighborhood Conditions") and, together with romantic loss, may be a proximal risk factor for suicide (Marttunen et al., 1993). Poor family environment and the presence of risk behaviors, such as physical fighting and alcohol abuse, were significantly associated with suicidal ideation and attempts in one study (King et al., 2001).

A third cluster is the presence of mental health problems and access to lethal means. Youths with comorbid psychiatric illness (Brent et al., 1991), CD, and previous mental health treatment (Shah et al., 2000), depression, and substance abuse (Brent et al., 1988) are at higher risk for suicide when a firearm is in the home.

In summary, the accumulation of risk factors and the presence of clusters of variables place adolescents at substantial risk for serious suicidal behaviors. Many of these variables present stressors that may independently elevate risk or accumulate to place children at heightened risk for suicide. Considerable evidence exists about the effects of stressors on children (chapter 2), but there is a great need for testing and developing research-based models of risk factors for youth suicide.

PROTECTIVE FACTORS

Studies have not yet reached a conclusion on why some youths commit suicide and others do not (American Academy of Child and Adolescent Psychiatry, 2001). Many youths with risk factors do not commit suicide. There has been little research about the factors that make youths resilient, and protect them from suicide. Much is speculative. A few of the common protective factors will be reviewed here and are summarized in Table 12-1.

Clinical care, both its availability and quality, appears to be a protective factor. In one study, suicidal ideation was negatively correlated with seeking professional help (Saunders, Resnick, Hoberman, & Blum, 1994). Furthermore, retention is often a problem, and treatment follow through is protective (King & Knox, 2000). A strong therapeutic alliance may be protective but has not been empirically tested with adolescents (Jacobs et al., 1999). Contact with helpful and responsible adults is a protective factor (Kalafat, 2000).

Another protective factor appears to be the restriction to lethal means of suicide. Removing this proximal risk factor helps to reduce risk among youths who are impulsive (Shaffer, Garland, Gould, Fisher, & Trautman, 1988).

Harmonious and supportive family relationships are protective (Goldman & Beardslee, 1999; Pfeffer et al., 1998). In one study, connection with a parent (for example, "mother who cheers me up when I am sad," "is able to make me feel better when I am upset," "is easy to talk to") had a negative correlation with suicidal ideation (Shagle & Barber, 1995). In another study, perceived family and parent connectedness was protective against suicide attempts (Borowsky et al., 2001). Among adolescents with learning disabilities, connectedness to parents and school has been associated with fewer suicide attempts (Svetaz, Ireland, & Blum, 2000).

Having reasons for living, and survival and coping beliefs appear to be protective. In one study, these factors protected against later suicidal behavior among youths with histories of suicide attempts but do not appear to be protective among those without histories of attempts (Goldston et al., 2001).

Among younger children, separation anxiety disorder (SAD) is found to be protective against suicide attempts (Strauss et al., 2000). Strauss and colleagues speculated that behavior inhibition that is associated with SAD may explain the lowered attempts rate.

Additional factors related to age, gender, and culture will be reviewed in the following section. In sum, the research is not sufficiently developed to draw conclusions about which protective factors (and in what measure) are needed to reduce which risk factors (and to what degree). For the most part, the protective factors cited in the literature are largely the absence or reduction of risk factors (that is, "promotive" factors; see chapter 2). There is a clear need for research on protective factors in the face of risk.

DIFFERENCES IN RISK AND PROTECTIVE FACTORS BY AGE, GENDER, RACE OR ETHNICITY, AND SEXUAL ORIENTATION

This section reviews the evidence that suggests variation of risk and protective factors across groups, including age, and other factors covered in Table 12-2.

Age

A consistent finding internationally is that children and young adolescents are at the lowest risk for youth suicide (Holinger et al., 1994; Klimes-Dougan et al., 1999). In the United States, older youths are at higher risk (Hussy, 1997), reaching a peak between the ages of 19 and 23 years (American Academy of Child and Adolescent Psychiatry, 2001). The higher rate of suicide among older youths is in part due to greater prevalence of psychopathology (for example, substance abuse) and greater suicidal intent (Brent et al., 1999). The lower rate among younger youths is likely due to fewer risk factors, rather than to a resilience to risk factors: "Children and young adolescents are just as liable as older adolescents to commit suicide when exposed to the risk factors we examined" (Groholt, Ekeberg, Wichstrom, & Haldorsen, 1998, p. 479).

Gender

Suicide is more common among males than females (Holinger et al., 1994). Males are 2.5 times more likely than females to commit suicide (Hussy, 1997). Suicide attempts are much higher for girls but taper off by age 19 to a level comparable with that of males (Lewinsohn et al., 2001). There are several reasons for the gender differences, including the lethality of methods among boys, accuracy of reports, higher rates of depression among girls, and "socialization regarding culturally acceptable forms of self-destructive behaviors" (Lewinsohn et al., 2001, p. 428).

Among girls, the largest risk factors for suicide are major depression (increasing the rate by 20 times in one study), followed by a previous suicide attempt (American Academy of Child and Adolescent Psychiatry, 2001; Shaffer et al., 1996). In one study,

Table 12-2. Risk and Protective Factors by Diverse Groups

GROUP	RISK FACTORS	PROTECTIVE FACTORS
Gender		
Females	• Mood disorder (suicide)[a] • Previous suicide attempt (suicide)[a] • Social phobia with comorbid depression (ideation, attempts) • Tobacco and over-the-counter drug use (girls; ideation, attempts) • Learning disability (attempts) • Chronic illness (ideation) • Low self-esteem and substantial family dysfunction (ideation) • Dangerous violence (ideation)	• Emotional well-being (attempts)
Males	• Previous suicide attempt (suicide)[a] • Mood disorder (suicide)a • AOD abuse (suicide)[a] • Aggressive behavior and violence (suicidal behavior) • Disruptive behavior (attempt) • Chronic stress (ideation)	• High grade-point average (attempts)
Race/Ethnicity		
African American	• Erosion of cultural distinctiveness, increase in SES, rise in secularism • Increased availability of firearms, separation from a parental figure, insomnia, neglect, AOD abuse, suicidal ideation, failing grades (attempts)	• Strong social support system, multigenerational support, strong religious beliefs and devotion (suicidal behaviors)
Hispanic/Latino American	• Acculturation stress, family, school, psychiatric problems (suicides, attempts) • Latinas: sociocultural, family variables, mother-daughter factors, psychological variables (depression, low self-concept; attempts)	• Family honor, familism
American Indian/ Alaska Native	• Friends/family members with suicidal behaviors, somatic symptoms, physical/sexual abuse, health problems, AOD use, special-education classes, treatment for emotional problems, gang involvement, access to a firearm (attempts)	• Discussing problems with family or friends, emotional health, attachment to family (attempts)
Gay, lesbian, and bisexual youth	• Psychiatric disorders (suicide) • Parent relations, school environment, and negative self-perception; gender nonconformity; early awareness and disclosure of homosexuality; stress; violence; lack of support; school dropout; family problems; acquaintances' suicide attempts; homelessness; substance abuse; loss of friends due to the youth's sexual orientation; loneliness; current suicidal ideation (attempts) • Problems with self-esteem and depression (ideation)	• Strong parent relations, favorable school environment, positive self-perception (attempts)

NOTE: Terms in parentheses indicate whether the risk is associated with suicide, attempted suicide, or suicidal ideation, if known. AOD = alcohol and other drugs; SES = socioeconomic status.

[a]These factors are considered at high risk for suicide by the American Academy of Child and Adolescent Psychiatry. (2001). Practice parameter for the assessment and treatment of children and adolescents with suicidal behavior. *Journal of the American Academy of Child and Adolescent Psychiatry, 40*(7 Suppl.), 24S–51S.

females with comorbid alcohol use and CD were about three times more likely to have attempted suicide than those with only one of those problems (Kelly et al., 2001). Girls with learning disabilities are at twice the risk for a suicide attempt than their peers (Svetaz et al., 2000). Other risk factors for suicidal ideation and attempts include social phobia with comorbid depression (Nelson et al., 2000); tobacco and over-the-counter drug use (Vannatta, 1997); family problems mediated by internalizing symptomatology (among AOD-abusing females; Mezzich et al., 1997); low self-esteem; and substantial family dysfunction (Kelly et al., 2001). Emotional well-being was a protective factor against suicide attempts (Borowsky et al., 2001).

The biggest risk factor for boys is a previous suicide attempt (increasing the rate more than 30 times), followed by depression, AOD abuse, and disruptive behavior (Brent, Perper, Moritz, Baugher, & Allman, 1993; Brent et al., 1999; Kelly et al., 2001; Shaffer et al., 1996). Disruptive disorders commonly co-occur with a mood disorder and AOD abuse. There has been speculation to account for these associations, including early deprivation or other childhood experiences that predispose the individual to both depression and antisocial behavior, a temperamental predisposition to violent or impulsive behavior, or the secondary consequences of the numerous stresses that often occur in the lives of young people with disruptive disorder (American Academy of Child and Adolescent Psychiatry, 2001, p. 32S).

Chronic stress has predicted male suicidal ideation (Kelly et al., 2001). In one study, a high grade-point average was found to be a protective factor against suicide attempts among boys (Borowsky et al., 2001; Table 12-2).

Race and Ethnicity

Racial and ethnic groups are diverse, and findings about suicide may hide subcultural differences. In addition, differences across cultures could be explained by suicide contagion within isolated groups rather than by cultural beliefs (American Academy of Child and Adolescent Psychiatry, 2001). The following is a review of some of the common risk and protective factors that are summarized in Table 12-2.

The suicide rate has increased rapidly among African American youths; the rate is now almost as high as that of white youths. Researchers have posited a number of explanations for the rise in rates, suggesting risk and protective factors. The factors generally relate to strengths within the traditional African American community and the problems associated with assimilating into the larger culture. Risk factors include the erosion of cultural distinctiveness through an accelerating pace of occupational, residential, political, and educational integration (Shaffer, Gould, & Hicks, 1994); an increase in socioeconomic status (SES), which introduces stress associated with the new social environment with its more acceptable method of coping with depression and hopelessness (Feldman & Wilson, 1997; Gould et al., 1996); a rise in secularism (Neeleman, Wessely, & Lewis, 1998); the increased availability and use of firearms (CDC, 1998; O'Donnell, 1995); and reporting bias (Monk, 1987; Sorenson & Shen, 1996).

Empirical studies have identified the following risk factors for suicide attempts among African American youths: separation from a parental figure, insomnia, neglect, AOD abuse, suicidal ideation, and failing grades (Jones, 1997; Lyon et al., 2000; Vega, Gil, Warheit, Apospori, & Zimmerman, 1993).

Factors that protect youths from suicidal behaviors include a strong social support system, multigenerational support, and strong religious beliefs and devotion (Gibbs, 1997; Neeleman et al., 1998), all of which are characteristic of the traditional, insular African American community. Rates of suicide tend to be lower in areas of traditional African American settlements (Shaffer et al., 1994).

Among Hispanic American groups, risk factors for suicides and attempts include acculturation stress and family, school, and psychiatric problems (Queralt, 1993; Roberts & Chen, 1995; Vega et al., 1993). Among Latinas, risk factors for suicide attempts include sociocultural variables (for example, acculturation, generational issues, socioeconomic conditions), general family variables (for example, low cohesiveness, family conflict and violence, rigidity, little parental support and warmth, parent–adolescent conflict, and absence of the father), specific mother–daughter variables (for example, diffused generational boundaries and maternal social isolation), developmental struggles with mother (for example, conflicts surrounding autonomy and dependence), and psychological variables (for example, depression and low self-concept; Zayas, Kaplan, Turner, Romano, & Gonzalez-Ramos, 2000). Zayas and colleagues proposed that acculturation and generational issues act as background variables but do not sufficiently explain why some attempt suicide while others do not (Zayas et al., 2000). In addition, the factors interrelate to heighten risk (for example, sociocultural with family).

Researchers have suggested that protective factors among Hispanic Americans include family honor and familism: "One behavioral referent to familism is family members' obligation to help one another. Working together, family honor and the strength of family cohesion may act as disincentives for suicides or suicide attempts" (Zayas, 1987, p. 9).

Some research among American Indians has failed to find common risk factors for suicidal ideation because of the heterogeneity across culturally distinct tribes (Novins, Beals, Roberts, & Manson, 1999). Other research involving American Indians and Alaska Natives has found common risk factors. Attempting suicide was correlated with having friends or family members with suicidal behaviors, somatic symptoms, physical or sexual abuse, health problems, AOD use, a history of being in a special education class, treatment for emotional problems, gang involvement, and having access to a firearm (Borowsky, Resnick, Ireland, & Blum, 1999). Borowsky and colleagues found that, as the number of risk factors increased, so did the risk of an attempted suicide. Protective factors included discussing problems with family or friends, being emotionally healthy, and being attached to the family. The study noted that "increasing protective factors was more effective at reducing the probability of a suicide attempt than was decreasing risk factors" (Borowsky et al., 1999, p. 573).

In sum, a common protective factor appears to be attachment to culture and family. Some of the risk factors result from the loss of the protective elements of the community, which occurs either because of immigration or assimilation.

GLB Youths

Researchers have noted that GLB youths are at risk for suicide (Garofalo et al., 1998; Proctor & Groze, 1994; Remafedi, 1999b; Safren & Heimberg, 1999). Males are particularly at risk (McDaniel et al., 2001). In one of the few studies of suicide among GLB adolescents, Shaffer and colleagues (Shaffer, Fisher, Hicks, Parides, & Gould, 1995) found that significant psychiatric disorders, but not stigmatization or lack of support, preceded the deaths. Some of the risk factors among GLB youths who have attempted suicide include problems in parent relations, school dropout, and negative self-perception, gender nonconformity, early awareness and disclosure of homosexuality, stress, violence, lack of support, acquaintances' suicide attempts, homelessness, substance abuse, and other psychiatric symptoms (Anhalt & Morris, 1998; Proctor & Groze, 1994; Remafedi, 1999a). Other studies have noted that the loss of friends due to the youth's sexual orientation, loneliness, and current suicidal ideation are strong predictors of attempted suicide (Grossman & Kerner, 1998b; Hershberger, Pilkington, & D'Augelli, 1997).

With respect to protective factors, research has found that GLB youths who have strong parent relations, school environment, and self-perception are less likely to attempt suicide (Proctor & Groze, 1994).

Although there have been advances in the research on the risk and protective factors among GLB youths, more work is needed. To address these limitations, "Future population-based surveys should routinely inquire about sexual orientation to retest prior findings in diverse settings. Prospective, longitudinal studies are needed to examine the evolving risk of suicide across the life span of homosexual persons" (Remafedi, 1999a, p. 1291).

METHODS OF ASSESSING RISK AND PROTECTIVE FACTORS

Due to its limited usefulness (Garrison, Lewinsohn, Marsteller, Langhinrichsen, & Lann, 1991), instrumentation should not be the sole basis for determining the risk of suicide. Instruments should form part of a comprehensive assessment derived from multiple sources and methods (American Academy of Child and Adolescent Psychiatry, 2001), including a face-to-face meeting with the young person (Grossman & Kruesi, 2000; Holinger et al., 1994; Miller & Glinski, 2000). To be complete, the assessment should include a plan of action for the youth, family, peers, and service providers (Grossman & Kruesi, 2000).

A number of assessment protocols are available. Some are unstructured clinical interviews that use decision trees or tables of risk factors and resources to determine severity of suicidality (for example, American Academy of Child and Adolescent Psychiatry, 2001, p. 26S; Goldman & Beardslee, 1999, pp. 430–433; Holinger et al., 1994, pp. 113–117). A more rigorous approach is to use a semistructured or structured diagnostic interview. Four instruments that have been well reviewed (Goldston, 2000) are (1) the Diagnostic Interview Schedule for Children and Adolescents (DICA; Reich, 2000), (2) the Diagnostic Interview Schedule for Children (DISC; Shaffer, Fisher, Lucas, Dulcan, & Schwab-Stone, 2000), (3) the Interview Schedule for Children and Adolescents (ISCA; Kovacs, 1997; Sherrill & Kovacs, 2000), and (4) the Child Suicide Potential Scales (CSPS; which include the Spectrum of Suicidal Behavior Scale and the Concepts of Death Scale; Pfeffer, Conte, Plutchik, & Jerrett, 1979).

Practitioners may use specific measures of suicidality. Two instruments for measuring suicide ideation that have favorable psychometric properties (Goldston, 2000; Range & Knott, 1997) are (1) the Beck Scale for Suicide Ideation (BSI; Beck & Steer, 1991) and (2) the Suicide Ideation Questionnaire (SIQ; Reynolds, 1988).

Practitioners should examine suicide plans when attempting to gauge the possibility of suicide attempts (Jacobs et al., 1999, pp. 24–25). In general, plans that are more detailed indicate a higher risk for suicide. Practitioners may administer a specific measure for suicide attempts. One with promising psychometric properties (Goldston, 2000) is the Lethality of Suicide Attempt Rating Scale (Smith, Conroy, & Ehler, 1984).

As noted earlier in the section "Individual Characteristics," hopelessness is a key risk factor for suicide. Two instruments to assess this risk factor are (1) the Beck Hopelessness Scale (BHS; Beck & Steer, 1988; Steer & Beck, 1988) and, for younger children, the Hopelessness Scale for Children (Kazdin, Rodgers, & Colbus, 1986), both of which have been well reviewed (Goldston, 2000). Practitioners can assess depression using the Children's Depression Inventory (CDI; Kovacs, 1985, 1992), which also has favorable properties (Goldston, 2000).

CULTURALLY RELEVANT MEASURES

Although a number of the instruments noted previously under "Methods of Assessing Risk and Protective Factors" have been tested cross-culturally, only a few have been developed specifically for certain population groups. The Indian Health Service Adolescent Health Survey (Pharris, Resnick, & Blum, 1997), which has been extensively used among both American Indian and Alaskan Native youths (Goldston, 2000), includes a number of protective factors. A screening tool for GLB youths is the Challenges and Coping Survey for Lesbian, Gay, and Bisexual Youth (D'Augelli & Hershberger, 1993; Hershberger & D'Augelli, 1995; Hershberger et al., 1997); it is the only measure developed specifically for this population (Goldston, 2000). These measures have relatively unknown psychometric properties (Goldston, 2000) and should be used judiciously.

IMPLICATIONS FOR PREVENTION, INTERVENTION, AND TREATMENT

What are some practice implications based on the risk and protection evidence? Clearly, a continuum of responses—from prevention to treatment—must address the multiple factors related to youth suicide. If we focus on proximal risk factors alone, we could overlook the important role of distal factors, such as underlying mental disorders or family factors (McKeown et al., 1998). This section briefly reviews the evidence for preventing suicide (for an expanded discussion, readers may consult Macgowan, 2004, and Macgowan, in press), describes a model for interrupting risk process, and provides some general guidelines for practice.

PREVENTION PROGRAMS

Efforts to prevent suicidality generally target all youths rather than selected subpopulations. Few directly target the broad environmental risk factors (for example, increasing opportunities for resources or increasing employment) and tend to involve risk factors in systems more directly in contact with the youths (for example, school, peer, neighborhood). Some commonly used prevention methods include gatekeeper training, means reduction, crisis hotlines, media guidelines, and direct screening.

Gatekeeper training aims to increase awareness of risk factors and involve persons in direct contact with youths, including school personnel, social workers, students, clergy, and health care professionals and to increase awareness of risk factors and procedures for getting help. Recent reviews conclude that student and teacher education strategies appear to be effective in improving knowledge about risk factors and intentions to intervene and refer potentially suicidal youths (Kalafat, 2000; King & Knox, 2000, p. 254). However, more research is needed to determine efficacy (that is, reduction in suicidal behavior) and unintended negative effects (for example, normalizing suicide as an option to problems) among some youths (King & Knox, 2000). Reviews of training of community gatekeepers conclude that there is some success in improving attitudes toward intervention after training, but there is no evidence for efficacy in reducing suicidal behavior (Burns & Patton, 2000; CDC, 1992).

Means restriction may include reducing the availability of firearms, medications, and alcohol. The evidence suggests means restriction may reduce suicides, especially impulsive ones (CDC, 1992; Grossman & Kruesi, 2000; Shaffer et al., 1988). However, gun security laws have not had a significant affect on suicides, although they have had an affect on accidental deaths (American Academy of Child and Adolescent Psychiatry, 2001; Cummings, Grossman, Rivara, & Koepsell, 1997).

Crisis hot lines are commonly thought to reduce the potential for suicide, but the evidence is limited and fails to show the effect on the incidence of suicide (American Academy of Child and Adolescent Psychiatry, 2001; Burns & Patton, 2000).

Media education has been used to address contagion and imitation. Although media guidelines have been developed (American Academy of Child and Adolescent Psychiatry, 2001, pp. 47S), there is no evidence that they are efficacious.

Direct screening (also known as direct case finding or proactive screening) is an approach to identify at-risk youths in schools and other settings. Youths are asked to respond to questions about mood, AOD use, and suicidal thoughts and behaviors. Once identified, these youths are referred for services. This approach has been widely recommended as an efficient and effective method for assessing risk and the need for treatment (American Academy of Child and Adolescent Psychiatry, 2001; CDC, 1992; King & Knox, 2000; Shaffer & Craft, 1999). However, its success is limited to schools that participate and to youths who attend those schools (King & Knox, 2000). In sum, these prevention efforts appear promising but lack substantial empirical support.

INTERVENTION AND TREATMENT

Recent reviews of the outcome literature (Hawton et al., 1998; King & Knox, 2000; Rudd, 2000) found only one study of actual suicidal behaviors (that is, suicidal attempts) involving a sample made up exclusively of adolescents. In that study, Cotgrove, Zirinsky, Black, and Weston (1995) randomly assigned youths who were being discharged from the hospital either to a treatment group consisting of standard treatment and a token ("green card") allowing readmission to the hospital on demand or to a control group with standard treatment only. The treatment group had a lower suicide attempt rate, but the rate was not statistically different from that of the control group.

Four recent, randomized studies involving high-risk youths appear promising. The first three include measures of both risk and protective factors.

Two studies tested two interventions: (1) a brief interview (C-CARE) condition and (2) C-CARE plus a 12-session peer-group intervention (CAST; Randell, Eggert, & Pike, 2001; Thompson, Eggert, Randell, & Pike, 2001). C-CARE consisted of three elements: (1) a two-hour, computer-assisted suicide assessment; (2) a brief motivational counseling session; and (3) a social network intervention to link each youth with a case manager and to contact a parent or guardian to enhance support. CAST is a skills-training and social support intervention targeting mood management (depression and anger management), school performance, and drug involvement. Researchers randomly assigned students at risk of both dropping out of school and of suicidal behaviors to C-CARE, to C-CARE plus CAST, or to usual services. In one study, attitudes toward suicidality (thoughts, threats, attempts) significantly declined in the experimental groups (Thompson et al., 2001). C-CARE and CAST were also effective in reducing depression and hopelessness. CAST was most effective in building and maintaining personal control and problem-solving coping. Randall and colleagues (2001) observed equally encouraging findings in the second study. C-CARE and CAST led to increased personal control, problem-solving coping, and perceived family support. Both C-CARE plus CAST and C-CARE led to decreases in depression and to enhanced self-esteem and family goals met. However, all three conditions showed the same decreases in suicide risk behaviors, anger control problems, and family distress. These findings are encouraging because the two interventions not only reduced attitudes toward suicide and suicidal ideation, but also reduced associated risk factors.

A third study examined the effects of group leader support on peer group support and personal control (Thompson, Eggert, & Herting, 2000). The researchers hypothesized that personal control would mediate between leader and peer group support to reduce depression and suicidal risk behaviors (frequency of ideation; and threats or attempts, or both). They compared three groups: two treatment groups consisting of a one- and two-semester personal growth class and an assessment-only comparison group. The treatment groups included materials on social support resources, and life-skills training. The study revealed that group leader support enhanced peer-group support and that peer-group support increased personal control and directly reduced suicide risk behaviors in the two-semester group. Furthermore, personal control directly influenced depression and suicidal risk behaviors.

A fourth experimental study examined the effects of three approaches: (1) individual cognitive behavior therapy, (2) systemic behavior family therapy, or (3) nondirective supportive therapy (Brent et al., 1997). All three methods reduced suicidal ideation among depressed youths over the 12 to 16 weeks of treatment, but cognitive therapy was more effective at reducing major depression than the other treatments.

Although mostly small scale and in need of replication, these four studies provide clues about how to prevent youths suicide. Figure 12-5 incorporates these studies and provides a heuristic model for interrupting the risk processes in youth suicide. The model is based on the best evidence, but the chain of events is largely speculative because the research is limited and mostly correlational. However, it illustrates a few points of intervention in the process to prevent youth suicide.

Figure 12-5

Model for Interrupting Risk Processes in Youth Suicidality

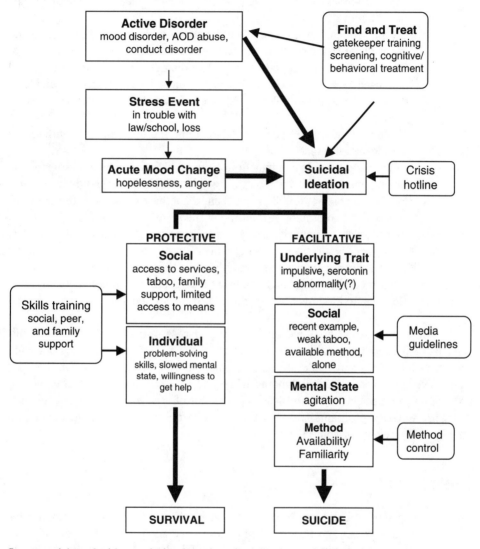

SOURCE: Adapted with permission from American Academy of Child and Adolescent Psychiatry. (2001). Practice parameter for the assessment and treatment of children and adolescents with suicidal behavior. *Journal of the American Academy of Child and Adolescent Psychiatry, 40*(7 Suppl.), 34S.

Suicide prevention should include the following elements, as revealed in the review in this chapter and in other sources (Kalafat, 2000, p. 242; Móscicki, 1999, p. 51; Thompson et al., 2000, p. 253):

- Identify and target high-risk groups or individuals (such as Latinas and GLB youths).

- Include and test theory-based prevention models linking both risk and protective factors related to adolescent suicidality (see Table 12-1).
- Target and include the unique risk and protective factors of diverse groups (see Table 12-2).
- Be comprehensive. Include a long-term approach designed to address the major distal risk factors in an integrated manner—prevention and appropriate treatment of mental and addictive disorders at the clinical level and increased restrictions on access to the most lethal means of suicide at the public health and policy levels (see the multiple approaches noted in Figure 12-1).
- Use an ecological perspective. Address the multiple contexts with which participants interact.
- Be intense. Provide a sufficient dose to build new behavioral repertoires.
- Include mechanisms for monitoring suicide risk. In one study by Pfeffer, Peskin, and Siefker (1992), more than half of the youths who attempted suicide were in treatment at the time of the study.
- Articulate components clearly, including appropriate instructional principles.
- Incorporate empirically verified health-promotion strategies including social support enhancement and life-skills training.
- Conform to the culture and values of the target participants and organization.
- Be implemented over sufficient time to show effects.

In sum, researchers have made much progress in understanding youth suicide. We know more about what factors put youths at risk of suicide and about what protective influences may moderate risk. Although more outcome studies are needed, gains have been made in understanding what may be effective (and not effective) in preventing youth suicide. Research-based guidelines offer ways of improving the quality of preventative programs and how they may be delivered. These developments offer hope in preventing youth suicide.

REFERENCES

American Academy of Child and Adolescent Psychiatry. (2001). Practice parameter for the assessment and treatment of children and adolescents with suicidal behavior. *Journal of the American Academy of Child and Adolescent Psychiatry, 40* (7 Suppl.), 24S–51S.

Andrews, J. A., & Lewinsohn, P. M. (1992). Suicidal attempts among older adolescents: Prevalence and co-occurrence with psychiatric disorders. *Journal of the American Academy of Child and Adolescent Psychiatry, 31*(4), 655–662.

Anhalt, K., & Morris, T. (1998). Developmental and adjustment issues of gay, lesbian, and bisexual adolescents: A review of the empirical literature. *Clinical Child and Family Psychology Review, 1*(4), 215–230.

Apter, A., Gothelf, D., Orbach, I., Weizman, R., Ratzoni, G., Har-Even, D., & Tyana, S. (1995). Correlation of suicidal and violent behavior in different diagnostic categories in hospitalized adolescent patients. *Journal of the American Academy of Child and Adolescent Psychiatry, 34*(7), 912–918.

Beautrais, A. L., Joyce, P. R., & Mulder, R. T. (1999). Personality traits and cognitive styles as risk factors for serious suicide attempts among young people. *Suicide and Life-Threatening Behavior, 29*(1), 37–47.

Beck, A., & Steer, R. (1988). *Beck Hopelessness Scale Manual*. San Antonio, TX: Psychological Corporation.

Beck, A., & Steer, R. (1991). *Manual for the Beck Scale for Suicidal Ideation*. San Antonio, TX: Psychological Corporation.

Birckmayer, J., & Hemenway, D. (1999). Minimum-age drinking laws and youth suicide, 1970–1990. *American Journal of Public Health, 89*(9), 1365–1368.

Bollen, K. A., & Philips, D. P. (1982). Imitative studies: A national study of the effects of television news stories. *American Sociological Review, 47,* 802–809.

Borowsky, I. W., Ireland, M., & Resnick, M. D. (2001). Adolescent suicide attempts: Risks and protectors. *Pediatrics, 107*(3), 485–493.

Borowsky, I. W., Resnick, M. D., Ireland, M., & Blum, R. W. (1999). Suicide attempts among American Indian and Alaska Native youth: Risk and protective factors. *Archives of Pediatric Adolescent Medicine, 153*(6), 573–580.

Brener, N., Krug, E., & Simon, T. (2000). Trends in suicidal ideation and behavior among high school students in the United States. *Suicide and Life-Threatening Behavior, 30,* 304–312.

Brent, D. A. (1986). Overrepresentation of epileptics in a consecutive series of suicide attempters seen at a children's hospital, 1978–1983. *Journal of the American Academy of Child Psychiatry, 25*(2), 242–246.

Brent, D. A., Baugher, M., Bridge, J., Chen, T., & Chiappetta, L. (1999). Age- and sex-related risk factors for adolescent suicide. *Journal of the American Academy of Child and Adolescent Psychiatry, 38*(12), 1497–1505.

Brent, D. A., Bridge, J., Johnson, B. A., & Connolly, J. (1996). Suicidal behavior runs in families. A controlled family study of adolescent suicide victims. *Archives of General Psychiatry, 53*(12), 1145–1152.

Brent, D. A., Holder, D., Kolko, D., Birmaher, B., Baugher, M., Roth, C., Iyengar, S., & Johnson, B. A. (1997). A clinical psychotherapy trial for adolescent depression comparing cognitive, family, and supportive therapy. *Archives of General Psychiatry, 54*(9), 877–885.

Brent, D. A., Johnson, B. A., Perper, J., Connolly, J., Bridge, J., Bartle, S., & Rather, C. (1994). Personality disorder, personality traits, impulsive violence, and completed suicide in adolescents. *Journal of the American Academy of Child and Adolescent Psychiatry, 33*(8), 1080–1086.

Brent, D. A., Perper, J. A., Allman, C. J., Moritz, G. M., Wartella, M. E., & Zelenak, J. P. (1991). The presence and accessibility of firearms in the homes of adolescent suicides: A case-control study. *Journal of the American Medical Association, 266*(21), 2989–2995.

Brent, D. A., Perper, J. A., Goldstein, C. E., Kolko, D. J., Allan, M. J., Allman, C. J., & Zelenak, J. P. (1988). Risk factors for adolescent suicide: A comparison of adolescent suicide victims with suicidal inpatients. *Archives of General Psychiatry, 45*(6), 581–588.

Brent, D. A., Perper, J. A., Moritz, G., Allman, C., Friend, A., Roth, C., Schweers, J., Balach, L., & Baugher, M. (1993). Psychiatric risk factors for adolescent suicide: A case-control study. *Journal of the American Academy of Child and Adolescent Psychiatry, 32*(3), 521–529.

Brent, D. A., Perper, J. A., Moritz, G., Baugher, M., & Allman, C. (1993). Suicide in adolescents with no apparent psychopathology. *Journal of the American Academy of Child and Adolescent Psychiatry, 32*(3), 494–500.

Brent, D. A., Perper, J. A., Moritz, G., Baugher, M., Roth, C., Balach, L., & Schweers, J. (1993). Stressful life events, psychopathology, and adolescent suicide: A case control study. *Suicide and Life-Threatening Behavior, 23*(3), 179–187.

Brent, D. A., Perper, J. A., Moritz, G., Baugher, M., Schweers, J., & Roth, C. (1993). Firearms and adolescent suicide. A community case-control study. *American Journal of Diseases of Children, 147*(10), 1066–1071.

Brent, D. A., Perper, J. A., Moritz, G., Liotus, L., Schweers, J., Balach, L., & Roth C. (1994). Familial risk factors for adolescent suicide: A case-control study. *Acta Psychiatrica Scandinavica, 89*(1), 52–58.

Burge, V., Felts, M., Chenier, T., & Parrillo, A. V. (1995). Drug use, sexual activity, and suicidal behavior in U.S. high school students. *Journal of School Health, 65(6),* 222–227.

Burns, J., & Patton, G. (2000). Preventive interventions for youth suicide: A risk factor based approach. *Australian and New Zealand Journal of Psychiatry, 34*(3), 388–407.

Carlson, G. A., & Cantwell, D. P. (1982). Suicidal behavior and depression in children and adolescents. *Journal of the American Academy of Child Psychiatry, 21*(4), 361–368.

Centers for Disease Control and Prevention. (1992). *Youth suicide prevention programs: A resource guide*. Atlanta: Author.

Centers for Disease Control and Prevention. (1998). Suicide among black youths—United States, 1980–1995. *Morbidity and Mortality Weekly Report, 47*(10), 193–196.

Centers for Disease Control and Prevention. (2000). Youth risk behavior surveillance—United States, 1999. *Morbidity and Mortality Weekly Report, 49*.

Centers for Disease Control and Prevention. (2001a). Temporal variations in school-associated student homicide and suicide events—United States, 1992–1999. *Morbidity and Mortality Weekly Report, 50*(31), 657–660.

Centers for Disease Control and Prevention. (2001b). Youth Risk Behavior Survey 99 (Version 2) [CD-ROM]: U.S. Department of Health and Human Services, Centers for Disease Control and Prevention.

Centers for Disease Control and Prevention. (2002). *Web-based Injury Statistics Query and Reporting System (WISQARS)* [Online]. National Center for Injury Prevention and Control, Centers for Disease Control and Prevention (producer). Retrieved from: http://webapp.cdc.gov/sasweb/ncipc/mortrate.html on January 24, 2002.

Cotgrove, A. J., Zirinsky, L., Black, D., & Weston, D. (1995). Secondary prevention of attempted suicide in adolescence. *Journal of Adolescence, 18*(5), 569–577.

Culp, A. M., Clyman, M. M., & Culp, R. E. (1995). Adolescent depressed mood, reports of suicide attempts, and asking for help. *Adolescence, 30*(120), 827–837.

Cummings, P., Grossman, D. C., Rivara, F. P., & Koepsell, T. D. (1997). State gun safe storage laws and child mortality due to firearms. *Journal of the American Medical Association, 278*(13), 1084–1086.

D'Augelli, A. R., & Hershberger, S. L. (1993). Lesbian, gay, and bisexual youth in community settings: Personal challenges and mental health problems. *American Journal of Community Psychology, 21*(4), 421–448.

de Anda, D., & Smith, M. A. (1993). Difference among adolescent, young adult, and adult callers of suicide help lines. *Social Work, 38*(4), 421–428.

Donaldson, D., Spirito, A., & Farnett, E. (2000). The role of perfectionism and depressive cognitions in understanding the hopelessness experienced by adolescent suicide attempters. *Child Psychiatry and Human Development, 31*(2), 99–111.

Ettinger, A. B., Devinsky, O., Weisbrot, D. M., Ramakrishna, R. K., & Goyal, A. (1999). A comprehensive profile of clinical, psychiatric, and psychosocial characteristics of patients with psychogenic nonepileptic seizures. *Epilepsia, 40*(9), 1292–1298.

Feldman, M., & Wilson, A. (1997). Adolescent suicidality in urban minorities and its relationship to conduct disorders, depression, and separation anxiety. *Journal of the American Academy of Child and Adolescent Psychiatry, 36*(1), 75–84.

Fergusson, D. M., Horwood, L. J., & Lynskey, M. T. (1996). Childhood sexual abuse and psychiatric disorder in young adulthood: 2. Psychiatric outcomes of childhood sexual abuse. *Journal of the American Academy of Child and Adolescent Psychiatry, 35*(10), 1365–1374.

Flannery, D. J., Singer, M. I., & Wester, K. (2001). Violence exposure, psychological trauma, and suicide risk in a community sample of dangerously violent adolescents. *Journal of the American Academy of Child and Adolescent Psychiatry, 40*(4), 435–442.

Flisher, A. J., Kramer, R. A., Hoven, C. W., King, R. A., Bird, H. R., Davies, M., Gould, M. S., Greenwald, S., Lahey, B. B., Regier, D. A., Schwab-Stone, M., & Shaffer, D. (2000). Risk behavior in a community sample of children and adolescents. *Journal of the American Academy of Child and Adolescent Psychiatry, 39*(7), 881–887.

Fowler, R. C., Rich, C. L., & Young, D. (1986). San Diego Suicide Study: 2. Substance abuse in young cases. *Archives of General Psychiatry, 43*(10), 962–965.

Fritsch, S., Donaldson, D., Spirito, A., & Plummer, B. (2000). Personality characteristics of adolescent suicide attempters. *Child Psychiatry and Human Development, 30*(4), 219–235.

Garnefski, N., Diekstra, R. F., & de Heus, P. (1992). A population-based survey of the characteristics of high school students with and without a history of suicidal behavior. *Acta Psychiatrica Scandinavica, 86*(3), 189–196.

Garofalo, R., Wolf, R., Kessel, S., Palfrey, J., & DuRant, R. (1998). The association between health risk behaviors and sexual orientation among a school-based sample of adolescents. *Pediatrics, 101*(5), 895–902.

Garrison, C. Z., Lewinsohn, P. M., Marsteller, F., Langhinrichsen, J., & Lann, I. (1991). The assessment of suicidal behavior in adolescents. *Suicide and Life-Threatening Behavior, 21*(3), 217–230.

Garrison, C. Z., McKeown, R. E., Valois, R. F., & Vincent, M. L. (1993). Aggression, substance use, and suicidal behaviors in high school students. *American Journal of Public Health, 83*(2), 179–184.

Gibbs, J. T. (1997). African-American suicide: A cultural paradox. *Suicide and Life-Threatening Behavior, 27*(1), 68–79.

Goldman, S., & Beardslee, W. R. (1999). Suicide in children and adolescents. In D. Jacobs (Ed.), *The Harvard Medical School guide to suicide assessment and intervention* (pp. 417–442). San Francisco: Jossey-Bass.

Goldston, D. (2000). *Assessment of suicidal behaviors and risk among children and adolescents*. Bethesda, MD: National Institute of Mental Health.

Goldston, D. B., Daniel, S. S., Reboussin, B. A., Reboussin, D. M., Frazier,

P. H., & Harris, A. E. (2001). Cognitive risk factors and suicide attempts among formerly hospitalized adolescents: A prospective naturalistic study. *Journal of the American Academy of Child and Adolescent Psychiatry, 40*(1), 91–99.

Gould, M. S. (2001). Suicide and the media. *Annals of the New York Academy of Sciences, 932,* 200–221.

Gould, M. S., Fisher, P., Parides, M., Flory, M., & Shaffer, D. (1996). Psychosocial risk factors of child and adolescent completed suicide. *Archives of General Psychiatry, 53*(12), 1155–1162.

Gould, M. S., Petrie, K., Kleinman, M. H., & Wallenstein, S. (1994). Clustering of attempted suicide: New Zealand national data. *International Journal of Epidemiology, 23*(6), 1185–1189.

Gould, M. S., Shaffer, D., Fisher, P., & Garfinkel, R. (1998). Separation/divorce and child and adolescent completed suicide. *Journal of the American Academy of Child and Adolescent Psychiatry, 37*(2), 155–162.

Gould, M. S., Wallenstein, S., & Kleinman, M. (1990). Time-space clustering of teenage suicide. *American Journal of Epidemiology, 131*(1), 71–78.

Gould, M. S., Wallenstein, S., Kleinman, M. H., O'Carroll, P., & Mercy, J. (1990). Suicide clusters: An examination of age-specific effects. *American Journal of Public Health, 80*(2), 211–212.

Groholt, B., Ekeberg, O., Wichstrom, L., & Haldorsen, T. (1998). Suicide among children and younger and older adolescents in Norway: A comparative study. *Journal of the American Academy of Child and Adolescent Psychiatry, 37*(5), 473–481.

Grossman, A., & Kerner, M. (1998a). Self-esteem and supportiveness as predictors of emotional distress in gay male and lesbian youth. *Journal of Homosexuality, 35*(2), 25–39.

Grossman, A., & Kerner, M. (1998b). Support networks of gay male and lesbian youth. *Journal of Gay, Lesbian, and Bisexual Identity, 3*(1), 27–46.

Grossman, J. A., & Kruesi, M. J. (2000). Innovative approaches to youth suicide prevention: An update of issues and research findings. In R. Maris, S. Cannetto, J. Macintosh, & M. Silverman (Eds.), *Review of Suicidology* (pp. 170–201). New York: Guilford Press.

Handwerk, M. L., Larzelere, R. E., Friman, P. C., & Mitchell, A. M. (1998). The relationship between lethality of attempted suicide and prior suicidal communications in a sample of residential youth. *Journal of Adolescence, 21*(4), 407–414.

Hawton, K., Arensman, E., Townsend, E., Bremner, S., Feldman, E., Goldney, R., Gunnell, D., Hazell, P., van Heeringen, K., House, A., Owens, D., Sakinofsky, I., & Traskman-Bendz, L. (1998). Deliberate self-harm: Systematic review of efficacy of psychosocial and pharmacological treatments in preventing repetition. *British Medical Journal, 317,* 441–447.

Head, B. (2001, June 4). Lost in the shadows. *People, 55,* p. 59.

Hendin, H. (1991). Psychodynamics of suicide, with particular reference to the young. *American Journal of Psychiatry, 148*(9), 1150–1158.

Hershberger, S., & D'Augelli, A. (1995). The impact of victimization on the mental health and suicidality of lesbian, gay, and bisexual youths. *Developmental Psychology, 31*(65–74).

Hershberger, S., Pilkington, N., & D'Augelli, A. (1997). Predictors of suicide attempts among gay, lesbian, and bisexual youth. *Journal of Adolescent Research, 12*(40), 477–497.

Hibbard, R. A., Brack, C. J., Rauch, S., & Orr, D. P. (1988). Abuse, feelings, and health behaviors in a student population. *American Journal of Diseases of Children, 142*(3), 326–330.

Holinger, P., Offer, D., Barter, J., & Bell, C. (1994). *Suicide and homicide among adolescents.* New York: Guilford Press.

Hollis, C. (1996). Depression, family environment, and adolescent suicidal behavior. *Journal of the American Academy of Child and Adolescent Psychiatry, 35*(5), 622–630.

Hussy, J. (1997). The effects of race, socioeconomic status, and household structure on injury mortality in children and young adults. *Maternal and Child Health Journal, 1*(4), 217–227.

Jacobs, D., Brewer, M., & Klein-Benheim, M. (1999). Suicide assessment: An overview and recommended protocol. In D. G. Jacobs (Ed.), *The Harvard Medical School guide to suicide assessment and prevention* (pp. 3–39). San Francisco: Jossey-Bass.

Johnson, B. A., Brent, D. A., Bridge, J., & Connolly, J. (1998). The familial aggregation of adolescent suicide attempts. *Acta Psychiatrica Scandinavica, 97*(1), 18–24.

Jones, G. D. (1997). The role of drugs and alcohol in urban minority adolescent suicide attempts. *Death Studies, 21*(2), 189–202.

Kalafat, J. (2000). Issues in the evaluation of youth suicide prevention initiatives. In T. E. Joiner & M. D. Rudd (Eds.), *Suicide science: Expanding the boundaries* (pp. 241–249). Norwell, MA: Kluwer Academic.

Kaplan, S. J., Pelcovitz, D., Salzinger, S., Mandel, F., & Weiner, M. (1997). Adolescent physical abuse and suicide attempts. *Journal of the American Academy of Child and Adolescent Psychiatry, 36*(6), 799–808.

Kazdin, A., Rodgers, A., & Colbus, D. (1986). The Hopelessness Scale for Children: Psychometric characteristics and concurrent validity. *Journal of Consulting and Clinical Psychology, 54,* 241–245.

Kelly, T. M., Lynch, K. G., Donovan, J. E., & Clark, D. B. (2001). Alcohol use disorders and risk factor interactions for adolescent suicidal ideation and attempts. *Suicide and Life-Threatening Behavior, 31*(2), 181–193.

King, C. A. (1997). Suicidal behavior in adolescence. In R. Maris, M. Silverman, & S. Canetto (Eds.), *Review of Suicidology* (pp. 61–95). New York: Guilford Press.

King, C. A., & Knox, M. (2000). Recognition and treatment of suicidal youth: Broadening our research agenda. In T. Joiner & M. D. Rudd (Eds.), *Suicide science: Expanding the boundaries* (pp. 251–269). Norwell, MA: Kluwer Academic.

King, R. A., Schwab-Stone, M., Flisher, A. J., Greenwald, S., Kramer, R. A., Goodman, S. H., et al. (2001). Psychosocial and risk behavior correlates of youth suicide attempts and suicidal ideation. *Journal of the American Academy of Child and Adolescent Psychiatry, 40*(7), 837–846.

Klimes-Dougan, B., Free, K., Ronsaville, D., Stilwell, J., Welsh, C. J., & Radke-Yarrow, M. (1999). Suicidal ideation and attempts: a longitudinal investigation of children of depressed and well mothers. *Journal of the American Academy of Child and Adolescent Psychiatry, 38*(6), 651–659.

Kovacs, M. (1985). The Children's Depression Inventory (CDI). *Psychopharmacology Bulletin, 21,* 995–998.

Kovacs, M. (1992). *Children's Depression Inventory manual.* North Tonawanda, NY: Multi-Health Systems.

Kovacs, M. (1997). *The Interview Schedule for Children and Adolescents (ISCA): Current and Lifetime (ISCA—C & L) and Current and Interim (ISCA—C & I) versions.* Unpublished instruments, University of Pittsburgh School of Medicine, Western Psychiatric Institute and Clinics, Pittsburgh.

Kovacs, M., Goldston, D., & Gatsonis, C. (1993). Suicidal behaviors and childhood-onset depressive disorders: A longitudinal investigation. *Journal of the American Academy of Child and Adolescent Psychiatry, 32*(1), 8–20.

Kraemer, H. C., Kazdin, A. E., Offord, D. R., Kessler, R. C., Jensen, P. S., & Kupfer, D. J. (1997). Coming to terms with the terms of risk. *Archives of General Psychiatry, 54*(4), 337–343.

Kumar, G., & Steer, R. A. (1995). Psychosocial correlates of suicidal ideation in adolescent psychiatric inpatients. *Suicide and Life-Threatening Behavior, 25*(3), 339–346.

Levy, J. C., & Deykin, E. Y. (1989). Suicidality, depression, and substance abuse in adolescence. *American Journal of Psychiatry, 146*(11), 1462–1467.

Lewinsohn, P. M., Rohde, P., Seeley, J. R., & Baldwin, C. L. (2001). Gender differences in suicide attempts from adolescence to young adulthood. *Journal of the American Academy of Child and Adolescent Psychiatry, 40*(4), 427–434.

Lyon, M. E., Benoit, M., O'Donnell, R. M., Getson, P. R., Silber, T., & Walsh, T. (2000). Assessing African American adolescents' risk for suicide attempts: Attachment theory. *Adolescence, 35*(137), 121–134.

Macgowan, M. J. (2004). Prevention and intervention in youth suicide. In P. Allen-Meares & M. W. Fraser (Eds.), *Intervention with children and adolescents: An interdisciplinary perspective* (pp. 282–310). Boston: Allyn & Bacon.

Macgowan, M. J. (in press). Psychosocial treatment of youth suicide: A systematic review of the research. *Research on Social Work Practice.*

Mann, J. J., & Arango, V. (1999). The neurobiology of suicidal behavior. In D. G. Jacobs (Ed.), *Harvard Medical School guide to suicide assessment and interventions* (pp. 98–114). San Francisco: Jossey-Bass.

Marcenko, M., Fishman, G., & Friedman, J. (1999). Reexamining adolescent suicidal ideation: A developmental perspective applied to a diverse population. *Journal of Youth and Adolescence, 28*(1), 121–138.

Marttunen, M. J., Aro, H. M., & Lonnqvist, J. K. (1993). Precipitant stressors in adolescent suicide. *Journal of the American Academy of Child and Adolescent Psychiatry, 32*(6), 1178–1183.

McDaniel, J. S., Purcell, D. W., & D'Augelli, A. R. (2001). The relationship between sexual orientation and risk for suicide: Research findings and future directions for research and prevention. *Suicide and Life-Threatening Behavior, 31*(1), 84–105.

McIntosh, J. L. (2000). Epidemiology of adolescent suicide in the United States. In R. Maris, S. Cannetto, J. Macintosh, & M. Silverman (Eds.), *Review of Suicidology* (pp. 3–33). New York: Guilford Press.

McKeown, R. E., Garrison, C. Z., Cuffe, S. P., Waller, J. L., Jackson, K. L., & Addy, C. L. (1998). Incidence and predictors of suicidal behaviors in a longitudinal sample of young adolescents. *Journal of the American Academy of Child and Adolescent Psychiatry, 37*(6), 612–619.

Mezzich, A. C., Giancola, P. R., Tarter, R. E., Lu, S., Parks, S. M., & Barrett, C. M. (1997). Violence, suicidality, and alcohol/drug use involvement in adolescent females with a psychoactive substance use disorder and controls. *Alcoholism, Clinical and Experimental Research, 21*(7), 1300–1307.

Miller, A., & Glinski, J. (2000). Youth suicidal behavior: Assessment and intervention. *Journal of Clinical Psychology, 56*(9), 131–1152.

Molin, R. S. (1986). Covert suicide and families of adolescents. *Adolescence, 21*(81), 177–184.

Monk, M. (1987). Epidemiology of suicide. *Epidemiologic Reviews, 9,* 51–69.

Móscicki, E. K. (1999). Epidemiology of suicide. In D. G. Jacobs (Ed.), *The Harvard Medical School guide to suicide assessment and prevention* (pp. 40–51). San Francisco: Jossey-Bass.

Muehrer, P. (1995). Suicide and sexual orientation: A critical summary of recent research and directions for future research. *Suicide and Life-Threatening Behavior, 25*(Suppl.) 72–81.

National Center for Health Statistics. (2000). *Leading cause of death reports, 1998 United States, ages 10–19, all races, both sexes* [Online]. Retrieved from http://webapp .cdc.gov/sasweb/ncipc/leadcaus.html on March 14, 2001.

National Center for Injury Prevention and Control. (2001). *Customized injury mortality report* [Online]. Retrieved from http://webapp.cdc.gov/sasweb/ncipc/mortrate. html on August 15, 2001.

Neeleman, J., Wessely, S., & Lewis, G. (1998). Suicide acceptability in African- and white Americans: The role of religion. *Journal of Nervous and Mental Diseases, 186*(1), 12–16.

Nelson, E. C., Grant, J. D., Bucholz, K. K., Glowinski, A., Madden, P.A.F., Reich, W., & Heath, A. C. (2000). Social phobia in a population-based female adolescent twin sample: Co-morbidity and associated suicide-related symptoms. *Psychological Medicine, 30*(4), 797–804.

Nilsson, L., Tomson, T., Farahmand, B. Y., Diwan, V., & Persson, P. G. (1997). Cause-specific mortality in epilepsy: A cohort study of more than 9,000 patients once hospitalized for epilepsy. *Epilepsia, 38*(10), 1062–1068.

Novins, D. K., Beals, J., Roberts, R. E., & Manson, S. M. (1999). Factors associated with suicide ideation among American Indian adolescents: Does culture matter? *Suicide and Life-Threatening Behavior, 29*(4), 332–346.

O'Carroll, P. W., Berman, A. L., Maris, R. W., Móscicki, E. K., Tanney, B. L., & Silverman, M. M. (1996). Beyond the Tower of Babel: A nomenclature for suicidology. *Suicide and Life-Threatening Behavior, 26,* 237–252.

O'Carroll, P. W., & Potter, L. B. (1994). Suicide contagion and the reporting of suicide: Recommendations from a national workshop. U.S. Department of Health and Human Services. *Morbidity and Mortality Weekly Report, 43*(RR-6), 9–17.

O'Donnell, C. R. (1995). Firearm deaths among children and youth. *American Psychologist, 50*(9), 771–776.

Orbach, I., Rosenheim, E., & Hary, E. (1987). Some aspects of cognitive functioning in suicidal children. *Journal of the American Academy of Child and Adolescent Psychiatry, 26*(2), 181–185.

Patsiokas, A. T., Clum, G. A., & Luscomb, R. L. (1979). Cognitive characteristics of suicide attempters. *Journal of Consulting and Clinical Psychology, 47*(3), 478–484.

Pfeffer, C., Conte, H., Plutchik, R., & Jerrett, I. (1979). Suicidal behavior in latency age children: An empirical study. *Journal of the American Academy of Child Psychiatry, 18,* 679–692.

Pfeffer, C., Normandin, L., & Kakuma, T. (1998). Suicidal children grow up: Relations between family psychopathology and adolescents' lifetime suicidal behavior. *Journal of Nervous and Mental Disease, 186*(5), 269–275.

Pfeffer, C. R. (2000). Suicidal behavior in prepubertal children: From the 1980s to the new millennium. In R. Maris, S. Cannetto, J. Macintosh, & M. Silverman (Eds.), *Review of Suicidology* (pp. 159–169). New York: Guilford Press.

Pfeffer, C. R., Peskin, J. R., & Siefker, C. A. (1992). Suicidal children grow up: Psychiatric treatment during follow-up period. *Journal of the American Academy of Child and Adolescent Psychiatry, 31*(4), 679–685.

Pharris, M. D., Resnick, M. D., & Blum, R. W. (1997). Protecting against hopelessness and suicidality in sexually abused American Indian adolescents. *Journal of Adolescent Health, 21*(6), 400–406.

Phillips, D. P., & Carstensen, L. L. (1988). The effect of suicide stories on various demographic groups, 1968–1985. *Suicide and Life-Threatening Behavior, 18*(1), 100–114.

Potter, L., Powell, K., & Kachur, S. (1995). Suicide prevention from a public health perspective. *Suicide and Life-Threatening Behavior, 25*(1), 82–91.

Poussaint, A. F., & Alexander, A. (2001). *Lay my burden down: Suicide and the mental health crisis among African Americans* (rev. ed.). Boston: Beacon Press.

Proctor, C. D., & Groze, V. K. (1994). Risk factors for suicide among gay, lesbian, and bisexual youths. *Social Work, 39*(5), 504–513.

Queralt, M. (1993). Psychosocial risk factors associated with a small community of Latino adolescent attempters. *Social Work in Education, 15*(2), 91–103.

Randell, B. P., Eggert, L. L., & Pike, K. C. (2001). Immediate post-intervention effects of two brief youth suicide prevention interventions. *Suicide and Life-Threatening Behavior, 31*(1), 41–61.

Range, L. M., Goggin, W. C., & Steede, K. K. (1988). Perception of behavioral contagion of adolescent suicide. *Suicide and Life-Threatening Behavior, 18*(4), 334–341.

Range, L. M., & Knott, E. C. (1997). Twenty suicide assessment instruments: Evaluation and recommendations. *Death Studies, 21,* 25–58.

Reich, W. (2000). Diagnostic Interview for Children and Adolescents (DICA). *Journal of the American Academy of Child and Adolescent Psychiatry, 39,* 59–66.

Remafedi, G. (1999a). Sexual orientation and youth suicide. *Journal of the American Medical Association, 282*(13), 1291–1292.

Remafedi, G. (1999b). Suicide and sexual orientation: Nearing the end of controversy? *Archives of General Psychiatry, 56*(10), 885–886.

Remafedi, G., Farrow, J. A., & Deisher, R. W. (1993). Risk factors in attempted suicide in gay and bisexual youth. In L. D. Garnets & D. C. Kemmel (Eds.), *Psychological perspectives on lesbian and gay studies* (pp. 486–499). New York: Columbia University Press.

Renaud, J., Brent, D. A., Birmaher, B., Chiappetta, L., & Bridge, J. (1999). Suicide in adolescents with disruptive disorders. *Journal of the American Academy of Child and Adolescent Psychiatry, 38*(7), 846–851.

Reynolds, W. M. (1988). *Suicidal Ideation Questionnaire, professional manual.* Odessa, FL: Psychological Assessment Resources.

Roberts, R. E., & Chen, Y. W. (1995). Depressive symptoms and suicidal ideation among Mexican-origin and Anglo adolescents. *Journal of the American Academy of Child and Adolescent Psychiatry, 34*(1), 81–90.

Rotheram-Borus, M. J., Trautman, P. D., Dopkins, S. C., & Shrout, P. E. (1990). Cognitive style and pleasant activities among female adolescent suicide attempters. *Journal of Consulting and Clinical Psychology, 58*(5), 554–561.

Rudd, M. D. (2000). Integrating science into the practice of clinical suicidology: A review of the psychotherapy literature and a research agenda for the future. In R. Maris, S. Cannetto, J. Macintosh, & M. Silverman (Eds.), *Review of Suicidology* (pp. 47–83). New York: Guilford Press.

Safren, S. A., & Heimberg, R. G. (1999). Depression, hopelessness, suicidality, and related factors in sexual minority and heterosexual adolescents. *Journal of Consulting and Clinical Psychology, 67*(6), 859–866.

Saunders, S. M., Resnick, M. D., Hoberman, H. M., & Blum, R. W. (1994). Formal help-seeking behavior of adolescents identifying themselves as having mental health problems. *Journal of the American Academy of Child and Adolescent Psychiatry, 33*(5), 718–728.

Schmidtke, A., & Schaller, S. (1998). What do we know about media effects on imitation of suicidal behavior: State of the art. In D. DeLeo, A. Schmidtke, & R.F.W. Diekstra (Eds.), *Suicide prevention: A holistic approach* (pp. 121–137). Dordrecht, Netherlands: Kluwer.

Schwartz, J. A., Kaslow, N. J., Seeley, J., & Lewinsohn, P. (2000). Psychological, cognitive, and interpersonal correlates of attributional change in adolescents. *Journal of Clinical Child Psychology, 29*(2), 188–198.

Shaffer, D. (1988). The epidemiology of teen suicide: An examination of risk factors. *Journal of Clinical Psychiatry, 49*(Suppl.), 36–41.

Shaffer, D., & Craft, L. (1999). Methods of adolescent suicide prevention. *Journal of Clinical Psychiatry, 60*(Suppl. 2), 70–74.

Shaffer, D., Fisher, P., Hicks, R. H., Parides, M., & Gould, M. (1995). Sexual orientation in adolescents who commit suicide. *Suicide and Life-Threatening Behavior,* 25(Suppl.), 64–71.

Shaffer, D., Fisher, P., Lucas, C., Dulcan, M., & Schwab-Stone, M. (2000). NIMH Diagnostic Interview Schedule for Children, Version IV (NIMH DISC-IV): Description, differences from previous versions, and reliability of some common diagnoses. *Journal of the American Academy of Child and Adolescent Psychiatry, 39,* 28–38.

Shaffer, D., Garland, A., Gould, M., Fisher, P., & Trautman, P. (1988). Preventing teenage suicide: A critical review. *Journal of the American Academy of Child and Adolescent Psychiatry, 27*(6), 675–687.

Shaffer, D., Gould, M., & Hicks, R. C. (1994). Worsening suicide rate in black teenagers. *American Journal of Psychiatry, 151*(12), 1810–1812.

Shaffer, D., Gould, M. S., Fisher, P., Trautman, P., Moreau, D., Kleinman, M., & Flory, M. (1996). Psychiatric diagnosis in child and adolescent suicide. *Archives of General Psychiatry, 53*(4), 339–348.

Shagle, S. C., & Barber, B. K. (1995). A social-ecological analysis of adolescent suicidal ideation. *American Journal of Orthopsychiatry, 65*(1), 114–124.

Shah, S., Hoffman, R. E., Wake, L., & Marine, W. M. (2000). Adolescent suicide and household access to firearms in Colorado: Results of a case-control study. *Journal of Adolescent Health, 26*(3), 157–163.

Shaunesey, K., Cohen, J. L., Plummer, B., & Berman, A. (1993). Suicidality in hospitalized adolescents: Relationship to prior abuse. *American Journal of Orthopsychiatry, 63*(1), 113–119.

Sherrill, J., & Kovacs, M. (2000). The Interview Schedule for Children and Adolescents (ISCA). *Journal of the American Academy of Child and Adolescent Psychiatry, 39*, 67–75.

Smith, K., Conroy, R., & Ehler, B. (1984). Lethality of Suicide Attempt Rating Scale. *Suicide and Life-Threatening Behavior, 14*, 214–242.

Sorenson, S. B., & Shen, H. (1996). Youth suicide trends in California: An examination of immigrant and ethnic group risk. *Suicide and Life-Threatening Behavior, 26*(2), 143–154.

Spirito, A., Overholser, J., & Stark, L. J. (1989). Common problems and coping strategies: 2. Findings with adolescent suicide attempters. *Journal of Abnormal Child Psychology, 17*(2), 213–221.

Spirito, A., Williams, C. A., Stark, L. J., & Hart, K. J. (1988). The Hopelessness Scale for Children: Psychometric properties with normal and emotionally disturbed adolescents. *Journal of Abnormal Child Psychology, 16*(4), 445–458.

Steer, R., & Beck, A. (1988). Use of the Beck Depression Inventory, Hopelessness Scale, Scale for Suicidal Ideation, and Suicidal Intent Scale with adolescents. *Advances in Adolescent Mental Health, 3*, 219–231.

Strauss, J., Birmaher, B., Bridge, J., Axelson, D., Chiappetta, L., Brent, D., & Ryan, N. (2000). Anxiety disorders in suicidal youth. *Canadian Journal of Psychiatry, 45*(8), 739–745.

Suris, J. C., Parera, N., & Puig, C. (1996). Chronic illness and emotional distress in adolescence. *Journal of Adolescent Health, 19*(2), 153–156.

Svetaz, M. V., Ireland, M., & Blum, R. (2000). Adolescents with learning disabilities: Risk and protective factors associated with emotional well-being: Findings from the National Longitudinal Study of Adolescent Health. *Journal of Adolescent Health, 27*(5), 340–348.

Swedo, S. E., Rettew, D. C., Kuppenheimer, M., Lum, D., Dolan, S., & Goldberger, E. (1991). Can adolescent suicide attempters be distinguished from at-risk adolescents? *Pediatrics, 88*(3), 620–629.

Thompson, E., Eggert, L., & Herting, J. (2000). Mediating effects of an indicated prevention program for reducing youth depression and suicide risk behaviors. *Suicide and Life-Threatening Behavior, 30*(3), 252–271.

Thompson, E. A., Eggert, L. L., Randell, B. P., & Pike, K. C. (2001). Evaluation of indicated suicide risk prevention approaches for potential high school dropouts. *American Journal of Public Health, 91*(5), 742–752.

Topol, P., & Reznikiff, M. (1982). Perceived peer and family relationships, hopelessness, and loss of control as factors in adolescent suicide attempts. *Suicide and Life-Threatening Behavior, 13,* 141–150.

U.S. Department of Health and Human Services. (2000). *Trends in the well-being of America's children and youth: 1999.* Rockville, MD: U.S. Department of Health and Human Services.

U.S. Department of Health and Human Services. (2001). *National strategy for suicide prevention: Goals and objectives for action.* Rockville, MD: U.S. Department of Health and Human Services.

U.S. Public Health Service. (1999). *The Surgeon General's call to action to prevent suicide: At a glance: Suicide among the young* [Online]. Retrieved from http://www.surgeongeneral.gov/library/calltoaction/fact3.htm on July 18, 2001.

Vannatta, R. (1997). Adolescent gender differences in suicide related behaviors. *Journal of Youth and Adolescence, 26*(5), 559–568.

Vega, W. A., Gil, A., Warheit, G., Apospori, E., & Zimmerman, R. (1993). The relationship of drug use to suicide ideation and attempts among African American, Hispanic, and white non-Hispanic male adolescents. *Suicide and Life-Threatening Behavior, 23*(2), 110–119.

Velting, D. M., Rathus, J. H., & Miller, A. L. (2000). MACI personality scale profiles of depressed adolescent suicide attempters: A pilot study. Million Adolescent Clinical Inventory. *Journal of Clinical Psychology, 56*(10), 1381–1385.

Vossekuil, B., Reddy, M., Fein, R., Borum, R., & Modzeleski, W. (2000). *U.S.S.S. Safe School Initiative: An interim report on the prevention of targeted violence in schools.* Washington, DC: U.S. Secret Service, National Threat Assessment Center.

Wagner, B., Cole, R., & Schwartzman, P. (1995). Psychosocial correlates of suicide attempts among junior and senior high school youth. *Suicide and Life-Threatening Behavior, 25*(3), 358–372.

Wagner, K. D., Rouleau, M., & Joiner, T. (2000). Cognitive factors related to suicidal ideation and resolution in psychiatrically hospitalized children and adolescents. *American Journal of Psychiatry, 157*(12), 2017–2021.

Weinberger, L. E., Sreenivasan, S., Sathyavagiswaran, L., & Markowitz, E. (2001). Child and adolescent suicide in a large, urban area: Psychological, demographic, and situational factors. *Journal of Forensic Sciences, 46*(4), 902–907.

Woods, E., Lin, Y., Middleman, A., Beckford, P., Chase, L., & DuRant, R. (1997). The association of suicide attempts in adolescents. *Pediatrics, 99*(6), 791–796.

Yang, B., & Clum, G. A. (2000). Childhood stress leads to later suicidality via its effect on cognitive functioning. *Suicide and Life-Threatening Behavior, 30*(3), 183–198.

Young, S. E., Mikulich, S. K., Goodwin, M. B., Hardy, J., Martin, C. L., Zoccolillo, M. S., & Crowley, T. J. (1995). Treated delinquent boys' substance use: Onset, pattern, relationship to conduct and mood disorders. *Drug and Alcohol Dependence, 37*(2), 149–162.

Zayas, L. (1987). Toward an understanding of suicide risks in young Hispanic females. *Journal of Adolescent Research, 2*(1), 1–11.

Zayas, L. H., Kaplan, C., Turner, S., Romano, K., & Gonzalez-Ramos, G. (2000). Understanding suicide attempts by adolescent Hispanic females. *Social Work, 45,* 53–63.

13

Risk and Resilience in Childhood: Toward an Evidence-Based Model of Practice

Mark W. Fraser and Maeda J. Galinsky

Social work and other helping professions have embraced ecological and systems theories as inclusive frames of reference for education and practice (Council on Social Work Education, 2001; Germain, 1991). Because they constantly remind us that behavior is shaped by both individual and environmental factors, these theories are important for understanding the experience of childhood. Children live in nested settings of influence that range from family and school to neighborhood and the broader community. It is the interplay of a child's individual characteristics with contextual influences that ultimately yields behavior and, in the long run, developmental outcomes.

Although they establish essential groundwork for understanding human behavior, ecological and systems theories are insufficiently specific for practice. These theories are insufficient for articulating explicit information, which is a prerequisite for conducting case assessments and developing intervention plans. Theories and frames of reference that provide more specific knowledge about childhood depression, delinquency, teenage pregnancy, and other problems are needed to guide action.

RISK AND RESILIENCE PERSPECTIVE

This book has traced the elements of an emerging risk and resilience perspective, one that holds the potential to provide social work and other professions with an improved frame of reference for the design of child and family services. This book defines risk factors as any influences that increase the probability of harm or—more specifically—that increase the probability of the onset, digression to a more serious state, or maintenance of a problem condition. It defines protective factors as both the internal and external resources that modify risk. Resilience is defined as adaptive behavior that produces positive social and health outcomes arising from the interplay of risk and protective factors. On the basis of these concepts, the risk and resilience perspective has two essential elements.

First, it consists of a growing body of knowledge on individual and environmental conditions that appear to underlie many childhood social and health problems. In aggregate, these markers, correlates, and possible causes can be thought of as elements of a common or cross-cutting model for risk and protective factors for a variety of childhood disorders. They can be classified ecologically as environmental conditions, including neighborhood, school, and peer-related contextual factors; family conditions;

and individual, psychosocial, and biological conditions, including genetic liability. Table 13-1 gives common risk and protective factors, as they were described in chapter 2, for each of the three system levels.

Second, building on these common factors, the risk and resilience perspective recognizes that some risk factors contribute uniquely to particular problems and that some protective factors provide safeguards against particular problems. Thus, to better understand childhood problems, not only must we consider common risk and protective mechanisms, we also need to develop a list of problem-specific risk and protective factors. Chapters 4 through 12 presented problem-specific risk conditions that combine with common risk conditions to give rise to specific childhood problems. These chapters also initiated discussion of the protective resources—assets and strengths—associated with resistance to and amelioration of specific problems.

The essence of the risk and resilience perspective is the articulation of multiple pathways, comprised of interwoven chains of risk and protective factors that lead to developmental outcomes in childhood. By extending the ecological and systems perspectives, with whom to intervene, when to intervene, and how to intervene can be decided more accurately.

Table 13-1 shows selected problem-specific risk and protective factors for sexually transmitted infections (STIs), which is the topic of chapter 9. As can be seen in Table 13-1, STIs are clearly affected by a combination of common and STI-specific risk and protective factors. It is also evident that there is overlap between the common and specific factors. For example, child maltreatment and harsh discipline are common risk factors related to many of the problem-specific risk and protective factors—poor parental monitoring, family norms that accept early initiation of sexual intercourse and multiple partners, early initiation of sexual activity, sexual abuse, and substance use. The problem-specific risk and protective factors, however, provide significantly more information about the etiology of STIs. In addition, compared with the common factors, the problem-specific factors provide more precise clues for the design of intervention and prevention programs.

MULTIDETERMINISM

This risk and resilience perspective is based on the idea that childhood problems are multidetermined. That is, problems have many causes, whether at the level of the individual, the family or school, or the broader environment (see, for example, Henggeler, Schoenwald, Borduin, Rowland, & Cunningham, 1998). For example, some children may have a genetically related predisposition to a problem such as attention deficit hyperactivity disorder; yet, familial and environmental conditions, as well as other individual factors, strongly affect whether and how the disorder is manifested. Most childhood problems have multiple individual and contextual determinants. This concept of multideterminism is central to a risk and resilience orientation to practice.

ACCUMULATED RISK VERSUS SPECIFIC PATHWAYS

Furthermore, risks are thought to accumulate, or "bundle" together, and we conceptualize many relationships between risk factors and outcomes as being reciprocal.

Table 13-1. Common and Selected Problem-Specific Risk and Protective Factors for Sexually Transmitted Infections: An Ecological and Multisystems Perspective

SYSTEM LEVEL	RISK FACTORS	PROTECTIVE FACTORS
Environmental and Contextual Conditions, including Neighborhood, School, and Peers	**Common Risk Factors** Few opportunities for education and employment Racial discrimination and injustice Poverty **Problem-Specific Risk Factors** Lack of access to universal health care Lack of emphasis on prevention Media that sexualize women and promote unsafe sexual practices Limited opportunities for sexuality education Neighborhood and peer norms that accept early initiation of sexual intercourse and multiple partners	**Common Protective Factors** Many opportunities for education, employment, growth, and achievement Collective efficacy Presence of caring adult **Problem-Specific Protective Factors** Access to culturally and developmentally sensitive health care and prevention Public awareness of sexual health and responsible sexual behavior
Family Factors	**Common Risk Factors** Child maltreatment Interparental conflict Parental psychopathology Harsh discipline **Problem-Specific Risk Factors** Family norms that accept early initiation of sexual intercourse and multiple partners Older siblings who are sexually active Poor parental monitoring	**Common Protective Factors** Effective parenting Positive parent–child relationship **Problem-Specific Protective Factors** Partner or friend supportive of safer sex Effective parental monitoring Communication regarding sexuality
Individual, Psychosocial and Biological Factors	**Common Risk Factors** Gender Biomedical conditions and problems **Problem-Specific Risk Factors** Early puberty Early initiation of sexual activity Inability to say no or negotiate safer sex Intention to initiate intercourse Negative attitudes and beliefs about safer sex practices Substance use Having been sexually abused	**Common Protective Factors** Easy temperament as an infant Self-esteem and hardiness High intelligence Normative competence in roles: Self efficacy **Problem-Specific Protective Factors** Formal operational thinking Positive attitudes and beliefs about safer sex practices

NOTE: Each of the problem-specific risk and protective factors is adapted from chapter 9 and focuses on sexually transmitted infections. Common factors remain the same for different types of problems, but the content of problem-specific factors changes. See chapters 4 through 12 for summaries of problem-specific content.

Although individual, family, peer, school, neighborhood, and environmental factors clearly influence behavior, the causal order and relative strength of each in producing life course outcomes are often unclear. Specific pathways that generalize to large numbers of children are hard to isolate. Consider, for instance, aggressive, violent behavior. Youth violence may be strongly influenced by the neighborhood rate of violence, but the rate of neighborhood violence is often bundled with major risk factors such as association with delinquent peers, parental criminality, poor parental supervision of children, and school risk conditions (Sampson, Raudenbush, & Earls, 1997). Factors at the individual, family, school, and neighborhood levels are intertwined. Which comes first? And what is the strength of competing contextual and other influences? Because violent behavior occurs across neighborhoods with different levels of violence, and because children may be exposed to a variety of neighborhood, school, family, and other systems-level effects, the causal order of relationship is difficult to untangle (Duncan & Raudenbush, 2001). Given the complexity of relationships, some scholars are beginning to argue that many relationships are best characterized as reciprocal and that it is accumulated risk, rather than a particular risk sequence, that most compromises child development (see, for example, Rutter, 2000a, 2000b, 2001; Sameroff & Fiese, 2000; Thornberry, Lizotte, Krohn, Farnsworth, & Jang, 1991).

Because child development is subject to so many influences, no single theory is likely to account fully for the many different factors that affect substance abuse, mood disorders, truancy, academic failure, and other childhood problems. The factors that may trigger or untrigger a condition, such as conduct disorder, do not appear to operate equivalently at all points in a child's development. And they may vary by gender, sexual orientation, race and ethnicity, and other factors. Absent dramatic new discoveries in cognitive, labeling, psychodynamic, social control, social disorganization, social learning, structural opportunity, and other theories that are often applied to the problems of childhood, the risk and resilience perspective provides a mechanism for beginning to organize the multitude of factors that affect children and, as described in the section that follows, for improving the precision of social programs through evidence-based practice (EBP).

TOWARD EVIDENCE-BASED PRACTICE

EBP is a concept with European roots and is characterized by a process of systematically identifying and employing the strongest evidence in making practice decisions (Jaeschke, Guyatt, & Meade, 1998). It is "the conscientious, explicit, and judicious use of current best evidence in making decisions" in developing and implementing practice strategies (Sackett, Rosenberg, Gray, Haynes, & Richardson, 1996, p. 71). This perspective incorporates the wide range of information that practitioners use routinely in developing understandings of problems and devising intervention plans. EBP integrates accumulated expertise—practice wisdom—and individual and family preferences with current research findings.

EBP requires knowledge of risk factors giving rise to problems and corresponding knowledge of the effectiveness of alternative interventions. Practitioners are not required to have all this knowledge in their heads! Rather, they must simply have a means to access it. The EBP perspective differs from an empirically based practitioner model in which the social worker is expected to collect, to analyze, and to evaluate data in conjunction with day-to-day practice. In EBP, the practitioner does not engage in research, but rather is expected to understand and use research knowledge in defining practice problems and in selecting interventions matched to risk and protective factors. This knowledge is systematically collected by groups of professionals and made available to practitioners. Using this "best available" information ensures that practice strategies will represent the best current thinking and be rooted in research. By extension it implies that, in the application of research findings or in the absence of research related to a specific problem or issue, the worker is expected to use theory with a research basis, knowledge of risk mechanisms associated with related social and health problems, knowledge derived from clinical supervision, and knowledge from practical experience.

EBP is collaborative in the sense that the child and his or her family are involved in defining the problem, selecting and tailoring practice strategies, and assessing outcomes. The steps may be summarized as follows:

- Defining the problem collaboratively with the child, his or her family, or the primary caregivers.
  Practice Question: What are the risk factors for the problems and the protective resources we can mobilize to deal with these risks?
  In other words, identifying through careful assessment the conditions giving rise to problems and the protective resources that are or may be mobilized to deal with those conditions.
- Identifying a set of practice questions with the child and his or her family.
  Practice Question: What outcomes do we want to achieve?
- Selecting and searching for appropriate resources to answer the questions.
  Practice Questions: What interventions reduce the identified risk factors and promote protective resources? What interventions are associated with the desired outcomes?
- Integrating and applying the evidence to the design of an initial practice strategy.
  Practice Question: After considering local conditions and knowledge of race and ethnicity, gender, and age, which interventions seem developmentally appropriate for the current situation?
- Modifying further the initial practice strategy on the basis of client preference and practice expertise, including adjusting practice strategies for unique or local conditions.
  Practice Questions: What does the child or his or her family want? How can the best available interventions be tailored on the basis of consumer preference and practice experience? Are there special local conditions on which practice should be conditioned?
- Applying a case-specific, well-designed practice strategy.
  Practice Question: Are there practice resources—for example, treatment manuals or practice guides—that clearly specify the central elements of the best available strategy?
- Evaluating outcomes with the client.
  Practice Question: What measures can be used to assess desired outcomes—both proximal and distal?

EBP places control in the hands of the practitioner and the family: it is not a top-down hierarchical or a paint-by-the-numbers mechanistic perspective (Sackett, Richardson, Rosenberg, & Haynes, 1997). From the beginning, it requires a careful assessment to identify risk or protective factors; then it requires selection of strategies that, on the basis of the evidence, are likely to reduce risk and promote protection. Practitioners involve consumers in defining the problem and in determining the relevance of evidence, integrate consumer preferences with practice experience and evidence to form a strategy, and manage how and when a strategy is implemented. Practitioners must have access to published knowledge and must be able to appraise critically and give practical meaning to the published literature. This is a tall order. However, because practitioners rarely have access to the range of information produced by other practitioners and practice researchers, online databases (such as the established Cochrane Library in medicine and the newly developing Campbell Collaboration Library, 2001, in social work and the social sciences), published practice guidelines (such as those developed by the American Psychological Association and the American Academy of Pediatrics), and other practice resources (such as NASW's *Practice Resources Book Series*) are being developed and disseminated for use by practitioners (see, for example, Cochrane Library, 2001; Herrerias, Perrin, & Stein, 2001; Rosen & Proctor, 2002; Woolfenden, Williams, & Peat, 2001).

Two Basic Strategies: Reduce Risk and Promote Protection

In our view, the risk and resilience perspective offers an important clue for answering the question, How do we make profound differences in the lives of children? To make a difference, we must simultaneously adopt and implement two evidence-based strategies. First, risk must be reduced. Risk factors should guide intervention efforts, and the goal of intervention should be to reduce the effect of specifically targeted risk factors. Second, protection must be strengthened. Because some risk factors cannot be changed quickly, the protective mechanisms that operate for children who are in high-risk circumstances but who do not manifest problems must be understood and used to construct preventive interventions. Interventions that strengthen protection and concomitantly reduce the effects of risk form the basis of a risk and resilience orientation. Coupled with "local" knowledge, they are core ingredients of EBP.

Identifying Local Risk and Protective Chains

Because environmental resources, local traditions, and cultural practices vary widely, no single risk chain for a childhood condition is likely to apply to all children. Furthermore, risk chains may differentially apply to children, depending on how groupings of personal characteristics (race or ethnicity, gender, and age, for instance) are approached in each community. Thus, specific risk and protective factors, as they occur in specific communities, must be identified for specific childhood conditions. As shown throughout the book, cross-cutting information on risk and, to a lesser degree, on protection, is beginning to emerge; this information is necessary in planning evidence-based interventions—but it is not sufficient. If we adopt an ecological perspective, we implicitly adopt the idea that the local environment significantly influences behavior, and knowledge of environmental conditions must be incorporated into intervention planning.

Building on knowledge of common risk and protective factors and findings from studies of problem-specific risk and protective factors, intervention must integrate from the start an understanding of local risk and protective conditions. Knowledge of these conditions comes from community studies, from practitioners who work in the community, from community members, and from consumers of services (see, for example, Hawkins, Catalano, & Associates, 1992). Thus, a resilience-based intervention is founded on the specification of risk and protective chains for a presenting problem: these chains should link common and problem-specific knowledge with carefully gathered and sifted information about local conditions, values, practices, and beliefs. This knowledge, then, is combined with knowledge of the comparative effectiveness of different change strategies; the combined knowledge then allows practitioners to develop plans for assessment and intervention and thus to address risks and use strengths.

Fitting Change Strategies to Keystone Risk Factors

Because risks vary in influence and because we often cannot mount change strategies that affect all risk conditions, keystone risk factors are frequently used as the basis for devising interventive strategies. Keystone risks are those conditions and social processes that are thought to be predominantly causal in etiologic chains and subject to change via intervention (Loeber & Stouthamer-Loeber, 1996). How might the idea of keystone risks be applied to delinquency? Much delinquency never progresses beyond a first offense. It makes little sense to intervene if a large number of children will desist without intervention. However, we know that some first offenders do not desist and in fact go on to engage in behaviors that endanger others. Consequently, the challenge we face is to identify the risk factors that distinguish those who will desist from those who will escalate their delinquent involvement. Then we must note which of these risk factors might be malleable through intervention. Keystone risks are those conditions or processes that cause a child to be most vulnerable to problems and that, if left unattended, will cause such problems to exacerbate. On balance, then, keystone risks are targets for intervention.[1]

The development of risk chains and the designation of keystone influences enable practitioners and program planners to identify appropriate interventive goals. Most goals will focus on reducing risk and strengthening protective factors. Practitioners must match keystone risk factors to interventive strategies. Whenever possible, identified strategies should be supported by research. When research evidence is not available, practitioners must rely on experience, on clinical judgment, and on consultation with peers as "the best current evidence." In this same manner, they should also develop strategies to strengthen protective processes.

To use an EBP perspective, one needs to know which interventions work and which do not. Fortunately, there is a growing multidisciplinary literature on the

---

[1]Keystone protective factors also may exist, but because so little is known about protective mechanisms, it makes sense for interventions to seek to strengthen all protective factors and processes. As knowledge about protective factors increases, it may be possible to identify keystone protective factors that warrant special attention.

effectiveness of interventions, increasingly available through the Cochrane Library, Campbell Collaboration, NASW Press, the American Psychological Association, and the American Psychiatric Association. As we develop this practice base, we can begin to identify intervention strategies, or practice guidelines, that address particular risk and protective factors. Interventive knowledge combined with practice experience and knowledge derived from systematic assessment (of risk and protective factors), along with careful analyses of consumer preferences, are the bases for defining service activities related to intervention goals and activities. A risk and resilience perspective therefore requires:

- skill in assessing risk and protective factors and in engaging clients in the process of assessment;
- skill in identifying cultural and local conditions affecting or conditioning risk and protection
- skill in specifying risk and protective mechanisms that are malleable (subject to change through intervention)
- skill in accessing practice resources (for example, guidelines and treatment manuals) that are indexed to risk and protective factors and that describe alternative interventive strategies
- skill in engaging client participation in the choice of interventions
- skill in using practice guidelines and treatment manuals to provide a "tailored" intervention that accounts for keystone and local risk factors, while strengthening protection.

IMPLICATIONS FOR PRACTICE

This risk and resilience perspective on child development is part of an evidence-based perspective on practice that conjoins experience accrued from practice and knowledge of culture and local conditions with burgeoning literatures on the causes of social and health problems and the effectiveness of various interventive strategies. The practitioner must have skills in assessing risk and protective factors, in accessing databases that summarize practice knowledge, and in employing systematic change strategies. The practitioner must also be able to use this information in the context of practice experience, of case supervision, and of client wishes. Use of this perspective requires skills in risk assessment and in developing a hierarchy of change strategies that address the factors affecting children in the context of their families, schools, and neighborhoods. At once, EBP accepts empirically validated information, reflects a judicious use of clinical experience, and embraces the inclusion of consumer opinions.

RISK ASSESSMENT

Risk assessment is a linchpin of EBP. It involves gathering information from children and their families on a wide array of individual, familial, and extrafamilial factors. It concentrates on prediction and on the cumulative odds of a negative future outcome, such as a child's vulnerability for future conduct problems, depression, suicide, or other poor developmental outcomes. In child welfare, risk assessment often focuses on the likelihood of future maltreatment. In juvenile justice, it usually focuses on the likelihood of future offenses or on "dangerousness." In mental health, it focuses on the likelihood of relapse or medications compliance. In research designed to identify risk factors, risk assessment typically involves hundreds of potential risk factors. A study of risk factors for violence among 939 people ages 18 to 40 who had serious mental disorders included 134 measures—scales for psychopathy, anger, delusions, violent thoughts, hallucinations, diagnosis, self-harm thoughts, and social support network. In addition, it included dozens of measures of history of child abuse, prior violence, parental criminality, and contextual variables (Monahan et al., 2001). Although this type of research is the basis for clinical risk assessment, parsimony must be the rule in agency-level practice. Risk assessment is usually more delimited at that level, more targeted, and less time consuming.

To be sure, clinicians have always done risk assessment, but in the past, it was more anecdotal. Today, we are aided by new risk assessment instruments that have undergone extensive validation. Risk assessment involves the use of structured interview guides that are scored using actuarial anchors from prior research. The North Carolina Juvenile Court Risk Assessment Scale was adopted by juvenile courts in North Carolina and used by court counselors to advise the Court on dispositions. It exemplifies this new type of clinical tool and contains nine measures predictive of future offending. Tools such as this scale are usually scored additively. That is, a summated "total risk score" reflects aggregate risk. In some scales, keystone risks will receive double or triple weighting to reflect the fact that they are more predictive of outcomes than other risk factors in an instrument. Based on cut points—often arbitrarily determined—total risk scores are broken down into several levels of risk, such as high, medium, and low risk. These types of risk assessment instruments, combined with practice experience and knowledge of local conditions, will enhance our ability to intervene in problematic situations and to develop prevention strategies. Although we are at a relatively early stage in the development of instruments, knowledge of particular risk and protective factors for specific conditions, as illustrated in chapters 4 to 12, will contribute to this process of development. In each chapter, we have presented examples of promising assessment instruments that are currently available.

The risk assessment instrument used in North Carolina's juvenile courts is relatively simple to use. Researchers are also developing more complex measures to deal with the array of information needed for treatment planning. A relatively new method, contingent risk assessment, is based on the idea that many pathways lead to poor outcomes—that a particular social or health problem can be caused by a different combination of factors—and that these different pathways are associated with different levels of risk. This approach classifies children into groups with different risk factors and different levels of risk. Monahan and colleagues (2001) have constructed a hypothetical classification tree for violence, using the contingent risk-assessment approach.

Risk assessment instruments are often based more on knowledge of risk factors than on knowledge of protective factors. There are several reasons for this. First, our knowledge of protective factors is more limited than our knowledge of risk factors. Second, the measurement of protection is profoundly affected by the lack of conceptual clarity about protection itself. Finally, the few studies comparing risk and protective factors suggest that risk factors may be more predictive than protective factors of future difficulties (Pollard, Hawkins, & Arthur, 1999). In any event, we need to continuously update our risk assessment instruments. As our knowledge of protective factors increases and as we identify more potent risk factors, we will have to systematically add these factors to our assessment protocols.

Arguably, the core features of EBP are systematic assessment and the selection of interventions that reduce risk and promote protection. The actuarial methods of risk assessment are based on studies of samples of youths and are useful in summarizing risk as we understand it *on average*. That is, risk estimates whether applied to all youths or subgroupings of youths—of the sort that emerge from classification trees—are likelihoods based on average tendencies. They are not conditioned on unique circumstances. We have argued that workers must use their knowledge of culture and local conditions to assess risk and to devise intervention plans. Our position asks, To what degree should workers "adjust" results from systematic risk assessments based on local knowledge?

In our view, *prudent clinical judgment that is informed by knowledge of the unique circumstances affecting children and their families should always temper actuarial risk assessment*. This approach is consistent with the principles of EBP, which call for the incorporation of practitioner experience and assessment skill into any intervention plan. Research samples rarely reflect the diversity of children who are in need and who receive social and health services. The most at-risk families are difficult to recruit and retain in research. Consequently, research samples are often biased toward lower-risk subjects. Research, to date, is also inadequate in sampling of girls and children from minority and low-income families. As a result, important risk factors for children from, say, Latino populations may not be included in commercially available risk assessment instruments. Finally, because they are based on what happens on average, risk assessment instruments do not account for factors that are specific to a particular individual, family, or community.

In this chapter, we have highlighted the importance of local knowledge and practice experience in EBP. Systematic risk assessment and prudent clinical judgment are both needed. EBP uses risk assessment as a basis for treatment planning, but it also incorporates the idea that the clinician may have knowledge of culture and local conditions and experience with individual cases that will improve the accuracy of risk assessment. Lacking research to the contrary, our view is that the effectiveness of services will be improved when workers augment actuarially based risk assessment by using knowledge of unique conditions affecting children and their families.

Strengths or Assets Perspective

A risk and resilience orientation to practice builds also on the strengths and assets perspectives in social work, psychology, education, and other fields (Chapin, 1995; Fraser, Richman, & Galinsky, 1999; McQuaide & Ehrenreich, 1997; Saleebey, 1996, 1997, 2000; Seligman & Csikszentmihalyi, 2000; Weick, Rapp, Sullivan, & Kisthardt, 1989). In chapters 4 through 12, we described protective factors for many childhood conditions; one may think of these protective factors and processes as strengths. A resilience perspective ensures that the strengths of individuals, families, and communities are assessed and that assets that may exist in the environment are activated in ways that prevent problems and ameliorate existing difficulties. Assets that are not used cannot function protectively. In employing the term "protection," then, we imply that there is a dynamic relationship between risk and potential resources such that assets and strengths actively modify risk. Assets and strengths become protective factors when they reduce risk. They function protectively to earn the label of protective factor. Assets and strengths may also affect children independent of risk and promote, in an additive sense, positive developmental outcomes for children. When they function to promote positive outcomes regardless of a child's risk level, assets and strengths are sometimes called "promotive" factors (Sameroff, Bartko, Baldwin, Baldwin, & Seifer, 1998).

A resilience perspective is founded on the idea that risk as well as protective (and promotive) factors must be systematically included in change efforts. Recent data suggest that children at high risk may have few assets on which to build (Pollard et al., 1999). It is hard to imagine an intervention that would fail to address risk under such circumstances. Although many experts argue that traditional practice has focused excessively on deficits, dysfunctions, and pathology, we argue that practice should devote energy to both risk and protection. The study of protective factors among children who face high risks but who avoid negative outcomes is a distinguishing feature of resilience-based practice. Practitioners must be knowledgeable about the ways protective mechanisms operate if they are to design intervention strategies for those children whose exposure to risk factors has already placed them in jeopardy. Moreover, they must be knowledgeable if they are to design prevention strategies for children who are likely to be exposed to risk in the future.[2]

Empowerment

The risk and resilience perspective is closely linked to empowerment. Theorists and practitioners have used the concept of empowerment in a variety of ways (Gutierrez, 1990; Gutierrez & Lewis, 1999; Gutierrez, Parsons, & Cox, 1998). We use the broadest meaning of empowerment, which, according to Gutierrez (1990):

> includes combining a sense of personal control with the ability to affect the behavior of others, a focus on enhancing existing strengths in individuals or communities, a goal of establishing equity in the distribution of resources, an ecological (rather than individual) form of analysis for understanding individual and community phenomena, and a belief that power is not a scarce commodity but rather one that can be generated. (p. 150)

Empowerment denotes a partnership between the practitioner and the client or consumer. It involves the development and use of the capacities of the individual, family, organization, and community. Drawing on these capacities helps the consumer

---

[2] A word of caution is in order, however. Because protective factors have been studied primarily in the context of the resilient—those who have avoided or minimized the negative consequences of risk factors—we need to examine whether strengthening the same protective factors lowers risk for children who were not formerly resilient.

of services fully realize his or her own abilities and goals (Cowger, 1994; Gutierrez, 1990; Gutierrez, GlenMaye, & DeLois, 1995; Gutierrez & Lewis, 1999; Simon, 1994). EBP calls for consumer collaboration at every stage of the intervention process, from assessment to action to evaluation. When practitioners present current evidence on risk, protection, and intervention effectiveness to consumers, they engage them as active partners and empower them with knowledge to make decisions about their care.

Our focus on the local community—including differences based on gender, culture, ethnicity, race, religion, and sexual orientation—as an axiomatic aspect of intervention, is rooted in this concept of empowerment. At the community level, stakeholders—representing a diversity of peoples and organizations—must be involved in the design of services, and services should be based on an understanding of local risk and protective factors. In turn, stakeholders need to have access to the best available evidence on risk and protective factors. This combination of access to published information and use by intervention planners of local wisdom about factors operative in the communities is a central element of developing EBP strategies. Many states have area mental health authorities, crime prevention councils, county child welfare boards, and other local planning authorities. But few of these authorities make use of the increasingly rich array of data on risk factors that could inform planning. Some states, however, have created interagency task forces to aggregate data and make geographically identified information on risk factors available to planning councils through the Internet. This is an essential feature, for example, of the multistate Communities That Care Program (Harachi, Ayers, Hawkins, & Catalano, 1996; Hawkins et al., 1992). The closer we can come to gathering and using local information, the greater will be the ability of communities to affect targeted services for their own areas. By understanding risk and matching risk to intervention, we are potentially able to alter the configuration of ser-vices; this affects the immediate contextual forces as well as the individual influences on children and their families.

Discrimination and Empowerment

As we have seen throughout this book, risk and protective factors related to specific childhood problems often differ according to gender, race and ethnicity, and sexual orientation (see, for example, Henry, Tolan, & Gorman-Smith, 2001). Boys and girls from African American, Hispanic American, and other racial and ethnic backgrounds are subject to differential direct and indirect effects of discrimination, compounding and exacerbating their risk for many kinds of problems. The empowerment process is one means by which discrimination can be addressed for children at risk. It includes the involvement of members of the community in the identification of local risk and protective factors, among which are those related to discrimination and combating discrimination. It also emphasizes attention to the strengths of local community beliefs, traditions, and practices. It invites members of the local community to focus on their strengths and to devise solutions to their own problems. And it encourages communities to acquire power to act in their own behalf and to affect broader environmental conditions (Gutierrez, 1990; Gutierrez & Lewis, 1999; Gutierrez & Ortega, 1991; Gutierrez et al., 1998). Successful intervention from this perspective relies on recognition of diversity and on empowerment.

EVIDENCE-BASED PRACTICE AND INTERVENTION RESEARCH

Knowledge of risk and protective factors is not sufficient to address the problems that confront youths and their families. Knowledge of how to change individual behavior, family processes, and contextual conditions is also essential. Though far from adequate, a growing body of literature in social work is devoted to evaluation of intervention strategies. Since the start of the profession, social workers have evaluated interventions—efforts to produce meaningful differences in the lives of children and their families. There are numerous descriptive accounts of practice at the individual, group, family, organizational, and community levels. These descriptions have proved useful in informing others of work that is being done by skilled and creative professionals. Witness, for example, Edith Abbott's description of efforts to reform housing in the tenements of Chicago from 1908 to 1935:

> Minimum standards have been laid down in the tenement-house code [of 1902] regarding the size of rooms and the size of windows, but the Health Department seems to have found it impossible to apply these minimum standards to the dreary rows of old tenements that line one street after another in deteriorated areas. Approximately one-fourth of the rooms visited by our investigators did not have the minimum area of 70 square feet prescribed by the ordinance, and 19 per cent did not have the minimum height of 8½ feet, with the percentage below the minimum running very much higher than this in some of the poorest housing areas. (Abbott, 1936, pp. 480–481)

Recently, systematic studies focus both on the outcomes of interventions, such as changes in housing codes or the provision of a special after-school program to promote academic achievement in high-risk children, and on the change process. Early social workers discovered that changing laws and codes did not necessarily produce positive outcomes. Specific interventions ranging from the community mobilizations of the Chicago Area Projects to individually focused behaviorally oriented treatment plans came to be seen as the means for producing significant social change. In the past 25 years, studies of practice have become increasingly rigorous. Outcomes are carefully measured and interventions, which can be conceived as systematic change strategies, are developed on the basis of prior research and theory. Although studies of interventions are still relatively few, they contribute to a developing body of evidence on the effectiveness of practice. (For a review of these studies, see Reid & Fortune, 2004.) The findings from these studies will contribute to the design of more effective interventions. It is essential that we begin to codify and systematize these findings in a way that is accessible and usable for practitioners.

Based on knowledge gleaned from research and practice, social work practitioners and educators are calling for the creation of practice guidelines and treatment manuals (Rosen & Proctor, 2004). These guides for practice have enormous detail. From a growing base of interdisciplinary knowledge about the effectiveness of various interventions, they outline practice principles, describe effective programs, and discuss common implementation issues (Fraser, 2004; Howard & Jensen, 1999; Richey & Roffman, 1999). Unfortunately, we are just starting to develop these resources. In some areas of social work practice, we have begun the process of translating research findings into practice resources. For example, based on knowledge of social information processing and its influence on aggressive behavior, Fraser and others developed a *Making Choices* group work manual for use with eight- and nine-year-old children in school and after-school settings. They have tested the effectiveness of this approach in a variety of situations, from after-school church-based programs and Boys and Girls Clubs, to third-grade classrooms (Fraser, Nash, Galinsky, & Darwin, 2000; Fraser et al., 2001). As information on risk and protective factors and on ways to intervene are increased, it will be increasingly important to translate research into practice resources such as *Making Choices*. To achieve the promises of EBP, the scholarly capabilities of the profession will need to focus on intervention research and on translating findings from intervention research into practice guidelines and treatment manuals.

CAN WE MAKE MEANINGFUL DIFFERENCES?

Although it is increasingly clear that the presence of adversity in a child's environment does not always lead to negative outcomes, it is still clearer that the presence of risk, especially multiple risks, is a marker for negative outcomes. We need to incorporate this knowledge in the design of public programs and policies. If a program or policy successfully reduces those risks, the odds of making meaningful differences in the lives of children will go up. Public health workers have already used knowledge of risk factors to implement programs of prevention. For example, this approach gave rise to effective prevention programs that warned people about the spread of AIDS. Can this approach be used in such fields as delinquency, where parents, professionals, and others are concerned about youth violence? Can it be used to develop early intervention programs in child welfare, where mandated services focus on investigation and substitute care rather than on early intervention and prevention? More generally, can knowledge of risk and protective factors be built into programs of intervention on a policy level, on a community level, on a family level, and on an individual level to make positive changes for children who are already deeply involved in chains of disadvantage and alienation?

Recent progress in the understanding of human behavior holds out promise that meaningful differences can be made. This progress, which has been described throughout this book, is beginning to be realized in many fields. The elements of an EBP strategy are taking shape, and they rely on understanding risk and protective factors. These elements include aspects of community practice often associated with community mobilization and neighborhood organization. These elements are extending, or perhaps reincorporating, the strategies of Edith Abbott, Jane Addams, Mary Richmond, and other early social workers, and involve

- understanding both the common and problem-specific risk and protective factors for various childhood problems
- employing systematic methods for the assessment of risk and protective factors at the individual, family, school, neighborhood, and broader environmental levels
- targeting specific risk and protective mechanisms

- selecting intervention strategies on the basis of the "best available" evidence, including research information and practice wisdom
- collaborating with consumers at every stage, from assessment to intervention to evaluation.

Although the risk and resilience perspective is beginning to work its way into the curricula of professional schools and into the strategic planning of state and local agencies where services are developed and implemented, progress is slow. It must become a higher priority for us to apply knowledge of risk and resilience to policy and practice.

CONCLUSION

Children are placed at risk by many individual and environmental conditions, so the processes that are likely to improve their status must involve changing these conditions. Change strategies should combine community practice with policy, organizational, group, family, and individual interventions. These strategies must build on emerging knowledge to identify local risk and protective factors through a process that involves community as well as individual and family assessment. They require specification of risk chains that increase the odds of poor developmental outcomes and the specification of protective mechanisms that appear to help children prevail over adversity. They require that children or groups of children with many risks be identified and comprehensive strategies be developed to reduce risk. And, whether at the community or the individual level, they require matching risk profiles with effective change strategies that capitalize on and strengthen protective mechanisms. Ecologically focused and evidence-based interventions and public policies, which reduce risk and build resilience, offer new promise for millions of children and their families across the country.

REFERENCES

Abbott, E. (1936). *The tenements of Chicago, 1908–1935*. Chicago: University of Chicago Press.

Campbell Collaboration Library. (2001). [Database]. Retrieved from http://www .campbellcollaboration.org/Fralibrary.html on July 14, 2003.

Chapin, R. K. (1995). Social policy development: The strengths perspective. *Social Work, 40,* 506–514.

Cochrane Library. (2001). [Database]. Retrieved from http://www.update-software.com/ cochrane/default.htm on July 7, 2003.

Council on Social Work Education. (2001). *Educational policy and accreditation standards*. Washington, DC: Author.

Cowger, C. D. (1994). Assessing client strengths: Clinical assessment for client empowerment. *Social Work, 39,* 262–268.

Duncan, G. J., & Raudenbush, S. W. (2001). Neighborhoods and adolescent development: How can we determine the links? In A. Booth & A. C. Crouter (Eds.), *Does it take a village?* (pp. 105–136). Mahwah, NJ: Lawrence Erlbaum.

Fraser, M. W. (2004). Intervention research in social work: A basis for evidence-based practice and practice guidelines. In A. Rosen & E. K. Proctor (Eds.), *Developing practice guidelines for social work interventions: Issues, methods, and research agenda*. New York: Columbia University Press.

Fraser, M. W., Galinsky, M. J., Hodges, V. G., Smokowski, P. R., Day, S. H., Abell, M., & Nash, J. K. (2001). *The effectiveness of an Early Intervention Program for Aggressive Behavior: The Making Choices and Strong Families Programs*. Atlanta: Society for Social Work and Research.

Fraser, M. W., Nash, J. K., Galinsky, M. J., & Darwin, K. M. (2000). *Making choices: Social problem-solving skills for children*. Washington, DC: NASW Press.

Fraser, M. W., Richman, J. M., & Galinsky, M. J. (1999). Risk, protection, and resilience: Toward a conceptual framework for social work practice. *Social Work, 3*, 131–142.

Germain, C. B. (1991). *Human behavior in the social environment: An ecological view*. New York: Columbia University Press.

Gutierrez, L., GlenMaye, L., & DeLois, K. (1995). The organizational context of empowerment practice: Implications for social work administration. *Social Work, 40*, 249–258.

Gutierrez, L., & Lewis, E. (Eds.). (1999). *Empowering women of color*. New York: Columbia University Press.

Gutierrez, L., & Ortega, R. (1991). Developing methods to empower Latinos: The importance of groups. *Social Work with Groups, 14*(2), 23–44.

Gutierrez, L., Parsons, R., & Cox, E. O. (1998). *Empowerment in social work practice: A sourcebook*. Belmont, CA: Wadsworth.

Gutierrez, L. M. (1990). Working with women of color: An empowerment perspective. *Social Work, 35*, 149–154.

Harachi, T. W., Ayers, C. D., Hawkins, J. D., & Catalano, R. F. (1996). Empowering communities to prevent adolescent substance abuse: Process evaluation results from a risk- and protection-focused community mobilization effort. *Journal of Primary Prevention, 16*(3), 233–254.

Hawkins, J. D., Catalano, R. F., Jr., & Associates. (1992). *Communities that care*. San Francisco: Jossey-Bass.

Henggeler, S. W, Schoenwald, S. K., Borduin, C. M., Rowland, M. D., & Cunningham, P. B. (1998). *Multisystemic treatment of antisocial behavior in children and adolescents*. New York: Guilford Press.

Henry, D. B., Tolan, P. H., & Gorman-Smith, D. (2001). Longitudinal family and peer group effects on violence and nonviolent delinquency. *Journal of Clinical Child Psychology, 30*(1), 172–186.

Herrerias, C. T., Perrin, J. M., & Stein, M. T. (2001). The child with ADHD: Using the AAP clinical practice guideline. *American Family Physician, 63*(9), 1803–1811.

Howard, M. O., & Jenson, J. M. (1999). Clinical practice guidelines: Should social work develop them? *Research on Social Work Practice, 9*(3), 283–301.

Jaeschke, R., Guyatt, G., & Meade, M. (1998). Evidence-based practice: What it is, why we need it. *Advances in Wound Care, 11*(5), 214–218.

Loeber, R., & Stouthamer-Loeber, M. (1996). The development of offending. *Criminal Justice and Behaviour, 23*(1), 12–24.

McQuaide, S., & Ehrenreich, J. H. (1997). Assessing client strengths. *Families in Society: The Journal of Contemporary Human Services, 78*(2), 201–212.

Monahan, J., Steadman, H. J., Silver, E., Appelbaum, P. S., Robbins, P. C., Roth, L. H., Grisso, T., & Banks, S. (2001). *Rethinking risk assessment: The MacArthur study of mental disorder and violence*. New York: Oxford University Press.

Pollard, J. A., Hawkins, J. D., & Arthur, M. W. (1999). Risk and protection: Are both necessary to understand diverse behavioral outcomes in adolescence? *Social Work Research, 23*(3), 145–158.

Reid, W. J., & Fortune, A. E. (2004). Harbingers, origins, and approximations of evidence-based practice in current social work knowledge. In A. Rosen & E. K. Proctor (Eds.), *Developing practice guidelines for social work interventions: Issues, methods, and research agenda*. New York: Columbia University Press.

Richey, C. A., & Roffman, R. A. (1999). Further thoughts on the fit between clinical guidelines and social work practice. *Research on Social Work Practice, 9*(3), 311–321.

Rosen, A., & Proctor, E. K. (Eds.). (2004). *Developing practice guidelines for social work interventions: Issues, methods, and research agenda*. New York: Columbia University Press.

Rutter, M. (2000a). Psychosocial influences: Critiques, findings, and research needs. *Development and Psychopathology, 12,* 375–405.

Rutter, M. (2000b). Resilience reconsidered: Conceptual considerations, empirical findings, and policy implications. In J. P. Shonkoff & S. J. Meisels (Eds.), *Handbook of early childhood intervention* (2nd ed., pp. 651–682). New York: Cambridge University Press.

Rutter, M. (2001). Psychosocial adversity: Risk, resilience, and recovery. In J. M. Richman & M. W. Fraser (Eds.), *The context of youth violence: Resilience, risk, and protection* (pp. 13–41). Westport, CT: Praeger Publishers.

Sackett, D. L., Richardson, W. S., Rosenberg, W., & Haynes, R. B. (1997). *Evidence-based medicine: How to practice and teach EBM*. New York: Churchill Livingstone.

Sackett, D. L., Rosenberg, W.M.C., Gray, J.A.M., Haynes, R. B., & Richardson, W. S. (1996). Evidence-based medicine: What it is and what it isn't. *British Medical Journal, 312,* 71–72.

Saleebey, D. (1996). The strengths perspective in social work practice: Extensions and cautions. *Social Work, 41,* 296–305.

Saleebey, D. (Ed). (1997). *The strengths perspective in social work practice: Power in the people* (2nd ed.). White Plains, NY: Longman.

Saleebey, D. (2000). Power in the people: Strengths and hope. *Advances in Social Work, 1*(2), 127–136.

Sameroff, A. J., Bartko, W. T., Baldwin, A., Baldwin, C., & Seifer, R. (1998). Family and social influences on development of child competence. In M. Lewis & C. Feiring (Eds.), *Families, risk, and competence* (pp. 161–185). Mahwah, NJ: Lawrence Erlbaum.

Sameroff, A. J., & Fiese, B. H. (2000). Transactional regulation: The developmental ecology of early intervention. In J. P. Shonkoff & S. J. Meisels (Eds.), *Handbook of early childhood intervention* (2nd ed., pp. 135–159). New York: Cambridge University Press.

Sampson, R. J., Raudenbush, S., & Earls, F. (1997). Neighborhoods and violent crime: A multilevel study of collective efficacy. *Science, 277,* 918–924.

Seligman, M.E.P., & Csikszentmihalyi, M. (2000). Positive psychology: An introduction. *American Psychologist, 55*(1), 5–14.

Simon, B. L. (1994). *The empowerment tradition in American social work: A history.* New York: Columbia University Press.

Thornberry, T. P., Lizotte, A. J., Krohn, M. D., Farnsworth, M., & Jang, S. J. (1991). Testing interactional theory: An examination of reciprocal causal relationships among family, school, and delinquency. *Journal of Criminal Law and Criminology, 82*(1), 3–35.

Weick, A., Rapp, C., Sullivan, W. P., & Kisthardt, W. (1989). A strengths perspective for social work practice. *Social Work, 34,* 350–354.

Woolfenden, S. R., Williams, K., & Peat J. (2001, February 28). *Family and parenting interventions in children and adolescents with conduct disorder and delinquency aged 10–17* (Cochrane Review) [Online]. Retrieved from http://www.update -software.com/abstracts/ab003015.htm on October 22, 2001.

Index

About the Editor

Mark W. Fraser, MSW, PhD, holds the John A. Tate Distinguished Professorship for Children in Need at the School of Social Work, University of North Carolina, Chapel Hill. He directs the Making Choices Project, a school-based prevention program focused on third-grade children and their families in ethnically diverse and rapidly growing communities. This project has two components: (1) the development of a social problem–solving curriculum focused on children's skills in processing social information and regulating emotions and (2) the development of a set of parent workshops designed to promote academic achievement and reduce aggressive behavior in third-grade children. Dr. Fraser is also the editor of the NASW Practice Resources Series. He has written numerous chapters and articles on risk and resilience, child behavior, child and family services, and research methods. With colleagues, he is the coauthor or editor of five books that include *Families in Crisis*, a study of intensive family-centered services, and *Evaluating Family-Based Services*, a text on methods for family research. In *Making Choices*, Dr. Fraser and his coauthors outline a program to help children build enduring social relationships with peers and adults. In *The Context of Youth Violence*, he and his colleagues explore violence from the perspective of resilience, risk, and protection. His most recent book is *Intervention with Children and Adolescents: An Interdisciplinary Perspective*.

About the Contributors

Michael W. Arthur, PhD, received his degree in community psychology from the University of Virginia in 1990. His research includes community interventions to prevent adolescent antisocial behavior and to promote social competency, prevention research methodology, and prevention needs assessment methods. His recent publications have appeared in *Social Work Research*; and he has contributed chapters to *Serious and Violent Juvenile Offenders: Risk Factors and Successful Interventions, Handbook of Antisocial Behavior,* and *Building a Safer Society: Strategic Approaches to Crime Prevention.* He is a research associate professor at the University of Washington, School of Social Work and a researcher at the Social Development Research Group in Seattle.

Charles D. Ayers, MSW, is the executive director of Cascade Bicycle Club, a not-for-profit organization in Seattle. His current interests include environmental advocacy, community development, risk and protective factors related to delinquency, youth developmental assets, and experiential and adventure-based programming for children and adolescents at elevated risk for involvement in delinquent activities. His current publications have appeared in *Social Work Research, Journal for Juvenile Justice & Detention Services,* and *Journal of Quantitative Criminology.*

Gary L. Bowen, PhD, ACSW, is the Kenan Distinguished Professor in the School of Social Work at the University of North Carolina at Chapel Hill. He also holds a joint appointment in the Department of Communication Studies. Dr. Bowen chairs the Direct Practice Concentration in the MSW program and serves as an appointed member of the Academic Affairs Institutional Review Board at the university level. Dr. Bowen is the author or coauthor of numerous journal articles, book chapters, monographs, and technical reports. He recently served as guest editor with Dr. Jack Richman of a special issue of *Children & Schools: A Journal of Social Work Practice,* which addresses schools in the context of communities. With support from the Knight Foundation and the National Institute on Drug Abuse, he codirects the School Success Profile Project with Dr. Jack Richman and Dr. Natasha Bowen. His honors include an Alumni Pacesetter Award in 1998 from the University of North Carolina, School of Environmental Sciences, Greenboro, "for actively making a difference in the lives of others and the world around them," where he received his doctorate in 1981.

Jacqueline Corcoran, PhD, is an assistant professor at Virginia Commonwealth University, School of Social Work. She was previously a faculty member at the University of Texas at Arlington School of Social Work, where she served as codirector of the Community Service Clinic at the School of Social Work. She received her PhD from the University of Texas at Austin in 1996. Dr. Corcoran teaches courses in direct social work practice and human behavior in the social environment. She has published numerous articles in the areas of family practice, solution-focused therapy, crisis intervention, and adolescent pregnancy. Her book *Evidence-Based Social Work Practice with Families: A Lifespan Approach* was published in 2000, and she has two forthcoming books with Oxford University Press.

Cynthia Franklin, PhD, is a professor at the University of Texas at Austin, School of Social Work, where she serves as coordinator of Clinical Social Work concentration. She teaches courses on clinical practice, family therapy, and research methods. Dr. Franklin specializes in clinical practice with children and families and is especially known for her expertise in school social work and practice–research integration. She has over 100 publications in the professional literature. Her publications focus on clinical assessment, the effectiveness of solution-focused therapy, alternative school programs, and teen pregnancy prevention. Dr. Franklin is author of several books including *Clinical Assessment for Social Workers: Quantitative and Qualitative Methods* published by the Lyceum Press and *Family Practice: Brief Systems Methods for Social Work* published by Brooks/Cole Publications. Dr. Franklin is a clinical member of the American Association of Marriage and Family Therapy and holds practices licenses in clinical social work (LMSW-ACP) and Marriage and Family Therapy (LMFT).

Maeda J. Galinsky, MSW, PhD, is Kenan Distinguished Professor at the School of Social Work, University of North Carolina at Chapel Hill. Her research interests center on the design, analysis, and evaluation of social interventions, particularly group services. She has published widely in the area of group work research and practice, including articles on support groups, open-ended groups, and evaluation of innovative group interventions. Her recent publications focus on technology-based groups, use of the risk and resilience framework as a foundation for social work practice, and a structured group intervention geared to the prevention and reduction of aggressive behavior in children. She is coprincipal investigator of the Making Choices Project, a program aimed at the prevention of violence in elementary-school children.

M. Carlean Gilbert, MSW, DSW, is assistant professor in the School of Social Work, Loyola University Chicago. Her scholarship and teaching focus on health and mental disorders of children and families, social group work, and spirituality. Her most recent publications have appeared in *Social Work in Health Care, Social Work with Groups*, and *Child & Adolescent Social Work Journal*. Dr. Gilbert serves on the editorial board of *Social Work in Health Care* and represents health care practice as a member of the Commission on Social Work Practice of the Council of Social Work Education. She also maintains a part-time consultation and clinical practice.

Mary Beth Harris, PhD, is on the faculty of New Mexico Highlands University, School of Social Work. She teaches direct and macropractice with an emphasis on the Hispanic and Native American populations of the New Mexico–West Texas region. Dr. Harris is a well-known trainer for social workers and other professionals working with vulnerable child and adolescent populations. Her current work focuses on outcome research related to skills building with adolescent mothers. Dr. Harris holds the social work clinical practice license in Texas (LMSW-ACP) and in New Mexico (LISW).

Jeffrey M. Jenson, MSW, PhD, is Bridge Professor of Children, Youth, and Families at the Graduate School of Social Work, University of Denver. Dr. Jenson's interests include the etiology, prevention, and treatment of adolescent substance abuse and juvenile delinquency. His current research includes a longitudinal study examining the effects of a school-based prevention curriculm on risk and protective factors associated with antisocial behavior among elementary-school children. Dr. Jenson is the author of more than 50 articles and books on topics related to adolescent problem behavior.

Laura D. Kirby, MSW, MPH, graduated in 1996 from the Schools of Social Work and Public Health at the University of North Carolina at Chapel Hill. She has interests in child maltreatment, family support, and early intervention.

Mark J. Macgowan, PhD, LCSW, is on the faculty of the School of Social Work at Florida International University in Miami where he teaches direct practice. Dr. Macgowan's research centers on reducing suicidality, substance abuse, and violence among youths. His funded research projects include multisite, community-based randomized designs involving culturally diverse groups. Dr. Macgowan's recent publications have appeared in *Research on Social Work Practice, Violence and Victims, Journal of Social Service Research,* and *Small Group Research.* He is a Licensed Clinical Social Worker with many years of practice experience working with adolescents in juvenile justice and clinical settings.

James K. Nash, MSW, PhD, is assistant professor at the Graduate School of Social Work at Portland State University in Portland, Oregon. He received the MSW and PhD in social work at the University of North Carolina. His research interests include understanding and preventing youth violence, promoting optimal behavior and development in children and adolescents, intervention research, and quantitative research methods.

Karen A. Randolph, PhD, is an assistant professor at the Florida State University School of Social Work. She received her PhD in social work from the University of North Carolina at Chapel Hill. Her research area is youth development and risk and resilience during adolescence. Substantive areas of interest include adolescent substance use prevention and promoting academic success in high school. Her recent publications appear in *Social Service Review* and *Children and Youth Services Review.*

Jack M. Richman, MSW, PhD, is the dean and professor at the School of Social Work at the University of North Carolina at Chapel Hill. He received his MSW in social work from the State University of New York at Albany and his PhD in counseling psychology from Florida State University. His teaching areas for PhD and MSW students are in social work theory and practice with individuals, couples, and families. He also teaches courses that prepare doctoral students for university teaching roles. His research is focused in the areas of at-risk students, social support, and violence and trauma in childhood. He is coprincipal investigator and codeveloper, with Gary Bowen, of The School Success Profile, an evaluation and practice-monitoring instrument for practitioners, youths at risk of school failure, and their families. Dr. Richman, a frequent contributor to the professional literature, is on the editorial board for *Children & Schools* and *The American Journal of Hospice and Palliative Care.* He and Mark Fraser are the editors of *The Context of Youth Violence: Resilience, Risk and Protection* published by Praeger Press. Dr. Richman is a recipient of the University of North Carolina School of Social Work Award for Teaching Excellence.

Kathleen A. Rounds, PhD, MPH, MSW, is a professor at the School of Social Work, University of North Carolina at Chapel Hill. Her research has included evaluation of support services for people with HIV, treatment interventions for pregnant and post-partum women using drugs and alcohol, and adolescent pregnancy prevention pro-grams. Her practice interests focus on social work in public health and community health settings, particularly in the area of maternal and child health. Dr. Rounds directs the Public Health Social Work Leadership Training Program and codirects the Behavioral Healthcare Resource Program at the School of Social Work.

Rune J. Simeonsson, PhD, MSPH, is a psychologist, professor of education, and research professor of psychology at the University of North Carolina at Chapel Hill. He has graduate teaching responsibilities in the areas of psychological assessment and child development and disability. He is a fellow at the FPG Child Development Institute, with major research interests in measurement of children's functional status, health and quality of life, outcome evaluation, and international issues related to assessment and intervention of childhood disability. His major research interests are measurement of functional status, health and quality of life, outcome evaluation, and international issues in assessment and classification of childhood disability. He has recently published *Psychological and Developmental Assessment of Children with Disabilities and Chronic Conditions* (2001).

Paul R. Smokowski, MSW, PhD, is an assistant professor at the University of North Carolina at Chapel Hill School of Social Work. He has held pre- and postdoctoral fel-lowships in Social Welfare and Child Development that were funded by the National Institutes of Health. Dr. Smokowski received his doctorate in Social Welfare from the University of Wisconsin–Madison and performed his postdoctoral work at the Institute of Child Development, University of Minnesota–Twin Cities. He is currently coprinci-pal investigator of the Making Choices Project, a youth violence prevention program for elementary-school children and a collaborator on the *Chicago Longitudinal Study*. His research focuses on resilience development.

Barbara Thomlison, PhD, is a professor in the School of Social Work and director of the Institute for Children and Families at Risk. She obtained her PhD in social work from the University of Toronto and has a lengthy interdisciplinary practice history with children, families, and policy services research. Her teaching experiences involve both undergrad-uate and graduate programs in other universities. Her academic interests include child welfare, foster care, mental health, field education, program evaluation, working with fam-ilies, and evidence-based services. At the Florida International University School of Social Work, she teaches courses on child welfare, child maltreatment, and practice interven-tions. Her current research projects are in the area of school readiness and kinship care. Dr. Thomlison's publications include articles in the areas of child welfare practice, family preservation, foster care, treatment foster care, family reunification, and social work field education. Dr. Thomlison is actively involved as a board and community member in local and national child welfare and family service organizations.

Richard A. Van Dorn, PhD, is currently a postdoctoral research fellow at Duke University in the Department of Psychiatry and Behavioral Sciences. Dr. Van Dorn received his PhD in social work from the School of Social Work at the University of North Carolina at Chapel Hill, where he was a Spencer Fellow in Education Policy Research and a predoctoral fellow at the Center for Developmental Science. His current research includes risk and protective factors for violence and victimization in both youths and adults and contextual processes of educational outcomes. His current publications have appeared in *Social Work, Journal of Adolescent Health, Children & Schools, Violence and Victims*, and *Families in Society*.

James Herbert Williams, PhD, is the E. Desmond Lee Professor of Racial and Ethnic Diversity and associate dean for Academic Affairs at the George Warren Brown School of Social Work, Washington University, St. Louis, Missouri. He received a PhD in social welfare from the University of Washington School of Social Work in Seattle in 1994. His research interests includes children mental health services, service utilization in African American communities, racial differences in risk and protective factors for childhood and adolescent antisocial behavior, race disproportionality and disparities in juvenile justice, youth development, cross-sector systems of care, and prevention programming. His current publications have appeared in *Social Work Research, Social Work, Journal of Family Issues, Violence and Victims, Journal of Quantitative Criminology, Journal of Youth and Adolescence, Urban Education*, and *Families in Society*. He.

Michael E. Woolley, MSW, PhD, is an assistant professor with a joint appointment in the School of Social Work and the School of Education at the University of Michigan at Ann Arbor. Dr. Woolley received his doctorate from the School of Social Work at the University of North Carolina at Chapel Hill, where he was awarded a Weiss, Senior Weiss, and Spencer Fellowship. He is a Diplomate in Clinical Social Work from the National Association of Social Workers and has 11 years of post-MSW practice experience working with children and families in school, health, and mental health settings. Dr. Woolley's interests revolve around research into the provision of social work services to children and families in schools and the development of assessment instruments for direct practice.

Irene Nathan Zipper, MSW, PhD, is clinical associate professor at the School of Social Work, University of North Carolina at Chapel Hill. Her teaching and research interests are in the areas of childhood disability, family support, children's mental health services, and service coordination. Her recent publications have addressed service coordination and the use of technology in personnel preparation.

RISK AND RESILIENCE IN CHILDHOOD:
AN ECOLOGICAL PERSPECTIVE (2ND EDITION)

Cover design by Eye to Eye Design Studio, Bristow, VA
Composed by MidAtlantic Books and Journals,
Baltimore, MD, in Century Old Style
Printed by Phoenix Color Corp., Hagerstown, MD, on 50# Phoenix

MORE RESOURCES FROM NASW PRESS!

Risk and Resilience in Childhood: *An Ecological Perspective, 2nd Edition, Mark W. Fraser, Editor.* Why are some children so resilient when others are not? Building on the concepts and models presented in the best-selling first edition, *Risk and Resilience in Childhood* takes a major leap forward from other social work texts to probe both risk and resilience and the protective factors that promote positive developmental outcomes. Firmly research based, it bridges the gap between ecological theory and strengths-based practice and provides a foundation for developing case-specific interventions.

ISBN: 0-87101-356-8. 2003. Item #3568. $49.99.

Making Choices: *Social Problem-Solving Skills for Children, Mark W. Fraser, James K. Nash, Maeda J. Galinsky, and Kathleen M. Darwin.* Based on a cognitive problem-solving approach, *Making Choices* addresses the urgent need for children to acquire competence in meeting the demands of childhood within social, school, and family parameters. The book is designed for children from kindergarten through middle school whose behavior is impulsive, oppositional, or aggressive. Recognizing that a great deal of children's behavior is tied to problem solving, the volume focuses on how children solve instrumental and relational issues in different social settings.

ISBN: 0-87101-323-1. 2000. Item #3231. $33.99.

Resiliency: *An Integrated Approach to Practice, Policy and Research, Roberta R. Greene, Editor.* Social workers require both the understanding of how people successfully meet life challenges and the knowledge to build client strengths, adaptation, healing, and self-efficacy. This comprehensive volume integrates social work theory, policy, research, and method to promote and improve resilience-based practice. Faculty across curriculum, students, and practitioners will find this timely book an invaluable text.

ISBN: 0-87101-350-9. January 2002. Item #3509. $44.99.

Children & Schools: *A Journal of Social Work Practice, Wilma Peebles-Wilkins, Editor-in-Chief. Children & Schools* (formerly *Social Work in Education*) is a trusted tool for those who provide critical social work services in education for children. Articles present innovations in practice, interdisciplinary efforts, research, program evaluation, policy, and planning. Topics include student-authority relationships, multiculturalism, early intervention, needs assessment, violence, and ADHD. It is a valuable practitioner-to-practitioner resource that assists readers in developing relevant courses and curricula and encourages multidisciplinary collaboration. Available online at www.naswpressonline.org.

ISSN: 1532-8759. Published quarterly in January, April, July, and October. NASW Member (#6001) $49.00; NASW Student Member (#6101) $33.00; Individual Nonmember (#6201) $83.00; Library/Institution (#6301) $115.00.

Peace Power for Adolescents: *Strategies for a Culture of Nonviolence, Mark A. Mattaini with the PEACE POWER Working Group.* This groundbreaking book looks at the wide range of risk factors and indicators for violence among our children and translates the findings into an effective prevention and intervention system. The *PEACE POWER* method recognizes that we can find peaceful solutions to strengthen our communities and takes a positive and practical approach that respects the divergent cultures and values in our society.

ISBN: 0-87101-329-0. 2001. Item #3290. $39.99.

Multisystem Skills and Interventions in School Social Work Practice, *Edith M. Freeman, Cynthia G. Franklin, Rowena Fong, Gary L. Shaffer, and Elizabeth M. Timberlake, Editors. Multisystem Skills* is a practical guide that covers interventions that work on all levels, from school to family to community agencies to the policy level. Using case examples, this practice-oriented text investigates difficult challenges such as curbing aggressive behavior, improving attendance in at-risk children, empowering families, preventing youth suicide, participating in post-traumatic event debriefing, and developing new strategies for emerging areas of concern.

ISBN: 0-87101-295-2. 1998. Item #2952. $39.99.

(Order form and information on reverse side)

ORDER FORM

Qty.	Title	Item #	Price	Total
__	Risk and Resilience in Childhood	3568	$49.99	_____
__	Making Choices	3231	$33.99	_____
__	Resiliency	3509	$44.99	_____
	Children & Schools			
__	NASW Member	6001	$49.00	
__	NASW Student Member	6101	$33.00	
__	Individual Nonmember	6201	$83.00	
__	Library/Institution	6301	$115.00	_____
__	Peace Power for Adolescents	3290	$39.99	_____
__	Multisystem Skills and Interventions in School Social Work Practice	2952	$39.99	_____

POSTAGE AND HANDLING
Minimum postage and handling fee is $4.95. Orders that do not include appropriate postage and handling will be returned.

DOMESTIC: Please add 12% to orders under $100 for postage and handling. For orders over $100 add 7% of order.

CANADA: Please add 17% postage and handling.

OTHER INTERNATIONAL: Please add 22% postage and handling.

Subtotal _____
Postage and Handling _____
DC residents add 6% sales tax _____
MD residents add 5% sales tax _____
NC residents add 4.5% sales tax _____
Total _____

❑ **Check** or **money order** (payable to NASW Press) for $ _____.

❑ **Credit card**
    ❑ Visa ❑ MasterCard ❑ American Express

_____   _____
Credit Card Number   Expiration Date

Signature _____

Name _____

Address _____

City _____ State/Province _____

Country _____ Zip _____

Phone _____ E-mail _____

NASW Member # (if applicable) _____

(Please make checks payable to NASW Press. Prices are subject to change.)

NASW PRESS
P. O. Box 431
Annapolis JCT, MD 20701
USA

Credit card orders call
1-800-227-3590
(In the Metro Wash., DC, area, call 301-317-8688)
Or fax your order to 301-206-7989
Or order online at www.naswpress.org